Social Cognition

Edited by

Marilynn B. Brewer

and

Miles Hewstone

Blackwell
Publishing

Editorial material and organization © 2004 by Blackwell Publishing Ltd

350 Main Street, Malden, MA 02148-5020, USA
108 Cowley Road, Oxford OX4 1JF, UK
550 Swanston Street, Carlton, Victoria 3053, Australia

First published 2004 by Blackwell Publishing Ltd.

Library of Congress Cataloging-in-Publication Data

Social cognition / edited by Marilynn Brewer and Miles Hewstone.
p.   cm. – (Perspectives on social psychology)
Includes bibliographical references and index.
ISBN 1-4051-1070-8 (pbk. : alk. paper)
1. Mental representation–Social aspects.   2. Social perception.
I. Brewer, Marilynn B., 1942–   II. Hewstone, Miles.   III. Series.

BF316.6.S65 2003
302′.1–dc21
2003004956

A catalogue record for this title is available from the British Library.

Set in 10/12½pt Adobe Garamond
by Graphicraft Limited, Hong Kong
Printed and bound in the United Kingdom
by MPG Books, Bodmin, Cornwall

For further information on
Blackwell Publishing, visit our website:
http://www.blackwellpublishing.com

Social Cognition

WITHDRAWN

Perspectives on Social Psychology

The four volumes in this series collect readings from the *Blackwell Handbooks of Social Psychology* and present them thematically. The results are course-friendly texts in key areas of social psychology – *Social Cognition, Self and Social Identity, Motivation and Emotion,* and *Applied Social Psychology*. Each volume provides a representative sample of exciting research and theory that is both comprehensive and current and cross-cuts the levels of analysis from intrapersonal to intergroup.

Social Cognition, edited by Marilynn B. Brewer and Miles Hewstone
Self and Social Identity, edited by Marilynn B. Brewer and Miles Hewstone
Applied Social Psychology, edited by Marilynn B. Brewer and Miles Hewstone
Emotions and Motivation, edited by Marilynn B. Brewer and Miles Hewstone

Contents

Part II: Cognition in Social Interaction

Preface

When the *Blackwell Handbooks of Social Psychology* project was conceived, we sought to go beyond a simple topical structure for the content of the volumes in order to reflect more closely the complex pattern of cross-cutting theoretical perspectives and research agendas that comprise social psychology as a dynamic enterprise. The idea we developed was to represent the discipline in a kind of matrix structure, crossing levels of analysis with topics, processes, and functions that recur at all of these levels in social psychological theory and research. Taking inspiration from Willem Doise's 1986 book (*Levels of Explanation in Social Psychology*) four levels of analysis – intrapersonal, interpersonal, intragroup, and intergroup – provided the basis for organizing the Handbook series into four volumes. The two co-editors responsible for developing each of these volumes selected content chapters on the basis of cross-cutting themes represented by basic social psychological processes of social cognition, attribution, social motivation, affect and emotion, social influence, social comparison, and self and identity.

The four-volume handbook that resulted from this organizational framework represents the collective efforts of two series editors, eight volume editors, and 191 contributing authors. The *Intraindividual Processes* volume edited by Abraham Tesser and Norbert Schwarz provides a comprehensive selection of work on social cognition, affect, and motivation, which focuses on the individual as the unit of analysis. The *Interpersonal Processes* volume edited by Garth Fletcher and Margaret Clark also covers the cognition, affect, and motivation themes as they are played out in the context of close interpersonal relationships and dyadic exchanges. Again in the volume on *Group Processes*, edited by Michael Hogg and Scott Tindale, the themes of cognition, affect, and motivation are well represented in work on collective behavior in small groups and social organizations. Finally, the volume on *Intergroup Processes* edited by Rupert Brown and Samuel Gaertner covers work that links cognitive, affective, and motivational processes to relationships between social groups and large collectives.

Across all four volumes and levels of analysis, *social cognition* occupies a prominent position in explanatory theories for all of the phenomena of interest to social psychologists. Given the central role of social cognition to the study of all social psychological phenomena, research on social cognition is well represented among the chapters in all four volumes of the *Blackwell Handbooks of Social Psychology*. Because of the matrix structure of the handbooks, it is possible to draw from all four volumes to create a selection of readings on social cognition that cross-cuts the levels of analysis from intrapersonal to intergroup. This book contains a set of such readings, which we have selected for the purpose of providing a representative sampling of exciting research and theory on social cognition that is both comprehensive and current.

Marilynn Brewer and Miles Hewstone

Acknowledgments

The editor and publishers gratefully acknowledge the following for permission to reproduce copyright material:

Brown, Rupert and Gaertner, Sam (Eds.) (2001). *Blackwell Handbook of Social Psychology: Intergroup Processes*. Oxford: Blackwell Publishing. Reprinted with permission.

Fletcher, Garth J. O. and Clark, Margaret S. (Eds.) (2001). *Blackwell Handbook of Social Psychology: Interpersonal Processes*. Oxford: Blackwell Publishing. Reprinted with permission.

Hogg, Michael A. and Tindale, Scott (Eds.) (2001). *Blackwell Handbook of Social Psychology: Group Processes*. Oxford: Blackwell Publishing. Reprinted with permission.

Tesser, Abraham and Schwarz, Norbert (Eds.) (2001). *Blackwell Handbook of Social Psychology: Intraindividual Processes*. Oxford: Blackwell Publishing. Reprinted with permission.

The publishers apologize for any errors or omissions in the above list and would be grateful to be notified of any corrections that should be incorporated in the next edition or reprint of this book.

Introduction

Broadly speaking, social cognition refers to the mental representations that people hold of their social world, including beliefs about the causes of social events, beliefs about the characteristics of persons and social groups, and general knowledge about relationships among social actors and patterns of social behavior. Social cognition also encompasses the study of social information processing – how events and experiences are attended to, encoded (interpreted), stored in memory, and retrieved or remembered. Much of the interest in social cognition theory is focused on how our cognitive representations of past experience and learning (e.g., stereotypes, expectations, and specific memories) interact with new, incoming information and experiences to determine how we understand and interpret what is going on in our social world.

At the individual level, social cognition is the mental "filter" through which objective events and experiences are subjectively represented and remembered. It is a basic premise of the "cognitive revolution" in psychology that individuals do not respond directly to stimuli from the external environment but to their *perceptions* and cognitive interpretations of those stimuli. Cognition mediates the effects of external events on the decisions and behaviors individuals make in response to those experiences. Further, cognitions – as mental representations or images of past experience and learning – can direct behavior in the absence of current environmental input. People can respond to memories of the past or expectations about the future without the referents of those images being physically present. Thus, any attempt to understand and explain social behavior requires first an understanding of how individuals process and organize information about social events, themselves, and other people.

Social cognition extends beyond the understanding of individual behavior to the level of interpersonal relationships, group processes, and intergroup behavior. First of all, individuals have cognitions *about* relationships and social groups that influence how they behave in the context of specific relationships or in the presence of particular social groups or group members. More important, cognitions about the world and ideas are *shared* in the course of interpersonal interactions and group dynamics. Social interaction provides a source of indirect knowledge or vicarious experience that extends an individual's cognitive understandings of the world beyond the confines of his or her own personal experience. Further, the knowledge that information and ideas are shared by others provides a kind of "meta-cognition" that facilitates social coordination and guides our expectations about our own and others' behaviors. In many ways, then, cognition itself *is* socially determined and *for* social functioning (Fiske, 1992; Levine, Resnick, & Higgins, 1993), as the readings in this volume suggest.

We have organized the selected reading for this volume around two broad themes. The first part deals with cognitive representations of the social world, focusing on cognitions *about* the social world. The second part deals with cognition in social interaction, showing how cognition takes place and develops within social relationships and other forms of social exchange.

REFERENCES

Fiske, S. T. (1992). Thinking is for doing: Portraits of social cognition from Daguerreotype to laserphoto. *Journal of Personality and Social Psychology, 63,* 877–889.

Levine, J. M., Resnick, L. B., & Higgins, E. T. (1993). Social foundations of cognition. *Annual Review of Psychology, 44,* 585–612.

PART I

Cognitive Representations of the Social World

Introduction

The selections in this Part are representative of current theory and research on cognitions *about* the social world. Within social psychology, mental representations of the self, other persons, and social groups are particularly important topics of study. Our readings include reviews of research on how such representations are constructed and stored in memory (Smith & Queller; Operario & Fiske), the structure and content of these social representations (Smith & Queller; Operario & Fiske; Collins & Allard), when they are activated and used in processing new social information (Martin, Strack, & Stapel; Operario & Fiske), and how they are changed by new learning (Rothbart).

Several interesting themes run through the various readings, reflecting current foci of interest in the social psychological literature. The first is the role of unconscious processes in our understanding and interpretation of the social world (see especially, Banaji, Lemm, & Carpenter; Oakes). The second – and related – theme is the role of affect and motivation in social cognition (Collins & Allard; Martin, Strack, & Stapel). Representations of the social world are inevitably laden with affect and emotion. Social categorization involves dividing the world into ingroups and outgroups – "us" and "them" – with associated motives to protect and enhance what is associated with the self. In addition to self-esteem motivations, human cognition is influenced by motives to achieve meaning and coherence (Oakes; Operario & Fiske) and to preserve important attachments to others (Collins & Allard). Each of these motives affects what information is attended to, how it is interpreted and remembered, and when it is accessed from memory.

Finally, a third important theme in the study of social cognition is the mutual relationship between mental representations of the world, acquired from past experience and learning, and the processing and interpretation of new information and social experiences (see especially Operario & Fiske; Rothbart). Past learning is stored in the form of social stereotypes, person memory, and attitudes and beliefs, all of which function as filters through which new persons and social events are perceived and understood. To some extent, these mental structures are resistant to change – a kind of cognitive conservatism that helps preserve meaning and consistency in our understanding of the world. But human beings are not simply passive information processors. We actively seek new information and modify our mental representations in the light of new experience. Further, we may become aware of how our prior knowledge may bias our perception of incoming information and actively correct for such biases in our judgments and decisions (Martin, Strack, & Stapel). The complex interactions among mental representations, new experience, and social motivations provide the challenge for modern theories of social cognition.

CHAPTER ONE

Mental Representations

Eliot R. Smith and Sarah Queller

Introduction

Many of the core concepts of social psychology, including attitudes, the self-concept, stereo-types, and impressions of other persons, are mental representations. Thus, most theories in social psychology, because they deal with these concepts, implicitly or explicitly make assumptions about how mental representations are constructed, stored in memory, changed, and used to make judgments or plan actions. This chapter aims to explicate and clarify the most popular general conceptions of mental representation and their respective assumptions, which in many theories remain implicit and unelaborated. We review four types of representation: associative networks, schemas, exemplars, and distributed representations. The review focuses on types of representations rather than on "theories," for a single theory often incorporates several types of representation for distinct purposes. For example, Wyer and Srull's (1989) well-known theory includes both associative networks and schemas.

For each of the four types of representation, the chapter will first review basic assumptions regarding representation formation and use. Next, a number of key empirical effects will be described and each mechanism's ability to account for these effects will be discussed. We will discuss explicit, intentional forms of memory as well as the more implicit, unintended effects of mental representations that occur when past experiences influence current perceptions or judgments. Through this discussion, cases where several mechanisms can equally account for existing data will become apparent. The chapter ends with some more general comments on the relations between the different types of representation.

Psychologists generally define a representation as an encoding of information in memory. An individual can create, retain, and access representations. Once accessed, the individual can then use the representation in various ways. For example, your impression of your neighbor is a mental representation that describes your feelings about her and your beliefs about what she is like. You might draw on your impression of your neighbor to describe her

Preparation of this chapter was facilitated by a research grant (R01 MH48640) and a Research Scientist Development Award (K02 MH01178) to the first author and an NRSA postdoctoral fellowship to the second author, from the National Institute of Mental Health.

to a friend, evaluate her as a potential dog-sitter, or decide how to behave when she says something offensive.

Effects of a representation can be explicit in that a previously stored representation is intentionally retrieved from memory, or implicit in that a previously stored representation affects current perceptions or judgments without intention, and perhaps even without conscious awareness (Schacter, 1987, 1994). We typically say "I remember" to denote explicit recall. In contrast, phrases like "I know" or "I believe" are common when implicit memory effects are at work. We rely on explicit memory when remembering a friend's phone number, for example. Explicit memory is often conceptualized using metaphors involving search and retrieval, as if memory was a warehouse filled with different objects. It is implicit memory, on the other hand, that causes us to avoid approaching a person who looks like our childhood tormentor, even if the resemblance is not consciously recognized. Implicit memory fits less well with the notion of search, and instead evokes metaphors like "resonance" to describe the way a stored representation subconsciously influences the way the individual processes new information and makes judgments.

The explicit/implicit memory distinction is one between tasks or ways in which memory has effects rather than between "memory systems" such as semantic versus episodic memory (Tulving, 1972). It is tempting to assume that semantic memory (general knowledge about the world) shows itself in implicit tasks whereas episodic memory (autobiographical memory for specific events located in time and place) affects explicit tasks. But this is misguided. A specific episode can have implicit memory effects. For example, in the phenomenon of repetition priming, reading "elephant" can improve a person's ability to complete the word fragment E – E – – A – T even when the person does not consciously remember reading the word (Tulving, Schacter, & Stark, 1982). In addition, general knowledge can influence explicit memories through reconstructive processes (Ross & Conway, 1986). Thus, the explicit/implicit distinction refers to *uses* of memory – the consciously recollective use of memory versus its use in performing some other task without conscious awareness of memory *per se* (Jacoby & Kelley, 1987).

We now turn to descriptions of the four types of representation, and then discuss how each type accounts for a number of explicit and implicit memory effects.

Associative Networks

Influential theories of associative network representation in non-social cognition can be found in Collins and Quillian (1969), Collins and Loftus (1975), and Anderson and Bower (1973). Within social psychology, the assumptions of associative networks have been described in a number of reviews (Carlston & Smith, 1996; Ostrom, Skowronski, & Nowak, 1994; Fiske & Taylor, 1991; Wyer & Carlston, 1994). The assumptions are as follows:

1 *Fundamental representational assumption*: Representations are constructed from discrete nodes connected by links.
2 *Interpretation of nodes*: Each node stands for a concept. Part of the meaning of each concept is derived from the pattern of linkages to other nodes.

3 *Formation of links through contiguity*: Links are formed between nodes when the concepts the nodes represent are experienced or thought about together.

4 *Link strength*: Existing links are strengthened to the extent the objects they link are experienced or thought about together. Strength changes only slowly with time.

5 *Activation and its spread*: Nodes have a property termed activation, which can vary rapidly over time. A node can become activated if it is perceptually present or actively thought about. An activated node spreads activation to connected nodes via the intervening links, increasing activation of the connected nodes. This process is called "spreading activation" (for a quantitative model, see Anderson, 1983).

6 *Activation in long-term memory*: Long-term memory is a single, large, interconnected associative structure. Short-term memory is the currently activated subset of this structure. Memory retrieval amounts to raising a node's activation level above some threshold.

7 *Links as pathways for retrieval in free recall*: Activating one node may result in the spread of enough activation to a neighboring node to elicit its retrieval. As a direct implication, the more links connected to a particular node, the greater its probability of retrieval.

Though they tend to share the above assumptions in some form, associative network models in social psychology also have some points of variation. First, activation on a node decays with time, but estimates of the rate of decay vary widely (Anderson, 1983; Higgins, 1996; Ostrom et al., 1994, p. 225). Second, some conceptualize retrieval as resulting from the parallel spread of activation across all links connected to currently activated nodes (Anderson, 1983, ch. 3), and others as sequential traversal of links where activation spreads along only one of several possible links at a time (Hastie, 1988). Third, theorists disagree regarding the conceptual level of nodes (see Wyer & Carlston, 1994, p. 7). A node could be a feature, a concept, or a whole body of knowledge ("schema"). And finally, theorists disagree as to whether the links are labeled (e.g. Fiske & Taylor, 1991, p. 297) or unlabeled (Wyer & Srull, 1989, ch. 7). Unlabeled links limit the representational power of associative structures (Carlston & Smith, 1996). For example, if links for subjects versus objects are not distinguished, the representation of the proposition "Sean killed the tiger" would be the same as that of "The tiger killed Sean."

Schemas

Influential works on schematic representation in non-social cognition include Bartlett (1932), Bruner (1957), Bransford & Franks (1971), Anderson & Pichert (1978), and Schank & Abelson (1977). Schematic mechanisms in social psychology, as reviewed by Markus & Zajonc (1985), Carlston & Smith (1996), Fiske & Taylor (1991), and Wyer & Carlston (1994), generally share the following assumptions:

1 *Fundamental representational assumption*: A schema is a structured unit of knowledge about some object or concept. Schemas represent abstract or generalized knowledge as opposed to detailed knowledge about episodes tied to a specific time or context (Fiske & Taylor, 1991; Markus & Zajonc, 1985).

2 *Activation*: A schema can be activated by explicit thought about its topic or by an encounter with relevant information. Making the schema active renders readily accessible all the structured knowledge contained therein.

3 *Level of accessibility*: A schema is likely to become activated and used to the extent that it is accessible. Accessibility is increased by recent or frequent use.

4 *Independence of units*: Schemas are independent entities. Thus, if one schema becomes active this has no necessary implications for other, related schemas.

5 *Interpretive effect of schemas*: Schemas affect the interpretation of perceptual stimuli. That is, the way ambiguous information is construed and the default values that are assumed for unavailable information are influenced by active schemas. The schema-consistent interpretation of a stimulus may be encoded in memory as if it were perceptually present in the stimulus.

6 *Attentional effect of schemas*: Activated schemas direct attention, sometimes to schema-consistent information and sometimes to unexpected or inconsistent information, depending on the circumstances.

7 *Retrieval cueing/reconstructive function of schemas*: Schemas can also influence memory retrieval and judgment. A schema can serve as a source of cues, generally facilitating retrieval of schema-consistent information. It can also serve as a guide for guessing and reconstruction when retrieval attempts fail or produce ambiguous results.

Different theorists' assumptions about schematic mechanisms differ in some respects. First, schemas are typically assumed to represent information about the typical characteristics of particular concepts, such as restaurant dining or doctors. However, in some cases, schemas are assumed to represent general rules of inference independent of any particular content domain (e.g. Heiderian balance can be viewed as a schema.) Second, theorists have modeled schema accessibility in various ways, including Storage Bins, battery, and synapse models (Wyer & Srull, 1989; Higgins, 1996).

Exemplars

Exemplar representations trace directly back to exemplar models of categorization, such as the seminal work by Medin and Schaffer (1978). These models downplay the role of abstractions (such as summaries of the average characteristics of categories) and emphasize instead the role of specific experiences. In non-social cognition, influential works include Brooks (1978), Jacoby & Brooks (1984), and Whittlesea (1987), and in social psychology see Lewicki (1985), Smith (1988, 1990), and Linville, Fischer, & Salovey (1989). Exemplar mechanisms share the following core ideas:

1 *Fundamental representational assumption*: Representations record information about specific stimuli or experiences, rather than abstracted summaries or generalizations. Such a representation may be constructed on the basis of veridical perception of a stimulus object, misperception of it, inference about it, imagination of it, second-hand communication about it, etc.

2 *Representations record feature co-occurrences*: Representations of specific stimuli record patterns of feature co-occurrences. Such representations support people's observed sensitivity to the correlation of features within categories (e.g. they know that small birds are more likely to sing than large ones; Malt & Smith, 1984). In contrast, a schema would contain only information about the typical values of features (i.e. that birds are typically small and that they typically sing), not about feature co-occurrences.

3 *Activation of exemplars by retrieval cues*: Retrieval cues (whether self-generated or external in origin) activate all stored exemplars in parallel. Each exemplar is activated to the extent that it is similar to the retrieval cue. Activation is not synonymous with retrieval, but instead makes the activated exemplars available to influence judgments or impressions (Hintzman, 1986).

4 *Parallel on-line computation*: When a new stimulus is to be evaluated, judged, or categorized, it is compared in parallel to many activated exemplar traces. Similarly, when generalizations about a type of stimulus are required they can be computed by activating all exemplars of that type and summarizing them.

5 *Effects on interpretation, attention, and judgment*: The effects of an activated mass of exemplars are assumed to be the same as those attributed to schemas. That is, the activated exemplars influence interpretation, attention, retrieval, and reconstruction at a preconscious level.

Exemplar theories differ regarding whether only exemplars are stored or, alternately, whether both abstractions and exemplars are stored.

Distributed or PDP representations

Detailed introductions to the newest category of models of mental representation, which have been termed distributed memory, connectionist, or parallel distributed processing (PDP) models, can be found in Churchland & Sejnowski (1992), Smolensky (1988), Rumelhart, McClelland, et al. (1986), as well as McClelland, Rumelhart, et al. (1986). Smith (1996) provides a brief overview oriented toward social psychologists. Distributed representation generally embodies these assumptions:

1 *Fundamental representational assumption*: A concept or object is represented by a distributed representation, where each representation is a different pattern of activation across a common set of simple nodes or units within a network. A useful analogy is a TV screen. No individual pixel has any specific meaning but different patterns of illumination over the entire array of pixels can produce a large number of different meaningful images. This assumption contrasts with associative representations, where individual nodes are semantically meaningful.

2 *Unity of representation and process*: A connectionist network is responsible for both processing and storing information. In contrast, other types of representation require additional assumptions about processes that operate on static representations.

3 *Computing with distributed representations*: Units are interconnected and send activation to each other across weighted connections. A given unit's activation level at a particular

time is a function of its previous activation level as well as the total activation flowing to it from other units across the weighted connections. Thus, the pattern of activation taken on by a given set of units is determined by the initial inputs to the network of units and the weights on the inter-unit connections.

4 *Positive or negative activation*: In most models, both the weights on inter-unit connections and the activation that flows between units can be either positive or negative. Negative activation decreases the activity level of the unit to which it flows (i.e. it has an inhibitory effect). This assumption contrasts with most associative-network models, in which "spreading activation" is always positive.

5 *Learning*: Connection weights are initially assigned random values, which are then shaped by a learning procedure that incrementally changes the weights as the network processes many stimuli.

6 *Connection weights as long-term memory*: The weights on the connections are assumed to change only slowly, in contrast to the quickly changing activation values. Thus, the connection weights are the repository of the network's long-term memory.

7 *Pattern transformation*: Networks with a feed-forward architecture (in which all connections run in one direction from inputs to outputs) can transform representations from one domain into another (Anderson, 1995). Examples are the transformation of input patterns representing behaviors into output patterns representing trait concepts, or inputs of letter sequences into output patterns representing a word's meaning or pronunciation. When the input pattern is presented to input units, activation flows over the connections and eventually produces a new pattern of activation on the network's output units.

8 *Pattern completion or memory*: Networks using a different type of architecture (recurrent connections that link units bidirectionally) can do pattern completion. After the network learns a set of patterns, when the inputs constitute a subset or an approximation of one of those patterns, flows of activation cause the network to reconstruct the entire pattern as output. Pattern completion can be viewed as a form of memory. However, the potential patterns are not explicitly "stored" anywhere. Instead, the network stores connection strengths that allow many patterns to be reproduced given the right cues.

9 *Reconstruction, not retrieval*: When a network must encode several patterns, the connection strengths are a compromise. Hence, reproduction of any given pattern from input cues will be imperfect and will be influenced by the other patterns encoded in the network. As new patterns are learned by the network, the representation of previously learned patterns may change. Thus, distributed representations are *evoked* or *reconstructed* rather than *searched for* or *retrieved* in invariant form (McClelland, Rumelhart, & Hinton, 1986, p. 31).

10 *Parallel constraint satisfaction*: In a network in which bidirectional flows of activation between units are possible, the network can be thought of as converging on a final pattern of activation that simultaneously satisfies the constraints represented by the current inputs (representing external stimuli) and the network weights (representing learned constraints) (Barnden, 1995). Constraint satisfaction is "soft"; learned constraints and current inputs may conflict and each can only be satisfied as well as possible.

There are also points on which various models differ. Some related models accept most of these assumptions but use localist representational schemes in which single nodes have meaningful interpretations (Thorpe, 1995). A node may be interpreted as a feature, an object or concept, or a whole proposition. A connection between nodes is interpreted as encoding past experiences of covariation between the nodes (if nodes represent features or objects) or logical constraints such as consistency or inconsistency between propositions (if nodes represent propositions). Such networks perform parallel satisfaction of multiple constraints (Read & Marcus-Newhall, 1993; Kunda & Thagard, 1996). However, they lack other properties that stem from distributed representation, such as the ability to learn to represent new concepts (new concepts require the explicit addition of new nodes).

Within the class of distributed representation models, literally hundreds of competing models have been proposed with various architectures (numbers and interconnection patterns of nodes), activation equations, and learning rules (see Hertz, Krogh, & Palmer, 1991). In contrast, in each of the three types of representation considered to this point – exemplar, schematic, and associative network – there are perhaps a handful of serious, well-specified competing models. The properties of these diverse distributed models are being actively explored in ongoing theoretical and simulation studies.

Key Memory Effects in Social Psychology

With a basic understanding of the four memory mechanisms in hand, we now turn to describing how each of these mechanisms might account for a number of established effects of mental representations.

Related concepts or contextual factors as retrieval cues

One aspect of memory involves how information that has been learned in the past is retrieved at a later date. Suppose you are introduced to Arturo at a party. How can you recall Arturo's name when you meet him again? This amounts to retrieval of some information (name) from associated information (his appearance). Or how can you recall that he was among the people who attended that particular party? This is retrieval based on contextual cues (the party). These types of memory retrieval are central in most explicit memory tests including paired-associate and list-learning paradigms.

Associative representation   Nodes representing concepts that are perceived together or thought about together become linked. When one of the concepts is experienced later, its node becomes active. Activation then spreads across the link to the associated node, potentially raising the activation of this node above the threshold required for retrieval. In this manner, spreading activation explains how related concepts or contextual factors can act as retrieval cues.

The counter-intuitive finding that people recall more behaviors that are inconsistent with their impression of a person than behaviors that are consistent with their impression (Hastie & Kumar, 1979) has been explained in terms of associative representations. When an impression-inconsistent behavior is encountered, the perceiver may try to resolve or explain away the inconsistency. In doing so, the perceiver thinks about the relation of the impression-inconsistent behavior to previously stored impression-consistent and inconsistent behaviors. This process establishes additional links between the inconsistent behavior and other behaviors. These additional links provide more paths along which activation can spread, thus increasing the probability of retrieval of an impression-inconsistent behavior relative to that of recalling an impression-consistent behavior (Hastie, 1980; Srull, 1981).

Recognition of expectation-inconsistent items is also enhanced relative to expectation-consistent items, but only when recognition sensitivity measures are used (measures that correct for a guessing bias; Stangor & McMillan, 1992). Perceivers will guess they have seen consistent items before even when they do not actually recall having seen them, leading to a recognition advantage for consistent items when this bias is not taken into account. While associative representations deal nicely with the finding that expectation-inconsistent items are better *recalled*, the associative representation does not offer an explanation for why *recognition* of expectation-inconsistent behaviors is also enhanced. In recall, a cue is activated and activation spreads across links until an item reaches sufficient activation for retrieval. However, in recognition, an item is presented and the perceiver is asked if he or she previously studied the item. Inter-item associative links are not required as retrieval pathways when the item is directly thought about, so the inconsistency effect for recognition does not seem to be well explained by associative memory mechanisms.

Schematic representation   Schematic representations can easily account for the retrieval of items of information that are meaningfully related – that is, are part of the same schema – such as "bread" and "butter." Encountering one of these items activates the schema, which includes the other item. However, schematic models have more difficulty in accounting for a newly learned association (formed by meeting someone for the first time). One could assume that a new schema representing the person is created, but accounts of schema construction (as opposed to retrieval and use) are underdeveloped or entirely absent in most schema theories. In any case, one could argue that forming a new schema to represent a specific occurrence violates the definition of a schema as a representation of abstract, generic knowledge. The definition of schemas as abstract and generic also leads to the conclusion that schema representations do not account well for contextual cueing of retrieval.

Exemplar representation   An exemplar representation may preserve information about the specific context in which a stimulus was encountered as well as information about the stimulus characteristics. Therefore an exemplar representation (e.g. incorporating a person's appearance, name, and context) could account for these types of explicit memory retrieval. However, exemplars have more often been invoked to account for implicit rather than explicit memory effects.

Distributed representation   When a cue consisting of a partial pattern is presented as input to the network, retrieval occurs via reconstruction of the complete pattern that best satisfies the constraints of the cues provided as input (e.g. Chappell & Humphreys, 1994). In this explanation, a number of stimulus attributes and contextual details are all components of one large pattern, so any of these can act as retrieval cues for the entire pattern.

Accessibility

One important property of memory is that all mental constructs are not equally likely to be used. One determinant of whether a construct is applied is its fit to a current stimulus (Bruner, 1957; Higgins, 1996). Beyond that, mental representations vary in *accessibility*, affecting how readily a perceiver can apply them to the processing of an input. Thus, for example, a professor might tend to evaluate all new acquaintances in terms of intelligence. Intelligence would be an accessible construct for this person.

Associative representation   In associative representations, increased accessibility in response to recent use is explained as residual activation on a recently used node. This residual activation puts the node closer to the threshold activation for conscious recall and thus facilitates retrieval of the recently used concept. Increased accessibility in response to frequent use of a concept is explained in terms of link strength. The more a concept is thought about in relation to other concepts, the stronger the links between the corresponding nodes become. Since activation flows more readily over stronger links, retrieval via spreading activation is more likely for frequently used concepts.

Applying these principles, Fazio (1986) suggests that attitudes are represented by an attitude object node linked to an evaluative node. If the attitude is expressed frequently, the link can get strong enough that simply perceiving the object can result in automatic activation of the evaluation. This in turn can lead to evaluative priming effects where a prime facilitates processing of same-valence target items relative to opposite-valence targets (Fazio, Sanbonmatsu, Powell, & Kardes, 1986).

Schema representation   Higgins, Rholes, & Jones (1977) showed that recently used traits are more accessible and thus more likely to impact judgments. This finding can be interpreted in terms of increased accessibility of a trait schema due to recent use. In contrast to the short-lived effects of priming, chronic accessibility of a schema is assumed to result from frequent use of a schema over a long period of time (Higgins, King, & Mavin, 1982). For example, some people habitually interpret new information in terms of its implications for gender (Frable & Bem, 1985).

Effects of recency and frequency of use on schema accessibility do not follow directly from the basic assumptions of schema representation. Instead, schema theories have incorporated additional assumptions to account for accessibility. Wyer & Srull (1980) account for accessibility using a "Storage Bin" metaphor. Schemas are thought of as stacked in a Storage Bin and a search for a schema that is applicable to the current stimulus occurs in a top-down fashion. A schema that is nearer the top of the Storage Bin is more accessible. They accounted for the effects of recent use by assuming that a schema was replaced at the top of the Storage Bin after each use, increasing the schema's probability of future use. To account for effects of frequent use, a copying function was later added (Wyer & Srull, 1989), such that when a schema is used, one copy stays in the original location in the Storage Bin and another copy is placed at the top. For frequency effects to be observed, the copies below the top must contribute to accessibility so the probability of using an applicable schema in the top-down search was restricted to $p < 1$ in the revised model.

A "synapse" metaphor was suggested by Higgins, Bargh, & Lombardi (1985) that likened the activation of a schema to a charge that decays with time. Use of a schema fully charges it with activation. The activation subsequently decays. More recently used concepts have more residual activation and are thus more accessible. In order to account for the effect of frequent use on accessibility, the "synapse" model proposes that frequency of use decreases the rate of decay of activation. Note that these authors proposed two distinct mechanisms to deal with recency and frequency effects.

Exemplar representation   Frequent or recent use of a concept adds additional exemplar representations to the store in memory. This means that when these exemplars are activated (when a new judgment concerning the concept is required) their summed impact on judgment or memory retrieval is greater. Smith (1988) showed that Hintzman's (1986) MINERVA exemplar model could account for accessibility effects through this mechanism.

Distributed representation   Recall that distributed representations are formed through incremental changes in the common set of weights in a connectionist network. If a particular stimulus is presented frequently, the weights will be repeatedly adjusted, becoming better able to reconstruct the pattern corresponding to that stimulus. Consequently, the network will more accurately process frequently encountered patterns compared to less frequently encountered patterns. Recent exposure will also facilitate pattern recognition. In this case, the advantage in accessibility derives from a lessened opportunity for subsequent weight changes that would move the weight values away from those that best process the recent stimulus. Smith and DeCoster (1998) showed that typical effects of recency and frequency on accessibility can be modeled in a connectionist network through this mechanism.

Semantic priming

Semantic priming occurs when perceiving or thinking about one concept makes it easier to process related concepts. Thus, for example, the target word "nurse" is more quickly identified following the prime word "doctor" than following "tree" (Meyer & Schvaneveldt, 1971). The priming effect only lasts a brief period of time (Anderson, 1983; Ostrom et al., 1994, p. 225; Higgins, 1996) and it can be wiped out through the presentation of a single word intervening between prime and target (Masson, 1991; Ratcliff & McKoon, 1988). We know this is an implicit process because it occurs when the prime to target interval is too short for strategic generation of expectations about what is coming next (Neely, 1977) and because it occurs even when the prime is presented subliminally (Wittenbrink, Judd, & Park, 1997).

Associative representation   If two nodes are connected with a link then activation from one node can spread across the link to the associated node. When the prime node is activated, the linked target node increases in activation but, unlike the case of explicit recall, the node does not reach the threshold necessary for retrieval. Instead, the target becomes more retrievable in a subsequent task. (Although similar, the explanation of semantic priming should not be confused with that of recency. With recency, the target concept is directly activated and becomes more accessible at a later time. With semantic priming, a concept related to the target concept is directly activated and activation is spread to produce the sub-threshold activation of the target concept.)

Associative representations typically have been relied upon in explaining priming phenomena within social psychology. For example, white subjects responded more quickly to positive trait words following the prime word "white" than following the prime word "black" (Dovidio, Evans, & Tyler, 1986). The associative explanation is that "white" is semantically linked to positive concepts to a greater extent than is "black." This finding and the related suppositions about representation have relevance for racial stereotyping. Another effect that has been explained in associative terms is evaluative priming (Fazio et al., 1986). Processing of an evaluatively laden prime ("cockroach") results in facilitated processing of evaluatively similar targets ("death") and inhibited processing of evaluatively dissimilar targets ("beautiful"). This finding is robust, although there is debate regarding whether it holds only for objects about which the perceiver holds fairly strong attitudes (Bargh, Chaiken, Raymond, & Hymes, 1996; Fazio, 1993).

Schema representation   Semantic priming in schema representations occurs because a schema-relevant stimulus can activate the whole schema. Thus, for example, if the word "doctor" activates the schema for hospital or medical care, processing of the word "nurse" might be facilitated since it would be activated as part of that schema. In contrast, the word "tree" would not activate a hospital schema so "tree" would not facilitate processing of "nurse."

Exemplar representation   A mass of similar exemplars can function like a schematic general knowledge structure, since the respects in which they are similar reinforce each other while contextual or nonessential differences cancel out (Hintzman, 1986). Therefore numerous exemplars of medical care or hospital situations, most of which included both doctors and nurses, might account for semantic priming in the same way as a "medical care" schema.

Distributed representation   Semantically related concepts tend to share features and, thus, semantically related prime/target pairs will have overlapping patterns of activation in a distributed network. To the extent that the target's pattern of activation overlaps with the previously processed prime's pattern of activation, the network will more quickly and accurately process the target pattern. As activation is a short-lived property, the distributed mechanism accurately predicts that the priming effect should be wiped out by presentation of an unrelated stimulus between prime and target (Masson, 1991).

Repetition priming

Processing of a stimulus is facilitated when the same stimulus has been processed in the same way on a previous occasion. This phenomenon is long lasting (as long as months: Sloman,

Hayman, Ohta, Law, & Tulving, 1988), in contrast with short-lived semantic priming effects. The previous exposure does not have to be consciously remembered for repetition priming to occur (Schacter, 1987; Smith, Stewart, & Buttram, 1992). For example, Smith, Stewart, & Buttram (1992) had subjects quickly decide if each of hundreds of behaviors were friendly or intelligent. Some of the behaviors were repeated and some were not. Repetition of behaviors resulted in faster judgment times, even when the delay following the initial exposure was a week. Faster judgment times occurred even when subjects could not recall the previous exposure to the behavior. Because repetition priming is so long lasting, it cannot be explained in terms of residual activation because in all four types of representation, activation is relatively short lived.

Associative representation   Repetition priming can be explained by assuming that a new association is formed linking the specific stimulus being judged or processed to the results of that processing. For example, attributes of a particular behavior would become associated with a trait like "friendly." When the same behavior is encountered again, activation would spread to the trait concept, facilitating a repetition of the same judgment.

Schema representation   The basic assumptions of schema representation do not readily lead to an explanation for repetition priming. Activation of a trait schema might occur when the trait judgments are made in the Smith, Stewart, & Buttram (1992) study, but the effect would be to speed *all* later judgments using that trait, rather than only judgments about specific repeated behaviors (which is what is empirically observed).

Exemplar representation   When an exemplar is judged in a particular way (say a behavior is judged on a trait) that judgment becomes part of the exemplar representation that is stored in memory (e.g. the trait implications become part of the behavior representation). This illustrates the general principle that exemplar representations are always stored *as processed* or interpreted by the perceiver, not in veridical form (Whittlesea & Dorken, 1993). When the same behavior is presented again at a later time, if the exemplar can be retrieved from memory the judgment is already available. Consequently, a second judgment is performed faster than an identical first judgment (Logan, 1988; Smith, 1990).

Distributed representation   Weight changes after exposure to a specific pattern will facilitate later processing of the same pattern. However, as additional patterns are presented to the network, they cause further weight changes, overwriting those that provide an advantage to the repeated stimulus. This argument is similar to that for accessibility of a pattern due to recent use. (See Wiles & Humphreys, 1993, pp. 157–163 for a quantitative analysis.)

Filling in default values and resolving ambiguity

Theorists have long understood that perceivers do not process new information in a strictly unbiased manner but, instead, rely on prior knowledge to help make sense of new information (Arbib, 1995; Bartlett, 1932; Bruner, 1957; Markus & Zajonc, 1985; Minsky, 1975;

Neisser, 1976). Prior knowledge is helpful in resolving ambiguities in incoming information or filling in default values for unobserved characteristics. These effects of prior experience are implicit: we don't "remember," for example, that the bird we saw standing in the tall grass had feet, we just "know" it. As an example, imagine observing a car that does not slow down as a pedestrian crosses in front of it. The pedestrian raises his hand and a moment later, the driver extends his arm out the window. They might be waving at each other or they might be exchanging rude gestures.

Associative representation   Spreading activation across links makes linked nodes available for use in resolving ambiguity. In an associative framework, the way you interpret a situation and make assumptions about unknown aspects would depend on the concepts you have strongly linked together based on past experience (Anderson, 1983). If you thought the driver had been careless, links from that concept to the concept of anger might lead you to interpret the hand gestures as insults. You might also think that the driver shouted a curse, even though you could not hear the driver.

Schema representation   Schemas are activated in an all or none fashion and the content of an activated schema is applied to incoming information in an implicit manner. The ready explanation of the resolution of ambiguous information and the use of default values to fill in missing information have led to the popularity of schema models within social psychology. Stereotypes are often conceived of as schemas that allow us to generate expectations about types of people. For example, a girl who turned in a mixed performance on a test was rated as more academically talented by subjects who believed she came from an upper-middle-class background than by subjects who thought she was working-class (Darley & Gross, 1983). Similarly, scripts are schemas that store generalized knowledge about a type of event, such as going to a birthday party or dining at a restaurant (Schank & Abelson, 1977). If a script for "road rage" is activated by the driver-pedestrian encounter, it may lead to interpretations and inferences that are consistent with an angry interchange.

Exemplar representation   The common characteristics of the mass of exemplars called to mind when making a judgment may be applied to the novel stimulus (Hintzman, 1986; Smith & Zarate, 1992). The effect is similar to that of a schema and the difference is only that a set of exemplars serve as the prior knowledge instead of a schema that contains generalized knowledge.

Distributed representation   The filling in of default values and resolution of ambiguities occurs in distributed representations through the flow of activation in a connectionist network whose weights have been tuned by past experiences (Rumelhart, Smolensky, McClelland, & Hinton, 1986). The input to the network may be a partial pattern with only a few characteristics filled in. But as activation flows through the connection weights, the network outputs a complete pattern that best satisfies the constraints of the input and the knowledge currently stored in the connection weights (Smith & DeCoster, 1998). Thus, default values are automatically generated and ambiguities are resolved through constraint satisfaction in distributed networks.

Flexibility and context sensitivity

Recent thinking in social psychology has emphasized flexibility and context sensitivity in the areas of the self-concept (Markus & Wurf, 1987; Linville & Carlston, 1994; Higgins, Van Hook, & Dorfman, 1988; Turner, Oakes, Haslam, & McGarty, 1994), attitudes (Wilson & Hodges, 1992; Tourangeau & Rasinski, 1988; Strack & Martin, 1987; Schwarz & Clore, 1983; Wilson, 1990), and even stereotypes (Bodenhausen, Schwarz, Bless, & Wanke, 1995). Not only the accessibility of a representation, but the content of the representation can be altered by contextual information. That is, particular features are emphasized or de-emphasized in different contexts. In addition, Barsalou (1987) has shown that ad hoc concepts such as "things that might fall on your head" are structured in the same way as concepts with which one has had a great deal of experience and prior learning. Extending this finding to the social domain, people may easily generate stereotypes (summaries of and feelings about a group's typical characteristics) for previously unconsidered groups such as "people who fly only at night" or "adopted Latinos."

Associative representation   Associative representations are flexible to the extent that distinct sets of cues may activate different sets of associates. Thus, for example, the cue "bird" plus the cue "barnyard" might activate the concept "chicken," whereas the cue "bird" plus the cue "suburban backyard" may activate the concept "robin" (see Barsalou, 1987). This is consistent with research showing that although people rate "robin" as a better exemplar of the bird category than "chicken" without context, they rate "chicken" higher in a barnyard context. Interestingly, however, if the cue "bird" alone activates the concept "robin," in associative terms it seems that the compound cue "bird" plus "barnyard" should activate "robin" in addition to "chicken." (The same activation should spread from the "bird" node regardless of whether the "barnyard" node is also active.) Only if assumptions about spreading inhibition as well as activation are added might the "chicken" concept be retrieved without also retrieving the "robin" concept. Classic models using associative representations and spreading activation did not invoke inhibition (e.g. Anderson, 1983). However, recent associative formulations within social psychology have assumed that associative links can be inhibitory as well as facilitative (e.g. Carlston, 1994).

Schema representation   Schematic representations have difficulty accounting for context sensitivity. One would have to postulate, for instance, that distinct "bird-in-suburbs" and "bird-in-barnyard" schemas exist instead of a single "bird" schema. However, this leads to an explosion of the number of concepts that must be represented. Alternatively one could assume that general "bird" and "barnyard" schemas are combined on-line in some fashion to yield the new context-specific concept representation, but models of schema combination have received little attention (Wisniewski, 1997), and none in social psychology.

Exemplar representation   Exemplar representations can accommodate flexible use of prior knowledge (Smith, 1990). Different sets of exemplars may be activated when making different judgments, depending on context or other details of the specific set of cues provided. Judgments are then based on the activated set of exemplars.

Distributed representation   Distributed representations also allow fluid use of prior knowledge. The set of cues provided can include incidentally activated goals (e.g. enhancing
self-esteem), context, mood, perceptually present objects, and/or objects of current thought.
All of these cues are represented in the common set of weight values so retrieval is influenced
by all of them (Rumelhart, Smolensky, McClelland, & Hinton, 1986; Clark, 1993).

Dissociations between recall, recognition, and judgment

If different memory tasks such as recall, recognition, and judgment all access the same
underlying representational structure, one would expect dependence between the different
tasks. For example, if a specific representation can be demonstrated to influence judgment,
such as through a priming effect, the representation would be expected also to be available to
explicit retrieval. However, this is not always the case. For example, priming manipulations
often have similar or even greater effects on judgment when they cannot be consciously
remembered as when they are explicitly retrievable (Lombardi, Higgins, & Bargh, 1987;
Martin, Seta, & Crelia, 1990). And although a person might be judged to be honest, recall
of the person's behaviors might include a large number of dishonest behaviors (Hastie &
Kumar, 1979).

These and other dissociations have been shown to be a function of how the information
was processed at learning (Carlston & Smith, 1996; Hastie & Park, 1986; Jacoby, 1983).
For example, whether a target is processed perceptually (read the word "honest") or conceptually (read several honest behaviors and generate the relevant trait) will affect performance
on different memory tasks. Fragment completion (complete the word "H – N – – T") is
more strongly enhanced following a perceptual task, whereas recall (recall the trait words
from the previous task) and category accessibility (read an ambiguous behavior and pick a
trait that fits) show greater effects of a previous conceptual task (Smith & Branscombe,
1988). For a review of dissociations among implicit and explicit memory measures in non-
social cognition, see Richardson-Klavehn & Bjork (1988) and Hintzman (1990).

Associative representation   With associative representations, dissociations occur when different cognitive structures are drawn on for different tasks. As Hastie and Park (1986) suggest,
perceivers create different types of representations in memory depending on whether they
initially process the incoming information in a "memory-based" fashion or in an "on-line"
fashion. "Memory-based" processing initially stores representations of the input stimuli.
When a judgment is called for, the stimulus details are recalled and summarized at the time
of retrieval. In this case, recall of the details and the judgment should correspond, since the
judgment is based directly on what can be recalled. With "on-line" processing, abstraction or
summarization of the stimuli occurs as the stimuli are encountered, resulting in a summary
representation as well as stimulus-specific details being stored in memory. When a judgment
is required, the summary representation is accessed. When recall is performed, the detailed
representations are accessed. Dissociation is explained by the use of these two distinct representations that may not contain exactly the same content. Similarly, Wyer and Gordon
(1984) suggested that people store a target's behaviors in both trait-based associative clusters

and an evaluative summary, stored independently in the "Storage Bin." An evaluative judgment task accesses the evaluative summary, whereas explicit recall of behaviors accesses the trait based clusters. Because the two tasks access different cognitive representations, there may be little relationship between the judgment and the behaviors recalled.

Schema representation　　As noted earlier, models of schema formation are typically weak or underdeveloped, making schema models poor candidates for explaining phenomena that involve the creation of new representations. Leaving this issue aside, one could explain dissociations by suggesting that people form multiple schemas organized along different lines (as in the Wyer & Gordon model just described) as they process stimulus inputs.

Exemplar representation　　Dissociations are assumed to be due to the distinct subsets of exemplars that are activated by the different cues provided by different tasks (such as implicit versus explicit memory tasks; Roediger & McDermott, 1993). Thus the exemplar representations that can be explicitly retrieved (e.g. the members of a category that one can recall or recognize) may not be the same as those that implicitly influence categorization judgments.

Distributed representation　　Dissociations among different memory tasks may be due to differences in tasks that cause the perceiver to draw on distinct network representations. For example, Wiles and Humphreys (1993) suggest that explicit recall and semantic priming draw on pattern completion networks that reconstruct the features of past stimuli when partial cues are presented. In contrast, they suggest that repetition priming is due to changes in weights in pattern transformation networks that translate from perceptual (e.g. visual) to internal (e.g. semantic) types of representations. This proposal explains why repetition priming is specific to a given perceptual modality such as visual or auditory, while semantic priming is not modality specific. Another explanation for dissociations in distributed representations is that different cues might be presented in different types of memory tasks and this may give rise to independence between tasks (Humphreys, Bain, & Pike, 1989).

Summary and Conclusions

The two types of representation most frequently invoked in social psychology are associative and schema representations. Comparison of these two is informative. First, although associative representations focus on the acquisition of new knowledge as well as its use, schema models emphasize the use of existing general knowledge. Loosely, we might say that the construction of new associative representations accounts for episodic memory for particular events or stimuli, whereas schematic representations seem better aligned with semantic or generic memory. In other words, these different types of representation may be complementary rather than competing. Indeed, a number of theorists (McClelland, McNaughton, & O'Reilly, 1995; Humphreys, Bain, & Pike, 1989; Hirst, 1989; Masson, 1989; Macleod & Bassili, 1989; Squire, 1994; Schacter, 1994; Moscovitch, 1994) have recently posited two functionally independent memory systems. One system handles one-shot learning by constructing new representational structures (akin to social psychological assumptions regarding associative representations). The other system learns slowly, gradually building representations of the general characteristics of objects or events. These dual memory theories are supported by a number of psychological and neuropsychological studies of different types. For example, evidence suggests that rapid, episodic learning is mediated by the hippocampus and related structures whereas slow, semantic learning relies on cortical structures (Squire, 1994).

Comparison between associative and schematic representations also suggests that associative representations can mimic schema representations. A schema can be conceptualized in associative terms as a set of units that are so strongly interlinked that activating any one of them necessarily activates them all (Ostrom et al., 1994, p. 221; Anderson, 1983). As discussed above, exemplar and distributed representations can also mimic the effects of schemas that are typically emphasized in social psychology, such as using prior knowledge to interpret new inputs. Thus, we suggest that in social psychology, a schema is more a description of a *function* that can be performed by a learned knowledge representation, rather than a description of an actual entity inside our heads.

In fact, associative and exemplar representations as well as schemas may be more descriptions of memory function than they are accounts of actual underlying representations and processes. This consideration raises a distinction between associative, schema, and exemplar representations on the one hand and distributed representations on the other. The former three have all been formulated based on specific empirical phenomena. That is, a function was observed (e.g. accessibility) and a mechanism of memory was proposed to account for that function (e.g. position in a Storage Bin). This leads to a one-to-one correspondence between empirical evidence and theoretical mechanisms that makes theories relatively clear and understandable. Distributed representations tend to proceed in the opposite direction. Instead of starting from psychological findings, theorists who use distributed representations begin with a theoretical vocabulary (computationally simple units and interconnections, modeled very loosely on the properties of biological neurons). They then use this vocabulary to build specific models and see whether they can replicate known memory findings. It is possible that distributed representations may turn out to more often predict novel empirical effects, precisely because they are not originally formulated to provide a one-to-one correspondence with known phenomena.

This distinction between empirical observations and theoretical vocabulary as starting points for modeling may be regarded as a distinction between levels of theory (Smith, 1998; Smolensky, 1988). If a higher level of theory is sufficient to explain social psychological phenomena of interest, it might be argued that we need not consider the lower-level details of mental representations. However, there are several counterarguments. First, the details of how mental representations are formed and used necessarily constrain higher level theories. As an analogy, a theory about the chemical reactions between molecules will not stand if it is inconsistent with known properties of atoms. Second, new mechanisms display new properties. Distributed representations are certainly new to social psychology but have already been shown to generate novel predictions regarding social psychological issues such as accessibility (DeCoster & Smith, 1998) and stereotype learning and change (Queller & Smith, 1998). Third, distributed representations provide a dynamic approach that emphasizes learning. Many of the most interesting social psychological questions – about attitude change and stereotype change, for example – involve *changes* in representation. Finally, modeling at a lower level can lead to greater integration and parsimony. Traditionally within social psychology, theories have been developed and refined to account for the specifics of a relatively small domain. Taken to extremes, this approach can lead to a profusion of fragmentary mini-theories that have unclear relations with one another and no common basis of assumptions. Connectionist models offer the possibility of a broad integration not only within social psychology, but beyond, including areas of cognition, perception, development, and neuroscience (Elman, Bates, Johnson, Karmiloff-Smith, Parisi, & Plunkett, 1995; McClelland, McNaughton, & O'Reilly, 1995).

REFERENCES

Anderson, J. A. (1995). Associative networks. In M. A. Arbib (Ed.), *Handbook of brain theory and neural networks* (pp. 102–107). Cambridge, MA: MIT Press.

Anderson, J. R. (1983). *The architecture of cognition.* Cambridge, MA: Harvard University Press.

Anderson, J. R., & Bower, G. H. (1973). *Human associative memory.* Washington, DC: Winston & Sons.

Anderson, R. C., & Pichert, J. W. (1978). Recall of previously unrecallable information following a shift in perspective. *Journal of Verbal Learning and Verbal Behavior, 17,* 1–12.

Arbib, M. A. (1995). Schema theory. In M. A. Arbib (Ed.), *Handbook of brain theory and neural networks* (pp. 830–834). Cambridge, MA: MIT Press.

Bargh, J. A., & Thein, R. D. (1985). Individual construct accessibility, person memory, and the recall–judgment link: The case of information overload. *Journal of Personality and Social Psychology, 49,* 1129–1146.

Bargh, J. A., Lombardi, W. J., & Higgins, E. T. (1988). Automaticity of chronically accessible constructs in person X situation effects on person perception: It's just a matter of time. *Journal of Personality and Social Psychology, 55,* 599–605.

Bargh, J. A., Lombardi, W. J., & Tota, M. E. (1986). The additive nature of chronic and temporary sources of construct accessibility. *Journal of Personality and Social Psychology, 50,* 869–879.

Bargh, J. A., Chaiken, S., Raymond, P., & Hymes, C. (1996). The automatic evaluation effect: Unconditional automatic attitude activation with a pronunciation task. *Journal of Experimental Social Psychology, 22,* 104–128.

Barnden, J. A. (1995). Artificial intelligence and neural networks. In M. A. Arbib (Ed.), *Handbook of brain theory and neural networks* (pp. 98–102). Cambridge, MA: MIT Press.

Barsalou, L. (1987). The instability of graded structure: Implications for the nature of concepts. In U. Neisser (Ed.), *Concepts and conceptual development* (pp. 101–140). Cambridge, UK: Cambridge University Press.

Bartlett, F. C. (1932). *Remembering.* Cambridge, UK: Cambridge University Press.

Bodenhausen, G. V., Schwarz, N., Bless, H., & Wanke, M. (1995). Effects of atypical exemplars on racial beliefs: Enlightened racism or generalized appraisals? *Journal of Experimental Social Psychology, 31,* 48–63.

Bransford, J. D., & Franks, J. J. (1971). The abstraction of linguistic ideas. *Cognitive Psychology, 2,* 331–350.

Brooks, L. (1978). Nonanalytic concept formation and memory for instances. In E. Rosch & B. B. Lloyd (Eds.), *Cognition and categorization* (pp. 169–211). Hillsdale, NJ: Lawrence Erlbaum Associates.

Bruner, J. S. (1957). Going beyond the information given. In H. Gruber, G. Terrell, & M. Wertheimer (Eds.), *Contemporary approaches to cognition*. Cambridge, MA: Harvard University Press.

Carlston, D. E. (1994). Associated systems theory: A systematic approach to cognitive representations of persons. In T. K. Srull & R. S. Wyer (Eds.), *Advances in social cognition: A dual process model of impression formation* Vol. 7 (pp. 1–78). Hillsdale, NJ: Lawrence Erlbaum Associates.

Carlston, D. E., & Smith, E. R. (1996). Principles of mental representation. In E. T. Higgins & A. Kruglanski (Eds.), *Social psychology: Handbook of basic principles* (pp. 184–210). New York: Guilford Press.

Chappell, M., & Humphreys, M. S. (1994). An auto-associative neural network for sparse representations: Analysis and application to models of recognition and cued recall. *Psychological Review, 101*, 103–128.

Churchland, P. S., & Sejnowski, T. J. (1992). *The computational brain*. Cambridge, MA: MIT Press.

Clark, A. (1993). *Associative engines: Connectionism, concepts, and representational change*. Cambridge, MA: MIT Press.

Collins, A., & Loftus, E. F. (1975). A spreading activation theory of semantic memory. *Journal of Verbal Learning and Verbal Behavior, 8*, 240–247.

Collins, A. M., & Quillian, M. R. (1969). Retrieval time from semantic memory. *Journal of Verbal Learning and Verbal Behavior, 8*, 240–247.

Darley, J. M., & Gross, P. H. (1983). A hypothesis-confirming bias in labelling effects. *Journal of Personality and Social Psychology, 44*, 20–33.

DeCoster, J., & Smith, E. R. (1998). Rapid recovery of accessibility: Empirical tests of a novel prediction of a connectionist memory. Unpublished paper, Purdue University.

Dovidio, J. F., Evans, N., & Tyler, R. B. (1986). Racial stereotypes: The content of their cognitive representations. *Journal of Experimental Social Psychology, 22*, 22–37.

Elman, J. L., Bates, E. A., Johnson, M. H., Karmiloff-Smith, A., Parisi, D., & Plunkett, K. (1995). *Rethinking innateness: A connectionist perspective on development*. Cambridge, MA: MIT Press.

Fazio, R. H. (1986). How do attitudes guide behavior? In R. M. Sorrentino & E. T. Higgins (Eds.), *Handbook of motivation and cognition* (pp. 204–243). New York: Guilford Press.

Fazio, R. H. (1993). Variability in the likelihood of automatic attitude activation: Data reanalysis and commentary on Bargh, Chaiken, Govender, and Pratto (1992). *Journal of Personality and Social Psychology, 64*, 753–758.

Fazio, R. H., Sanbonmatsu, D. M., Powell, M. C., & Kardes, F. R. (1986). On the automatic activation of attitudes. *Journal of Personality and Social Psychology, 50*, 229–238.

Fiske, S., & Taylor, S. (1994). *Social cognition*. 2nd. edn. Reading, MA: Addison-Wesley.

Frable, D. E. S., & Bem, S. L. (1985). If you are gender schematic, all members of the opposite sex look alike. *Journal of Personality and Social Psychology, 49*, 459–468.

Hastie, R. (1980). Memory for information which confirms or contradicts a general impression. In R. Hastie, T. M. Ostrom, E. B. Ebbesen, R. S. Wyer, D. Hamilton, & D. E. Carlston (Eds.), *Person memory* (pp. 155–177). Hillsdale, NJ: Lawrence Erlbaum Associates.

Hastie, R. (1988). A computer simulation model of person memory. *Journal of Experimental Social Psychology, 24*, 423–447.

Hastie, R., & Kumar, P. A. (1979). Person memory: Personality traits as organizing principles in memory for behaviors. *Journal of Personality and Social Psychology, 37*, 25–38.

Hastie, R., & Park, B. (1986). The relationship between memory and judgment depends on whether the judgment task is memory-based or on-line. *Psychological Review, 93*, 258–268.

Hertz, J., Krogh, A., & Palmer, R. G. (1991). *Introduction to the theory of neural computation*. Redwood City, CA: Addison-Wesley.

Higgins, E. T. (1996). Knowledge activation: Accessibility, applicability, and salience. In E. T. Higgins & A. W. Kruglanski (Eds.), *Social psychology: Handbook of basic principles* (pp. 133–168). New York: Guilford Press.

Higgins, E. T., Bargh, J. A., & Lombardi, W. (1985). Nature of priming effect on categorization. *Journal of Experimental Psychology: Learning, Memory and Cognition, 11*, 59–69.

Higgins, E. T., King, G. A., & Mavin, G. H. (1982). Individual construct accessibility and subjective impressions and recall. *Journal of Personality and Social Psychology, 43*, 35–47.

Higgins, E. T., Rholes, W. S., & Jones, C. R. (1977). Category accessibility and impression formation. *Journal of Experimental Social Psychology, 13*, 141–154.

Higgins, E. T., Van Hook, E., & Dorfman, D. (1988). Do self-attributes form a cognitive structure? *Social Cognition, 6*, 177–207.

Hintzman, D. L. (1986). "Schema abstraction" in a multiple-trace memory model. *Psychological Review, 93*, 411–428.

Hintzman, D. L. (1990). Human learning and memory: Connections and dissociations. *Annual Review of Psychology, 41*, 109–140.

Hirst, W. (1989). On consciousness, recall, recognition, and the architecture of memory. In S. Lewandowsky, J. C. Dunn, & K. Kirsner (Eds.), *Implicit memory: Theoretical issues* (pp. 33–46). Hillsdale, NJ: Lawrence Erlbaum Associates.

Humphreys, M. S., Bain, J. D., & Pike, R. (1989). Different ways to cue a coherent memory system: A theory for episodic, semantic, and procedural tasks. *Psychological Review, 96*, 208–233.

Jacoby, L. L. (1983). Perceptual enhancement: Persistent effects of an experience. *Journal of Experimental Psychology: Learning, Memory, and Cognition, 9*, 21–38.

Jacoby, L. L., & Brooks, L. R. (1984). Nonanalytic cognition: Memory, perception and concept learning. In G. Bower (Ed.), *The psychology of learning and motivation: Advances in research and theory* Vol. 18. New York: Academic Press.

Jacoby, L. L., & Kelley, C. M. (1987). Unconscious influences of memory for a prior event. *Personality and Social Psychology Bulletin, 13*, 314–336.

Kunda, Z., & Thagard, P. (1996). Integrating stereotypes with individuating information: A parallel constraint satisfaction model of impression formation. *Psychological Review, 103*, 284–308.

Lewicki, P. (1985). Nonconscious biasing effects of single instances of subsequent judgments. *Journal of Personality and Social Psychology, 48*, 563–574.

Linville, P. W., & Carlston, D. E. (1994). Social cognition of the self. In P. G. Devine, T. M. Ostrom, & D. L. Hamilton (Eds.), *Social cognition: Impact on social psychology* (pp. 143–193). Orlando, FL: Academic Press.

Linville, P. W., Fischer, G. W., & Salovey, P. (1989). Perceived distributions of the characteristics of in-group and out-group members: Empirical evidence and a computer simulation. *Journal of Personality and Social Psychology, 57*, 165–188.

Logan, G. D. (1988). Toward an instance theory of automatization. *Psychological Review, 95*, 492–527.

Lombardi, W. J., Higgins, E. T., & Bargh, J. A. (1987). The role of consciousness in priming effects on categorization: Assimilation versus contrast as a function of awareness of the priming task. *Personality and Social Psychology Bulletin, 13*, 411–429.

McClelland, J. L., McNaughton, B. L., & O'Reilly, R. C. (1995). Why there are complementary learning systems in the hippocampus and neocortex: Insights from the successes and failures of connectionist models of learning and memory. *Psychological Review, 102*, 419–457.

McClelland, J. L., Rumelhart, D. E., & Hinton, G. E. (1986). The appeal of parallel distributed processing. In D. E. Rumelhart, J. L. McClelland, et al. (Eds.), *Parallel distributed processing* Vol. 1 (pp. 3–44). Cambridge, MA: MIT Press.

McClelland, J. L., Rumelhart, D. E., et al. (Eds.) (1986). *Parallel distributed processing* Vol. 2. Cambridge, MA: MIT Press.

MacLeod, C. M., & Bassili, J. N. (1989). Are implicit and explicit tests differentially sensitive to item-specific vs. relational information? In S. Lewandowsky, J. C. Dunn, & K. Kirsner (Eds.), *Implicit memory: Theoretical issues* (pp. 159–172). Hillsdale, NJ: Lawrence Erlbaum Associates.

Malt, B. C., & Smith, E. E. (1984). Correlated properties in natural categories. *Journal of Verbal Learning and Verbal Behavior, 23,* 250–269.

Markus, H., & Wurf, E. (1987). The dynamic self-concept: A social psychological perspective. *Annual Review of Psychology, 38,* 299–337.

Markus, H., & Zajonc, R. B. (1985). The cognitive perspective in social psychology. In G. Lindzey & E. Aronson (Eds.), *Handbook of social psychology.* 3rd. edn., Vol. 1 (pp. 137–230). New York: Random House.

Martin, L. L., Seta, J. J., & Crelia, R. A. (1990). Assimilation and contrast as a function of people's willingness and ability to expend effort in forming an impression. *Journal of Personality and Social Psychology, 59,* 38–49.

Masson, M. E. J. (1989). Fluent reprocessing as an implicit expression of memory for experience. In S. Lewandowsky, J. C. Dunn, & K. Kirsner (Eds.), *Implicit memory: Theoretical issues* (pp. 123–138). Hillsdale, NJ: Lawrence Erlbaum Associates.

Masson, M. E. J. (1991). A distributed memory model of context effects in word identification. In D. Besner & G. W. Humphreys (Eds.), *Basic processes in reading: Visual word recognition* (pp. 233–263). Hillsdale, NJ: Lawrence Erlbaum Associates.

Medin, D. L., & Schaffer, M. M. (1978). Context theory of classification learning. *Psychological Review, 85,* 207–238.

Meyer, D. E., & Schvaneveldt, R. W. (1971). Facilitation in recognizing pairs of words: Evidence of a dependence between retrieval operations. *Journal of Experimental Psychology, 90,* 227–234.

Minsky, M. (1975). A framework for representing knowledge. In P. H. Winston (Ed.), *The psychology of computer vision.* New York: McGraw-Hill.

Moscovitch, M. (1994). Memory and working with memory: Evaluation of a component process model and comparisons with other models. In D. L. Schacter & E. Tulving (Eds.), *Memory systems 1994* (pp. 269–310). Cambridge, MA: MIT Press.

Neely, J. H. (1977). Semantic priming and retrieval from lexical memory: Roles of inhibitionless spreading activation and limited-capacity attention. *Journal of Experimental Psychology: General, 1,* 226–254.

Neisser, U. (1976). *Cognition and reality.* San Francisco: Freeman.

Ostrom, T. M., Skowronski, J. J., & Nowak, A. (1994). The cognitive foundation of attitudes: It's a wonderful construct. In P. G. Devine, T. M. Ostrom, & D. L. Hamilton (Eds.), *Social cognition: Impact on social psychology* (pp. 195–257). Orlando, FL: Academic Press.

Queller, S., & Smith, E. R. (1998). Stereotype change from dispersed and concentrated disconfirming information: New insights from connectionist models. Unpublished paper, Purdue University.

Ratcliff, R., & McKoon, G. (1988). A retrieval theory of priming in memory. *Psychological Review, 95,* 385–408.

Read, S. J., & Marcus-Newhall, A. (1993). Explanatory coherence in social explanations: A parallel distributed processing account. *Journal of Personality and Social Psychology, 65,* 429–447.

Richardson-Klavehn, A., & Bjork, R. A. (1988). Measures of memory. *Annual Review of Psychology, 39,* 475–544.

Roediger, H. L., & McDermott, K. B. (1993). Implicit memory in normal human subjects. In F. Boller & J. Erafman (Eds.), *Handbook of neuropsychology* Vol. 8 (pp. 63–131). Amsterdam: Elsevier.

Ross, M., & Conway, M. (1986). Remembering one's own past: The construction of personal histories. In R. M. Sorrentino & E. T. Higgins (Eds.), *Handbook of motivation and cognition* (pp. 122–144). New York: Guilford Press.

Rumelhart, D. E., McClelland, J. L., et al. (Eds.). (1986). *Parallel distributed processing* Vol. 1. Cambridge, MA: MIT Press.

Rumelhart, D. E., Smolensky, P., McClelland, J. L., & Hinton, G. E. (1986). Schemata and sequential thought processes in PDP models. In J. L. McClelland & D. E. Rumelhart (Eds.), *Parallel distributed processing: Explorations in the microstructure of cognition* Vol. 2 (pp. 7–57). Cambridge, MA: MIT Press.

Schacter, D. L. (1987). Implicit memory: History and current status. *Journal of Experimental Psychology: Learning, Memory, and Cognition, 13*, 501–518.

Schacter, D. L. (1994). Priming and multiple memory systems: Perceptual mechanisms of implicit memory. In D. L. Schacter & E. Tulving (Eds.), *Memory systems 1994* (pp. 233–268). Cambridge, MA: MIT Press.

Schank, R., & Abelson, R. P. (1977). *Scripts, plans, goals, and understanding.* Hillsdale, NJ: Lawrence Erlbaum Associates.

Schwarz, N., & Clore, G. L. (1983). Mood, misattribution, and judgments of well-being: Informative and directive functions of affective states. *Journal of Personality and Social Psychology, 45*, 513–523.

Sloman, S. A., Hayman, C. A. G., Ohta, N., Law, J., & Tulving, E. (1988). Forgetting in primed fragment completion. *Journal of Experimental Psychology: Learning, Memory, and Cognition, 14*, 223–239.

Smith, E. R. (1988). Category accessibility effects in a simulated exemplar-only memory. *Journal of Experimental Social Psychology, 24*, 448–463.

Smith, E. R. (1990). Content and process specificity in the effects of prior experiences. Target Article in T. K. Srull & R. S. Wyer (Eds.), *Advances in social cognition* Vol. 3 (pp. 1–60). Hillsdale, NJ: Lawrence Erlbaum Associates.

Smith, E. R. (1996). What do connectionism and social psychology offer each other? *Journal of Personality and Social Psychology, 70*, 893–912.

Smith, E. R. (1998). Mental representation and memory. In D. Gilbert, S. Fiske, & G. Lindzey (Eds.), *Handbook of social psychology.* 4th. edn., Vol. 1 (pp. 391–445). New York: McGraw-Hill.

Smith, E. R., & Branscombe, N. R. (1988). Category accessibility as implicit memory. *Journal of Experimental Social Psychology, 24*, 490–504.

Smith, E. R., & DeCoster, J. (1998). Knowledge acquisition, accessibility, and use in person perception and stereotyping: Simulation with a recurrent connectionist network. *Journal of Personality and Social Psychology, 74*, 21–35.

Smith, E. R., & Zárate, M. A. (1992). Exemplar-based model of social judgment. *Psychological Review, 99*, 3–21.

Smith, E. R., Stewart, T. L., & Buttram, R. T. (1992). Inferring a trait from a behavior has long-term, highly specific effects. *Journal of Personality and Social Psychology, 62*, 753–759.

Smolensky, P. (1988). On the proper treatment of connectionism. *Behavioral and Brain Sciences, 11*, 1–74.

Squire, L. R. (1994). Declarative and nondeclarative memory: Multiple brain systems supporting learning and memory. In D. L. Schacter & E. Tulving (Eds.), *Memory systems 1994* (pp. 203–232). Cambridge, MA: MIT Press.

Srull, T. K. (1981). Person memory: Some tests of associative storage and retrieval models. *Journal of Experimental Psychology: Human Learning and Memory, 7*, 440–463.

Stangor, C., & McMillan, D. (1992). Memory for expectancy-congruent and expectancy-incongruent information: A review of the social and social developmental literatures. *Psychological Bulletin, 111*, 42–61.

Strack, F., & Martin, L. L. (1987). Thinking, judging, and communicating: A process account of context effects in attitude surveys. In H.-J. Hippler, N. Schwarz, & S. Sudman (Eds.), *Social information processing and survey methodology* (pp. 123–148). New York: Springer-Verlag.

Thorpe, S. (1995). Localized and distributed representations. In M. A. Arbib (Ed.), *Handbook of brain theory and neural networks* (pp. 549–552). Cambridge, MA: MIT Press.

Tourangeau, R., & Rasinski, K. A. (1988). Cognitive processes underlying context effects in attitude measurement. *Psychological Bulletin, 103*, 299–314.

Tulving, E. (1972). Episodic and semantic memory. In E. Tulving & W. Donaldson (Eds.), *Organization of memory*. New York: Academic.

Tulving, E., Schacter, D. L., & Stark, H. (1982). Priming effects in word-fragment completion are independent of recognition memory. *Journal of Experimental Psychology: Learning, Memory, and Cognition, 8*, 336–342.

Turner, J. C., Oakes, P. J., Haslam, S. A., & McGarty, C. (1994). Self and collective: Cognition and social context. *Personality and Social Psychology Bulletin, 20*, 454–463.

Whittlesea, B. W. A. (1987) Preservation of specific experiences in the representation of general knowledge. *Journal of Experimental Psychology: Learning, Memory, and Cognition, 13*, 3–17.

Whittlesea, B. W. A., & Dorken, M. D. (1993). Incidentally, things in general are particularly determined: An episodic-processing account of implicit learning. *Journal of Experimental Psychology: General, 122*, 227–248.

Wiles, J., & Humphreys, M. S. (1993). Using artificial neural nets to model implicit and explicit memory test performance. In P. Graf & M. E. J. Masson (Eds.), *Implicit memory: New directions in cognition, development, and neuropsychology* (pp. 141–165). Hillsdale, NJ: Lawrence Erlbaum Associates.

Wilson, T. D. (1990). Self-persuasion via self-reflection. In J. M. Olson & M. P. Zanna (Eds.), *Self-inference processes: The Ontario Symposium* Vol. 6 (pp. 43–68). Hillsdale, NJ: Lawrence Erlbaum Associates.

Wilson, T. D., & Hodges, S. D. (1992). Attitudes as temporary constructions. In L. L. Martin & A. Tesser (Eds.), *The construction of social judgments* (pp. 37–65). Hillsdale, NJ: Lawrence Erlbaum Associates.

Wisniewski, E. J. (1997). When concepts combine. *Psychonomic Bulletin and Review, 4*, 167–183.

Wittenbrink, B., Judd, C. M., & Park, B. (1997). Evidence for racial prejudice at the implicit level and its relationship with questionnaire measures. *Journal of Personality and Social Psychology, 72*, 262–274.

Wyer, R. S., & Carlston, D. E. (1994). The cognitive representation of persons and events. In R. S. Wyer & T. K. Srull (Eds.), *Handbook of Social Cognition.* 2nd. edn. (pp. 41–98). Hillsdale, NJ: Lawrence Erlbaum Associates.

Wyer, R. S., & Gordon, S. E. (1984). The cognitive representation of social information. In R. S. Wyer & T. K. Srull (Eds.), *Handbook of social cognition* Vol. 2 (pp. 73–150). Hillsdale, NJ: Lawrence Erlbaum Associates.

Wyer, R. S., & Srull, T. K. (1980). The processing of social stimulus information: A conceptual integration. In R. Hastie, T. M. Ostrom, E. B. Ebbesen, R. S. Wyer, D. Hamilton, & D. E. Carlston (Eds.), *Person memory* (pp. 227–300). Hillsdale, NJ: Lawrence Erlbaum Associates.

Wyer, R. S., & Srull, T. K. (1989). *Memory and cognition in its social context*. Hillsdale, NJ: Lawrence Erlbaum Associates.

CHAPTER TWO

The Social Unconscious

Mahzarin R. Banaji, Kristi M. Lemm, and Siri J. Carpenter

Contemporary social psychologists are aware that long before concepts of cognitive mediation were admissible in scientific psychology, their predecessors had been sufficiently entranced with matters of mind to study them even at risk of marginalization by the then dominant antimentalists. The first social psychologists were bold not so much in their recognition that thinking, feeling, and motivation were fundamental mental systems – for hundreds of years, thinkers even in the western world, had known the same. The unique audacity of these psychologists was in the belief that thought, feeling, and motive could be scrutinized, manipulated, and subjected to experimentation in a manner not unlike the treatment accorded to particles, ions, and bacteria. It should be of little surprise then, that a field so confident a century ago that processes of conscious mental life could indeed be measured is now equally confident about measuring mental life that lies beyond consciousness.

Johnson-Laird's (1983) question "What should a theory of consciousness explain?" produced four components, *awareness*, *control*, *intention*, and *self-reflection*, that a tractable theory of consciousness must explain. The focus of this chapter is on the hidden side of consciousness, which leads us to focus on the inverse of these components: thoughts, feelings, and actions performed outside conscious awareness, without conscious control, or without intention. At this stage, research on unconscious processes reflects a basic attempt to demonstrate that particular unconscious processes occur at all, to trace the boundary conditions of their operation, to document the full richness of the systems that are engaged (cognition, affect, motivation) and the levels of social objects they include (e.g. self, other, social group). With a strong emphasis on developing robust and replicable methods for investigation, researchers have asked: can knowledge that resides outside conscious awareness influence social thinking, feeling, and action? Is unawareness actually a precondition for observing particular effects? How should we characterize attitudes that are fully within awareness but relatively outside conscious control? Is it possible to consider the unconscious activation of goals and motives as we have come to accept unconscious cognition and affect? What do these investigations

This research was supported by grant number SBR 9709924 from the National Science Foundation. We thank Richard Hackman and Aiden Gregg for their helpful comments and suggestions.

imply regarding the notion of free-will, particularly as it concerns assumptions about the freedom or constraints to think, feel, and act toward one's self and others? These are among the questions that have mattered to contemporary psychologists interested in the analysis of the social unconscious.

Research on unconscious processes does not, unfortunately, reflect a sensible observance of terminology of constructs and processes. Terms like *automatic, implicit, unconscious,* and *indirect* are often used interchangeably, and sometimes to refer to divergent underlying processes (e.g. awareness versus control). In recognition of our own complicity in creating this confusion, we attempt to restore some order for future discussions by using the term *unconscious* to refer to the family of processes that occur outside conscious awareness, without conscious control, or without intention to perform. The use of the term *unconscious* reflects a deliberate attempt to capture its usage from still largely psychodynamic meaning. In addition, we use the term *implicit* to refer to those processes that operate without the actor's conscious awareness, and the term *automatic* to refer to processes that operate without the actor's conscious control. In time, these issues and concerns about predictive validity and relationships among families of measures will be resolved. However, progress will be greatly speeded-up by charting a clear research agenda and encouraging greater collaboration across laboratories with divergent perspectives and methodological allegiances.

Much social psychological research can be said to be, in essence, the study of processes that operate outside conscious awareness and intention. After all, experiments must routinely create circumstances in which the behavior that is observed and measured is free of the concerns of social desirability and demand characteristics, and in that sense unawareness about the source of influence on behavior is the norm. Yet, it is only more recently that unconscious processes in social behavior have been examined in their own right, rather than as a methodological by-product of social psychological experimentation. This review revolves around those experiments that bring a deliberate focus to unconscious processes because of a genuine interest in the limits on introspection, in understanding the extent and nature of the social unconscious, and in using the study of unconscious processes as the basis to challenge commonplace notions of individual responsibility on the part of social actors, and assumptions of justice in interpersonal treatment of social targets.

Over two hundred years ago, Immanuel Kant wrote:

> We can reduce all the powers of the human mind, without exception, to these three: the *cognitive power*, the *feeling of pleasure and displeasure*, and the *power of desire*. It is true that philosophers who otherwise deserve unlimited praise for the thoroughness in their way of thinking have asserted that this distinction is only illusory, and have tried to bring all powers under nothing but the cognitive power. Yet it is quite easy to establish, and has in fact been realized for some time, that this attempt to bring unity into that diversity of powers, though otherwise undertaken in the genuine philosophic spirit, is futile. (Kant, 1790/1987, p. 394; italics in original)

Two centuries later, we find it worthwhile to retain this triumvirate, and are bemused by the similar dominance of the "cognitive power" then, as it is now. We include research on unconscious forms of affect, and note that research on unconscious motives is at such an early stage of development that it would be hard to provide a responsible review of such work at this time.

This chapter brings together selected samples of research on unconscious processes as they inform cognition and affect (for reviews see Bargh, 1997; Bornstein & Pittman, 1992; Greenwald, 1992; Kihlstrom, 1990; Kihlstrom, Mulvaney, Tobias, & Tobis, in press; Uleman & Bargh, 1989; Wegener & Bargh, 1998). By necessity, the treatment here is not historical, and the attention to any single area is superficial. Should the review reflect a sense of the potential pervasiveness and emerging lawfulness of unconscious processes as they are revealed in social life, it will have succeeded.

Unconscious Cognition

By far the most research attention has been devoted to the study of unconscious social cognition. This is not surprising because of disproportionate attention given to the study of social perception, attention, memory, categorization, and judgment more generally. In this section, we devote our attention to three aspects of unconscious social cognition: the study of self, other, and social group. Admittedly, the demarcation is somewhat arbitrary, but it will allow us to build the case that a wide bandwidth of learning has become possible within a relatively short time on how humans think about themselves, others individuals, and the social groups of their species.

Self

Proposals to study the self as a cognitive structure have appeared since the 1970s (see Banaji & Prentice, 1994; Markus, 1977; Greenwald & Pratkanis, 1984; Kihlstrom, Cantor, Albright, Chew, Klein, & Niedenthal, 1988; Klein & Loftus, 1990; Linville & Carlston, 1994) and these set the stage for contemporary research on unconscious processes involving the self. These position papers and experimental accounts placed the study of self firmly in cognitive space, often using the dominant language of models that allowed a connection to established constructs such as memory (e.g. Greenwald & Banaji, 1989; Klein, Loftus, & Kihlstrom, 1996). The language of these models and the demystification of self that emerged out of these accounts permitted unconscious self processes to also be measured. The research may roughly be separated into analyses of the unconscious manner by which shifts in self-related processes such as self-presentation and self-evaluation occur, and the role of unconscious self-related processes in guiding an understanding of the social world.

The most illustrative findings that show that unconscious activation of significant others can have implications for self-evaluation come from studies in which the priming procedure uses subliminal presentation. Baldwin (1994) used subliminal primes to activate representations of a significant other (one's adviser) who is critical or accepting in orientation and showed parallel shifts in views of self; also, that approval or disapproval from unconsciously activated others can influence one's evaluation of one's own work (Baldwin, Carrell, & Lopez, 1990). Besides the role accorded to significant others, the idea that membership in social groups has repercussions for individual psychological functioning has been of perennial interest to social scientists (see Walsh & Banaji, 1997, for a review). In its most recent form, this idea has led to research suggesting a potential link between activated knowledge of beliefs about one's group and performance on ability tests. Steele and Aronson (1995, p. 808) point out that "the existence of a negative stereotype about a group to which one belongs . . . means that in situations where the stereotype is applicable, one is at risk of confirming it as a self-characterization, both to one's self and to others who know the stereotype. That is what is meant by stereotype threat." In their experiments, Black Americans underperformed on tests of intellectual ability, and women underperformed on tests of mathematical ability (Steele, 1997) when subtly made aware of their group membership or the link between the group and the negative attribute. Several additional demonstrations of this finding now exist. For example, Levy (1996) showed that subliminally activated negative stereotypes about old age creates decrements in memory performance among elderly subjects; Croizet & Claire (1998) showed that eliciting information about parents' level of education led to a decrement in verbal ability among low SES students; Shih, Pittinsky, & Ambady (1999) showed that activating gender identity or ethnic identity among Asian women shifted performance to be respectively inferior or superior on a math test. Evidence about the robustness and ease of replication of these effects is only just beginning to be determined, and the mechanisms by which such effects are produced are not yet identified. Yet their implications for the ease with which equality and fairness in treatment can be compromised by group membership are sufficiently shocking to require particularly intensive study by investigators with varying theoretical perspectives.

In other research we learn that who one is and how one assesses oneself can implicitly influence views of others, just as we observed previously that significant others and social groups can influence judgments of self. Spencer, Fein, Wolfe, Fong, and Dunn (1998) showed that threat to self-image can automatically activate stereotypes of social groups even under conditions that otherwise do not produce such activation. And Sedikides & Skowronski (1993) showed the role of self in forming impressions of others more generally, by demonstrating that central dimensions of the self-concept were influential in judgments of others. Perhaps the most impressive corpus of research showing the role of one's significant others in shaping social perception has been obtained by Andersen and her colleagues (Andersen & Glassman, 1996). In providing the first experimental evidence for transference, they show that activation of information pertaining to significant others implicitly lead to inferences about new individuals that mimic representations of significant others and self. Moreover, such activation can also elicit facial affect that captures the evaluation of the significant other and produces behavioral confirmation in interpersonal interaction.

To demonstrate the role of unconscious processes in short-cuts to self-evaluation, Swann, Hixon, Stein-Seroussi, & Gilbert (1990) demonstrated that under conditions of limited cognitive capacity, participants showed a simpler preference for self-enhancing social agents, whereas the availability of resources led to more informative self-verifying strategies. It also appears that processes of social comparison occur with minimal cognitive resources or intention to compare, and even when the source of comparison is nondiagnostic for self-assessment. Social comparison can lead to decrements in self-evaluation in such cases when resources are unavailable to adjust for the inappropriate comparison (Gilbert, Giesler, & Morris, 1995).

Studies showing the involvement of unconscious self-related processes are numerous, and these examples are selected to show that lack of both awareness and control play a role in assessments of self, and that self-knowledge and personal relationships can unconsciously influence assessments of the surrounding social world. The breakdown of simple distinctions between thinking and feeling are quite obvious in many analyses of self, and examining the role of unconscious processes shows such interrelations among mental systems to be fundamental, and defying of our imposed separation of these systems for expository purposes.

Other

Few topics in social psychology can be regarded as more central to the field's mission of understanding the stuff of human relations than the processes involved in one person observing, understanding, and assessing another. Although Katz and Braly (1933) and Icheiser (1949) explicitly recognized the role of unconscious processes in person and group perception, it was a later generation of experimenters who with their newfangled technologies studied the unconscious operation of person perception: to what degree and in what manner, they asked, are awareness, control, and intention components of the pervasive act of judging others? It is now clear that spontaneous, fluid, and effortless acts of person perception, when brought under scientific scrutiny, reveal the operation of a vastly intricate thought system, able to perform social gymnastics of incredible speed and elegance. The social gymnast, however, does not always land on the balance beam. The research we review shows also a more clumsy side of person perception: susceptibility to situational intrusions, the constraints of routinized thought patterns, of errors in computation and application that create costs of varying magnitude.

Implicit perception of others stems from the constructs in the perceiver's mind   Among the highlights of this research literature are experiments conducted by Higgins, Rholes, & Jones (1977) which appeared without heralding the study of unconscious processes in person perception. Yet it ushered in a wave of research that has produced what some regard to be a law of social perception: constructs that are active in a perceiver's mind implicitly shape perception and judgment of others (Sedikides & Skowronski, 1990). Participants read material that served to activate knowledge about personality qualities such as "stubborn" or "persistent." Later, in a test of reading comprehension ostensibly unrelated to the previous session, participants judged an ambiguously described target to be more in line with the previously activated knowledge; those who had been primed with "stubborn" were inclined to find the target to be relatively stubborn, and others who had been primed with "persistent" judged the identical target to be more persistent. Participants in such experiments were not *aware* of the influence of previous experience in shaping their judgment, and in the absence of such awareness, there was no opportunity to *control* judgment. Certainly, we assume that participants *intended* to provide an unbiased judgment, on the basis of the actions of the target. Yet, as this experiment and the countless others using variations of this procedure suggest, person perception can be guided by factors that may emanate elsewhere, outside consciously accessible cognition (see Higgins, 1996, and Sedikides & Skowronski, 1990, for reviews).

The many experiments that followed on the heels of Higgins, Rholes, & Jones (1977) served as more than just the clean-up crew. These experiments, continuing up to the present, reveal a rich understanding of unconscious person perception. Additionally, theoretical frameworks of various levels of specificity have been proposed that offer working explanations, suggest useful metaphors, and specify mechanisms (Higgins, Bargh, & Lombardi, 1985; Higgins, 1989; Herr, Sherman, & Fazio, 1983; Martin, 1986; Wyer & Srull, 1980). While we cannot review the theoretical models here, it is clearly the case that the experimental findings and theoretical attempts to understand unconscious person perception (e.g. recency, frequency, awareness, specificity, chronicity, contrast) have allowed hidden aspects of unconscious processes themselves to be revealed. Together, they have created a view of person perception that is altogether more complex and complete, and more troubling in its implications: perceivers believe that their judgments of others reflect properties of the target, and not of the thoughts that are implicitly active in their mind. That such influences on judgment occur without the intention to create bias in the judgment process, and without awareness that such bias may even exist, starkly raises the question of the extent to which "mental due process" (Banaji & Bhaskar, in press) in interpersonal interaction can be assumed.

The robustness of a theoretical construct is evident when a diversity of applications provide supporting evidence for the principle. The activation of constructs, either temporary or chronic, have been shown to influence behavior in a variety of domains: desire to work with a gay person (Johnson, Bryant, Jackson, Gatto, Nowak, & MacVittie, 1994); reducing risk of pregnancy (Norris & Devine, 1992); increasing the assessment of "alcoholic" (Southwick, Steele, & Lindell, 1986); explaining the cognitive states of depressives (Gotlib & McCann, 1984); priming aggression by sports (Wann & Branscombe, 1989); explaining individual differences in aggression (Graham & Hudley, 1994); increasing judgments of women as sexual objects (Rudman & Borgida, 1995); implicating television viewing as a vehicle of priming (Shrum & O'Guinn, 1993); the role of chronic accessibility in electoral choice (Lau, 1989); and the role of priming self-interest in political reasoning (Young, Thomsen, Borgida, Sullivan, & Aldrich, 1991).

Implicit perception of others follows from spontaneous trait inferences   The construct accessibility literature shows that our judgments of others are influenced by the concepts that are active in our own minds at the time of perception. But what exactly is perceived when we observe others' behavior? Knowing that there may be multiple causes for behavior, to what do we attribute a particular action? Following decades of research in person perception beginning with Lewin and Heider, we know that the most common inference made is a trait attribution – we encounter a behavior, and infer that some trait about the actor must be associated with its occurrence.

Uleman and colleagues (Newman & Uleman, 1989) kicked off a controversy in the field of person perception by suggesting that traits are inferred spontaneously, or possibly automatically, upon encountering a behavior. In an early demonstration, Winter and Uleman (1984) had participants study descriptions of people performing behaviors that implied traits, such as "the sailor leaves his wife with 20 pounds of laundry." Later, participants were asked to recall the sentences they had previously read, given recall cues that were either traits that had been implied by the sentences (e.g. inconsiderate), non-trait semantic associates of the sentences (e.g. sea or wash), or no cue. Trait cues facilitated sentence recall better than no cue, and as well as or better than strong semantic associates, suggesting that participants had automatically made trait inferences at the time of learning about the behavior.

The original STI effect has been replicated in many iterations, providing convincing evidence that traits are inferred outside of conscious awareness (Moskowitz & Roman, 1992) and without conscious impression-formation goals (e.g. Skowronski, Carlston, Mae, & Crawford; 1998; Uleman, Newman, & Winter, 1992; Whitney, Waring, & Zingmark, 1992). Although the trait-cued recall paradigm has been challenged methodologically (D'Agostino & Beegle, 1996), evidence that traits are inferred spontaneously at encoding has been provided by research using methods other than cued recall, including probe recognition (Uleman, Hon, Roman, and Moskowitz, 1996), savings in a relearning task (Carlston & Skowronski, 1994), and using blatant or subtle priming at encoding to inhibit or facilitate STI (Newman & Uleman, 1990).

Spontaneous trait inferences may provide input to dispositional inference processes   The bulk of the evidence suggests that most trait inferences made without intention are inferences about *behavior*, not dispositional inferences directly linked to the actor (e.g. Carlston, Skowronski, & Sparks, 1995; Moskowitz, 1993; Uleman, Moskowitz, Roman, & Rhee, 1993; Whitney, Davis, & Waring, 1994). However, STI may play an essential role in the formation of personality inferences. Several models of person perception have proposed that dispositional inference proceeds in multiple stages, the first of which requires minimal cognitive resources or control, and may thus be considered spontaneous or automatic (e.g. Burnstein & Schul, 1982; Brewer, 1988; Higgins, Strauman, & Klein, 1986; Ross & Olson, 1981).

Trope's two-stage inference model (Trope, 1986; Trope & Liberman, 1993) and Gilbert's three-stage model (Gilbert, Pelham, & Krull, 1988; Gilbert & Krull, 1988; Gilbert & Osborne, 1989) propose that observed behavior, the situation in which it occurs, and prior information about the actor are automatically identified in terms of underlying traits (e.g. "this is a friendly behavior"). The output of this automatic identification stage in turn becomes the input for the dispositional inference, in which behavioral, situational, and prior information that has been identified in terms of traits is combined to form a trait attribution about the actor. Experimental evidence shows that people make behavioral identifications even under conditions of diminished cognitive resources, whereas conscious correction for situational contributions to behavior may be inadequate if perceivers do not have adequate cognitive resources (Trope & Alfieri, 1997; Gilbert, Pelham, & Krull, 1988). The implications about human nature and nurture from these models are also troubling: because people are so often engaged in concurrent activities, behavior characterizations are often not appropriately adjusted for situational contributions to behavior. This can tilt toward trait- (rather than situation-) correspondent inferences, a phenomenon also termed the fundamental attribution error (Ross, 1977).

What early attribution theorists had predicted, research over the last twenty years has confirmed about the swift and remarkably sophisticated inferences that are made about individual others in one's social world. The methods that are used are reliable, and this has allowed a healthy exporting of methods outside the laboratories in which they were developed. The theories of human inference processes in social context that have emerged are creative and continuously generative of research. All in all, research on unconscious processes in perceiving, understanding, and judging others shows how intelligent but fallible systems operate within the constraints of the cognitive architecture that evolution and learning allows and the demands of daily social life.

Social group

Perhaps the most distinguishing mark of social psychological research on unconscious processes is its interest in the social group as a legitimate unit of analysis. In the previous sections, we discussed how judgments about individual personality qualities can arise from unconsciously perceived sources. In this section, we discuss research on the unconscious activation of stereotypes and their application in judgments of individuals and groups. In the next section on unconscious affect, we will review related research on attitudes of prejudice that reside outside of conscious control or awareness.

As has often been argued, stereotypes about social groups are heuristics that simplify and organize perception of the social world. In so doing, beliefs about social groups and their use in individual judgment merely reveal ordinary processes of learning and generalization. Our discussion of these particular short-cuts will show the various ways in which unconscious processes reveal their presence. Our discussion will also point out the moral question that emerges from this rather ordinary discovery about category learning, generalization, and inferences. Stereotypes exact a toll by subsuming individuals into the larger social categories and by giving to individuals privileges and punishments that are not their due. We noted previously that social judgment may not reflect the actions of the target but of unconsciously applied constructs in the perceiver's mind. It is unsettling, at least in societies that consciously affirm that judgments ought to be based on the "content of one's character," to discover the extent to which judgments of individuals may reflect beliefs about their social group.

Unconscious stereotypes are rooted in social categorization   A rich literature on social categorization processes indicates that such processes are automatically prompted by the mere presence of a stimulus target (Banaji & Hardin, 1996; Blair & Banaji, 1996; Blascovich, Wyer, Swart, & Kibler, 1997; Brewer, 1988; Eckes, 1994; Fiske & Neuberg, 1990; Ford, Stangor, & Duan, 1994; Hamilton & Sherman, 1994; Perdue, Dovidio, Gurtman, & Tyler, 1990; Pendry & Macrae, 1996; Stangor & Lange, 1994; Stroessner, 1996; Zárate, Bonilla, & Luévano, 1995). And in the mind of the social perceiver, stereotypes that accompany a particular category automatically accrue to its members.

Unconscious stereotyping is ubiquitous   In an influential demonstration of unconscious race stereotyping, Devine (1989) found that subliminally presenting race information influenced how participants subsequently judged the ambiguous behavior of a race-unspecified target. Both high- and low-prejudiced participants rated the target as more hostile when they had been presented with a list containing 80 percent stereotypically black words (e.g. jazz, basketball, Africa) than when the list contained only 20 percent stereotypically black words. Devine's evidence that stereotypes could be automatically activated by presenting cues about a stereotyped group inspired research on how stereotypes operate without conscious awareness, control, and intention (see Fiske, 1998, and Greenwald & Banaji, 1995, for reviews). This body of research provides strong evidence that beliefs about social groups are readily activated, and influence perception of the target. What's more, the research suggests that unconscious processes not only facilitate stereotyped responding but also inhibit counterstereotypical associations, perhaps making stereotypes additionally resistant to changing in the face of atypical group exemplars (Trope & Thompson, 1997; Van Knippenberg & Dijksterhuis, 1996).

Gender, as a category, has received much attention, in part because of its fundamental nature and presence in all human societies and in part for its convenience in not attracting attention to social category as the focus of the experiment (Banaji & Greenwald, 1995; Banaji & Hardin, 1996; Blair & Banaji, 1996; Dunning & Sherman, 1997; Lambert, 1995; Macrae, Bodenhausen, Milne, & Thorn, 1997; Nelson, Acker, & Manis, 1996; Pratto & Bargh, 1991). This research has shown that information about one's gender, whether conveyed through names, pictures, or gender stereotypical words, exerts an unconscious influence on judgment. For example, Banaji and Greenwald (1995) found that more male names than female names were identified as famous under conditions of memory uncertainty, suggesting that stereotypical beliefs about fame were implicitly applied in assigning fame to people. In other research, using traditional semantic priming procedures, participants were found to more quickly identify male and female target names (Blair & Banaji, 1996) or pronouns (Banaji & Hardin, 1996) when the names matched the gender stereotypicality of the primes than when they were incongruent with the primes.

Support is also found for the unconscious operation of race stereotypes (Bodenhausen, Schwarz, Bless, & Wänke, 1995; Dovidio, Evans, & Tyler, 1986; Gilbert and Hixon, 1991; Glaser & Banaji, 1998; Kawakami, Dion, & Dovidio, 1998; Lepore & Brown, 1997; Spencer, Fein, Wolfe, Fong, & Dunn, 1998; Von Hippel, Sekaquaptewa, & Vargas, 1997; Wittenbrink, Judd, & Park, 1997). These studies show, for example, that race stereotypes are easily activated upon encountering members of stereotyped groups (e.g. Gilbert & Hixon, 1991; Gaertner & McLaughlin, 1983; Lepore & Brown, 1997). Other research has indicated that activating unconscious stereotypes can influence not only individuals' judgments of others but also their overt behavior (Bargh, Chen, & Burrows, 1996). Such experiments starkly reveal that perceivers may have less control over the knowledge they use in social interaction than they or even the scientists who study them may have assumed. When knowledge about the social groups to which one belongs enters into the equation of social judgment early and with force, it can shape the cumulative record of social interaction without the hindrance of awareness or hence responsibility.

Is unconscious stereotyping unavoidable?   Despite the preponderance of evidence that unconscious stereotypes hold a tight grasp over everyday thinking, the extent to which they are related to explicit beliefs and attitudes, the circumstances under which they are activated, and the degree to which unconscious stereotypes can be brought under deliberate control remain less certain. The question of the relationship between conscious and unconscious measures emerged early. Are those who hold weaker forms of conscious stereotypes also likely to evidence weaker forms of unconscious stereotypes? Early attempts to address this question suggested that unconscious stereotypes, assessed indirectly by examining nonverbal behavior, social perception, memory, and speeded reactions to social stimuli, are often unrelated or only slightly related to explicitly expressed stereotypes assessed by self-report measures (Banaji & Greenwald, 1995; Banaji & Hardin, 1996; Devine, 1989; Dunning & Sherman, 1997; Gaertner & McLaughlin, 1983; Hense, Penner, & Nelson, 1995; Von Hippel, Sekaquaptewa, & Vargas, 1997; Wittenbrink, Judd, & Park, 1997). However, there is also a body of recent evidence that suggests the contrary (Augoustinos, Innes, & Ahrens, 1994; Dovidio, Brigham, Johnson, & Gaertner, 1996; Hense, Penner, & Nelson, 1995; Kawakami, Dion, & Dovidio, 1998; Lepore & Brown, 1997; Locke, MacLeod, & Walker, 1994; Wittenbrink, Judd, & Park, 1997).

Lepore and Brown (1997, 1999) argued that individual differences in consciously expressed prejudice should predict unconscious stereotyping. Using a procedure similar to that used by Devine (1989), Lepore and Brown subliminally primed high- and low-prejudiced participants either with evaluatively neutral words that connoted the social category Blacks (without connoting particular stereotypes), or with nonsense syllables. Then, participants read behavioral descriptions of a race-unspecified target person and rated the target on a number of traits stereotypic of Blacks. Participants who had scored high in prejudice against Blacks employed more negative stereotypes and fewer positive stereotypes in the prime condition than in the no-prime condition. In contrast, low-prejudiced participants used more positive stereotypes in the prime condition than in the no-prime condition, but showed no difference on the negative scales. Lepore and Brown concluded that when race *category* information is primed but race *stereotypes* are not, unconscious race stereotyping is contingent upon how much one explicitly endorses prejudice.

Recently, Kawakami, Dion, & Dovidio (1998) proposed an additional explanation for the murky relationship between implicit and explicit beliefs. They noted that even in research in which implicit and explicit measures are associated, the association is relatively weak, and proposed that highly sensitive procedures may be necessary to pick up relationships between implicit stereotyping and explicit beliefs and attitudes. In addition, Cunningham, Nezlak, & Banaji (1999) have shown that a general ethnocentric personality disposition is related to specific unconscious prejudices (toward foreigners, Black Americans, the poor, Jews, and gays). Such efforts represent initial strides in identifying the conditions under which implicit and explicit beliefs converge and diverge, by identifying methodological, statistical, and theoretical hurdles that need to be set aside before a more complete picture regarding the relationship between conscious and unconscious stereotypes or prejudice may be observed.

Can unconscious stereotypes be controlled? The controllability of unconscious stereotypes has sparked considerable theoretical debate and empirical research. There is abundant evidence that stereotypes that operate unconsciously defend their territory fiercely, influencing social interactions even when perceivers are consciously vigilant and motivated to defeat them (Banaji & Greenwald, 1995; Bargh, in press; Blair & Banaji, 1996; see Greenwald & Banaji, 1995). Indeed, conscious attempts to purge stereotypic thoughts can easily backfire, bringing stereotypes to the fore with redoubled force (Macrae, Bodenhausen, Milne, & Ford, 1997; Nelson, Acker, & Manis, 1996; Nelson, Biernat, & Manis, 1990; Sherman, Stroessner,

Loftus, & Deguzman, 1997). Bargh (in press) has proposed a metaphor to characterize unconscious stereotyping, comparing it to a monster whose influence cannot be restrained once it is set into motion. The solution may lie in motivated individuals' ability to develop, over time, chronically accessible *egalitarian* beliefs that can counter the effects of unconscious stereotypes.

Our assessment of the issue of controlling automatic processes is in line with Bargh (in press). When a process operates unconsciously, there is little, if anything, that can be done to retract, revoke, or rescind. If this message from basic research on unconscious stereotypes is to make contact with the world it seeks to improve, the responsible suggestion at the present time is not the simplistic one to "just say no." Automatic stereotypes can and will influence perception, memory, and judgment. If the goal of judging individuals by the content of their character is one that this and other societies wish to take seriously, this body of social psychological research suggests two radical strategies. First, create the social conditions that allow new associations and new learning about social groups that blur the bright line that demarcates social groups. Second, generate individual and group-based strategies for compensation in conscious recognition of the stark and pervasive unconscious biases that operate in social judgment.

Unconscious Affect

Whereas no uncertainty is expressed about the existence of an unconscious form of cognition and whether it can be reliably assessed, there is still active debate regarding the existence of unconscious affect (Clore, 1994; Clore & Ketelaar, 1997; Kihlstrom, Mulvaney, Tobias, & Tobis, in press; LeDoux, 1994, 1996; Zajonc, 1994, 1998). Research on unconscious affect (and related concepts better recognized by the labels emotion, evaluation, attitude, and prejudice) has acquired increased prominence in social psychology in part from the desire to provide more complete models of social behavior, and in part from the availability of tractable methods to measure these warm and wet constructs. Perhaps a rigorous analysis of unconscious affect is naturally located in social psychology because of the field's long-standing interest in constructs that tap feeling, most obviously that of attitude and esteem (see Greenwald & Banaji, 1995). Research on unconscious evaluation, attitudes, and affect has its origins in a multitude of experimental traditions necessitating tough choices regarding selection for review. However, no attempt is made here to distinguish between the various terms that are used to refer to slightly differing aspects of the basic construct. For additional coverage and differing emphases see Kihlstrom, et al. (in press) and Zajonc (1998).

Physiological measures of evaluation and attitude

Among the reasons to probe evaluation and attitudes in their physiological form, Cacioppo, Crites, Gardner, & Berntson (1994, p. 121) offer the following rationale: "Unfortunately, the attitudes that individuals are least willing to report are often those that are most important to measure accurately, as they may differentiate individuals along theoretically important dimensions." Autonomic measures of unconscious evaluation were initially viewed with hope, but such assessments failed to separate intensity and valence of attitude (see Petty and Cacioppo, 1983; Zanna, Detweiler, & Olson, 1984). Facial EMG responses have also been obtained (Cacioppo, Martzke, Petty, & Tassinary, 1988) but again, their disadvantages have been noted, including the inability of such measures to protect against masking and distortion (see Cacioppo, Petty, Losch, & Kim, 1986). Recently, experiments in which a late positive potential (LPP) of the event-related brain potential (ERP) was related to evaluative categorization have been reported (Cacioppo, Crites, Berntson, & Coles, 1993). Further, the amplitude of LPP increases as a function of the mismatch between evaluative categorization and expectation of evaluative significance through salient contextual cues (Cacioppo et al., 1994). The amplitude of LPP is larger when a negative (rather than positive) attitude stimulus is presented within a sequence of positive stimuli, and such measures also appear to show sensitivity to intensity of negative stimuli. The obvious utility of such a measure to provide a marker of individual differences (e.g. fear responses to social situations implicated in phobia or negative responses to members of social groups as revealed in prejudice) will be realized in future experiments to test the construct and predictive validity of the measure.

Sensory-motor processes in evaluation and attitude

Evidence suggesting the involvement of motor processes and their sensory consequences in attitude formation merits attention here, because it points to yet another path that can reveal the role of unconscious evaluative processes in social cognition. Wells and Petty (1980) showed that the motor action of shaking versus nodding one's head while listening to persuasive messages resulted in lesser or greater agreement with the message. Likewise, Strack, Martin, & Stepper (1988) showed that motor activity that facilitated smiling increased ratings of the humor of cartoons compared with slightly differing motor activity that inhibited smiling. Such effects emerged in spite of subjects' being unaware of the meaning of the contractions of the zygomaticus muscle. Other research supports these findings that manipulations of facial expressions create affective states or influence attitudinal responses outside conscious awareness (Martin, Harlow, & Strack, 1992; Zajonc, Murphy, & Inglehart, 1989). Stepper & Strack (1993) have shown that proprioceptive cues from body posture (upright versus slumped) can influence the affective experience of pride, just as it can influence nonaffective judgments of effort, and Förster and Strack (1996) have shown that head nodding versus shaking increases memory for valence-consistent words. A distinction has been proposed between *experiential* knowledge, in which "feelings are 'immediately given' to the individual and have a distinct phenomenal quality" (Stepper & Strack, 1993, p. 218) versus *noetic* representations which reflect inferred, indirect knowledge, with the former being implicated in the information that is obtained from bodily posture or facial expression without conscious awareness. Finally, there is suggestive evidence that somatic manipulations involved in arm flexion versus arm extension can have small but reliable effects on the evaluation of attitudinally neutral stimuli such as ideographs, leading the authors to conclude that "attitudinal effects involve active motor processes and that a person does not need to know the evaluative or motivational significance of the motor process for it to have attitudinal effects" (Cacioppo, Priester, & Berntson, 1993, p. 16). This intriguing research needs to be nurtured and developed further, for it has the potential to inform about the role of unconscious processes in a most fundamental association of body and mind, and the potential for the products of such unconscious operation to influence feeling and social behavior.

Perception and memory reveal unconscious forms of affect

With the increased usage of indirect measures of *perception* and *memory*, a welcome blurring of the sharp distinction between these two processes has occurred. Viewing unconscious processes of memory and perception as they inform about the nature of affective experience and expression has contributed to a broadening of our understanding of consciousness.

Mere exposure   Among the most influential ideas linking perception and affect comes from the discovery that exposure to a stimulus leads to enhanced liking for it (Zajonc, 1968). There have been over two hundred published experiments testing this hypothesis (Bornstein, 1989; Bornstein & D'Agostino, 1994) that verify the reliability and robustness of the basic effect across a wide variety of stimulus forms, dependent variable formats, methods of exposure, and experimental settings. The finding that mere exposure produces liking has also been extended to research on interpersonal interaction (Bornstein, Leone, & Galley, 1987). The literature on category accessibility (see previous section on unconscious cognition) showed the peculiar effect of awareness on unconscious thought and social judgment (i.e. the influence of the priming event is most visible when that event is least available to conscious recollection). Research on the mere exposure effect has pointed up a parallel finding regarding unconscious affect: the magnitude of the effect is greater under conditions of subliminal rather than supraliminal exposure (Bornstein, 1989, 1992; Bornstein & D'Agostino, 1992). Theoretically, the mere exposure effect has shifted from being considered a phenomenon unique to the expression of affect to one that most parsimoniously fits into the broader landscape of familiarity and its effect on judgment more generally (Bornstein & D'Agostino, 1994; Jacoby & Kelley, 1987; Jacoby, Toth, Lindsay, & Debner, 1992; Mandler, Nakamura, and Van Zandt, 1987). Whatever the interpretational leaning, the mere exposure effect will remain among the most important discoveries of twentieth-century psychology. Here, its importance is in having identified a dissociation between what is consciously known and what is unconsciously felt.

Automatic evaluation   In the early 1970s the discovery was made that meaning is automatically activated upon the mere presentation of a word (Meyer & Schvaneveldt, 1971; Posner & Snyder, 1975). Efforts to resist activation of default meaning are moot when conditions do not permit the exerting of conscious control (Neely, 1977). The evidence to be reviewed here pertains to the finding that just as semantic meaning is extracted automatically upon presentation of a word, the evaluative meaning of information is also grasped without conscious control. Fazio, Sanbonmatsu, Powell, & Kardes (1986) showed that judgments of a target were facilitated when its valence was congruent rather than incongruent with that of the prime. Bargh, Chaiken, Govender, & Pratto (1992; Bargh, Chaiken, Raymond, &

Hymes, 1996) replicated and extended this finding, additionally proposing that autol evaluation occurs regardless of the strength (extremity) of prime valence, a claim about w there is debate (Chaiken & Bargh, 1993; Fazio, 1993), and even in the absence of a focus on the evaluative properties of information in judgment. Glaser & Banaji (1998) have reported a series of studies in which contrast effects in automatic evaluation appear when primes are of extreme valence, and they interpret this finding as an automatic correction for the implicitly perceived biasing influence of the prime.

In an effort to test the reliability, robustness, and boundary conditions of automatic evaluation, Greenwald, Draine, & Abrams (1996) and Greenwald, Klinger, & Liu (1989) effectively showed that the evaluative meaning of words is automatically registered by pre- senting the prime subliminally. In their most recent research they did this by inventing a variation of the technique called the "response window" that reliably produces the effect. As this research reveals, experiments have relied on time (measured in milliseconds) to respond to the target as an indicator of automatic evaluation. A second procedure has also been used in which evaluative primes, usually in the form of evaluative facial expressions, are briefly flashed (on the order of 4 milliseconds to prevent conscious registration) following which a neutral target (e.g. a Chinese ideograph) is to be rapidly judged. The replicated finding is that judgments of the neutral stimuli shift in the direction of the evaluative position of the prime (Murphy & Zajonc, 1993; Niedenthal, Setterlund, & Jones, 1994). Pratto & John (1991) used a Stroop color-naming task with evaluative stimuli in place of color names to extend the generality of automatic evaluation, showing that automatic evaluation can inter- fere with a conscious cognitive task.

Together, these experiments on automatic evaluation have changed our thinking about the existence and tractability of unconscious affect. First, they demonstrate that the affect- ive quality of information registers without conscious awareness of the stimulus (as in the subliminal presentation studies) and without conscious control over the response (Murphy, Monahan, & Zajonc, 1995). Second, it appears that automatic evaluations are sensitive only to gross distinctions of polarity and not to anything that can be considered to be a more fine-grained evaluative assessment (see Pratto, 1994; Zajonc, 1994). Finally, although the experiments have examined unconscious perception and memory for evaluative material, they have been interpreted as revealing an attitude. This is a noteworthy shift in social psychology's understanding of the concept of attitude. In commenting on research on un- consciously activated attitudes, Cacioppo, et al. (1993, p. 16) which one? note that "Indeed, the day may come when we regard attitudes as being 'evaluative perceptions' . . . aroused by stimuli." Because conceptions of attitudes as necessarily accessible to conscious awareness and control are difficult to shake off, the research summarized here will come to be viewed as historically important – as the first robust and reliable demonstrations that permitted a sufficient breakthrough to allow us to conceptualize attitudes as automatic evaluations.

Attitudes of prejudice

Experts who study attitudes and beliefs toward social groups have emphasized the need to treat attitude (prejudice) with the same importance as has been accorded to belief (stereotype), and have resisted the merging of these two constructs both in theory and in experimental practice. In part, this desire has stemmed from the conviction that attitudes of prejudice represent a unique and separable component from stereotypic beliefs. The organization of this chapter allows that distinction to continue even at the expense of separating research on unconscious prejudice from its cousin, unconscious stereotypes (see previous section). Just as the study of unconscious cognition has received greater attention than the study of unconscious affect, the parallel constructs of unconscious stereotype and unconscious prejudice have received similarly differential treatment. For evidence of this, see the greater coverage allowed to research on unconscious stereotypes compared with unconscious prejudice in a recent review (Fiske, 1998). Even since that review, however, attention to the study of unconscious prejudice has increased, largely from straightforward extensions of techniques to study automatic attitudes more generally. As with the study of stereotypes, such research is already challenging accepted notions of what prejudice means and raising troubling questions regarding the implications for how to regard human nature and human nurture (see Banaji & Bhaskar, 1999).

Indirect measures of prejudice have been of interest for over two decades (Crosby, Bromley, & Saxe, 1980), with continuing interest in related issues such as physiological indicators of prejudice (Vanman, Paul, Ito, & Miller, 1997; Vrana & Rollock, 1998), the relationship between public and private expressions of prejudice (Lambert, Cronen, Chasteen, & Lickel, 1996), and the impact of single direct or indirect exposure to negative behavior on judgments of groups and members of groups (Henderson-King & Nisbett, 1996). Yet a rigorous analysis of the role of consciousness and the disjunction between the unconscious roots of prejudice and its conscious manifestations has only just become possible. With methods to measure automatic evaluation and automatic stereotypes in place, it was only a matter of time before such techniques were used to study applications to prejudice. In fact, research to show that priming of race stereotypes produced evidence of linking evaluatively positive information with White compared with Black has been available for some time (Dovidio, Evans, & Tyler, 1986), in addition to evidence of a more general liking for one's own group. Associating neutral syllables with "we," "us," "ours" versus "they," "them," "theirs" produced greater liking for syllables attached to ingroup compared with outgroup primes (Perdue, Dovidio, Gurtman, & Tyler 1990).

With the first publication in 1998, the Implicit Association Test (IAT; Greenwald, McGhee, & Schwartz, 1998) has already attracted attention as a measure of automatic association, most notably in the investigation of automatic *evaluative* associations toward social groups and self. The attraction of the method lies in two of its most salient properties: (a) the ability to obtain large effects compared with priming methods of automatic evaluation, and (b) the ability to compellingly reveal a lack of control over automatic evaluative associations. Like related measures of automatic association (e.g. semantic priming) the technique is based on the assumption that if two concepts have come to be associated in memory, they will be associated more quickly when they are encountered. The IAT procedure operationalizes this assumption by requiring participants to swiftly associate exemplars of categories such as "old" and "young" along with exemplars of the evaluative category "bad" or "unpleasant." The speed with which old–good and young–bad are classified compared to the speed with which old–bad and young–good are classified produces a robust measure of the relative automatic evaluation of young and old. The original research demonstrated that the method is capable of detecting robust positive automatic associations toward flowers compared with insects, toward White compared with Black Americans (among non-Black subjects), and automatic ingroup positivity among Korean and Japanese Americans. (Reports of ongoing explorations with the technique are available at <www.yale.edu/implicit> or <depts.washington.edu/iat>, showing the wide application of the technique to investigate the attitudinal basis of depression or smoking, and attitudes toward a variety of social groups, e.g. Turks/Germans, Jews/Christians, East/West Germans, old/young, omnivore/vegetarian, male/female, overweight/thin.)

Research with the technique has explored attitudes toward self and social groups: female/male, feminine/masculine, or female leader/male leader, and the relationship between self-identity and gender attitude (Carpenter & Banaji, 1998; Lemm & Banaji, 1998; Mitchell, Nosek, & Banaji, 1998; Rudman & Glick, 1998; Rudman & Kilianski, 1998; Rudman, Greenwald, & McGhee, 1998); attitudes toward math/science versus arts and the relationship among automatic gender identity, gender stereotypes about math/science, self-math identity, and performance (Nosek, Banaji, & Greenwald, 1998); race identity, group-esteem, and self-esteem (Rosier, Banaji, & Greenwald, 1998); dissociated attitudes toward multiply categorizable objects (Mitchell, Nosek, & Banaji, 1998); attitudes regarding age, nationality, and religion (Rudman, Greenwald, Mellot, & Schwartz, 1998); and the role of personality in automatic prejudice (Cunningham, Nezlak, & Banaji, 1999). New designs for research have been suggested, based on a unified view of social cognition that draws on consistency theories (especially the Heiderian notion of balance) and associationist networks (Greenwald, et al., in press). However, several questions regarding its construct validity are only beginning to be addressed. The theoretical questions of utmost interest concern the predictive validity of this and other measures of automatic association (see Fazio, Jackson, Dunton, & Williams, 1995; Bessenoff & Sherman, 1998), developing measures of motivation to control prejudice (Dunton & Fazio, 1997; Plant & Devine, 1998), the relationship between automatic and controlled prejudice (Dovidio, Kawakami, Johnson, Johnson, & Howard, 1997; Kawakami, Dion, & Dovidio, 1998; Lepore & Brown, 1997; Von Hippel, Sekaquaptewa, & Vargas, 1997; Wittenbrink, Judd, & Park, 1997), and the malleability of automatic evaluative associations (Carpenter & Banaji, 1999; Dasgupta & Greenwald, 1999). Research on unconscious forms of prejudice elicits attention, in part because it speaks to a problem of great social significance. Because of this, and because of the potential to challenge many assumptions about the propensity to create harm without intention and awareness, this research requires the attention of a diversity of methodological and theoretical perspectives.

Conclusion

Beings with consciousness have the luxury to speculate that their own mind and behavior may also operate in a strikingly different mode, detached from consciousness. For hundreds of years, lay people and experts have believed that not only is there a mental world that remains hidden from consciousness, but that the workings of this world have important and far-reaching consequences for understanding who we are and who we aspire to be. Yet it is only in the last hundred years, beginning with experiments on humans and other animals, that a science of the unconscious was attempted and succeeded. In this chapter, we attended to the work of those who grounded their investigations firmly in the social world, the ether in which mental life operates.

The assumption that human social behavior can only be understood by asking those capable of language to say, preferably in grammatical English, what they think, feel, and intend to do about themselves and others in their world is a limiting one. In the last two decades, social psychology has shown the advances that are possible when such an assumption is momentarily set aside. In another context, we made the point that it is not difficult to imagine why it is that social perceivers and social psychologists have trouble imagining and investigating those processes that lie outside conscious awareness (Banaji, Blair, & Glaser, 1997). We argued that when the source of an action emanates in time and space unconnected to the observed action, it is difficult to grasp the connection between the source and target of influence. It took Newton's genius to discover that light, a source unattached to physical objects, was responsible for producing the subjective experience of color. Likewise, sources of influence on thoughts, affect, and motives are not likely to be discerned easily because their causes lie in places that are unreachable by conscious awareness. In addition, as we observed, even under conditions that permit awareness, the ability to control thoughts, feelings, and motives may be weaker than assumed. The problem here is more complex than contemplating an understanding of the physical world, for unlike the physical world, the object of inquiry (unconscious mind) is a part of the thinking system that must conduct the inquiry. The limits on being able to look inward are serious, and here the social world offers a solution for theory and praxis: a rich array of events, situations, and opportunities to explore the manner in which unconscious processes operate, in contexts in which they have significant impact on happiness, liberty, and justice. It is perhaps the case that as we discover the extent to which unconscious processes control social thought, feeling, and behavior, we will arrive at a fuller appreciation of the unique role played by consciousness in a species with the capability to evaluate the nature of the social unconscious.

REFERENCES

Andersen, S. M., & Glassman, N. S. (1996). Responding to significant others when they are not there: Effects on interpersonal interference, motivation, and affect. In R. M. Sorrentino & E. T. Higgins (Eds.), *Handbook of motivation and cognition* Vol. 3 (pp. 262–321). New York: Guilford Press.

Augoustinos, M., Innes, J. M., & Ahrens, C. (1994). Stereotypes and prejudice: The Australian experience. *British Journal of Social Psychology, 33*, 125–141.

Baldwin, M. W. (1994). Primed relational schemas as a source of self-evaluative reactions. *Journal of Social and Clinical Psychology, 13*, 380–403.

Baldwin, M. W., Carrell, S. E., & Lopez, D. F. (1990). Priming relationship schemas: My advisor and the Pope are watching me from the back of my mind. *Journal of Experimental Social Psychology, 26*, 435–454.

Banaji, M. R., & Bhaskar, R. (1999). Implicit stereotypes and memory: The bounded rationality of social beliefs. In D. L. Schacter and E. Scarry (Eds.), *Belief and memory*. Cambridge, MA: Harvard University Press.

Banaji, M. R., & Greenwald, A. G. (1995). Implicit gender stereotyping in judgments of fame. *Journal of Personality and Social Psychology, 68*, 181–198.

Banaji, M. R., & Hardin, C. (1996). Automatic stereotyping. *Psychological Science, 7* (3), 136–141.

Banaji, M. R., & Prentice, D. A. (1994). The self in social contexts. *Annual Review of Psychology, 45,* 297–332.

Banaji, M. R., Blair, I. V., & Glaser, J. (1997). Environments and unconscious processes. In R. S. Wyer (Ed.), *The automaticity of everyday life: Advances in social cognition,* vol. 10 (pp. 63–74). Mahwah, NJ: Erlbaum.

Banaji, M. R., Hardin, C., & Rothman, A. J. (1993). Implicit stereotyping in person judgment. *Journal of Personality and Social Psychology, 65,* 272–281.

Bargh, J. A. (1997). The automaticity of everyday life. In R. S. Wyer, Jr. (Ed.), *The automaticity of everyday life: Advances in social cognition* Vol. 10 (pp. 1–61). Mahwah, NJ: Lawrence Erlbaum Associates.

Bargh, J. A. (1999). The cognitive monster: The case against the controllability of automatic stereotype effects. In S. Chaiken & Y. Trope (Eds.), *Dual process theories in social psychology.* New York: Guilford Press.

Bargh, J. A., Chen, M., & Burrows, L. (1996). Automaticity of social behavior: Direct effects of trait construct and stereotype activation on action. *Journal of Personality and Social Psychology, 71,* 230–244.

Bargh, J. A., Chaiken, S., Govender, R., & Pratto, F. (1992). The generality of the automatic attitude activation effect. *Journal of Personality and Social Psychology, 62,* 893–912.

Bargh, J. A., Chaiken, S., Raymond, P., & Hymes, C. (1996). The automatic evaluation effect: Unconditional automatic attitude activation with a pronunciation task. *Journal of Experimental Social Psychology, 32,* 104–128.

Beck, A. T. (1976). *Cognitive therapy and the emotional disorders.* New York: Penguin Books/Meridian.

Bessenoff, G. R., & Sherman, J. W. (1998). Automatic and controlled components of prejudice toward the overweight: Evaluation versus stereotype activation. Unpublished manuscript, Northwestern University.

Blair, I. V., & Banaji, M. R. (1996). Automatic and controlled processes in stereotype priming. *Journal of Personality and Social Psychology, 70,* 1142–1163.

Blascovich, J., Wyer, N. A., Swart, L. A., & Kibler, J. L. (1997). Racism and racial categorization. *Journal of Personality and Social Psychology, 72,* 1364–1372.

Bodenhausen, G. V., Schwarz, N., Bless, H., & Wänke, M. (1995). Effects of atypical exemplars on racial beliefs: Enlightened racism or generalized appraisals? *Journal of Experimental Social Psychology, 31,* 48–63.

Bornstein, R. F. (1989). Exposure and affect: Overview and meta-analysis of research, 1968–1987. *Psychological Bulletin, 106,* 265–289.

Bornstein, R. F. & D'Agostino, P. R. (1992). Stimulus recognition and the mere exposure effect. *Journal of Personality and Social Psychology, 63,* 545–552.

Bornstein, R. F., & D'Agostino, P. R. (1994). The attribution and discounting of perceptual fluency: Preliminary tests of a perceptual fluency/attributional model of the mere exposure effect. *Social Cognition, 12,* 103–128.

Bornstein, R. F., & Pittman, T. S. (1992). *Perception without awareness: Cognitive, clinical, and social perspectives.* New York: Guilford Press.

Bornstein, R. F., Leone, D. R., & Galley, D. J. (1987). The generalizability of subliminal mere exposure effects: Influence of stimuli perceived without awareness on social behavior. *Journal of Personality and Social Psychology, 53,* 1070–1079.

Brewer, M. B. (1988). A dual process model of impression formation. In T. K. Srull & R. S. Wyer (Eds.), *Advances in social cognition* Vol. 1 (pp. 1–36). Hillsdale, NJ: Erlbaum.

Burnstein, E., & Schul, Y. (1982). The informational basis of social judgments: Operations in forming an impression of another person. *Journal of Experimental Social Psychology, 18,* 217–234.

Cacioppo, J. T., Priester, J. R., & Berntson, G. G. (1993). Rudimentary determinants of attitudes: II. Arm flexion and extension have differential effects on attitudes. *Journal of Personality and Social Psychology, 65*, 5–17.

Cacioppo, J. T., Crites, S. L., Berntson, G. G., & Coles, M. G. (1993). If attitudes affect how stimuli are processed, should they not affect the event-related brain potential? *Psychological Science, 4*, 108–112.

Cacioppo, J. T., Crites, S. L., Gardner, W. L., & Berntson, G. G. (1994). Bioelectrical echoes from evaluative categorizations: I. A late positive brain potential that varies as a function of trait negativity and extremity. *Journal of Personality and Social Psychology, 67*, 115–125.

Cacioppo, J. T., Martzke, J. S., Petty, R. E., & Tassinary, L. G. (1988). Specific forms of facial EMG response index emotions during an interview: From Darwin to the continuous flow hypothesis of affect-laden information processing. *Journal of Personality and Social Psychology, 54*, 592–604.

Cacioppo, J. T., Petty, R. E., Losch, M. E., & Kim, H. S. (1986). Electromyographic activity over facial muscle regions can differentiate the valence and intensity of affective reactions. *Journal of Personality and Social Psychology, 50*, 260–268.

Carlston, D. E., & Skowronski, J. J. (1994). Savings in the relearning of trait information as evidence for spontaneous inference generation. *Journal of Personality and Social Psychology, 66*, 840–856.

Carlston, D. E., Skowronski, J. J., & Sparks, C. (1995). Savings in relearning: II. On the formation of behavior-based trait associations and inferences. *Journal of Personality and Social Psychology, 69*, 420–436.

Carpenter, S. J., & Banaji, M. R. (1998). Implicit attitudes and behavior toward female leaders. Paper presented at Midwestern Psychological Association meeting, Chicago.

Chaiken, S., & Bargh, J. A. (1996). Occurrence versus moderation of the automatic attitude activation effect: Reply to Fazio. *Journal of Personality and Social Psychology, 64*, 759–765.

Clore, G. L. (1994). Why emotions are never unconscious. In P. Ekman & R. J. Davidson (Eds.), *The nature of emotion: Fundamental questions* (pp. 285–190). New York: Oxford University Press.

Clore, G. L., & Ketelaar, T. (1997). Minding our emotions: On the role of automatic, unconscious affect. In R. S. Wyer (Ed.), *The automaticity of everyday life: Advances in social cognition* Vol. 10 (pp. 105–120). Mahwah, NJ: Lawrence Erlbaum Associates.

Croizet, J., & Claire, T. (1998). Extending the concept of stereotype threat to social class: The intellectual underperformance of students from low socioeconomic backgrounds. *Personality and Social Psychology Bulletin, 24*, 588–594.

Crosby, F., Bromley, S., & Saxe, L. (1980). Recent unobtrusive studies of Black and White discrimination and prejudice: A literature review. *Psychological Bulletin, 87*, 546–563.

Cunningham, W. A., Nezlak, J. B., & Banaji, M. R. (1999). The roots of prejudice. Unpublished manuscript, Yale University.

D'Agostino, P. R., & Beegle, W. (1996). A reevaluation of the evidence for spontaneous trait inferences. *Journal of Experimental Social Psychology, 32*, 153–164.

Dasgupta, N., & Greenwald, A. G. (1999). Exposure to admired group members reduces implicit prejudice. Paper presented at the annual meetings of the American Psychological Society, Denver, CO.

Devine, P. G. (1989). Stereotypes and prejudice: Their automatic and controlled components. *Journal of Personality and Social Psychology, 56*, 5–18.

Dovidio, J. F., Evans, N., & Tyler, R. B. (1986). Racial stereotypes: The contents of their cognitive representations. *Journal of Experimental Social Psychology, 22*, 22–37.

Dovidio, J. F., Brigham, J., Johnson, B., & Gaertner, S. (1996). Stereotyping, prejudice, and discrimination: Another look. In N. Macrae, C. Stangor, & M. Hewstone (Eds.), *Stereotypes and stereotyping* (pp. 1276–1319). New York: Guilford Press.

Dovidio, J. F., Kawakami, K., Johnson, C., Johnson, B., & Howard, A. (1997). On the nature of prejudice: Automatic and controlled processes. *Journal of Experimental Social Psychology, 33*, 510–540.

Dunning, D., & Sherman, D. A. (1997). Stereotypes and tacit inference. *Journal of Personality and Social Psychology, 73*, 459–471.

Dunton, B. C., & Fazio, R. H. (1997). An individual difference measure of motivation to control prejudiced reactions. *Personality and Social Psychology Bulletin, 23*, 316–326.

Eckes, T. (1994). Explorations in gender cognition: Content and structure of female and male subtypes. *Social Cognition, 12* (1), 37–60.

Fazio, R. H. (1993). Variability in the likelihood of automatic attitude activation: Data reanalysis and commentary on Bargh, Chaiken, Govender & Pratto (1992). *Journal of Personality and Social Psychology, 64*, 753–758.

Fazio, R. H., Jackson, J. R., Dunton, B. C., & Williams, C. J. (1995). Variability in automatic activation as an unobtrusive measure of racial attitudes: A bona fide pipeline? *Journal of Personality and Social Psychology, 69*, 1013–1027.

Fazio, R. H. Sanbonmatsu, D. M., Powell, M. C., & Kardes, F. R. (1986). On the automatic activation of attitudes. *Journal of Personality and Social Psychology, 50*, 229–238.

Fiske, S. T. (1998). Stereotyping, prejudice, and discrimination. In D. T. Gilbert, S. T. Fiske, & G. Lindzey (Eds.), *The handbook of social psychology* Vol. 2 (pp. 357–411). Boston: Mcgraw-Hill.

Fiske, S. T., & Neuberg, S. L. (1990). A continuum of impression formation, from category-based to individuating processes: Influences of information and motivation on attention and interpretation. In M. P. Zanna (Ed.), *Advances in experimental social psychology* Vol. 23 (pp. 1–74). New York: Academic Press.

Ford, T. E., Stangor, C., & Duan, C. (1994). Influence of social category accessibility and category-associated trait accessibility on judgments of individuals. *Social Cognition, 12* (2), 149–168.

Förster, J., & Strack, F. (1996). Influence of overt head movements on memory for valenced words: A case of conceptual–motor compatibility. *Journal of Personality and Social Psychology, 71*, 421–430.

Gaertner, S. L., & McLaughlin, J. P. (1983). Racial stereotypes: Associations and ascriptions of positive and negative characteristics. *Social Psychology Quarterly, 46*, 23–30.

Gilbert, D. T., & Hixon, J. G. (1991). The trouble of thinking: Activation and application of stereotypic beliefs. *Journal of Personality and Social Psychology, 60*, 509–517.

Gilbert, D. T., & Krull, D. S. (1988). Seeing less and knowing more: The benefits of perceptual ignorance. *Journal of Personality and Social Psychology, 54*, 93–102.

Gilbert, D. T., & Osborne, R. E. (1989). Thinking backward: The curable and incurable consequences of cognitive busyness. *Journal of Personality and Social Psychology, 57*, 940–949.

Gilbert, D. T., Giesler, R. B., & Morris, K. A. (1995). When comparisons arise. *Journal of Personality and Social Psychology, 69*, 227–236.

Gilbert, D. T., Pelham, B. W., & Krull, D. S. (1988). On cognitive busyness: When person perceivers meet persons perceived. *Journal of Personality and Social Psychology, 54*, 733–740.

Glaser, J., & Banaji, M. R. (1998). Assimilation and contrast in automatic evaluation and prejudice. Paper presented at the annual meeting of the Society for the Psychological Study of Social Issues, Ann Arbor, MI.

Gotlib, I. H., & McCann, C. D. (1984). Construct accessibility and depression: An examination of cognitive and affective factors. *Journal of Personality and Social Psychology, 93*, 19–30.

Graham, S., & Hudley, C. (1994). Attributions of aggressive and nonaggressive African–American male early adolescents: A study of construct accessibility. *Developmental Psychology, 30*, 365–373.

Greenwald, A. G. (1992). New look 3: Unconscious cognition reclaimed. *American Psychologist, 47*, 766–779.

Greenwald, A. G., & Banaji, M. R. (1989). The self as a memory system: Powerful, but ordinary. *Journal of Personality and Social Psychology, 57*, 41–54.

Greenwald, A. G., & Banaji, M. R. (1995). Implicit social cognition: Attitudes, self-esteem, and stereotypes. *Psychological Review, 102* (1), 4–27.

Greenwald, A. G., & Pratkanis, A. R. (1984). The self. In R. S. Wyer & T. K. Srull (Eds.), *Handbook of social cognition* Vol. 3 (pp. 129–178). Hillsdale, NJ: Erlbaum.

Greenwald, A. G., Banaji, M. R., Rudman, L. A., Farnham, S. D., Nosek, B. A., & Rosier, M. (in press). Prologue to a unified theory of attitudes, stereotypes, and self-concept. In J. P. Forges (Ed.), *Feeling and thinking: The role of affect in social cognition and behavior.* New York: Cambridge University Press.

Greenwald, A. G., Draine, S. C., & Abrams, R. L. (1996). Three cognitive markers of unconscious semantic activation. *Science, 283*, 1699–1702.

Greenwald, A. G., Klinger, M. R., & Liu, T. J. (1989). Unconscious processing of dichoptically masked words. *Memory & Cognition, 17*, 35–47.

Greenwald, A. G., McGhee, D. E., & Schwartz, J. K. (1998). Measuring individual difference in implicit cognition: The Implicit Association Test. *Journal of Personality and Social Psychology.*

Hamilton, D. L., & Sherman, J. W. (1994). Stereotypes. In R. S. Wyer, Jr., & T. K. Srull (Eds.), *Handbook of social cognition* Vol. 2 (pp. 1–68). Hillsdale, NJ: Erlbaum.

Henderson-King, E. I., & Nisbett, R. E. (1996). Anti-black prejudice as a function of exposure to the negative behavior of a single black person. *Journal of Personality and Social Psychology, 71*, 654–664.

Hense, R. L., Penner, L. A., & Nelson, D. L. (1995). Implicit memory for age stereotypes. *Social Cognition, 13* (4), 399–415.

Herr, P. M., Sherman, S. J., & Fazio, R. H. (1983). On the consequences of priming: Assimilation and contrast efforts. *Journal of Experimental Social Psychology, 19*, 323–340.

Higgins, E. T. (1989b). Knowledge accessibility and activation: Subjectivity and suffering from unconscious sources. In J. S. Uleman & J. A. Bargh (Eds.), *Unintended thought* (pp. 75–123). New York: Guilford Press.

Higgins, E. T. (1996). Knowledge activation: Accessibility, applicability, and salience. In E. T. Higgins & A. W. Kruglanski (Eds.), *Social psychology: Handbook of basic principles* (pp. 133–168). New York: Guilford Press.

Higgins, E. T., Bargh, J. A., & Lombardi, W. (1985). The nature of priming effects on categorization. *Journal of Experimental Psychology: Learning, Memory, and Cognition, 11*, 59–69.

Higgins, E. T., Rholes, W. S., & Jones, C. R. (1977). Category accessibility and impression formation. *Journal of Experimental Social Psychology, 13*, 141–154.

Higgins, E. T., Strauman, T., & Klein, R. (1986). Standards and the process of self-evaluation. In R. M. Sorrentino & E. T. Higgins (Eds.), *Handbook of motivation and cognition: Foundation of social behavior* Vol. 1 (pp. 23–63). New York: Guilford Press.

Icheiser, G. (1949). Misunderstandings in human relations: A study in false social perception. *American Journal of Sociology, 55*, Part 2.

Jacoby, L. L. & Kelley, C. M. (1987). Unconscious influences of memory for a prior event. *Personality and Social Psychology Bulletin, 13*, 314–336.

Jacoby, L. L., Toth, J. P., Lindsay, D. S., & Debner, J. A. (1992). Lectures for a layperson: Methods for revealing unconscious processes. In R. F. Bornstein and T. S. Pittman (Eds.), *Perception without awareness: Cognitive, clinical, and social perspectives* (pp. 81–120). New York: Guilford Press.

Johnson, J., Bryant, M., Jackson, L. A., Gatto, L., Nowak, A., & MacVittie, T. (1994). Construct accessibility, AIDS, and judgment. *Journal of Social Behavior and Personality, 9*, 191–198.

Johnson-Laird, P. N. (1983). A computational analysis of consciousness. *Cognition and Brain Theory, 6*, 499–508.

Kant, I. (1790/1987). *Critique of judgment*. Trans. W. S. Pluhar. Indianapolis, IN: Hackett Publishing.

Katz, D., & Braly, K. (1933). Racial stereotypes of one hundred college students. *Journal of Abnormal and Social Psychology*, *28*, 280–290.

Kawakami, K., Dion, K. L., & Dovidio, J. F. (1998). Racial prejudice and stereotype activation. *Personality and Social Psychology Bulletin*, *24* (4), 407–416.

Kihlstrom, J. F. (1990). The psychological unconscious. In L. A. Pervin (Ed.), *Handbook of personality: Theory and research* (pp. 445–464). New York: Guilford Press.

Kihlstrom, J. F., Mulvaney, S., Tobias, B. A., & Tobis, I. P. (in press). The emotional unconscious.

Kihlstrom, J. F., Cantor, N., Albright, J. S., Chew, B. R., Klein, S. B., & Niedenthal, P. M. (1988). Information processing and the study of the self. In. L. Berkowitz, et al. (Eds.), *Advances in experimental social psychology* Vol. 21 (pp. 145–178). San Diego: Academic Press.

Klein, S. B., & Loftus, J. (1990). The role of abstract and exemplar-based knowledge in self-judgments: Implications for a cognitive model of the self. In T. K. Srull & R. S. Wyer (Eds.), *Content and process specificity in the effects of prior experiences: Advances in social cognition* Vol. 3 (pp. 131–139). Hillsdale, NJ: Lawrence Erlbaum Associates.

Klein, S. B., Loftus, J., & Kihlstrom, J. F. (1996). Self-knowledge of an amnesic patient: Toward a neuropsychology of personality and social psychology. *Journal of Experimental Psychology: General*, *125*, 250–260.

Lambert, A. (1995). Stereotypes and social judgment: The consequences of group variability. *Journal of Personality and Social Psychology*, *68*, 388–403.

Lambert, A. J., Cronen, S., Chasteen, A. L., & Lickel, B. (1996). Private vs. public expressions of racial prejudice. *Journal of Experimental Social Psychology*, *32*, 437–459.

Lau, R. R. (1989). Construct accessibility and electoral choice. *Political Behavior*, *11*, 5–32.

LeDoux, J. E. (1994). Emotional processing, but not emotions, can occur unconsciously. In P. Ekman & R. J. Davidson (Eds.), *The nature of emotion: Fundamental questions* (pp. 291–292). New York: Oxford University Press.

LeDoux, J. E. (1996). *The emotional brain*. New York: Simon & Schuster.

Lemm, K., & Banaji, M. R. (1998). Implicit and explicit gender identity and attitudes toward gender. Paper presented at the Midwestern Psychological Association meeting, Chicago.

Lepore, L., & Brown, R. (1997). Category and stereotype activation: Is prejudice inevitable? *Journal of Personality and Social Psychology*, *72*, 275–287.

Lepore, L., & Brown, R. (1999). Exploring automatic stereotype activation: A challenge to the inevitability of prejudice. In D. Abrams & M. A. Hogg (Eds.), *Social identity and social cognition* (pp. 141–163). Oxford: Blackwell Publishers.

Levy, B. (1996). Improving memory in old age through implicit self-stereotyping. *Journal of Personality and Social Psychology*, *71*, 1092–1107.

Linville, P. W., & Carlston, D. E. (1994). Social cognition of the self. In P. G. Devine, D. C. Hamilton, & T. M. Ostrom (Eds.), *Social cognition: Impact on social psychology* (pp. 143–193). New York: Academic Press.

Locke, V., MacLeod, C., & Walker, I. (1994). Automatic and controlled activation of stereotypes: Individual differences associated with prejudice. *British Journal of Social Psychology*, *33*, 29–46.

Macrae, C. N., Bodenhausen, G. V., Milne, A. B., & Ford, R. L. (1997). On the regulation of recollection: The intentional forgetting of stereotypical memories. *Journal of Personality and Social Psychology*, *72*, 709–719.

Macrae, C. N., Bodenhausen, G. V., Milne, A. B., Thorn, T. M. J., & Castelli, L. (1997). On the activation of social stereotypes: The moderating role of processing objectives. *Journal of Experimental Social Psychology*, *33*, 471–489.

Mandler, G., Nakamura, Y., & Van Zandt, B. J. S. (1987). Nonspecific effects of exposure on stimuli that cannot be recognized. *Journal of Experimental Psychology: Learning, Memory, & Cognition, 13,* 646–648.

Markus, H. (1977). Self-schemata and processing information about the self. *Journal of Personality and Social Psychology, 3,* 445–450.

Martin, L. L. (1986). Set/reset: Use and disuse of concepts in impression formation. *Journal of Personality and Social Psychology, 51,* 493–504.

Martin, L. L., Harlow, T. F., & Strack, F. (1992). The role of bodily sensations in the evaluation of social events. *Personality & Social Psychology Bulletin, 18,* 412–419.

Meyer, D. E., & Schevaneveldt, R. W. (1971). Facilitation in recognizing pairs of words: Evidence of a dependence between retrieval operations. *Journal of Experimental Psychology, 90,* 227–234.

Mitchell, J., Nosek, B., & Banaji, M. R. (1998). A rose by any other name? Dissociated attitudes toward social group members. Paper presented at the American Psychological Society meeting, Washington, DC.

Moskowitz, G. B. (1993). Person organization with a memory set: Are spontaneous trait inferences personality characteristics or behaviour labels? *European Journal of Personality, 7,* 195–208.

Moskowitz, G. B., & Roman, R. J. (1992). Spontaneous trait inferences as self-generated primes: Implications for conscious social judgment. *Journal of Personality and Social Psychology, 62,* 728–738.

Murphy, S. T., & Zajonc, R. B. (1993). Affect, cognition, and awareness: Affective priming with suboptimal and optimal stimulus. *Journal of Personality and Social Psychology, 64,* 723–739.

Murphy, S. T., Monahan, J. L., & Zajonc, R. B. (1995). Additivity of nonconscious affect: Combined effects of priming and exposure. *Journal of Personality and Social Psychology, 69,* 589–602.

Neely, J. H. (1977). Semantic priming and retrieval from lexical memory: Roles of inhibitionless spreading activation and limited-capacity attention. *Journal of Experimental Social Psychology, 26,* 505–527.

Nelson, T. E., Acker, M., & Manis, M. (1996). Irrepressible stereotypes. *Journal of Experimental Social Psychology, 32,* 13–38.

Nelson, T. E., Biernat, M. B., & Manis, M. (1990). Everyday base rates (sex stereotypes): Potent and resilient. *Journal of Personality and Social Psychology, 59,* 664–675.

Newman, S. L., & Uleman, J. S. (1989). Spontaneous trait inference. In J. Uleman & J. A. Bargh (Eds.), *Unintended thought* (pp. 155–188). New York: Guilford Press.

Newman, L. S., & Uleman, J. S. (1990). Assimilation and contrast effects in spontaneous trait inference. *Personality and Social Psychology Bulletin, 16,* 224–240.

Niedenthal, P. M., Setterlund, M. B., & Jones, D. E. (1994). Emotional organization of perceptual memory. In P. M. Niedenthal & S. Kitayama (Eds.), *The heart's eye: Emotional influences in perception and attention* (pp. 87–113). San Diego: Academic Press.

Norris, A. E., & Devine, P. G. (1992). Linking pregnancy concerns to pregnancy risk avoidant action: The role of construct accessibility. *Personality and Social Psychology Bulletin, 18,* 118–127.

Nosek, B., Banaji, M. R., & Greenwald, A. G. (1998). Math = Bad + Male, Me = Good + Female, therefore Math – Me. Paper presented at the American Psychological Society meeting, Washington, DC.

Pendry, L. F., & Macrae, C. N. (1996). What the disinterested perceiver overlooks: Goal-directed social categorization. *Personality and Social Psychology Bulletin, 22,* 249–256.

Perdue, C. W., Dovidio, J. F., Gurtman, M. B., & Tyler, R. B. (1990). "Us" and "Them": Social categorization and the process of intergroup bias. *Journal of Personality and Social Psychology, 59,* 475–486.

Petty, R. E., & Cacioppo, J. T. (1983). The role of bodily responses in attitude measurement and change. In J. T. Cacioppo and R. E. Petty (Eds.), *Social psychophysiology: A sourcebook* (pp. 51–101). New York: Guilford Press.

Plant, E. A., & Devine, P. A. (1998). Internal and external motivation to respond without prejudice. *Journal of Personality and Social Psychology, 75*, 811–832.

Posner, M. I., & Snyder, C. R. R. (1975). Attention and cognitive control. In R. L. Solso (Ed.), *Information processing and cognition: The Loyola Symposium* (pp. 55–85). Hillsdale, NJ: Lawrence Erlbaum Associates.

Pratto, F. (1994). Consciousness and automatic evaluation. In P. M. Niedenthal and S. Kitayama (Eds.), *The heart's eye: Emotional influences in perception and attention* (pp. 115–143). San Diego: Academic Press.

Pratto, F., & Bargh, J. A. (1991). Stereotyping based on apparently individuating information: Trait and global components of sex stereotypes under attention overload. *Journal of Experimental Social Psychology, 27*, 26–47.

Pratto, F., & John, O. P. (1991). Automatic vigilance: The attention-grabbing power of negative social information. *Journal of Personality and Social Psychology, 61*, 380–391.

Rosier, M., Banaji, M. R., & Greenwald, A. G. (1998). Implicit and explicit self-esteem & group membership. Paper presented at the Midwestern Psychological Association meetings, Chicago.

Ross, L. (1977). The intuitive psychologist and his shortcomings. In L. Berkowitz (Ed.), *Advances in experimental social psychology* Vol. 10 (pp. 173–220). New York: Academic Press.

Ross, M., & Olson, J. M. (1981). An expectancy-attribution model of the effects of placebos. *Psychological Review, 88*, 408–437.

Rudman, L. A., & Borgida, E. (1995). The afterglow of construct accessibility: The behavioral consequences of priming men to view women as sexual objects. *Journal of Experimental Social Psychology, 31*, 493–517.

Rudman, L. A., & Glick, P. (1998). Implicit gender stereotypes and backlash toward agentic women: The hidden costs to women of a kinder, gentler image of managers. Unpublished manuscript, Rutgers University.

Rudman, L. A., & Kilianski, S. (1998). Implicit and explicit attitudes toward female authority. Unpublished manuscript, Rutgers University.

Rudman, L. A., Greenwald, A. G., & McGhee, D. E. (1998). Sex differences in gender stereotypes revealed by the Implicit Association Test. Unpublished manuscript, Rutgers University.

Rudman, L. A., Greenwald, A. G., Mellot, D. S., & Schwartz, J. L. K. (1998). Automatic prejudices: Flexibility and generality of the Implicit Association Test. Unpublished manuscript, Rutgers University.

Sedikides, C., & Skowronski, J. J. (1990). Towards reconciling personality and social psychology: A construct accessibility approach. *Journal of Social Behavior and Personality, 5*, 531–546.

Sedikides, C., & Skowronski, J. J. (1993). The self in impression formation: Trait centrality and social perception. *Journal of Experimental Social Psychology, 29*, 347–357.

Sherman, J. W., Stroessner, S. J., Loftus, S. T., & Deguzman, G. (1997). Stereotype suppression and recognition memory for stereotypical and nonstereotypical information. *Social Cognition, 15* (3), 205–215.

Shih, M., Pittinsky, T. L., & Ambady, N. (1999). Stereotype susceptibility: Identity salience and shifts in quantitative performance. *Psychological Science, 10*, 81–84.

Shrum, L. J., & O'Guinn, T. C. (1993). Processes and effects in the construction of social reality: Construct accessibility as an explanatory variable. *Communications Research, 20*, 436–471.

Skowronski, J. J., Carlston, D. E., Mae, L., & Crawford, M. T. (1998). Spontaneous trait transference: Communicators take on the qualities they describe in others. *Journal of Personality and Social Psychology, 74*, 837–848.

Southwick, L., Steele, C., Lindell, M. (1986). The roles of historical experience and construct accessibility in judgments about alcoholism. *Cognitive Therapy and Research, 10*, 167–186.

Spencer, S. J., Fein, S., Wolfe, C. T., Fong, C., & Dunn, M. A. (1998). Automatic activation of stereotypes: The role of self-image threat. *Personality and Social Psychology Bulletin, 24* (11), 1139–1152.

Stangor, C., & Lange, J. E. (1994). Mental representations of social groups: Advances in understanding stereotypes and stereotyping. *Advances in Experimental Social Psychology, 26,* 357–416.

Steele, C. M. (1997). A threat in the air: How stereotypes shape the intellectual identities and performance of women and African Americans. *American Psychologist, 52,* 613–629.

Steele, C. M., & Aronson, J. (1995). Stereotype threat and the intellectual test performance of African Americans. *Journal of Personality and Social Psychology, 69,* 797–811.

Stepper, S., & Strack, F. (1993). Proprioceptive determinants of emotional and nonemotional feelings. *Journal of Personality and Social Psychology, 64,* 211–220.

Strack, F., Martin, L. L., & Stepper, S. (1988). Inhibiting and facilitating conditions of the human smile: Unobtrusive test of the facial feedback hypothesis. *Journal of Personality and Social Psychology, 54,* 768–777.

Stroessner, S. J. (1996). Social categorization by race or sex: Effects of perceived non-normalcy on response times. *Social Cognition, 14* (3), 247–276.

Swann, W. B., Hixon, J. G., Stein-Seroussi, A., & Gilbert, D. T. (1990). The fleeting gleam of praise: Cognitive processes underlying behavioral reactions to self-relevant feedback. *Journal of Personality and Social Psychology, 59,* 17–26.

Trope, Y. (1986). Identification and inferential processes in dispositional attribution. *Psychological Review, 93,* 237–257.

Trope, Y., & Alfieri, T. (1997). Effortfulness and flexibility of dispositional judgment processes. *Journal of Personality and Social Psychology, 73,* 662–674.

Trope, Y., & Liberman, A. (1993). The use of trait conceptions to identify other people's behavior and draw inferences about their personalities. *Personality and Social Psychology Bulletin,* 553–562.

Trope, Y., & Thompson, E. P. (1997). Looking for truth in all the wrong places? Asymmetric search of individuating information about stereotyped group members. *Journal of Personality and Social Psychology, 73,* 229–241.

Uleman, J. S., & Bargh, J. A. (Eds.) (1989). *Unintended thought.* New York: Guilford Press.

Uleman, J. S., Newman, L., & Winter L. (1992). Can personality traits be inferred automatically? Spontaneous inferences require cognitive capacity at encoding. *Consciousness and Cognition, 1,* 77–90.

Uleman, J. S., Hon, A., Roman, R. J., & Moskowitz, G. B. (1996). On line evidence for spontaneous trait inferences at encoding. *Personality and Social Psychology Bulletin, 22,* 377–394.

Uleman, J. S., Moskowitz, G. B., Roman, R. J., & Rhee, E. (1993) Tacit, manifest, and intentional reference: How spontaneous trait inferences refer to persons. *Social Cognition, 11,* 321–351.

Van Knippenberg, A., & Dijksterhuis, A. (1996). A posteriori stereotype activation: The preservation of stereotypes through memory distortion. *Social Cognition, 14* (1), 21–53.

Vanman, E. J., Paul, B. Y., Ito, T. A., & Miller N. (1997). The modern face of prejudice and structural features that moderate the effect of cooperation on affect. *Journal of Personality and Social Psychology, 73,* 941–959.

Von Hippel, W., Sekaquaptewa, D., & Vargas, P. (1997). The linguistic intergroup bias as an implicit indicator of prejudice. *Journal of Experimental Social Psychology, 33,* 490–509.

Vrana, S. R., & Rollock, D. (1998). Physiological response to a minimal social encounter: Effects of gender, ethnicity, and social context. *Psychophysiology, 35,* 462–469.

Walsh, W. A., & Banaji, M. R. (1997). The collective self. In J. G. Snodgrass & R. L. Thompson (Eds.), *The self across psychology: Self-recognition, self-awareness, and the self concept. Annals of the New York Academy of Sciences* Vol. 818 (pp. 193–214). New York: New York Academy of Sciences.

Wann, D. L., & Branscombe, N. R. (1990). Person perception when aggressive or nonaggressive sports are primed. *Aggressive Behavior, 16*, 27–32.

Wegner, D. M., & Bargh, J. A. (1998) Control and automaticity in social life. In D. T. Gilbert, S. T. Fiske, & G. Lindzey (Eds.), *The handbook of social psychology* Vol. 2 (pp. 446–496). Boston: McGraw-Hill.

Wells, G. L., & Petty, R. E. (1980). The effects of overt head movement on persuasion: Compatibility and incompatibility responses. *Basic and Applied Social Psychology, 1*, 219–230.

Whitney, P., Davis, P. A., & Waring, D. A. (1994). Task effects on trait inference: Distinguishing categorization from characterization. *Social Cognition, 12*, 19–35.

Whitney, P., Waring, D. A., & Zingmark, B. (1992). Task effects on the spontaneous activation of trait concepts. *Social Cognition, 10*, 377–396.

Winter, L., & Uleman, J. S. (1984). When are social judgments made? Evidence for the spontaneousness of trait inferences. *Journal of Personality and Social Psychology, 47*, 237–252.

Wittenbrink, B., Judd, C. M., & Park, B. (1997). Evidence for racial prejudice at the implicit level and its relationship with questionnaire measures. *Journal of Personality and Social Psychology, 72*, 262–274.

Wyer, R. S., Jr., & Srull, T. K. (1980). The processing of social stimulus information: A conceptual integration. In R. Hastie, E. B. Ebbesen, T. M. Ostrom, R. S. Wyer, D. L. Hamilton, & D. E. Carlton (Eds.), *Person memory: The cognitive basis of social perception* (pp. 227–300). Hillsdale, NJ: Erlbaum.

Young, J., Thomsen, C. J., Borgida, E., Sullivan, J. L., & Aldrich, J. A. (1991). When self-interest makes a difference: The role of construct accessibility in political reasoning. *Journal of Experimental Social Psychology, 27*, 271–296.

Zajonc, R. B. (1968). The attitudinal effects of mere exposure. *Journal of Personality and Social Psychology*, Monograph Supplement, 9, (2, Pt. 2).

Zajonc, R. B. (1994). Evidence for nonconscious emotions. In P. Ekman and R. J. Davidson (Eds.), *The nature of emotion: Fundamental questions* (pp. 293–297). New York: Oxford University Press.

Zajonc, R. B. (1998). Emotions. In D. T. Gilbert and S. T. Fiske (Eds.), *The handbook of social psychology* Vol. 2, 4th. edn. (pp. 591–632). Boston: McGraw-Hill.

Zajonc, R. B., Murphy, S. T., & Inglehart, M. (1989). Feeling and facial efference: Implications of the vascular theory of emotions. *Psychological Review, 96*, 395–416.

Zanna, M. P., Detweiler, R. A., & Olson, J. M. (1984). Physiological mediation of attitude maintenance, formation, and change. In W. M. Waid (Ed.), *Sociophysiology* (pp. 163–196). New York: Springer-Verlag.

Zárate, M. A., Bonilla, S., & Luévano, M. (1995). Ethnic influences on exemplar retrieval and stereotyping. *Social Cognition, 13* (2), 145–162.

CHAPTER THREE

How the Mind Moves: Knowledge Accessibility and the Fine-tuning of the Cognitive System

Leonard L. Martin, Fritz Strack,
and Diederik A. Stapel

Two monks were arguing about the temple flag as it waved in the wind. One monk believed that it was the wind that was moving. The other believed that it was the flag that was moving. Despite considerable debate, neither monk was able to convince the other of his point of view. Finally, the Master arrived, and the two monks broached the issue with him. The Master noted, "It is not the wind that moves. It is not the flag that moves. It is your mind that moves." At this, the two monks were enlightened.

Zen parable

This chapter is about the mind moving. More precisely, it explores the general proposition that social perception is not a neutral registration of objective reality, but an active construction that is influenced by concurrent processes of thought, memory, feeling, and motivation (cf. Bruner, 1992; Martin & Tesser, 1992). In elaborating upon this proposition, we discuss some of the early research (e.g. Bruner, 1957) that demonstrated the constructive nature of social perception. Then, we discuss the theoretical advancements made with regard to this issue in some of the early social cognition research (e.g. Higgins, Rholes, & Jones, 1977). Finally, we discuss some recent findings that have helped to refine our understanding of the constructive nature of social perception. The chapter ends by suggesting that the processes involved in social perception are more complex than was reflected in the earlier research. Individuals are not cognitive misers who use whatever information is on the top of their heads. Rather, they are cognitive optimizers. They have access to a variety of different types of information and they use these selectively in the service of a range of processing objectives and motivations.

A Classic Example of the Mind Moving

The 1951 football game between Princeton and Dartmouth was an especially rough one. A large number of penalties were called, and Princeton's star quarterback had to leave the game because of a broken nose and a concussion. Although students from both schools agreed that the game had been rough, they did not agree on exactly how rough it had been, and on which team had started the rough play. To gain a better understanding of this lack of agreement, Hastorf & Cantril (1954) conducted a study. First, they assessed the attitudes of some Princeton and Dartmouth students toward the game. Then, they showed these students a film of the game, and asked them some questions about the film they had just seen.

Not surprisingly, the attitudes of the students at the two schools differed. The Princeton students generally thought that the game was rough and dirty, and that the Dartmouth team had started the dirty play. The Dartmouth students also thought that the game was rough, but they were more likely than the Princeton students to see the game as fair and to see both sides as to blame for the rough play. More interestingly, though, for present purposes, was the way in which these differences in attitudes reflected themselves in the two groups' perceptions of the game film. Although students from the two schools watched the exact same film, the Princeton students saw the Dartmouth team make many more infractions than their own team, whereas the Dartmouth students saw both teams make about the same number of infractions, with their team making half the number of infractions attributed to it by the Princeton students.

In explaining these different perceptions in the face of the same objective information, Hastorf & Cantril (1954) proposed that "there is no such 'thing' as a 'game' existing 'out there' in its own right which people merely 'observe'" (ibid., p. 133). Rather, "an 'occurrence' on the football field or in any other social situation . . . becomes an 'event' only when the happening . . . reactivates learned significances already registered in what we have called a person's assumptive form-world" (ibid., p. 132). Stated differently, the objective reality of the game resulted in different subjective experiences because students from the two schools viewed the game using different previously stored knowledge structures, which, in turn, led them to attend selectively to different occurrences and to interpret the same occurrences in different ways.

This general conclusion has been supported in a variety of subsequent studies (for a review, see Martin & Tesser, 1992). What these studies have shown is that individuals do not make judgments (e.g. How much do I like my mother?) by retrieving a single invariant score from memory (e.g. my evaluation of my mother). Rather, individuals construct their judgments as needed, using previously stored information as well as information from the current context (e.g. my evaluation of my mother given that I am in a bad mood and that she just grounded me). Thus, judgment of the same stimulus by the same individual can differ depending on the context in which the judgment is rendered.

It should be noted, though, that from a constructivist perspective, these context dependent changes in judgment do not reflect an inability on the part of the perceiver to retrieve his or her *real* evaluation. Rather, context dependency is assumed to be a natural by-product of the processes by which evaluations are rendered. After all, a person who is home alone *should* have a different interpretation of the sound of a window breaking than a person who is home with children playing in the next room. The children provide a ready explanation for the window breaking, but who is breaking the window if the person is home alone? From a constructivist perspective, this example does not reflect different interpretations of the same stimulus. It reflects different interpretations of different stimuli. This is because, from a constructivist perspective, the stimulus is not "the sound of a window breaking." It is "the sound of a window breaking while I am home alone" or "the sound of a window breaking while children are playing in the next room." People respond contextually. By the same reasoning, an individual who has had a heart attack *should* interpret a chest pain differently than a person who has recently eaten a bowl of extra spicy jambalaya. The stimulus is not "a chest pain," but "a chest pain in the light of my memory of what has just happened" (i.e. heart attack versus jambalaya). The more general point is that individuals bring aspects of themselves (e.g. memories, motivations), as well as aspects of the current context, to bear in evaluating any given target stimulus. This is what is meant by saying that social judgments are constructed.

It is important to point out that in assuming that social judgments are constructed, one need not assume that such judgments are arbitrary or that there are no general rules. In fact, quite the opposite is true. There are general rules, and these rules are beginning to be understood. For example, research has shown that social judgments depend, in predictable ways, not only on the particular knowledge that individuals bring to the judgment, but also on factors such as the relation between this knowledge and the target stimulus, the timing of the activation of the knowledge, the method by which the knowledge was activated, and the perceiver's motivational state. These are the kinds of issues we examine in this chapter. We begin by briefly reviewing some of the early research that emphasized the constructive nature of perception.

The Role of Accessibility: Some Initial Considerations

The research that is most often cited as the prime influence on the study of knowledge accessibility in social psychology today is that of Bruner (1957). The goal of this early work was to show that individuals do not respond to a direct copy of the objective world, but to their categorization of the objective world (Bruner, 1992). This is the case, according to Bruner, because most information is relatively meaningless until it has been identified with a mental category. A dark tubular object, for example, would elicit little reaction in an individual until he or she had categorized the object as a snake or a stick. Perhaps the main contribution of Bruner's early work was highlighting some of the factors that make individuals more likely to interpret information in terms of one category as opposed to another.

According to Bruner, the central factor in determining which category individuals use to interpret information was the relative accessibility of the relevant categories (i.e. the ease with which the individual could retrieve the category). The greater the accessibility of a category the less the stimulus input needed for categorization to occur in terms of that category, the wider the range of input characteristics accepted as belonging in the category, and the more likely it was that categories that provide a better or equally good fit for the input would be masked. Category accessibility was assumed to be a function of the expectancies of the perceiver and the search requirements imposed by the perceiver's processing objectives. Thus, a dark tubular shape would be more likely to be categorized as a stick if the perceiver were walking through the snow looking for firewood than if he or she were wading through a jungle stream looking for zoo specimens.

In sum, Bruner proposed that stimulus information was generic until it had been interpreted in terms of a mental category. When individuals have more than one category they could use to interpret information, they use the one whose accessibility had been increased by their motivational state (e.g. hunger) and/or their expectancy (e.g. being in an orchard).

The Classic Social Cognition View: Accessibility X Applicability

Current interest in category accessibility in social psychology can be traced to a study by Higgins, Rholes, & Jones (1977). The initial interest of these investigators was in understanding the way in which the accessibility of trait concepts could influence a person's interpretation of behaviors as he or she attempted to form an impression of another person. The assumption was that the implications of any given behavior (e.g. skydiving) would depend on the concept (e.g. adventurous versus reckless) used to interpret that behavior. They also assumed, following Bruner, that when behavioral information was interpretable in terms of more than one concept, individuals would use the one that was most accessible. Unlike Bruner, however, Higgins, et al. did not emphasize the role of motivation and expectancy in heightening accessibility. Rather, they emphasized the role of previous activation, which they referred to as priming. They proposed that if a concept had been recently used for almost any processing whatsoever (i.e. if it had been primed), then this concept would be more accessible and thus be more likely to be used to interpret subsequently encountered target information – provided the concepts were applicable to that information. Applicability, in this case, referred to denotative similarity.

To test this passive priming X applicability hypothesis, Higgins, Rholes, & Jones (1977) had participants perform in what, ostensibly, were two unrelated experiments. In the first, participants had to name the color of ink in which various words were written. Then, in the second, participants were presented with a description of a person and were asked to form an impression of this person. This description contained behaviors that were open to several interpretations. For example, the target person was described as being "well aware of his ability to do things well." This behavior could be interpreted as either self-confident or conceited.

To prime different concepts, Higgins, et al. embedded different words in the color naming task. For some participants, these words were positive and were descriptively relevant to interpreting the target's behaviors (e.g. self-confident). For other participants, the words were negative yet descriptively relevant to interpreting the target's behaviors (e.g. conceited). Other participants were exposed to words that were either positive (e.g. neat) or negative (e.g. listless) but that were not relevant to interpreting the target's behaviors. Consistent with the passive priming X applicability hypothesis, participants rendered more favorable impressions of the target following activation of the positive compared to the negative concepts, but only when the concepts were denotatively related to the information in the target paragraph.

These results were consistent with Bruner's formulation in the sense that participants used the most accessible, relevant category to interpret target information. The results extended Bruner's formulation, however, by emphasizing the passive possibilities in priming. In the Higgins, Rholes, & Jones (1977) study, participants used the relevant primed concepts even though they were not motivated to do so, had no reason to expect the primed concepts more than their alternatives, and the primed concepts were relevant to the target information only by virtue of their denotative relatedness. It seemed that merely activating a trait concept was sufficient to increase the likelihood that the concept would be used to interpret information to which it was denotatively related.

This view of priming was fleshed out in a number of subsequent studies. Srull & Wyer (1980), for example, demonstrated that primed concepts are used to interpret target information at the time this information is initially encoded. Priming a concept after participants have interpreted the target information has no effect at all on the subsequently formed impression (see also Wyer & Martin, 1986). Higgins, Bargh, & Lombardi (1985) suggested that if a concept is primed frequently enough it can become chronically accessible. When this occurs, the concept is likely to be used in interpreting information even when the concept has not been recently primed by contextual stimuli. Moreover, mental operations performed on information related to a chronically accessible concept may be performed automatically (Bargh & Thein, 1985). Finally, priming effects are not restricted to mental operations or to pencil-and-paper measures. Priming can also affect overt behavior. Priming the concept *aggressive*, for example, can lead individuals to behave more aggressively (Berkowitz, 1993; Carver, Ganellen, Froming, & Chambers, 1983).

Taken together, these early studies painted a very clear and coherent picture of concept priming. The picture was so compelling in fact that a large number of researchers were motivated to use this conceptualization to help make sense of phenomena in a wide variety of areas. For example, researchers applied this passive priming X applicability view of accessibility to stereotypes (Devine, 1989), attitudes (Fazio, Sanbonmatsu, Powell, & Kardes, 1986), goals (Bargh, 1997), relationships (Baldwin, Carrell, & Lopez, 1990), death concerns (Greenberg, Simon, Pyszczynski, & Solomon, 1992), aggression (Berkowitz, 1993), the answering of questions on surveys (Sudman, Bradburn, & Schwarz, 1996), explanations (Wilson, Hodges, & LaFleur, 1995), and anchoring effects (Strack & Mussweiler, 1997).

The advantage of this explosion in research was that the field gained a great deal of knowledge about priming as well as about phenomena that seemed to have priming as one of its underlying components. The flip side of this explosion, of course, was that researchers also became aware of areas of incompleteness. As Smith, Stewart, & Buttram (1992, p. 759) noted, "the familiar conceptualization that categorization is a function of Accessibility X Fit now appears to be inadequate." In the remainder of this chapter, we address these inadequacies. More specifically, we present research showing that (a) concept applicability involves more than the denotative fit between the concept and the target; (b) information can be accessible and applicable yet not used to interpret information; (c) increasing the accessibility of different types of knowledge structures (e.g. traits versus exemplars) produces different effects; and (d) priming can do more than increase the likelihood that a concept will be used to interpret information. We also examine the role of awareness, accuracy motivation, and correction processes in determining the use of primed information.

Non-motivational Qualifications of the Passive Accessibility X Fit View

When distilled to its essence, the passive accessibility X fit view can be seen to consist of five elements: *trait concepts* are used to *interpret* information to the extent that these concepts are *accessible* and *applicable* with applicability being defined in terms of the *denotative similarity* between the primed concept and the target information. In the following sections, we describe qualifications on each of these five elements.

Beyond denotative applicability

As just noted, the initial work on concept accessibility (e.g. Higgins, Rholes, & Jones, 1977) emphasized the denotative fit between the primed knowledge and the target information as a determinant of the likelihood that a primed concept would be used to categorize target information. Subsequent research has suggested, however, that denotative relatedness may not be the only determinant of concept applicability. Stapel & Koomen (1999), for example, had participants form an impression of an ambiguously described target person. As in Higgins, Rholes, & Jones (1977), some participants were primed with concepts that were either denotatively applicable or inapplicable to interpreting the subsequent target information, and that had moderate evaluative connotations (e.g. applicable: assured versus arrogant; inapplicable: unrealistic versus idealistic). With these primes, the results would presumably parallel those of Higgins, Rholes, & Jones (1977). Participants would assimilate their impressions of the target behavior toward the implications of the applicable concepts but not the inapplicable ones.

What would happen, though, if participants were primed with concepts that had no clear denotative implications but that had relatively broad and strong evaluative implications (good versus bad)? Similarly, what would happen if participants were primed with concepts that were denotatively inapplicable to the target information but that had relatively narrow but strong evaluative implications (aggressive versus sweet)? Stapel and Koomen hypothesized that in these cases participants might use the strong evaluative implications to help disambiguate the target information, even though the denotative applicability is low. If so, then participants should assimilate their impression of the target toward the implications of the primed information even though this information is not denotatively relevant to interpreting the target behaviors.

The results of Stapel & Koomen (1999) supported this reasoning. They found that participants' impressions were assimilated toward the implications of the primed concepts not only when these were denotatively applicable, but also when they were generally evaluative with no clear denotative implications and when they were denotatively inapplicable but possessing strong evaluative implications. It is only when the primed concepts were denotatively inapplicable and both relatively narrow and evaluatively weak that participants' impressions did not assimilate toward the implications of the primed concepts (e.g. Higgins, Rholes, & Jones, 1977). What these results suggest is that denotative applicability is not a necessary ingredient of concept applicability (see also Martin, 1986; Martin, Seta, & Crelia, 1990). In some cases, strong connotation may be sufficient to allow target information to be interpreted in a manner consistent with the implications of primed information, even when this information consists of denotatively inapplicable concepts.

Different types of representations produce different effects

Another feature of the passive priming X applicability view was its emphasis on the use of trait concepts to interpret target information. We know, however, that individuals possess knowledge structures other than trait concepts. These include exemplars, scripts, and procedural knowledge. Subsequent research has begun to explore the effects of priming these knowledge structures. The question is whether effects like those obtained with the priming of trait concepts would also be obtained if one of these other knowledge structures were activated. There is some reason to think not.

Consider, for example, that trait concepts represent diffuse semantic information that can be applicable to a wide range of behaviors. The trait "aggressive," for example, could be used to characterize behaviors as diverse as shoving, verbal abuse, and cutting someone off in traffic. An exemplar, on the other hand, reflects knowledge about a specific person (e.g. Hitler), and this may be less likely to generalize to thoughts about another specific person. An exemplar, however, might make a useful standard of comparison (e.g. Herr, Sherman, & Fazio, 1983). For example, almost anyone would appear less aggressive compared to Hitler. It is possible, therefore, that with the same degree of denotative applicability, priming a trait concept may give rise to assimilation, whereas priming an exemplar may give rise to contrast. These hypotheses were tested, and supported, by Stapel, Koomen, & Van der Pligt (1997). They found that participants primed with trait concepts assimilated their impressions of the target toward the implications of the primed concepts, whereas participants primed with exemplars contrasted their target impressions away from the implications of these exemplars.

If it is true that exemplar priming produces contrast because exemplars make good standards of comparison, then it should be possible to eliminate exemplar-induced contrast by undermining the comparison relevance of the exemplar. This hypothesis was tested by Stapel, Koomen, & Van der Pligt (1997). They primed participants with hostility-related but *non-person* exemplars such as "Shark" and "Tiger" or "Puppy" and "Bunny." These exemplars reflect distinct entities associated with varying degrees of hostility, making them, at least in principle, good candidates for standards of comparison. The exemplars also represent animals, however, and animals are generally not relevant standards of comparison when judging humans. As a result, priming of these non-person exemplars may not lead to contrast of the target person.

These exemplars, however, are associated with different levels of hostility. So, it is possible that when this hostility-related information is made accessible, the result may be assimilation. That is, participants primed with non-person exemplars may assimilate their impression of an ambiguously described hostile/friendly target person toward the implications of the primed (non-relevant) hostile or friendly exemplars. These were in fact the results obtained by Stapel, Koomen, & Van der Pligt (1997).

In sum, it appears that with the same degree of denotative applicability, priming a trait concept or a non-relevant exemplar is likely to give rise to assimilation, whereas priming a relevant exemplar is likely to give rise to contrast. The former two knowledge structures appear to influence participants' interpretations of the target information, whereas the latter one seems to facilitate a comparison process.

Different effects of primes at encoding versus output

If traits and exemplars play different roles in the impression formation process (i.e. interpretation versus comparison), then priming these different knowledge structures at different times should produce different effects. Recall Srull & Wyer's (1980) finding that priming trait concepts before participants had interpreted the target information resulted in assimilation, whereas priming these same concepts after participants had interpreted the target information had no effect on participants' judgments (see also Wyer & Martin, 1986). What these results suggest is that primed traits are used to disambiguate target information at the time participants first encode that information. When are exemplars used? According to Stapel, Koomen, & Van der Pligt (1997), exemplars may be used as a standard of comparison either at encoding or after individuals have formed an impression and are attempting to translate it into an overt response. What this means is that priming of a trait concept is likely to produce assimilation if the priming occurs before, but not after, participants have encoded the target information, whereas the priming of an exemplar is likely to produce contrast regardless of whether it is primed before or after participants have encoded the information.

To test these ideas, Stapel, Koomen, & Van der Pligt (1997) primed participants with either trait concepts or exemplars, and this occurred either before or after participants had read the target information. In replication of Srull & Wyer (1980), they found assimilation when a trait concept was primed before but not after participants had read the target information. With the priming of exemplars, however, they found contrast regardless of whether the priming occurred before or after participants had read the target information. This pattern of results suggests that trait concepts are generally used in interpreting or disambiguating information as individuals first encode it, whereas exemplars are used as standards of comparison either as individuals are interpreting information or after they have already formed their impression.

The role of procedural knowledge

Another feature common to most early priming research was the tendency to explain priming effects in terms of what might be called structural changes in semantic knowledge. The synapse model (Higgins, et al., 1985), for example, suggested that use of a concept increases its hypothetical charge, which, in turn, made the concept more likely to be used. The bin model (Wyer & Srull, 1989) suggested that use of a concept causes that concept to get placed, metaphorically, on the top of a semantic bin in memory. Because of this placement, the concept would be encountered more quickly than a less recently used concept in any subsequent search of that bin. This, in turn, would make a recently activated concept more likely to be used. As can be seen, despite their differences, both models assumed that priming effects were the result of a change in the status of semantic information. Smith & Branscombe (1987) suggested an alternative. They proposed that at least some category accessibility effects might reflect the operation of procedural knowledge.

Procedural knowledge can be thought of as cognitive structures that represent skills or "how to" knowledge. Such knowledge can be represented hypothetically as production systems or if–then statements. These systems are selected for execution when their conditions (i.e. the "if") match the current contents of working memory or the perceptual environment. The execution of the action part of a production system (i.e. the "then") can result automatically in the performance of cognitive tasks, such as generating inferences. For example, a person may have a production system that specifies something like the following:

IF you observe one <*person*> <*exert power over*> <*another*>,
THEN interpret that behavior as hostile.

The variables (i.e. *person*, *exert power*, *another*) within the production system become instantiated with the values in a given situation. So, if an individual has practiced the production system described above, and if this individual has just observed Donald giving orders to Jamal, then the individual is likely to interpret Donald's action as hostile even though the action might simply reflect Donald's attempt to be efficient. Production systems are assumed to develop out of practice. The basic assumption is that people typically get better at doing things they do frequently.

It is interesting in this context to note that in many priming studies, the priming tasks gave participants repeated practice at interpreting behaviors in terms of a trait. For example, it was not uncommon to prime participants by asking them to construct meaningful sentences out of scrambled words (e.g. "hit he the it"). In performing this task, participants may gain practice in generating trait based interpretations (e.g. hostile) of ambiguous behavior. Could it be that practice of this interpretation procedure (rather than a change in the activation status of concept in semantic memory) was responsible for the subsequent assimilation of the target information? In other words, when presented with a target who engaged in behavior that was relatively ambiguous with regard to its level of hostility, participants may have used the interpretational procedure they had just practiced in the priming task to interpret the target behavior in terms of a hostile concept.

How can we tell if any given priming effect is the result of procedural knowledge or changes in the accessibility of semantic knowledge? According to Smith and Branscombe, the effects of procedural knowledge are more specific and longer lasting than those of semantic priming. To test these hypotheses, Smith & Branscombe (1987, Experiment 2) had participants perform a task that either allowed them to practice the procedure of interpreting behavior in terms of a concept or that increased the accessibility of semantic knowledge. In the first case, participants were asked to construct meaningful sentences from a scrambled list of words. In the second case, participants were asked to judge pairs of words (e.g.

hostile—crude) in terms of whether or not the words had the same meaning. Then, either immediately following these tasks or three minutes later, participants were presented with a behavioral description that was ambiguous with regard to the trait (or procedure) that had been primed in the earlier tasks.

Consistent with the hypothesis that procedurally mediated priming effects last longer than semantically mediated priming effects, Smith and Branscombe found that when the priming task consisted of unscrambling sentences, participants' impressions assimilated toward the implications of the primed concepts in both the short and the long delay. When the priming task consisted of judging the meaning of words, participants' impressions assimilated toward the implications of the primed concepts only in the short delay condition.

In a second study, Smith and Branscombe found some evidence consistent with their second proposed distinction between procedurally mediated and semantically mediated priming effects. They found that the effects of procedural priming are more specific than those of semantic trait priming. Taken together, the results of these two studies suggest that the activation of procedural knowledge can account for at least some priming effects, and that theoretical conceptualizations of priming that focus only on the activation of semantic concepts are incomplete.

Priming does more than facilitate categorization

We have seen that information other than traits (e.g. exemplars, procedures) can be primed and that effects other than interpretation (e.g. contrast) can occur. Such results suggest that priming does more than increase the probability that individuals will use primed trait concepts to interpret behaviors. It appears, instead, that priming increases the likelihood that the primed knowledge will be used in whatever processing occurs at the time, whether this be interpretational or otherwise. This more general view of priming may be best illustrated in research showing that priming can influence quantitative judgments that do not even involve interpretation. Strack & Mussweiler (1997), for example, used priming to explain the anchoring and adjustment effect.

In one demonstration of the anchoring and adjustment effect, Tversky & Kahneman (1974) asked participants whether the percentage of African nations in the United Nations was higher or lower than 80 percent (or 20 percent). Then, they asked these same participants to estimate the actual percentage of African nations in the United Nations. Tversky and Kahneman found that participants given the high standard (e.g. 80 percent) in the comparison task provided higher estimates on the absolute judgment task than did participants given the low standard (e.g. 20 percent).

Explanations of this effect have focused on the numerical value provided as a standard in the initial comparison task. More specifically, it has been suggested (e.g. Jacowitz & Kahneman, 1995) that participants start their estimation of the absolute value at the value presented in the comparison task. Then, they adjust upward or downward (depending on the condition) until they encounter the outer limits of their acceptable range of responses. This results in higher estimates when participants are adjusting downward than when they are adjusting upward.

Strack & Mussweiler (1997) explored the possibility that performing the initial comparison task might do more than leave a numerical standard salient. It might also prime a more general mental representation relevant to rendering the subsequent absolute judgment. Specifically, Strack and Mussweiler proposed that in performing the comparison task, participants might create a representation of the target as possessing the standard. For example, if participants were asked whether the Mississippi River is longer or shorter than 3,000 miles, they might imagine the north–south extension of the United States and use their geographic knowledge to compute the answer. If they do this using a positive test strategy (Klayman & Ha, 1987), then they are likely to bring to mind information consistent with the target possessing the value supplied in the standard. This standard-consistent information may then be consulted when participants make the subsequent absolute judgment, and it is this information that leads to the anchoring and adjustment effect.

Note that this standard-consistent information would not be brought to mind if the standard provided by the comparison task were clearly implausible (e.g. "Is the Mississippi River longer or shorter than 1 mile?"). In this case, the standard would be so clearly wrong that participants could generate an answer to the comparison question without bringing a great deal of related information to mind. If this theoretical analysis is correct, then participants should take longer to make the initial comparison judgment when a plausible rather than implausible standard is provided.

The effects of standard plausibility should be different, however, on the time it takes participants to render the absolute judgment. Because participants presented with a plausible standard would already have brought related information to mind, they should perform the absolute judgment relatively quickly. Participants presented with an implausible standard, on the other hand, will not have brought such information to mind, so they must do so when they make the absolute judgment. This could take time. This reasoning implies a crossover interaction in response times. Relative to participants who have been primed with an implausible standard, those primed with a plausible standard will take more time to make the initial comparison judgment but less time to make the subsequent absolute judgment. This crossover pattern was in fact obtained by Strack and Mussweiler.

If, as these results suggest, informational priming plays a role in (at least some) anchoring and adjustment effects, then these effects might not be seen if the primed information were inapplicable to the absolute judgment. This is because primed information is applied only to the extent it is applicable (Higgins, Rholes, & Jones, 1977; Stapel & Koomen, 1999). To test this idea, Strack and Mussweiler asked participants to render a comparison judgment (e.g. "Is the Brandenburg Gate taller or shorter than 50 (or 150) meters?") followed by an absolute judgment. The absolute judgment was either related to the information primed in the comparison task (e.g. "How tall is the Brandenburg Gate?") or it was not (e.g. "How wide is the Brandenburg Gate?"). Consistent with the priming applicability hypothesis, an anchoring and adjustment effect was observed only when the information primed in the comparison task was applicable to the absolute judgment (e.g. both judgments involved height).

Taken together, these studies suggest that at least some anchoring and adjustment effects are not due simply to participants starting from a numerical standard and then adjusting upward or downward to an insufficient degree. Rather, priming of more general, judgment relevant information seems to be involved. This primed information is not a trait concept, however, and it is not used to interpret target information. It is a mental representation of the target possessing the value primed in the standard, and it can influence subsequent quantitative judgments to the extent that it is applicable to those judgments.

Content or Phenomenology?

The studies we have discussed so far were concerned primarily with the nature of the content that had been made accessible. These studies examined the effects of priming concepts, exemplars, or procedures that varied in their applicability to the target information. In each case, the general assumption was that target judgments are affected because of the implications of the content that has been brought to mind. Note, however, that priming not only brings information to mind, it also increases the ease with which this information comes to mind. Could the subjective experience of ease of retrieval also be informative? This possibility was first raised by Tversky & Kahneman (1974) in their discussion of the availability heuristic. They suggested that individuals sometimes assess the frequency of an occurrence (e.g. words beginning with the letter k) by assessing the ease with which they can retrieve instances of that occurrence.

Schwarz, Bless, Strack, & Klumpp (1991) examined the effects of priming in a condition in which the implications of the primed content were at odds with the implications of subjective ease of retrieval. Specifically, they had participants recall either 6 or 12 instances of either assertive or submissive behaviors they had performed. Then, they had participants rate themselves in terms of how assertive–submissive they were. Participants who recalled 12 instances of the target behavior would have twice as much evidence that they possessed the target trait than participants who only recalled 6 instances. So, we might expect participants who recalled 12 instances to rate themselves higher in the direction of the recalled instances than participants who recalled only 6. This would reflect the impact of information accessibility.

On the other hand, it is more difficult to recall 12 instances than 6 instances. So, if participants used ease of retrieval to estimate frequency, then we might expect those who recalled 12 instances to rate themselves as possessing less of the trait than participants who recalled only 6. If participants really were assertive (or submissive), then why would it be so hard for them to recall 12 instances in which they displayed this trait? Or so their thinking would go.

The results suggested that both accessibility and ease of retrieval were informative. When participants recalled only 6 instances, those who recalled the assertive behaviors rated themselves as more assertive than those who recalled the submissive behaviors. When participants recalled 12 instances, however, those who recalled the assertive behaviors rated themselves as less assertive than those who recalled the submissive behaviors. In short, individuals can gain information not only from what comes to mind but also from *how* that information comes to mind.

Motivated Limits on the Passive Priming X Fit View

What we have seen so far is that the familiar conceptualization of accessible, applicable trait concepts being used to interpret information can be qualified in each of its major components.

Different knowledge structures activated at different times can have different effects. Note, however, that each of the qualifications we discussed were non-motivational. That is, they were based on the nature of the knowledge structure primed and/or the time at which the structures were primed. There is evidence, however, that motivational factors can also determine the nature of priming effects. We can take a trait concept with a given level of accessibility and applicability, for example, and influence the extent to which participants are likely to use that concept to interpret information by manipulating variables such as accuracy motivation (Thompson, Roman, Moskowitz, Chaiken, & Bargh, 1994) and cognitive effort (Martin, Seta, & Crelia, 1990). One implication of such findings is that a distinction needs to be maintained between a concept's accessibility and its use in interpreting information (Martin, 1986).

To the extent that a concept's accessibility and its use are distinct, it should be possible to manipulate the two orthogonally. This was accomplished by Stapel & Koomen (under review). They hypothesized that priming a concept would lead to different judgments among participants who approached the judgment task with an interpretational mindset compared to participants who approached the task with a comparison mindset. To induce an interpretational set, Stapel and Koomen presented participants with a list of different behaviors and asked the participants to describe each behavior with a single word. To induce a comparison mindset, participants were asked to compare the persons performing the behaviors to different standards (e.g. the average woman, the average student). Following this task, participants were primed with either a positive or a negative concept and asked to form an impression of a target whose behavior was relatively ambiguous with regard to the primed traits.

Consistent with the idea that priming of the same trait can have different effects on judgments of the same behavior depending on one's mindset, participants who had completed the interpretation task assimilated their impressions toward the implications of the primed concepts, whereas participants who had completed the comparison task contrasted their impressions with the implications of the primed concepts. Thus, motivational variables can influence priming effects even when the structural properties of the situation (e.g. the applicability and accessibility of the primed concepts) are held constant.

Epistemic motivation

Within social psychology, motivation has often been identified with the irrational, such as dissonance or ego-defensive biases, and it has typically been contrasted with cold, analytical, logical thinking such as that typified in attribution theory. From a general information processing perspective, however, there can also be motivations toward accuracy and analytic thinking. Moreover, these kinds of motivations can moderate the effects of concept priming.

Ford & Kruglanski (1995) and Thompson, et al. (1994), for example, found that participants with no particular incentive to be accurate while forming an impression assimilated their impression of an ambiguous target person toward the implications of the primed traits. The impressions of participants who were highly motivated to form an accurate impression, on the other hand, showed no influence of the primed concepts. Apparently, the motivation to be accurate can, at least in some cases, inoculate participants from the assimilative effects of concept priming.

In a conceptually related study, Sedikides (1990) found that the more specific motivation of communicating a particular impression can also attenuate the assimilative effects of concept priming. Participants who thought they were to communicate their impression of an ambiguously described target person to an audience that liked the target rendered more favorable impressions of the target than participants who thought they had to convey their impression to an audience that disliked the target. More importantly, for present purposes, these differences in judgment occurred even when participants were primed with concepts that were opposite in valence to the presumed attitudes of the audience. In other words, participants communicating an impression to an unfavorable audience formed a negative impression despite being primed with a positive, applicable concept. Taken together, these studies suggest that certain processing objectives (e.g. be accurate, communicate a specific impression) can override the effects of passive contextual priming.

Not all priming effects are susceptible to moderation by accuracy motivations, however. Stapel, Koomen, & Zeelenberg (1998) found that accuracy motives were less likely to overcome contrastive influences than assimilative influences. These investigators induced assimilation or contrast by priming a trait concept or an exemplar, respectively (cf. Stapel, Koomen, & Van der Pligt, 1997). Following this, they had participants form an impression of an ambiguously described target person. To manipulate accuracy motivation, half of the participants were told that the tasks they were performing were merely part of a pilot study and might possibly be used in some future study. The remaining participants were told that they should try to be as accurate as possible in their judgments. In replication of earlier work, trait priming led to assimilation among low accuracy participants, but had no effect among the high accuracy participants. Unlike earlier studies, however, exemplar priming led to contrast in both the low accuracy and the high accuracy participants. Taken together, the studies discussed in this section suggest that different motivations have different consequences for different types of knowledge accessibility effects.

Awareness of a bias

Another type of motivation that has been studied is more specific, namely, removing perceived bias from the target judgment. Note that the initial priming research (e.g. Higgins, Rholes, & Jones, 1977) emphasized the passive nature of priming. This was true, in part, because the initial studies used disguised priming tasks in the so-called "two-experiment" paradigm. These steps were taken to rule out the possibility that the results were due to demand characteristics. They were successful in doing this, but they may also have ruled out the possibility that participants would engage in other theoretically important psychological processes. As Martin (1986, p. 494) noted:

> When a concept is primed very subtly, individuals may not even be aware that it has been activated in them (Bargh & Pietromonaco, 1982). Consequently, when this concept comes to

mind in the subsequent impression formation task they have no reason to believe that it is anything other than their own spontaneous reaction to the target. This means that they have no reason not to use the primed concept in interpreting the target information, provided that it is consistent with the implications of that information.

The same may not hold true, however, when a concept is primed more blatantly. Under these conditions, individuals may associate the activation of the concept with their exposure to the priming stimuli rather than with the target stimulus. As a result, they may actually avoid using the primed concept to interpret the target information, as its use would appear to bias their independent evaluation of the target.

In short, a quite different set of processes may come into play when concepts are primed more blatantly, and these processes may produce quite different effects than those found in the initial priming studies. Evidence for this possibility has been obtained in a variety of studies. Strack, Schwarz, Bless, Kübler, & Wänke (1993), for example, had participants perform what they thought were a series of cognitive and perceptual tasks. In one of these tasks, participants heard a series of tones paired with words. Participants were asked to classify the tones as high or low and to write down the words. For half of the participants, the words were positive (e.g. friendship), whereas for the other half, the words were negative (e.g. dishonest). Following the tone–word task, participants were asked to form an impression of a person whose actions (e.g. stole exam questions for a desperate friend) were interpretable in terms of either the positive or the negative primed concepts.

To manipulate the blatancy of the priming stimuli, Strack, et al. (1993) had some participants perform the tone–word task and then form their impression. Other participants were asked to answer some questions about the tone–word task (e.g. how well they were able to discriminate the tones) prior to forming their impressions. The point of this questioning was to remind participants of the priming stimuli (i.e. the positive or negative words used in the tone–word task).

In replication of earlier priming studies (e.g. Higgins, Rholes, & Jones, 1997), Strack, et al. (1993) found that impressions of the target assimilated toward the primed concepts when participants were not reminded of the priming task. When participants were reminded, however, their impressions were contrasted with the implications of the primed concepts. What these results suggest is that a concept may be highly accessible and applicable to interpreting information, but if participants are aware that this concept has been primed by a non-target event (i.e. the priming stimuli), then they may not use this concept in interpreting the target information (see also Lombardi, Higgins, & Bargh, 1987). The next question, of course, is why. Why do participants avoid the use of blatantly primed concepts?

Several explanations have been offered (Lombardi, Higgins, & Bargh, 1987; Martin, 1986; Strack & Hannover, 1996; Wegener & Petty, 1995; Wilson & Brekke, 1994). Despite their differences, these explanations generally agree that, in some way or another, participants sense a threat to the genuineness of their evaluation of the target and (in some form or another) they take steps to remove the perceived bias from their evaluation of the target. So, now we can ask, what is the nature of the bias that is sensed? How do people correct for this bias? One possible answer to both questions entails naive theories, that is, beliefs about the effects of a context on a target.

Theory Based Correction

According to Wilson & Brekke (1994), individuals generally have weak introspective abilities (see also Nisbett & Wilson, 1977). One implication of this weakness is that individuals may generally fail to appreciate the influence of contextual factors on their judgments. In other words, individuals may not be able to discriminate reliably between biased and unbiased judgments merely by turning inward. So, if they are to remove the bias from their judgments, then they must look elsewhere for guidance.

One source of guidance may be naive theories. Consider, for example, a person who is asked to rate a moderately attractive face after having just rated some extremely attractive faces. In this context, the moderately attractive face may appear to the person to be unattractive (i.e. a contrast effect). Although this is a biased judgment, the person may not realize it. The assessment of the face as unattractive may feel like the person's genuine assessment of the target. Suppose, however, that the person retrieved a theory that suggested that ratings of moderately attractive faces could be lowered by previously rating more attractive faces. Armed with this knowledge, the person would be in a position to correct for the biasing influence of the context. In this way, individuals' naive theories could potentially alert them to biases that they might miss if they relied solely on introspection.

It appears, further, that naive theories may help people to remove the perceived bias from their judgments. Specifically, it has been suggested (Strack, 1992; Strack & Hannover, 1996; Wegener & Petty, 1995; Wilson & Brekke, 1994) that when people believe that their judgments are being biased, they consult their naive theories to determine the extent and direction of the bias. Then, they adjust their target ratings in a direction that is opposite to the theorized bias and to an extent that is commensurate with the theorized amount of bias. As Strack (1992, p. 269) put it, "People can apply norms, rules, or theories to adjust their response for the effect of the pernicious influence. . . . It is important, however, that judges have such rules at the ready; otherwise, they would not know how to alter their responses."

Evidence suggestive of a role for naïve theories in the correction of contextual bias has been obtained in a series of studies by Wegener and Petty (for a review, see Wegener & Petty, 1997). They began by providing participants with a series of context–target configurations and asking participants to indicate what effect the context might have on ratings of the target. In this way, Wegener and Petty were able to find sets of stimuli for which participants held theories of either assimilation or contrast. For example, most participants believed that their ratings of a product would be biased toward desirability if the product were endorsed by attractive as compared to unattractive women (i.e. an assimilation effect). Most also believed that ratings of moderately attractive women would be biased away from ratings of extremely attractive or extremely unattractive women (i.e. a contrast effect).

After establishing that there were sets of stimuli for which participants held theories of either assimilation or contrast, Wegener & Petty (1995) had participants actually make their ratings of these stimuli. Half of the participants were asked without further elaboration to rate the context and target items, whereas half were given an explicit warning not to let their judgments of the context influence their judgments of the target. This warning informed participants of a possible bias, but it did not specify the direction or magnitude of that bias. It was assumed that this information would be gleaned by participants from their naïve theories. The results were consistent with this hypothesis.

When participants simply rated the context and target stimuli, their target judgments reflected assimilation when participants rated stimuli they had earlier theorized would lead to assimilation, but reflected contrast when they rated stimuli they had earlier theorized would lead to contrast. When participants had been instructed to remove the contextual bias, however, their judgments showed the opposite pattern. There was assimilation when participants rated stimuli they had earlier theorized would lead to contrast, but contrast when they had rated stimuli they had earlier theorized would lead to assimilation. This pattern is consistent with the hypothesis that when individuals are alerted to a potential bias in their judgments, they consult their naive theories in order to understand the nature of the contextual influence, and then they adjust their judgments in a direction opposite to the theorized influence.

Target Based Correction

According to the theory based models of correction, individuals cannot correct for a contextual influence without having some sort of understanding of the nature of that influence. Although this assumption is plausible, it is not entirely clear that the knowledge individuals need to correct their judgments has to come from a theory that specifies the context–target relation. As Stapel, Martin, & Schwarz (1998) noted, the blatant warning used in the Wegener and Petty studies may have allowed participants to by-pass their use of theories. The warning (i.e. "Please don't let your ratings of the target be influenced by your rating of the context") essentially told participants that the contextual stimuli were likely to be biasing their target judgments. As a result, participants did not have to consult their theories to determine if the context were biasing their judgments. They already had reason to believe it was. So, a blatant warning may allow participants to by-pass the first step of theory-guided correction (i.e. use theory to detect bias).

Of course, even if participants do not use their theories to detect the contextual bias, then they may still consult their theories when correcting for the bias. After all, participants still need to know the direction and extent of the influence if they are to correct for it. Stapel, Martin, & Schwarz (1998) hypothesized, however, that participants may even be able to correct without recourse to a theory that specifies the relation between the context and the target. If participants experience an inclination to evaluate the target favorably and are told that there may be a bias in their judgments, then participants may infer that an unbiased judgment would be one that was less favorable. Conversely, if they experience an inclination to evaluate the target unfavorably and are told that there may be a bias in their judgments, then participants may infer that an unbiased judgment would be one that was more favorable. In this way, participants' evaluative inclinations in the context of a blatant warning may allow participants to adjust their judgments without consulting theories to assess bias or guide correction.

Stapel, Martin, & Schwarz (1998) addressed this issue by examining the nature of correction induced by blatant and subtle warnings. All participants were asked to rate some target stimuli in a context that typically produced contrast (e.g. they rated the desirability of the weather in Midwestern US cities after having rated the desirability of the weather in vacation spots). One group of participants was asked merely to rate the context and target stimuli. Two other groups rated these same stimuli, but received a warning between their ratings of the context and the targets. For some participants, this warning was the blatant one used by Wegener and Petty. Specifically, these participants were instructed to "Make sure that your perceptions of the weather in the vacation spots above do not influence your ratings of the following places." The remaining participants received a conditional warning. They read "When you feel there is something that may have an unwanted influence on your ratings, please try to adjust for that influence." The first warning implies that there is a bias; the second allows participants to determine on their own whether or not there is a bias.

The next step was to manipulate the amount of bias participants perceived to be coming from the context. This was accomplished by having half of the participants rate the context and target stimuli on the same dimension, but having half rate the context on one dimension and the targets on another dimension (e.g. job satisfaction verus desirability of weather). The potential biasing influence of the context should be more obvious when the stimuli are considered on the same dimension than when they are considered on different dimensions (cf. Brown, 1953). So, if participants correct only when they perceive a bias, then they are likely to correct only when they rate the context and target on the same dimension.

The results indicated a clear difference between the effects of the subtle and blatant warnings. When participants received no warning, their judgments reflected contrast regardless of whether they rated the targets on the same dimension as the contextual stimuli or on different dimensions. This suggests that the uncorrected effect of this context was contrast. What this also means is that if the warned participants correct for the contextual influence, then their judgments will shift toward assimilation. When participants were given the conditional warning, such a shift toward assimilation was seen, but only when the perceived influence of the context was obvious.

Judgments of participants who had been blatantly warned, on the other hand, reflected a correction toward assimilation regardless of the dimension on which the contextual stimuli had been judged. In other words, the blatantly warned participants adjusted their responses regardless of whether the level of bias coming from the contextual stimuli was salient or non-salient. More importantly, the blatantly warned participants adjusted their target evaluations even in a condition in which the conditionally warned participants did not perceive any bias. If the conditionally warned participants did not detect a bias coming from this context, then what were the blatantly warned participants correcting for?

These data raise the possibility that correction may take place without reference to a theory that specifies the context–target influence. Participants may simply consider their target judgment in the context of a blatant warning. If they experience an inclination to render a favorable judgment, then they might make their judgments less positive. If they experience an inclination to render an unfavorable judgment, then they might make their judgments more positive.

Summary and Conclusions

The early priming research depicted the processes involved in priming as rather simple. It was generally assumed that individuals used whatever concepts were accessible and applicable with applicability being defined in terms of denotative similarity. Subsequent research, however, has qualified this view. In fact, it appears that this view of priming holds only under the conditions used in the initial studies. When changes, even relatively small ones, are made to the procedures used in the early studies, quite different results are obtained. The recent studies highlight the sophisticated and conditional nature of priming effects. These effects depend on the type of knowledge structure activated, the timing of the activation, and the motivation level and mental set of the participants.

Although social judgments that have been influenced by priming are not always accurate in an objective sense, this should not take away from the function of priming, which is to fine-tune individuals' processing to the specific judgment task at hand. It is in the nature of judgment that individuals bring aspects of themselves (memories, processing objectives) to bear and these aspects influence the individuals' judgments in predictable ways. We should continue to explore the regularities governing the construction of social judgments and we should give the social perceiver his or her due as sophisticated processors of social information.

REFERENCES

Baldwin, M. W., Carrell, S. E., & Lopez, D. F. (1990). Priming relationship schemas: My advisor and the pope are watching me from the back of my mind. *Journal of Experimental Social Psychology, 26*, 435–454.

Bargh, J. A. (1997). The automaticity of everyday life. In R. S. Wyer, Jr. (Ed.), *Advances in social cognition* Vol. 10 (pp. 1–61). Mahwah, NJ: Lawrence Erlbaum Associates.

Bargh, J. A., & Pietromonaco, P. (1982). Automatic information processing and social perception: The influence of trait information presented outside of conscious awareness on impression formation. *Journal of Personality and Social Psychology, 43*, 437–449.

Bargh, J. A., & Thein, R. D. (1985). Individual construct accessibility, person memory, and the recall–judgment link: The case of information overload. *Journal of Personality and Social Psychology, 49*, 1129–1146.

Berkowitz, L. (1993). Towards a general theory of anger and emotional aggression: Implications of the cognitive–neoassociationistic perspective for the analysis of anger and other emotions. In R. S. Wyer, Jr., & T. K. Srull (Eds.), *Advances in social cognition* Vol. 6 (pp. 1–46). Hillsdale, NJ: Lawrence Erlbaum Associates.

Brown, D. R. (1953). Stimulus–similarity and the anchoring of subjective scales. *American Journal of Psychology, 66*, 199–214.

Bruner, J. S. (1957). On perceptual readiness. *Psychological Review.*

Bruner, J. S. (1992). Another look at New Look 1. *American Psychologist, 47*, 780–783.

Carver, C. S., Ganellen, R. J., Froming, W. J., & Chambers, W. (1983). Modelling: An analysis in terms of category accessibility. *Journal of Experimental Social Psychology, 16*, 779–804.

Devine, P. G. (1989). Stereotypes and prejudice: Their automatic and controlled components. *Journal of Personality and Social Psychology, 56*, 5–18.

Fazio, R. H., Sanbonmatsu, D. M., Powell, M. C., & Kardes, F. R. (1986). On the automatic activation of attitudes. *Journal of Personality and Social Psychology, 50*, 229–238.

Ford, T. E., & Kruglanski, A. W. (1995). Effects of epistemic motivations on the use of accessible constructs in social judgment. *Personality and Social Psychology Bulletin, 21*, 950–962.

Greenberg, J., Simon, L., Pyszczynski, T., & Solomon, S. (1992). Terror management and tolerance: Does mortality salience always intensify negative reactions to others who threaten one's worldview? *Journal of Personality and Social Psychology, 63*, 212–220.

Hastorf, A. H., & Cantril, H. (1954). They saw a game: A case study. *Journal of Abnormal and Social Psychology, 49*, 129–14.

Herr, P. M., Sherman, S. J., & Fazio, R. H. (1983). On the consequences of priming: Assimilation and contrast effects. *Journal of Experimental Social Psychology, 19*, 323–340.

Higgins, E. T., Bargh, J. A., & Lombardi, W. (1985). Nature of priming effects on categorization. *Journal of Experimental Psychology: Learning, Memory, and Cognition, 11*, 59–69.

Higgins, E. T., Rholes, W. S., & Jones, C. R. (1977). Category accessibility and impression formation. *Journal of Experimental Social Psychology, 13*, 141–154.

Jacowitz, K. E., & Kahneman, D. (1995). Measures of anchoring in estimation tasks. *Personality and Social Psychology Bulletin, 21*, 1161–1166.

Klayman, J., & Ha, Y. W. (1987). Confirmation, disconfirmation, and information in hypotheses testing. *Psychological Review, 94*, 211–228.

Lombardi, W. J., Higgins, E. T., & Bargh, J. A. (1987). The role of consciousness in priming effects on categorization: Assimilation versus contrast as a function of awareness of the priming task. *Personality and Social Psychology Bulletin, 13*, 411–429.

Martin, L. L. (1986). Set/reset: The use and disuse of concepts in impression formation. *Journal of Personality and Social Psychology, 51*, 493–504.

Martin, L. L., & Achee, J. W. (1992). Beyond accessibility: The role of processing objectives in judgment. In L. L. Martin & A. Tesser (Eds.), *The construction of social judgments* (pp. 195–216). Hillsdale, NJ: Erlbaum.

Martin, L. L., & Tesser, A. (1992). *The construction of social judgment.* Hillsdale, NJ: Lawrence Erlbaum Associates.

Martin, L. L., Seta, J. J., & Crelia, R. (1990). Assimilation and contrast as a function of people's willingness and ability to expend effort in forming an impression. *Journal of Personality and Social Psychology, 59*, 27–37.

Nisbett, R. E., & Wilson, T. D. (1977). Telling more than we can know: Verbal reports on mental processes. *Psychological Review, 84*, 231–259.

Schwarz, N., Bless, H., Strack, F., & Klumpp. G. (1991). Ease of retrieval as information: Another look at the availability heuristic. *Journal of Personality and Social Psychology, 61*, 195–202.

Sedikides, C. (1990). Effects of fortuitously activated constructs versus activated communication goals on person impressions. *Journal of Personality and Social Psychology, 58*, 397–408.

Smith, E. R., & Branscombe, N. R. (1987). Procedurally mediated social inferences: The case of category accessibility effects. *Journal of Experimental Social Psychology, 23*, 361–382.

Smith, E. R., Stewart, T. L., & Buttram, R. T. (1992). Inferring a trait from a behavior has long-term, highly specific effects. *Journal of Personality and Social Psychology, 62*, 753–759.

Srull, T. K., & Wyer, R. S. (1979). The role of category accessibility in the interpretation of information about persons: Some determinants and implications. *Journal of Personality and Social Psychology, 37*, 1660–1672.

Srull, T. K., & Wyer, R. S. (1980). Category accessibility and social perception: Some implications for the study of person memory and interpersonal judgments. *Journal of Personality and Social Psychology, 38*, 842–856.

Stapel, D. A., & Koomen, W. (1997). Using primed exemplars during impression formation: Interpretation or comparison? *European Journal of Social Psychology, 27*, 357–367.

Stapel, D. A., & Koomen, W. (in press). How far do we go beyond the information given? The impact of knowledge activation on interpretation and inferences. *Journal of Personality and Social Psychology.*

Stapel, D. A., & Koomen, W. (under review). The impact of interpretation versus comparison goals on knowledge accessibility effects. Manuscript under review.

Stapel, D. A., Koomen, W., & Van der Pligt, J. (1997). Categories of category accessibility: The impact of trait concept versus exemplar priming on person judgments. *Journal of Experimental Social Psychology, 33*, 47–76.

Stapel, D. A., Koomen, W., & Zeelenberg, M. (1998). The impact of accuracy motivation in interpretation, comparison, and correction processes: Accuracy X knowledge accessibility effects. *Journal of Personality and Social Psychology, 74*, 878–898.

Stapel, D. A., Martin, L. L., & Schwarz, N. (1998). The smell of bias: What instigates correction processes in social judgments? *Personality and Social Psychology Bulletin, 24*, 797–806.

Strack, F. (1992). The different routes to social judgments: Experiential vs. informational strategies. In L. L. Martin & A. Tesser (Eds.), *The construction of social judgment* (pp. 249–275). Hillsdale: Erlbaum.

Strack, F., & Hannover, B. (1996). Awareness of influence as a precondition for implementing correctional goals. In P. M. Gollwitzer & J. A. Bargh (Eds.), *The psychology of action: Linking cognition and motivation to behavior* (pp. 579–596). New York: Guilford Press.

Strack, F., & Mussweiler, T. (1997). Explaining the enigmatic anchoring effect: Mechanisms of selective accessibility. *Journal of Personality and Social Psychology, 73*, 437–446.

Strack, F., Schwarz, N., Bless, H., Kübler, A., & Wänke, M. (1993). Awareness of the influence as a determinant of assimilation vs. contrast. *European Journal of Experimental Social Psychology, 23*, 53–62.

Sudman, S., Bradburn, N. M., & Schwarz, N. (1996). *Thinking about answers: The application of cognitive processes to survey methodology.* San Francisco: Jossey-Bass Publishers.

Thompson, E. P., Roman, R. J., Moskowitz, G. B., Chaiken, S., & Bargh, J. A. (1994). Accuracy motivation attenuates covert priming: The systematic reprocessing of social information. *Journal of Personality and Social Psychology, 66*, 474–489.

Tversky, A., & Kahneman, D. (1974). Judgment under uncertainty: Heuristics and biases. *Science, 185*, 1124–1131.

Wegener, D. T., & Petty, R. E. (1995). Flexible correction processes in social judgment: The role of naive theories in corrections for perceived bias. *Journal of Personality and Social Psychology, 68*, 36–51.

Wegener, D. T., & Petty, R. E. (1997). The flexible correction model: The role of naive theories of bias in bias correction. In M. P. Zanna (Ed.), *Advances in experimental social psychology* Vol. 29 (pp. 141–208). San Diego: Academic Press.

Wilson, T. D., & Brekke, N. (1994). Mental contamination and mental correction: Unwanted influences on judgments and evaluations. *Psychological Bulletin, 116*, 117–142.

Wilson, T. D., Hodges, S. D., & LaFleur, S. J. (1995). Effects of introspecting about reasons: Inferring attitudes from accessible thoughts. *Journal of Personality and Social Psychology, 69*, 16–28.

Wyer, R. S., Jr., & Martin, L. L. (1986). Person memory: The role of traits, group stereotypes, and specific behaviors in the cognitive representation of persons. *Journal of Personality and Social Psychology, 50*, 661–675.

CHAPTER FOUR

Cognitive Representations of Attachment: The Content and Function of Working Models

Nancy L. Collins and Lisa M. Allard

As individuals enter new relationships, they bring with them a history of social experiences and a unique set of memories, beliefs, and expectations that guide how they interact with others and how they construe their social world. Of course, these representations continue to evolve as individuals encounter new people and develop new relationships throughout their lives. Nevertheless, attachment theory suggests that cognitive models that begin their development early in one's personal history are likely to remain influential. First proposed by Bowlby (1973), and then refined by other scholars (Bretherton, 1985; Collins & Read, 1994; Main, 1991; Main, Kaplan, & Cassidy, 1985), internal "working models" of attachment are thought to be core features of personality that shape the manner in which the attachment system is expressed by directing cognitive, emotional, and behavioral response patterns in attachment-relevant contexts. Furthermore, individual differences in "attachment style" observed between children and adults are attributed to systematic differences in underlying models of self and others, and whatever continuities exist in these styles across the lifespan are proposed to be largely a function of the enduring quality of these models.

The purpose of this chapter is to provide a review and analysis of working models with regard to adult attachment. We begin by considering the content and structure of these models, including how they may differ for adults with different attachment styles. Next, we consider how these models function, and the processes through which they shape cognitive, emotional, and behavioral response patterns in adulthood.

Preparation of this chapter was supported by National Science Foundation Grant No. SBR-9870524 to the first author. Please address correspondence to Nancy L. Collins, Department of Psychology, University of California, Santa Barbara, CA 93106-9660. Electronic mail may be sent via internet to ncollins@psych.ucsb.edu.

The Content and Structure of Working Models

What are working models? What are they composed of? How are they structured in memory? These are all critical questions for attachment scholars. To answer these questions, we begin by briefly reviewing the major propositions outlined by Bowlby and others on the early development and nature of working models.[1] Our goal is not to review the developmental literature, but to use that literature as a point of departure for understanding how working models may be characterized in adulthood. Next, we specify the components of working models and discuss how these components can be useful for mapping out differences in adult attachment styles. Finally, we discuss how working models are likely to be structured in memory, focusing on some important issues regarding the complex and multidimensional nature of attachment representations.

Working models from infancy to adulthood

Bowlby (1973) used the term "working models" to describe the internal mental representations that children develop of the world and of significant people within it, including the self. These representations evolve out of experiences with attachment figures and center around the regulation and fulfillment of attachment needs – namely, the maintenance of proximity to a nurturing caregiver and the regulation of felt security (Bretherton, 1985; Sroufe & Waters, 1977). Of course, not all infants will have access to caretakers who respond to their attachment needs in a consistent and loving manner. Thus, the quality of the infant– caretaker relationship, and hence the nature of one's working models, are expected to be largely determined by the caregiver's emotional availability and responsiveness to the child's needs. Working models are hypothesized to include two complementary components, one referring to the attachment figure and the other referring to the self. The former characterizes whether the caregiver will be available, sensitive, and responsive when needed, and the latter characterizes the self as either worthy or unworthy of love and care. For example, children whose caretakers are sensitive and consistently available when needed should develop a working model in which others are characterized as responsive and trustworthy and the self is characterized as lovable and worthy of care. In contrast, children who have inconsistent or rejecting caregivers are likely to develop a working model in which others are characterized as unresponsive and the self is characterized either as unworthy of care or as self-sufficient and not in need of such care.

Early working models are thus composed of schemata that reflect a child's attempts to gain comfort and security along with the typical outcome of those attempts (Main, Kaplan, & Cassidy, 1985). That is, working models contain a summary of the child's interactions with the caregiving environment and are expected to be fairly accurate reflections of social reality as experienced by the developing child (Bowlby, 1973). One central aspect of working models adopted by Bowlby is the idea that working models are used to predict the behavior of others and to plan one's own behavior in social interaction. Working models shape the nature in which the attachment behavioral system is expressed, and are dynamic and functional. For this reason, individual differences in infant *behavioral* patterns, as displayed in diagnostic situations, are used to infer underlying differences in internal working models (Main et al., 1985), and serve as the basis for categorizing infants into secure and various forms of insecure attachment styles (Ainsworth, Blehar, Waters, & Wall, 1978).

In early childhood, attachment models appear to be relatively open to change if the quality of caregiving changes (Egeland & Farber, 1984; Thompson, Lamb, & Estes, 1982; Vaughn, Egeland, Sroufe, & Waters, 1979). However, given a fairly consistent pattern of caregiving throughout childhood and adolescence, working models are expected to become solidified through repeated experience and increasingly generalized over time. Thus, what begins as a schema of a specific child–caretaker relationship results in the formation of more abstract representations of oneself and the social world (Shaver, Collins, & Clark, 1996). Once formed, these representations are likely to operate automatically and unconsciously, thereby making them resistant to dramatic change (Bowlby, 1979). As such, working models of self and others that take root in childhood are carried forward into adulthood where they continue to shape social perception and behavior in close relationships.

On the basis of this assumption, attachment theory has become a widely used model for understanding interpersonal behavior and romantic experience in adult close relationships. Inspired by Hazan and Shaver's (1987) seminal paper on romantic love as an attachment process, much of the empirical work in social psychology has focused on individual differences in adult attachment style. These styles reflect chronic differences in the way individuals think, feel, and behave in close relationships and they are believed to be rooted in systematic differences in working models of self and others.

Adult attachment researchers typically define four prototypic attachment styles (secure, preoccupied, dismissing, fearful) derived from two underlying dimensions – *anxiety* and *avoidance* (Bartholomew & Horowitz, 1991; Brennan, Clark, & Shaver, 1998; Fraley & Waller, 1998). The anxiety dimension refers to one's sense of self-worth and acceptance (vs. rejection) by others, and is believed to reflect the positive or negative nature of one's model of self. The avoidance dimension refers to the degree to which one approaches (vs. avoids) intimacy and interdependence with others and is believed to reflect the positive or negative nature of one's model of others. *Secure* adults are low in both attachment-related anxiety and avoidance; they are comfortable with intimacy, willing to rely on others for support, and confident that they are valued by others. *Preoccupied* adults (also called *anxious–ambivalent*) are high in anxiety and low in avoidance; they have an exaggerated desire for closeness and dependence, coupled with a heightened concern about being rejected. *Dismissing avoidant* individuals are low in attachment-related anxiety but high in avoidance; they view close relationships as relatively unimportant and they value independence and self-reliance. Finally, *fearful avoidant* adults are high in both attachment anxiety and avoidance; although they desire close relationships and the approval of others, they avoid intimacy because they fear being rejected. Although this four-category typology (Bartholomew & Horowitz, 1991) is widely used, many attachment researchers rely on the original three-category typology (Hazan & Shaver, 1987), which includes a single avoidant category.

Attachment styles represent theoretical prototypes that individuals can approximate to varying degrees (Bartholomew & Horowitz, 1991), and they are most often assessed through self-report scales or semi-structured interviews.[2] Although there are a number of unresolved issues concerning how best to conceptualize and measure individual differences in adult attachment style, attachment researchers agree that these styles are rooted in fundamental differences between people in the content and nature of their working models of self and others. Until recently, however, the concept of working models has remained vague and ill-defined, and the precise mechanisms through which they operate have not been well understood. Fortunately, attachment scholars have begun to develop more detailed theories about the nature of working models, and have employed more sophisticated techniques for studying them (e.g., Baldwin, Keelan, Fehr, Enns, & Koh-Rangarajoo, 1996; Collins & Read, 1994; Shaver, Collins, & Clark, 1996). We begin our discussion of working models by identifying their components and suggesting how these components can be useful for mapping out differences in adult attachment styles.

Building blocks of working models

Internal working models of attachment are similar in many ways to other cognitive structures studied by social psychologists, including schemas, scripts, and prototypes. Like all such constructs, working models are hypothetical structures that are presumed to be stored in long-term memory. They organize past experience and provide a framework for understanding new experiences and guiding social interaction.

Although working models share many features with other social-cognitive structures, they are also unique in some respects (Shaver, Collins, & Clark, 1996). First, unlike traditional approaches to schemas, which tend to focus on semantic knowledge and verbal propositions, attachment theory places greater emphasis on the representation of motivational elements (needs and goals) and behavioral tendencies. Second, because working models are formed in the context of emotional experiences and center around the fulfillment of emotional needs, they are more heavily affect-laden than other knowledge structures typically studied by cognitive social psychologists. Third, working models differ from other schemas in that they are explicitly interpersonal and relational in nature (Baldwin, 1992). Finally, working models of attachment are thought to be broader, more multidimensional, and more complex than other social representations typically studied by social psychologists.

What are working models composed of? Because working models are built within the context of the attachment behavioral system, they should contain the history of experiences of that system, beliefs about the self and others based on those experiences, and the resulting motivational and behavioral strategies that have evolved for the expression of this system. Collins and Read (1994) propose that working models include four interrelated components: (1) memories of attachment-related experience; (2) beliefs, attitudes, and expectations about self and others in relation to attachment; (3) attachment-related goals and needs; and (4) strategies and plans associated with achieving attachment goals. Below we describe the four components of working models in greater detail. In doing so, we suggest some ways in which the contents of each might differ for adults with different attachment styles and we review recent empirical work where available.

Attachment-related memories An important component of working models is memories and accounts of attachment-related experiences. These should include not only representations of specific interactions and concrete episodes, but also constructions placed on those episodes, such as appraizsals of experience and explanations for one's own and others' behavior. Because these memories should be based, in part, on actual experience, we would expect that secure and insecure adults would represent their attachment experiences differently. In general, secure adults should be more likely than insecure adults to report positive relationship experiences with key attachment figures (parents, peers, romantic partners). Some preliminary evidence for this idea has been obtained in studies involving retrospective reports of relationships with parents. For example, Hazan and Shaver (1987) found that secure adults remembered their relationships with their parents as more affectionate and warm than did avoidant or anxious adults; avoidant adults were especially likely to report their mothers as having been cold and rejecting (see also Feeney & Noller, 1990).

More recently, Mikulincer and his colleagues have used a response latency paradigm to explore attachment style differences in the cognitive accessibility of emotional memories. In one study (Mikulincer & Orbach, 1995), young adults were asked to recall childhood experiences in which they felt a particular emotion (anger, sadness, anxiety, and happiness). The time taken to retrieve each episode was then recorded. When comparisons were made across groups, avoidant adults showed the lowest accessibility (slowest responding) to sadness and anxiety memories, whereas anxious-ambivalent adults showed the highest accessibility (fastest responding). When comparisons were made within groups, secure individuals were faster to retrieve positive memories than negative memories, whereas anxious-ambivalent individuals showed the opposite pattern. In another study, Mikulincer (1998b, Study 1) asked young adults to recall a series of positive and negative experiences related to trust (e.g., "remember a time when your mother behaved in such a way that she increased the trust you felt toward her"). Secure individuals were quicker to retrieve positive trust-related memories whereas avoidant and anxious adults were quicker to retrieve negative memories.

Attachment-related beliefs, attitudes, and expectations. A person's knowledge about self, others, and relationships is likely to be extremely complex in adulthood. It will include not only static *beliefs* (e.g., "relationships require a lot of work"), but also *attitudes* (e.g., "relationships are not worth the effort") and *expectations* (e.g., "I am unlikely to find someone who will love me completely"). This knowledge is abstracted, in part, from concrete experiences during childhood, adolescence, and adulthood, and may be altered through reflection and reevaluation. Beliefs about oneself and others can also vary in level of abstraction. Some will be associated with particular attachment figures (e.g., "my mother is emotionally distant"), others will be broader generalizations about relationships (e.g., "friends can be counted on for support") or about people (e.g., "people are trustworthy").

Although empirical work is still in its early stages, important links have been found between self-reported attachment style and general beliefs about the self and the social world. For example, Hazan and Shaver (1987) reported that secure adults viewed themselves as having fewer self-doubts and as being better liked by others compared to anxious and avoidant adults. They were also more likely to think that other people are generally well-intentioned and good-hearted. In a more extensive study, Collins and Read (1990) found that individuals with a secure attachment style viewed people in general as trustworthy, dependable, and altruistic. Anxious adults thought that others were complex and difficult to understand and that people have little control over the outcomes in their lives. Avoidant adults reported largely negative beliefs about human nature; they were suspicious of human motives, viewed others as not trustworthy and not dependable, and doubted the honesty and integrity of social role agents such as parents. Important differences were also found in participants' self-concepts. Secure adults were higher in self-worth, saw themselves as more confident in social situations, more interpersonally oriented, and more assertive as compared to anxious individuals. Avoidant individuals did not differ from the secure group in their self-worth or assertiveness, but they did view themselves as less confident in social situations and as not interpersonally oriented.

In addition to identifying the content of one's beliefs about self and others, secure and insecure adults are also likely to differ in the way their social knowledge is organized. Consistent with this idea, Clark, Shaver, and Calverley (1994; described in Shaver & Clark, 1996) found that adults with different attachment styles differed in the degree to which positive and negative features of the self were central or peripheral in their self-schema. For instance, although secure adults reported both positive and negative features in their self-concept, their positive features were more central and their negative features were more peripheral; fearful avoidant individuals showed the opposite pattern. In an impressive series of studies, Mikulincer (1995) provided further evidence for attachment style differences in the structure of self-models by using a variety of measures developed in the self-concept literature. Among the many interesting findings, secure participants were found to have more balanced, complex, and coherent self-structures than anxious and avoidant participants. Secure individuals also reported fewer discrepancies between their *actual* self and their *ideal* self, and between their actual self and their *ought* self.

Finally, Baldwin, Fehr, Keedian, Seidel, and Thomson (1993) have shown that attachment-related beliefs may be stored as "if–then" propositions that reflect a person's expectations about their social interactions with others (e.g., "If I trust others, they will hurt me"). In one study, they asked participants to consider a number of hypothetical, attachment-relevant behaviors (e.g., "If I depend on my partner") and then to rate the likelihood that their partner would respond in various positive and negative ways (e.g., "then my partner will leave me" or "then my partner will support me"). Results indicated that secure participants held more positive if–then expectancies than did avoidant or anxious-ambivalent participants. In a second study, they used a response latency paradigm and a lexical decision task to extend their findings beyond self-reports and to examine spreading activation between elements of relational schemas. Reaction times provided further evidence that insecure adults hold more pessimistic interpersonal expectations than secure adults. For example, when participants with an avoidant attachment style were given a prime that involved trusting a romantic partner, they showed particularly quick reactions to the negative outcome word "hurt."

Response latency paradigms, such as those used by Baldwin et al. and by Mikulincer and his colleagues are especially useful because they provide opportunities to uncover implicit or unconscious aspects of working models that might not be accessible through self-report. Other methods for investigating implicit mental representations that are being developed in the social cognition literature (e.g., Greenwald, McGhee, & Schwartz, 1998) may also prove useful for attachment scholars.

Attachment-related goals and needs.   Although the attachment behavioral system serves the broad goal of maintaining felt-security, a person's history of achieving or failing to achieve this goal is expected to result in a characteristic hierarchy of attachment-related social and emotional needs. For example, individuals differ in the extent to which they are motivated to develop intimate relationships, avoid rejection, maintain privacy, seek approval from others, and so on. As such, the goal structures of secure and insecure individuals should differ considerably. For example, secure adults are likely to desire intimate relationships with others and, within relationships, to seek a balance of closeness and autonomy. Preoccupied (anxious-ambivalent) adults also desire close relationships but their additional need for approval and fear of rejection may lead them to seek high levels of intimacy and lower levels of autonomy. Avoidant adults are guided by a need to maintain distance; dismissing avoidants seek to limit intimacy in the service of satisfying their desire for autonomy and independence, but fearful avoidants do so to avoid rejection (Bartholomew & Horowitz, 1991). Avoidant adults may also place greater weight on non-attachment-related goals, such as achievement in school or in a career (Brennan & Bosson, 1998; Brennan & Morris, 1997; Hazan & Shaver, 1990). Individuals with different attachment styles may also differ in the extent to which certain goals are salient or chronically accessible. For example, although most people are presumed to have a need for acceptance by others, the chronic accessibility of this need should differ considerably between people, being most chronically activated for preoccupied adults.

There is little empirical work that directly assesses the goal structures of adults with different attachment styles, but a few studies point to some potentially important patterns. Collins and Allard (1999) asked participants in dating relationships to rate the importance of their romantic partner fulfilling specific attachment-related needs (e.g., "how important is it that your partner comfort you when you are feeling down?"). They found that attachment-related anxiety was positively associated with importance ratings whereas avoidance was negatively associated with these ratings.

In a series of studies, Mikulincer (1998b) found evidence of attachment style differences in the accessibility of interpersonal goals related to trust. In one study (Study 2) he asked young adults to describe the benefits associated with trusting one's partner. These narratives were then coded for the presence of specific trust-related goals. Secure adults were most likely to spontaneously mention increases in intimacy as a trust-related goal; anxious-ambivalent adults were most likely to mention increases in security; and avoidant adults were most likely to mention increases in the attainment of control. In another study (Study 4), Mikulincer used a lexical decision task to explore the accessibility of trust-related goals. Following a trust-related prime, anxious-ambivalent individuals reacted more quickly to the word "security," whereas avoidant adults reacted more quickly to the word "control."

Plans and strategies.   Plans and strategies are organized sequences of behavior aimed at the attainment of some goal. Individuals are expected to have encoded as part of their working models a set of plans and strategies for regulating their attachment-related social and emotional needs, and these strategies should be contingent upon a person's history of experiences with key attachment figures (Main, 1981). Thus important attachment-style differences are expected in one's plans and strategies for managing socio-emotional needs and goals and maintaining felt security. Among many behavioral strategies, this should include strategies for regulating emotional distress (Kobak & Sceery, 1988), obtaining comfort when needed, maintaining autonomy, developing intimacy with others, giving comfort to others, and so on.

Identifying individual differences in plans and strategies poses some difficulties because such representations are likely to be stored as procedural knowledge, which may be difficult to articulate and which may operate largely outside of awareness. One way to identify different plans and strategies is to examine how individuals behave in response to the *same* social stimuli. For example, in a series of studies, Collins (Collins, 1996; Collins & Allard, 1999) asked respondents to imagine a series of attachment-relevant events in which their partner behaved in a potentially negative manner (e.g., "imagine that your partner didn't responde when you tried to cuddle"). Respondents were then asked to describe in detail how they would behave in response to each event. Content coding of these descriptions revealed important individual differences in behavioral strategies. Relative to insecure adults, secure adults tended to choose behavioral strategies that were less punishing toward their partner and less likely to lead to conflict. (These patterns remained even after controlling for relationship satisfaction.) In another study, Ognibene and Collins (1998) asked young adults to describe how they would cope with a series of hypothetical stressful life events. Results revealed systematic difference in the coping styles of adults with different attachment styles. For example, secure and preoccupied adults were more likely than avoidant adults to seek social support as a coping strategy.

Another useful research strategy is to employ response latency paradigms to uncover differences in the *accessibility* of specific behavioral strategies. For example, Mikulincer (1998b, Study 5) used a lexical decision task to study attachment style differences in the way individuals cope with trust violations. When participants were presented with a prime that involved a violation of trust, secure and anxious-ambivalent adults responded more quickly than avoidant adults to the word "talk," and avoidant adults responded more quickly to the word "escape".

Of course, another method for identifying differences in plans and strategies is to observe actual behavior in attachment-relevant contexts. Although observational research is still somewhat rare in the adult attachment literature, a growing number of studies reveal differences in a variety of attachment-relevant behaviors including support seeking and caregiving (Collins & Feeney, 2000; Simpson, Rholes, & Nelligan, 1992), conflict and problem solving (Feeney, Noller, & Callan, 1994; Simpson, Rholes, & Phillips, 1996), self-disclosure (Mikulincer & Nachshon, 1991), and responses to separation from one's partner (Fraley & Shaver, 1998).

Summary.   In summary, internal working models are attachment-related knowledge structures concerning the self and the social world that include cognitive as well as affective components. They are developed through attachment experience and stored in long-term memory. Working models are composed of a number of elements including episodic memories, beliefs, goals, and plans. Finally, individual differences in attachment styles can be defined in terms of characteristic configurations of these various components. In the section that follows, we continue our discussion of working models by considering how multiple models may be structured in memory.

The structure of working models:
a complex representational network

There is a strong tendency to discuss working models and attachment style in the singular, as if an individual can have only one. However, there are good reasons to question this assumption. Because adult representations of attachment are based on a variety of relationships both within and outside the family, they are apt to be complex and multifaceted (Baldwin et al., 1996; Bretherton, Biringen, Ridgeway, Maslin, & Sherman, 1989; Crittenden, 1990; George & Solomon, 1989). Moreover, it is unreasonable to assume that a single, undifferentiated working model can effectively guide the full range of attachment behavior in adulthood. Multiple models of attachment are necessary for adults to function adaptively in diverse circumstances and to satisfy their attachment goals across a variety of relationships.

For these reasons, Collins and Read (1994) have suggested that adult representations of attachment are best considered as a network of interconnected models that may be organized as a *default hierarchy*. At the top of the hierarchy is the default model that corresponds to the most general representations about people and the self, abstracted from a history of relationship experiences with caretakers and peers. This default model can apply to a wide range of relationships and situations, although it may not describe any one of them very well. Further down in the hierarchy are models that correspond to particular kinds of relationships (parent–child relationships, friendships, romantic relationships), and lowest in the hierarchy are the most specific models corresponding to particular partners and particular relationships ("my husband Michael," "my friend Sandra"). It is important to note that models within the network are probably linked through a rich set of associations and are likely to share many elements. Thus, although each model may be somewhat distinct, we would expect a fair amount of overlap between various models.

Consistent with these ideas, a number of recent studies provide evidence for the multidimensional nature of attachment representations in adulthood. Bartholomew and Horowitz (1991, Study 2) compared adult representations of attachment with parents and with peers using a set of parallel interviews. Scores derived from the two interviews were only moderately correlated with each other, and each uniquely contributed to the prediction of interpersonal problems involving warmth. Similar findings were obtained by Crowell and Owens (1996) who developed an interview to assess security of attachment in a specific romantic relationship (the Current Relationship Interview, CRI). The CRI was designed to parallel the Adult Attachment Interview (AAI; George, Kaplan, & Main, 1984), which assesses adults' representations of their attachment experiences with parents. In a sample of young adults who were about to be married, they found a moderate correlation between security scores on the CRI and the AAI. Furthermore, in a series of studies (summarized in Crowell, Fraley, & Shaver, 1999) in which both assessments were used to predict relationship functioning over time, each assessment accounted for unique variance in outcomes. For example, premarital CRI scores uniquely predicted feelings of commitment, intimacy, and aggression 18 months later, and AAI scores uniquely predicted intimacy, threats to abandon the partner, and partner's physical aggression.

Evidence for the multidimensional nature of attachment representations has also been found using self-report measures of attachment style. Baldwin et al. (1996, Study 1) asked young adults to report their general attachment style in romantic relationships and their attachment orientation in their ten most significant relationships. Consistent with the idea of multiple models, the vast majority of participants reported two or more different attachment patterns across their ten relationships. At the same time, however, people with different general styles reported more individual relationships that matched their general style. For example, compared to their secure counterparts, anxious-ambivalent adults were more likely to report having experienced relationships that matched the anxious-ambivalent prototype. These data are consistent with the idea that individuals possess a complex associative network of working models that contains abstract representations (a general model or style) as well as specific exemplars (relationship-specific models or orientations). Further support for this idea was provided in a study by Beer and Kihlstrom (1999) in which they used a cognitive priming procedure to examine how various working models are encoded in long-term memory. Cognitive models of relationships with parents showed evidence of being stored in terms of abstract traits, whereas models of a current relationship showed evidence of being more episodic and autobiographical.

Given the multidimensional nature of attachment representations, how can we predict which model(s) will be activated and used to guide social perception and behavior? As summarized by Collins and Read (1994), activation is likely to depend on characteristics of the models themselves and features of the prevailing social situation. Some models will be more accessible than others, where accessibility depends on a variety of factors including the amount of experience on which the model is based, the number of times it has been applied in the past, and the density of its connections to other knowledge structures. This implies that general working models (which are abstracted from a history of relationship experiences and are likely to be densely connected) are likely to be highly accessible. Consistent with this speculation, Baldwin et al. (1996, Study 2) asked people with different chronic attachment styles (general orientations in romantic relationships) to think of *specific* relationships that matched each of the three attachment style prototypes. Participants then rated how easy it was for them to think of these specific exemplars. Although most participants reported relationships that matched all three attachment prototypes, the ease with which a person could generate a specific exemplar was predicted by their general attachment style. For example, relative to their secure counterparts, adults who rated themselves as avoidant (in general) found it much easier to think of specific relationships in which they were avoidant. Baldwin et al. suggest that although most individuals possess multiple attachment models (or *relational schemas*) a person's general attachment style may represent their best-articulated and most accessible knowledge structure.

Whether or not features of the situation match features of the working model will also affect its likelihood of use. Among the features that should be important are characteristics of the interaction partner, the nature of the relationship, and the goals that are salient in the situation. For instance, characteristics of the interaction partner such as gender and physical appearance should be important cues in matching. In support of this idea, Collins and Read (1990) have shown that in romantic relationships, one's model of the opposite sex parent is a better predictor of aspects of the relationship than is the model of the same sex parent. Presumably the nature of one's current relationship should also be an important cue. For example, models based on relationships with parents may be more relevant when interacting with one's own children than when interacting with one's peers. This functional specificity was illustrated in a study by Kobak and Sceery (1988) in which young adults' representations of their childhood experiences with parents predicted the extent to which they perceived that social support was currently available from their family, but did not predict their judgments about available support from their friends.

The specificity of the match should also be important in determining which models are activated and used. All other things being equal, more specific models should be preferred because they provide more accurate guides for responding to particular partners and relationships. However, a recent study in our lab suggests that the tendency to prefer specific models may differ for people with different attachment styles (Collins & Allard, 1999). We asked respondents to provide attributions for a series of potentially negative partner behaviors. The attributional patterns of secure adults were strongly predicted by their relationship-specific expectations (a relationship-specific working model), such that individuals in better functioning relationships endorsed more benign attributions, whereas those in poorly functioning relationships endorsed more negative attributions. In contrast, insecure adults tended to endorse the negative attributions regardless of the quality of their current relationship. These preliminary findings suggest that adults with insecure chronic models may find it difficult to set aside their doubts and may rely on their pessimistic models even when a more positive relationship-specific model is available.

As the above discussion makes clear, attachment researchers will need to be more precise in specifying which aspect of the attachment network they are concerned with in a given line of research. Just as it is incorrect to speak of a single model of self or others, it may also be incorrect to speak of a single corresponding attachment style. Although this idea has not been made explicit in the literature, it is already reflected in the various approaches used to measure individual differences in adult attachment styles (e.g., Bartholomew & Horowitz, 1991; Brennan, Clark, & Shaver, 1998; George, Kaplan, & Main, 1984; Kobak & Hazan, 1991; Crowell & Owens, 1996). These approaches differ in the particular content that they target (e.g., parents, peers, romantic partners), and in the general versus specific nature of that content (e.g., relationships in general versus one specific relationship). We believe that no one approach is more or less "correct," but that each approach assesses a different aspect of the attachment network. Nevertheless, the notion that someone has a particular attachment "style" in close relationships implies that they are predisposed to think, feel, and behave in certain ways in all such relationships. Thus, Collins and Read (1994) suggest that the term "attachment style" should be reserved for models that are more general (abstract) and chronic. The term "attachment quality" can then be used to describe the model one develops within a specific close relationship: a *relational schema* in Baldwin's (1992) terms. A more detailed understanding of the interrelationships between attachment style and attachment quality will be facilitated by empirical studies that employ multiple methods of assessing adult attachment orientations.

Summary. In summary, individuals possess multiple models of attachment that differ in their level of specificity and accessibility, and which may be structured in memory as a hierarchical network that provides maximum flexibility in regulating attachment needs. In the next section of the chapter, we turn our attention to the mechanisms through which working models guide social perception and behavior. In doing so, we limit our discussion to a consideration of attachment style as studied by most social psychologists, who define attachment styles in terms of one's general orientation toward intimate relationships. However, the processes we describe below should also be applicable to relationship-specific working models.

The Functions of Working Models in Adulthood

> Every situation we meet with in life is construed in terms of the representational models we have of the world about us and of ourselves. Information reaching us through our sense organs is selected and interpreted in terms of those models, its significance for us and for those we care for is evaluated in terms of them, and plans of action conceived and executed with those models in mind. On how we interpret and evaluate each situation, moreover, turns also how we feel.
>
> (Bowlby, 1980, p. 229)

As reflected in Bowlby's statement, working models are central components of the attachment behavioral system that are expected to play an important role in shaping how individuals operate in their relationships and how they construe their social world. Empirical support for this assumption is beginning to accumulate as a growing body of research finds that adults with different attachment styles differ markedly in the nature and quality of their close relationships (see Feeney, 1999, for a comprehensive review of this literature). Although the correlational nature of these studies prevents us from drawing firm conclusions about causality, the underlying assumption throughout this research is that working models of attachment directly contribute to relationship outcomes by shaping cognitive, emotional, and behavioral response patterns. Unfortunately, the specific mechanisms through which this occurs remain poorly understood. In this section of the chapter, we turn our attention to this issue by considering some of the important ways in which working models function. In doing so, we use current research and theory in cognitive social psychology as a guide for suggesting how each process will be shaped by working models, and we review attachment research where available.

Framework for studying the functions of working models

How do working models operate? One way to approach this question is to consider working models of attachment as part of a broader system of cognitive, affective, and behavioral processes that enable people to make sense of their experiences and to function in ways that meet their personal needs. Based on existing research and theory in personality and social psychology, Collins and Read (1994) proposed a very general model for understanding how such a system might operate. They argue that working models of attachment are highly accessible cognitive constructs that will be activated automatically in memory whenever attachment-relevant events occur. Once activated, they are predicted to have a direct impact on both the cognitive processing of social information and on emotional appraisal. The outcome of these processes will then determine one's choice of behavioral strategies. In short, the impact of working models on *behavior* in any given situation is likely to be mediated by the *cognitive interpretation* of the situation along with the person's *emotional response*. Moreover, we need not assume that people are consciously directing these processes, or even that they are aware of them. In fact, we expect that much of this system will operate "automatically"; that is, spontaneously, with little effort, and outside of awareness (Bargh & Chartrand, 1999).

This model is intended to be a general framework for exploring a number of more specific cognition–emotion–behavior linkages. Our task in the following sections is to specify these links in greater detail. To accomplish this, we discuss each component separately, keeping in mind the broader model that ties them together.

Cognitive response patterns

Working models of attachment contain a rich network of memories, beliefs, and goals that should play a critical role in shaping how individuals think about themselves and their relationships. Although cognitive processes are only just beginning to be studied in the adult attachment literature, support for these ideas is provided by a large body of research in social psychology on the role of prior knowledge in social information processing and social judgment. Empirical work in social psychology clearly demonstrates that social perception is heavily influenced by top-down, theory-driven processes in which existing goals, schemas, and expectations shape the way people view new information. Although most of this research involves thinking about strangers, these processes are increasingly being explored in the context of close relationships (e.g., Fletcher & Fincham, 1991; Fletcher & Fitness, 1996; Martin, 1991; Holmes & Rempel, 1989). Below, we consider three processes that should be strongly influenced by working models and should have important implications for personal and interpersonal functioning: (a) selective attention, (b) memory, and (c) social construal.

Selective attention. Empirical as well as anecdotal evidence indicates that two people viewing or experiencing the same event rarely agree about what took place. This tendency toward divergent perceptions suggests that perceivers are predisposed to attend to particular features of their environment and to disregard others. Indeed, Bargh (1984) concludes that social perception "involves an interaction between the environmental stimuli that are currently present and the individual's readiness to perceive some over others" (p. 15). But what determines a person's readiness to attend to particular information? One important factor is one's currently active goals. Goals and personal needs provide an orienting framework for the direction of cognitive resources, and evidence indicates that people become highly sensitized to goal-related stimuli (Srull & Wyer, 1986). Individuals are also more likely to notice information that can be easily assimilated into their existing knowledge about self and others (Cohen, 1981; Markus, 1977; Roskos-Ewoldsen & Fazio, 1992), especially when that knowledge is chronically accessible (Bargh, 1984; Higgins, King, & Mavin, 1982). As a result, people are apt to attend to information that is relevant to their goals and consistent with their existing beliefs or attitudes about self and others.

This literature suggests that working models of attachment will play an important role in directing cognitive resources in attachment-relevant situations. For example, anxious-ambivalent (preoccupied) adults are expected to have "seeking approval" and "avoiding rejection" as chronically active goals. As a result, they are likely to have a threat- or rejection-oriented attentional focus that keeps them vigilant for signs of disapproval by others. In addition, because they expect the worst, they will easily notice evidence that confirms their fears. The attentional focus of avoidant adults should be characterized by a very different pattern. Their motivation to maintain autonomy should make them highly sensitive to signs of intrusion or control by others. In addition, their desire to minimize attachment concerns will tend to direct their attention away from features of the environment that make attachment needs salient (Fraley, Davis, & Shaver, 1998). In sum, at the earliest stages in the perceptual process attachment style differences in working models will direct attention toward certain features of the environment and away from others. As a result, information available for further processing may tend to be biased in a goal-relevant and expectation-consistent manner.

Although these specific hypotheses have not yet been tested, a study by Mikulincer (1997) provides preliminary evidence that attachment-related goals can shape information seeking. In this study (1997, Study 2), participants were asked to evaluate a new product and were given the opportunity to select how much information they wanted to hear about the product. In addition, they were told that time spent listening to this information would affect how much time they had left for a second task. Half of the participants were told that this second task was a social interaction, and the other half were told that it was a sensory test. Within-group comparisons revealed that avoidant adults selected more information during the first task when the second task was social than non-social; anxious-ambivalent adults showed the opposite pattern. In contrast, secure adults requested the same amount of information regardless of the second task. These data suggest that insecure participants allocated their attention in ways that served their personal goals. Anxious-ambivalent adults – who value social connection and social approval – limited their attention to a competing task when it interfered with a social task. In contrast, avoidant adults – who value social distance – increased their attention to a non-social task, thereby decreasing their available attention for a social task.

Memory.   One of the most robust findings in the social cognitive literature is that existing knowledge structures shape what gets stored in memory, and what is later recalled or reconstructed. In general, aspects of experience that can be interpreted in terms of easily accessible concepts are more likely to be encoded into memory than aspects that cannot be easily assimilated (Srull & Wyer, 1989). As a result, strong, well-established schemas bias memory toward schema-relevant, and often schema-consistent, information (Hastie, 1981; Higgins & Bargh, 1987). In addition, once information is stored in memory, further processing gives consistent material an advantage over inconsistent material (Srull & Wyer, 1989; Tesser, 1978).

While existing representations improve memory for relevant features of an experience, they may also lead one to recall or reconstruct features that never took place. One reason for this effect is that, as memory for an event fades over time, people may rely more on their generic schemas and less on the particular encounter (Graesser & Nakamura, 1982). As a result, people will sometimes reconstruct experiences and "remember" schema-consistent material that was never encountered. For example, Andersen and her colleagues (Andersen &

Cole, 1990; Andersen, Glassman, Chen, & Cole, 1995) have shown that people can mistakenly remember characteristics of a new person when that person resembles someone close to them.

Research on schema-driven memory has clear implications for working models of attachment. Because their social knowledge and prior experiences differ, adults with different attachment styles will be predisposed to remember different kinds of information. In general, individuals should be more likely to store, recall, and reconstruct attachment-related experiences in ways that are consistent with their existing models of self and others.[3]

Support for this idea was provided in a series of studies conducted by Mikulincer and Horesh (1999), who adapted Andersen's (Andersen & Cole, 1990) transference paradigm to explore how models of *self* influence memory for other people. In two studies, participants were presented with descriptions of targets persons who were systematically varied (idiographically) to be similar to or different from the participants' actual self and unwanted self. The ease with which the targets were recalled (Study 2), and false-positive memory intrusions (recalling a characteristic that was not actually presented; Study 3), were measured. Both studies revealed that insecure adults projected their own self-models onto their memory for new people. Avoidant individuals found it easier to remember the target who resembled their *unwanted* self, and they also made more false-positive memory errors for that target. Anxious-ambivalent individuals found it easier to remember the target who resembled their *actual* self, and they also made more false-positive errors for that target. Secure adults showed no memory biases. Mikulincer and Horesh (1999) suggest that these patterns may result from "defensive-projection" on the part of avoidant adults (heightened awareness of a feared self) and "projective identification" on the part of anxious-ambivalent adults (similarity in the search for connection to others).

Mikulincer and Horesh's findings raise the possibility that attachment style differences in memory may be partly due to schema-driven processes and partly due to strategic or motivational processes. Further support for these dual processes is provided by Miller and Noirot's (1999) study in which participants were asked to remember a story after being primed with a supportive or a rejecting friendship memory. Secure attachment was associated with better recall of positive story events, but only when participants were primed by rejecting memories prior to reading the story. Fearful attachment was associated with better recall of negative story events regardless of the prime. These data suggest that secure adults may have been motivated to attend to and remember positive events in an effort to manage or repair the threat presented by the rejecting prime. However, the pattern for fearful participants is more consistent with a schema-driven interpretation. Although these interpretations are speculative, they highlight the importance of exploring both schema-driven and motivational processes – both of which are important to understanding the impact of working models on memory. (See also Fraley & Shaver, 1997.)

Social construal. A large body of research in social psychology indicates that people's existing concepts and expectations play an active role in shaping the way they perceive others and interpret their social experiences. Social information is filtered through existing knowledge structures, such as social stereotypes and self-schemas, which then guide social inference processes. Although these processes are only just beginning to be explored in the context of close relationships (Fletcher & Fitness, 1993; Holmes & Rempel, 1989; Pierce, Sarason, &

Sarason, 1992), these studies illustrate how interpersonal expectations, once established, may be difficult to overcome.

Like other social knowledge structures, working models of attachment should play an important role in guiding how individuals make sense of their relationships. One process that is especially important for relationship functioning, and which is expected to be strongly influenced by working models, is the construction of explanations and attributions (Bradbury & Fincham, 1990). Because adults with different attachment styles hold very different models of themselves and others, they should be predisposed to explain and interpret events in characteristic ways. In a series of studies, Collins (1996; Collins & Allard, 1999) tested this idea by examining attachment style differences in patterns of explanation for relationship events. In these studies, participants were presented with a set of potentially negative partner behaviors (e.g., "imagine that your partner didn't comfort you when you were feeling down") and were asked to provide explanations and attributions for their partner's behavior. Overall, secure adults tended to provide more benign and more relationship-enhancing attributions than their insecure counterparts. For example (Collins, 1996, Study 1), the explanations provided by secure participants reflected stronger perceptions of love and security in their relationship, greater confidence in their partner's responsiveness, and stronger belief in their partner's warmth and desire for closeness. In contrast, anxious-ambivalent participants were more likely to explain events in ways that revealed low self-worth and self-reliance, less confidence in their partner's love and in the security in their relationship, less trust, and a belief that their partner was purposely rejecting closeness. Effects such as these emerged even after controlling for relationship satisfaction (Collins, 1996, Study 2), depressed mood, and attributional style (Collins & Allard, 1999).

By presenting participants with a controlled set of social stimuli, these initial studies provided strong evidence that social construal was colored by existing expectations about self and others. Nevertheless, because participants in these studies were asked to explain hypothetical events on the basis of very little information, the results may not generalize to more natural settings. To address this limitation, Collins and Feeney (1999; 2000) examined biased perceptions in the context of actual social interactions between romantic partners. In one study (Collins & Feeney, 2000) they videotaped couples while one member of the couple (the support-seeker) disclosed a personal problem or worry to his or her partner (the support-provider). Both members of each couple then evaluated the quality and supportiveness of their interaction. Two independent observers also rated each interaction. Results indicated that support-providers who were higher in attachment-related anxiety and avoidance perceived their interactions more negatively (relative to those who were lower in anxiety and avoidance), even after controlling for their partner's perceptions of the interaction and ratings made by independent observers. Although support-seekers' perceptions were not predicted by their general attachment models, they were predicted by their *relationship-specific* working models. Support-seekers who felt closer to their partner and more satisfied with their relationship perceived their interactions as more supportive (relative to those who had less positive models of their current relationship), even after controlling for their partner's perceptions and ratings made by independent observers.

In another series of studies, Collins and Feeney (1999) brought couples into the lab and asked one member of the couple to engage in a stressful task (giving a speech). While preparing alone for their speech task, participants were given a note written by their partner in another room. In the first study, the content of this note was manipulated by asking partners to copy a specific message designed to be either supportive or mildly unsupportive. In the second study, partners were allowed to write a genuine note, which was then rated by the participant and by three independent coders. Results from both studies provided further evidence for biased perceptions; insecure participants perceived their partner's note less favorably than did secure participants.

Taken together, these studies offer compelling evidence that insecure working models pose a cognitive vulnerability; they predispose insecure individuals to construe their social interactions in pessimistic ways, which may have important implications for relationship functioning. At the same time, secure working models appear to offer a cognitive strength or resource that enables secure individuals to arrive at more generous interpretations of their partner's behavior.

In addition to schema-driven processes such as those illustrated above, it is also important to explore *motivated* construal processes. Evidence for attachment style differences in strategic social construal is beginning to accumulate. For example, after receiving failure feedback, avoidant adults tend to inflate their self-views while anxious-ambivalent adults tend to emphasize their negative self-aspects (Mikulincer, 1998a). Along similar lines, under conditions of threat, anxious-ambivalent individuals increase their perceptions of self–other similarity, whereas avoidant individuals decrease self–other similarity (Mikulincer, Orbach, & Iavnieli, 1998). Mikulincer suggests that these strategic patterns reflect chronic emotion-regulation strategies: avoidant adults manage threat by avoiding recognition of personal weaknesses and by distancing self from others; anxious-ambivalent adults manage threat by becoming overly attentive to inner sources of distress and by seeking closeness and connection to others. (See also Fraley & Shaver, 1997; Mikulincer, 1997.) Studies such as these point to the dynamic and functional nature of working models, and they highlight the importance of studying *motivated* social construal processes in close relationships.

Emotional response patterns

The second general function of working models is to guide affective response patterns. Emotional processes are a central feature of attachment theory and individual differences in attachment style are associated with variations in emotion regulation and emotional expression (e.g., Kobak & Sceery, 1988; Shaver, Collins, & Clark, 1996). Collins and Read (1994) suggest that working models of attachment may shape emotional responses through two different pathways. The first is a direct path, which they label primary appraisal, and the second is an indirect pathway, which they label secondary appraisal.

Primary appraisal. When an attachment-related event occurs, working models are likely to initiate an immediate emotional response. Two primary mechanisms are proposed to operate here. First, attachment representations are heavily affect-laden and this affect should be automatically evoked whenever working models are activated in memory, a process referred to as "schema-triggered affect" (Fiske & Pavelchak, 1986; see also Andersen & Baum, 1994).

The second mechanism linking working models and emotional appraisal involves goals and needs. In general, individuals respond with positive emotions when a goal is achieved or facilitated, and negative emotions when a goal is blocked (Berscheid, 1983). Collins and Read (1994) suggest that events are initially appraised for the extent to which they fulfill one's currently active attachment-related goals and needs. Because adults with different attachment styles have different personal and interpersonal goals, they will tend to respond to the same event with different emotions. For example, an avoidant individual is likely to feel pleased when their partner desires to be alone for the evening because it facilitates their own need for distance. In contrast, an anxious-ambivalent individual may feel angry and frustrated because being left alone is inconsistent with their desire for closeness and interdependence. Thus, understanding attachment style differences in emotional response patterns will be facilitated by mapping out the goal structures of secure and insecure adults. Consistent with this idea, Collins and Allard (1999) asked young adults to imagine a series of potentially negative partner behaviors (e.g., "your partner left you standing alone at a party"). They found that attachment style differences in emotional distress in response to the vignettes were mediated by the importance of the needs/goals being violated by their partner.

The outcome of the primary appraisal process is especially important because of its impact on further information processing. Affect has been shown to influence information processing in several ways. First, affect appears to influence what is attended to in the environment. For example, negative arousal will alert one to potential threat and will create a negatively biased search process. Mood will also make mood-congruent events more easily noticed and more salient (Forgas, Bower, & Krantz, 1984). Affect has also been shown to influence memory. In general, people tend to better encode material that is consistent with their current mood (Bower, Monteiro, & Gilligan, 1978). In addition, memory will be enhanced when our mood while storing the material is matched to our mood when retrieving it (Gilligan & Bower, 1984). Finally, high levels of arousal may have a general effect on information processing by restricting cognitive resources (Sarason, 1975). This will make readily retrieved material from memory even more accessible (Eysenk, 1977; Kihlstrom, 1981), and may reduce the likelihood that individuals will do an adequate search of internal and external cues in explaining and interpreting a partner's behavior (Bradbury & Fincham, 1987). As a result, strong emotional responses may lead to a tendency to rely on over-learned schemas at the expense of conducting more "controlled" and effortful processing of information (Kim & Baron, 1988).

Consistent with these ideas, two recent studies suggest that attachment-related anxiety may interfere with information processing. Miller and Noirot (1999) found that, when participants were asked to write about a rejecting (versus a supportive) friendship experience, fearful avoidance was associated with impaired performance on a subsequent (non-attachment-relevant) task. In a second study, Miller (1996) tested the hypothesis that a rejection prime would interfere with insecure adults' ability to effectively solve social problems. In this study, participants read a series of scenarios describing difficult interpersonal interactions and then rated the likelihood of using different strategies. Results revealed that anxious attachment was associated with less problem-solving flexibility, but only after writing about a negative friendship experience. Taken together, these findings provide preliminary evidence that the activation of chronic worries about rejection (for fearful and anxious-ambivalent adults) can interfere with effective problem solving.

Secondary appraisal.   An individual's initial emotional response to an event can be maintained, amplified, or altered depending on how the experience is construed (Lazarus & Folkman, 1984; Weiner, 1986). Collins and Read (1994) suggest that people respond to attachment experiences not just on the basis of whether or not they like the outcome, but also on what the outcome means, at a symbolic level, for themselves and their relationship (Kelley, 1984). And, because adults with different attachment styles will tend to differ in the way they interpret events, they should also differ in the way they feel in response to them.

Consistent with this idea, Collins (1996; Collins & Allard, 1999) found that participants who interpreted their partner's behavior as caused by a lack of responsiveness and caring were much more likely to respond with feelings of anger and distress. Moreover, path analysis indicated that attachment style differences in emotional distress were largely mediated by attributions. These data suggest that individuals who were high in attachment-related anxiety experienced greater distress, in part, because they interpreted their partner's behavior in more threatening ways.

Behavioral response patterns

Thus far we have proposed a number of ways in which working models of attachment direct information processing and emotional response patterns. Although these outcomes are themselves important for understanding social experience, they are also the key to understanding interpersonal behavior. Collins and Read (1994) have suggested that working models shape behavior primarily by shaping the way people think and feel about themselves and their relationships. That is, adults with different attachment styles behave differently precisely *because* they think and feel differently.

Consistent with this idea, Collins (1996) found that attachment style differences in behavioral strategies (in response to hypothetical relationship events) were mediated by the attributions people made for these events and by their emotional responses to them. For example, in two studies, path analyses indicated that individuals who were higher in attachment-related anxiety (relative to those low in anxiety) tended to write explanations that were more negative and to respond to the events with greater emotional distress; these explanatory patterns and emotional responses then strongly predicted their tendency to engage in more conflictual behavior. These patterns emerged even after controlling for relationship satisfaction, and were replicated in a third study using similar methodology (Collins & Allard, 1999). Although these studies did not involve behavioral observations, they provide preliminary evidence for the role that social construal and emotional response patterns may play in explaining attachment style differences in interpersonal behavior. These findings also point to the need for more work that incorporates cognition, emotion, and behavior in ways that allow for the exploration of mediational processes.

What are the specific mechanisms through which working models shape behavioral responses? First, working models contain a rich source of knowledge that can be used to plan one's behavior in social interaction. Indeed, Bowlby (1982) suggested that working models can be used to run "small scale experiments within the head" for making predictions about how attachment goals can be achieved. Thus, once activated in memory, individuals can rely on their social knowledge, along with their construal of the current situation, to develop a plan of action. Because individuals with different attachment styles will draw from different social knowledge, they will tend to develop different plans and strategies for meeting their attachment-related needs.

Of course, planning requires time and cognitive resources, which are not always readily available. Individuals are often required to react immediately and under conditions of high stress and arousal (such as during an argument), when processing capacity is limited. Evidence suggests that under such conditions, individuals may rely on readily accessible, over-learned strategies and behavioral scripts (Clark & Isen, 1982; Ellis, Thomas, & Rodriguez, 1984; Kihlstrom, 1981). In these circumstances, working models may guide behavior by providing ready-made plans and behavioral strategies for the attainment of attachment-related goals. It is important to remember that adults with different attachment styles will draw from different behavioral repertoires and will be motivated to achieve different interpersonal goals. More-over, it is likely that particular social construals and particular emotions are linked directly to particular plans and strategies. That is, behavioral strategies may be stored in terms of "if–then" contingencies (Baldwin, 1992) that specify which strategies to use in particular circum-stances (e.g., if stressed, seek support; if hurt, seek emotional distance). As a result, once a social situation is appraised, a person's behavioral response may be largely over-determined.

The idea that behavioral strategies can be automatically evoked raises the possibility that the mere activation of an attachment model is sufficient for eliciting a behavioral response, without having to posit an intervening cognitive and emotional mediator. To be sure, some situations are so familiar, and some behaviors so over-learned, that behavioral responses can be elicited by particular features of the environment alone (Bargh, Chen, & Burrows, 1996). This may be especially likely to occur in long-term relationships for which people have highly elaborate and strongly held relational schemas. Nevertheless, we suspect that this is unlikely to represent the majority of interpersonal behavior. Many social situations are ambiguous and require at least some degree of cognitive processing to identify the nature of one's social environment. This processing could be as minimal as categorizing the situation as threatening or benign, forming a rapid impression of another's personal goals and motives, or retrieving a past experience from memory. All of these processing activities are likely to occur rapidly and outside awareness, yet they play an important role in determining behavior. We also believe that emotional appraisals are highly influential in guiding behavior and critical to understanding attachment style differences in social interaction.

Attachment style differences in behavior, then, result from a combination of biased cognit-ive processing and emotional response tendencies. However, under some conditions, behaviors may be evoked automatically when working models are activated in memory. There may also be individual differences in the relative importance of cognition and emotion in directing behavior. We might speculate, for example, that secure adults are better able to integrate cognitive and emotional cues when planning their behavior. In contrast, anxious adults may tend to weight emotional cues more heavily, whereas avoidant adults may over-rely on cognitive cues.

Summary

Working models of attachment operate as part of a broader system of cognitive, emotional, and behavioral response processes that help individuals understand their social world and behave in ways that meet their personal needs. The specific mechanisms are undoubtedly complex, but we have highlighted a few that can be studied using existing methodologies in social and cognitive psychology. Such investigations include studying the role of attachment representations in selective attention, memory encoding and retrieval, social construal, and emotional response tendencies. Future research should also investigate the dynamic and reciprocal relationship between cognitive and emotional processes, and the ways in which these processes work together to guide behavior.

Concluding Comments

Many of the ideas presented in this chapter remain untested and we suspect they will be elaborated, refined, and modified as empirical work on attachment representations continues to grow. Our goal has been to encourage attachment researchers to think about working models in a more precise and systematic way, and to stimulate interesting and thoughtful research on the topic. We hope also to develop links between attachment theory and the literature in cognitive social psychology, which offers research methodologies that might prove useful for attachment scholars. As our review makes clear, a number of attachment scholars have already begun to use these methodologies to uncover important features of working models and to explore their role in social information processing.

As we have highlighted throughout this chapter, individuals do not enter relationships as *tabulae rasae*. Instead they bring with them a rich network of representations that shape how they construct their lives and how they find meaning in their personal and interpersonal experiences. Of course, features of the environment and qualities of particular interaction partners will also make an important contribution to one's social experience, and a full understanding of social functioning requires that we consider the ways in which these factors interact with already existing personal strengths and vulnerabilities. Our intention was not to minimize the importance of situations, or unique person-by-situation interactions, but to clarify some of the ways in which working models operate on an *intra*personal level, and thereby contribute to what are surely very complex *inter*personal systems. Attachment theory reminds us that close relationships in adulthood cannot be fully understood without reference to the long history of social and emotional experiences that precede such relationships.

NOTES

1   The interested reader is directed to Bowlby (1973) for a more complete discussion of working models in infancy and childhood, and to the following sources for comprehensive reviews and elaborations on these original ideas: Bretherton (1985); Bretherton & Munholland (1999); Crittendon (1990); and Main, Kaplan, & Cassidy (1985).

2   A full discussion of measurement issues is beyond the scope of this chapter, but excellent reviews can be found in several recent chapters (Bartholomew & Shaver, 1998; Brennan, Clark, & Shaver, 1998; Crowell, Fraley, & Shaver, 1999).

3   Although our discussion of attention and memory has focused on schema-consistent effects, people are also likely to attend to and remember events that are highly inconsistent with their prior expectations. Improved memory may occur because unexpected events require explanation, which results in more effortful processing of social information. This deeper processing, in turn, facilitates encoding and retrieval (see Fiske & Taylor, 1991, for a more complete discussion of this issue). Thus, attachment style differences in attention and memory may result, in part, from differences in the type of social information that is surprising or unexpected for people with different working models.

REFERENCES

Ainsworth, M. D., Blehar, M. C., Waters, C., & Wall, S. (1978). *Patterns of attachment: A psychological study of the strange situation*. Hillsdale, NJ: Erlbaum.

Andersen, S. M., & Baum, A. (1994). Transference in interpersonal relations: Inferences and affect based on significant-other representations. *Journal of Personality, 62*, 459–497.

Andersen, S. M., & Cole, S. W. (1990). "Do I know you?": The role of significant others in general social perception. *Journal of Personality and Social Psychology, 59*, 384–399.

Andersen, S. M., Glassman, N. S., Chen, S., & Cole, S. W. (1995). Transference in social perception: The role of chronic accessibility in significant-other representations. *Journal of Personality and Social Psychology, 69*, 41–57.

Baldwin, M. W. (1992). Relational schemas and the processing of social information. *Psychological Bulletin, 112*, 461–484.

Baldwin, M. W., Fehr, B., Keedian, E., Seidel, M., & Thomson, D. W. (1993). An exploration of the relational schemas underlying attachment styles: Self-report and lexical decision approaches. *Personality and Social Psychology Bulletin, 19*, 746–754.

Baldwin, M. W., Keelan, J. P. R., Fehr, B., Enns, V., & Koh-Rangarajoo, E. (1996). Social cognitive conceptualization of attachment working models: Availability and accessibility effects. *Journal of Personality and Social Psychology, 71*, 94–104.

Bargh, J. A. (1984). Automatic and conscious processing of social information. In R. S. Wyer & T. K. Srull (Eds.), *Handbook of social cognition* (Vol. 3, pp. 1–44). Hillsdale, NJ: Erlbaum.

Bargh, J. A., & Chartrand, T. L. (1999). The unbearable automaticity of being. *American Psychologist, 54*, 462–479.

Bargh, J. A., Chen, M., & Burrows, L. (1996). Automaticity of social behavior: Direct effects of trait construct and stereotype activation on action. *Journal of Personality and Social Psychology, 71*, 230–244.

Bartholomew, K., & Horowitz, L. M. (1991). Attachment styles among young adults: A test of a four-category model. *Journal of Personality and Social Psychology, 61*, 226–244.

Bartholomew, K., & Shaver, P. R. (1998). Methods of assessing adult attachment: Do they converge? In J. Simpson & W. S. Rholes (Eds.), *Attachment theory and close relationships* (pp. 25–45). New York: Guilford Press.

Beer, J. S., & Kihlstrom, J. F. (1999). *Representations of self in close relationships: A test of continuity in internal working models in child and adult attachment*. Unpublished manuscript, University of California at Berkeley.

Berscheid, E. (1983). Emotion. In H. H. Kelley, E. Berscheid, A. Christensen, J. Harvey, T. Huston, G. Levinger, E. McClintock, L. A. Peplau, & D. Peterson (Eds.), *Close relationships* (pp. 110–168). San Francisco: Freeman.

Bower, G. H., Monteiro, K. P., & Gilligan, S. G. (1978). Emotional mood as a context for learning and recall. *Journal of Verbal Learning and Verbal Behavior, 17,* 573–585.

Bowlby, J. (1973). *Attachment and loss, vol. 2: Separation: Anxiety and anger.* New York: Basic Books.

Bowlby, J. (1979). *The making and breaking of affectional bonds.* London: Tavistock.

Bowlby, J. (1980). *Attachment and loss, vol. 3: Loss.* New York: Basic Books.

Bowlby, J. (1982). *Attachment and loss, vol. 1: Attachment* (2nd edition). New York: Basic Books.

Bradbury, T. N., & Fincham, F. D. (1987). Affect and cognition in close relationships: Towards an integrative model. *Cognition and Emotion, 1,* 59–87.

Bradbury, T. N., & Fincham, F. D. (1990). Attribution in marriage: Review and critique. *Psychological Bulletin, 107,* 3–33.

Brennan, K. A., & Bosson, J. K. (1998). Attachment-style differences in attitudes toward and reactions to feedback from romantic partners: An exploration of the relational bases of self-esteem. *Personality and Social Psychology Bulletin, 24,* 699–714.

Brennan, K. A., Clark, C. L., & Shaver, P. R. (1998). Self-report measurement of adult attachment: An integrative overview. In J. Simpson & W. S. Rholes (Eds.), *Attachment theory and close relationships* (pp. 46–76). New York: Guilford Press.

Brennan, K. A., & Morris, K. A. (1997). Attachment styles, self-esteem, and patterns of seeking feedback from romantic partners. *Personality and Social Psychology Bulletin, 23,* 23–31.

Bretherton, I. (1985). Attachment theory: Retrospect and prospect. *Monographs of the Society for Research in Child Development, 50,* 3–35.

Bretherton, I., Biringen, Z., Ridgeway, D., Maslin, C., & Sherman, M. (1989). Attachment: The parental perspective. *Infant Mental Health Journal, 10,* 203–221.

Bretherton, I., & Munholland, K. A. (1999). Internal working models in attachment relationships. In J. A. Cassidy & P. R. Shaver (Eds.), *Handbook of attachment: Theory, research, and clinical applications* (pp. 434–465). New York: Guilford Press.

Clark, M. S., & Isen, A. M. (1982). Toward understanding the relationship between feeling states and social behavior. In A. Hastorf & A. Isen (Eds.), *Cognitive social psychology.* New York: Elsevier North-Holland.

Cohen, C. E. (1981). Person categories and social perception: Testing some boundaries of the processing effects of prior knowledge. *Journal of Personality and Social Psychology, 40,* 441–452.

Collins, N. L. (1996). Working models of attachment: Implications for explanation, emotion, and behavior. *Journal of Personality and Social Psychology, 71,* 810–832.

Collins, N. L., & Allard, L. M. (1999). *Working models of attachment and social construal processes in romantic relationships.* Unpublished manuscript, University of California at Santa Barbara.

Collins, N. L., & Feeney, B. C. (1999). *Attachment style and social construal processes in dyadic interaction: Biased perceptions of social support.* Unpublished manuscript, University of California at Santa Barbara.

Collins, N. L., & Feeney, B. C. (2000). A safe haven: An attachment theory perspective on support-seeking and caregiving in intimate relationships. *Journal of Personality and Social Psychology, 75,* 1053–1073.

Collins, N. L., & Read, S. J. (1990). Adult attachment, working models, and relationship quality in dating couples. *Journal of Personality and Social Psychology, 58,* 644–663.

Collins, N. L., & Read, S. J. (1994). Cognitive representations of attachment: The structure and function of working models. In K. Bartholomew & D. Perlman (Eds.), *Attachment processes in adulthood* (pp. 53–90). London: Jessica Kingsley.

Crittenden, P. M. (1990). Internal representational models of attachment relationships. *Infant Mental Health Journal, 11,* 259–277.

Crowell, J. A., Fraley, R. C., & Shaver, P. R. (1999). Measurement of individual differences in adolescent and adult attachment. In J. A. Cassidy & P. R. Shaver (Eds.), *Handbook of attachment: Theory, research, and clinical applications* (pp. 434–465). New York: Guilford Press.

Crowell, J. A., & Owens, G. (1996). *Current relationships interview and scoring system.* Unpublished manuscript, State University of New York at Stony Brook.

Egeland, B., & Farber, E. (1984). Infant-mother attachment: Factors related to its development and change over time. *Child Development, 55,* 753–771.

Ellis, H. C., Thomas, R. L., & Rodrigues, I. A. (1984). Emotions, mood states and memory: Elaborative encoding, semantic processing, and cognitive effort. *Journal of Experimental Psychology: Learning, Memory, and Cognition, 10,* 470–482.

Eysenk, M. W. (1977). *Human memory: Theory, research, and individual differences.* Elmsford, NY: Pergamon.

Feeney, J. A. (1999). Adult romantic attachment and couple relationships. In J. A. Cassidy & P. R. Shaver (Eds.), *Handbook of attachment: Theory, research, and clinical applications* (pp. 355–377). New York: Guilford Press.

Feeney, J. A., & Noller, P. (1990). Attachment style as a predictor of adult romantic relationships. *Journal of Personality and Social Psychology, 58,* 281–291.

Feeney, J. A., Noller, P., & Callan, V. J. (1994). Attachment style, communication and satisfaction in the early years of marriage. In K. Bartholomew & D. Perlman (Eds.), *Attachment processes in adulthood* (pp. 269–308). London: Jessica Kingsley.

Fiske, S. T., & Pavelchak, M. A. (1986). Category-based versus piecemeal-based affective responses: Developments in schema-triggered affect. In R. M. Sorrentino & E. T. Higgins (Eds.), *Handbook of motivation and cognition: Foundations of social behavior* (pp. 167–203). New York: Guilford Press.

Fiske, S. T., & Taylor, S. E. (1991). *Social cognition.* New York: McGraw-Hill.

Fletcher, G. J. O., & Fincham, F. D. (1991). *Cognition in close relationships.* Hillsdale, NJ: Erlbaum.

Fletcher, G. J. O., & Fitness, J. (1993). Knowledge structures and explanations in intimate relationships. In S. Duck (Ed.), *Individuals in relationships* (pp. 121–143). Newbury Park, CA: Sage.

Fletcher, G. J. O., & Fitness, J. (Eds.). (1996). *Knowledge structures in close relationships: A social psychological approach.* Mahwah, NJ: Erlbaum.

Forgas, J. P., Bower, G. H., & Krantz, S. E. (1984). The influence of mood on perceptions of social interactions. *Journal of Experimental Social Psychology, 20,* 497–513.

Fraley, R. C., Davis, K. E., & Shaver, P. R. (1998). Dismissing-avoidance and the defensive organization of emotion, cognition, and behavior. In J. A. Simpson & W. S. Rholes (Eds.), *Attachment theory and close relationships* (pp. 249–279). New York: Guilford Press.

Fraley, R. C., & Shaver, P. R. (1997). Adult attachment and the suppression of unwanted thoughts. *Journal of Personality and Social Psychology, 73,* 1080–1091.

Fraley, R. C., & Shaver, P. R. (1998). Airport separations: A naturalistic study of adult attachment dynamics in separating couples. *Journal of Personality and Social Psychology, 75,* 1198–1212.

Fraley, R. C., & Waller, N. G. (1998). Adult attachment patterns: A test of the typological model. In J. A. Simpson & W. S. Rholes (Eds.), *Attachment theory and close relationships* (pp. 77–114). New York: Guilford Press.

George, C., Kaplan, N., & Main, M. (1984). *Attachment interview for adults.* Unpublished manuscript, University of California at Berkeley.

George, C., & Solomon, J. (1989). Internal working models of caregiving and security of attachment at age six. *Infant Mental Health Journal, 10,* 222–237.

Gilligan, S. G., & Bower, G. H. (1984). Cognitive consequences of emotional arousal. In C. E. Izard, J. Kagan, & R. B. Zajonc (Eds.), *Emotions, cognition, and behavior* (pp. 547–588). Cambridge, England: Cambridge University Press.

Graesser, A. C., & Nakamura, G. V. (1982). The impact of a schema on comprehension and memory. In G. H. Bower (Ed.), *The psychology of learning and motivation* (Vol. 16, pp. 60–109). New York: Academic Press.

Greenwald, A. G., McGhee, D. E., & Schwartz, J. L. K. (1998). Measuring individual differences in implicit cognition: The implicit association test. *Journal of Personality and Social Psychology, 74*, 1464–1480.

Hastie, R. (1981). Schematic principles in human memory. In E. T. Higgins, C. P. Herman, & M. P. Zanna (Eds.), *Social cognition: The Ontario symposium* (Vol. 1, pp. 39–88). Hillsdale, NJ: Erlbaum.

Hazan, C., & Shaver, P. (1987). Romantic love conceptualized as an attachment process. *Journal of Personality and Social Psychology, 52*, 511–524.

Hazan, C., & Shaver, P. (1990). Love and work: An attachment theoretical perspective. *Journal of Personality and Social Psychology, 59*, 270–280.

Higgins, E. T., & Bargh, J. A. (1987). Social cognition and social perception. In M. R. Rosensweig & L. W. Porter (Eds.), *Annual review of psychology* (Vol. 38, pp. 369–425). Palo Alto, CA: Annual Reviews.

Higgins, E. T., King, G. A., & Mavin, G. H. (1982). Individual construct accessibility and subjective impressions and recall. *Journal of Personality and Social Psychology, 43*, 35–47.

Holmes, J. G., Rempel, J. K. (1989). Trust in close relationships. In C. Hendrick (Ed.), *Review of personality and social psychology: Vol. 10. Close relationships* (pp. 187–220). London: Sage.

Kelley, H. H. (1984). Affect in interpersonal relations. In P. Shaver (Ed.), *Review of personality and social psychology* (Vol. 5, pp. 89–115). Beverly Hills, CA: Sage.

Kihlstrom, J. F. (1981). On personality and memory. In N. Cantor & J. Kihlstrom (Eds.), *Personality, cognition, and social interaction* (pp. 123–149). Hillsdale, NJ: Erlbaum.

Kim, H., & Baron, R. S. (1988). Exercise and the illusory correlation: Does arousal heighten stereotypic processing? *Journal of Experimental Social Psychology, 24*, 366–380.

Kobak, R. R., & Hazan, C. (1991). Attachment in marriage: The effects of security and accuracy of working models. *Journal of Personality and Social Psychology, 60*, 861–869.

Kobak, R. R., & Sceery, A. (1988). Attachment in late adolescence: Working models, affect regulation, and perception of self and others. *Child Development, 59*, 135–146.

Lazarus, R. S., & Folkman, S. (1984). *Stress, appraisal, and coping.* New York: Springer.

Main, M. (1981). Avoidance in the service of attachment: A working paper. In K. Immelmann, G. Barlow, L. Petrinovich, & M. Main (Eds.), *Behavioral development: The Bielefeld interdisciplinary project* (pp. 651–693). New York: Cambridge University Press.

Main, M. (1991). Metacognitive knowledge, metacognitive monitoring, and singular (coherent) vs. multiple (incoherent) model of attachment. In C. M. Parkes, J. Stevson-Hinde, & P. Marris (Eds.), *Attachment across the life cycle* (pp. 127–159). London: Tavistock/Routledge.

Main, M., Kaplan, N., & Cassidy, J. (1985). Security in infancy, childhood, and adulthood: A move to the level of representation. *Monographs of the Society for Research in Child Development, 50*, 66–104.

Markus, H. (1977). Self-schemata and processing information about the self. *Journal of Personality and Social Psychology, 35*, 63–78.

Martin, R. (1991). Examining personal relationship thinking: The relational cognition complexity instrument. *Journal of Social and Personal Relationships, 8*, 467–480.

Mikulincer, M. (1995). Attachment style and the mental representation of the self. *Journal of Personality and Social Psychology, 69*, 1203–1215.

Mikulincer, M. (1997). Adult attachment style and information processing: Individual differences in curiosity and cognitive closure. *Journal of Personality and Social Psychology, 72,* 1217–1230.

Mikulincer, M. (1998a). Adult attachment style and affect regulation: Strategic variations in self-appraisals. *Journal of Personality and Social Psychology, 75,* 420–435.

Mikulincer, M. (1998b). Attachment working models and the sense of trust: An exploration of inter-action goals and affect regulation. *Journal of Personality and Social Psychology, 74,* 1209–1224.

Mikulincer, M., & Horesh, N. (1999). Adult attachment style and the perception of others: The role of projective mechanisms. *Journal of Personality and Social Psychology, 76,* 1022–1034.

Mikulincer, M., & Nachshon, O. (1991). Attachment styles and patterns of self-disclosure. *Journal of Personality and Social Psychology, 61,* 321–331.

Mikulincer, M., & Orbach, I. (1995). Attachment styles and repressive defensiveness: The accessibility and architecture of affective memories. *Journal of Personality and Social Psychology, 68,* 917–925.

Mikulincer, M., Orbach, I., & Iavnieli, D. (1998). Adult attachment style and affect regulation: Strategic variations in subjective self-other similarity. *Journal of Personality and Social Psychology, 75,* 436–448.

Miller, J. B. (1996). Social flexibility and anxious attachment. *Personal Relationships, 3,* 241–256.

Miller, J. B., & Noirot, M. (1999). Attachment memories, models and information processing. *Journal of Social and Personal Relationships, 16,* 147–173.

Ognibene, T. C., & Collins, N. L. (1998). Adult attachment styles, perceived social support and coping strategies. *Journal of Social and Personal Relationships, 15,* 323–345.

Pierce, G. R., Sarason, B. R., & Sarason, I. G. (1992). General and specific support expectations and stress as predictors of perceived supportiveness: An experimental study. *Journal of Personality and Social Psychology, 63,* 297–307.

Roskos-Ewoldsen, D. R., & Fazio, R. H. (1992). On the orienting value of attitudes: Attitude accessib-ility as a determinant of an object's attraction to visual attention. *Journal of Personality and Social Psychology, 63,* 198–211

Sarason, I. G. (1975). Anxiety and self-preoccupation. In I. G. Sarason & C. D. Spielberger (Eds.), *Stress and Anxiety, Vol 2.* New York: Wiley.

Shaver, P. R., & Clark, C. L. (1996). Forms of adult romantic attachment and their cognitive and emotional underpinnings. In G. G. Noam & K. W. Fischer (Eds.), *Development and vulnerability in close relationships* (pp. 29–58). Mahwah, NJ: Erlbaum.

Shaver, P. R., Collins, N. L., & Clark, C. L. (1996). Attachment styles and internal working models of self and relationship partners. In G. J. O. Fletcher & J. Fitness (Eds.), *Knowledge structures in close relationships: A social psychological approach* (pp. 25–61). Mahwah, NJ: Erlbaum.

Simpson, J. A., Rholes, W. S., & Nelligan, J. S. (1992). Support-seeking and support-giving within couple members in an anxiety-provoking situation: The role of attachment styles. *Journal of Person-ality and Social Psychology, 62,* 434–446.

Simpson, J. A., Rholes, W. S., & Phillips, D. (1996). Conflict in close relationships: An attachment perspective. *Journal of Personality and Social Psychology, 71,* 899–914.

Sroufe, L. A., & Waters, E. (1977). Attachment as an organizational construct. *Child Development, 48,* 1184–1199.

Srull, T. K., & Wyer, R. S., Jr. (1986). The role of chronic and temporary goals in social information processing. In R. M. Sorrentino & E. T. Higgins (Eds.), *Handbook of motivation and cognition: Foundations of social behavior* (pp. 503–549). New York: Guilford Press.

Srull, T. K., & Wyer, R. S., Jr. (1989). Person memory and judgement. *Psychological Review, 96,* 58–83.

Tesser, A. (1978). Self-generated attitude change. In L. Berkowitz (Ed.), *Advances in experimental social psychology* (Vol. 11, pp. 289–338). New York: Academic Press.

Thompson, R. A., Lamb, M. E., & Estes, D. (1982). Stability of infant-mother attachment and its relationship to changing life circumstances in an unselected middle-class sample. *Child Development*, *53*, 144–148.

Vaughn, B., Egeland, B., Sroufe, L. A., & Waters, E. (1979). Individual differences in infant-mother attachment at twelve and eighteen months: Stability and change in families under stress. *Child Development*, *50*, 971–975.

Weiner, B. (1986). Attribution, emotion, and action. In R. Sorrentino & E. T. Higgins (Eds.), *Handbook of motivation and cognition: Foundations of social behavior* (pp. 281–312). New York: Guilford Press.

CHAPTER FIVE

The Root of all Evil in Intergroup Relations? Unearthing the Categorization Process

Penelope Oakes

1 Introduction

The social psychology of intergroup processes has a long and venerable history. As evidenced by this volume, our understanding of intergroup phenomena is rich, complex, and ripe with possibility in both scientific and social terms. At the heart of all this lies one pivotal process without which the modern social psychology of intergroup relations is almost impossible to imagine – categorization.

We can define categorization as "the process of understanding what some thing is by knowing what other things it is equivalent to and what other things it is different from" (McGarty, 1999, p. 1). It is through categorization that we identify things, *know what they are*. Henri Tajfel, viewed by many as laying the foundations of the categorization analysis of intergroup relations, always emphasized this elaborative, meaning-giving function of the process. He argued that social categorization works to "structure the causal understanding of the social environment" as a guide to action. Importantly, it also provides a system of orientation for *self-reference*, creating and defining the individual's place in society. Our "self-definition in a social context" (1978, p. 61) always depends upon social categorization. Where the relevant categorization produces a subjective division into social groups – we are Australians, you are New Zealanders; we are police, you are protesters – *action within that context will take on the distinct meaning and significance of intergroup relations*.

Developing the legacy of theorists such as Asch (1952) and Sherif (1967), Tajfel urged recognition of a qualitative discontinuity between interpersonal and intergroup behavior.

Grateful thanks to Alex Haslam, Kate Reynolds, and the editors for comments on an earlier draft, and to Kate Reynolds and Peter Reid for their invaluable support and encouragement during the writing of this chapter.

At the same time, the subdiscipline of social cognition was developing apace. With it came discussions of the categorization process, which had more to say about distortion and bias than they did about self-definition and behavior. Indeed, it has been as a source of *bias* rather than contextually variable knowledge and understanding that categorization has featured so centrally in the social psychology of intergroup processes. For example, in 1986 David Wilder published an influential paper entitled, "Social categorization: Implications for creation and reduction of intergroup bias", in which he comments that "categorization, per se, propels the individual down the road to bias" (p. 292). And this view has prevailed. Retaining the road metaphor, Bodenhausen and Macrae recently commented that "the road to . . . discrimination begins with the simple act of categorization" (1998, p. 7). Essentially, categorization stands accused of leading us to perceive something other than reality, of generating efficient but inaccurate interpretations of social life.

Is this what happens when perceivers categorize? Does categorization place us out of touch with reality, almost helplessly propelled down roads to bias and discrimination? Can it therefore be held accountable, at least in part, for the real evils of social mistreatment and bigotry which, though sometimes in mutated forms, continue to pervade society?

This chapter addresses these questions by *unearthing* social categorization, in the sense of laying bare, making explicit, its role within both the social psychology of group processes and the social reality of intergroup relations. The "road to bias" is thought to pass through three vital staging posts: activation, construal, and discrimination (see Bodenhausen, Macrae, & Garst, 1998). We visit each of these in turn, asking questions about what categorization is actually *doing* at each stage. Importantly, are categories activated automatically, without due regard for the realities of context? Do the known manifestations of category-based construal – accentuation and assimilation to category meaning – constitute bias? And is categorization responsible for intergroup discrimination?

2 Activation

In a highly influential paper published in 1978, Taylor, Fiske, Etcoff, and Ruderman presented seven hypotheses concerning "the perceptual and cognitive underpinnings" of intergroup discrimination. Building on the groundbreaking work of Tajfel (1969; Tajfel, Billig, Bundy, & Flament, 1971; Tajfel & Wilkes, 1963), Taylor and colleagues contributed to the development of a categorization approach to intergroup behaviour and stereotyping. In particular, they raised the issue of the "contextual bases" of group phenomena, suggesting that stereotyping would only happen when categorization happened. Thus, understanding the factors responsible for activating social categories became a priority.

Taylor et al. (1978, p. 779) hypothesized that perceivers would use "physical and social discriminators such as race and sex" to categorize people, and that this was especially likely when the relevant cues were highly distinctive, novel, within the current social context. Moreover, activation of the category would lead to an accentuation of within-group similarity and between-group difference (following Tajfel & Wilkes, 1963) and stereotypical interpretation of targets' behavior (see section 3 below). While the specific hypothesis about the prepotence of distinctive cues has attracted some controversy (Biernat & Vescio, 1993,

1994; Oakes, 1994), the basic idea that certain stimulus cues can almost automatically (at least, with conditional automaticity; Bargh, 1989) activate social categories has remained highly influential – "theories of stereotyping generally hold that stereotype activation is an automatic process that operates when the appropriate situational cue is present" (Blair & Banaji, 1996, p. 1143).

In recent work the unconscious automaticity of social category activation has been emphasized. For example, Blair and Banaji (1996) measured how long it took for participants to identify first names as either male or female. Presentation of the names was preceded by a 150-millisecond prime which was male stereotypical (e.g., strong, mechanic), female stereotypical (e.g., gentle, ballet) or gender-neutral. As predicted, reaction times were significantly reduced when primes were stereotypic (e.g., gentle – Jane) rather than counterstereotypic (e.g., gentle – John), providing evidence of the "automatic activation of gender stereotypes" (p. 1148) by the preconscious gender-relevant primes.

Work initiated by Devine (1989) has argued that the automatic activation of categories is so powerful it can produce "prejudice-related discrepancies" (Monteith, 1993, p. 469) in which category content that the perceiver does not actually endorse or believe in is activated by highly salient cues (such as skin color). Thus, perceivers become the victims of "spontaneous, unintentional stereotype use" (ibid.), applying beliefs which are not their own but are foisted upon them by cultural currency. Similarly, Bodenhausen and Macrae suggest that the effects of automatic categorization are "typically not consciously intended by perceivers; rather, they arise spontaneously because of basic properties of the information processing system" (1998, p. 20). Thus, we have a view of categorization as the root cause of "unwanted thoughts" which might lead individuals to act in ways counter to their real beliefs (e.g., to appear prejudiced when they believe they are not; but see Haslam & Wilson, 2000). Other recent work has, however, questioned aspects of this evidence of automaticity (e.g., Lepore & Brown, 1997), and the true significance of these "semantic priming" type effects is unclear, once real social contexts and pressing perceiver goals enter the analytic picture.

The effects of perceiver goals on category activation receive serious consideration in the continuum model of impression formation developed and tested by Fiske and her colleagues (Fiske, Lin, & Neuberg, 1998; Fiske & Neuberg, 1990). Briefly, the model distinguishes between individuated impressions formed through piecemeal integration of attributes and stereotyping based on categorization, placing these at opposite ends of an impression formation continuum. Movement along the continuum is dependent upon attention: the more attention perceivers invest in the impression formation process the more they will analyze current attribute information rather than rely on predigested category-based information, increasing the likelihood of individuation over stereotyping. Conversely, lack of attentional investment increases reliance on available cues to categorization and produces stereotyping.

One factor thought to increase attentional investment in impression formation, and therefore reduce the likelihood of categorization, is interdependence. Neuberg and Fiske (1987) suggest that interdependence motivates perceivers to discover the other's "true attributes" (e.g., see Ruscher, Fiske, Miki, & Van Manen, 1991; cf. Reynolds & Oakes, 2000). This argument has been extended (Fiske, 1993) to provide an account of the way in which power differentials affect categorization. Fiske suggests that, because of their dependence on the powerful, the powerless direct their attention up the hierarchy and don't categorize those with power. The powerful, on the other hand, are too busy, too unconcerned with accuracy, and possibly too dominance-oriented to invest any attention in their appraisals of the powerless. They tend, therefore, to categorize and to form highly stereotypical impressions of those over whom they can exert power (Fiske & Dépret, 1996).

Fiske views social perceivers as "versatile, flexible . . . remarkably skilled and often quite attuned in their use of situation-appropriate strategies" (Fiske & Neuberg, 1990, p. 62), and her work on the way in which categorization is responsive to perceiver goals and motives (through, she believes, their effects on attention) is consistent with this emphasis. None the less, Fiske and her colleagues remain convinced of categorization's tendency to *over*simplify and thus distort, bias, and otherwise degrade impressions.

Thus far, the exemplar-category relationship, the ability of given cues to trigger given categories, has been presented as relatively unproblematic. Straightforward associations are assumed between the isolated attributes of isolated stimuli (e.g., an Irish accent) and a category ("Irish") with fairly fixed meaning. It is not difficult to see how this contributes to ideas about the biasing effects of categorization – many of these cues and the categories they relate to may be *irrelevant* in the present context, but it seems that the cues spark the categories regardless. Indeed, some argue that the attribute-category trigger is so automatic, some cued categories have to be actively inhibited in order for one single category to emerge as a clear basis for impression formation (Bodenhausen & Macrae, 1998).

We turn now to ideas generated mainly within the study of stereotype change, ideas about the conditions under which the presence of "consistent" or "confirming" cues is more or less likely to trigger the relevant categorization. This work is important because it moves us towards consideration of the *relationships between* attributes and between categorizable stimuli as potentially important influences on the categorization process.

In their cognitive analysis of intergroup contact Rothbart and John (1985) comment on "the often autonomous relationship between category attributes and the attributes of individual category members" (p. 101). They are referring to a syndrome we all know about – the homophobe who declares that some of his best friends are gay, the White member of an explicitly racist political organization who gets along perfectly well with her Asian work-mates. The presumably positive attributes of some individual category members appear unrelated to the presumably negative defining attributes of the category. Rothbart and John's analysis of this shaky exemplar-category relationship, and more specifically of the conditions under which exemplar atypicality might succeed in challenging category meaning, has been elaborated by Hewstone and colleagues into a cognitive model of stereotype change (see Hewstone, 1996). The model is founded on a prototype approach to categorization in which "goodness of fit" to the category prototype, rather than the simple presence of relevant cues, determines whether or not a stimulus is perceived in terms of a given category. This is important for stereotype change because by definition potential change agents are some-what aprototypical and thus likely to be seen as individual exceptions, or categorized as members of some group other than the one targeted for change. Change requires that exemplars with some degree of aprototypicality gain acceptance as category members. When does this happen?

Hewstone's research manipulates the way in which constant amounts of category confirming and disconfirming information are distributed across a number of category members (e.g., Johnston & Hewstone, 1992). This work has consistently demonstrated that the dispersal of disconfirming information across several members, such that each remains *relatively* proto-typical, produces significantly more change than does concentrated disconfirmation which defines some highly typical but also some highly atypical category members. The lack of change under concentrated conditions is attributed to a process of subtyping, in which atypical members are corralled into a subdivision within the overall category, leaving the latter intact (Hantzi, 1995).

This work clearly demonstrates that categorization is not a matter of isolated cues trigger-ing given categories (cf. Blair & Banaji, 1996, p. 1143, cited above). Individuals can carry crucial cues (e.g., appropriate uniform) to the categorization of interest ("police officer") but under certain conditions may be categorized in ways that the presence of the cue, in itself, could not predict (e.g., as more of a "welfare worker" than an agent of law enforcement; see Hewstone, Hopkins, & Routh, 1992). Findings of the kind reported by Hewstone suggest that relations between stimulus aspects contribute to categorization in two ways. First, the role of each "cue" in the categorization process is clearly conditioned by its relationship to other cues characterizing the target (cf. Kunda & Thagard, 1996). A police uniform does not mean the same when it is on a person talking about road safety in a classroom as it does when it is on someone exercising their move-on powers on a Saturday night (Hewstone et al., 1992), and "Black skin" is not the same thing when it appears in conjunction with "highly educated, famous biochemist" (Rothbart & John, 1985, p. 88) as when it character-izes a cool and groovy blues singer (Asch, 1946; Reynolds, 1996).

Second, the characteristics of *other people* within the salient context affect the categoriza-tion of any given target. In other words, being a police officer in comparison with welfare workers is not the same thing as being a police officer in comparison with prison guards, and this obviously affects the "cues" relevant for category "activation" (cf. Haslam, Turner, Oakes, McGarty, & Hayes, 1992). We have recently explored this issue in experiments which have introduced explicit comparison outgroups into Hewstone's dispersed/concen-trated disconfirmation paradigm (Oakes, Haslam, & Reynolds, 1999). In one study students at the Australian National University (ANU) read about six students at a Catholic university who were generally believed to be conservative and conventional. The information presented included both confirming and disconfirming traits, the latter portraying the Catholic stu-dents as progressive, frivolous, and rebellious. This information was either concentrated in three of the stimulus students or dispersed across all six (cf. Johnston & Hewstone, 1992). Half of the participants also expected to read about members of the Call to Australia Party, an extremely conservative, fundamentalist right-wing religious group.

As we had predicted, under these "extended context" conditions the usual dispersed/concentrated effect was reversed, i.e., presentation of concentrated disconfirmation produced *more* stereotype change than did dispersed disconfirmation. Our interpretation of these findings focused on the variable definition of social categories across different comparative contexts. Indeed, it was evident from the data provided by control subjects, who received no information about individual category members, that the "typical attributes" of Catholic students were different – more progressive – under comparison with Call to Australia than when only the ANU participants and the Catholic targets defined the comparative context. Under these conditions the rebellious, frivolous concentrated disconfirmers had more impact on definition of the Catholic student category than did the (now rather atypical) largely conservative, tradition-loving dispersed disconfirmers.

This brings us to the self-categorization theory (SCT) analysis of category activation, or "salience", in which features of the current comparative context play a crucial role (Oakes, 1987). In fact, there are two important ways in which the category activation question as asked by SCT researchers is different from that posed by the approaches discussed so far. First, the question for SCT is not "when do we categorize, when don't we?" The theory regards all person perception as the outcome of a process of categorization, but a process which operates at varying *levels of abstraction*. The difference between individuated and stereotypical impression formation is that the latter is more abstract, more inclusive, than the former, defining differences between and similarities within *groups* of people. Categorization at the individual level, on the other hand, defines interpersonal differences and intra-individual consistency, and there can be social categorization both more and less abstract than these two intergroup and interpersonal levels.

Second, SCT places a strong emphasis on categorization as context-specific *process* rather than activation of cognitive structure (Turner, Oakes, Haslam, & McGarty, 1994). Together with Medin and colleagues, it considers the attribute-matching approach to categorization untenable in both its classical and prototype forms, because relevant "attributes" cannot be defined without reference to perceivers' purposes and prior understandings (see Medin, Goldstone, & Gentner, 1993). Relevant evidence comes from Medin and Wattenmaker (1987) who presented participants with a set of children's drawings divided into two categories and asked them to explain the basis of the categorization. In addition, participants were given a "theory" to guide this rule induction process; some were told that the pictures had been drawn by farm versus city children, others that they came from mentally healthy versus disturbed children, and so forth. It was found that the theories altered the meaning of "attributes", such that they had to be seen as emergent products of, rather than fixed inputs to, the categorization process. For example, uniformly smiling faces in one group of drawings was often used to explain their attribution to mentally healthy (versus disturbed) children in the appropriate condition. In another condition, exactly the same attribute was used as evidence that the drawings were done by noncreative (versus creative) children: "the faces show little variability in expression". Medin concludes that judgments of similarity are emergent and variable rather than based on a hit-or-miss attribute matching process: "similarity is always dynamic . . . and discovers and aligns features rather than just adding them up . . . the constituents are determined in the context of the comparison, not prior to it" (Medin et al., 1993, p. 275).

SCT views "relevant attributes" (see Medin et al., 1993) and salient categories as mutually emergent outcomes of an inherently *comparative* process working towards the resolution of the stimulus field that is most meaningful to the perceiver. To this end, categorization operates to maximize perceived similarity within and difference between categories in terms of contextually and normatively relevant dimensions. Formally, the hypothesis is that categorization is determined by an interaction between category-stimulus *fit* (both comparative and normative; i.e., in terms of both the pattern and the substantive content of perceived similarity and difference) and *perceiver readiness*. These factors define a dynamic interplay between stimulus information and the perceiver's perspective, values and motives which produces highly variable outcomes. *It is this complete dependence on variable features of both perceivers and contexts that enables categorization to fulfil its meaning-giving, identity-conferring function in perception.* We know that meaning varies with context – tears at a wedding are not the same as tears at a funeral. Accordingly, if categorization is to serve the knowledge function with which it is credited it too has to vary with context. The fixed cue-category relationships implied in cognitive structure/attribute-matching approaches do not easily accommodate the fact that meaning, identity, always varies with context. No wonder that categorization thus understood has been considered a hindrance to valid perception rather than a help.

In terms of the important differentiation between individuated and intergroup categorization, the prediction is that where perceived similarities and differences covary with a potential division into social groups in a way that makes sense in terms of the perceiver's motives and his or her background theories about the contextual significance or purpose of those groups, an ingroup-outgroup categorization will become salient and attitudes and actions will become inter*group* rather than interpersonal (or interspecies, or whatever). On the other hand, where individuals are perceived to vary within more than between groups categorization will be interpersonal and impression formation individuated (for relevant evidence see Oakes, Turner, & Haslam, 1991; Van Knippenberg, Van Twuyver, & Pepels, 1994; Yzerbyt, Rogier, & Fiske, 1998).

Two important assumptions underlying the SCT analysis of category salience deserve emphasis here. First, the crucial role of *self*-categorization (cf. Tajfel, 1978, discussed above). The self always features in the categorization work of the perceiver, is always an element of the to-be-categorized domain – "categorization works to *align the person with the realities of the social context*, to produce dynamic, context-specific definitions of self and others which both reflect and make possible the almost infinitely variable pattern of human social relations" (Oakes et al., 1999, p. 58, emphasis in original).

Second, distinctive amongst the approaches we have discussed in this section (with the exception of Hewstone's work) SCT follows Tajfel in emphasizing a qualitative discontinuity between interpersonal and intergroup contexts. The difference between categorization at the interpersonal and intergroup levels, as a cognitive process, is inalienably related to an assumed difference between interpersonal and intergroup *social reality* (see Oakes, 1996; Oakes, Reynolds, Haslam, & Turner, in press). Life – social life, work, political processes, cultural activity, and so forth – proceeds through the coordinated actions of groups as well as the private or idiosyncratic acts of individuals, and in order to be *accurate*, our social perceptions must register this distinctive group reality. This point was perhaps best expressed by Solomon Asch:

> Group-properties are the forms that interrelated activities of individuals take, not simply the actions of separate individuals. A flying wedge of policemen has a quality of power or threat that is a direct consequence of its organization. A picket line in front of a plant has a quality of unity that is a product of its organization. In each of these instances the group property cannot be rediscovered in the individuals taken singly (1952, p. 225).

Note that Asch locates distinctive group properties in the "*interrelated* activities of individuals", in other words it is the contextual relations between people which must be apprehended in order to access these group properties. SCT argues that, through comparative and normative fit, it is precisely these context-specific relationships which categorization represents.

To summarize the work discussed in this section, many argue that category activation is essentially a matter of an appropriate cue triggering a category and its contents, and impression formation proceeding accordingly. Motives and context are considered in some variants of this approach, but all endorse the idea of a cognitive category activated by given attributes. In an explicitly alternative view, SCT argues that cue-category relations are not enough, and indeed do not exist independent of context. Further, the theory insists that social categorization is not just about cognitive events; it is also always about social reality. To apply a category to an individual (e.g., "police officer") is not to *stereotype* them unless relevant aspects of the current context lead the category to be applied at an ingroup-outgroup level of inclusiveness, indicating interchangeability with other "police officers" and contrast from an appropriate outgroup.

3 Construal

Does the mere act of categorizing actors into a group lead to a different set of inferences than if they are perceived to be unrelated to one another? (Wilder, 1986, p. 296)

The answer, of course, is yes. That categorization into groups transforms inference is not in doubt, and we shall discuss two basic manifestations of this – accentuation and assimilation to category meaning. These effects demonstrate that both the perceived structure and the substantive meaning of input are significantly affected by categorization, and because they have been understood as instances of bias and distortion in social perception it is these effects (together with ingroup favouritism, discussed in the next section) that have earned social categorization such a bad name.

In one of the most famous categorization experiments in social psychology, Tajfel and Wilkes (1963) found that division into categories can produce "a tendency to exaggerate the difference . . . between items which fall into distinct classes, and to minimize these differences within each of the classes" (Tajfel, 1969, p. 83). Numerous studies explored the potential for extrapolation of Tajfel and Wilkes' findings to the social domain (see McGarty, 1999, for review and a critical discussion of the robustness of this effect). For example, Allen and Wilder (1979; following Tajfel et al., 1971, see below) divided participants into two groups, in fact randomly but allegedly on the basis of preferences for paintings, then assessed their beliefs on a range of topics including art, politics, and college life. Participants also completed the beliefs measure as if they were either another ingroup member or an outgroup member. Responses revealed an assumed within-group similarity and between-group difference of opinion on both relevant (art) and entirely irrelevant (e.g., politics) dimensions. Put simply, accentuation effects reveal that when we believe (on whatever basis) that individuals share a salient group membership we expect them to be similar, more so than when such a shared identity is not salient (see McGarty & Turner, 1992). We also expect people divided by categorization to be different from each other, more so than when they are not distinguished from each other in this way.

One development of this basic accentuation finding has been exploration of the *outgroup homogeneity effect*. This refers to the apparent tendency for within-group accentuation of similarity to apply to outgroups rather more than it does to ingroups – "*they* all look alike to me" (e.g., Park & Rothbart, 1982; for review see Haslam, Oakes, Turner, & McGarty, 1996). Symptomatic of the assumed robustness of this pattern of asymmetrical perceived homogeneity, Park and Rothbart refer to it as "the *principle* of outgroup homogeneity" (1982, p. 1051, emphasis added) which, together with the "principle" of ingroup favoritism (see below) they see as a major cause of negative outgroup stereotypes and intergroup conflict. Attempts to explain the asymmetry have focused on identifying fundamental differences in the way in which ingroup and outgroup categories are represented.

Tajfel understood the accentuation effects of categorization as a distortion of perception – stimuli are being perceived as more similar and different *than they really are*, than they would appear to be if the perceiver made more effort or took "a closer look" (Tajfel, 1972). However, in recent work, Haslam and Turner (e.g., 1992) have turned our understanding of accentuation effects on its head, and argued that an *absence* of what we have come to know as "accentuation" would indicate distortion, would reflect perception which was insufficiently sensitive to context. At the heart of their argument is a point we have already emphasized – that, through categorization, *all perception is relative to context*. If this is the case, how can we establish a "standard" in comparison to which other impressions are "distorted" or "accentuated"? Theoretically, we could just as well define participants' awareness of interindividual differences in interpersonal contexts as an accentuated distortion of the "real" similarities perceived when group memberships are salient. The fact that stereotyping and individuation have not been construed in this way simply indicates that researchers have, without explicit justification, defined interpersonal differences as the objectively accurate "standard".

Haslam and Turner argue that it is inappropriate to refer to the judgment effects of ingroup-outgroup categorization as "accentuation", because this suggests that to be nonaccentuated (i.e., accurate) impression formation should always proceed as if it were operating in an interpersonal context, with reference to individual differences (see Fiske & Neuberg, 1990; cf. Oakes & Reynolds, 1997). However, once we accept the real distinctiveness of group-level behavior, we can understand that it would make no sense to see people as individuals when they were behaving as group members, or as group members when they were behaving idiosyncratically. At the same time, Haslam and Turner emphasize that their re-analysis of accentuation is not restricted to conditions where group influences do in fact transform the character of individual "stimuli", such as where conformity processes produce relatively homogeneous behavior within groups. This is, of course, part of a clear dynamic within which stereotyping processes operate, but even where the stimulus is incapable of effecting change itself (as in most studies of social judgment), veridical perception will still involve accentuation (at some level of categorization), because accentuation simply reflects cognizance of the *relational* properties of stimuli within the current context.

Returning briefly to the outgroup homogeneity (OGH) effect mentioned above, recall that the apparently asymmetrical pattern of accentuation observed was held partially responsible for unwarranted derogation of outgroups and social conflict. Work by Simon and colleagues (e.g., Simon, 1992) and by self-categorization researchers (e.g., Haslam et al., 1996) has now produced extensive evidence inconsistent with a generalized OGH "effect" and consequently inconsistent with its proposed basis in entrenched differences between ingroup and outgroup representations. This work demonstrates that perceived group homogeneity – both ingroup and outgroup – is a predictable outcome of the categorization process as driven by the comparative, normative, and motivational principles specified in SCT and social identity theory. Again, the view of accentuation effects as distortions of a sovereign individuated, interpersonal social reality can be challenged – homogenization of both ingroups and outgroups occurs in a predictable manner which indicates that social perception is sensitive to the comparative and normative realities of the social context, and individuals' goals within that context.

In addition to findings of categorical accentuation effects, there is much accumulated evidence that the encoding, retrieval and interpretation of stimulus information is affected by category content (see Kunda & Thagard, 1996 for review). Wilder (1986, p. 294) refers to this as evidence of "categorical blinders" which restrict perceivers' perspectives on new information producing confirmation of pre-existing category-based expectations, sometimes even when disconfirming, inconsistent evidence is available and particularly when the available evidence is ambiguous (e.g., Kunda & Sherman-Williams, 1993).

The classic example comes from Duncan (1976) who manipulated the race (Black/White) of both the perpetrator and the victim of an "ambiguous shove". White participants tended to see the shove as fooling around when perpetrated by a White actor, but as violent behavior when perpetrated by a Black actor, particularly when the victim was White. Interpretation of the Black actor's behavior was guided by category content that defined Blacks as "impulsive and given to crimes and violence" (Duncan, 1976, p. 591).

Also widely cited under this heading is the work of Snyder and his colleagues (e.g., Snyder & Swann, 1978) which demonstrates that category-based expectations can affect the way in which perceivers structure their intake of information from the environment and the way in which they behave towards others, such that those expectations tend to be confirmed rather than disconfirmed (for discussion of limitations on this effect see Neuberg, 1994). Further, patterns of recall indicate information processing that favours category confirmation (e.g., Snyder & Uranowitz, 1978). Given the longstanding assumption that social category content is an inaccurate misrepresentation of the characteristics of group members (e.g., Judd & Park, 1993), it is not surprising that this sort of construal through categorization has been defined as a distortion of the "true attributes" of individuals. Again, it is assumed that these true attributes would be apparent to a motivated perceiver prepared to take "a closer look."

But is this a defensible assumption? As with accentuation, it appears to require some un-construed form of social perception as an accurate standard against which the outcomes of categorization can be defined as "biased". Indeed, this idea is quite explicit in Fiske and Neuberg's (1990) continuum model, which proposes that fully individuated impression formation involves a piecemeal, bottom-up appreciation of "true attributes", "uncontaminated" by categorization. It is in comparison with this effortful accuracy that the quick-fix categorical alternative is defined as "unfortunate", oversimplified and distorted.

In contrast, as we outlined above, SCT explicitly rejects the idea of uncategorized social perception. It argues that all impression formation involves categorization, that categorization varies with context, and therefore that the validity (accuracy) of *all* impression formation is relative to context (Oakes & Reynolds, 1997). It is, moreover, relative to the currently salient *self*-categorization of the perceiver, a perceiver who approaches every perceptual act armed with the theories, motives, values, and so forth that are relevant to that salient identity (Turner & Oakes, 1997).

Who is to establish the "correct" interpretation of Duncan's explicitly *ambiguous* shove? Apparently, it is the experimenter and the social-scientific community, people who are not placed in a salient relationship with the stimulus individuals, and who reject the stereotype of Blacks as violent. The White participants in the study, on the other hand, were asked to engage with, and make sense of, the scenario. Their potentially differing relationships to the White and to the Black protagonists – respectively, intragroup and intergroup (especially when the victim was White) – evidently did affect their own salient identity and therefore the motives, values, background theories that they brought to bear in interpreting events. At least some of the White participants experienced the encounter as one involving "a Black person and a White person" (rather than two individuals, or two students, or whatever) and the meaning that those categories had for them included an expectation of conflict and hostility. The Black actor's "ambiguous shove" was given meaning within that theoretical context, while the same action from a White actor was interpreted with reference to different expectations and theories. Note that *both* judgments require categorization – the conclusion that the White actor was "fooling around" was a product of his categorization as "ingroup", just as the judgment of "violence" followed from categorization of the Black actor as "outgroup".

What are we really doing when we interpret Duncan's findings as evidence that categorization produces bias and distortion? In fact, we are making value judgments about the *end products* of categorization. We want to say that race shouldn't matter, and that Blacks certainly shouldn't be stereotyped as violent. We are making a *political* statement, as is our right, but we cannot condemn categorization as a source of *psychological* inadequacy simply because we don't like some of its outcomes.

We have discussed these issues at length in the context of the question of stereotype accuracy (Oakes et al., 1994; Oakes & Reynolds, 1997) and of the general validity of social perception (Turner & Oakes, 1997). Our aim is not to defend political or social relativ*ism* (the fatal stumbling block for social-constructionist analyses with which we disagree in some fundamental ways) but to emphasize the inherent, inescapable *relativity* of human social perception. The categorization process is heavily implicated in this, as it produces the variable, context-dependent identities from which perceptual relativity flows. However, it cannot, in our view, be indicted as producing *bias* through this process. If it does, then all human perception, all human life, is bias because we are not computers or omniscient, all-seeing beings and there is no neutral, disinterested thought – "perception and thought . . . are actively involved in representing and understanding the world *from the point of view of the participating perceiver*" (Turner & Oakes, 1997, p. 367, emphasis added). As active participants in the political processes of social life, we may well wish to reject and protest "the point of view of the participating perceiver" in Duncan's study, but that is a matter of politics rather than psychology.

Finally, recent work also indicates that the influence of category content is more a matter of context-dependent, emergent interpretation than the imposition of fixed, oversimplified preconceptions on a complex reality. First, early indications of the context-dependence of stereotype content (e.g., Diab, 1963) have been confirmed (e.g., Haslam et al., 1992; Verkuyten, 1997). Consistent with both SCT and the analysis offered by Medin, discussed above, the attribute-category relationship appears to be far more fluid than had been presumed, with categories and attributes mutually emergent products of an "interaction of intelligent systems with aspects of their perceptual world" (Medin & Wattenmaker, 1987, p. 50). Second, it has been argued (often with direct reference to Medin's work) that categorization does not represent the efficient but relatively brutal wielding of the blunt instrument so frequently selected from the toolbox of the cognitive miser (Macrae, Milne, & Bodenhausen, 1994). On the contrary, this categorical deployment of knowledge is actually a highly complex interpretive, explanatory process with fairly hefty resource requirements (e.g., Nolan, Haslam, Spears, & Oakes, 1999; Spears & Haslam, 1997; Wittenbrink, Park, & Judd, 1998; Yzerbyt et al., 1998). Typical of the tone of this work, Wittenbrink and colleagues treat stereotypes as "a kind of shorthand for a *more elaborate theory* of what a group is like" (1998, p. 192, emphasis added).

In summary, we have discussed two major aspects of categorical influence in the construal of social stimuli – accentuation and assimilation to category content. In both instances, we have argued that the "bias" perspective can be usefully, and without great difficulty, jettisoned in favour of a more dynamic view in which the categorization process, in all its forms, is simply doing its job of producing *meaning* by defining stimuli in context-dependent, relational and self-relative terms.

4   Discrimination

In what must stand as one of the most influential and provocative experiments in the study of intergroup processes, Tajfel and colleagues (1971) divided schoolboys into minimal groups and asked them to distribute rewards between two anonymous others, an ingroup member and an outgroup member (see Bourhis & Gagnon, 2001). The results are well known. This apparently meaningless division into groups was sufficient to provoke ingroup-favoring responses in the allocation of rewards, even at the expense of absolute ingroup gain.

It was the fact that the "the mere act of categorizing" (Wilder, 1986, p. 296) apparently produced these ingroup-favoring responses that drew researchers' attention. Conclusions about the irrationality and meaninglessness of intergroup conflict and discrimination were drawn by some, but not by Tajfel, who insisted that it was the very need to create meaning in an "otherwise empty situation", particularly meaning for the *self* – identity – that led participants to act in terms of the minimal categories (see 1972, pp. 39–40). In fact, one can turn the triviality argument on its head and argue that the power of minimal categorizations to produce group-based behavior reflects the customary significance and usefulness of categorical perception which participants import to the laboratory – when a context is defined in social-categorical terms *participants expect the categories to mean something*. McGarty and colleagues have used this argument in interpretation of the illusory correlation effect, presenting evidence that what had been seen as an automatic bias in social perception actually reflects "normal sense-making processes involving differentiation between groups which can be seen as both sensible and logical in the unusual context in which subjects are asked to make judgments" (McGarty & De la Haye, 1997, p. 169).

The crucial link Tajfel had drawn between social categorization and the self helped to make sense of minimal intergroup discrimination; insofar as participants' identities became engaged with the minimal groups ingroup favoritism could be seen as positive *self*-evaluation. This interpretation catalyzed the development of social identity theory, Tajfel and Turner's (1979) more general analysis of intergroup relations, and it is the subtle complexity of this analysis that stands as the true legacy of the minimal categorization experiments.

The social identity analysis of intergroup relations has been outstandingly fruitful. Perhaps most importantly it has challenged researchers, provoking disagreement and debate from which new clarity has emerged. We shall not discuss this work here because it is reviewed in detail elsewhere (see Turner & Reynolds, 2001). For present purposes we shall simply note that the intergroup literature abounds with attempts to psychologize intergroup conflict by misusing aspects of the social identity analysis (see Turner, in press). Most relevant for the present discussion, many conclude from both minimal categorization findings and social identity theory that categorization, minimal or otherwise, automatically and inevitably produces intergroup discrimination (e.g., Stangor & Jost, 1997; Stephan, 1985). In fact, it was always clear that this was not the case. The first essential step is psychological identification, the engagement of the self such that a category is transformed into an *ingroup* (in contrast to a relevant outgroup) and this does not always occur within the minimal group paradigm (Turner, 1975) or elsewhere. What one then does about, with and in relation to that ingroup, discrimination or otherwise, emerges in interaction with both perceived social-structure (as discussed in social identity theory; e.g., see Ellemers, 1993) and other contextual and social-psychological factors (e.g., Ellemers, Spears, & Doosje, 1999). Again, as we noted in section 2, the workings of social categorization are always about social reality as much as they are about cognition.

Thus, the social identity analysis describes a road from categorization to discrimination that is rather more circuitous, offering many more possibilities for alternative destinations, than some commentaries on this literature have suggested. We cannot hold categorization, *per se*, responsible for intergroup discrimination. Indeed, we know that *exactly the same process of categorical self-definition* can, under appropriate conditions, *reduce* hostility (e.g., Gaertner, Mann, Murrell, & Dovidio, 1989; Hewstone & Brown, 1986) and produce cooperation (Morrison, 1997), a sense of justice and fairness (Tyler & Dawes, 1993), and the potential for extreme heroism and individual self-sacrifice. Recognition of the all-round validity of this process might prove more fruitful than persisting with the good cop/bad cop routine.

5 Conclusions: Categorization and Intergroup Conflict

This chapter has discussed the pivotal role of categorization in the social psychology of intergroup processes. We have followed the sequence of category activation, category-based construal, and (as one possible outcome of such construal) intergroup discrimination. Our mission has been to dispute the widely endorsed view that what categorization does, at every stage of this process, is to impose both informational and motivational "blinders" through cognitive laziness and self-interest which produce distorted perception and social hostility.

The explanation of conflict has always been at the top of the agenda for social theorists. Harmony and peaceful coexistence are desired and straightforwardly acceptable, but conflict is usually seen as a problem that needs to be dealt with. It falls to our discipline to specify the psychological underpinnings of social hostility, and our main response has been to identify various scapegoats (dysfunctions of the personality, shortcomings of cognition) which serve to disconnect human social conflict from human rationality – we don't *mean* to fight, we just can't help it. Categorization has been the most successful scapegoat thus far, a universally essential process, often automatic and mindless, but with negative side effects.

We can see that the starting point of this analysis is the definition of conflict as pathology, as problematic. We reject conflict and then portray its psychological underpinnings as themselves pathological and irrational. In effect, social psychology has defined some of the most significant events of history and some of the most engaging and forceful of human motivations as, in psychological terms, unintended byproducts, irrational, pathological, meaningless. There is, however, an alternative view in which intergroup conflict is taken seriously as a normal and perfectly healthy aspect of the political process that is social life. Consistent with this meta-theoretical perspective, social identity and self-categorization theories have presented categorization as the process through which individuals achieve "self-definition in a social context" (Tajfel, 1978, p. 61), context-specific identities which are emergent outcomes of human cognition engaging in the active interpretation of social reality. There is nothing irrational, distorting, oversimplifying, or biased about this process. It works to align the individual with the current social context and the outcome is that perception and thought operate from the specific vantage point, the singular perspective, of the self currently salient. Inevitably, then, there are differences of opinion, varying interpretations of reality.

It seems ironic that subjectivity, "the notion . . . that we actively construe reality instead of passively registering our environment" (Wittenbrink, Gist, & Hilton, 1997, p. 526), has been one of the defining principles of social psychology, and yet we have condemned what is probably its major basis, categorization, as a source of *bias*. We seem to pay lip service to subjectivity when we should be taking it seriously as a basic element of the human condition. Perhaps this is because social categorization can produce, within a single social context, not one, consensual subjectivity but a plethora of conflicting, contradictory statements of "fact" (e.g., see Bar-Tal, 1990). How can this be? Many have cried "bias"; others have argued that the reality of social disagreement cannot be defused in this way, and that we must "fac[e] the specific political, historical, and ideological facts of society" (Turner, 1999, p. 34) – conflict, contempt, disagreement, and denigration included. In this chapter I have advocated an analysis of categorization which, in my view, allows social psychology to do this. Our discipline may, in the process, become a far more powerful force in opposition to the real social injustices with which intergroup theorists have been rightly preoccupied.

REFERENCES

Allen, V. L., & Wilder, D. A. (1979). Group categorization and attribution of belief similarity. *Small Group Behaviour, 10*, 73–80.

Asch, S. E. (1946). Forming impressions of personality. *Journal of Personality and Social Psychology, 41*, 258–290.

Asch, S. E. (1952). *Social Psychology*. New York: Prentice-Hall.

Bar-Tal, D. (1990). *Group beliefs*. New York: Springer-Verlag.

Bargh, J. (1989). Conditional automaticity: Varieties of automatic influence on social perception and cognition. In J. S. Uleman & J. A. Bargh (Eds.), *Unintended thought* (pp. 3–51). New York: Guilford Press.

Biernat, M., & Vescio, T. K. (1993). Categorization and stereotyping: Effects of group context on memory and social judgement. *Journal of Experimental Social Psychology, 29*, 166–202.

Biernat, M., & Vescio, T. K. (1994). Still another look at the effects of fit and novelty on the salience of social categories. *Journal of Experimental Social Psychology, 30*, 399–406.

Blair, I. V., & Banaji, M. (1996). Automatic and controlled processes in stereotype priming. *Journal of Personality and Social Psychology, 70*, 1142–1163.

Bodenhausen, G., & Macrae, C. N. (1998). Stereotype activation and inhibition. In R. S. Wyer (Ed.), *Stereotype activation and inhibition* (Advances in social cognition Vol. XI) (pp. 1–52). Mahwah, NJ: Erlbaum.

Bodenhausen, G., Macrae, C. N., & Garst, J. (1998). Stereotypes in thought and deed: Social-cognitive origins of intergroup discrimination. In C. Sedikides, J. Schopler, & C. A. Insko (Eds.), *Intergroup cognition and intergroup behaviour* (pp. 311–336). Mahwah, NJ: Erlbaum.

Bourhis, R. Y., & Gagnon, A. (2001). Social orientations in the minimal group. In R. Brown and S. Gaertner (Eds.), *Blackwell Handbook of Social Psychology: Intergroup Processes* (pp. 89–111). Oxford, UK: Blackwell.

Devine, P. G. (1989). Stereotypes and prejudice: Their automatic and controlled components. *Journal of Personality and Social Psychology, 56*, 5–18.

Diab, L. N. (1963). Factors determining group stereotypes. *Journal of Social Psychology, 61*, 3–10.

Duncan, B. L. (1976). Differential social perception and attribution of intergroup violence: Testing the lower limits of stereotyping of Blacks. *Journal of Personality and Social Psychology, 34*, 590–598.

Ellemers, N. (1993). The influence of socio-structural variables on identity enhancement strategies. *European Review of Social Psychology, 4*, 27–57.

Ellemers, N., Spears, R., & Doosje, B. (Eds.), (1999). *Social identity: Context, commitment, content*. Oxford, UK: Blackwell.

Fiske, S. T. (1993). Controlling other people: The impact of power on stereotyping. *American Psychologist, 48*, 621–628.

Fiske, S. T., & Dépret, E. (1996). Control, interdependence and power: Understanding social cognition in its social context. In W. Stroebe & M. Hewstone (Eds.), *European review of Social psychology* (Vol. 7, pp. 31–61). Chichester, UK: Wiley.

Fiske, S. T., Lin, M., & Neuberg, S. L. (1998). The continuum model: Ten years later. In S. Chaiken & Y. Trope (Eds.), *Dual process theories in social psychology*. New York: Guilford Press.

Fiske, S. T., & Neuberg, S. L. (1990). A continuum of impression formation, from category-based to individuating processes: Influences of information and motivation on attention and interpretation. In M. P. Zanna (Ed.), *Advances in experimental social psychology* (Vol. 23, pp. 1–73). New York: Random House.

Gaertner, S. L., Mann, J., Murrell, A., & Dovidio, J. F. (1989). Reducing intergroup bias: The benefits of recategorization. *Journal of Personality and Social Psychology, 57*, 239–249.

Hantzi, A. (1995). Change in stereotypic perceptions of familiar and unfamiliar groups: The pervasiveness of the subtyping model. *British Journal of Social Psychology, 34*(4), 463–477.

Haslam, S. A., Oakes, P. J., Turner, J. C., & McGarty, C. (1996). Social identity, self-categorization and the perceived homogeneity of ingroups and outgroups: The interaction between social motivation and cognition. In R. M. Sorrentino & E. T. Higgins (Eds.), *Handbook of Motivation and Cognition* (Vol. 3). New York: Guilford Press.

Haslam, S. A., & Turner, J. C. (1992). Context-dependent variation in social stereotyping 2: The relationship between frame of reference, self-categorization, and accentuation. *European Journal of Social Psychology, 22*, 251–278.

Haslam, S. A., Turner, J. C., Oakes, P. J., McGarty, C. A., & Hayes, B. K. (1992). Context-dependent variation in social stereotyping 1: The effects of intergroup relations as mediated by social change and frame of reference. *European Journal of Social Psychology, 22*, 3–20.

Haslam, S. A., & Wilson, A. (2000). In what sense are prejudiced beliefs *personal*? The importance of an ingroup's shared stereotypes. *British Journal of Social Psychology, 39*, 45–63.

Hewstone, M. (1996). Contact and categorization: Social psychological interventions to change intergroup relations. In C. N. Macrae, C. Stangor, & M. Hewstone (Eds.), *Foundations of stereotypes and stereotyping* (pp. 323–368). New York: Guilford. Press.

Hewstone, M. and Brown, R. (1986). *Contact and conflict in intergroup encounters.* Oxford: Blackwell Publishers.

Hewstone, M., Hopkins, N., & Routh, D. A. (1992). Cognitive models of stereotype change: (1) Generalization and subtyping in young people's views of the police. *European Journal of Social Psychology, 22*, 219–234.

Johnston, L., & Hewstone, M. (1992). Cognitive models of stereotype change: (3) Subtyping and the perceived typicality of disconfirming group members. *Journal of Experimental Social Psychology, 28*, 360–386.

Judd, C., & Park, B. (1993). Definition and assessment of accuracy in social stereotypes. *Psychological Review, 100*, 109–128.

Kunda, Z., & Sherman-Williams, B. (1993). Stereotypes and the construal of individuating information. *Personality and Social Psychology Bulletin, 19*, 90–99.

Kunda, Z., & Thagard, P. (1996). Forming impressions from stereotypes, traits and behaviors: A parallel-constraint-satisfaction theory. *Psychological Review, 103*, 284–308.

Lepore, L., & Brown, R. (1997). Category and stereotype activation: Is prejudice inevitable? *Journal of Personality and Social Psychology, 72*, 275–287.

Macrae, C. N., Milne, A. B., & Bodenhausen, G. V. (1994). Stereotypes as energy-saying devices: A peck inside the cognitive toolbox. *Journal of Personality and Social Psychology, 66*, 37–47.

McGarty, C. (1999). *The categorization process in social psychology.* London: Sage.

McGarty, C., & de la Haye, A.-M. (1997). Stereotype formation: Beyond illusory correlation. In R. Spears, P. Oakes, N. Ellemers, & S. A. Haslam (Eds.), *The social psychology of stereotyping and group life* (pp. 144–170). Oxford, UK: Blackwell.

McGarty, C., & Turner, J. C. (1992). The effects of categorization on social judgement. *British Journal of Social Psychology, 31*, 147–157.

Medin, D. L., Goldstone, R. L., & Gentner, D. (1993). Respects for similarity. *Psychological Review, 100*, 254–278.

Medin, D. L., & Wattenmaker, W. D. (1987). Category cohesiveness, theories, and cognitive archeology. In U. Neisser (Ed.), *Concepts and conceptual development: Ecological and intellectual factors in categorization.* Cambridge, UK: Cambridge University Press.

Monteith, M. J. (1993). Self-regulation of prejudiced responses: Implications for progress in prejudice-reduction efforts. *Journal of Personality and Social Psychology, 65*, 469–485.

Morrison, B. E. (1997). *Social cooperation: Re-defining the self in self-interest.* Unpublished Ph.D. thesis, The Australian National University.

Neuberg, S. L. (1994). Stereotypes, prejudice, and expectancy confirmation. In M. P. Zanna & J. M. Olson (Eds.), *Psychology of prejudice: The seventh Ontario symposium on personality and social psychology.* Hillsdale, NJ: Erlbaum.

Neuberg, S. L., & Fiske, S. T. (1987). Motivational influences on impression formation: Outcome dependency, accuracy-driven attention, and individuating processes. *Journal of Personality and Social Psychology*, *53*, 431–444.

Nolan, M. A., Haslam, S. A., Spears, R., & Oakes, P. J. (1999). An examination of resource-based and fit-based theories of stereotyping under cognitive load and fit. *European Journal of Social Psychology*, *29*, 641–664.

Oakes, P. J. (1987). The salience of social categories. In J. C. Turner et al., *Rediscovering the social group: A self-categorization theory*. Oxford, UK: Basil Blackwell and Madrid: Ediciones Morata (1990).

Oakes, P. J. (1994). The effects of fit versus novelty on the salience of social categories: A response to Biernat & Vescio (1993). *Journal of Experimental Social Psychology*, *30*, 390–398.

Oakes, P. J. (1996). The categorization process: Cognition and the group in the social psychology of stereotyping. In P. Robinson (Ed.), *Social groups and identity: Developing the legacy of Henri Tajfel*. Oxford, UK: Butterworth-Heinemann.

Oakes, P. J., Haslam, S. A., & Reynolds, K. J. (1999). Social categorization and social context: Is stereotype change a matter of information or of meaning? In D. Abrams & M. A. Hogg (Eds.), *Social identity and social cognition* (pp. 55–79). Oxford, UK: Blackwell.

Oakes, P. J., & Reynolds, K. J. (1997). Asking the accuracy question: Is measurement the answer? In R. Spears, P. Oakes, N. Ellemers, & S. A. Haslam (Eds.), *The social psychology of stereotyping and group life*. Oxford, UK: Blackwell.

Oakes, P. J., Reynolds, K. J., Haslam, S. A., & Turner, J. C. (in press). Part of life's rich tapestry: Stereotyping and the politics of intergroup relations. In E. Lawler & S. Thye (Eds.), *Advances in group processes* (Vol. 16) Greenwich, CT: JAI Press.

Oakes, P. J., Turner, J. C., & Haslam, S. A. (1991). Perceiving people as group members: The role of fit in the salience of social categorizations. *British Journal of Social Psychology*, *30*, 125–144.

Park, B., & Rothbart, M. (1982). Perception of outgroup homogeneity and levels of social categorization: Memory for the subordinate attributes of ingroup and outgroup members. *Journal of Personality and Social Psychology*, *42*, 1051–1068.

Reynolds, K. J. (1996). Beyond the information given: Capacity, context, and the categorization process in impression formation. Unpublished Ph.D. thesis, The Australian National University.

Reynolds, K. J., & Oakes, P. J. (2000). Variability in impression formation: Investigating the role of motivation, capacity, and the categorization process. *Personality and Social Psychology Bulletin*, *26*, 355–373.

Rothbart, M., & John, O. P. (1985). Social categorization and behavioral episodes: A cognitive analysis of the effects of intergroup contact. *Journal of Social Issues*, *41*, 81–104.

Ruscher, J. B., Fiske, S. T., Miki, H., & Van Manen, S. (1991). Individuating processes in competition: Interpersonal versus intergroup. *Personality and Social Psychology Bulletin*, *17*, 595–605.

Sherif, M. (1967). *Group conflict and co-operation: Their social psychology*. London: Routledge and Kegan Paul.

Simon, B. (1992). The perception of ingroup and outgroup homogeneity: Re-introducing the social context. In W. Stroebe & M. Hewstone (Eds.), *European review of social psychology*, (Vol. 3). Chichester, UK: Wiley.

Snyder, M., & Swann, W. B. (1978). Hypothesis-testing processes in social interaction. *Journal of Personality and Social Psychology*, *36*, 1202–1212.

Snyder, M., & Uranowitz, S. W. (1978). Reconstructing the past: Some cognitive consequences of person perception. *Journal of Personality and Social Psychology*, *36*, 941–950.

Spears, R., & Haslam, S. A. (1997). Stereotyping and the burden of cognitive load. In R. Spears, P. Oakes, N. Ellemers, & S. A. Haslam (Eds.), *The social psychology of stereotyping and group life* (pp. 171–207). Oxford, UK: Blackwell.

Stangor, C., & Jost, J. T. (1997). Commentary: Individual, group, and system level of analysis and their relevance for stereotyping and intergroup relations. In R. Spears, P. Oakes, N. Ellemers, & S. A. Haslam (Eds.), *The social psychology of stereotyping and group life* (pp. 336–358). Oxford, UK: Blackwell.

Stephan, W. G. (1985). Intergroup relations. In G. Lindzey & E. Aronson (Eds.), *Handbook of social psychology* (Vol. 2). New York: Random House.

Tajfel, H. (1969). Cognitive aspects of prejudice. *Journal of Social Issues, 25,* 79–97.

Tajfel, H. (1972). Social categorization. In S. Moscovici (Ed.), *Introduction à la psychologie sociale* (Vol. 1). Paris: Larousse.

Tajfel, H. (Ed.), (1978). *Differentiation between social groups: Studies in the social psychology of intergroup relations.* London: Academic Press.

Tajfel, H., Billig, M. G., Bundy, R. E., & Flament, C. (1971). Social categorization and intergroup behaviour. *European Journal of Social Psychology, 1,* 149–177.

Tajfel, H., & Turner, J. C. (1979). An integrative theory of intergroup conflict. In W. G. Austin & S. Worschel. (Eds.), *The social psychology of intergroup relations.* Monterey, CA: Brooks/Cole.

Tajfel, H., & Wilkes, A. L. (1963). Classification and quantitative judgement. *British Journal of Psychology, 54,* 101–114.

Taylor, S. E., Fiske, S. T., Etcoff, N. L., & Ruderman, A. J. (1978). Categorical and contextual bases of person memory and stereotyping. *Journal of Personality and Social Psychology, 36,* 778–793.

Turner, J. C. (1975). Social comparison and social identity: Some prospects for intergroup behaviour. *European Journal of Social Psychology, 5,* 149–178.

Turner, J. C. (1999). Some current issues in research on social identity and self-categorization theories. In N. Ellemers, R. Spears, & B. Doosje (Eds.), *Social identity: Context, commitment, content* (pp. 6–34). Oxford, UK: Blackwell.

Turner, J. C., & Oakes, P. J. (1997). The socially structured mind. In C. McGarty & S. A. Haslam (Eds.), *The message of social psychology.* Oxford, UK: Blackwell.

Turner, J. C., Oakes, P. J., Haslam, S. A., & McGarty, C. M. (1994). Self and collective: Cognition and social context. *Personality and Social Psychology Bulletin, 20,* 454–463.

Turner, J. C., & Reynolds, K. J. (2001). The social identity perspective in intergroup relations: Theory, themes, and controversies. In R. Brown and S. Gaertner (Eds.), *Blackwell handbook of social psychology: Intergroup processes* (pp. 133–152). Oxford, UK: Blackwell.

Tyler, T. R., & Dawes, R. M. (1993). Fairness in groups: Comparing the self-interest and social identity perspectives. In B. A. Mellers & J. Baron (Eds.), *Psychological perspectives on justice: Theory and applications.* Cambridge, UK: Cambridge University Press.

Van Knippenberg, A., Van Twuyver, M., & Pepels, J. (1994). Factors affecting social categorization processes in memory. *British Journal of Social Psychology, 33,* 419–432.

Verkuyten, M. (1997). Discourses of ethnic minority identity. *British Journal of Social Psychology, 36,* 565–586.

Wilder, D. A. (1986). Social categorization: Implications for creation and reduction of intergroup bias. In L. Berkowitz (Ed.), *Advances in experimental social psychology* (Vol. 19). New York: Academic Press.

Wittenbrink, B., Gist, P. L., & Hilton, J. L. (1997). Structural properties of stereotypic knowledge and their influences on the construal of social situations. *Journal of Personality and Social Psychology, 72,* 526–543.

Wittenbrink, B., Park, B., & Judd, C. (1998). The role of stereotypic knowledge in the construal of person models. In C. Sedikides, J. Schopler, & C. A. Insko (Eds.), *Intergroup cognition and intergroup behaviour* (pp. 177–202). Mahwah, NJ: Erlbaum.

Yzerbyt, V. Y., Rogier, A., & Fiske, S. T. (1998). Group entitativity and social attribution: On translating situational constraints into stereotypes. *Personality and Social Psychology Bulletin, 24,* 1089–1103.

CHAPTER SIX

Stereotypes: Content, Structures, Processes, and Context

Don Operario and Susan T. Fiske

> For the real environment is altogether too big, too complex, and too fleeting for direct acquaintance. We are not equipped to deal with so much subtlety, so much variety, so many permutations and combinations. And although we have to act in that environment, we have to reconstruct it on a simpler model before we can manage it.
>
> Lippmann (1922, p. 16)

Walter Lippmann introduced the word "stereotypes" to the social sciences in his groundbreaking text *Public Opinion* (1922), referring to them as "Pictures in our heads" that simplify how people think about human groups. Lippmann argued that people rely on simplistic pictures and images when forming and expressing opinions about others. Accordingly, thus derives the basis for social misunderstanding, tension, and conflict: People's stereotypes of human groups cloud reality, distorting actual experience with biased preconceptions. Lippmann argued, "For the most part we do not first see, and then define, we define first and then see" (1922, p. 81).

Almost 80 years later, the concept of stereotypes has spread throughout popular discourse. Discussion of stereotypes abounds: Newspaper and magazine articles describe how stereotypes impede social progress; college orientation programs inform new students about stereotypes permeating the culture; and business organizations provide workshops urging employees to suppress their stereotypes. Although most popular discussions of stereotypes recognize their destructive potential, few explicitly address what they communicate, why they exist, how they operate, and where they originate.

Does social psychology research enlighten this ubiquitous discussion of stereotypes? Indeed, following the publication of Lippmann's classic work, social psychologists have investigated almost every facet of stereotypes and stereotyping, from the cultural contexts that shape their meaning to the mental structures that shape their use. Literally thousands of studies published in psychological journals have addressed the bases for stereotypes and stereotyping, and dozens of review articles summarize the conclusions derived along the way. This wealth of knowledge is intellectually inspiring, yet intimidating in scope. A thorough review of this work leaves even the most expert reader wondering, "What core messages can be extracted from this corpus of knowledge?"

This chapter advances two core principles derived from a review of this literature. First, stereotypes are more ambivalent than people commonly recognize; stereotypes contain both positive and negative attributes about social groups, and, thus, their potency is largely determined by the social context within which they arise. Second, stereotypes are an inherent byproduct of the human cognitive system, yet controllable with personal motivation and effort. The novelty of this framework lies in explicit disentanglement of stereotypes as *a constellation of beliefs* about members of social groups, versus stereotyping as *a manner of thinking* about people and the groups to which they belong. Although both principles are intimately interconnected – each embedded in Lippmann's (1922) original treatise – most work focuses on one theme (thinking) exclusively, treating the other (beliefs) as an assumption. We argue that social scientists and lay people alike must consider both dimensions to appreciate the problem of stereotypes and seek solutions for their effects.

This chapter proceeds with four sections addressing, respectively, the what, why, how, and where of stereotypes: The content of stereotypes, the cognitive structures of stereotypes, the processes of stereotyping, and the context of stereotypes. The first and fourth sections, on content and context, argue that stereotyping involves negative or ambivalent belief systems that vary in potency according to the situation. The second and third sections, on structures and processes, argue that stereotyping is inherent to the cognitive system. Organized thus, each section supports either or both of our two core principles.

Several limitations (mostly space and feasibility) preclude an exhaustive discussion of relevant literature. Interested readers can seek recent work published elsewhere, for example, Fiske's (1998) chapter on stereotyping, prejudice, and discrimination (a companion piece to the present article, with a thorough examination of specific findings); as well as outstanding reviews, including Bodenhausen and Macrae (1998), Hilton and von Hippel (1996), and Stangor and Lange (1994).

Stereotype Content

Most lay discussions of stereotypes focus on content. In American culture, stereotypic content describes the "characteristics" of people who are ethnic minorities, women, elderly, overweight, and homosexual, among other categories. Stereotypes overgeneralize, misattribute, prescribe, and often condemn the behavior and personal characteristics associated with these categories. As this section discusses, such is the nature of stereotype content.

In contrast to popular discussion, social psychology has devoted considerably less research to content, focusing more on structures and processes (discussed in subsequent sections). However, studies of stereotype content matter just as much, for they illuminate *what*, rather than how and why, people think about others. Insight into stereotype content can elucidate intergroup relations, political attitudes, social tension, and other societal phenomena, whereas knowledge of process and structure may be less helpful in these domains.

One of the first studies to address the content of stereotypes was Katz and Braly's (1933) classic examination of ethnic stereotypes, which concluded that ethnic stereotypes were uniformly negative and consensually shared. However, follow-up studies observed over time diminishing negative attitudes toward minorities, concluding that these stereotypes were fading (Gilbert, 1951; Karlins, Coffman, & Walters, 1969). Prior research was claimed ungeneralizable (cf. Gergen, 1973); stereotype content allegedly provided historically sensitive descriptions of social attitudes, but fell outside the purview of general psychological principles.

The thesis in this section, however, is that stereotype content indeed follows general psychological principles. A review of research reveals basic principles that underlie stereotype content. These principles are that (a) stereotypes contain ambivalent beliefs reflecting relationships between groups, (b) stereotypes augment perceptions of negative and extreme behavior, and (c) stereotypes maintain division between ingroups ("us") and outgroups ("them"). This section briefly addresses the issue of stereotype accuracy and the debates about whether a "kernel of truth" underlies the content of stereotypes.

Ambivalent belief systems: Competence versus niceness

The content of stereotypes described in Allport's (1954) groundbreaking text *The Nature of Prejudice* reflects antipathy toward members of derogated groups. However, emerging perspectives in social psychology indicate that stereotype-based antipathy is rare. Instead, stereotypes more likely contain ambivalent beliefs, with a mixture of mostly negative but some positive attributes. The blend of these traits indeed reflects overall disparagement, but not utter repugnance.

For example, the Black stereotypes endorsed in Katz and Braly's (1933) study included *superstitious, lazy, happy-go-lucky, ignorant, musical, ostentatious*, and *religious*. Thus, even when explicit endorsement of negative Black stereotypes was somewhat acceptable, Katz and Braly's respondents in 1933 reported more ambivalent disapproval than outright antipathy. However, some stereotypes, even today, remain resolutely negative, including beliefs about terrorists and criminals. But again, ambivalence is more common than antipathy in stereotypes of outgroups.

The ambivalence of most social stereotypes reflects the structural relationship between groups, determined by (a) groups' relative status and (b) the nature of interdependence between groups. Relative status predicts whether the target group is perceived as competent or incompetent, and interdependence (cooperation versus competition) predicts whether the target group is perceived as nice or not (Fiske, Xu, Cuddy, & Click, in press). In this view, competence and niceness represent core dimensions of ambivalent belief systems.

Stereotypes ensue from groups' structural relationships, such that non-majority groups tend to be viewed as high on one domain but low on the other: either highly competent but not nice, or extremely incompetent but nice. Stereotype content adheres to this pattern. Recent data (Fiske et al., in press) indicate that people believe the following groups are nice but incompetent: retarded people, housewives, elderly people, disabled people, and blind people. In contrast, people believe the following groups are not nice but competent: feminists, business women, Black professionals, Asians, and Jews. The beliefs associated with these two clusters reflect their relationship with the dominant majority (White, male, middle-class, able-bodied). The first group presents no threat to the majority, whereas the second group presents significant threat.

The tradeoff between perceived niceness and competence corroborates many common cultural stereotypes about categories and their subtypes (Rosenberg, Nelson, & Vivkananthan, 1968). Business women are stereotypically industrious and aggressive (high competence–low niceness), whereas "pink-collar" workers are stereotypically nice but not very smart. Middle-class or wealthy African Americans are often viewed as ambitious but defensive about racism (high competence–low niceness). According to this analysis, only members of the dominant majority profit from being both competent and nice.

The dimensions of competence and niceness, which derive from groups' status and inter-dependence, reflect a trans-historical principle of stereotyping. Most common stereotypes contain ambivalent, rather than purely negative, beliefs about outgroup categories, which can influence perceivers' attitudes and behaviors in subtle yet powerful ways (e.g., Gaertner & Dovidio, 1986). Situational context can determine the overall valence and potency of ambivalent stereotypes (Oakes, Haslam, & Reynolds, 1999). An example of stereotypes about Asians demonstrates this point. Recent findings (Lin & Fiske, 1999) showed that some Anglo-Americans believe Asians are intelligent, shy, upwardly mobile, hardworking, and socially awkward – truly a heterogeneous combination of traits. Social context can trigger how perceivers use this stereotype: In a social situation, Asians are irrelevant and non-threatening, but in a competitive situation, Asians are dominating and menacing.

Negative and extreme behavior

A second principle of stereotype content is that stereotypes augment negative and extreme behavior. This simple principle has permeated social cognition research for decades (see Fiske, 1980), and impacts how people think about outgroup members.

Negative and extreme information captures people's attention (Skowronski & Carlston, 1989; Taylor, 1991). For example, research on salience (Taylor & Fiske, 1978) indicates that attention flows to negative and extreme stimuli – such as inappropriate behavior (crimes) or unanticipated accidents (car accidents). This occurs because people generally expect other people and events to be slightly positive or benign (Matlin & Stang, 1978), and in contrast, negative and extreme stimuli stand out. Consequently, perceivers assume that negative and extreme stimuli are diagnostic of a person or situation, and thus become central to sub-sequent formed impressions (Skowronski & Carlston, 1989).

Perceptions of outgroups are particularly vulnerable to the cognitive effects of negative and extreme behavior. Perceivers associate minority groups with negative or extreme behavior – known as the illusory correlation (Hamilton & Sherman, 1989) – because both are rare occurrences that represent exceptions to the rules (i.e., the majority group and positive events). When encountering both an unusual group and a rare event, perceivers assume the two are directly associated. For example, people tend to view AIDS as a homosexual disease because both are novel stimuli – homosexuals are a minority group and AIDS is a negative occurrence – when they happen to co-occur. Although the incidence of AIDS is higher among other groups (e.g., heterosexual women), the illusory correlation between AIDS and homosexuality persists. Other examples include the illusory correlation between African Americans and welfare recipients (most recipients are White) and between Mexicans and illegal immigration to the United States (just as many, if not more, illegal immigrants come from Canada, Europe, and Asia).

Stereotypes capitalize on the distinctiveness of negative and extreme concepts stored in people's mental representations. Minority group members tend to be novel or unique to majority group members, so are vulnerable to the cognitive processes that pair their distinctiveness with socially undesirable traits and behavior.

Us and them

The third principle of stereotype content is the advantage given to the ingroup and relative disadvantage given to the outgroup. This principle is the cornerstone of social identity theory (Tajfel & Turner, 1986), and an elementary concept in social psychology (see also Brewer & Brown, 1998).

People allocate more rewards to ingroup members than outgroup members (Brewer, 1979), have more positive reactions to ingroup versus outgroup stimuli presented unconsciously (Perdue, Dovidio, Gurtman, & Tyler, 1990), and engage in more cooperative rather than competitive behavior with ingroup members (Schopler & Insko, 1992). Stereotypic beliefs of the outgroup are implicated in all of these findings (Fiske, 1998). Although most laboratory evidence reveals ingroup favoritism rather than outgroup derogation *per se*, the realities of social life and resource scarcity suggest that the two are at least partially correlated (Brewer & Brown, 1998). Moreover, mere presence of an outgroup might suggest that one's own personal goals are at risk (Fiske & Ruscher, 1993), thereby prompting motivated stereotyping.

Stereotype accuracy?

Recent years have witnessed increased studies addressing the relative accuracy of stereotypes. Do they reflect a "kernel of truth" about outgroups? This perspective was highlighted in a volume by Lee, Jussim, and McCauley (1995), which countered the dominant view of stereotypes as incorrect, biased, and socially harmful. Lee, Jussim, and their colleagues argue that stereotype content has some factual basis. They cite evidence indicating that societies consensually agree about groups' traits and attributes; that minority group members themselves endorse stereotypes about their group; and that objective criteria, such as grades, standardized test scores, and job evaluations, corroborate the validity of stereotypes (see Ottati & Lee, 1995, for a summary of this evidence).

The perspective gleaned from our review of the literature, however, is less accommodating of the stereotype accuracy movement. Several lines of research indicate the sheer difficulty in establishing accuracy criteria. Judd, Park, and their colleagues have shown wide variability in people's judgments of what constitutes accuracy (Judd & Park, 1993; Ryan, Park, & Judd, 1996). For example, how could one measure whether African Americans conform to stereotypes that they are athletic, loud, superstitious, and academically unmotivated? Would accuracy be determined by group differences on these traits, by the amount of within-group variability on these traits, or by the trans-situational endurance of these traits among different subgroups? Judgments of accuracy are indeed complex, and the "kernel of truth" criteria will likely remain elusive.

Rather than focus on the a priori veracity of stereotype content, more compelling evidence supports behavioral confirmation of stereotype content. Research on self-fulfilling prophecies (Snyder, 1992) reveals that people who hold stereotypes about others can elicit confirmatory behavior, making their biases appear grounded in reality. For example, a biased individual who believes "Black people are hostile" might act cold, distant, and suspicious when interacting with an African American (Chen & Bargh, 1997). The African-American person might respond reciprocally, displaying resentment and hostility toward the biased perceiver. The stereotype thus becomes confirmed in the perceiver's eyes.

Another line of research by Steele and Aronson (1995) shows that members of stereotyped groups can be vulnerable simply to the awareness of their group's stereotype, and act in ways that support the stereotype (see Crocker & Quinn, 2001). For example, African Americans who are reminded of their group membership (and therefore made aware of alleged academic deficiencies) and women who are reminded about women's alleged math deficiencies, perform significantly worse on standardized tests compared to other group members who are not reminded of the stereotype (see also Steele, 1997). In this instance, stereotype-confirming behavior is not elicited by a biased perceiver; simply knowing that the stereotype exists can lead a target group member to confirm it.

Understanding *what* people do with the content of their stereotypes, rather than whether the content of those stereotypes is true or not, supports a social psychological account of influence processes, rather than degenerating into measurement debates.

Stereotype Structures

A second way of understanding stereotypes examines cognitive structures from which they arise. The preceding discussion of stereotype content assumed existence of internal structures that store stereotypic beliefs and information. This section explores the nature of these cognitive structures to understand how stereotypes draw support from basic mental architecture.

Earlier discussion focused on content rules of category-based beliefs. By categorizing people into groups – such as women, Blacks, Asians, college professors – people ascribe qualities associated with the group to the individual target. One might wonder, What exactly is a cognitive category? Is it a theoretical abstraction, or an actual mental construct? This section addresses these questions by surveying four major social cognitive approaches that clarify how people store information in their minds – that is, how they mentally represent the world as it exists "out there" – and how that organization of information influences subsequent perception and judgment. These four approaches are prototype, exemplar, associative network, and connectionist models of mental representation (see also Fiske & Taylor, 1991; Smith, 1998, for more discussion).

Prototype models

A prototype refers to the average or most typical member of a category. According to prototype models, people organize category information around the category's statistical average. However, the prototype of a category need not represent a veridical instance or member of the category; in most cases, the prototype does not actually exist (Posner & Keele, 1968; Reed, 1972). One would be hard-pressed to identify the embodiment of the average professor, African American, or lawyer, although one can describe the average attributes associated with these categories.

Prototype models posit that people represent categorical information in "fuzzy sets." That is, attributes about the category have no definite boundaries or systematic organizing criteria, except for mere association with the prototype. Category attributes cluster around the prototype according to family resemblance, wherein attributes share similar features, but their direct association makes sense only in the context of the prototype (Fiske & Taylor, 1991). For example, the attributes *intelligent, disorganized, distinguished*, and *awkward* make little sense as a coherent personality description, but organized professor prototype can describe many familiar individuals.

Prototypes have important implications for forming impressions and making judgments about group members. When forming impressions of people, perceivers compare the target individual with a category prototype; if the target overlaps sufficiently with the prototypical representation, perceivers assimilate the target into the category (Fiske & Neuberg, 1990). Stereotypes take hold when perceivers assume that fuzzy-set attributes associated with the general category describe the target individual. Following this logic, prototypes can influence all stages of social cognition, from initial impressions people form of others, to the way they interpret subsequent information, to the way they recall targets' attributes (Fiske, Lin, & Neuberg, 1999).

Prototype-based stereotyping is strongest when perceivers have little direct experience with the category yet possess strong group expectancies (Smith & Zàrate, 1990), for example, when people learn about an outgroup through cultural socialization rather than actual interaction. Such might be the case for racial stereotypes, wherein perceivers hold strong beliefs transmitted by culture, yet have little intergroup interaction due to racial segregation (cf. Pettigrew, 1997). According to prototype models, changing perceivers' beliefs about typical members of a given category (e.g., the "average" African American or woman) can dilute the stereotype (Hantzi, 1995).

Exemplar models

Exemplar models emphasize the role of concrete examples in mental representation (Medin & Schaffer, 1978), and are based on actual experience with category members (Carlston & Smith, 1996). Accordingly, perceivers compare target individuals with mental representations of actual category members when forming impressions and judgments (e.g., "He reminds me of my graduate school advisor"), rather than relying on prototypical abstractions (e.g., "He reminds me of the typical professor").

Exemplar models suggest that mental representations involve variability – that is, several discrete instances of the category – rather than typicality and homogeneity, as in the case for prototype models (Linville, Fischer, & Salovey, 1989). Exemplar models resonate with the notion of subgroups of general categories, which acknowledge within-group heterogeneity and allude to the potential for stereotype change via the accumulation of sufficient group variability (Maurer, Park, & Rothbart, 1995; Rothbart, 1996).

According to exemplar models, stereotyping ensues from the match between individual target and category exemplar (Smith & Zàrate, 1990, 1992). When targets resemble the exemplar, perceivers impute characteristics of the exemplar to the target. Although similar to prototype-based processes, exemplar-based stereotypes involve the application of concrete attributes associated with the exemplar, rather than abstract attributes associated with a prototype (Smith, 1998). Research suggests that exemplar-based stereotyping is strongest when perceivers have undeveloped beliefs about the general category (Sherman, 1996), and when discrete exemplars are highly accessible in the perceiver's memory (see Higgins, 1996 for review). However, stereotyping diminishes when perceivers use an exemplar as a frame of reference for forming impressions, and when targets contrast with the exemplar (Stapel & Koomen, 1998).

Associative networks

Associative network models can clarify basic assumptions of prototype and exemplar models, meanwhile offering unique predictions about stereotyping. According to associative network models (e.g., Anderson, 1983), information is stored in discrete mental structures called nodes. Each node corresponds to one and only one concept, whether it be a name, place, object, visual concept, personality trait, affective response, evaluation, or any other form of raw data (Carlston, 1994). Nodes are systematically interconnected by links, which map out meaningful associations between the concepts contained in each node. Inter-nodal linkages structure people's mental representations. Some links are particularly strong, denoting significant association between concepts, whereas others are relatively weak. The nature of nodal linkages fluctuates according to perceivers' experiences: Links increase or decrease in strength depending on the perceived correlation between concepts, and new nodal links can develop according to new associations between previously unpaired concepts.

Network models suggest that all knowledge and experiences are cognitively represented and organized by interlinked nodes. But most nodes lie dormant – that is, stored in long-term memory – and only a small portion are currently active, thus influencing conscious or unconscious cognition (Carlston & Smith, 1996). Impressions, judgments, and memories depend on which nodes are active at any given time, and the activation of one particular node implies the activation of closely related concepts (see also Smith, 1998, for more discussion).

Associative network models can explain how stereotypes ensue from mere categorization. According to prototype and exemplar models, perceivers infer targets' attributes associated with either a typical member (prototype) or a discrete instance (exemplar) of the general category. Network models extend this analysis, suggesting that stereotypes occur from spread of activation (Collins & Loftus, 1975), whereby the excitation of one node (e.g., the social category "professor") flows across links to stimulate other nodes (e.g., attributes such as intelligent and forgetful, visual concepts such as eyeglasses and disorganized desks, affective responses such as feeling intimidated). According to network models, excitation travels rapidly across strong links, triggering automatic associations between linked concepts.

This analysis resonates with findings in the stereotyping literature, particularly priming studies that measure response latency and strength of judgment (e.g., rapidly identifying the word "good") following the presentation of a single concept (e.g., seeing the word "white"). Some of the best-known studies in the stereotyping literature (e.g., Devine, 1989; Higgins, Bargh, & Lombardi, 1985; Perdue et al., 1990) employ this technique, suggesting that stereotypes represent the strength between two or more conceptual nodes stored in people's mental representations. Because of the emphasis on micro-level cognitive structures, network models suggest that stereotyping via associated nodes occurs largely outside of the perceiver's awareness (see also Banaji & Hardin, 1996, for discussion).

Parallel-distributed processing (PDP) models

Emerging from cognitive and neuroscience laboratories over the past decade (e.g., McClelland, Rumelhart, & Hinton, 1986), PDP, or connectionist, models of mental representation have infused social psychological research with new theoretical perspectives on the structures guiding thought (see Smith, 1996, for review). Like associative network models, PDP models posit that knowledge is represented in nodes, which are interconnected by associative links. But whereas network models focus on the information contained in activated nodes, PDP models suggest that a given node has no inherent meaning by itself, and nodes are not category specific. Rather, meaning comes from the patterns of activation across nodes, and nodes are general mental structures non-specific to any particular category. The focus, then, moves away from the discrete properties of each particular node, and is instead on the blend of impulses that arise from activation across a pattern of nodes.

With the focus now on the patterns across nodes, research emphasizes the properties of pattern activation, which has implications for research on stereotypes (see Smith, 1996, 1998, for more general discussion). Activation patterns – for example, from node a to nodes b, c, and d – function from the excitation level of initial node a and the weight of $a–b$, $a–c$, $a–d$ nodal connections (as well as $b–c$, $b–d$, and $c–d$ connections). Activation between nodes can be positive or negative; positive activations facilitate the connection between nodes, and negative connections inhibit connection. Given repeated stimulus exposure and experience, the activation of a few nodes within a pattern can lead to the completion of prior learned patterns; triggering nodes a and b alone can complete the pattern by stimulating c and d. Pattern activation is constrained by the initial information input, and by prior weights (positive or negative) between nodes. Multiple simultaneous patterns of activation occur at the same time, reflecting people's capacity for concurrent on-line cognitions.

Applications of PDP models to social psychology have been few thus far, largely because theoretical models are still developing. However, a few programs of research apply PDP models to stereotyping phenomena. One particular new trend in the stereotyping literature is the focus on both facilitatory and inhibitory mechanisms that underlie stereotypic thought (see Bodenhausen & Macrae, 1998, for review). Extending the emphasis on both positive and negative nodal connections, recent research has examined the variables that undermine or dampen stereotypes (e.g., Macrae, Bodenhausen, & Milne, 1998; Macrae, Bodenhausen, Milne, & Ford, 1997; Monteith, 1993), rather than focusing solely on variables that set them in motion. Another new trend in stereotyping research, derived from PDP models, is the explicit focus on constraint satisfaction processes (Kunda & Thagard, 1996; Miller & Read, 1991), in which activated nodes (e.g., individuating traits or personal motives) can counter the overwhelming effects of other nodes (e.g., categorical beliefs) when forming impressions and making judgments.

Social and cognitive psychology offer several models of mental representation, each model overlapping significantly with others, yet providing unique explanations and predictions. Prototype, exemplar, associative network, and PDP models have contributed valuable insight into the cognitive structures that sustain stereotypes. They indicate that stereotypes emerge from basic cognitive units that store prior beliefs and expectations, and are thus embedded within our mental architecture.

Stereotyping Processes

Another way of understanding stereotypes looks at the mental processes involved when people think about members of other groups. The thesis here: That the process of stereotyping – independent of the specific content of stereotypes – is a fundamental human mechanism for perceiving and making sense of the world. This idea traces back to the earliest theorizing on stereotyping (e.g., Lippmann, 1922; Allport, 1954), and counters the notion that stereotyping is entirely destructive, for the perceiver, at least.

This section reviews research on the functional properties of stereotyping processes, focusing on the automatic nature of categorization and stereotype activation, the cognitive and motivational processes that guide subsequent perception, and the mechanisms of stereotype maintenance and change. Viewed as such, stereotyping can be a pragmatic human process, controllable by motivation and attention to additional information, and not entirely faulty. Stereotypes are most detrimental for their targets, but can also disserve perceivers when accuracy or interdependence matters.

The utility of social categories

As Lippmann (1922) remarked in the chapter's opening quotation, humans cannot handle the complexity of their environment, and therefore "reconstruct it on a simpler model" (p. 16) to function within such complexity. Gordon Allport's (1954) *The Nature of Prejudice* elaborated on Lippmann's theme of simplifying the world, introducing a cognitive perspective to the stereotyping literature. So remarkable were his insights on the mental processes guiding stereotypes that even the most recent empirical findings can trace their theoretical origins to his text, and his insights are taken for granted.

Allport (1954) argued, in a now familiar analysis, that categorization of objects is adaptive and necessary to function effectively: "A new experience must be redacted into old categories. We cannot handle each event freshly in its own right" (p. 19). People categorize furniture such as tables and chairs; kitchen devices such as cookware and eating utensils; places such as restaurants and office buildings; and people such as professors, lawyers, and housewives. Categorization allows people to extract meaning from environmental objects by attending to a few diagnostic cues, rather than perceiving every attribute of every object – a time-consuming and labor-intensive task. In Allport's words, "All categories engender meaning upon the world. Like paths in a forest, they give order to our life-space" (1954, p. 171).

According to Allport's analysis, the processes guiding categorization are the same for all objects. Upon encountering objects in the environment – whether furniture, utensils, locations, or people – individuals first *select* certain characteristics that define the object, then *accentuate* those characteristics in their formed impressions (overlooking other characteristics), and finally *interpret* the object by generalizing from those particular characteristics (see Allport, 1954, chapter 10 for more discussion). Although subsequent research refined this outline of stages (e.g., Brewer, 1988; Fiske & Neuberg, 1990, reviewed shortly), Allport's initial work suggested that stereotyping follows basic rules associated with mere categorization, from which no perceivers or objects are exempt.

Although by now most current stereotyping research hinges on the role of categorization, Allport noted a fundamental distinction between categories and stereotypes. Categories refer to associated concepts, properties, or objects that overlap in meaning or purpose. Stereotypes refer to exaggerated beliefs associated with a category of people that function to rationalize behavior toward that category (see Allport, 1954, chapter 12). Stereotypes are specific consequences of the more general categorization process. The importance of this distinction lies in the difference between basic mental processes ensuing from categorization, versus interpersonal and social processes ensuing from generalized beliefs about group members.

Models of category-based stereotyping

Social cognition researchers developed models to track the progression of people's perceptions about others, from initial categories that promote stereotypes to piecemeal impressions that incorporate detailed information. The two most commonly cited models are Brewer's (1988) dual process model of impression formation and Fiske and Neuberg's (1990) continuum model of impression formation. Superficially, both share similar features, particularly their emphasis on categorization and its effects on subsequent information processing, but vary in specific theoretical postulates (Fiske, 1988). This subsection extracts the core themes from the vast empirical research supporting one or both of these models: (a) Perceivers automatically categorize other people; and (b) whenever possible, perceivers interpret information about others according to their initial categorization, which can result in stereotypes. However, when motivated, perceivers can (c) make use of category-inconsistent information to revise their categorical beliefs; as well as (d) view others as individuated beings, rather than as stereotyped category members. Note the temporal nature of these themes – as proposed in the original theoretical models, each theme represents a discrete stage in the impression formation process.

Automatic categorization. Perceivers categorize other people immediately upon meeting them. Repeated findings, using computer-aided timing techniques, reveal that initial categorization can occur within milliseconds after first encounter (Banaji & Hardin, 1996; Devine, 1989; Dovidio, Evans, & Tyler, 1986; Zàrate & Smith, 1990). Perceivers typically categorize others using obvious, visually salient cues, usually based on race, gender, and age (McCann, Ostrom, Tyner, & Mitchell, 1985; Perdue & Gurtman, 1990; Stangor, Lynch, Duan, & Glass, 1992); but other initial categories are also common, such as body size (Crandall, 1994; Ryckman, Robbins, Kaczor, & Cold, 1989), physiognomy (Kleck & Strenta, 1980; Zebrowitz, 1997), and social roles (Macrae, Bodenhausen, & Milne, 1998). Initial categorization often occurs outside of perceivers' awareness, and the effects of categories on perception can go unnoticed (Macrae, Milne, & Bodenhausen, 1994).

Once a target is placed within a category, numerous cognitive effects that facilitate stereotyping can take immediate hold (see Fiske & Taylor, 1991). For example, perceivers minimize differences between the target and other category members (Taylor, 1981), and ascribe stereotypic attributes to the person (Devine, 1989; Dovidio et al., 1986). Hence, upon categorizing a new acquaintance as a lawyer, perceivers might infer that he or she possesses stereotypical characteristics, such as ambition, intelligence, dishonesty, and greed.

The effects of initial categorization can have undeniably negative consequences for targets, who are perceived as interchangeable category members rather than as unique individuals, but this process confers advantages to the perceivers. By using automatic categories to assist their perceptual processes, people can make quick judgments and conserve cognitive energy for other tasks (Macrae et al., 1994). Thus, initial categorization organizes perceivers' complex environments, directing attentional flow along an orderly trajectory.

Information interpretation. After automatic initial categorization, perceivers sometimes engage in more thoughtful processing. This depends on motivation to exert cognitive effort beyond the categorization stage, as well as available information for forming impressions (Fiske & Neuberg, 1990). With modest amounts of motivation, perceivers make use of additional information (Erber & Fiske, 1984; Neuberg & Fiske, 1987; Ruscher & Fiske, 1990), but are biased by their initial categories.

Following categorization, perceivers' attention flows primarily to category-consistent information (Hamilton, Sherman, & Ruvolo, 1990). So after categorizing someone as "Black" or "female," perceivers tend to pay close attention to attributes consistent with those, categories. Category-based information processing increases when perceivers have limited attentional resources – that is, when they have little time or energy to think accurately (Macrae, Milne, & Bodenhausen, 1994).

Although perceivers bias information processing toward category-consistent information, other types of information exert influence on impression formation. Perceivers can encounter three types of information when forming impressions of others: information that matches the category, information irrelevant to the category, and information that disconfirms the category. When information matches the category, expectations are confirmed and categories strengthened (Hamilton et al., 1990; Oakes, Turner, & Haslam, 1991); stereotypes proceed from the alleged fit between target information and prior beliefs (cf. Snyder, 1984). When information is irrelevant to the category, perceivers either overlook it (Belmore, 1987; Fiske,

Neuberg, Beattie, & Milberg, 1987) or interpret it according to category-based expectations (Hilton & Von Hippel, 1990; Nelson, Biernat, & Manis, 1990); stereotypes thus capitalize on informational ambiguity. When information disconfirms the category, perceivers tend to perceive that information as non-representative of the general category (Krueger & Rothbart, 1990; Kunda & Oleson, 1995); stereotypes can thus "explain away" deviant information (e.g., Weber & Crocker, 1983). According to meta-analyses, perceivers tend to recall expectancy-inconsistent information only under very specific conditions (Stangor & McMillan, 1992), for example, when expectancies are weak, when incongruencies are strong, and when perceivers have explicit impression formation goals.

People assimilate information into their pre-existing beliefs about the category. This work resonates with Fiske and Ncuberg's (1990) idea of confirmatory categorization, whereby perceivers preserve their categories and prior beliefs via selected information searches. Stereotypes appear resilient to irrelevant and incongruent information, as perceivers find creative ways of reinterpreting discrepant information. But as we will see, stereotyping is not inevitable. Provided sufficiently disconfirming information and sufficient motivation to pay attention, perceivers can alter their categorical beliefs and view others as individuals, not only as category members.

Revising categorical beliefs. When highly motivated to attend and when provided adequate information, perceivers can modify both their a priori expectations and the very nature of their categories. Thus, stereotype change can occur by revising categorical beliefs through motivated attention to information (Hilton & Von Hippel, 1996).

Several models postulate the processes by which categories can change. An early model of change contrasted two processes (Rothbart, 1981). According to the bookkeeping process, people change their stereotypes gradually over time, by attending to categorydiscrepant targets and incorporating new information into that category. Categorical expectations change incrementally by averaging new information with prior beliefs. According to the conversion process, people change their stereotypes more rapidly, as a result of encountering highly discrepant category members. Accordingly, one prominent category member can individually alter the nature of the category (see Weber & Crocker, 1983, for empirical tests of this distinction).

Therefore, stereotypes can change when people attend to and incorporate new information into prior categories. Perceivers can form more specific categories subsumed within the broader stereotype, known as subtyping. Conversely, they can develop elaborated beliefs about the category, referred to as subgrouping (see Rothbart, this volume, chapter 7), which can ultimately dilute the stereotype. The latter process, wherein category variability diminishes stereotypic beliefs, presents the more promising avenue for stereotype change.

Forming individuated impressions. Models of impression formation posit that perceiving individuals according to their unique personal traits, rather than category-consistent attributes, represents the most individuated form of person perception (Brewer, 1988; Fiske & Neuberg, 1990). However, these models suggest that individuation occurs under rare instances; even subtyping and subgrouping processes prioritize categories over individual traits. Category-based perception is more common because full individuation takes enormous effort from the perceiver.

Under rare conditions, perceivers are motivated to form piecemeal impressions that integrate all the target's attributes. This motivation can come from outcome dependency (Erber & Fiske, 1984; Neuberg & Fiske, 1987), accountability (Tetlock, 1992), accuracy goals (Chen, Schechter, & Chaiken, 1996; Neuberg, 1989), and personal values of fairness (Monteith, 1993), in addition to other social motives (see Fiske, 1998, for review).

To arrive at an individuated impression, perceivers must proceed through all stages of perception just described – from categorization to information search and interpretation to recategorization. When no single category can explain the target person, perceivers treat the category as just another attribute. Perceivers appraise the individual's unique attributes, incorporating them into a piecemeal impression (cf. Anderson, 1981). Categories, thus, reduce to just another piece of information, and carry equal weight with other idiosyncratic information in the impression formation process (Fiske & Neuberg, 1990; see also Kunda & Thagard, 1996).

Stereotype Context

A discussion of stereotypes would be incomplete without reference to the social context of stereotype agents and targets. The first section of this paper focused on the interpersonal level, suggesting that stereotype content adheres to basic psychological principles of interpersonal and intergroup relations. The next two sections focused on the cognitive level, indicating that stereotypes arise from basic mental structures and processes that allow people to simplify the world and think efficiently. This final section argues that the larger context of stereotypes, reflected in social hierarchy and history, defines their truly insidious nature.

Two facets of social context determine the potency of stereotypes: (a) power dynamics and group hierarchy, plus (b) status quo justification. Macro-level contextual variables can have profound psychological effects that influence all levels of stereotyping – from formation of mental representations to endorsement and legitimization of their descriptive content.

Power and hierarchy

The nature of societal power dynamics and group hierarchy render stereotypes particularly oppressive for certain individuals and groups (Operario, Goodwin, & Fiske, 1998). In particular, individuals whose outcomes are controlled by others, and groups low in the social hierarchy, are vulnerable to the demeaning content of their stereotypes. Conversely, individuals who control others' outcomes, and groups near the top of the social hierarchy, are more likely to employ stereotypes about others, and even benefit from their own stereotypes (Fiske, 1993).

Individuals who have power over others are likely to engage in more stereotyping processes (Dépret & Fiske, 1993), because powerful people simply pay less individuating attention to their subordinates (Goodwin, Gubin, Fiske, & Yzerbyt, in press). Rather than examine subordinates' unique traits and attributes, powerful perceivers often rely on categorical assumptions to guide their inferences and judgments. Three mechanistic explanations account for this effect. First, powerful perceivers might lack motivation to form accurate impressions of their subordinates, and instead remain satisfied with categorical sketches of subordinates' personalities. Second, powerful perceivers might lack cognitive capacity, allocated elsewhere, to attend to their subordinates. And third, powerful perceivers who prefer to dominate others might simply desire to stereotype their subordinates (see Goodwin et al., in press; Lee-Chai, Bargh, & Chen, 1998; Operario & Fiske, 1999, for support of these postulates). In addition, people who identify with powerful groups tend to assume the cognitive and attitudinal tendencies associated with that group (Turner, Hogg, Oakes, Reicher, & Wetherell, 1987), and thus are prone to stereotyping their subordinates (see also Sachdev & Bourhis, 1985, 1991). Some findings suggest that stereotyping increases under threat or resource scarcity, wherein powerholders must protect their privileged status (Ellemers, Doosje, van Knippenberg, & Wilke, 1992). However, when people with power have communal orientations with their subordinates, they stereotype less (Lee-Chai et al., 1998).

Subordinate individuals or groups are less likely to stereotype the powerful (Fiske & (Dépret 1996). Subordinates pay more scrutinizing attention to powerholders' individuating attributes compared to their categorical attributes, and they sometimes form unrealistically positive impressions of powerholders (Stevens & Fiske, in press), ostensibly in an effort to increase their sense of prediction and control about future outcomes (see also Erber & Fiske, 1984; Neuberg & Fiske, 1987).

Thus, although all perceivers are prone to stereotyping, power increases the tendency to form category-based judgments, and likewise decreases the need to form individuated impressions. Aggregated across individuals and over time, the psychological effects of power on stereotyping can have profound societal effects (Martell, Lane, & Emrich, 1996). Not only does power perpetuate beliefs associated with social subordinates and minority groups, it also enables people to act upon stereotypic beliefs through legislation, economic policies, and institutional practices (Banks & Eberhardt, 1998; Goodwin, Operario, & Fiske, 1998; Sidanius, Levin, & Pratto, 1998).

Status quo justification

As noted, powerful people's stereotypes of social subordinates can have long-term ramifications for the status quo. Powerholders who consensually agree that disadvantaged groups possess negative or undesirable traits tend to act in ways that maintain power differentials (Pratto, Sidanius, Stallworth, & Malle, 1994; Sidanius, 1993). But given our understanding of the stereotyping content, structures, and processes, the tendency for powerholders to stereotype makes some intuitive sense: People strive to protect themselves and their ingroup, and consequently must derogate or impair the outgroup, at least relatively, if not absolutely.

A counterintuitive finding is the tendency for powerless or disadvantaged people to express outgroup favoritism and show biases that justify and maintain their group's low status (Jost, in press; Mlicki & Ellemers, 1996). Some explanations for the phenomenon suggest that members of disadvantaged groups accept the status quo when they perceive that their societal or institutional context follows appropriate social justice standards (Major, 1994; Martin, 1986). Social injustice can endure within cultures or contexts that outwardly endorse egalitarianism and equity. People in those contexts may believe hierarchy-maintaining stereotypes reflect the truth about social groups, rather than see stereotypes as myths that perpetuate power differentials (Sidanius, 1993).

Although people all along the social hierarchy might accept the status quo, members of low-status groups do not necessarily internalize negative stereotypes (see Crocker, Major, & Steele, 1998, for review). Members of low-power groups tend to acknowledge their groups' disadvantaged status, but minimize perceptions of personal vulnerability to discrimination (e.g., Taylor, Wright, Moghaddam, & Lalonde, 1990). In doing so, members of disadvantaged groups can maintain levels of self-esteem and personal control (Ruggiero & Taylor, 1997), and avoid feeling personally victimized. Future research on how members of disadvantaged groups react to prejudice can clarify the apparent tension between acknowledging societal bias and preserving perceptions of self-efficacy.

Stereotypes can be powerful tools for maintaining social hierarchies, rationalizing societal inequalities, and advocating intergroup hostility. Social context can "get inside the head" by influencing the very nature of people's cognitions about group members all along the social hierarchy.

Conclusion

This chapter has argued that stereotypes must be understood at multiple levels of analysis to appreciate their complexity and understand their universality At the cognitive level, stereotypes are functional mechanisms for thinking about the world. At the interpersonal level, stereotypes reflect the structural relationships between groups – particularly groups' relative status and interdependence. At the societal level, stereotypes reflect the larger context of group life. This analysis of stereotype content, structures, processes, and context indicates that stereotypes are both (a) basic human tendencies, inherent within our mental architecture; and (b) potentially damaging belief systems, depending on the power of the situation. Both principles of stereotypes must be acknowledged in theory, research, or intervention.

Social psychology's understanding of stereotypes and stereotyping has evolved considerably from Lippmann's (1922) introduction of the word. Aided by advances in theory and technology, more complex and multifaceted models guide our insight into stereotyping and group phenomena. Future research will undoubtedly capitalize on the recent body of work, spanning levels of analysis to understand and ameliorate the dilemmas rooted in stereotypes. But while social psychologists continue to seek sophisticated resolutions for stereotype-based problems, we are reminded of Lippmann's (1922) earlier wisdom:

What matters is the character of the stereotypes, and the gullibility with which we employ them. . . . If our philosophy tells us that each man is only a small part of the world, that his intelligence catches at best only phases and aspects in a coarse net of ideas, then, when we use our stereotypes, we tend to know that they are only stereotypes, to hold them lightly, to modify them gladly. (p. 90)

Social psychologists and lay people alike, we hope, will uncover ways to achieve Lippmann's ideal.

REFERENCES

Allport, G. W (1954). *The nature of prejudice.* Reading, MA: Addison-Wesley.

Anderson, J. R. (1983). *The architecture of cognition.* Cambridge, MA: Harvard University Press.

Anderson, N. H. (1981). *Foundations of information integration theory.* New York: Academic Press.

Banaji, M. R., & Hardin, C. (1996). Automatic stereotyping. *Psychological Science, 7,* 136–141.

Banks, R. R., & Eberhardt, J. L. (1998). Social psychological processes and the legal bases of racial categorization. In J. L. Eberhardt & S. T. Fiske (Eds.), *Confronting racism: The problem and the response* (pp. 54–75). Thousand Oaks, CA: Sage.

Belmore, S. M. (1987). Determinants of attention during impression formation. *Journal of Experimental Psychology: Learning, Memory, and Cognition, 13,* 480–489.

Bodenhausen, G. V., & Macrae, C. N. (1998). Stereotype activation and inhibition. In R. S. Wyer (Ed.), *Advances in social cognition* (Vol. 11, pp. 1–52). Mahwah, NJ: Erlbaum.

Brewer, M. B. (1979). Ingroup bias in the minimal intergroup situation: A cognitive motivational analysis. *Psychological Bulletin, 86,* 307–324.

Brewer, M. B. (1988). A dual process model of impression formation. In R. Wyer & T. Srull (Eds.), *Advances in social cognition* (Vol. 1, pp. 1–36). Hillsdale, NJ: Erlbaum.

Brewer, M. B., & Brown, R. J. (1998). Intergroup relations. In D. T. Gilbert, S. T. Fiske, & G. Lindzey (Eds.), *Handbook of social psychology* (4th ed., Vol. 2, pp. 554–594). New York: McGraw-Hill.

Carlston, D. E. (1994). Associated systems theory: A systematic approach to cognitive representations of persons. In T. K. Srull & R. S. Wyer (Eds.), *Advances in social cognition* (Vol. 7, pp. 1–78). Mahwah, NJ: Erlbaum.

Carlston, D. E., & Smith, E. R. (1996). Principles of mental representation. In E. T. Higgins & A. W. Kruglanski (Eds.), *Social psychology: Handbook of basic principles* (pp. 184–210). New York: Guilford Press.

Chen, M., & Bargh, J. A. (1997). Nonconscious behavioral confirmation processes: The selffulfilling consequences of automatic stereotype activation. *Journal of Experimental Social Psychology, 33,* 541–560.

Chen, S., Schechter, D., & Chaiken, S. (1996). Getting the truth or getting along: Accuracy- vs. impression-motivated heuristic and systematic processing. *Journal of Personality and Social Pychology, 71,* 262–275.

Collins, A. M., & Loftus, E. F. (1975). A spreading-activation theory of semantic processing. *Psychological Review, 82,* 407–428.

Crandall, C. S. (1994). Prejudice against fat people: Ideology and self-interest. *Journal of Personality and Social Psychology, 66,* 882–894.

Crocker, J., Major, B., & Steele, C. (1998). Social stigma. In D. T. Gilbert, S. T. Fiske, & G. Lindzey (Eds.), *The handbook of social psychology* (4th ed., pp. 504–553). New York: McGraw-Hill.

Crocker, J., & Quinn, D. M. (2001). Psychological consequences of devalued identities. In R. Brown & S. Gaertner (Eds.), *Blackwell handbook of social psychology: Intergroup processes.* (pp. 238–257) Oxford, UK: Blackwell.

Dépret, E. F., & Fiske, S. T. (1993). Social cognition and power: Some cognitive consequences of social structure as a source of control deprivation. In C. Weary, F. Gleicher, & K. Marsh (Eds.), *Control motivation and social cognition.* New York: Springer-Verlag.

Devine, P. G. (1989). Stereotypes and prejudice: Their automatic and controlled components. *Journal of Personality and Social Psychology, 56,* 5–18.

Dovidio, J. F., Evans, N., & Tyler, R. B. (1986). Racial stereotypes: The contents of their cognitive representations. *Journal of Experimental Social Psychology, 22,* 22–37.

Ellemers, N., Doosje, B. J., Knippenberg, A. V., & Wilke, J. (1992). Status protection in high status minority groups. *European Journal of Social Psychology, 22*, 123–140.

Erber, R., & Fiske, S. T. (1984). Outcome dependency and attention to inconsistent information. *Journal of Personality and Social Psychology, 47*, 709–726.

Fiske, S. T. (1980). Attention and weight in person perception: The impact of negative and extreme behavior. *Journal of Personality and Social Psychology, 38*, 889–906.

Fiske, S. T. (1993). Controlling other people: The impact of power on stereotyping. *American Psychologist, 48*, 621–628.

Fiske, S. T. (1998). Stereotyping, prejudice, and discrimination. In D. T. Gilbert, S. T. Fiske, & G. Lindzey (Eds.), *The handbook of social psychology* (4th ed., Vol. 2, pp. 357–411). New York: McGraw-Hill.

Fiske, S. T., & Dépret, E. (1996). Control, interdependence, and power: Understanding social cognition in its social context. *European Review of Social Psychology, 7*, 31–61.

Fiske, S. T., Lin, M., & Neuberg, S. L. (1999). The continuum model: Ten years later. In S. Chaiken (Ed.), *Dual-process theories in social psychology* (pp. 231–254). New York: Guilford Press.

Fiske, S. T., & Neuberg, S. L. (1990). A continuum model of impression formation: From category-based to individuating processes as a function of information, motivation, and attention. In M. P. Zanna (Ed.), *Advances in experimental social psychology* (Vol. 23, pp. 1–74). New York: Academic Press.

Fiske, S. T., Neuberg, S. L., Beattie, A. E., & Milberg, S. J. (1987). Category-based and attribute-based reactions to others: Some informational conditions of stereotyping and individuating processes. *Journal of Experimental Social Psychology, 23*, 399–427.

Fiske, S. T., & Ruscher, J. B. (1993). Negative interdependence and prejudice: Whence the affect? In D. M. Mackie, & D. L. Hamilton (Eds.), *Affect cognition, and stereotyping: Interactive processes in group perception* (pp. 239–268). New York: Academic Press.

Fiske, S. T., & Taylor, S. E. (1991). *Social cognition* (2nd ed.). New York: McGraw-Hill.

Fiske, S. T., Xu, J., Cuddy, A. J. C., & Glick, P. (in press). Respect versus liking: Status and interdependence underlie ambivalent stereotypes. *Journal of Social Issues.*

Gaertner, S. L., & Dovidio, J. F. (1986). The aversive form of racism. In J. F. Dovidio & S. L. Gaertner (Eds.), *Prejudice, discrimination, and racism* (pp. 61–89). Orlando, FL: Academic Press.

Gergen, K. (1973). Social psychology as history. *Journal of Personality and Social Psychology, 26*, 309–320.

Gilbert, G. M. (1951). Stereotype persistence and change among college students. *Journal of Abnormal and Social Psychology, 46*, 245–254.

Goodwin, S. A., Gubin, A., Fiske, S. T., & Yzerbyt, V. (in press). Power can bias impression formation: Stereotyping subordinates by default and by design. *Group Processes and Intergroup Relations.*

Goodwin, S. A., Operario, D., & Fiske, S. T. (1998). Situational power and interpersonal dominance: Factors that perpetuate bias and inequality. *Journal of Social Issues, 54*, 677–698.

Hamilton, D. L., & Sherman, S. J. (1989). Illusory correlations: Implications for stereotype theory and research. In D. Bar-Tal, C. F. Graumann, A. W. Kruglanski, & W. Stroebe (Eds.), *Stereotypes and prejudice: Changing conceptions* (pp. 59–82). New York: Springer-Verlag.

Hamilton, D. L., Sherman, S. J., & Ruvolo, C. M. (1990). Stereotype-based expectancies: Effects on information processing and social behavior. *Journal of Social Issues, 46*, 35–60.

Hantzi, A. (1995). Change in stereotypic perceptions of familiar and unfamiliar groups: The pervasiveness of the subtyping model. *British Journal of Social Psychology, 34*, 463–477.

Higgins, E. T. (1996). Knowledge activation: Accessibility, applicability, and salience. In E. T. Higgins, & A. W. Kruglanski (Eds.), *Social psychology: Handbook of basic principles* (pp. 133–168). New York: Guilford Press.

Higgins, E. T., Bargh, J. A., & Lombardi, W. (1985). The nature of priming effects of categorization. *Journal of Experimental Psychology: Learning, Memory, and Cognition, 11*, 59–69.

Hilton, J. L., & von Hippel, W. (1990). The role of consistency in the judgment of stereotype-relevant behaviors. *Personality and Social Psychology Bulletin, 16*, 430–448.

Hilton, J. L., & von Hippel, W. (1996). Stereotypes. In J. T. Spence, J. M. Darley, & D. J. Foss (Eds.), *Annual review of psychology* (Vol. 47, pp. 237–271). Palo Alto, CA: Annual Reviews.

Jost, J. T. (in press). Outgroup favoritism and the theory of system justification. In G. Moskowitz (Ed.), *Future directions in social cognition.* Hillsdale, NJ: Erlbaum.

Judd, C. M., & Park, B. (1993). Definition and assessment of accuracy in social stereotypes. *Psychological Review, 100*, 109–128.

Karlins, M., Coffman, T. L., & Waiters, G. (1969). On the fading of social stereotypes: Studies in three generations of college students. *Journal of Personality and Social Psychology, 13*, 1–16.

Katz, D., & Braly, K. (1933). Racial stereotypes in one hundred college students. *Journal of Abnormal and Social Psychology, 28*, 280–290.

Kleck, R. E., & Strenta, A. (1980). Perceptions of the impact of negatively valued physical characteristics on social interactions. *Journal of Personality and Social Psychology, 39*, 861–873.

Krueger, J., & Rothbart, M. (1990). Contrast and accentuation effects in category learning. *Journal of Personality and Social Psychology, 59*, 651–663.

Kunda, Z., & Oleson, K. C. (1995). Maintaining stereotypes in the face of disconfirmation: Constructing grounds for subtyping deviants. *Journal of Personality and Social Psychology, 68*, 565–579.

Kunda, Z., & Thagard, P. (1996). Forming impressions from stereotypes, traits, and behaviors: A parallel-constraint-satisfaction theory. *Psychological Review, 103*, 284–308.

Lee, Y., Jussim, L., & McCauley, C. R. (Eds.). (1995). *Stereotype accuracy.* Washington, DC: American Psychological Association.

Lee-Chai, A. Y., Bargh, J. A., & Chen, S. (1998, August). *Questioning the metamorphosis effec: A longitudinal study of social power.* Paper presented at the meeting of the Society for the Psychological Study of Social Issues, Ann Arbor, Michigan.

Lin, M. H., & Fiske, S. T. (1999). *Attitudes toward Asian Americans: Developing a prejudice scale.* Unpublished manuscript, University of Massachusetts at Amherst.

Linville, P. W., Fischer, G. W., & Salovey, P. (1989). Perceived distributions of the characteristics of in-group and out-group members: Empirical evidence and a computer simulation. *Journal of Personality and Social Psychology, 57*, 165–188.

Lippmann, W. (1922). *Public opinion.* New York: Harcourt Brace.

Macrae, C. N., Bodenhausen, G. V., & Milne, A. B. (1998). Saying no to unwanted thoughts: Self-focus and the regulation of mental life. *Journal of Personality and Social Psychology, 74*, 578–589.

Macrae, C. N., Bodenhausen, G. V., Milne, A. B., & Ford, R. (1997). On the regulation of recollection: The intentional forgetting of stereotypical memories. *Journal of Personality and Social Psychology, 72*, 709–719.

Macrac, C. N., Milne, A. B., & Bodenhausen, G. V. (1994). Stereotypes as energy-saying devices: A peek inside the cognitive toolbox. *Journal of Personality and Social Psychology, 66*, 37–47.

Major, B. (1994). From social inequality to personal entitlement: The role of social comparisons, legitimacy appraisals, and group membership. *Advances in Experimental Social Psychology, 26*, 293–355.

Martell, R. F., Lane, D. M., & Emrich, C. (1996). Male-female differences: A computer simulation. *American Psychologist, 51*, 157–158.

Martin, J. (1986). The tolerance of injustice. In J. M. Oleson, C. P. Herman, & M. P. Zanna (Eds.), *Relative deprivation and social comparison: The Ontario symposium* (Vol. 4, pp. 217–242). Hillsdale, NJ: Erlbaum.

Matlin, S., & Stang, D. (1978). *The Pollyanna principle.* Cambridge, MA: Schenkman.

Maurer, K. L., Park, B., & Rothbart, M. (1995). Subtyping versus subgrouping processes in stereotype representation. *Journal of Personality and Social Psychology, 69,* 812–824.

McCann, C. D., Ostrom, T. M., Tyner, L. K., & Mitchell, M. L. (1985). Person perception in heterogeneous groups. *Journal of Personality and Social Psychology, 49,* 1449–1459.

McClelland, J. L., Rumelhart, D. E., & Hinton, G. E. (1986). The appeal of parallel distributed processing. In D. E. Rumelhart, J. L. McClelland, & the PDP Research Group (Eds.), *Parallel distributed processing: Explorations in the microstructure of cognition* (Vol. 1, pp. 3–44). Cambridge, MA: MIT Press.

Medin, D. L., & Schaffer, M. M. (1978). Context theory of classification learning. *Psychological Review, 85,* 207–238.

Miller, L. C., & Read, S. J. (1991). On the coherence of mental models of persons and relationships: A knowledge structure approach. In G. J. O. Fletcher & E Fincham (Eds.), *Cognition in close relationships* (pp. 69–99). Hillsdale, NJ: Erlbaum.

Mlicki, P. P., & Ellemers, N. (1996). Being different or being better? National stereotypes and identifications of Polish and Dutch students. *European Journal of Social Psychology, 26,* 97–114.

Monteith, M. J. (1993). Self-regulation of prejudiced responses: Implications for progress in prejudice-reduction efforts. *Journal of Personality and Social Psychology, 64,* 198–210.

Nelson, T. E., Biernat, M. R., & Manis, M. (1990). Everyday base rates (sex stereotypes): Potent and resilient. *Journal of Personality and Social Psychology, 59,* 664–675.

Neuberg, S. L. (1989). The goal of forming accurate impressions during social interactions: Attenuating the impact of negative expectancies. *Journal of Personality and Social Psychology, 56,* 374–386.

Neuberg, S. L., & Fiske, S. T. (1987). Motivational influences on impression formation: Outcome dependency; accuracy-driven attention, and individuating processes. *Journal of Personality and Social Psychology, 53,* 431–444.

Oakes, P. J., Haslam, S. A., & Reynolds, K. J. (1999). Social categorization and social context: Is stereotype change a matter of information or of meaning? In D. Abrams (Ed.), *Social identity and social categorization* (pp. 55–79). Malden, MA: Blackwell.

Oakes, P. J., Turner, J. C., & Haslam, S. A. (1991). Perceiving people as group members: The role of fit in the salience of social categorizations. *British Journal of Social Psychology, 30,* 125–144.

Operario, D., & Fiske, S. T. (1999). *Effects of trait dominance on powerholders' judgments of subordinates.* Unpublished manuscript, University of California, San Francisco.

Operario, D., Goodwin, S. A., & Fiske, S. T. (1998). Power is everywhere: Social control and personal control both operate as stereotype activation, interpretation, and response. In R. S. Wyer (Ed.), *Advances in social cognition* (Vol. 11, pp. 169–176). Hillsdale, NJ: Erlbaum.

Ottati, V., & Lee, Y. (1995). Accuracy: A neglected component of stereotype research. In Y. Lee, L. J. Jussim, & C. R. McCauley (Eds.), *Stereotype accuracy: Toward appreciating group differences* (pp. 29–59). Washington, DC: American Psychological Association.

Perdue, C. W., Dovidio, J. F., Gurtman, M. B., & Tyler, R. B. (1990). Us and them: Social categorization and the process of intergroup bias. *Journal of Personality and Social Psychology, 59,* 475–486.

Perdue, C. W., & Curtman, M. B. (1990). Evidence for the automaticity of ageism. *Journal of Experimental Social Psychology, 26,* 199–216.

Pettigrew, T. F. (1997). Generalized intergroup contact effects on prejudice. *Personality and Social Psychology Bulletin, 5,* 461–476.

Posner, M. I., & Keele, S. W. (1968). On the genesis of abstract ideas. *Journal of Experimental Psychology, 77,* 353–363.

Pratto, F., Sidanius, J., Stallworth, L. M., & Malle, B. F. (1994). Social dominance orientation: A personality variable predicting social and political attitudes. *Journal of Personality and Social Psychology, 67,* 741–763.

Reed, S. K. (1972). Pattern recognition and categorization. *Cognitive Psychology, 3*, 382–407.

Rosenberg, S., Nelson, C., & Vivkananthan, P. S. (1968). A multidimensional approach to the study of personality impressions. *Journal of Personality and Social Psychology, 9*, 283–294.

Rothbart, M. (1981). Memory processes and social beliefs. In D. L. Hamilton (Ed.), *Cognitive processes in stereotyping and intergroup behavior* (pp. 145–181). Hillsdale, NJ: Erlbaum.

Rothbart, M. (1996). Category-exemplar dynamics and stereotype change. *International Journal of Intercultural Relations, 20*, 305–321.

Ruggiero, K. M., & Taylor, D. M. (1997). Why minority group members perceive or do not perceive the discrimination that confronts them: The role of self-esteem and perceived control. *Journal of Personality and Social Psychology, 72*, 373–389.

Ruscher, J. B., & Fiske, S. T. (1990). Interpersonal competition can cause individuating impression formation. *Journal of Personality and Social Psychology, 68*, 826–838.

Ryan, C. S., Park, B., & Judd, C. M. (1996). Assessing stereotype accuracy: Implications for understanding the stereotyping process. In C. N. Macrae, C. Stangor, & M. Hewstone (Eds.), *Stereotypes and stereotyping* (pp. 121–157). New York: Guilford Press.

Ryckman, R. M., Robbins, M. A., Kaczor, L. M., & Gold, J. A. (1989). Male and female raters' stereotyping of male and female physiques. *Personality and Social Psychology Bulletin, 15*, 244–251.

Sachdev, I., & Bourhis, R. Y. (1985). Social categorization and power differentials in group relations. *European Journal of Social Psychology, 15*, 415–434.

Sachdev, I., & Bourhis, R. Y. (1991). Power and status differentials in minority and majority group relations. *European Journal of Social Psychology, 21*, 1–24.

Schopler, J., & Insko, C. A. (1992). The discontinuity effect in interpersonal and intergroup situations: Generality and mediation. In W. Stroebe & M. Hewstone (Eds.), *European review of social psychology* (Vol. 3, pp. 121–151). Chichester, UK: Wiley.

Sherman, J. W. (1996). Development and mental representation of stereotypes. *Journal of Personality and Social Psychology, 70*, 1126–1141.

Sidanius, J. (1993). The psychology of group conflict and the dynamics of oppression: A social dominance perspective. In S. Iyengar & W. J. McGuire (Eds.), *Explorations in political psychology* (pp. 183–219). Durham, NC: Duke University Press.

Sidanius, J., Levin, S., & Pratto, F. (1998). Hierarchical group relations, institutional terror, and the dynamics of the criminal justice system. In J. L. Eberhardt & S. T. Fiske (Eds.), *Confronting racism: The problem and the response* (pp. 136–165). Thousand Oaks, CA: Sage.

Skowronski, J. J., & Carlston, D. E. (1989). Negativity and extremity biases in impression formation: A review of explanations. *Psychological Bulletin, 105*, 131–142.

Smith, E. R. (1996). What do connectionism and social psychology offer each other? *Journal of Personality and Social Psychology, 70*, 893–912.

Smith, E. R. (1998). Mental representation and memory. In D. T. Gilbert, S. T. Fiske, & G. Lindzey (Eds.), *Handbook of social psychology* (4th ed., Vol. 1, pp. 391–445). New York: McGraw-Hill.

Smith, E. R., & Zàrate, M. A. (1990). Exemplar and prototype use in social categorization. *Social Cognition, 8*, 243–262.

Smith, E. R., & Zàrate, M. A. (1992). Exemplar-based model of social judgment. *Psychological Review, 99*, 3–21.

Snyder, M. (1984). When beliefs create reality. In L. Berkowitz (Ed.), *Advances in experimental social psychology* (Vol. 18, pp. 248–306). New York: Academic Press.

Snyder, M. (1992). Motivational foundations of behavioral confirmation. In M. P. Zanna (Ed.), *Advances in experimental social psychology* (Vol. 25, pp. 67–114). San Diego, CA: Academic Press.

Stangor, C., & Lange, J. E. (1994). Mental representations of social groups: Advances in understanding stereotypes and stereotyping. In M. P. Zanna (Ed.), *Advances in experimental social psychology* (Vol. 26, pp. 357–416). San Diego, CA: Academic Press.

Stangor, C., Lynch, L., Duan, C., & Glass, B. (1992). Categorization of individuals on the basis of multiple social features. *Journal of Personality and Social Psychology, 62*, 207–218.

Stangor, C., & McMillan, D. (1992). Memory for expectancy-congruent and expectancyincongruent information: A review of the social and social developmental literatures. *Psychological Bulletin, 1*, 42–61.

Stapel, D. A., & Koomen, W. (1998). When stereotype activation results in (counter) stereotypic judgments: Priming stereotype-relevant traits and exemplars. *Journal of Personality and Social Psychology, 34*, 136–163.

Steele, C. M. (1997). A threat in the air: How stereotypes shape intellectual identity and performance. *American Psychologist, 52*, 613–629.

Steele, C. M., & Aronson, J. (1995). Stereotype vulnerability and the intellectual test performance of African-Americans. *Journal of Personality and Social Psychology, 69*, 797–811.

Stevens, L. E., & Fiske, S. T. (in press). Forming motivated impressions of a powerholder: Accuracy under task dependency and misperception under evaluative dependency. *Personality and Social Psychology Bulletin.*

Tajfel, H., & Turner, J. C. (1986). The social identity theory of intergroup behaviour. In S. Worchel & W. G. Austin (Eds.), *Psychology of intergroup relations* (pp. 7–24). Chicago, IL: Nelson.

Taylor, D. M., Wright, S. C., Moghaddam, F. M., & Lalonde, R. N. (1990). The personal/group discrimination discrepancy: Perceiving my group, but not myself, to be a target for discrimination. *Personality and Social Psychology Bulletin, 16*, 254–262.

Taylor, S. E. (1981). A categorization approach to stereotyping. In D. L. Hamilton (Ed.), *Cognitive processes in stereotyping and intergroup behavior* (pp. 88–114). Hillsdale, NJ: Erlbaum.

Taylor, S. E. (1991). Asymmetrical effects of positive and negative events: The mobilization/minimization hypothesis. *Psychological Bulletin, 110*, 67–85.

Taylor, S. E., & Fiske, S. T. (1978). Salience, attention, and attribution: Top of the head phenomena. In L. Berkowitz (Ed.), *Advances in experimental social psychology* (Vol. 11, pp. 249–288). New York: Academic Press.

Tetlock, P. E. (1992). The impact of accountability on judgment and choice: Toward a social contingency model. In M. P. Zanna (Ed.), *Advances in experimental social psychology* (Vol. 23, pp. 331–376). San Diego, CA: Academic Press.

Turner, J. C., Hogg, M. A., Oakes, P. J., Reicher, S. D., & Wetherell, M. S. (1987). *Rediscovering the social group: A self-categorization theory.* Oxford, UK: Blackwell.

Weber, R., & Crocker, J. (1983). Cognitive processes in the revision of stereotypic beliefs. *Journal of Personality and Social Psychology, 45*, 961–977.

Zàrate, M. A., & Smith, E. R. (1990). Person categorization and stereotyping. *Social Cognition, 8*, 161–185.

Zebrowtiz, L. A. (1997). *Reading faces: Windows to the soul?* Boulder, CO: Westview.

CHAPTER SEVEN

Category Dynamics and the Modification of Outgroup Stereotypes

Myron Rothbart

The tendency to disparage groups different from our own represents a social problem of enormous proportion, and one whose solution needs little justification. The last hundred years of this millennium may come to be described as a century of genocide, in which mass murder of outgroup members, thought to be a monopoly of impoverished third world countries, reached peak efficiency when practiced by the most advanced and civilized nation on earth. Few nations of the world, whether first or third world, remain untarnished by the dehumanization or mistreatment of outgroups. The goal of this chapter is to explore the nature and modifiability of outgroup stereotypes, with particular emphasis on the role of categorization processes in stereotype change. Given the strength – and often the fury – of outgroup hostility, is it possible to do justice to this by focusing on those causal mechanisms most removed from human emotion and from the conflictual nature of intergroup relations? No single approach is adequate to explain the complex, multi-faceted nature of intergroup hostility. Stereotypes play an important role in intergroup relations, and categorization processes play an important role in stereotyping. The approach taken in this chapter regards categorization as playing a very important – although by no means exclusive – role in the process of stereotype change.

The focus of this chapter is on the modification of outgroup rather than ingroup stereotypes. It is not assumed that the processes governing ingroup and outgroup stereotypes are fundamentally different, but that the more negative and more homogeneous image of the outgroup is in greater need of change.

This chapter explores three basic, related questions about the nature of outgroup stereotypes: (1) To what degree do image and reality correspond in our perception of outgroups? (2) When does our contact and/or experience with individual outgroup members alter our

This research was supported by National Institute of Mental Health Grant MH40662. I wish to thank Ellen Peters and Mary Rothbart for their astute comments on an earlier draft of this manuscript.

perceptions of the outgroup? (3) Are there some general strategies for making our perceptions of the outgroup more like our perceptions of the ingroup? The first two questions are closely linked, since there is evidence that our perceptions of the outgroup are unrealistically extreme, and that these extreme images are often not moderated by our experiences with outgroup members who do not fit the stereotype. It will be argued that categorization processes play an important role in insulating the stereotype from disconfirming information. The third question examines whether categorization processes can be recruited for the purpose of changing outgroup stereotypes to make them more like our images of the ingroup – that is, more favorable and more complex.

Image and Reality

Assessing the accuracy of stereotypic perception is a daunting task (Judd & Park, 1993; Judd, Ryan, & Park, 1991; Lee, Jussim, & McCauley, 1995), and it is not surprising that there is significant disagreement about the definition and assessment of stereotype accuracy. Judges may show accuracy in their ordering of social objects or in terms of absolute discrepancy of their estimates from "known" characteristics. This approach immediately raises the problem of deciding what benchmark of "reality' is to be used in assessing accuracy. Consider two important studies in this area. During the Vietnam War, samples of self-described Doves and Hawks on the War were obtained, based on advertisements placed in the campus newspaper (Dawes, Singer, & Lemons, 1972). Each subject was asked to write attitude statements that would accurately describe both Doves' and Hawks' views on the war. Since each subject was either a Dove or a Hawk, they were writing one set of statements to describe their ingroup and one to describe the outgroup. The statements were then given to outgroup members or other ingroup members to be rated for accuracy. Judges could rate the statements along a continuum from "too mild" to "too extreme" in describing their own attitudes, with the midpoint of the scale reflecting an accurate assessment.

The clearest prediction, based on the Gestalt principle of contrast from an anchoring stimulus (Sherif & Hovland, 1966) – where one's own position serves as the anchor – was that each group of subjects would write statements that "overshot" the actual attitudes of the outgroup, and this prediction was strongly confirmed. Statements describing the attitudes of Doves were more likely to be judged as too extreme when they were written by Hawks than by Doves, and statements describing the attitudes of Hawks were more likely to be judged as too extreme when written by Doves than Hawks. Although the perceptions of the outgroup were exaggerated in this work, there was evidence that ingroup members also overestimated the extremity of their own group – although not as much as for the outgroup. That is, both ingroup and outgroup members were viewed as more extreme than they really were, but this "distortion" was clearly stronger for outgroup than ingroup.

The problem of the criterion for accuracy is evident in this study. Judges are inaccurate only if the sample of Doves and of Hawks in this study is truly representative of their respective populations. That is, perhaps this particular sample of Doves and Hawks is "in reality" less extreme than Doves and Hawks in general, in which case the judges would have been accurate had the stimulus groups been the general population of Doves and Hawks.

Judd et al. (1991) corrected this problem in an analogous study, in which business and engineering majors were *randomly* sampled from their respective populations and used as judges (and stimulus groups) in their study. Using measures of both central tendency and dispersion, and using each subject's own judgments about the self as the criterion, Judd et al. obtained the same basic findings as Dawes et al. (1972). That is, both business and engineering majors were estimated as more extreme than they really were by both ingroup and outgroup judges, but the effect was clearly stronger for the latter. Since these groups were selected to be representative of their parent populations, a stronger inference of inaccuracy can be made. Moreover, Judd et al. found that the two effects – a general tendency to exaggerate the position of the target group, and a greater tendency to exaggerate the outgroup than the ingroup – were found for measures of both central tendency and dispersion. That is, the outgroup in particular was viewed as both more extreme and more homogeneous than it really was (with the criterion for reality being the aggregated self-judgments).

It should be emphasized that the Judd et al. research strongly corroborates and extends the Dawes et al. findings with different measures and different groups. Dawes et al. used two groups that were strongly opposed to each other's views, while Judd et al. used two relatively mundane college majors who, although not in conflict, had somewhat contrasting characteristics. The tendency to view a group in a way that is both more extreme and more homogeneous than warranted by reality can be thought of as a form of "idealization," and this idealization is clearly stronger for outgroup than for ingroup. Note that the difference between the perception of ingroup and outgroup resides not only in the degree of idealization but in the direction of the differences as well. That is, when the overwhelming tendency to judge the ingroup more favorably than the outgroup (Brewer, 1979) is combined with the tendency to extremitize the outgroup as well, the outgroup is idealized in an unfavorable direction while the ingroup tends to be idealized in a favorable direction.

There is reason to think that this idealization works for many different stimulus groups. First, there is a great deal of evidence indicating that a group is viewed as more homogeneous and monolithic by outgroup than ingroup members (Judd & Park, 1988; Park & Judd, 1990; Park & Rothbart, 1982). Second, Mauro (1981) noted the same inaccuracy and simplification in an important social context. To explain jurors' strong support for the death penalty in the abstract, and their strong reluctance to impose the death penalty in a specific case, Mauro argued that jurors' abstract image of "murderers" is extreme, corresponding to such serial killers as Charles Manson, for whom they would impose the death penalty. Garden-variety defendants accused of murder, however, typically have killed only their spouse, are not serial killers, have children and a job, and generally do not fit the extreme image that jurors associate with the category "murderers." Given what we know about crime statistics, the typical murderer is far less extreme than is the public image of murderers. More generally, the tendency to idealize outgroups is strong, we suspect, not only for such emotionally charged categories as murderers, rapists, schizophrenics, and Republicans, but for mundane categories as well, such as business majors, engineering majors, librarians, cab drivers, and professors.

Lakoff (1987) argued that social categories can be represented by a number of different structures, where the "characteristic" exemplar is not necessarily the most frequent or typical instance, and may well be the paragon, or most extreme, exemplar of the category (e.g.,

"Mother Teresa," when used as a category name, defines the extreme example of the altruistic, nurturing individual). Although category structure based strictly on paragons may be uncommon, it seems probable that the "characteristic" category member is displaced toward extreme instances, and away from the statistically frequent exemplars, for the same reason that people estimate death by fire to be more probable than death by a bee sting (Lichtenstein, Slovic, Fischhoff, Layman, & Combs, 1978). The media is far more likely to describe deaths caused by spectacular fires than by bee stings, and serial killers receive more coverage than do the more frequent, but less dramatic, spouse murderers. The availability of dramatic instances may be only one of several possible reasons for the displacement of "characteristic" members toward the extreme (cf. Lakoff, 1987).

Data from the Dawes et al. (1972) and the Judd et al. (1991) research indicate that the discrepancy between image and reality – the idealization of group impressions – is present for both ingroup and outgroup judges, but is considerably stronger for the latter. One way to approach the question of changing outgroup stereotypes, then, is to ask how we can make our perceptions of outgroup members less discrepant from reality and more like our perceptions of ingroup members. As the research above indicates, stereotypes are not absent in our perceptions of the ingroup, but they are less extreme and more complex (i.e., more heterogeneous) than are our perceptions of the outgroup. The question of how we can reduce the discrepancy between the image and the reality of the outgroup will be addressed after examining the question of how experiences with outgroup members influence perceptions of the outgroup as a whole.

When does contact with individual outgroup members modify the stereotype of the outgroup?

Newcomb (1947) used the concept of "autistic hostility" to describe the self-amplifying nature of interpersonal and intergroup conflict. He proposed that mutually antagonistic parties avoid contact and the isolation between the parties then allows each to generate unrealistically negative attributions about the other – since isolation does not allow the attributions to be tempered by reality. The cycle of hostility, isolation, and unrealistically negative attributions constitutes a positive feedback loop which putatively can be reversed by re-established contact. Through contact, the disparity between image and reality is reduced, with a corresponding reduction in hostility. In the case of intergroup hostility, the individual members of the category are recognized as being less negative than the category as a whole, and it is assumed that the latter is adjusted in the direction of the former.

Whereas Newcomb assumed that unrealistically negative group images would naturally be ameliorated by contact, Allport, in his *Nature of Prejudice*, made a more complex argument (Allport, 1954; Pettigrew, 1986, 1998). Allport argued that contact does not always lead to favorable attitude change, and posited four necessary conditions for favorable, contact-induced change: equal status, common goals, intergroup cooperation, and support from legal authorities and/or custom (Pettigrew, 1998).

The problem of contact-induced stereotype change may be even more difficult than commonly assumed given the nature of category-exemplar relations (Rothbart, 1996; Rothbart &

John, 1985; Rothbart, John, & Duncan, in prep.; Rothbart & Lewis, 1988; Rothbart, Sriram, & Davis-Stitt, 1996). The reader is referred to Rothbart (1996) for a general statement of the argument; a brief summary follows.

Responding to a call by Amir (1976) and by Cook (1970) for a theoretical analysis of the psychological factors involved in contact-induced stereotype change, Rothbart and John (1985) proposed a multi-step model for stereotype change. First, it was deemed necessary that category members engage in behaviors perceived as counter to the stereotype. This is a simple point, but its importance is frequently ignored. Some stereotypic attributions are more susceptible to behavioral disconfirmation than others (Rothbart & Park, 1986) and behavior itself is frequently ambiguous and thus easily assimilable to the group stereotype (Kunda & Sherman-Williams, 1993). Stereotypes are unlikely to be changed by contact if the contact is perceived as consistent with the stereotype. This may be one of the severest shortcomings of Newcomb's assumption: As inaccurate as our images may be, ambiguous behaviors are easily assimilable to the stereotype. Allport recognized that contact may support rather than negate the stereotype, and indeed the first three of his four facilitating factors (equal status, common goals, and intergroup cooperation) can be viewed as conditions most likely to bring out behaviors counter to the stereotype. That is, for low-status outgroups, equal status violates the stereotype; and for outgroups with whom we have a competitive relation, common goals and cooperative interactions also conflict with expectation.

Assuming, then, that the first step is satisfied in which behaviors engaged in by outgroup members are perceived as violating the stereotype, the second step becomes of cardinal importance. When do the stereotype-disconfirming attributes of the category member generalize to the category as a whole? Rothbart and John argued that the positions taken by Newcomb and Allport assume an Aristotelean view of category structure. That is, since all category members have the same status and are all "equally good" exemplars, generalization is as likely to occur for members with stereotype-disconfirming attributes as it is for members with stereotype-confirming attributes. The contact hypothesis is specifically concerned, of course, with the impact of category members whose attributes are inconsistent with the category, and assumes strong generalizability from poor-fitting examples of the category.

An alternative view of categorization, based on a graded view of category structure – in which members differ in their goodness of fit to the category – is more consistent with the psychological literature (Rosch, 1973, 1978), but has serious implications for the problem of generalization associated with the contact hypothesis. At the level of mechanism, as the goodness of fit between category and exemplar decreases, there would be less inference from category to exemplar, and from exemplar to category (cf. Rips, 1975; Rothbart & Lewis, 1988). At the level of phenomenology, a logical member of the category thus may not be perceived as a member of the category. The question of what is meant by "perceived" deserves elaboration. A fraternity member, Doug, who is shy, quiet, writes poetry, and plays the oboe may be a card-carrying member of his fraternity, but is not thought of as a member, given the poor fit between his attributes and the public image of fraternity members. Doug does not spontaneously activate the category "fraternity men" in others' thoughts, nor is the category "fraternity men" likely to activate Doug as an exemplar.

Rothbart and John argued that poor-fitting exemplars often become "functionally isolated," or compartmentalized, from the category, and thus the stereotype-disconfirming attributes do not generalize to the category as a whole. In essence, stereotype-disconfirming attributes are thought to have two contradictory effects. First, they increase the disparity between image and reality (category and exemplar), exerting force on the stereotype to moderate and to move into line with the exemplar (à la Newcomb). Second, the decreasing goodness of fit between exemplar and category psychologically removes the exemplar from the category-making generalization less likely. There is now a great deal of experimental evidence indicating that as an exemplar's stereotype-disconfirming attributes increase, the likelihood of those attributes being incorporated into the stereotype decrease (Brown, Vivian, & Hewstone, 1999; Desforges, Lord, & Pugh, 1997; Hewstone, 1994; Johnston & Hewstone, 1992; Kunda & Oleson, 1995; Lord, Desforges, Ramsey, Trezza, & Lepper, 1991; Weber & Crocker, 1983).

To summarize to this point, Rothbart and John (1985) argued simply that not all category members are "equally good," and that inference between exemplar and category is directly related to the goodness of fit between the two; in short, generalization will be proportional to an exemplar's typicality. The importance of typicality as an important determinant of contact-induced stereotype change was presaged by Lewin half a century ago (Lewin & Grabbe, 1945). Referring to research combating prejudice based on age and race, they argued:

> ... [these studies] indicate that favorable experiences with members of another group, even if they are frequent, do not necessarily diminish prejudices toward that group ... Only if a psychological linkage is made between the image of specific individuals and the stereotype of a certain group, only when the individuals can be perceived as "typical representatives" of the group, is the experience with individuals likely to affect the stereotype. (Lewin & Grabbe, 1945, p. 58)

The problem, of course, is that the same member characteristics that disconfirm the stereotype also serve to reduce the typicality of that group member. The challenge is to pair stereotype-disconfirming information with an otherwise "typical representative of the group" despite the inverse relation between disconfirming attributes and typicality – a difficult but not impossible task that will be discussed later (for an excellent, recent review of this issue, see Hewstone & Lord, 1998).

Because Rothbart and John expect generalization to be more likely for good than for poor-fitting category members, they predict a bias in information processing that favors stereotype stability over stereotype change. Whether the model is too pessimistic about the possibilities for contact-induced stereotype change will depend largely upon the findings of field research, preferably using a longitudinal design. Hovland's (1959) early analysis of attitude change research showed considerable change within the laboratory, but little change in the field – an analysis that may be as applicable today in the domain of stereotype change as in the earlier analysis of attitude change.

To assess the degree of stability and change in stereotypic beliefs, Rothbart and John conducted a four-year, four-panel, longitudinal study of the stereotypic beliefs of University of Oregon college students from their freshman to senior year (Rothbart & John, 1993; Rothbart, John, & Duncan, in prep.). Subjects judged 14 target groups on a number of stereotype measures, and provided us with detailed self-reports of the nature and extent of contact with each target group, as well as providing demographic and attitudinal data. For each target group, subjects rated approximately 40–50 trait descriptive terms at each of the four testing sessions. One measure of stereotype change is agreement over time in the ordering of the trait terms, corresponding to the test-retest reliability of the traits. Using aggregated means (computed across subjects, but within target groups), we found the average test-retest for the 14 different target groups over a four-year period – from the beginning of their freshman year to the end of their senior year – to be .92. A base-rate against which this can be judged is a comparable, non-longitudinal sample over a seven-day period, which produced a correlation of .96. The drop from .96 to .92 can be thought of as one measure of change over a four-year period – clearly very strong evidence for stability. This correlation is not the only measure of stability, however, and there was evidence of change for some of the target groups. Interestingly, the one group for which there was a great deal of change – in an unfavorable direction – was also the group for which there was a great deal of contact. Indeed, across all subjects, changes in the degree of self-reported direct contact (an index of amount and closeness of contact) correlated – .01 with changes in the favorability of the stereotype. There is considerable complexity to this data set, but thus far no strong evidence has emerged indicating that the *amount*, as opposed to judged quality of contact, is related to favorable stereotype change. Judged favorability of the contact did correlate significantly with changes in favorability toward the group, but the measure of favorability was based on retrospective self-report and may overlap conceptually with other indices of group favorability. In summary, at least one measure of stereotype change – consistency in the ordering of stereotypic attributes – showed enormous stability over an important four-year period in subjects' lives, providing evidence generally consistent with predictions from Rothbart and John (1985).

In the author's view, the Rothbart and John model is not an argument against contact in the amelioration of intergroup relations. Providence has given us rather few weapons in the fight against outgroup hostility, and contact is one of the few that has been effective, although not universally so. The arguments made by Rothbart and John attempt to define those conditions that might increase the likelihood of generalization for atypical exemplars. The first of these is that because the association of the category with the exemplar is a necessary condition for generalization to occur, it is especially important for atypical exemplars to be presented as clear – if not typical – members of the category. Second, if possible, disconfirming information should be associated with otherwise typical, rather than atypical members of the category. Finally, it may be useful to differentiate between group attributes that are more central or essential to group membership from those that are more peripheral. Greater generalization may be possible when highly typical peripheral attributes are presented to remind us of category membership, and atypical but central attributes are presented to challenge the more central aspects of the stereotype. To use an example (based more on fantasy than reality), assume that the image of a typical campus fraternity member is of a male who (1) wears a baseball cap backwards, (2) is clean shaven, (3) is politically conservative, and (4) conforms to the group. Assume the first two features are peripheral and the latter two are more central to group membership. If we were to try to change either of the more essential features, by presenting a liberal and/or nonconforming fraternity member, it would be useful to have the member typical on the peripheral features. Having group membership salient, even when presented with atypical members, is particularly helpful in weakening the stereotype (e.g., Maurer, Park, & Rothbart, 1995).

Individuation and Decategorization

What happens when we acquire individuating information about a category member? A number of thoughtful models have been proposed to account for the complex relation between individuating and categorical information (Brewer, 1988; Fiske & Neuberg, 1990; Locksley, Hepburn, & Ortiz, 1982; Nisbett, Zukier, & Lemley, 1981; Rothbart & John, 1985). This relation is important because one putative effect of sustained contact with a category member is the acquisition of information that is either irrelevant to or incongruent with the category. This newly acquired information about a category member should result, through generalization, in stereotype change. Indeed, at least two models hold individuation/decategorization to be an important component of stereotype change (Brewer & Miller, 1984; Pettigrew, 1998).

According to Rothbart and John, individuation and generalization may work against each other to produce stereotype change. The same counter-stereotypic behavior that disconfirms the stereotype also reduces the goodness of fit between category and category member, making generalization less likely. Qualms about the efficacy of personalization and decategorization in producing stereotype change are shared by Brown and Turner (1981), Hewstone and Brown (1986), and Brown et al. (1999), albeit for somewhat different theoretical reasons. Change at the interpersonal level is not necessarily mirrored by change at the intergroup level, and indeed there is reason to think that decategorizing an outgroup member may inhibit stereotype change.

Two recent sets of studies examine the effect of individuating information on categorical judgments. The first re-examines the interesting work by Nisbett et al. (1981) on the dilution effect. Nisbett et al. argued that information nondiagnostic of a target behavior could none the less dilute the predictive power of diagnostic information. For example, consider a target behavior "child abuse," which is predicted by "having a drinking problem," but not by "managing a hardware store." The category "having a drinking problem" is diagnostic of child abuse, but the behavior "managing a hardware store" is not. Nisbett et al. found that the addition of nondiagnostic information systematically decreased (diluted) the predictive strength of diagnostic information. Tversky's (1977) features of similarity model, which assumes similarity to be a function of common minus distinctive features, was invoked to account for dilution. The addition of nondiagnostic information increases the number of distinctive features, and thus reduces perceived similarity.

Peters and Rothbart (2000) argued that the dilution effect may be intimately related to category-exemplar dynamics, rather than to Tversky's features of similarity. Specifically, they argued that the nondiagnostic information may have influenced the perceived strength of the diagnostic information, which in turn influenced prediction. Thus, a person who "has a drinking problem *and* who manages a hardware store" may be viewed as less of an alcoholic than a person who is simply described as "having a drinking problem." Peters and Rothbart argued that the specific nondiagnostic behaviors used may have inadvertently reduced the strength of the diagnostic category by making the exemplar less typical of the category. If so, then it ought to be possible to create nondiagnostic behaviors that increase, decrease, or do not change the typicality of the stimulus person vis-à-vis the diagnostic category. Peters and Rothbart provided subjects with either 1, 3, or 5 pieces of nondiagnostic, individuating information that were either typical, atypical, or unrelated to the diagnostic category. Consistent with the Nisbett et al. research, as the amount of atypical information increased, the impact of the diagnostic information decreased, entirely consistent with the dilution effect. However, contrary to the dilution effect, as typical nondiagnostic information increased, enhanced categorical prediction – the opposite of dilution – was obtained. With irrelevant nondiagnostic information, there was no change in prediction as the amount of that information increased. Thus the critical variable – the typicality of the categorical information – seemed to be an essential ingredient in determining whether dilution would or would not occur.

In general, however, it was easier to dilute than to enhance the diagnostic category. Although there were a number of possible reasons for this finding, one explanation is based on the nature of categorical representation, as discussed earlier (Lakoff, 1987). A pure category alone may already contain a large number of typical elements, making it difficult, for example, to make an "alcoholic" even more alcoholic, although it is relatively easy to reduce the degree of alcoholism by including incongruent elements. This means that dilution may be the most frequently observed effect – as originally argued by Nisbett et al. – but for reasons related to the dynamics of stereotyping rather than to Tversky's model of similarity.

Are mothers women?

Given the idealized nature of category labels, in which features consistent with the category predominate, it is probable that the addition of individuating information is more likely to weaken than strengthen the link between category and exemplar. Although at first blush the ease of "decategorizing" a category member may seem desirable, since it "releases" the individual from the tyranny of the category, it may be undesirable from the point of view of generalization.

There is a story told by an eminent developmentalist studying the gender role expectations of young girls whose mothers were employed in highly atypical occupations. In one case, where the mother's job was driving a tractor-trailer cross country for a large trucking company, the daughter provided a list of the usual occupations appropriate for women: Secretaries, nurses, librarians, etc. When asked whether women could be truck drivers, the daughter said no. When the interviewer called attention to her mother's own occupation, the daughter commented that "that is my mother, that is not women." This anecdote illustrates the inverse relation between the amount of individuating information and the amount of generalization. Those category members about whom we have the greatest amount of individuating information, and who could potentially exert the greatest force for humanizing our abstract impressions of social categories, may well be those individuals whose attributes are least likely to generalize to the category as a whole.

An interesting experiment that examines this question directly was conducted by Scarberry, Ratcliff, Lord, Lanicek, and Desforges (1997). They created an experience with a category member (a male homosexual) under conditions that were most likely to show generalization to the category as a whole. The factors identified by Allport to facilitate contact-induced stereotype change were included in the present experiment. Subjects interacted cooperatively with a confederate under equal-status conditions to work interdependently on a task to achieve a mutually desired goal, and under conditions in which the confederate was viewed in a highly favorable way. On the cooperative task, the homosexual confederate provided help to the subject through the use of analogies, but the nature of the analogies was varied experimentally. For some subjects the analogies were given in the abstract, such as "like when someone squeezes every bit of toothpaste out of the tube"; in the other condition the analogies were given as self-examples, such as "like when I squeeze every bit of toothpaste out of the tube." Subjects' attitudes toward homosexuals and toward three other stigmatized groups were assessed both pre- and post-contact, and attitudes toward the homosexual confederate were also assessed. Confederates who used abstract or self-based analogies were both highly liked and, most importantly, equally well liked. However, favorable attitudes toward homosexuals in general were greater in the condition where the confederate used abstract, rather than personal, analogies. A nice feature of this experiment is the careful control of the nature of the information presented to subjects. The informativeness of the analogies was virtually the same across conditions, and only the referent (abstract vs. self) varied. When the analogies referred to the personal behavior of the homosexual confederate, there was less generalization than when the analogies were abstract and unrelated to the confederate. It appears that the individuating information, seemingly quite unrelated to the stereotype of homosexuals, succeeded in isolating the individual from the category.

There may be at least two ways to interpret the findings of Scarberry et al. One possibility is that some of the analogies used (e.g., woodworking) may actually be slightly disconfirming of the stereotype of homosexuals, and those analogies when personally associated with the confederate made him less typical of the category. This interpretation would be consistent with Peters and Rothbart's interpretation of Nisbett et al.'s dilution findings. It is also possible, however, that even mundane, truly stereotype-irrelevant information can reduce the goodness of fit between category and exemplar, particularly for "strong" categories, that is, categories which carry strong implication or have high "inductive potential" (Rothbart & Taylor, 1992). Strong categories, such as homosexual, often connote a highly limited, and evaluatively potent set of behaviors, and it is possible that even common, mundane, nondiagnostic behaviors may function to reduce the goodness of fit between category and exemplars for such strong categories.

When Allport (1954) wrote that some labels are ". . . exceedingly salient and powerful. They tend to prevent alternative classification, or even cross-classification. . . . 'labels of primary potency' . . . act like shrieking sirens, deafening us to all finer discriminations that we might otherwise perceive," he was referring to such strong categories, and his intuition is compelling: Once these categories are applied to individuals they may inhibit the application of other, even independent or neutral categories. Saltz and Medow (1971) found that young children have difficulty in applying more than one social category to an individual, and the same may be true for adults when the categories are strong (that is, have high inductive potential). For very strong categories, any individuating information that is not directly implied by the category label may serve to decategorize the individual by making the exemplar a less good fit to the category. If so, the fact that almost any information can liberate the individual from the stigma of category membership may be received as good news, but again the downside is that the unrealistically extreme image of such categories may remain unperturbed by the reality of the members who make up that category.

To summarize the argument thus far, there are powerful categorization processes that work against contact-induced stereotype change. The same processes that individuate the category member – that is, that distance the member from the category – work against generalization from the individual to the category. The limitations of contact-induced stereotype change are not in the author's view a moral imperative, but a theoretically derived prediction with considerable empirical support. Indeed, the arguments made can be used to inform research on contact to increase the likelihood of stereotype change, as shown by Hewstone and Lord (1998). Most generally, any techniques that remind an observer that atypical group members are none the less category members should increase the likelihood of generalization. The problem of intimately known outgroup members is particularly vexing, however, since high levels of individuating information about outgroup members may lead them to be only weakly associated with the category label. Emphasizing their category membership, and particularly their category attributes that are typical, may be of value, but the power to compartmentalize poor-fitting group members should not be underemphasized (cf. Kelman's (1992) work on small-group interactions between Jews and Arabs in Israel).

Our discussion thus far has been focused on the complex relation between a category and its members, and we now wish to turn to the basic question of how we define, explicitly or implicitly, the nature of category membership through the placement of category boundaries.

The nature of group boundaries

Any discussion of ingroup–outgroup relations accepts as a basic premise the importance of a boundary dividing one's own group from others. There is little need to remind social psychologists raised in the tradition of Asch (1948) and Lewin and Grabbe (1945) that the importance of such boundary markers lies, not necessarily in the reality of the external world, but in the phenomenal representation of that world. Two studies dealing with issues of boundary markers, one explicitly and the other implicitly, will be summarized and used to speculate on the relation of such boundary markers to the modification of outgroup stereotypes.

A study by Rothbart, Davis-Stitt, and Hill (1997) examined the impact of category labels and visual boundary markers on similarity judgments. In one experiment, they presented subjects with pairs of names of male actors located along a continous, percentile scale of political liberalism (e.g., Alan Alda was located at point that makes him more liberal than 85% of the population). Each subject judged the similarity between a number of pairs, some placed 10 units apart and others placed 15 units apart. The presence of boundary markers at the quartiles of the scale was systematically varied across subjects. Boundary markers were either verbal labels (e.g., "moderately conservative," "moderately liberal") or visual markers (solid vertical "tick" marks). One group received a continuum with no markers of any kind (a baseline control), another received a continuum with *both* verbal and visual boundary markers, and in the two other conditions there was the presence of one type of boundary marker but not the other. The results were clear: A given pair of actors was judged most similar to each other when no boundaries existed between them, and perceived similarity decreased as a function of the number of interposed boundary markers. The effects of the verbal and visual boundary markers were each significant and additive. Thus, even though the verbal and visual markers added nothing to the underlying reality of the scale, both types of markers – when interposed between stimulus persons – decreased the perceived similarity between them. A comparison between the baseline control condition and the condition with two boundary markers present indicates that there were two effects of category boundaries: 1) To increase the perceived similarity within categories, and 2) to decrease the perceived similarity between categories. These two effects constitute the phenomenon Turner, Hogg, Oakes, Reicher, and Wetherell (1987) have called "metacontrast" (cf. also Tajfel & Wilkes, 1963).

The design of the experiment also allowed a comparison between "reality" and categorization. Consider two different types of pairs: Those separated by 10 units and those separated by 15 units. The unit distance between the pairs represents the "reality" of the scale, and the judgments in the control baseline condition, where no boundaries are present, appropriately show greater similarity for the 10 unit than for the 15 unit pairs. Now consider the case in which the actors separated by 10 units are in different categories, and those separated by 15 units are present in the same category: Now the 15 unit pairs are judged more similar than are the 10 unit pairs. At least for this range of scale values, categorization is able to override the effects of reality. Category boundaries appear to be treated as informative even when they add little or no information to what is already known about the objects subsumed by the categories. If the opening example from that article is paraphrased, it is as if a farmer living at the boundary of Poland and Russia, after learning that his house is just inside the Polish border, exclaims with relief, "Thank God, no more Russian winters!" Similar findings have been obtained by Allison and Messick (1985) and Mackie and Allison (1987) in the context of group attributions, where the criterion for electoral success is varied.

Rothbart et al. explicitly manipulated the presence of boundary markers and examined the effects on perceived similarity. A study by Maurer, Park, and Rothbart (1995), although not explicitly designed to examine the effects of category boundaries, may usefully be interpreted in this way. Maurer et al. tested some important ideas put forth earlier by Park, Ryan, and Judd (1992) about subgrouping and perceived intragroup variability, and considered how subtyping may differ from subgrouping. Earlier work by Park et al. showed that subjects who first thought about the characteristics of the subordinate groups that make up the larger superordinate group then rated the superordinate group as *less* homogeneous. This phenomenon, referred to as subgrouping, has important implications for modifying the perceived complexity/heterogeneity of outgroups. How, then, does subgrouping differ from subtyping, where poor-fitting members of a category are also relegated to a subordinate category resulting in a *more* homogeneous view of the superordinate group (e.g., Johnston & Hewstone, 1992; Weber & Crocker, 1983)? The goal of the Maurer et al. research was to determine whether the creation of subgroups and subtypes – both of which involve the establishment of subordinate categories – leads to different effects on the perceived strength of the stereotype.

Subjects were given information about a group of 16 stimulus persons involved in a Big Brother program, where the group members varied in typicality. One group was given this information without any instructions (the control condition), and then were asked to make typicality judgments as well as judgments about the group as a whole (including judgments of intragroup variability). A second group was given "subtyping" instructions to sort the group members into those who fit and those who do not fit the image of the group before making the same judgments as did the control condition. A third group was given "subgrouping" instructions to sort the members into as many piles as they wished, trying to minimize differences within subgroups while maximizing differences between subgroups before making their judgments. Compared to the control condition, the subtyping condition had a more stereotyped and homogeneous image of the target group, while the subgrouping condition had a less stereotyped and more heterogeneous image. We believe the reason for this was that the subjects were implicitly drawing the group boundaries differently for the different conditions. In the subtyping condition, atypical members were functionally excluded from group membership, a conclusion which was supported by a mediational analysis based on typicality ratings; in the subgrouping condition, the boundaries enclosed all of the subgroups, and the heterogeneity of the included groups was apparent. Stated differently, the same atypical stimulus persons were functionally excluded from the group representation in the subtyping condition, while they were included in the subgrouping condition.

There are two potentially important implications of this research. One is that the perception of typicality is influenced not only by the "computation" of matching features between category and exemplar, but also by the processing goals of the subjects. Context can determine whether subjects do or do not include the atypical members in their implicit calculations of group impressions, and this is an important phenomenon that needs to be better understood. In this research, the subtyping and subgrouping instructions had very different effects on how subjects thought about the relation of group members to the group as a whole. The relatively simple dichotomous judgments (good fit vs. poor fit) required by the subtyping instructions may have led subjects to view group members in a unidimensional way, promoting an exaggerated difference between the attributes of good- and poor-fitting members (in comparison to the control condition). In contrast, the more complex subgrouping instructions, which encouraged subjects to examine similarities and differences between and among individual stimulus persons and between and among subgroups, may have had at least two important consequences. First, subjects may have been led to realize that each stimulus person was a complex set of attributes some of which fit and some of which did not fit the stereotype. In contrast to the subtyping instructions, the multiattribute nature of the stimulus persons was emphasized, leading to more moderate judgments of atypicality (cf. Judd & Lusk, 1984). Second, whereas the judgments under subtyping instructions may have led subjects to think of atypical members as outside the group, or as nonmembers of the group, the subgrouping instructions may have encouraged subjects to make discriminations *within* the context of an activated superordinate category. To state this somewhat differently, there is a difference between sorting a list of occupations into those that fit or do not fit our stereotype of women (the subtyping instructions) versus a task in which we classify a list of occupations, *all engaged in by women*, into subcategories (the subgrouping instructions). In the former case, the atypical exemplars may be *dissociated* from the superordinate category, and in the latter case may be actively *associated* with that category.

The second general implication of this work is the importance of implicit group boundaries. One way to think about the Maurer et al. (1995) results is that subjects in the subtyping
condition are implicitly drawing the group's boundaries in a way that is different from
subjects in the subgrouping condition. For the former, the boundaries appear to exclude
atypical group members, whereas for the latter, the boundaries appear to be drawn in a more
inclusive manner. Although the concept of "implicit group boundaries" remains vague, it
has precedence in Allport's concept of "refencing" (referring to the isolation of poor-fitting
group members outside the category) and in Lewin's treatment of psychological barriers. In
both cases, it is argued that one function of psychological boundaries is to seal off or isolate
one region of the "life-space" from another. The isolated regions may be individual group
members from the group as a whole, one social category from another, the ingroup from
the outgroup, or any concept or idea that remains isolated or inaccessible from another (cf.
Nissen, Ross, Willingham, Mackenzie, & Schacter, 1988).

Group Boundaries and Stereotype Change

In this last section, a number of general boundary-related strategies are considered that might
be useful in modifying perceptions of the outgroup, guided by the question: "How can we
make our images of the outgroup more like those of the ingroup?" Park and Rothbart (1982)
have provided one approach to answering this question. When asked to describe female dance
and female physics majors, female college students based their ratings primarily on college
major, whereas male college students based their ratings primarily on gender. For male
dance and male physics majors, now male judges used college major, while female judges
used gender. In other words, each group of judges used the more differentiating dimension
(college major) when rating its own gender and the less differentiating dimension (gender)
when rating the other gender. How can we get judges to think about outgroup members
in terms of their most differentiating rather than their least differentiating attributes?

Subgrouping

One strategy for making the outgroup more like the ingroup is to increase the perceived
variability of the outgroup, particularly with respect to increasing subordinate bases for
classification – that is, by making it clear that a number of subgroup category labels comprise
the superordinate group. This is exactly the program of research being carried out by Park
and her colleagues (e.g., Park, Judd, & Ryan, 1992). There may be a number of ways of
enhancing the perceived variability of a group, and consistent with the reasoning offered
earlier, presenting the subgroupings in the context of the superordinate grouping may be
particularly effective.

Augmentation of underrepresented subgroups.   One source of bias in the perception of
outgroups is the overrepresentation of particular subgroups for reasons of extremeness,
memorability, threat, etc. (Rothbart, Fulero, Jensen, Howard, & Birrell, 1978), and the

underrepresentation of others. For example, Whites' images of Blacks may be disproportionately influenced by the image of "young Black males." Even though violent behavior occurs in a minority of "young Black males," this subgroup itself represents only a minority of Blacks, a category which also includes Black females, elderly Blacks, middleclass Blacks, etc. Perhaps due to media attention directed at violent crime among young Black males, other subgroups are inadequately represented in our impressions of the group as a whole. This is an instance where increased public awareness of other Black subgroups may lead both to a more heterogeneous, and less negative, image of the group as a whole.

Aggregation of categories. Often an outgroup category retains its homogeneous, negative characteristics by remaining isolated or compartmentalized from both relevant category members and from other, affectively inconsistent, labels. In a classic study on the effects of consensual information, Asch (1948) had judges rank the favorability of a set of occupations, one of which was "politicians." In one condition, judges were informed that other subjects had rated politicians highly favorably, and in another condition, unfavorably. Judges were strongly influenced by these consensual ratings, but when Asch probed their thinking, it was clear that in the first condition, judges interpreted the category to mean "statesmen" and in the second condition to mean "political hacks" (cf. Sia, Lord, Blessum, Ratcliff, & Lepper, 1997, Lord & Lepper, 1999). Indeed, the exemplars activated in both conditions were politicians, by any reasonable definition of the term, and the categories "statesman' and "politician," although separated by an implicit boundary, could easily be aggregated to yield a single, more heterogeneous category.

Although there is little enthusiasm to change the public perception of politicians, there are many important social categories, such as "disabled" and "mentally ill," in which the categories retain their extreme character by virtue of excluding many other relevant classes of exemplars. The category "disabled" includes not only paraplegics or quadriplegics, but also individuals with less obvious impairments to hearing or vision. The mentally ill are not just dangerous psychotics, but include individuals with other disabling mental states (anxiety, fear, depression, etc.). Part of the problem with these categories is the ambiguity associated with category membership: How do we define a disability and how do we define mental illness? Although these two cases may constitute extreme examples of ambiguity, most social categories have fuzzy boundaries, and the consequence of such ambiguity is the exclusion or underrepresentation of more moderate exemplars. The process of aggregation joins together previously separated categories into a superordinate, but more heterogeneous grouping (cf. Abelson's (1959) concept of "transcendence").

Redefining category boundaries. Probably one of the clearest examples of altering category boundaries for the purpose of modifying outgroup stereotypes is the imposition of a superordinate category inclusive of ingroup and outgroup members, in effect removing the implicit boundary marker between the two groups. The classic research by M. Sherif, Harvey, White, Hood, & C. Sherif (1988) on the use of superordinate goals to reverse the destruction effects of intergroup competition can be thought of as an instance of removing category boundaries. Although Sherif preferred to explain the beneficial effects of cooperation on the "functional relations" between groups, it is also possible to interpret the results as due either to common fate (e.g., Rabbie & Horwitz, 1969) or to the redefinition of category boundaries to yield a single ingroup (Gaertner, Mann, Murrell, & Dovidio, 1989; Dovidio, Gaertner, Validzic, Matoka, Johnson, & Frazier, 1997; Gaertner, Mann, Dovidio, Murrell, & Pomare, 1990). These ideas are discussed extensively by Brewer and Gaertner (2001).

In summary, two possible routes to modifying the stereotypes of outgroup members have been considered in this chapter. One route, through contact with individual exemplars, can be problematic due to the dynamics of category-exemplar relations. Specifically, those exemplars most disconfirming of the stereotype are least likely to be associated with the category and least likely to produce generalization to the category as a whole. None the less, category-exemplar dynamics can also be exploited to increase the probability of generalization by making sure that atypical exemplars – through a variety of techniques – become strongly associated with the category. A second route attempts a modification of the relations among the categories themselves, by augmenting, combining, and redefining category boundaries in a way that yields a less extreme and more heterogeneous view of the outgroup. In the author's view, there is as yet no magic bullet that vanquishes the unfavorable, simplified images of the outgroup. Our categorical structures, which represent the mind's attempt to simplify the complexities of the social world, play a significant role in such stereotypes. The difficulty of modifying these categorical structures, to make them more complex and more reflective of the actual variety of the social world, should not be underestimated. The importance of achieving this goal also should not be underestimated.

REFERENCES

Abelson, R. P. (1959). Modes of resolution of belief dilemmas. *Journal of Conflict Resolution*, *3*, 343–352.

Allison, S. T., & Messick, D. M. (1985). The group attribution error. *Journal of Experimental Social Psychology*, *21*, 563–579.

Allport, G. W. (1954). *The nature of prejudice*. Cambridge, MA: Addison-Wesley.

Amir, Y. (1976). The role of intergroup contact in change of prejudice and ethnic relations. In P. A. Katz (Ed.), *Towards the elimination of racism* (pp. 245–308). New York: Pergamon Press.

Asch, S. E. (1948). The doctrine of suggestion, prestige, and imitation in social psychology. *Psychological Review*, *55*, 250–276.

Brewer, M. B. (1979). Ingroup bias in the minimal intergroup situation: A cognitive-motivational analysis. *Psychological Bulletin*, *86*, 307–324.

Brewer, M. B. (1988). A dual process model of impression formation. In T. K. Srull & J. Wyer (Eds.), *Advances in social cognition* (pp. 1–36). Hillsdale, NJ: Erlbaum.

Brewer, M. B., & Gaertner, S. L. (2001). Toward reduction of prejudice: Intergroup contact and social categorization. In R. Brown & S. Gaertner (Eds.), *Blackwell handbook of social psychology: Intergroup processes* (pp. 451–472). Oxford, UK: Blackwell.

Brewer, M. B., & Miller, N. (1984). Beyond the contact hypothesis: Theoretical perspectives on desegregation. In N. Miller & M. B. Brewer (Eds.), *Groups in contact: The psychology of desegregation*. New York: Academic Press.

Brown, R. J., & Turner, J. C. (1981). Interpersonal and intergroup behavior. In J. C. Turner & H. Giles (Eds.), *Intergroup behavior* (pp. 33–65). Chicago IL: University of Chicago Press.

Brown, R., Vivian, J., & Hewstone, M. (1999). Changing attitudes through intergroup contact: The effects of group membership salience. *European Journal of Social Psychology*, *29*(5–6), 741–764.

Cook, S. W. (1970). Motives in a conceptual analysis of attitude-related behavior. In W. J. Arnold & D. Levine (Eds.), *Nebraska symposium on motivation, 1969* (pp. 179–235). Lincoln, NE: University of Nebraska Press.

Dawes, R. M., Singer, D., & Lemons, F. (1972). An experimental analysis of the contrast effect and its implications for intergroup communication and the indirect assessment of attitude. *Journal of Personality and Social Psychology*, *21*(3), 281–295.

Desforges, D. M., Lord, C. G., & Pugh, M. A. (1997). Role of group representativeness in the generalization part of the contact hypothesis. *Basic and Applied Social Psychology*, *19*, 183–204.

Dovidio, J. F., Gaertner, S. L., Validzic, A., Matoka, K., Johnson, B., & Frazier, S. (1997). Extending the benefits of recategorization: Evaluations, self-disclosure, and helping. *Journal of Experimental Social Psychology*, *33*, 401–420.

Fiske, S. T., & Neuberg, S. L. (1990). A continuum of impression formation from category-based to individuating processes: Influences of information and motivation on attention and interpretation, *Advances in experimental social psychology* (Vol. 23). New York: Academic Press.

Gaertner, S. L., Mann, J., Murrell, A., & Dovidio, J. F. (1989). Reducing intergroup bias: The benefits of recategorization. *Journal of Personality and Social Psychology*, *57*, 239–249.

Gaertner, S. L., Mann, J. A., Dovidio, J. F., Murrell, A. J., & Pomare, M. (1990). How does co-operation reduce intergroup bias? *Journal of Personality and Social Psychology*, *59*, 692–704.

Hewstone, M. (1994). Revision and change of stereotypic beliefs: In search of the elusive subtyping model. In W. Stroebe & M. Hewstone (Eds.), *European review of social psychology* (Vol. 5, pp. 69–109). New York: Wiley.

Hewstone, M., & Brown, R. (1986). Contact is not enough: An intergroup perspective on the "Contact Hypothesis". In M. Hewstone & R. Brown (Eds.), *Contact and conflict in intergroup encounters* (pp. 1–44). Oxford, UK: Blackwell.

Hewstone, M., & Lord, C. G. (1998). Changing intergroup cognitions and intergroup behavior: The role of typicality. In C. Sedikides, J. Schopler, & C. A. Insko (Eds.), *Intergroup cognition and intergroup behavior*. Mahwah, NJ: Erlbaum.

Hovland, C. I. (1959). Reconciling conflicting results derived from experimental and survey studies of attitude change. *American Psychologist*, *14*, 8–17.

Johnston, L., & Hewstone, M. (1992). Cognitive models of stereotype change. 3. Subtyping and the perceived typicality of disconfirming group members. *Journal of Experimental Social Psychology*, *28*, 360–386.

Judd, C. M., & Lusk, C. M. (1984). Knowledge structures and evaluative judgments: Effects of structural variables on judgmental extremity. *Journal of Personality and Social Psychology*, *46*(6), 1193–1207.

Judd, C. M., & Park, B. (1988). Out-group homogeneity: Judgments of variability at the individual and group levels. *Journal of Personality and Social Psychology*, *54*, 778–788.

Judd, C. M., & Park, B. (1993). Definition and assessment of accuracy in social stereotypes. *Psychological Review*, *100*, 109–128.

Judd, C. M., Ryan, C. S., & Park, B. (1991). Accuracy in the judgment of in-group and out-group variability. *Journal of Personality and Social Psychology*, *61*, 366–379.

Kelman, H. C. (1992). Coalitions across conflict lines: The interplay of conflicts within and between the Israeli and Palestinian communities. In S. Worchel & J. A. Simpson (Eds.), *Conflict between people and groups* (pp. 236–258, 293–294). Chicago, IL: Nelson-Hall.

Kunda, Z., & Oleson, K. C. (1995). Maintaining stereotypes in the face of disconfirmation: Constructing grounds for subtyping deviants. *Journal of Personality and Social Psychology*, *68*, 565–579.

Kunda, Z., & Sherman-Williams, B. (1993). Stereotypes and the construal of individuating information. *Personality and Social Psychology Bulletin, 19*, 90–99.

Lakoff, G. (1987). Cognitive models and prototype theory. In U. Neisser (Ed.), *Concepts and conceptual development: ecological and intellectual factors in categorization* (pp. 63–100). New York: Cambridge University Press.

Lee, Y.-T., Jussim, J., & McCauley, C. R. (1995). *Stereotype accuracy: Toward appreciating group differences.* (1st ed.). Washington, DC: American Psychological Association.

Lewin, K., & Grabbe, P. (1945). Conduct, knowledge, and acceptance of new values. *Journal of Social Issues, 2*, 53–64.

Lichtenstein, S., Slovic, P., Fischhoff, B., Layman, M., & Combs, B. (1978). Judged frequency of lethal events. *Journal of Experimental Psychology: Human Learning and Memory, 4*, 551–578.

Locksley, A., Hepburn, C., & Ortiz, V. (1982). Social stereotypes and judgments of individuals: An instance of the base-rate fallacy. *Journal of Experimental Social Psychology, 18*, 23–42.

Lord, C. G., Desforges, D. M., Ramsey, S. L., Trezza, G. R., & Lepper, M. R. (1991). Typicality effects in attitude-behavior consistency: Effects of category discrimination and category knowledge. *Journal of Experimental Social Psychology, 27*, 550–575.

Lord, C. G., & Lepper, M. R. (1999). Attitude representation theory. In M. P. Zanna (Ed.), *Advances in Experimental Social Psychology* (Vol. 31). San Diego, CA: Academic Press.

Mackie, D. M., & Allison, S. T. (1987). Group attribution errors and the illusion of group attitude change. *Journal of Experimental Social Psychology, 23*, 460–480.

Maurer, K. L., Park, B., & Rothbart, M. (1995). Subtyping versus subgrouping processes in stereotype representation. *Journal of Personality and Social Psychology, 69*, 812–824.

Mauro, R. (1981). *Effects of the complexity and extremity of social prototypes on perceptions of individual category members.* Unpublished Masters, Yale University, New Haven, CT.

Newcomb, T. M. (1947). Autistic hostility and social reality. *Human Relations, 1*, 69–86.

Nisbett, R. E., Zukier, H., & Lemley, R. E. (1981). The dilution effect: Nondiagnostic information weakens the implications of diagnostic information. *Cognitive Psychology, 13*, 248–277.

Nissen, M. J., Ross, J. L., Willingham, D. B., Mackenzie, T. B., Schacter, D. L. (1988). Memory and awareness in a patient with multiple personality disorder. *Brain and Cognition, 8*, 117–134.

Park, B., & Judd, C. M. (1990). Measures and models of perceived group variability. *Journal of Personality and Social Psychology, 59*, 173–191.

Park, B., & Rothbart, M. (1982). Perception of out-group homogeneity and levels of social categorization: Memory for the subordinate attributes of in-group and out-group members. *Journal of Personality and Social Psychology, 42*(6), 1051–1068.

Park, B., Ryan, C. S., & Judd, C. M. (1992). Role of meaningful subgroups in explaining differences in perceived variability for in-groups and out-groups. *Journal of Personality and Social Psychology, 63*, 553–567.

Peters, E, & Rothbart, M. (2000). Typicality can create, eliminate, and reverse the dilution effect. *Personality and Social Psychology Bulletin, 26*, 177–187.

Pettigrew, T. F. (1986). The intergroup contact hypothesis reconsidered. In M. Hewstone & R. Brown (Eds.), *Contact and conflict in intergroup encounters* (pp. 169–195). Oxford, UK: Blackwell.

Pettigrew, T. F. (1998). Intergroup contact theory. *Annual Review of Psychology, 9*, 65–85.

Rabbie, J. M., & Horwitz, M. (1969). Arousal of ingroup-outgroup bias by a chance win or loss. *Journal of Personality and Social Psychology, 13*, 269–277.

Rips, L. J. (1975). Inductive judgments about natural categories. *Journal of Verbal Learning and Verbal Behavior, 14*, 665–681.

Rosch, E. H. (1978). Principles of categorization. In E. Rosch & B. Lloyd (Eds.), *Cognition and categorization* (pp. 27–48). Hillsdale, NJ: Erlbaum.

Rosch, E. H. (1973). On the internal structure of perceptual and semantic categories. In T. E. Moore (Ed.), *Cognitive development and the acquisition of language* (pp. 111–144). New York: Academic Press.

Rothbart, M. (1996). Category-exemplar dynamics and stereotype change. *International Journal of Intercultural Relations, 20*, 305–321.

Rothbart, M., Davis-Stitt, C., & Hill, J. (1997). Effects of arbitrarily placed category boundaries on similarity judgments. *Journal of Experimental Social Psychology, 33*(2), 122–145.

Rothbart, M., Fulero, S., Jensen, C., Howard, J., & Birrell, P. (1978). From individual to group impressions: Availability heuristics in stereotype formation. *Journal of Experimental Social Psychology, 14*, 237–255.

Rothbart, M., & John, O. P. (1985). Social categorization and behavioral episodes: A cognitive analysis of the effects of intergroup contact. *Journal of Social Issues, 41*, 81–104.

Rothbart, M., & John, O. P. (1993). Intergroup relations and stereotype change: A socialcognitive analysis and some longitudinal findings. In P. M. Sniderman, P. E. Tetlock, & E. C. Carmines (Eds.), *Prejudice, politics, and the American dream* (pp. 32–59, 307–332). Stanford, CA: Stanford University Press.

Rothbart, M., John, O., & Duncan, T. (in preparation). A longitudinal analysis of stereotype change.

Rothbart, M., & Lewis, S. (1988). Inferring category attributes from exemplar attributes: Geometric shapes and social categories. *Journal of Personality and Social Psychology, 55*, 861–872.

Rothbart, M., & Park, B. (1986). On the confirmability and disconfirmability of trait concepts. *Journal of Personality and Social Psychology, 50*, 131–142.

Rothbart, M., Sriram, N., & Davis-Stitt, C. (1996). The retrieval of typical and atypical category members. *Journal of Experimental Social Psychology, 32*, 309–336.

Rothbart, M., & Taylor, M. (1992). Category labels and social reality: Do we view social categories as natural kinds? In G. R. Semin & K. Fiedler (Eds.), *Language, interaction and social cognition* (pp. 11–36). London: Sage.

Saltz, E., & Medow, M. L. (1971). Concept conservation in children: The dependence of belief systems on semantic representation. *Child Development, 42*, 1533–1542.

Scarberry, N. C., Ratcliff, C. D., Lord, C. G., Lanicek, D. L., & Desforges, D. M. (1997). Effects of individuating information on the generalization part of Allport's contact hypothesis. *Society for Personality and Social Psychology, Inc., 23*, 1291–1299.

Sia, T., Lord, C., Blessum, K., Ratcliff, C., & Lepper, M. (1997). Is a rose always a rose? The role of social category exemplar change in attitude stability and attitude-behavior consistency. *Journal of Personality and Social Psychology, 72*, 501–514.

Sherif, M., Harvey, O. J., White, B. J., Hood, W. R., & Sherif, C. W. (1988/1961). *The Robbers Cave experiment: Intergroup conflict and cooperation.* Middletown, CT: Wesleyan University Press.

Sherif, M., & Hovland, C. I. (1966). *Social judgment: Assimilation and contrast effects in communication and attitude change.* New Haven, CT: Yale University Press.

Tajfel, H., & Wilkes, A. L. (1963). Classification and quantitative judgment. *British Journal of Social Psychology, 54*, 101–114.

Turner, J. C., Hogg, M. A., Oakes, P. J., Reicher, S. D., & Wetherell, M. S. (1987). *Rediscovering the social group: A self-categorization theory.* Oxford, UK: Blackwell.

Tversky, A. (1977). Features of similarity. *Psychological Review, 84*, 327–352.

Weber, R., & Crocker, J. (1983). Cognitive processes in the revision of stereotypic beliefs. *Journal of Personality and Social Psychology, 45*, 961–977.

PART II

Cognition in Social Interaction

Introduction

The focus of the first readings in Part I of this volume was the nature of cognition about the social world. But social cognition is not only about social relationships and groups; it also develops *within* the context of social relationships, social groups, and other forms of social intercourse. Part II shifts attention from the content and structure of social cognition to the functional relationships between cognition and social interaction.

Again, the readings encompass several current themes in the study of socially shared cognition and social influences on our experience of reality. One theme is the mutual influence of language and cognition (Fiedler & Schmid; Semin). Language is a tool of both cognitive representation and social communication, so there is an intimate connection between how we encode and represent our knowledge of the world and the need to share and communicate that understanding with others. A related second theme is the role of social influence and group processes in the construction of shared meaning and distributed knowledge (Cooper, Kelly, & Weaver; Tindale, Meisenhelder, Dykema-Engblade, & Hogg). Group consensus and shared cognitive representations influence our understanding of all aspects of the world, but they have particular importance in social psychology for our understanding of social stereotypes and the construction of beliefs about intergroup relations (Fiedler & Schmid; Lorenzi-Cioldi & Clémence).

Finally, a third theme in the study of social cognition and social interaction is the role that cognitive representations play in determining the course of interpersonal relationships (Fincham; Karney, McNulty, & Bradbury). The attributions we make about the intentions, motives, and dispositions of others (especially with regard to ourselves) are a critical ingredient in whether relationships are formed in the first place, how they develop, and whether they are maintained or dissolved.

Just as the selections in Part I addressed the complex interactions among internal psychological processes (cognitions, motives, and perception), the readings in Part II tackle the complex interrelationship between internal cognitions and the external context of social relationships and social interactions.

CHAPTER EIGHT

Attributions in Close Relationships: From Balkanization to Integration

Frank D. Fincham

Following Kelley's (1967) and Jones and Davis's (1965) important elaboration and system-atization of Heider's (1958) seminal ideas about the perceived causes of behavior, attribution research replaced dissonance as the major research topic in social psychology, accounting for 11 percent of all published social-psychological research during the 1970s (Pleban & Richardson, 1979). Although the focus of attention shifted to social cognition in the 1980s, the number of articles indexed with the term attribution as a descriptor continued to rise, tripling in number between 1974 and 1984 (Smith, 1994). The publication rate has not abated in the 1990s although it appears to have plateaued at approximately 300 articles per annum (1990–8; mean = 322.8, range = 291–366).

What the numbers do not reveal, however, is a shift in the nature of research on attribution that might account for the continued prodigious output. One shift has been increasing attention to Heider's broad concern with how a perceiver links observables to underlying stable or dispositional properties ("invariances") of the world to give meaning to phenomenal experience. From this perspective, attribution is synonymous with perception and compre-hension of the environment, and draws on a variety of domains (e.g., text comprehension, world knowledge) that might help elucidate the perceiver's causal construction of events. This emphasis fits well with social cognition research that also assumes continuity between inferences made about the social and nonsocial environment, and it places attribution in a broader framework of research on how people construct mental models of the world.

The second shift has concerned the narrower and more traditional focus on linking a person's behavior to underlying properties of the person (e.g., traits, motives). Basic attribution

The preparation of this manuscript was supported by a grant from the Templeton Foundation. The author thanks Steve Beach for his comments on an earlier draft of the manuscript. Correspondence concerning this chapter should be addressed to Frank Fincham, Department of Psychology, Park Hall, SUNY at Buffalo, Buffalo, NY 14260-4110 (e-mail: fincham@buffalo.edu) research on this topic, stimulated by the classic attribution statements of Kelley (1967) and Jones and Davis (1965), began to wane in the 1980s. However, the application of an attributional framework in emerging areas of inquiry such as close relationships, and to numerous applied problems (e.g., depression), maintained a steady output of research on this topic (see Hewstone & Fincham, 1996; Weiner, 1995).

The continued vitality of attribution research has, however, brought with it increased balkanization of the literature. The lack of interplay between the two new lines of attribution research just mentioned is striking. But even more striking is the relative isolation of research within closely related areas of inquiry. For example, the impact of attributions on individual and relational outcomes has been investigated but the literatures relating to each type of outcome remain distinct.

Like the broader literature on attribution, research on attributions in close relationships has continued to flourish. Although initially focused on marital relationships, the research has broadened to embrace other relationships. But this growth has again brought with it balkanization as there is limited cross-fertilization of attributional research on different topics within the same relationship (e.g., marital violence, distressed marriages) and across research on different types of relationships (e.g., marital, parent–child and peer/friendship relationships).

It is just over 20 years since the inception of marital attribution research in social (Orvis, Kelley, & Butler, 1976) and clinical (Wright & Fichten, 1976) psychology. As the field entered its adolescence, concerns were expressed about its "lack of focus and direction" (Baucom, Epstein, Sayers & Sher, 1989, p. 31). With the onset of adulthood, it behooves us to take stock of its development. In what ways have earlier expectations for the field come to fruition? Conversely, what promises remain unfulfilled and how might they now be realized? At a minimum, we need to recognize the price of balkanization and explore how integration among various domains of attribution research, and how links with a broader psychological literature, might enhance the study of attributions in marriage.

The chapter begins with a brief historical introduction to the study of attributions in marriage. It then evaluates the current state of the art in marital attribution research, paying particular attention to developments in the past decade. This serves as a springboard for examining the marital literature in relation to the two shifts in attribution research that have balkanized the literature. The chapter concludes with a summary of the main points.

Historical Context

A vast body of research on attributions for behavior existed at the time researchers turned to study attribution in close relationships. However, they did not build on this research. Why? One reason is that basic attribution research concerned attributions made about a stranger or hypothetical other on the basis of highly restricted information and for the purpose of complying with experimenter instructions. These characteristics cast doubt on the relevance of such research for understanding attributions in relationships. Empirical findings supported this doubt. For example, Knight and Vallacher (1981) showed that attributers who believed that they were interacting with another person showed the opposite pattern of attributions for that person's positive (situationally attributed) versus negative (disposition attributed) behavior compared to attributers who only expected to interact with the person at a later time. Detached observers did not make different attributions for these two forms of behavior. In a similar vein, persons tend to make stronger internal attributions for positive behavior performed by a friend or a spouse than for an acquaintance (Taylor & Koivumaki, 1976).

Interestingly, the discontinuity between the basic attribution research and research that emerged on attributions in close relationships extended to theory. Thus, for example, a seminal volume on close relationships published in the early 1980s (Kelley et al., 1983) makes no reference to Jones and Davis (1965) or to Kelley (1967). Reference to these works is also absent in recent, comprehensive overviews of the field (e.g., Berscheid & Reis, 1998; Hinde, 1997). This disjuncture is particularly surprising as both fields have an influential common ancestor in Hal Kelley.

What then were the historical antecedents of attributional research in marriage? Two general roots can be traced. In social psychology Kelley was struck by the frequency with which intimates mentioned stable, general properties of the partner (usually dispositions) when describing relationship problems (see Kelley, 1979). This led to the investigation of atttributional conflict or disagreement between a person and their partner about the cause of the person's behavior (Orvis et al., 1976; Passer, Kelley, & Michela, 1978; see also Harvey, Wells, & Alvarez, 1978)[1]. A major finding to emerge from this research was that actors preferred explanations for their negative behavior that reflected a positive attitude to the partner, whereas partners preferred explanations that reflected the actor's negative attitudes and/or traits. The characterization of attributions along an evaluative dimension suggested that satisfaction experienced by the partners may covary with attributions, a possibility which turned out to be the wellspring of marital attribution research in clinical psychology.

The origins of marital attribution research in clinical psychology did not, however, build on Kelley's work, even though Kelley had focused on marital conflict (see Braiker & Kelley, 1979), a topic that was central to clinical research (marital dysfunction was seen to result from a couple's ineffective response to conflict, Jacobson & Margolin, 1979). Instead, the attribution perspective was brought to bear on the dominant pursuit of the time, the attempt to understand what differentiates distressed from nondistressed spouses so as to better understand the determinants of marital satisfaction and thereby improve marital therapy. Accordingly, the focus of most studies tended to be some variant of the hypothesis that attributions are associated with marital satisfaction. Interestingly, this hypothesis was later shown to be consistent with Heider's (1958, pp. 207, 258) observations linking the liking of a person to the attributions made for his/her behavior (see Bradbury & Fincham, 1990).

Interest in the attribution–satisfaction association was facilitated by two factors. At the global level, it was stimulated by dissatisfaction with the limits of a behavioral account of marriage and a subsequent shift in research emphasis from the study of observed behavior to examination of intraindividual factors (cognition, emotions) that might enrich understanding of overt behavior. At a more specific level, excitement was generated by the implicit causal assumption that attributions for marital events (e.g., spouse arrives home late from work) can promote marital satisfaction (e.g., "s/he is working hard to make us financially secure") or distress (e.g., "s/he only cares about work and not about me," see Bagarozzi & Giddings, 1983).

Although originating in social and clinical psychology, the applied concerns of clinical researchers soon dominated the marital attribution literature. Before turning to this literature, it is worth noting some legacies of these historical origins as they inform the evaluation offered in the next section of the chapter.

First, marital researchers drew upon causal attribution dimensions in clinical psychology (e.g., Abramson, Seligman, & Teasdale's, 1978, attributional analysis of learned helplessness) rather than in social psychology (e.g., Weiner, Russel, & Lerman's, 1978, attributional analysis of emotion). This affected both the types of attributions initially investigated (causal attributions) as well as the manner in which they were investigated (in most research spouses rated causal dimensions). Ironically, however, it was not recognized that the locus, stability, and globality dimensions in the attributional reformulation of learned helplessness theory can be directly linked to Kelley's (1967) criteria of consensus, consistency, and distinctiveness.

Second, the evaluative implications of attributions in relationships were underscored by clinical observations that couples "typically view therapy as a way to demonstrate . . . that they are blameless and the other is at fault" (Jacobson & Margolin, 1979). This led to the suggestion that issues of responsibility and blame are particularly germane in relationships (Fincham, 1983). Whereas causal attributions concern who or what produced an event, responsibility entails assessment of who is accountable for the event once a cause is known. Blame, in turn, entails an assessment of responsibility (see Fincham & Jaspars, 1980; Shaver, 1985). As a consequence, responsibility attribution dimensions (e.g., intent, motivation) and blame attributions, in addition to causal attributions, became the subject of study in the marital literature. Figure 8.1 illustrates schematically the attribution hypothesis investigated in the marital literature showing that the pattern of attributions expected varies as a function of the valence of the event and the marital satisfaction of the attributer.

Third, the fact that attribution theory is one element of Heider's (1958) attempt to systematize common sense ("naïve psychology"), means that, as intuitive or lay psychologists, everyone has access to the ideas informing attribution theory. As a result, one can "set up studies without being very explicit about the attribution process" (Kelley in Harvey, Ickes, & Kidd, 1978, p. 375). This is particularly evident in marital attribution research. It manifested itself most obviously in the need to uncover unarticulated assumptions and build basic theory (Thompson & Snyder, 1986) and in measurement where dependent measures sometimes had nothing to do with attributions (e.g., estimates of behavioral frequency for assessment of causal stability, Holtzworth-Munroe & Jacobson, 1985, p. 1402). The upshot is remarkable variety in work that appears under the attribution rubric in the marital literature.

Attributions and Marriage: A Synopsis and Critique

The purpose of the present section is threefold. The first goal is to identify themes in marital attribution research that might reveal underlying coherence in the literature. The second is to provide a synopsis of the literature. As several earlier reviews are available (e.g., Bradbury & Fincham, 1990; Baucom, 1987; Harvey, 1987; Thomson & Snyder, 1986), the focus is on research that has appeared in the last decade. This leads naturally to the third goal, to evaluate progress by identifying both actualized and forgone opportunities as well as new

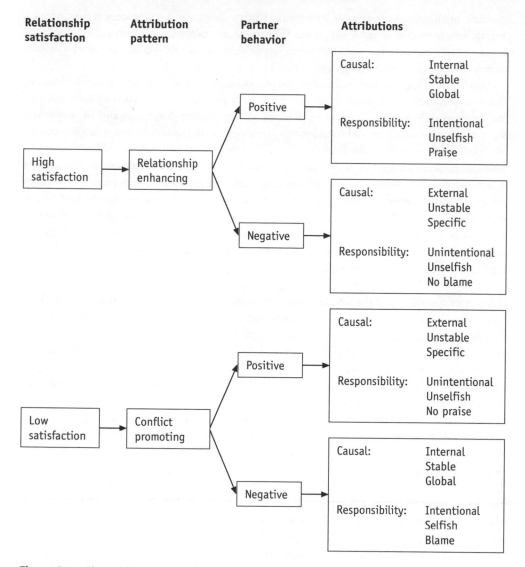

Figure 8.1 The attribution hypothesis in research on close relationships

lines of inquiry suggested by extant research. This, in turn, sets the stage for the next section of the chapter in which links are drawn with research outside of the marital area.

Taking stock

The attribution–satisfaction association. Early on, Thompson and Snyder (1986, p. 136) concluded that "research has supported a strong association between attributional processes and relationship satisfaction." Although perhaps premature, this conclusion was prescient. By the turn of the decade there were 23 relevant studies and across attributional dimensions an average of 80 percent of them supported the attribution hypothesis (Fincham, Bradbury, & Scott, 1990). Support for the attribution hypothesis has continued to accrue in the past decade and no data have emerged to contradict the hypothesis.

This is not to suggest that results obtained across measures and methodologies are identical. For example, Sabourin, Lussier, & Wright (1991), in a successful cross-cultural replication of the attribution hypothesis, found that attributions for marital difficulties and for hypothetical partner behaviors were only moderately correlated, with the former more often accounting for unique variance in satisfaction. They called for a standardized attribution measure to facilitate greater comparison of findings across studies, and the measurement of attributions is a topic that has received increased attention (see the section, "Delineating the domain of attributions," below). Although the relations among attributions obtained using different methodologies (e.g., thought listing, couple conversations, questionnaires) remain unknown, the association with satisfaction is robust. Indeed, the evidence for an association between attribution and marital satisfaction is overwhelming, making it possibly the most robust, replicable phenomenon in the study of marriage.

Threats to the validity of the attribution–satisfaction association. Concern about the validity of the attribution–satisfaction association has long been evident. Early work ruled out possible methodological artifacts (e.g., independent assessment of attributions and satisfaction, common method variance) and examined depression as a theoretically relevant variable that might account for the association (see Bradbury & Fincham, 1990). As the number of potentially relevant third variables can never be exhausted, it is not surprising to find continued work on this front throughout the 1990s.

Senchak and Leonard (1993) showed that demographic variables and anger did not account for the association and provided further evidence to show that the association was independent of depressive symptoms. They extended prior findings by demonstrating that with affect (anger and depression) of both self *and* partner controlled, attributions accounted for unique variance in satisfaction. In a similar vein, attributions for partner behavior have not been associated with the status of spouses as clinically depressed versus nondepressed (Bauserman, Arias, & Craighead, 1995; Bradbury, Beach, Fincham, & Nelson, 1996). It also appears that negative affectivity more generally (as indexed by neuroticism and depressive mood) does not account for the attribution–satisfaction relation; the association has emerged after controlling for the negative affectivity of both spouses and is independent of measurement error (Karney, Bradbury, Fincham, & Sullivan, 1994). Finally, the demonstration that the attribution–satisfaction association is independent of depression is consistent with findings obtained using dating couples (Fletcher, Fitness & Blampied, 1990).

A new third variable explanation for the attribution–satisfaction relation was raised in a study of marital violence. Holtzworth-Munroe and Hutchinson (1993) found that while violent husbands were more likely to attribute blame, negative intent, and selfish motivation to their wives than satisfied, nonviolent men, the attributions of maritally dissatisfied, nonviolent men did not differ from either of these two groups. If replicated, this finding would show that marital attribution phenomena may be attributable to the high rates of aggression and violence found in some married couples. However, the attribution–satisfaction association has been demonstrated in a sample of nonviolent husbands and also remains significant when marital violence is partialed out of the association (Fincham, Bradbury, Arias, Byrne, & Karney, 1997).

Ruling out threats to validity does not document the importance of attributions in marriage. Although robust, the attribution–satisfaction association may be unimportant for understanding marriage. Alternatively, it may simply reflect what Weiss (1980) has labeled "sentiment override" – the hypothesis that spouses respond noncontingently to partner behavior or questions about the marriage. In other words, spouses simply respond in terms of their dominant feeling or sentiment about the marriage and this is reflected "in as many tests as one chooses to administer" (Weiss & Heyman, 1990, p. 92). Belief in this position is so strong that attempts to explain variance in marital quality using self-reports have been characterized as "invalid from a scientific standpoint" (Gottman, 1990, p. 79). A fundamental task for the field therefore has been to show that attributions increase understanding of marriage and are not simply a proxy index of marital sentiment.

Documenting the importance of attributions in marriage. One way to address the importance of attributions in marriage is to provide evidence for the assumption that attributions influence marital satisfaction. Such evidence raises the question of how attributions might exert any causal influence. Although any effect may be direct, it may also occur indirectly through spouse behavior. Thus, certain attributions for partner behavior (e.g., rejection of a sexual advance) may be conflict promoting (e.g., "you don't really love me"). This highlights a second important assumption that stimulated interest in spousal attributions, the possibility that attributions may influence marital behavior. For example, attributions might explain interaction patterns (e.g., negative reciprocity) identified with marital distress. Each assumption is addressed in turn.

Attributions and marital satisfaction: A causal association? A possible causal association between attributions and satisfaction has been investigated primarily through longitudinal studies. Because only the variance that attributions do not share with marital quality is used to predict changes in marital quality, it is difficult to account for significant findings by arguing that attributions simply index marital quality.

Four new longitudinal studies supplement early findings showing that attributions predict later satisfaction in dating (Fletcher, Fincham, Cramer, & Heron, 1987) and married couples (Fincham & Bradbury, 1987a). In established marriages (mean length = 9.4 years) causal attributions predicted satisfaction 12 months later for both husbands and wives (Fincham & Bradbury, 1993). However, husbands' initial satisfaction also predicted change in their attributions suggesting a possible bidirectional causal relation between attributions and satisfaction. This study also ruled out depressive symptoms as a factor responsible for the longitudinal association and showed that the findings did not change when those who were chronically depressed or distressed were excluded from the sample. In a sample of newlywed husbands, conflict-promoting responsibility attributions contributed to declines in reported satisfaction 12 months later but not vice versa (Fincham, Bradbury, et al., 1997), thereby showing that the longitudinal pattern of findings extends beyond the population of established married couples.

The longitudinal association between attributions and satisfaction has also been replicated over an 18-month period and appears to be mediated by the impact of attributions on efficacy expectations which, in turn, influenced satisfaction (Fincham, Harold, & Gano-Phillips, in press). In this study, evidence was also obtained to support bidirectional effects in that satisfaction predicted attributions for both husbands and wives.

Finally, Karney and Bradbury (in press) provided novel data on the longitudinal relation through the application of growth curve modeling to eight waves of data collected over the first four years of marriage. They found intraindividual changes in attribution and in marital satisfaction covaried but found no evidence to suggest that either attributions or satisfaction were causally dominant. However, a different picture emerged at the between-subjects level of analysis. Controlling for within-subject covariation, initial attributions had greater effects on the trajectory of marital satisfaction than Time 1 satisfaction had on the trajectory of attributions. Specifically, more conflict-promoting attributions at Time 1 were associated with lower initial marital satisfaction, steeper declines in satisfaction, and satisfaction that covaried less with subsequent changes in attributions. Finally, wives' attributions improved prediction of marital dissolution and both husbands' and wives' changes in attributions were more strongly associated with deviations from the trajectory of marital satisfaction in marriages that dissolved.

In sum, there is a growing body of evidence consistent with the view that attributions influence marital satisfaction and increasing evidence that any causal relation between the two variables is bidirectional. Perhaps not surprisingly, attributions continue to be emphasized in newer, therapeutic interventions for couples (e.g., by offering a "formulation," an element of integrative couples therapy designed to promote non-blaming, Jacobson & Christensen, 1996, pp. 41–58). This highlights the opportunity to gain experimental evidence on the causal role of attributions but interest in such research appears to have evaporated (for an exception see Davidson & Horvath, 1997) following early demonstrations that supplementing standard therapies with an attribution intervention module did not improve therapeutic outcome (see Bradbury & Fincham, 1990). Unfortunately, the impact of attributions on therapeutic outcome has not been directly evaluated and nor has the importance of attributional change as a precursor to progress and positive change in marital therapy (see Fincham, Bradbury, & Beach, 1990). These considerations suggest that intervention research remains a potential source of important information (see the section, "Expressed emotion," below).

Attributions and behavior.   Despite its theoretical and applied significance, few studies have investigated the attribution–behavior link. Moreover, early attempts to do so were quite limited (see Bradbury & Fincham, 1990, p. 24). With the exception of an early experimental study in which manipulated attributions influenced subsequent observed behavior in distressed but not nondistressed spouses (Fincham & Bradbury, 1988), evidence bearing on the attribution–observed behavior relation is quite recent.

Five studies report data relating attributions to behavior observed during marital interaction (Bradbury, Beach, et al., 1996; Bradbury & Fincham, 1992, Study 1 & 2; Fincham & Bradbury, 1992, Study 3; G. E. Miller & Bradbury, 1995). Across 28 tests of the attribution–behavior association found in these studies, the mean effect size was .34; the "fail safe" number or number of unretrieved null findings that would allow one to attribute this effect size to sampling bias was 1,527. This moderate effect size, however, reflects a heterogeneous set of findings (chi-square (27) = 47, $p < .01$). One clear source of heterogeneity was spouse gender which was strongly associated with effect size ($r = .57$); the average effect size for men (mean $z = .23$) was smaller than that for women (mean $z = .45$). Although encouraging, these meta-analytic findings should be viewed with caution as they use a database that includes simple, bivariate correlations between attributions and rates of behavior. In view of earlier comments about sentiment override and the documented association between spousal satisfaction and behavior (Weiss & Heyman, 1997), it is important to show that an attribution–behavior association is independent of marital satisfaction.

With marital satisfaction partialed from the attribution–behavior relation, it has been shown that conflict-promoting responsibility attributions are related to: (1) wives' less effect-ive problem-solving behaviors (Bradbury & Fincham, 1992, Study 1); (2) more negative behaviors during problem-solving and support-giving tasks (G. E. Miller & Bradbury, 1995) and that this association is independent of level of depression (Bradbury, Beach, et al., 1996); (3) specific affects (whining and anger) displayed during problem solving (Fincham & Bradbury, 1992, Study 3); and (4) husbands' and wives' conflict-promoting attributions are related to increased rates of negative behavior during a problem-solving discussion (Bradbury & Fincham, 1992, Study 2). There is some evidence to suggest that the attribution–behavior association is moderated by marital quality in that it is stronger for distressed spouses and tends to occur more consistently for responsibility attributions (e.g., Bradbury & Fincham, 1992; G. E. Miller & Bradbury, 1995).

A recent study by Fletcher and Thomas (2000) provided the first longitudinal data on the relation between attributions and observed behavior. Using a sample of couples randomly selected from the New Zealand electoral rolls, they found that both husbands' and wives' conflict-promoting attributions for marital problems were associated with more negative interaction behavior over a 12-month period. Interestingly, earlier behavior was not related to later attributions, a pattern of findings consistent with the view that attributions influence behavior. A second important finding from this study was that attributions mediated the relation between marital satisfaction and behavior for both husbands and wives at Time 1 and again for husbands at Time 2. These mediational effects were shown to be independent of length of marriage and the seriousness of the problems from which observational data were obtained and for which spouses made attributions.

In sum, available evidence is consistent with the view that attributions influence behavior. This conclusion, however, rests on an important assumption. Because attributions are assessed at a global level rather than for the specific behaviors in the observed interaction, implicit is the view that these global attributions determine attributions for specific behaviors. It therefore remains to demonstrate that global attributions shape attributions for specific behaviors which, in turn, influence responses to the behavior (for a discussion of the issues in relating cognition to interactional behavior, see Fletcher & Kininmonth, 1991). Finally, the correlational nature of the data should not be overlooked.

Delineating the domain of attributions. Delineation of the domain to which the term attribution applies has been identified as the "single most significant barrier to progress" (Fincham, 1985, p. 205) in marital attribution research. Progress is facilitated on this task to the extent that attention is given to identifying the basic dimensions of underlying causal explanations in marriage, the measurement of these dimensions, and the types of attributions important in marriage.

Sayers and Baucom (1995) have attempted to identify underlying dimensions of causal explanations for marital problems. Using explanations offered by spouses, they employed college students' perceptions of the causes for a multidimensional scaling analysis to select a subset of causes to employ in a second multidimensional scaling analysis using spouses' perceptions of the causes. The use of college students is unfortunate as it undermines the study's attempt to document dimensions that are psychologically meaningful for spouses, and the solution they report for spouses is necessarily a function of the stimuli that were selected using student perceptions. The resulting complex set of findings with different, four-dimensional solutions for husbands and for wives, nonetheless identified a dimension in both spouses' solutions (relationship schism and disharmony versus other factors [husband]/family factors [wife]) that is consistent with one of Passer et al.'s. (1978) dimensions (positive versus negative attitude towards partner). This finding again emphasizes the implicit evaluative aspect of explanation in close relationships. Sayers and Baucom (1995) concluded that attributional assessment should move beyond assessment of traditional causal dimensions, a feature that is evident in progress to develop attribution measures.

Sabourin et al.'s (1991) earlier noted call for a standardized attribution measure has met with two quite different responses. One has been to develop measures to assess specific attributional content. For example, the development of a measure of dysfunctional attributions includes a subscale that assesses the extent to which partner behavior reflects "lack of love" (Pretzer, Epstein, & Fleming, 1991). Similarly, in their attributional assessment of problems in 12 domains of relationship functioning (e.g., finances, leisure) Baucom, Epstein, et al. (1996) inquire about attributional content (e.g., boundaries: "we disagree about how much of our lives to share with each other in this area of the relationship") and underlying attribution dimensions (as well as self-reported emotional and behavioral responses). Perhaps the most obvious problem with this approach is that it gives rise to nonindependent assessment of attributions and marital satisfaction (disagreement is assessed in both measures, see Fincham & Bradbury, 1987b), making reported associations (see Baucom, Epstein et al., 1996) tautologous. Second, there is a potentially vast domain of attributionally relevant content, a problem that led early attribution researchers to derive (both empirically and rationally) underlying attribution dimensions. Finally, this approach reinforces the earlier noted balkanization of the attribution literature as it militates against developing an attributional perspective that might transcend relationship type.

In contrast, the second response to the need for a broadly accepted, standard measure has been limited to assessment of attribution dimensions. However, it has also addressed the issue of attribution type by building on distinctions among causal, responsibility, and blame attributions documented in basic research. In fact, the presupposition or entailment model in which a blame attribution presupposes a judgment of responsibility, which, in turn, rests upon the determination of causality, was strongly supported among 206 cohabiting couples when they made judgments about relationship conflict (Lussier, Sabourin, & Wright, 1993). Unfortunately this study used single item measures of each attribution type. The use of multiple item measures has revealed that partners do not distinguish readily between responsibility and blame (Fincham & Bradbury, 1992). Although it is possible to imagine circumstances under which such distinctions may be made, only the distinction between causal (locus, stability, and globality) and responsibility dimensions (intent, motivation, blame) are incorporated in the measure resulting from this line of research – the *Relationship Attribution Measure* (RAM; Fincham & Bradbury, 1992). Advantages of this measure include its demonstrated relation to satisfaction and observed behavior, its brevity, its simplicity for respondents, the provision of indices for different types of attributions, and the potential to modify the scale in order to obtain analogous measures across relationship types (cf. *Children's Relationship Attribution Measure*, Fincham, Beach, Arias, & Brody, 1998). Although cause and responsibility attributions yielded by this measure are highly correlated ($r = .7-.8$), recent research confirms that a two-factor measurement model provides a significantly better fit to the data than a single-factor model (Davey, Fincham, Beach, & Brody, 1999).

In sum, there has been some progress in delineating the domain of attributions in marital research. However, this progress is largely a function of the attempt to develop measures and has been isolated from developments in a broader literature on attributions, leaving unresolved the importance of earlier, identified distinctions (e.g., interpersonal attributions, dyadic attributions, see Newman, 1981).

Some other developments. The foregoing themes capture much of the recent activity in the marital attribution literature. However, without mentioning two further themes the picture painted of developments over the past decade would be incomplete.

The first theme can be characterized in terms of the domain specificity of attributional phenomena. In marriage research it is manifest by the emergence of a quasi-independent literature on attributions for marital violence (for a review see Eckhardt & Dye, in press). Thus, for example, attributions for violent versus nonviolent partner behavior appear to differ (Holtzworth-Munroe, Jacobson, Fehrenbach & Fruzzetti, 1992), hostile attributions are evoked more readily in specific content domains (jealousy, spousal rejection, and potential public embarrassment) among violent men (Holtzworth-Munroe & Hutchinson, 1993), and are more likely to be spontaneously verbalized in this group (Eckhardt, Barbour, & Davison, 1998). Although the focus has been primarily on violent men, causal and responsibility attributions also correlate with wife-to-husband aggression (Byrne & Arias, 1997), mediate the relation between increased violence and wives' intentions to leave the relationship (Pape & Arias, in press), and responsibility attributions moderate the association between husband violence and wives' marital dissatisfaction (Katz, Arias, Beach, & Brody, 1995). Explicit recognition of possible domain specificity in relationship attribution phenomena is important. A move from content free to content specific inference rules would link marital attribution research to the broader cognitive literature in which specific knowledge of the world is central to understanding cognitive functioning.

A second theme, particularly evident in the early 1990s, was the development of general theoretical frameworks. These not only focused on the study of attribution/cognition in marriage (e.g., Epstein & Baucom, 1993; Fletcher & Fincham, 1991) but also integrated such study into a broader organizational framework for researching close relationships (e.g., Bradbury & Fincham, 1991). In these frameworks explicit links were drawn to broader literatures, particularly the social cognition literature, and we return to them in the section, "Social cognition," below.

Critique

The themes reviewed have already been critiqued and the present section therefore highlights some of the opportunities forgone in the marital attribution literature. In doing so, however, it is important to acknowledge the potential realized during the field's adolescence: confirmation of a robust attribution–satisfaction association, demonstration that this phenomenon is not an artifact, accumulation of systematic evidence that speaks to two central causal hypotheses, progress in identifying the types and underlying dimensions of attributions and how to measure them, careful theoretical specification of the role of attributions in understanding marriage, and attempts to locate marital attributional phenomena in broader, more comprehensive frameworks. Notwithstanding these achievements, a number of important topics received little or no attention in the 1990s.

Revisiting the beginnings of attributional research in close relationships is instructive. Orvis et al. (1976) studied attributions not as private events but as public behaviors. The implications are profound but remain relatively unexplored (see Bradbury & Fincham, 1990, p. 26–28). Three of these are highlighted. First, attributional understanding in relationships can result from dyadic interaction. However, we know relatively little about how spouses negotiate particular explanations to achieve a shared understanding of relationship events, yet such negotiated understanding is central to some accounts of marriage (see Berger & Kellner, 1970). Here a broader literature on accounts and their communication in relationships is relevant (e.g., Fincham 1992; Weber, Harvey, & Orbuch, 1992) but has not been tapped in marital attribution research possibly because the narratives studied in the accounts literature transcend the level of analysis found in attribution research.

Second, the identification of attributions as public events raises the question of their relation to attributions as private events. Early on, the relation between these two types of events was identified as an important issue (e.g., Bradbury & Fincham, 1988) along with the need to study public attributions (e.g., Holtzworth-Munroe & Jacobson, 1988) but neither have received attention in the marital attribution literature in the past decade.

Third, Orvis et al.'s (1976) work focused on self–partner discrepancies in attribution. Despite early evidence suggesting that discrepancies in attributions for self and partner behavior might advance understanding of the attribution–satisfaction association (e.g., Kyle & Falbo, 1985), self–partner attribution differences have not gained attention over the 1990s. Consideration of the relation between self and partner attributions highlights a further gap that is endemic to close relationships research, the need to study phenomena at the dyadic level. Although several studies have controlled for partner influence in examining the outcomes related to a spouse's attributions (e.g., Senchak & Leonard, 1993; Karney et al., 1994), evidence has only recently emerged to demonstrate the necessity of a dyadic model in examining attribution phenomena (Davey et al., 1999). Finally, study of attributions for self-behavior alerts one to the possibility that self-processes require consideration in a complete attributional account of marriage. Indeed, Kelley (1979, p. 109) notes attributions for partner behavior have implications for the self creating interdependence at the level of inferred dispositions of partners. In any event, it is clear that relating marital attribution research to research on self-processes is long overdue.

Perhaps more important than the relative lack of attention to the above implications, is the failure to systematically explore the assumption that spouses exhibit a tendency to make particular attributions "across different situations and across time" (Metalsky & Abramson, 1981, p. 38). As Karney and Bradbury (in press) point out, the presumed causal role of attributions in maintaining marital dissatisfaction, and attention to attributions in therapy, only make sense to the extent that spouses exhibit an "attribution style." Shifting attention from mean scores to consistency in attributions gives rise to an interesting variant of the attribution hypothesis in which variability in responses on attribution dimensions and patterns of responses across attributional dimensions is related to satisfaction. Although inconsistent findings have emerged for variability in responding on attribution dimensions, there is consistent evidence relating patterns in attributions across dimensions to marital satisfaction (Baucom, Sayers, & Duhe, 1989; Horneffer & Fincham, 1995). However, Karney and Bradbury's (in press) intraindividual analysis showed that attribution responses were not constant across time; wives' attributions became more conflict-promoting over the first four years of marriage and significant interindividual variability among husbands supported a linear change model even though group mean scores did not change. These findings suggest that attributional style does not operate as a trait. However, the conceptual status of "attributional style" is far from resolved.

Finally, a general feature of the marital attribution research is worth noting because it draws attention to a domain of inquiry that has yet to be exploited. Broadly speaking, marital researchers have been concerned with the consequences of attributions and can be said to have developed an attribution based approach to study marriage. Kelley and Michela (1980) distinguish such "attributional theory" from a second genre of attribution research that focuses on the antecedents and processes that lead to attributions. Although attention to this latter type of research is not entirely absent from the marital domain, attribution antecedents and processes have not been studied systematically. However, the events studied in marital attribution research may be important. For example, the feature-positive bias in which inferences about own attitude are influenced more by reactions to stimuli than by failures to react (Fazio, Sherman, & Herr, 1982) suggests that partner behaviors that prompt a reaction may be more likely to instigate attributional processing than those that do not prompt a reaction. In a similar vein, basic attribution research showing that people are considered more responsible for commissions than omissions (Fincham & Jaspars, 1980), may have implications for the demand–withdraw pattern of interaction. Specifically, attributions for demand behaviors (commissions) may differ from those for withdrawal behaviors (omissions).

This critique, like the review preceding it, is not intended to be exhaustive. Rather it serves as a springboard for the remainder of the chapter, which is intended as an antidote to the balkanization noted at the outset. As will soon be evident, the broader literature is relevant to many of the concerns noted in this critique and suggests several new directions for marital attribution research.

> **From Myopia to Presbyopia: Setting the**
> **Stage for an Attributional Analysis**
> **of Close Relationships**

In its youthful zest, marital attribution research has been somewhat egocentric, a characteristic that has served it well in focusing energy on establishing replicable phenomena, documenting their relevance, and so on. As it enters adulthood, however, the area has the opportunity to look further afield and fashion its identity in new ways. The purpose of this section is to draw connections with domains of inquiry that have the potential to enrich the study of attributions in marriage and contribute to an integrative, attributional account of close relationships. This will be done in relation to three domains of increasing generality, namely, relevant attribution research in family relationships, attribution research and adaptational outcomes, and research on social cognition.

Balkanization on the home front

Perhaps the most obvious starting point for enriching marital research is to examine overlooked areas of attributional research involving family relationships. Two examples with quite different origins and implications for the study of marriage are examined.

Expressed emotion.   In the late 1950s English researchers noted that the success of psychiatric patients released into the community was related to the kind of living group to which they returned, with those returning to the parental or matrimonial home faring worse than those who went to live in lodgings or with siblings (e.g., Brown, Carstairs, & Topping, 1958). Subsequent research identified the emotion expressed toward the patient by key relatives at the time of hospital admission, particularly hostility and criticism, to be a reliable predictor of the patient's relapse following hospital discharge (e.g., Vaughn & Leff, 1976; see Bebbington & Kuipers, 1994, for a review).

Attempts to understand the mechanism underlying the expressed emotion (EE)–relapse association led to an attributional analysis. Vaughn and Leff (1976) suggested that EE was associated with attributing patient behavior to personal characteristics of the patient rather than to the illness. Others went on to identify as critical the patient's perceived control over the causes of the symptoms (e.g., Hooley, 1987); undesirable patient behavior attributed to causes potentially under the patient's control were hypothesized to result in high EE whereas those attributed to the illness would lead to greater tolerance (low EE). Hooley, Richters, Weintraub, & Neale (1987) provided initial, indirect evidence consistent with this formulation in that spouses of patients with "positive" symptoms (those most easily attributed to illness, e.g., hallucinatory behaviors) were more maritally satisfied than those whose spouses displayed "negative" symptoms (behavioral deficits, e.g., lack of emotion). Direct assessment of attributions has confirmed the above predicted attributional difference in high and low EE relatives (Barrowclough, Johnston, & Tarrier, 1994; Brewin, MacCarthy, Duda, & Vaughn, 1991; Hooley & Licht, 1997).

Why is this research relevant? In addition to providing further, converging evidence that attributions may be important for understanding relationship behavior, it points to a major deficit in the marital attribution literature, the emotional dimension of marriage. It is difficult to imagine a comprehensive account of marriage that fails to accord emotion a central role, yet the marital attributional literature has little to say about emotion. This is all the more surprising given Weiner's (1986) attributional theory of emotion which again serves to underline discontinuity between marital and basic attribution research and theory.

One obvious implication is to consider how Weiner's theory can contribute to an understanding of marriage. According to Weiner, the valence of an event determines the initial emotional response (if positive, happy; if negative, frustrated and sad), but the perceived dimensions underlying the causes of the event determine the specific affect experienced. The focus on specific affect accords with developments in the marital domain where specific affects play a prominent role (Gottman, 1994). Specifically, Gottman (p. 184) contends that what makes marital conflict dysfunctional is "the response to one's partner with criticism, disgust, contempt, defensiveness and stonewalling" and he goes on to argue that his data support a chained effect in which complain/criticize → contempt → defensiveness → stonewalling.

An attributional analysis may facilitate an understanding of entry into, and initial movement along, this chain. Weiner's (1986) theory is helpful in understanding the initiation of overt conflict through the generation of anger towards the other (it follows the same logic outlined above in regard to EE). Anger, in Weiner's (1995, p. 18) writing is seen as an accusation that reflects the belief that the person could and should have behaved differently and "provides a bridge between thinking and conduct." Thus Weiner's analysis gets us to the point where overt conflict may arise but there is a subtle difference between disagreement and the initial step towards dysfunctional conflict.

It seems likely that it is the interplay among causal dimensions that may result in the shift from an initial complaint to criticism. Thus, prior experience with the partner in relation to the complaint or in related areas (which is likely to be reflected in causal globality and stability attribution ratings), would produce the shift from complaint to more global criticism. The further shift to contempt may reflect crossing a certain threshold in the configuration of responses on the causal dimensions. Although Gottman (1994, p. 415) believes the specific emotion cascade outlined above fits well "as a behavioral counterpart to attribution theories of marriage," the ultimate viability of the attributional analysis suggested here is less important than the goal of identifying a much needed integration. An integration of emotion and attribution research clearly transcends the scope of the present chapter.

Before leaving the topic of EE, it behooves us to note that this domain may provide one of the best opportunities to obtain experimental evidence on attributions and relationship outcomes. This is because intervention studies that reduce EE among relatives show significant decreases, relative to controls, in patient relapse rates at 6, 9, and 24 months and greater compliance with a medication regime (see Mari & Streiner, 1994, for a review). Such studies address only indirectly the attributional account of EE but it seems to be a small step to examine whether changes in relatives' attributions predict patient outcome. Brewin (1994) has made a promising start in showing that changes in relatives' hostility following intervention were associated with changed attributions and that these changes could not be ascribed to changes in the patient's behavior.

Parent–child relationships.   Unlike EE research, attributional analyses of parent–child relationships are rooted in attribution theory in social psychology. Thus, for example, Dix and
Grusec (1985) offer an exemplary application of Kelley (1967) and Jones and Davis's (1965)
models in their analysis of parent attributions in the socialization of children. Since then a
substantial literature has emerged on attributions in parent–child relationships. As reviews of
this literature are available elsewhere (e.g., Bugenthal & Goodnow, 1998; Joiner & Wagner,
1996; S. A. Miller, 1995), only selected aspects of this literature are highlighted to illustrate
a potential interplay with marital attribution research.

Perhaps the most obvious point to make in linking the two literatures is that study of the
parent–child relationship provides further evidence supporting phenomena documented in
the marital literature. Thus, for example, it is well established that parental attributions are
linked to parent satisfaction (e.g., Sacco & Murray, 1997) and to parenting behavior (e.g.,
Bugenthal & Shennum, 1984). Indeed, this literature provides much-needed experimental
data to show that attributions influence behavior. Slep and O'Leary (1998) showed that
mothers led to believe that their children were misbehaving voluntarily, and with negative
intent, were overreactive in observed discipline and reported somewhat more anger compared
to mothers who believed the misbehavior was due to the experimental situation. More
recently, children's attributions for parent behavior have also been shown to relate to their
satisfaction with the parent and to behavior observed with the parent (Fincham, Beach, et al.,
1998). The consistency of findings across relationship types is unusual and speaks to the
need to document pan-relational phenomena for a science of close relationships (Berscheid,
1994). Unfortunately, "thus far there has been little attempt to integrate findings from the
two literatures" (S. A. Miller, 1995, p. 1579).

Turning to the parent–child literature does more than provide additional evidence for
the themes studied by marital researchers; it also identifies new lines of inquiry as well as the
need to revisit exactly what is studied in attribution research. This can be illustrated by
focusing on two features of the parent–child relationship. First, there is a clear imbalance in
status and power that necessarily shapes attributional research on this relationship. The
specifics of the research are less important in the present context than the fact that power and
status have been ignored in marital attribution research. This oversight is emphasized by
Heider's (1958, p. 259) observation that "the power of *o* is an important determinant of *p*'s
general evaluation and reaction to an act of harm or benefit. Not only will *p*'s perception
of who is responsible for the act be influenced, but also his understanding of the reasons
motivating the act."

Attention to power provides a different perspective on sex differences in marital attributions. For example, the stronger association between wives' attributions and their behavior
may reflect the fact that women have typically commanded less power in marriage. This
could explain the attribution–behavior sex difference because, relative to less powerful actors,
more powerful actors are seen to be exerting their will and hence attributions for their
behavior are particularly diagnostic (and presumably can be more safely used to guide behavior).
If this account is correct, one might also postulate that wives are more likely to be attentive
to, and make attributions for, partner behavior.

Power and status are equally important for attributions in egalitarian marriages. This
is because making certain attributions for a partner behavior (e.g., "he's offering to help

because he thinks I'm incompetent") may imply a change in the power relation. As emphasized by the extension of self-evaluation maintenance process to marriage (e.g., Beach & Tesser, 1995), the implication may be more or less important depending on the relevance of the domain to the self and partner (e.g., for high partner/low self relevance it should have minimal impact). One resulting hypothesis is that acts with real or symbolic implications for status and power will be subject to close attributional analysis and that one class of such acts that can readily evoke issues of power/status are those that benefit another. Thus, contrary to the accepted view that only negative events evoke attribution processing (Weiner, 1985), in relationships certain positive events may also do so. The resulting attributions are likely to be critical for understanding why benefits may be rejected or have minimal impact (for an attributional analysis of social support, see Fincham & Bradbury, 1990).

A second, obvious feature of the parent–child relationship is that one partner is immature and constrained by developmental limitations. This necessarily draws attention to preconditions that have to be met before a child can be held responsible for their actions. For example, what mental capacities need to be present? Although marital researchers have paid attention to dimensions underlying responsibility, the parent–child literature invites us to revisit this attribution type. The issue of capacities necessary for inferring responsibility finds its analogue in marital relationships where a partner lacks the requisite skills or knowledge to act appropriately (e.g., be intimate, communicate freely). Such capacity criteria are utilized in clinical interventions where it is not uncommon to use a cognitive restructuring procedure called relabeling (e.g., Jacobson & Margolin, 1979). Hence a distressing spouse behavior that prompts a conflict-promoting attribution (e.g, "he won't tell me about his worries because he doesn't trust me") is reframed as a skill deficit (e.g., "he has never learned how to share things that he sees as weaknesses"). A good deal might be learned by determining what influences the criteria underlying responsibility attributions in marriage.

The more general and important point, however, is that it is timely to reconsider the study of responsibility in the marital domain. The discontinuity with basic attribution research has tended to isolate the study of responsibility in the marital literature from recent advances in the analysis of this construct (e.g., Schlenker, Britt, Pennington, Murphy, & Doherty, 1994; Shaver, 1985; Weiner, 1995). In this regard, it is worth noting that any analysis of responsibility in marriage will be enriched to the extent that it accords Heider's "ought forces" a central role. This is because partner behavior that violates expected standards is often experienced as upsetting the objective order or perceptions of the way things should work in the relationship even, and perhaps particularly, when spouses are unaware of the expectations that give rise to this response. As a result, attributed responsibility may not be seen as an interpretation regarding partner behavior but as something that is intrinsic to the behavior. General analyses of responsibility that fail to explicitly consider this element (e.g., Weiner, 1995), may nonetheless be helpful in relationship research (e.g., application to EE, see Hooley & Licht, 1997) to the extent that the behaviors studied implicitly violate generally accepted standards of behavior. However, making this assumption explicit allows it to be examined systematically.

To summarize, an attempt was made in this section to illustrate the value of linking marital attribution research and closely related, but independent, areas of inquiry. One outcome of this exercise is the potential to develop a more general attributional perspective that spans different close relationships. Success in achieving this ambitious goal is likely to be facilitated by willingness to benefit from developments outside of the field of close relationships. The remainder of the chapter is devoted to considering two such developments.

Leaving home

In moving further afield, we first visit an area that could be considered a family relative in that it arose from research on learned helplessness and investigates attributions and adaptational outcomes.

Attributions and adaptational outcomes.   Research on attributions and adaptational outcomes need only be briefly considered for the lessons to be learned are obvious, simple ones. Five characteristics of this literature are briefly considered.

First, in an interesting account of the evolution of research emanating from learned helplessness, Peterson, Maier, and Seligman (1993) accord the use of language an important role. The change in terminology from "attributional style" to "explanatory style" to "optimism" bears consideration. Although one can question the motivation to use "vivid language" and to distinguish the study of causal attribution in this literature "from any of a number of others with 'attributional' labels" (p. 302), the fact remains that the linguistic lens one uses as a researcher can have profound effects.

This point can be succinctly illustrated in the marital field. Because marital research has focused on the attributional analysis associated with helplessness, and because attributions tend to occur for negative events (Weiner, 1985), marital research has focused heavily on what could be labeled "pessimistic explanatory style." This highlights two points. First, explicit use of the term "style" crystallizes the often implicit view in marital research that the subject of study is a personality trait (see Karney & Bradbury, in press). Second, the descriptor, "pessimistic," draws attention to its opposite, "optimistic." Thinking in terms of optimism frees us from focusing on the negative. As marital researchers embrace study of how spouses link positive marital events to Heider's underlying "invariances," it is worth avoiding an assumption about psychological structure relating to optimism and pessimism implicit in the use of bipolar assessment scales. There is already evidence that marital quality, like affect and attitudes in general, comprises distinct and somewhat independent positive and negative dimensions (Fincham & Linfield, 1997), and similar structural independence may characterize explanatory optimism and pessimism.

A second general lesson to be drawn for the broader attribution/adapational outcome literature is the variety of adaptational outcomes studied. Thus, for example, explanatory style has been shown to be related to such outcomes as performance (e.g., in sports, in insurance sales, in academic tasks), death from coronary disease, victory in presidential elections, and physical health (see Buchanan & Seligman, 1995). The scope of outcomes studied contrasts with the limited range investigated in the marital domain. Investigation of additional relationship (e.g., commitment, intimacy) and individual (e.g., physical health, self-concept) outcomes represents an important avenue of future attributional research in marriage.

Third, the predictive power of the attributional style studied in the broader literature raises an important question for marital research. Is this attributional style sufficient to predict spouses' marital satisfaction? Stated differently, are the attributions studied in marriage simply a subset of a more generic attributional style rendering superfluous a distinct model of attributions in marriage? The single study to address this issue showed that marital attributions provided unique information in predicting both depressive symptoms and marital satisfaction and were significantly more powerful than general attributions in predicting marital satisfaction (Horneffer & Fincham, 1996). Although in need of replication, this study points to the potential value of marital attributions for understanding individual as well as relationship outcomes.

Fourth, the ubiquitous link between attributions and adaptational outcomes raises questions about the mechanisms that might account for this link. Although this is not the context in which to explore such mechanisms, there is an important, relevant lesson to be drawn. Specifically, there is a clear conceptual commitment to attributional style as a risk factor which forces consideration of what potentiates this risk. The resulting diathesis-stress framework in which attributional style is clearly situated as a moderating variable is instructive for marital researchers who have studied attributions independently of stressful events. Not surprisingly, the status of attributions in the marital literature as a mediating versus moderating variable has been unclear. On the one hand, attributions are treated as a mediating variable that "explain[s] how external physical events take on internal psychological significance" (Baron & Kenny, 1986; p. 1176), yet the standard means for testing a mediating variable have not been applied. On the other hand, attributions have also been treated as an individual difference factor that might function as a moderating variable, yet most studies examine only its "main effects." Clarifying the conceptual status accorded attributions in a study is therefore important in assessing the appropriateness of its methodology. One hypothesis worth exploring is whether attributions serve as a moderating variable when assessed globally via questionnaires and as a mediating variable when they pertain to inferences made in situ for partner behavior.

The fifth implication to be considered concerns measurement. Although the past decade has witnessed attention to attribution measurement in the marital domain, this effort has focused on questionnaire development with no attempt to follow up on earlier attention paid to unsolicited attributions (e.g., Holtzworth-Munroe & Jacobson, 1985). Questionnaire development has, however, been accompanied by development of the Content Analysis of Verbatim Explanations (CAVE) in the broader explanatory style literature (see Peterson, Schulman, Castellon, & Seligman, 1992; Reivich, 1995). The CAVE requires coders to identify and then rate causal attributions on the three dimensions (locus, stability, globality) represented in questionnaires. This has the advantage of allowing investigation of the convergence between questionnaire and coded attributions, although it should be noted that convergence is not a prerequisite. Each approach provides a legitimate perspective and source of data on attributions. It is also worth noting that a similar coding measure, the Leeds Attribution Coding System (LACS), has been more fully developed in the 1990s through its application in clinical, work, and consumer settings (see Munton, Silvester, Stratton, & Hanks, 1999). However, the LACS derives from a slightly different theoretical framework than the CAVE and provides a viable alternative to it.

These developments again highlight the need for a second strand to marital attribution research that focuses on coded attributions. This would allow the accrual of much-needed data on unsolicited and on spontaneous attributions that could allow for comparison of attributions that are made spontaneously with those that occur more deliberately (Berscheid & Reis, 1998). Developing a database on such attributions in relationships poses numerous challenges. These were discussed some time ago and that discussion remains pertinent (see Bradbury & Fincham, 1988). The need for developing such a database may not be apparent given the earlier noted link between the marital attribution literature and social cognition research. After all, the study of spontaneous attribution inferences is well represented in social cognitive research and hence the call for research on spontaneous attributions in marriage may appear anomalous. In turning to consider links with the field of social cognition that might advance marital attribution research, it will be seen that this anomaly is more apparent than real.

Social cognition.   Recall that at the beginning of the 1990s several conceptual analyses in the marital domain were influenced by ideas drawn from the social cognition literature (e.g., Fincham, Bradbury, & Scott, 1990; Fletcher & Fincham, 1991). For example, the distinction between automatic and controlled processes was used to deal with the observation that much interactional behavior unfolds rapidly and without mindful cognitive processing. As a result, one might reasonably have expected research on the spontaneous attribution inferences represented in social cognition research (e.g., Bassili, 1989) to be represented in the marital literature. However, during the 1990s clinical and social investigations of cognition in relationships began to diverge (Fincham & Beach, in press), which may account for the virtual absence of marital research that moves beyond the focus on conscious attributional content. Thus, there is no anomaly in calling for the development of a database on spontaneous attributions in marriage.

In light of the above observation, one purpose of this section is to reiterate the rallying call of the early 1990s for a rapprochement between the study of marital attributions and social cognition. In this regard, it takes its place alongside several similar calls for integrating a social cognitive perspective in the study of close relationships. For example, Reis and Knee (1996, p. 181) noted that relationship cognition research has focused "almost exclusively on 'what' questions" concerning conscious cognitive content and point to the need for research "to consider processes that occur outside of conscious awareness" (p. 175). Similarly, there is limited evidence of such research in a recent comprehensive survey of the close relationship literature where the section on automatic cognitive processes has the status of a promissory note (Berscheid & Reis, 1998). Lest it appear otherwise, one must hasten to add that there are a number of notable exceptions to these summary conclusions (see Chapter 2, by Karney et al., below) that augur well for the future. For the present, however, the social cognitive analyses of marriage offered earlier in the decade remain relevant (see Fincham, Bradbury, & Scott, 1990; Fletcher & Fincham, 1991; Scott, Fuhrman, & Wyer, 1991). Rather than repeat the observations made in them, the remainder of the section highlights two implications of social cognition research that have been overlooked in these analyses.

First, social cognition research shows that people access and use specific knowledge in making social judgments (e.g., Smith & Zarate, 1992). The implication is that marital attributions may vary depending on the stored knowledge that is accessed when the attribution is made. In the social cognition domain this is readily demonstrated through priming or making accessible a construct and then examining the effects of such priming. Although discussed in prior analyses, the complexity of priming effects in marriage has not been recognized. For example, Fincham and Beach (in press) report studies in which priming marital satisfaction did not influence subsequent judgments, whereas priming hostility did affect judgments of partner behavior, but in the direction opposite to that predicted. Spouses who had been primed rated subsequent partner behavior as *less* hostile. It is likely that a variety of such contrast effects, as well as assimilation effects, will be found as marital researchers examine the effects of stored knowledge on spouses' attributions. It will therefore be important to accommodate to the impact of a number of influences on priming effects, including the recency, frequency, and blatancy of the priming, awareness of the priming, exact relation between primed and target materials, and so on (see Higgins, 1996). It has been somewhat simpler to document the importance of chronically primed material; the attribution–marital satisfaction association has been shown to be significantly larger among spouses whose marital satisfaction was more accessible than among spouses where it was less accessible (Fincham, Garnier, Gano-Phillips, & Osborne, 1995).

A final, but important, point regarding the potential impact of accessing stored knowledge on attributions concerns domain specificity. Simply stated, the relevance of accessed knowledge for the event, subject to an attributional analysis, may influence its impact. From this perspective, further and perhaps more subtle, attribution phenomena may emerge from investigations that examine domain specific effects. There is initial evidence to suggest such phenomena. For example, Collins (1996) has found that internal working models of attachment are related to attributions independently of relationship satisfaction among dating students, but only for attachment-relevant partner behaviors. Documenting such domain-specific effects is consistent with the earlier call to broaden the correlates of attributions studied in marriage.

A second implication of social cognition research worth highlighting is the emphasis on goals. The impact of goals on information processing is ubiquitous in social cognition studies and is evident in basic research on spontaneous attribution – in contrast to other goals (e.g., remembering stimulus material), the goal of forming an impression results in spontaneous trait inferences (Smith, 1994). It is also apparent, however, that trait inferences can occur without a causal analysis of the behavior (cf. Smith & Miller, 1979, where trait inferences occur more rapidly than causal inferences), emphasizing the need to examine explicitly the impact of information processing goals on causal and responsibility attributions in marriage. Vorauer and Ross (1996) specifically address the role of information goals in close relationships thereby both extending the range of goals considered and providing a goal analysis specific to the relationship domain. They suggest that the goal of obtaining information about issues relevant to the perceiver leads to a diagnosticity bias that influences attributions; i.e., partner behavior is more likely to be attributed to the self. Their analysis identifies a number of factors likely to influence information goals (e.g., shifting circumstances, relationship development, coordination of partners' goal) that could profitably be used to examine the impact of information goals on attributions.

The value of pursuing a goal-based approach in marital attribution research is enhanced when it is recognized that goal obstruction or interruption may be critical to understanding the instigation of attribution processing. From this perspective, negative events occasion attributions because they are generally inimical to the goals people pursue, but it is the thwarting of the goal that is more fundamental. If correct, this raises a variety of questions about how different elements of goals may influence attributions. At the simplest level one could examine whether thwarting of approach versus avoidance goals are associated with different attributional outcomes in a manner analogous to attributions for commissions versus omissions. Similarly, does the generality of the goal constrain acceptable attributions? For example, is a conversational interruption (e.g., while a couple is trying to locate their destination) adequately explained by an attribution that speaks to goal content (e.g., "I just wanted to let you know I don't like asking for directions") when a relational goal (e.g., to experience mutual respect and equality) is seen to be thwarted? Goals have been found to vary along a number of dimensions that might be examined in relation to attributions (e.g., level of consciousness, importance-commitment, difficulty, specificity, temporal range and connectedness; see Austin & Vancouver, 1996).

Again the specific form of the link between goals and attributions is less important than its potential to yield integrative theory. First, the goal-thwarting hypothesis offered above is cut from the same cloth as Berscheid's (1983) theory of emotion in close relationships where interrupted goal pursuit gives rise to emotion. Goals may be a vehicle for minting the coin that displays affect and cognition on each side. Second, a goal analytic framework has been applied to marital conflict, the topic that simulated marital attribution research (Fincham & Beach, 1999). As this analysis attempts to incorporate research on marital phenomena, marital prevention, and intervention under a single goal theoretic framework, placing marital attribution research in the same framework represents a step towards increased theoretical integration that has been the legacy of social cognition in basic attribution research (Smith, 1994).

Conclusion

The chapter began by noting the continued vitality of attribution research and offered two reasons to account for this phenomenon. One was a broader study of attribution consistent with continuity between social and nonsocial cognition, and the second was the application of an attribution perspective to many new, and especially applied, areas. This provided a context for understanding the emergence and evolution of marital attribution research. An updated review of this field showed that it has realized a great deal of its early potential and several clear themes were evident. However, it was equally apparent that the balkanization accompanying the prodigious output of attribution research was also evident in the marital domain. Accordingly, links were made with other areas of research and with the broader social cognition literature. This analysis identified gaps in the marital attributional literature and pointed to ways in which these new avenues of inquiry might be pursued. The importance of pursuing this research is emphasized by the promise of yielding a more integrated theoretical account of attributions in close relationships.

NOTE

1   Harvey, Wells, and Alvarez's (1978) study of attribution for conflict and separation in relationships was also an important early influence. However, it gave rise to a broader literature on accounts that was not limited to attributions or relationship events but instead focused on the narratives that arise in reaction to severe stress (see Harvey, Weber, & Orbuch, 1990).

REFERENCES

Abramson, L. Y., Seligman, M. E. P., & Teasdale, J. (1978). Learned helplessness in humans: Critique and reformulation. *Journal of Abnormal Psychology, 87*, 49–74.

Austin, J. T., & Vancouver, J. B. (1996). Goal constructs in psychology: Structure, process, and content. *Psychological Bulletin, 120*, 338–375.

Bagarozzi, D. A., & Giddings, C. W. (1983). The role of cognitive constructs and attributional processes in family therapy. In L. R. Wolberg & M. L. Aronson, (Eds) *Group and family therapy 1983*. New York: Brunner/Mazel.

Baron, R. M., & Kenny, D. A. (1986). The moderator-mediator variable distinction in social psychological research: Conceptual, strategic, and statistical considerations. *Journal of Personality and Social Psychology, 51*, 1173–1182.

Barrowclough, C., Johnston, M., & Tarrier, N. (1994). Attributions, expressed emotion, and patient relapse: An attributional model of relatives' response to schizophrenic illness. *Behavior Therapy, 25*, 67–88.

Bassili, J. N. (1989). Trait encoding in behavior identification and dispositional inference. *Personality and Social Psychology Bulletin, 15*, 285–296.

Baucom, D. H. (1987). Attributions in distressed relations: How can we explain them? In S. Duck & D. Perlman (Eds.), *Intimate relationships: Development, dynamics, and deterioration* (pp. 177–206). London: Sage.

Baucom, D. H., Epstein, N., Duito, A. D., Carels, R. A., Rankin, L. A., & Burnett, C. K. (1996). Cognitions in marriage: The relationship between standards and attributions. *Journal of Family Psychology, 10*, 209–222.

Baucom, D. H., Epstein, N., Sayers, S., & Sher, T. G. (1989). The role of cognitions in marital relationships: Definitional, methodological, and conceptual issues. *Journal of Consulting and Clinical Psychology, 57*, 31–38.

Baucom, D. H., Sayers, S. L., & Duhe, A. (1989). Attributional style and attributional patterns among married couples. *Journal of Personality and Social Psychology, 56*, 596–607.

Bauserman, S. A., Arias, I., & Craighead, W. E. (1995). Marital attributions in spouses of depressed patients. *Journal of Psychopathology and Behavioral Assessment, 17*, 231–249.

Beach, S. R. H., & Tesser, A. (1995). Self-esteem and the extended self-evaluation model: The self in social context. In M. Kernis (Ed.), *Efficacy, Agency, and Self-esteem* (pp. 145–170). New York: Plenum.

Bebbington, P., & Kuipers, L. (1994). The predictive utility of expressed emotion in schizophrenia: An aggregate analysis. *Psychological Medicine, 21*, 1–11.

Berger, P., & Kellner, H. (1970). Marriage and the construction of reality. In H. P. Dreitzel (Ed.), *Recent sociology: Patterns of communicative behavior*. New York: Macmillan.

Berscheid, E. (1983). Emotion. In H. H. Kelley, E. Berscheid, A. Christensen, J. H. Harvey, T. L. Huston, G. Levinger, E. Mclintock, L. A. Peptan, & D. R. Peterson (Eds.), *Close Relationships* (pp.110–168). New York: W. H. Freeman.

Berscheid, E. (1994). Interpersonal relationships. *Annual Review of Psychology, 45,* 79–129.

Berscheid, E., & Reis, H. T. (1998). Attraction and close relationships. In D. T. Gilbert, S. T. Fiske & G. Lindsey (Eds.), *Handbook of Social Psychology* (Vol. 2, pp. 193–281). New York: McGraw Hill.

Bradbury, T. B., Beach, S. R. H., Fincham, F. D., & Nelson, G. M. (1996). Attributions and behavior in functional and dysfunctional marriages. *Journal of Consulting and Clinical Psychology, 64,* 569–576.

Bradbury, T. N., & Fincham, F. D. (1988). Assessing spontaneous attributions in marital interaction: Methodological and conceptual considerations. *Journal of Social and Clinical Psychology, 7,* 122–130.

Bradbury, T. N., & Fincham, F. D. (1990). Attributions in marriage: Review and critique. *Psychological Bulletin, 107,* 3–33.

Bradbury, T. N., & Fincham, F. D. (1991). A contextual model for advancing the study of marital interaction. In G. J. O. Fletcher & F. D. Fincham (Eds.), *Cognition in close relationships* (pp. 127–147). Hillsdale, NJ: Erlbaum.

Bradbury, T. N., & Fincham, F. D. (1992). Attributions and behavior in marital interaction. *Journal of Personality and Social Psychology, 63,* 613–628.

Braiker, H. B. & Kelley, H. H. (1979). Conflict in the development of close relationships. In R. L. Burgess & T. L. Huston (Eds.), *Social exchange in developing relationships* (pp. 135–168). New York: Academic Press.

Brewin, C. R. (1994). Changes in attribution and expressed emotion among the relatives of patients with schizophrenia. *Psychological Medicine, 24,* 905–911.

Brewin, C. R., McCarthy, B., Duda, K., & Vaughn, C. E. (1991). Attribution and expressed emotion in the relatives of patients with schizophrenia. *Journal of Abnormal Psychology, 100,* 546–554.

Brown, G. W., Carstairs, G. M., & Topping, G. C. (1958). The post hospital adjustment of chronic mental patients. *The Lancet, ii,* 685–689.

Buchanan, G. M., & Seligman, M. E. P. (Eds.). (1995). *Explanatory style.* Hillsdale, NJ: Erlbaum.

Bugental, D. B., & Goodnow, J. J. (1998). Socialization processes. In N. Eisenberg (Ed.), *Handbook of child psychology. Volume 3: Social, emotional, and personality development.* New York: Wiley.

Bugental, D. B., & Shennum, W. A. (1984). "Difficult" children as elicitors and targets of adult communication patterns: An attributional-behavior transactional analysis. *Monographs of the Society for Research in Child Development, 49* (1, Serial No. 205).

Byrne, C. A., & Arias, I. (1997). Marital satisfaction and marital violence: Moderating effects of attributional processes. *Journal of Family Psychology, 11,* 188–195.

Collins, N. L. (1996). Working models of attachment: Implications for explanation, emotion, and behavior. *Journal of Personality and Social Psychology, 71,* 810–822.

Davey, A., Fincham, F. D., Beach, S. R. H., & Brody, G. (1999). *Does a dyadic conceptualization expand our understanding of marital cognition?* Manuscript submitted for publication.

Davidson, G. N. S., & Horvath, A. O. (1997). Three sessions of brief couples therapy: A clinical trial. *Journal of Family Psychology, 11,* 422–435.

Dix, T. H., & Grusec, J. E. (1985). Parent attribution processes in the socialization of children. In I. E. Sigel (Ed.), *Parental belief systems* (pp. 201–234). Hillsdale, NJ: Erlbaum.

Eckhard, C. I., Barbour, K. A., & Davison, G. C. (1998). Articulated thoughts of maritally violent and nonviolent men during anger arousal. *Journal of Consulting and Clinical Psychology, 66,* 259–269.

Eckhard, C. I., & Dye, M. L. (in press). The cognitive characteristics of maritally violent men: Theory and evidence. *Cognitive Therapy and Research.*

Epstein, N., & Baucom, D. H. (1993). Cognitive factors in marital disturbance. In K. S. Dobson, and P. C. Kendall (Eds.), *Psychopathology and cognition. Personality, psychopathology, and psychotherapy series* (pp. 351–385). San Diego: Academic Press.

Fazio, R. H., Sherman, S. J., & Herr, P. M. (1982). The feature-positive effect in the self-perception process: Does not doing matter as much as doing? *Journal of Personality and Social Psychology, 42,* 404–411.

Fincham, F. D. (1983). Clinical applications of attribution theory: Problems and prospects. In M. Hewstone (Ed.), *Attribution theory: Social and functional extensions* (pp. 187–205). Oxford: Blackwell.

Fincham, F. D. (1985). Attributions in close relationships. In J. H. Harvey & G. Weary (Eds.), *Attribution: Basic issues and applications* (pp. 203–234). New York: Academic Press.

Fincham, F. D. (1992). The account episode in close relationships. In M. L. McLaughlin, M. Cody, & J. S. Read (Eds.), *Explaining one's self to others: Reason-giving in a social context* (pp. 167–182). Hillsdale, NJ: Erlbaum.

Fincham, F. D., & Beach, S. R. (1999). Marital conflict: Implications for working with couples. *Annual Review of Psychology, 50,* 47–77.

Fincham, F. D., & Beach, S. R. (in press). Marriage in the new millennium: Is there a place for social cognition in marital research? *Journal of Social and Personal Relationships.*

Fincham, F. D., Beach, S. R., Arias, I., & Brody, G. (1998). Children's attributions in the family: The Children's Relationship Attribution Measure. *Journal of Family Psychology, 12,* 481–493.

Fincham, F. D., & Bradbury, T. N. (1987a). The impact of attributions in marriage: A longitudinal analysis. *Journal of Personality and Social Psychology, 53,* 481–489.

Fincham, F. D., & Bradbury, T. N. (1987b). The assessment of marital quality: A reevaluation. *Journal of Marriage and the Family, 49,* 797–809.

Fincham, F. D., & Bradbury, T. N. (1988). The impact of attributions in marriage: An experimental analysis. *Journal of Social and Clinical Psychology, 7,* 147–162.

Fincham, F. D., & Bradbury, T. N. (1990). Social support in marriage: The role of social cognition. *Journal of Social and Clinical Psychology, 9,* 31–42.

Fincham, F. D., & Bradbury, T. N. (1992). Assessing attributions in marriage: The Relationship Attribution Measure. *Journal of Personality and Social Psychology, 62,* 457–468.

Fincham, F. D., & Bradbury, T. N. (1993). Marital satisfaction, depression, and attributions: A longitudinal analysis. *Journal of Personality and Social Psychology, 64,* 442–452.

Fincham, F. D., Bradbury, T. N., Arias, I., Byrne, & C. A., Karney, B. R. (1997). Marital violence, marital distress and attributions. *Journal of Family Psychology, 11,* 367–372.

Fincham, F. D., Bradbury, T. N., & Beach, S. R. (1990). To arrive where we began: A reappraisal of cognition in marriage and in marital therapy. *Journal of Family Psychology, 4,* 167–184.

Fincham, F. D., Bradbury, T. N., & Scott, C. K. (1990). Cognition in marriage. In F. D. Fincham & T. N. Bradbury (Eds.), *The psychology of marriage: Basic issues and applications* (pp. 118–149). New York: Guilford.

Fincham, F. D., Garnier, P. C., Gano-Phillips, S., & Osborne, L. N. (1995). Pre-interaction expectations, marital satisfaction and accessibility: A new look at sentiment override. *Journal of Family Psychology, 9,* 3–14.

Fincham, F. D., Harold, G., & Gano-Phillips, S. (in press). The longitudinal association between attributions and marital satisfaction: Direction of effects and role of efficacy expectations. *Journal of Family Psychology.*

Fincham, F. D., & Jaspars, J. M. (1980). Attribution of responsibility: From man the scientist to man as lawyer. In L. Berkowitz (Ed.), *Advances in experimental social psychology* (Vol. 13, pp. 81–138). New York: Academic Press.

Fincham, F. D., & Linfield, K. J. (1997). A new look at marital quality: Can spouses feel positive and negative about their marriage? *Journal of Family Psychology, 11,* 489–502.

Fletcher, G. J. O., & Fincham, F. D. (1991). Attribution processes in close relationships. In G. J. O. Fletcher & F. D. Fincham (Eds.), *Cognition in close relationships* (pp. 7–35). Hillsdale, NJ: Erlbaum.

Fletcher, G. J. O., Fincham, F. D., Cramer, L., & Heron, N. (1987). The role of attributions in the development of dating relationships. *Journal of Personality and Social Psychology, 53,* 510–517.

Fletcher, G. J. O., Fitness, J., & Blampied, N. M. (1990). The link between attributions and happiness in close relationships: The roles of depression and explanatory style. *Journal of Social and Clinical Psychology, 9,* 243–255.

Fletcher, G. J. O., & Kininmonth, L. (1991). Interaction in close relationships and social cognition. In G. J. O. Fletcher & F. D. Fincham (Eds.), *Cognition in close relationships* (pp. 235–256). Hillsdale, NJ: Erlbaum.

Fletcher, G. J. O., & Thomas, G. (2000). Behavior and on-line cognitions in marital interaction. *Personal Relationships, 7,* 111–130.

Gottman, J. M. (1990). How marriages change. In G. R. Patterson (Ed.), *Depression and aggression in family interaction* (pp. 75–102). Hillsdale, NJ: Erlbaum.

Gottman, J. M. (1994). *What predicts divorce?* Hillsdale, NJ: Erlbaum.

Harvey, J. H. (1987). Attributions in close relationships: Research and theoretical developments. *Journal of Social and Clinical Psychology, 5,* 420–434.

Harvey, J. H., Ickes, W., & Kidd, R. F. (1978). A conversation with Edward E. Jones and Harold H. Kelley. In J. H. Harvey, W. Ickes, & R. F. Kidd (Eds.), New directions in attribution research (Vol. 2, pp. 371–388). Hillsdale, NJ: Erlbaum.

Harvey, J. H., Weber, A. L., & Orbuch, T. L. (1990). *Interpersonal accounts: A social psychological perspective.* Cambridge, MA: Blackwell.

Harvey, J. H., Wells, G. L., & Alvarez, M. D. (1978). Attribution in the context of conflict and separation in close relationships. In J. H. Harvey, W. J. Ickes, & R. F. Kidd (Eds.), *New directions in attribution research* (Vol. 2, pp. 235–260). Hillsdale, NJ: Erlbaum.

Heider, F. (1958). *The psychology of interpersonal relations.* New York: Wiley.

Hewstone, M. R. H., & Fincham, F. D. (1996). Attribution theory and research. In M. Hewstone, W. Stroebe, & G. M. Stephenson (Eds.), *Introducing social psychology* (pp. 167–204). Oxford: Blackwell.

Higgins, E. T. (1996). Knowledge activation: Accessibility, applicability, and salience. In E. T. Higgins & A .W. Kruglanski (Eds.), *Social psychology: Handbook of basic principles* (pp. 133–168). New York: Guilford.

Hinde, R. A. (1997). *Relationships: A dialectical perspective.* Hove: Psychology Press.

Holtzworth-Munroe, A., & Hutchinson, G. (1993). Attributing negative intent to wife behavior: The attributions of maritally violent versus nonviolent men. *Journal of Abnormal Psychology, 102,* 206–211.

Holtzworth-Munroe, A., & Jacobson, N. S. (1985). Causal attributions of married couples: When do they search for causes? What do they conclude when they do? *Journal of Personality and Social Psychology, 48,* 1398–1412.

Holtzworth-Munroe, A., & Jacobson, N. S. (1988). Toward a methodology for coding spontaneous causal attributions: Preliminary results with married couples. *Journal of Social and Clinical Psychology, 7,* 101–112.

Holtzworth-Munroe, A., Jacobson, N. S., Fehrenbach, & P. A., & Fruzzetti, A. (1992).Violent married couples' attributions for violent and nonviolent self and partner behaviors. *Behavioral Assessment, 14,* 53–64.

Hooley, J. M. (1987). The nature and origins of expressed emotion. In M. J. Goldstein & K. Hahlweg (Eds.), *Understanding major mental disorder: The contribution of family interaction research* (pp. 176–194). New York: Family Process Press.

Hooley, J. M., & Licht, D. M. (1997). Expressed emotion and causal attributions in the spouses of depressed patients. *Journal of Abnormal Psychology, 106,* 298–306.

Hooley, J. M., Richters, J. E., Weintraub, S., & Neale, J.-M. (1987). Psychopathology and marital distress: The positive side of positive symptoms. *Journal of Abnormal Psychology, 96,* 27–33.

Horneffer, K. J., & Fincham, F. D. (1995). The construct of attributional style in depression and marital distress. *Journal of Family Psychology, 9,* 186–195.

Horneffer, K. J., & Fincham, F. D. (1996). Attributional models of depression and marital distress. *Personality and Social Psychology Bulletin, 22,* 678–689.

Jacobson, N. S., & Christensen, A. (1996). *Integrative couple therapy: Promoting acceptance and change.* New York: Norton.

Jacobson, N. S., & Margolin, G. (1979). *Marital therapy: Strategies based on social learning and behavior exchange principles.* New York: Brunner/Mazel.

Joiner, T. E., & Wagner, K. D. (1996). Parent, child-centered attributions and outcomes: A meta-analytic review with concepetual and methodological implications. *Journal of Clinical Child Psychology, 24,* 37–52.

Jones, E. E., & Davis, K. E. (1965). From acts to dispositions: The attribution process in person perception. In L. Berkowitz (Ed.), *Advances in experimental social psychology* (Vol. 2, pp. 219–266). New York: Academic Press.

Karney, B. R., & Bradbury, T. N. (in press). Attributions in marriage: State or trait? A growth curve analysis. *Journal of Personality and Social Psychology.*

Karney, B. R., Bradbury, T. N., Fincham, F. D., & Sullivan, K. T. (1994). The role of negative affectivity in the association between attributions and marital satisfaction. *Journal of Personality and Social Psychology, 66,* 413–424.

Katz, J., Arias, I., Beach, S. R. H., & Brody, G. (1995). Excuses, excuses: Accounting for the effects of partner violence on marital satisfaction and stability. *Violence & Victims, 10,* 315–326.

Kelley, H. H. (1967). Attribution theory in social psychology. In D. Levine (Ed.), *Nebraska symposium on motivation* (pp. 192–238). Lincoln, NE: University of Nebraska Press.

Kelley, H. H. (1979). *Personal relationships: Their structures and processes.* Hillsdale, NJ: Erlbaum.

Kelley, H. H., Berscheid, E., Christensen, A., Harvey, J. H., Huston, T. L., Levinger, G., McClintock, E., Peplau, L. A., & Peterson, D. R. (Eds.). (1983). *Close relationships.* New York: W. H. Freeman.

Kelley, H. H., & Michela, J. L. (1980). Attribution theory and research. *Annual Review of Psychology, 31,* 457–501.

Knight, J. A., & Vallacher, R. R. (1981). Interpersonal engagement in social perception: The consequences of getting into the action. *Journal of Personality and Social Psychology, 40,* 990–999.

Kyle, S. O., & Falbo, T. (1985). Relationships between marital stress and attributional preferences for own and spouse behavior. *Journal of Social and Clinical Psychology, 3,* 339–351.

Lussier, Y., Sabourin, S., & Wright, J. (1993). On causality, responsibility, and blame in marriage: Validity of the entailment model. *Journal of Family Psychology, 7,* 322–332.

Mari, J., & Streiner, D. L. (1994). An overview of family interventions and relapse on schizophrenia: Meta analysis of research findings. *Psychological Medicine, 24,* 565–578.

Metalsky, G. I., & Abramson, L. Y. (1981). Attributional style: Toward a framework for conceptualization and assessment. In P. Kendall & S. Hollon (Eds.), *Assessment strategies for cognitive-behavioral interventions* (pp. 13–58). New York: Academic Press.

Miller, G. E., & Bradbury, T. N. (1995). Refining the association between attributions and behavior in marital interaction. *Journal of Family Psychology, 9,* 196–208.

Miller, S. A. (1995). Parents' attributions for their children's behavior. *Child Development, 66,* 1557–1584.

Munton, A. G., Silvester, J., Stratton, P., & Hanks, H. (1999). *Attributions in action: A practical approach to coding qualitative data.* Chichester, England: Wiley.

Newman, H. M. (1981). Communication within ongoing intimate relationships: An attributional perspective. *Personality and Social Psychology Bulletin, 7,* 59–70.

Orvis, B. R., Kelley, H. H., & Butler, D. (1976). Attributional conflict in young couples. In J. H. Harvey, W. Ickes, & R. F. Kidd (Eds.), *New directions in attribution research* (Vol. 1, pp. 353–386). Hillsdale, NJ: Erlbaum.

Pape, K. T., & Arias, I. (in press). The role of perceptions and attributions in battered women's intentions to permanently end their violent relationships. *Cognitive Therapy and Research.*

Passer, M. W., Kelley, H. H., & Michela, J. L. (1978). Multidimensional scaling of the causes for negative interpersonal behavior. *Journal of Personality and Social Psychology, 36,* 951–962.

Peterson, C., Maier, S. F., & Seligman, M. E. P. (1993). *Learned helplessness: A theory for the age of personal control.* New York: Oxford University Press.

Peterson, C., Schulman, P., Castellon, C., & Seligman, M. E. P. (1992). The explanatory style scoring manual. In C. P. Smith (Ed.), *Handbook of thematic analysis* (pp. 383–392). New York: Cambridge University Press.

Pleban, R., & Richardson, D. C. (1979). Research and publication trends in social psychology: 1973–7. *Personality and Social Psychology Bulletin, 5,* 138–141.

Pretzer, J., Epstein, N., & Fleming, B. (1991). Marital Attitude Survey: A measure of dysfunctional attributions and expectancies. *Journal of Cognitive Psychotherapy, 5,* 131–148.

Reis, H. T., & Knee, C. R. (1996). What we know, what we don't know and what we need to know about relationship knowledge structures. In G. J. O. Fletcher & J. Fitness (Eds.), *Knowledge structures in close relationships: A social psychological approach* (pp. 169–194). Hillsdale, NJ: Erlbaum.

Reivich, K. (1995). The measurement of explanatory style. In G. M. Buchanan & M. E. P. Seligman (Eds.), *Explanatory style.* Hillsdale, NJ: Erlbaum.

Sabourin, S., Lussier, Y., & Wright, J. (1991). The effects of measurement strategy on attributions for marital problems and behaviors. *Journal of Applied Social Psychology, 21,* 734–746.

Sacco, W. P., & Murray, D. W. (1997). Mother-child relationship satisfaction: The role of attributions and trait conceptions. *Journal of Social and Clinical Psychology, 16,* 24–42.

Sayers, S. L., & Baucom, D. H. (1995). Multidimensional scaling of spouses' attributions for marital conflicts. *Cognitive Therapy and Research, 19,* 667–693.

Schlenker, B. R., Britt, T. W., Pennington, J., Murphy, R., & Doherty, K. (1994). The triangle model of responsibility. *Psychological Review, 101,* 632–652.

Scott, C. K., Fuhrman, R. W., & Wyer, R. S. (1991). Information processing in close relationships. In G. J. O. Fletcher & F. D. Fincham (Eds.), *Cognition in close relationships* (pp. 37–68). Hillsdale, NJ: Erlbaum.

Senchak, M., & Leonard, K. E. (1993). The role of spouses' depression and anger in the attribution–marital satisfaction relation. *Cognitive Therapy and Research, 17,* 397–409.

Shaver, K. G. (1985). *The attribution of blame: Causality, responsibility, and blameworthiness.* New York: Springer-Verlag.

Slep, A. M. S., & O'Leary, S. G. (1998). The effects of maternal attributions on parenting: An experimental analysis. *Journal of Family Psychology, 12,* 234–242.

Smith, E. R. (1994). Social cognition contributions to attribution theory and research. In P. Devine, D. L., Hamilton, & T. M. Ostrom (Eds.), *Social cognition: Impact on social psychology.* New York: Academic Press.

Smith, E. R., & Miller, F. D. (1979). Attributional information processing: A response time measure of causal subtraction. *Journal of Personality and Social Psychology, 37,* 1723–31.

Smith, E., R., & Zarate, M. A. (1992). Exemplar-based model of social judgment. *Psychological Review, 99,* 3–21.

Taylor, S. E., & Koivumaki, J. H. (1976). The perception of self and others: Acquaintanceship, affect, and actor–observer differences. *Journal of Personality and Social Psychology, 33*, 403–406.

Thompson, J. S., & Snyder, D. K. (1986). Attribution theory in intimate relationships: A methodological review. *American Journal of Family Therapy, 14*, 123–138.

Vaughn, C., & Leff, J. (1976). The influence of family and social factors on the course of psychiatric illness: A comparison of schizophrenic and depressed neurotic patients. *British Journal of Psychiatry, 129*, 125–137.

Vorauer, J. D., & Ross, M. (1996). The pursuit of knowledge structures in close relationships: An informational goals analysis. In G. J. O. Fletcher & J. Fitness (Eds.), *Knowledge structures in close relationships: A social psychological approach* (pp. 369–396). Hillsdale, NJ: Erlbaum.

Weber, A. L., Harvey, J. H., & Orbuch, T. L. (1992). What went wrong: Communicating accounts of relationship conflict. In M. L. McLaughlin, M. J. Cody, & S. J. Read (Eds.), *Explaining oneself to others*. Hillsdale, NJ: Erlbaum.

Weiner, B. (1985). "Spontaneous" causal search. *Psychological Bulletin, 97*, 74–84.

Weiner, B. (1986). *An attributional theory of motivation and emotion*. New York: Springer-Verlag.

Weiner, B. (1995). *Judgments of responsibility*. New York: Guilford Press.

Weiner, B., Russel, D., & Lehrman, D. (1978). An attributional model of achievement strivings, attributions and affective intensity. In J. H. Harvey, W. Ickes, & R. F. Kidd (Eds.), *New directions in attribution research* (Vol. 2, pp. 59–90). Hillsdale, NJ: Erlbaum.

Weiss, R. L. (1980). Strategic behavioral marital therapy: Toward a model for assessment and intervention. In J. P. Vincent (Ed.), *Advances in family intervention, assessment and theory* (Vol. 1, pp. 229–271). Greenwich, CT: JAI Press.

Weiss, R. L., & Heyman, R. E. (1990). Observation of marital interaction. In F. D. Fincham & T. N. Bradbury (Eds.), *The psychology of marriage* (pp. 87–117). New York: Guilford.

Weiss, R. L., & Heyman, R. E. (1997). A clinical-research overview of couple interactions. In W. K. Halford & H. J. Markman (Eds.), *The clinical handbook of marriage and couples interventions* (pp. 13–42). New York: Wiley.

Wright, J., & Fichten, C. (1976). Denial of responsibility, videotape feedback and attribution theory: Relevance for behavioral marital therapy. *Canadian Psychology Review, 17*, 219–230.

CHAPTER NINE

Cognition and the Development of Close Relationships

Benjamin R. Karney, James K. McNulty, and
Thomas N. Bradbury

Introduction

Although close relationships generally begin with each partner feeling positive and optimistic about the future, most nevertheless end with one or both partners deciding that the relationship is no longer rewarding. The disparity between initial and final evaluations is particularly dramatic in marriage. Although newlyweds presumably approach marriage as a source of satisfaction and fulfillment, nearly two thirds of all first marriages end in divorce or permanent separation (Castro-Martin & Bumpass, 1989), and the dissolution rate for remarriages is even higher (Cherlin, 1992). Thus, the modal course of relationship development indicates that partners in close relationships experience a significant cognitive shift. Somehow the thoughts and feelings that initially draw two people together transform, in a majority of cases, into thoughts and feelings that eventually push those same two people apart. This pattern suggests that a fundamental question for relationships researchers is a cognitive one: how do partner's initially positive evaluations of their relationships so frequently deteriorate and become negative?

For social psychologists, this question is especially perplexing, because a broad tradition of research on social cognition demonstrates that people possess effective techniques for maintaining beliefs that are rewarding to them (for a review, see Kunda, 1990). To protect a desired belief, people tend to ignore evidence that contradicts that belief (Miller, 1997a), generate narratives that support their belief (Murray & Holmes, 1993), and demonstrate better memory for events that are consistent with that belief (Sanitioso, Kunda, & Fong, 1990). Furthermore, people have been shown to adhere to desired beliefs even when confronted with evidence that logically should undermine those beliefs (Nisbett & Ross, 1980). The results of this work suggest that partners' initially positive beliefs about their close relationships, being highly desirable, should be especially resistant to change. This does not appear to be the case. Despite the often remarkable ability of people to believe what they wish to believe, partners in close relationships are frequently unable to avoid the decline of their initial satisfaction. Examining how evaluations of relationships change or remain stable is thus interesting not only for what it may reveal about the success and failure of close relationships, but also for how it may illuminate broader issues in the way strongly held beliefs can deteriorate despite powerful motivations to maintain them.

Addressing these issues requires understanding the role of cognitions and cognitive processes in the development of close relationships. Accordingly, the last two decades of the twentieth century witnessed a burgeoning interest in the study of cognition in interpersonal contexts (e.g., Baucom, Epstein, Sayers, & Sher, 1989; Berger & Roloff, 1982; Berscheid, 1994; Fincham, Bradbury, & Scott, 1990; Fletcher & Fincham, 1991; Fletcher & Fitness, 1996). Our goal in this chapter is to organize and review recent developments in this literature, with an explicit emphasis on research that has implications for how close relationships change or remain stable over time. We acknowledge at the outset that a focus on cognition alone is unlikely to provide a complete explanation of relationship development. Undoubtedly, interpersonal and environmental factors also play important parts in the success or failure of relationships and so need to be included in any comprehensive explanation of how they change (see Karney & Bradbury, 1995b). Nevertheless, a critical step towards understanding relationship development is to understand the nature of the associated cognitions and cognitive processes.

Chapter overview

Although researchers have examined cognition in close relationships for a relatively short time, already the field has grown to encompass a wide range of variables. As an organizing principle, this chapter divides the field into three aspects of cognition that may affect how close relationships develop and change. The first section addresses the *content* of cognition, i.e., the beliefs and values that make up an individual's mental representation of the relationship. The second section addresses the *structure* of cognition, i.e., how relationship-relevant knowledge is organized. The third deals with the *process* of cognition, i.e., the pursuit, integration, and assimilation of knowledge. Clearly, these three categories are not mutually exclusive. We do not propose them as definitive, but merely as a guide to this broad and complex literature. The last section ends the chapter by suggesting ways that future research might integrate these three areas to better explain how close relationships develop over time.

When possible, we review longitudinal research on aspects of cognition that have been shown to predict relationship outcomes over time. In most cases, however, research in this area has been cross-sectional, identifying the kinds of cognitions associated with satisfying and dissatisfying relationships, but neglecting to explain how disappointment comes about in relationships that begin as satisfying. As a result, many theoretical propositions linking cognition to relationship development have not yet been tested directly. In these cases, cross-sectional work will be reviewed, with suggestions for research still needed to support developmental hypotheses.

The Content of Cognition in Close Relationships

The overwhelming majority of research on cognition in close relationships has examined the content of partners' cognitions. This includes research on partners' enduring attachment models and beliefs, their perceptions of each other's traits and behaviors, and their specific and global impressions of the relationship. As a useful framework to organize this domain, Fletcher and Thomas (1996) distinguished between individuals' theories and beliefs about relationships in general and their theories and beliefs about specific relationships that they have experienced or are experiencing. Global evaluations of a given relationship are the primary dependent variable in this literature and are themselves cognitions that fall into the latter category. In exploring how cognitive content affects the development of relationships, the underlying issue is how general and specific knowledge structures account for change in one particular knowledge structure: a person's global evaluation of a relationship.

Theoretical perspectives

Early models of cognition in close relationships were concerned not with how evaluations of a relationship change but with how individuals integrate their evaluations of specific aspects of the relationship with their global impressions of the relationship. This question arose as a result of early research on marriage that obtained spouses' reports of specific behaviors that occur in the relationship. This research found that spouses who were generally satisfied with their relationships tended to report more positive behaviors and fewer negative ones, whereas spouses who were less satisfied tended to report fewer positive behaviors and more negative ones (e.g., Birchler, Weiss, & Vincent, 1975; Wills, Weiss, & Patterson, 1974). Such findings were taken as support for strictly behavioral models of relationship functioning, until comparisons between spouses' reports revealed that spouses were unreliable observers of what had actually occurred in the relationship (Christensen & Nies, 1980; Jacobson & Moore, 1981). To explain the discrepancies between spouses' reports, relationship researchers drew from existing social psychological models of person perception (e.g., Asch, 1946; Thorndyke, 1920) and suggested that partners rely on their global impressions when asked to evaluate specific aspects of the relationship (Weiss, 1980). As a result of a process of "sentiment override," partners who are generally satisfied with their relationships should tend to evaluate specific aspects of the relationship positively, whereas partners in generally distressed relationships should tend to evaluate specific aspects of the relationship negatively. This line of thinking indicated a need for further work on how partners perceive and interpret each other's behaviors (e.g., Bradbury & Fincham, 1987; Fincham & O'Leary, 1983; Weiss, 1984a), but by itself it said more about the cognitive consequences of global impressions than about the determinants of those impressions.

A subsequent line of thinking about cognition in close relationships shifted the focus from partners' perceptions of the relationship to their beliefs about how relationships function. Drawing from models of rational emotive therapy (Ellis & Grieger, 1977) and cognitive theories of depression (e.g., Abramson, Seligman, & Teasdale, 1978; Seligman, Abramson, Semel, & Von Baeyer, 1979), Epstein and his colleagues (Eidelson & Epstein, 1982; Epstein & Eidelson, 1981) were among the first to argue that certain beliefs about relationships may be dysfunctional. For example, individuals who hold the unrealistic belief that all disagreements are destructive to a relationship are likely to experience disappointment when disagreements arise in their own relationships. To evaluate these ideas, researchers have developed a number of self-report inventories that assess partners' general beliefs and theories about relationship functioning (e.g., Baucom, Epstein, Rankin, & Burnett, 1996; Eidelson & Epstein, 1982; Fletcher & Kininmonth, 1992; Hendrick & Hendrick, 1986; Knee, 1998; Sprecher & Metts, 1989). To date, evidence for a main effect of general beliefs on satisfaction in a particular relationship has been mixed. For example, a number of studies using Eidelson and Epstein's Relationship Belief Inventory (RBI) have found that married spouses who endorse more unrealistic beliefs about relationships also report lower marital satisfaction (e.g., Bradbury & Fincham, 1993; Epstein & Eidelson, 1981; Kurdek, 1992). In contrast, research with the Inventory of Specific Relationship Standards (ISRS), developed by Baucom and his colleagues (1996), found that spouses who endorse higher standards for relationships tend to report higher marital satisfaction. Furthermore, research on dating couples that has used other instruments to assess relationship theories and beliefs has failed to find any direct associations between beliefs and relationship satisfaction (e.g., Fletcher & Kininmonth, 1992; Knee, 1998). The inconsistency of the results across measures and populations suggests that general relationship beliefs may be associated with evaluations of a particular relationship only under certain conditions.

The nature of those conditions was finally suggested by models that integrated the two earlier lines of thinking. The roots of these models lie in Thibaut and Kelley's interdependence theory of interpersonal relationships (Kelley & Thibaut, 1978; Thibaut & Kelley, 1959). In this view, a specific relationship event or outcome will be perceived as satisfying or costly only to the extent that it exceeds or falls short of an individual's enduring values, or comparison level (CL), for relationships. Because standards for relationship functioning and perceptions of specific aspects of relationships vary across individuals, neither category of judgment should directly affect relationship satisfaction. Rather, general beliefs and values for relationships should *moderate* the impact of partners' perceptions of specific aspects of the relationship on their impressions of the relationship as a whole. In other words, a specific perception will have different effects on global evaluations of a relationship depending on the beliefs and values of the perceiver (cf. Kelley et al., 1983; Bradbury & Fincham, 1989, 1991).

Thus, current theories of cognition in close relationships emphasize the interplay between cognitive content and specific experience. To the extent that beliefs are confirmed and standards are met, then initially positive evaluations of a relationship should remain high. Satisfaction should decline, however, when partners' experiences do not coincide with their enduring beliefs and values. It is not the content of cognition itself, but rather the way cognitive content affects interpretations of specific events that determines the development of global relationship satisfaction.

Methodological considerations

Before reviewing empirical research on these issues, two methodological considerations should be noted. First, the reliance on self-report measures, common to much of this research, raises the potential problem of item overlap. For example, frequently used measures of relationship satisfaction, such as the Marital Adjustment Test (Locke & Wallace, 1959) and the Dyadic Adjustment Test (Spanier, 1976), include items assessing a wide range of constructs. In cases where instruments measuring cognitive constructs overlap with these measures, it is entirely possible that significant associations may result from the same construct being measured twice, rather than from an empirical relationship between independent constructs (see Fincham & Bradbury, 1987).

This problem may be exacerbated by a second methodological concern. The wide array of terms used to describe different aspects of cognitive content (e.g., beliefs, assumptions, standards, expectations, ideals, values, theories, etc.) have usually been defined vaguely and in ways that do not clearly distinguish one construct from another (see Baucom et al., 1989). For example, expectations have been described variously as standards for the relationship (e.g., "This is what I expect to receive and I will not settle for less") and as predictions for the relationship (e.g., "I expect that we will have children in a couple of years").

In this chapter, we distinguish between two broad classes of cognitive content: beliefs and values (see Baucom et al., 1996; Kurdek, 1992). Consistent with the distinction offered by Fletcher and Thomas (1996), beliefs can represent general ideas, theories, and assumptions about relationships, or they can represent specific expectations, narrowly defined as predictions for the future, about the functioning of a particular relationship. These types of cognition will be discussed together because both affect the specific experiences that individuals anticipate in their relationships (cf. Baldwin, 1992). In contrast, values encompass standards and ideals, which represent what individuals believe should occur and wish would occur, respectively. Although conceptual distinctions between standards and ideals have been articulated (e.g., Higgins, 1997), these constructs will be discussed together here because both affect how individuals evaluate their specific experiences in relationships (see Tangney, Niedenthal, Covert, & Barlow, 1998, for research that fails to find consequential differences between standards and ideals).

Empirical research

Beliefs.   Researchers have demonstrated at least two ways in which beliefs interact with specific experiences to affect relationship satisfaction. First, certain beliefs may motivate relationship maintenance behaviors that can bolster initial satisfaction. Early evidence for this idea came from experimental research on self-fulfilling prophecies. In a classic study by Snyder, Tanke, and Berscheid (1977), male participants engaged in a telephone conversation with a woman that they believed was either attractive or unattractive. Participants expected that attractive conversation partners would be more sociable, and so they were: those who believed they were conversing with attractive partners led their partners to behave in a more sociable manner. Correlational research on expectancies in close relationships has obtained similar results. For example, the burgeoning literature on adult attachment suggests that people's internal working models of relationships affect the way they approach and maintain their own relationships (e.g., Klohnen & Bera, 1998; Shaver, Collins, & Clark, 1996). Similarly, marital research has shown that spouses with high expectations of personal efficacy (i.e., spouses who believe that they have the ability to affect desired changes in their lives; see Doherty, 1981; Fincham, Bradbury, & Grych, 1990) exchange more positive behaviors during problem-solving discussions and maintain higher marital satisfaction over a one-year period, controlling for their initial satisfaction, compared to spouses who have lower expectations of personal efficacy (Bradbury, 1989). Downey, Freitas, Michaelis, and Khouri (1998) demonstrated more specifically, through daily diary reports and observations of conflict discussions in dating couples, that individuals who expect to be rejected in their personal relationships lead their partners to behave in a more rejecting manner towards them.

Which beliefs motivate relationship maintenance behaviors and which beliefs discourage them? The answer is not entirely clear because, as noted earlier, some positive beliefs, such as expectations of personal efficacy, are associated with efforts to maintain the relationship, whereas other positive beliefs, such as the expectation that partners can read each other's minds, are not. Research on behavior in other domains offers a possible explanation, suggesting that expectations of achievement through effort and expectations of achievement without effort have very different implications for goal-directed behavior (e.g., Henderson & Dweck, 1990; Pham & Taylor, 1999). To date, this distinction has not been examined directly in the context of close relationships.

A second way that beliefs and theories may affect the development of relationship satisfaction is through their effects on how partners interpret specific experiences in the relationship. The same experiences may have different implications for an individual's relationship satisfaction depending on the individual's beliefs about how relationships function. For example, Downey and Feldman demonstrated that individuals who expect to be rejected in their personal relationships are more likely to label an ambiguous interaction with a confederate as rejecting, compared to individuals who do not expect to be rejected. Ruvolo and Rotondo (1998) compared the association between specific views of a partner and overall relationship satisfaction among dating couples with varying beliefs about the malleability of personality. For individuals who believed that people's personalities are fixed and unlikely to change, specific impressions of the partner were strongly associated with global impressions of the relationship. However, for individuals who believed that people's personalities are malleable, the association between specific impressions of the partner and global impressions of the relationship was significantly weaker. In a related line of research, Knee (1998) examined dating partners who endorsed different theories about whether relationship outcomes were destined (i.e., determined by fate and the immutable characteristics of the partners) or grown (i.e., developed through effort and communication). Neither type of belief had any direct associations with relationship satisfaction. However, in response to relationship stressors, those who endorsed destiny beliefs reported reacting with disengagement and restraint, whereas those who endorsed growth beliefs reported reacting with more active coping strategies. Furthermore, for individuals who endorsed destiny beliefs, initial relationship satisfaction predicted the longevity of the relationship across six months, whereas for individuals endorsing a low belief in destiny, initial satisfaction was unrelated to the longevity of the relationship. In other words, the long-term implications of relationship stressors and initial relationship satisfaction may depend on whether partners believe that relationship outcomes can be affected by their own efforts.

A central issue may be whether a given experience is consistent with expectations or a violation of expectations (e.g., Afifi & Metts, 1998; Burgoon, 1993). Experiences that are consistent with general beliefs about how relationships function should require less adjustment than experiences that are inconsistent with those beliefs. To examine this idea, Helgeson (1994) examined relationship beliefs among dating couples coping with long-distance relationships. Not surprisingly, partners who endorsed positive beliefs about the relationship were more likely to stay together over the course of three months. However, for those couples who did not stay together, those initially endorsing positive relationship beliefs experienced greater distress, controlling for initial levels of distress and for which partner initiated the breakup. As Helgeson concludes: "Positive relationship beliefs might facilitate adjustment to a relationship stressor when beliefs are confirmed . . . but impede adjustment to a relationship stressor when beliefs are disconfirmed" (p. 254). Vanzetti, Notarius, & NeeSmith (1992) obtained additional evidence of an interaction between expectancies and experiences within the context of marital interactions. In this study, married couples who were high or low in perceptions of relational efficacy were asked to predict their partners' behaviors during an upcoming marital interaction, and then to make attributions for the behaviors that actually occurred during the interaction. The key analysis compared the two groups of couples on their attributions for the unpredicted negative behaviors of their partners. Spouses who reported low relational efficacy were likely to make dispositional attributions for their partners' unexpected negative behaviors during the interaction, thereby blaming their partners for the negative experiences. In contrast, spouses who reported high relational efficacy were significantly less likely to make dispositional attributions for their partners' unexpected negative behaviors during the interaction. Together, these studies suggest that individuals' beliefs about relationships affect the development of their satisfaction by determining whether specific negative experiences are expected, and thus likely to motivate adequate coping strategies, or unexpected, and thus likely to give rise to maladaptive coping strategies.

Values   The standards and ideals that partners use to evaluate experiences in their close relationships may affect their satisfaction in the same ways that beliefs and theories do. Specifically, relationship-relevant values should moderate the impact of specific experiences such that experiences consistent with an individual's values should enhance satisfaction, whereas experiences inconsistent with an individual's values should diminish satisfaction. A number of studies have supported this view. For example, Fletcher and Kininmonth (1992) examined standards, satisfaction, and self-reports of behavior in a sample of college students. Standards had no direct association with satisfaction, but standards did moderate the association between satisfaction and behavior. For individuals who held that a specific type of behavior was an important part of a good relationship, reports of that behavior were highly correlated with satisfaction. For individuals who held that a specific behavior was less important, reports of that behavior were less strongly associated with satisfaction (see also Simpson, Fletcher, & Campbell, 2001). Baucom et al. (1996) elaborated on the role of standards by assessing perceptions of whether or not those standards were being met among spouses in established marriages. Not surprisingly, spouses who perceived that their standards were being met were more satisfied with their relationships than spouses who did not perceive their standards being met. Kelley and Burgoon (1991) assessed violations of standards more directly by comparing spouses' standards for various specific aspects of a relationship with their perceptions of those aspects of their own relationships. The greater the discrepancy between standards and perceptions, the lower the spouses' satisfaction with the relationship.

Two limitations of these studies are that all have been cross-sectional and none have separated the main effects of high or low standards from the main effects of discrepancies between standards and perceptions. Ruvolo and Veroff (1997) addressed these limitations by using multiple regression to examine the unique effects of perceptions of the relationship, relationship-relevant ideals, and real–ideal discrepancies, on change in satisfaction over the first year of marriage. For wives, real–ideal discrepancies, but not perceptions or ideals by themselves, predicted change in satisfaction over the first year. None of these variables predicted changes for husbands, perhaps because husbands experienced relatively little change in their satisfaction over the study period.

The finding that discrepancies between perceptions of the relationship and standards for the relationship predict declines in satisfaction over time raises a provocative question: is it beneficial or harmful for individuals to hold high relationship standards? On one hand, Epstein and his colleagues (Eidelson & Epstein, 1982; Epstein & Eidelson, 1981) have argued that unrealistically high standards place initially satisfied partners at greater risk for disappointment. This logic has led some to argue (e.g., Miller, 1997b) that relationships would be more stable if partners lowered their standards and learned to accept less than their ideal relationships. On the other hand, Murray, Holmes, and Griffin (1996) have argued that high standards act as self-fulfilling prophecies, leading to happier relationships over time. The research reviewed in this section suggests that neither position is completely accurate. These studies support the view that the standards and ideals that individuals use to evaluate experiences in their relationships have negligible direct effects on the development of their marital satisfaction. Rather, high standards support the relationship only to the extent that the individual perceives these standards as being met. Modest standards protect the relationship only if the relationship provides experiences that surpass those standards. Rather than focusing on the cognitions themselves, current research suggests that it is the interaction between partners' values and their experiences that is likely to account for changes in satisfaction over time.

Agreement between partners.   Several researchers have raised the possibility that, in addition to the content of each partner's cognitions, the compatibility between partners' cognitions plays an important role in the development of their relationship. This is a possibility worth considering carefully, because research on cognition in relationships, as can be seen from the studies described above, has focused mostly on intrapsychic, rather than dyadic, analyses.

Despite the potential value of dyadic analyses, to date research that has examined the compatibility of spouses' cognitions has demonstrated few noteworthy effects compared with the effects of perceived discrepancies between values and perceptions within each partner. For example, Baucom et al. (1996) reported that between-spouse differences in relationship standards were negatively associated with relationship satisfaction. However, these associations were notably weaker than the main effects of standards and perceived discrepancies within each spouse. Using multiple regression, Kelley and Burgoon (1991) directly compared agreement between spouses and real–ideal discrepancies within each spouse for their ability to account for variance in spouses' relationship satisfaction. For both spouses, real–ideal discrepancies within each spouse accounted for significantly more variance than agreement between spouses. Finally, Acitelli, Kenny, and Gladstone (1996) noted that any two partners' standards are likely to agree with each other to some extent due to the general agreement among most people about certain values (see Kenny & Acitelli, 1994). Controlling for the stereotypical beliefs held by all couples, Acitelli et al. found no significant associations between spousal agreement on their ideals for marriage and their concurrent marital satisfaction.

Summary and critique

How does cognitive content affect the development of relationship satisfaction? The research and theory reviewed in this section suggest that cognitive content moderates the association between specific information and global evaluations of a relationship. A given experience or perception can contribute to or detract from an individual's initially positive evaluations depending on whether or not that experience or perception is consistent with the individual's beliefs and values. Relationships should remain satisfying to the extent that experiences in the relationship meet or exceed partners' standards for how relationships function. However, satisfaction should decline to the extent that experiences in the relationship fall short of partners' standards or fail to confirm their positive expectations.

An important limitation of this view is that it assumes that, compared to global impressions of the relationship, beliefs and values are relatively enduring aspects of each partner. This may be an accurate assumption, but to date there has been no empirical research to support it. As noted earlier, most of the research in this domain has been cross-sectional, and thus incapable of assessing the stability of cognitive content over time. The few longitudinal studies described in this section have measured cognitive content only at Time 1, using that assessment to predict changes in relationship satisfaction over time. In the absence of longitudinal data on the stability of relationship-relevant beliefs and values, the possibility remains that these cognitions are not stable, but rather may themselves change as a reaction to changes in the quality of the relationship. In other words, rather than beliefs and values determining the global meaning of specific experiences, it is equally likely that specific experiences may affect the development of beliefs and values within the individual. Within the literature on attachment models, there is at least tentative evidence that this can occur (Davila, Karney, & Bradbury, 1999; Kirkpatrick & Hazan, 1994). Before definitive statements can be made about the causal role of cognitive content in close relationships, longitudinal data are needed to evaluate this alternative possibility.

The Structure of Cognition in Close Relationships

There has been far less research on the structure of cognitions in close relationships than there has been on the content of those cognitions. Nevertheless, the way people organize relationship-relevant knowledge may have particular significance for explaining how evaluations of the relationship change or remain stable over time. For example, maintaining globally positive evaluations in the face of the specific challenges and vicissitudes of daily life requires the capacity to assimilate discordant information and respond appropriately to new situations (Raush, Barry, Hertel, & Swain, 1974). As Burgess, Wallin, and Schultz (1954) pointed out in their early research on marriage, "the ability to adjust to one's mate and to the responsibilities of the married state might be regarded, from one standpoint, as the most important factor of all in determining the success or failure of a marriage" (p. 313). The structure of partners' cognitive representations of the relationship may account for this ability.

In other areas of social psychology, research on cognitive structure is well developed (e.g., Scott, Osgood, & Peterson, 1979; Tetlock, 1983). Why has there been so little research on the structure of cognition in close relationships? One reason may be that structure has not played a large role in the theories guiding research in this field. Just as various aspects of cognitive content have been studied without regard to how these aspects may be organized and related to each other, so has the organization of relationship-relevant knowledge within the individual been all but overlooked as a topic of research interest. Another reason may be that studying cognitive structure requires a different repertoire of methods than are commonly employed in research on close relationships. Rather than relying on partners' direct reports of how their cognitions are organized, research on cognitive structure tends to use more indirect techniques, inferring aspects of cognitive structure through thought-listing tasks and assessments of reaction time.

Despite these theoretical and methodological obstacles, a number of researchers have explored the implications of how cognitions are structured for the development of close relationships. In this section, we review theory and research on two dimensions of cognitive structure that have been studied within this context: the complexity of partners' beliefs about the relationship, and the accessibility of certain beliefs and evaluations.

Cognitive complexity

Theoretical perspectives.   As noted earlier, relationship-relevant cognitions can vary from global beliefs about how relationships function to perceptions of specific partner characteristics (e.g., Fletcher & Thomas, 1996; Srull & Wyer, 1989; see also Baldwin, 1992). Cognitive complexity (also referred to as conceptual or integrative complexity) draws attention to how individuals differentiate and integrate these distinct cognitions (e.g., Crockett, 1965; Schroder, 1971). Differentiation refers to the number of categories or kinds of information taken into account in evaluating persons or events. For example, people with relatively undifferentiated beliefs about their relationship might evaluate their partners' behaviors by categorizing them as either selfish or unselfish. A person with a more differentiated set of beliefs would recognize that a specific behavior can be evaluated in multiple or even contradictory ways. Integration refers to the degree and quality of the connections among differentiated characteristics. For example, people with less integrated beliefs about their relationships may acknowledge differences of opinion with their partners, but people with highly integrated beliefs should both acknowledge differences and recognize the multiple levels at which different positions on an issue connect and interact. It follows that differentiation is a prerequisite for integration (Tetlock & Suedfeld, 1988).

A premise of research on cognitive complexity in close relationships is that more complex representations of a relationship, independent of the content of those representations, allow partners more flexibility in assimilating specific information about the relationship (R. W. Martin, 1991; Neimeyer, 1984). Thus, an initially complex view of the relationship may allow partners to distinguish their globally positive views of the relationship from the specific challenges of everyday life. In contrast, an initially simple view of the relationship may be more fragile and more likely to deteriorate in response to specific setbacks. In this way, greater cognitive complexity should be associated with more resilient relationship satisfaction over time (cf. also Linville, 1987; Showers, 1992a, 1992b, for similar ideas in research on self-concepts).

Empirical research.   Cross-sectional research suggests that the complexity of partners' cognitions about their relationships is associated with important relationship processes. For example, two studies have examined the association between cognitive complexity and satisfaction in established marriages (Crouse, Karlins, & Schroder, 1968; Neimeyer, 1984). Crouse et al. measured the complexity of spouses' beliefs about their marriage by asking each spouse to continue a series of sentences beginning with relationship-relevant phrases (e.g., "When my mate does not agree with me . . ."). The resulting paragraphs were then rated for differentiation and integration. Neimeyer used a different procedure, asking spouses to complete Kelly's (1955) Role Construct Repertory Test, an instrument that assesses spouses' views of their own families for level of differentiation only. In both studies, complexity scores were moderately associated with marital satisfaction. However, the lack of longitudinal data leaves the precise interpretation of these findings unclear. Although the findings raise the possibility that spouses with more complex views of the marriage are also more satisfied with their relationships, Tetlock and Suedfeld (1988) argue that the complexity of a set of cognitions at any one time should be independent of the content of those cognitions. An alternative explanation of these findings is that complexity predicts rates of change in satisfaction over time and that spouses in these established marriages had experienced different changes in their relationships by the time they were studied. Distinguishing between these possible effects requires longitudinal data and analyses capable of separating effects on levels of satisfaction from effects on rates of change (Karney & Bradbury, 1995a), but such data have not been reported in this area.

More recent research suggests that cognitive complexity may affect the development of close relationships through its association with the way partners communicate with each other. Spouses whose cognitions about relationships are more complex may possess a broader range of potential responses to specific experiences and so should be more likely to exchange adaptive behaviors during problem-solving discussions. Cross-sectional research offers some support for this idea. For example, Tyndall and Lichtenberg (1985) used Budner's (1962) Intolerance of Ambiguity Scale to measure how spouses in established marriages approached ambiguous or inconsistent information in their environments. Spouses describing themselves as more tolerant of ambiguity reported their interactions with their partners to be more adaptive and less rigid than spouses who described themselves as intolerant of ambiguity. Moving beyond self-report data, R. Martin (1992) assessed the complexity of spouses' open-ended descriptions of important relationships and then recorded spouses engaging in problem-solving discussions. The complexity of husbands, but not of wives, was associated with behavior during these discussions, such that husbands who were more complex tended to be more supportive than husbands who were less complex.

A limitation of both of these studies, however, is that neither one examined the simultaneous associations between relationship satisfaction and behavior, leaving open the possibility that associations between satisfaction and both complexity and behavior accounts for the previous findings. Denton, Burleson, and Sprenkle (1995) addressed this possibility by assessing marital satisfaction, cognitive complexity, and problem-solving behavior in a study of established marriages. Analyses indicated that the composite satisfaction of the couple moderated the association between cognitive complexity and problem-solving behaviors. In marriages where both partners were satisfied, complexity scores were unrelated to the quality of the interaction. However, in distressed marriages, spouses who were rated as more cognitively complex proved to be more effective communicators in that the intent of their behaviors matched the impact of those behaviors on the partner.

Summary.   Researchers examining cognitive complexity have yet to reach consensus on the appropriate operationalization of the construct. Thus, it is noteworthy that the findings of these studies have been fairly consistent so far. More complex representations of relationships in general appear to be associated with a more flexible and adaptive repertoire of problem-solving behaviors, and possibly with higher satisfaction in established marriages. Still to be addressed is the question of how the complexity of partners' representations of their relationships may influence the way those representations change or remain stable over time.

Accessibility

Theoretical perspectives.   In contrast to work on cognitive complexity, which examines the structure of a set of cognitions, research on accessibility examines the ease with which a particular cognition can be brought to mind (Bruner, 1957). A premise of research in this area is that different cognitions vary along this dimension (e.g., Higgins & King, 1981). For example, some beliefs and values are likely to be easily accessible. These cognitions may be chronically activated, or they may be so frequently activated that their reactivation is relatively automatic. Highly accessible cognitions should significantly affect interpretations of relevant specific experiences, increasing the likelihood that new information is assimilated to existing knowledge structures. Thus, highly accessible cognitions should be more stable over time. In contrast, some beliefs and values will be relatively inaccessible. To the extent that certain cognitions are difficult to bring to mind, those cognitions should be less likely to affect interpretations of new data. In this case, existing cognitions are more likely to accommodate to new information, and so should be more likely to change over time. In sum, this view suggests that the accessibility of a particular cognition should moderate the impact of the cognition on the interpretation of specific experiences and on the stability of the cognition over time.

Among relationship-relevant cognitions, satisfaction has been assumed to be highly accessible for most people and thus likely to influence perceptions of specific events across a variety of contexts (Weiss, 1980). Nevertheless, research in other domains has documented significant individual differences in the accessibility of even highly accessible beliefs (e.g., Markus & Smith, 1981). To measure these differences, some researchers have operationalized accessibility as the speed with which an individual uses a particular belief or value to judge a particular object, adjusted for individual differences in speed of responding (see Fazio, 1990). Research participants are typically presented with a range of stimuli and asked to judge whether each one is relevant or irrelevant to a particular cognition. The time to react to the stimulus, also called the response latency, is considered a measure of the accessibility of the cognition in question. Measured in this way, individual differences in construct accessibility tend to be small, a matter of milliseconds or less. Nevertheless, individual differences in accessibility have been associated with a number of important outcomes (e.g., Fazio, 1995).

Empirical research.   Does the accessibility of relationship-relevant cognitions moderate the effects of those cognitions on the relationship? Research conducted by Fincham and his colleagues offers preliminary evidence that it does. In this study, spouses in established marriages reported on their marital satisfaction, attributions, and expectations for their partners' behavior immediately prior to a marital interaction. Spouses also participated in a series of computer tasks in which the time to judge a series of relationship-relevant words (e.g., "your spouse," "your husband") as positive or negative was measured. For husbands, but not for wives, response latencies on the computer task were associated with the strength of the correlation between marital satisfaction and preinteraction expectations. In husbands whose marital satisfaction was highly accessible, marital satisfaction and preinteraction expectations were more strongly correlated than in husbands whose marital satisfaction was less accessible, controlling for overall levels of marital satisfaction. For both spouses, accessibility also moderated the association between marital satisfaction and attributions, such that satisfaction and attributions were more strongly associated in spouses for whom marital satisfaction was more accessible. Additional analyses of this data set (Fincham, 1998) revealed that the accessibility of spouses' marital satisfaction moderated the association between satisfaction and the actual behaviors that spouses exchanged during marital interactions. Behavior and satisfaction were significantly associated only for those spouses whose marital satisfaction was highly accessible. Finally, these effects appear to have implications for the development of relationship satisfaction over time. Through retrospective analyses of these couples, Fincham demonstrated that the accessibility of one spouse's marital satisfaction moderates the stability, measured by a test–retest correlation, of the other spouse's marital satisfaction over the previous 18 months, such that marital satisfaction is more stable for spouses whose partners' marital satisfaction is more accessible. It should be noted that all of these findings await replication in an independent sample. Yet the consistent pattern across dependent measures supports the idea that individual differences in the accessibility of relationship-relevant cognitions may moderate the effect of those cognitions on other relationship processes.

To the extent that this idea receives further confirmation, these data raise an additional important question: how do individual differences in the accessibility of these cognitions come about? Some have suggested that the accessibility of a belief or value is associated with its strength or extremity (e.g., Fazio, 1995). To evaluate this possibility, Fletcher, Rosanowski, and Fitness (1994) measured response latencies in a sample of dating partners with either strong or weak beliefs about the importance of intimacy and passion in relationships. Half of the individuals engaged in the response latency task while distracted by an irrelevant memory task, and half engaged in the task without distraction. For partners who endorsed strong beliefs, the addition of the memory task had no effect on response latencies, suggesting that the beliefs of these individuals could be activated automatically. In contrast, for partners who endorsed weak beliefs, the memory task significantly increased response latencies, suggesting that the beliefs of these individuals were less accessible and therefore more difficult to activate under conditions of distraction. These findings suggest that the cognitions of individuals with more extreme beliefs and values may also be highly accessible and thus likely to influence interpretations of specific experiences.

As an alternative explanation for individual differences in the accessibility of relationship cognitions, Baldwin and his colleagues (Baldwin, 1994; Baldwin, Carrell, & Lopez, 1990; Baldwin, Keelan, Fehr, Enns, & Koh-Rangarajoo, 1996) focused on the ability of different contexts to activate, or prime, specific beliefs and values from among the many that a person might apply to a given situation. For example, Baldwin and Fehr (1995) argued that individuals possess not one attachment model, as has been assumed in most research on attachment, but rather many models that are activated at different times depending on the specific context. In a study that supports this view, Baldwin et al. (1996) demonstrated that randomly assigning participants to be primed with a particular type of attachment experience significantly affected their attraction to different potential dating partners. Their explanation for this finding is that priming a specific attachment model made that model more accessible, thus allowing that model to exert a greater influence over subsequent evaluations. Presumably, different social environments are more or less likely to prime different available relationship cognitions.

Summary.   To the extent that aspects of cognitive content affect how an individual interprets and responds to specific experiences, the research reviewed in this section suggests that relatively accessible cognitions will exert a greater effect than relatively inaccessible ones. Yet research on the determinants of accessibility indicates that the same cognition may be more or less accessible in different contexts. Thus, a task for future research in this area is to determine the natural conditions under which important relationship-relevant cognitions are more or less accessible, and thus more or less likely to affect relationship development.

General critique

Research on the structure of cognitions in close relationships is still in its early stages. The two dimensions reviewed in this section – complexity and accessibility – have only begun to be examined in detail. Furthermore, there remain potentially important aspects of cognitive structure that have yet to be studied with respect to close relationships (Baldwin, 1992; Beach, Etherton, & Whitaker, 1995). For example, individuals may vary in the strength of the covariance between their global evaluations about their relationships and their perceptions of specific aspects of the relationship over time. A strong covariance between global evaluations and specific perceptions may indicate satisfaction that is relatively fragile and sensitive to negative experiences, whereas a weak covariance may indicate satisfaction that is robust to specific negative experiences. In addition, relationships among dimensions of cognitive structure are of potential interest. For example, the complexity of individuals' representations of their relationships may have implications for the accessibility of specific aspects of that representation. Within a more complex representation, the accessibility of any specific cognition may be diminished, leading to less schematic processing for those with more complex representations.

To understand the effects of any of these aspects of cognitive structure on the development of close relationships, longitudinal research is crucial for two reasons. Most obviously, such research is necessary to address the key hypothesis of this research: that the structure of individuals' cognitions about their close relationships affects the resiliency of those cognitions over time. Less obviously, longitudinal research is needed to answer important questions about the origins and development of cognitive structures. With respect to complexity and accessibility, for example, it seems likely that certain representations (such as my image of my spouse during an argument) may become more or less complex, and certain beliefs and values (such as the importance of intimacy and passion in a relationship) may become more or less accessible, depending on the experiences of each partner in the relationship over time.

The Process of Cognition in Close Relationships

Each aspect of cognitive content and cognitive structure reviewed so far can be seen as the product of cognitive processes. These processes include all of the ways in which individuals pursue, integrate, explain, evaluate, and recall general and specific information about their relationships. As many researchers have recognized, the nature of these processes may affect relationships independent of the products of these processes (e.g., Baucom et al., 1989; Fincham, Bradbury, & Scott 1990). The way spouses make attributions for each other's behaviors, for example, has been the most extensively studied cognitive process in this domain. A well-developed literature demonstrates that the nature of partners' attributions has important implications for how their global relationship satisfaction changes or remains stable over time (for reviews, see Baucom, 1987; Bradbury & Fincham, 1990; Harvey, 1987.

Aside from attributions, however, research on close relationships has not focused much attention on the details of specific cognitive processes and how they operate. Instead, this research has focused on the broad motives that may influence the processing of specific information (Kunda, 1990). A premise of this research is that the processing of relationship-relevant information is not strictly rational but rather biased towards the fulfillment of an individual's hopes and aspirations for themselves and their relationships. For example, most people strongly desire to be in a relationship that they perceive as satisfying. Thus, research on close relationships has identified specific cognitive processes that allow individuals to maintain and enhance their perceptions of satisfaction. Other processing goals have also been proposed, and some evidence suggests that these goals also affect the processing of relationship-relevant information. In this section, we review the evidence that the motivated processing of specific information in close relationships may affect the development of global satisfaction.

Maintenance and enhancement

One of the challenges of a long-term relationship is to preserve a positive global evaluation of the relationship despite the specific problems and disappointments that are likely to arise over time. For people who are constrained to remain in their relationships regardless of their satisfaction (e.g., by the presence of children or the lack of available alternatives), this challenge is especially poignant. Rather than confront the possibility that they are trapped in an unsatisfying situation, most people should be highly motivated, regardless of the objective quality of their relationships, to maintain the general belief that their relationships are rewarding and worth pursuing. Research on cognition in close relationships has identified a number of specific processes through which individuals might accomplish this goal.

Social comparison.   One way to justify remaining in an imperfect relationship is to engage in self-serving social comparisons (e.g., Wood & Taylor, 1991) and decide that one's own relationship, whatever its problems, is better than other people's relationships. Indeed, a number of researchers have shown that most people do believe their own relationships to be more supportive (Taylor, Wood, & Lichtman, 1983), more equitable (Buunk & Van Yperen, 1989), and less likely to end (Weinstein, 1980) than the relationships of other people. Buunk and van der Eijnden (1997) demonstrated that the degree of perceived superiority is associated with satisfaction, such that unsatisfied individuals are less likely than satisfied individuals to perceive their relationships as superior (cf. also Fowers, Lyons & Montel, 1996). Nevertheless, even in this study, a perception of superiority was reported by all but the most distressed individuals.

How might the perception of superiority come about? To explore processes that might give rise to the perception of superiority, van Lange and Rusbult (1995) asked undergraduates to list their spontaneous thoughts about their own dating relationships and those of unspecified others. When thinking about their own relationships, people tended to report more positive thoughts than negative ones. However, when thinking about the relationships of others, people tended to report more negative thoughts than positive ones. Furthermore, people were able to generate more positive thoughts about their own relationships than about other people's relationships, and more negative thoughts about other people's relationships than their own. To understand these findings, the authors proposed that people have a "tendency to focus selectively on attributes that make one's own relationship appear advantaged" (1995, p. 43). In other words, out of all the specific dimensions upon which people may compare their relationships to others, people may choose to make comparisons on the specific dimensions that will support the general conclusions they wish to reach.

Derogation of alternatives.   Another process that may contribute to the perception that one's own relationship is superior to others is the derogation of alternative relationship partners. Even for people in satisfying, committed relationships, the presence of an attractive alternative partner can be threatening, potentially raising questions about the value of one's own partner. To avoid having to face these questions, Thibaut and Kelley (1959) proposed that people can eliminate the threat "by taking a 'sour grapes' attitude toward the rewarding aspects of the [alternative] or by emphasizing the negative, cost-increasing aspects of it" (p. 175). Johnson and Rusbult (1989), in one of a series of studies, evaluated this idea by asking people in dating relationships to evaluate photographs of members of the opposite sex, ostensibly for use in a computer dating service. Half were told that their ratings would be used to match them with partners through the service (high threat condition); the other half were told that they would not be participating in the service (low threat condition). People's attitudes towards their own relationships were not generally associated with their ratings of the targets. However, when the targets were attractive and potentially threatening, people who were more committed to their own relationships rated the targets as significantly less desirable than people who were less committed to their own relationships (for replications and extensions of this work, see Lydon, Meana, Sepinwall, Richards, & Mayman, 1999; Simpson, 1987). These findings suggest that people may have considerable latitude in how they evaluate potential alternative partners. The desire to perceive one's own relationship as superior may lead individuals to evaluate alternatives in the most negative way possible.

Selective attention.   Baucom et al. (1989) suggested that one of the fundamental ways in which individuals maintain positive global impressions of their relationships is by selectively attending only to specific information consistent with that impression. In other words, the desire to believe that one is in a rewarding relationship should lead partners to focus on the positive aspects of the relationship and ignore the negative ones. This is a provocative suggestion, but to date there has been little research directly exploring this idea. The one relevant study that we are aware of examined selective attention not for positive and negative aspects of one's own relationship, but for attractive alternatives outside of one's relationship. Miller (1997a) asked subjects to review, at their own pace, a series of slides featuring attractive members of the opposite sex. People who were in relationships where they felt committed and close spent significantly less time reviewing the slides than people who did not feel committed and close to their partners, or who were not in relationships. These findings were interpreted as support for the idea that one way to maintain positive feelings about a relationship is to pay less attention to information, like the availability of attractive alternatives, that might threaten those feelings.

Rationalization.   Similar to the process of attending to positive aspects of a relationship and ignoring negative ones, people motivated to protect their globally positive impressions of their relationships may construct narratives that discount negative aspects of the relationship and augment positive ones. In a sophisticated program of research, Murray and Holmes (1993, 1994) have demonstrated that, when faced with specific threatening information about their relationship partners, people tell stories that minimize the impact of that information. In one study, members of satisfied dating couples who had rated their relationships as low in conflict were informed (falsely) that conflict was actually a sign of a healthy relationship. Participants were then given an opportunity to describe their relationships in an open-ended narrative. Compared to a control group who had not been given the false information, partners who believed conflict was a sign of strength told stories that exaggerated instances of conflict and discounted the conflict avoidance they had reported earlier. These findings suggest that people selectively recruit and weave together specific information to construct narratives that support the general impressions they desire to maintain.

Temporal comparison.   Most research on comparison processes in close relationships has focused on social comparisons. However, it is also possible that relationships are evaluated through temporal comparisons, i.e., through comparisons between the current state of the relationship and the state of the relationship at some point in the past (Albert, 1977). Carver and Scheier (1990) have suggested that the perceptions of change that arise from such comparisons drive people's affective responses to their current state, such that the perception of growth is rewarding and the perception of stagnation and decline is distressing (see also Aronson & Linder, 1965). With respect to relationships, one implication of this idea is that people should be motivated to perceive their relationships as growing more satisfying over time, and their recollections of the past may be biased in order to maintain this perception. Karney and Coombs (2000) evaluated this possibility in a longitudinal study of wives' perceptions of the emotional quality of their marriages. Prospective ratings of the relationship across ten years indicated that wives' perceptions of their marriages grew significantly less positive over time, consistent with other longitudinal research (e.g., Johnson, Amoloza, & Booth, 1992; Vaillant & Vaillant, 1993). However, retrospective reports indicated that the wives believed that their marriages had become significantly more positive over the same interval, and they justified this belief by negatively biasing their recollections of the past. This process had important implications for the future of the relationship, such that wives who did not perceive the present as an improvement over the past were more likely to divorce over the subsequent ten years. Together with other research on the malleability of memory in close relationships (Sprecher, 1999), these findings suggest that the way individuals recall the past may be influenced by the desire to preserve and enhance positive evaluations of the present.

Accuracy and verification

Supporting positive impressions is not the only goal that may drive the processing of information in close relationships. As partners in developing relationships grow more dependent on one another, their need to understand and predict each other's behavior should lead to a desire for accurate information about the relationship, regardless of whether that information is positive or negative (Newman & Langer, 1988). For individuals in unsatisfying relationships, this motive should lead individuals to process information very differently from those whose thinking is driven by the enhancement or maintenance motive. A number of researchers have explored specific implications of this idea. For example, Swann and his colleagues (e.g., de la Ronde & Swann, 1998; Swann, 1983, Swann, De La Ronde, & Hixon, 1994), in a lengthy program of research, have suggested that people attempt to verify their strongly held beliefs about themselves and their intimates, even when those beliefs are negative. Comparing partners' ratings of each other's specific attributes (Pelham & Swann, 1989), these researchers have shown that people feel closer to their partners when their partners view them as they view themselves (Swann et al., 1994) and that people tend to reject feedback that is inconsistent with their own views of their partners (de la Ronde & Swann, 1998). Vorauer and Ross (1996), adopting a similar position, have suggested that the desire for accurate information may vary at different stages of development, waxing during periods of transition or crisis and waning during periods of stability. Paradoxically, they propose that the desire for accurate information may at these times lead to a diagnosticity bias, i.e., the belief that specific information is more informative than it may actually be (Vorauer & Ross, 1993). To date, research on accuracy and verification motives has focused more on partners' preferences for different kinds of information than on the specific cognitive processes involved in pursuing these goals. Thus, it is not clear whether the specific processes these goals invoke are the same or different from the processes that support maintenance and enhancement goals.

Summary and critique

With few exceptions, there has been little longitudinal research on cognitive processes in close relationships. Therefore, understanding the role of these processes in the development of close relationships requires extrapolating from cross-sectional research. As our review indicates, this research emphasizes top-down or schematic processes, demonstrating how general goals and aspirations for a relationship determine the processing of specific relationship-relevant information. Regardless of the particular goal, each of the processes identified here serves to assimilate new information to existing cognitive structures. By diminishing the impact of inconsistent information and augmenting the impact of supportive information, these various processes protect and maintain rewarding beliefs and evaluations. Thus, the processes identified in this section should contribute to the stability of those beliefs and evaluations over time.

The problem with this conclusion is that it fails to account for the way close relationships actually develop. For most people, initially positive beliefs about a relationship do not endure over time. As noted at the outset of this chapter, the normative course of a close relationship is for cherished beliefs about the relationship to change and deteriorate. Although new information may be assimilated to existing beliefs in the short term, the fact that relationships change indicates that existing beliefs must accommodate to new information in the long term. Research on cognitive processes in close relationships has neglected to consider such bottom-up processes, and this oversight currently limits the ability of this research to contribute to an understanding of how close relationships develop over time.

One way to address this gap would be to explore factors that account for when individuals may be more or less likely to engage in top-down or bottom-up processing. For example, motives to protect existing beliefs may vary in strength at different stages of the relationship. During periods of stability, the preservation of current beliefs and evaluations may be a powerful motive, and so the processes described above may be more likely to occur. During periods of crisis or transition, however, the desire for accurate information may become more relevant, and so bottom-up processing might be more likely (Vorauer & Ross, 1996). Similarly, the motive to protect globally positive beliefs about the relationship may be more powerful for people who are constrained to remain in their relationships than for those who are not so constrained (Thibaut & Kelley, 1959). To the extent that contextual factors are associated with changes in the relative strength of different processing motives at different times, then such factors may also account for when global evaluations of a relationship should be maintained and when they may change in response to specific contradictory information.

Another avenue worth pursuing is the possibility that different individuals may differ in their ability to engage in motivated processes. To date, most research on cognitive processes in close relationships demonstrates merely that motivated reasoning does occur and is associated with relationship satisfaction. By this reasoning, people who are better at protecting their beliefs (e.g., more skilled at rationalization, derogating alternatives, etc.), should over time experience more stable satisfaction. People who are not as skilled should engage in less schematic processing, and so their global impressions of the relationship should be more responsive to specific information that contradicts their beliefs.

Towards an Integrated Theory of Cognition in Close Relationships

To the extent that most social phenomena involve individuals either processing, interpreting, or storing data, there are very few aspects of human behavior that are not in some way cognitive (Berkowitz & Devine, 1995). For researchers examining cognition in the development of close relationships, the vastness of this domain represents a strength and a potential limitation to research. The strength is that research on cognition in close relationships has the potential to integrate what have widely been viewed as disparate areas of investigation. Issues of culture, personality, stress, and behavior unite in that they are likely to influence close relationships through their effects on cognition. Cognitions and cognitive processes may indeed prove to be the "final common pathway" (Jacobson, 1985; Karney & Bradbury, 1995b) through which these other variables affect the outcomes of close relationships. The potential limitation, however, is that this domain may prove so vast that researchers examining particular aspects of cognition fail to recognize their common interests. In order to shed meaningful light on this field, most researchers have chosen to define their topic areas rather narrowly, identifying and examining specific types of beliefs, structures, or processes. The resulting research describes many dimensions of cognition in close relationships, but does not accumulate to support a coherent theory that explains how close relationships develop or remain stable over time (Baucom & Epstein, 1989; Sillars, 1985).

Furthermore, for want of a focus on the larger domain, important parts of this landscape remain unmapped. Researchers have described the elements of cognitive content in relationships, but it is unknown where beliefs and evaluations come from and how they may change over time. Research on the implications of cognitive structure is advancing in other domains (e.g., Read, Vanman, & Miller, 1997; Thagard, 1992), but research on the structure of cognitions in relationships is only beginning. Researchers have identified motives that may drive cognitive processes in relationships, but it remains unclear when different motives are more or less likely to operate. Finally, as we have repeated throughout this chapter, cross-sectional research is an important first step, but additional longitudinal and experimental research is critical to understanding the causal role of cognitions in close relationships. In its absence, the possibility remains that all of these variables do not predict changes in relationship satisfaction but merely follow from them.

Thus, it may be too early to propose an integrative theory of how initially positive beliefs about relationships remain stable or deteriorate over time. Constructing such a theory requires research that fills the gaps in our current knowledge, as well as research that spans the different aspects of cognition reviewed in this chapter. For example, Fincham, Garnier, Gano-Phillips, & Osborne (1995) have speculated that there may be important interactions between cognitive content and cognitive structure. Specifically, they suggest that the accessibility of particular cognitions may be more important for global beliefs about a relationship than for beliefs about more specific characteristics. Such ideas raise the possibility that the effects of different kinds of cognitive content may depend on how those cognitions are structured.

Similarly, research in other areas of social psychology offers evidence for interactions between cognitive content and cognitive processes. In a well-developed line of research, Dunning and his colleagues (e.g., Dunning, Leuenberger, & Sherman, 1995; Dunning & McElwee, 1995; Dunning, Meyerowitz, & Holzberg, 1989) have demonstrated that self-serving motives operate more strongly on perceptions of traits that are ambiguous than on traits that are concrete. Extrapolating to close relationships, these findings suggest that the cognitive processes reviewed here may have stronger effects on global evaluations of a relationship than on perceptions of specific aspects of a relationship. In response to negative experiences, specific perceptions of the relationship may change even when global evaluations do not. Thus, over time, specific negative perceptions may accumulate and ultimately overwhelm global satisfaction. In this way, exploring the interaction between levels of cognitive content and types of cognitive processes may help to explain how globally positive evaluations of a relationship so frequently change despite people's best efforts to maintain them.

KEY READINGS

Berscheid, E. (1994). Interpersonal relationships. *Annual Review of Psychology, 45,* 79–129.
Fincham, F. D., Bradbury, T. N., & Scott, C. K. (1990). Cognition in marriage. In F. D. Fincham & T. N. Bradbury (Eds.), *The psychology of marriage* (pp. 118–149). New York: Guilford.
Fletcher, G. J. O., & Fincham, F. D. (1991). *Cognition in close relationships.* Hillsdale, NJ: Erlbaum.
Fletcher, G. J. O., & Thomas, G. (1996). Close relationship lay theories: Their structure and function. In G. J. O. Fletcher & J. Fitness (Eds.), *Knowledge structures in close relationships: A social psychological perspective* (pp. 3–24). Mahwah, NJ: Erlbaum.

ACKNOWLEDGMENTS

Preparation of this chapter was supported by a Research Development Award from the College of Letters and Science at the University of Florida, by Grant 4-4040-199900-07 from the Committee on Research of the UCLA Academic Senate, and by Grant MH 48674 from the National Institute of Mental Health. The authors wish to express their appreciation to Jennifer Brown for her assistance in gathering references, and to Nancy Frye and Lisa Neff, for helpful comments on a previous draft of this chapter.

REFERENCES

Abramson, L. Y., Seligman, M. E. P., & Teasdale, J. F. (1978). Learned helplessness in humans: Critique and reformulation. *Journal of Abnormal Psychology, 87,* 49–74.

Acitelli, L. K., Kenny, D. A., & Gladstone, D. (1996). *Do relationship partners embrace the same ideals for marriage? (Yes, but their images of each other don't agree).* Paper presented at the International Network on Personal Relationships, Seattle, WA.

Afifi, W. A., & Metts, S. (1998). Characteristics and consequences of expectation violations in close relationships. *Journal of Social and Personal Relationships, 15,* 365–392.

Albert, S. (1977). Temporal comparison theory. *Psychological Review, 84,* 485–503.

Aronson, E., & Linder, D. (1965). Gain and loss of esteem as determinants of interpersonal attractiveness. *Journal of Experimental Social Psychology, 1,* 156–171.

Asch, S. E. (1946). Forming impressions of personality. *Journal of Abnormal and Social Psychology, 41,* 258–290.

Baldwin, M. W. (1992). Relational schemas and the processing of social information. *Psychological Bulletin, 112,* 461–484.

Baldwin, M. W. (1994). Primed relational schemas as a source of self-evaluative reactions. *Journal of Social and Clinical Psychology, 13,* 380–403.

Baldwin, M. W., Carrell, S. E., & Lopez, D. F. (1990). Priming relationship schemas: My advisor and the pope are watching me from the back of my mind. *Journal of Experimental Social Psychology, 26,* 435–454.

Baldwin, M. W., & Fehr, B. (1995). On the instability of attachment style ratings. *Personal Relationships, 2,* 247–261.

Baldwin, M. W., Keelan, J. P. R., Fehr, B., Enns, V., & Koh-Rangarajoo, E. (1996). Social-cognitive conceptualization of attachment working models: Availability and accessibility effects. *Journal of Personality and Social Psychology, 71,* 94–109.

Baucom, D. H. (1987). Attributions in distressed relations: How can we explain them? In S. Duck & D. Perlman (Eds.), *Intimate relationships: Development, dynamics, and deterioration* (pp. 177–206). London: Sage.

Baucom, D. H., & Epstein, N. (1989). The role of cognitive variables in the assessment and treatment of marital discord. In M. Hersen, R. M. Eisler, & P. M. Miller (Eds.), *Progress in behavior modification* (Vol. 24, pp. 223–248). Newbury Park: Sage.

Baucom, D. H., Epstein, N., Rankin, L. A., & Burnett, C. K. (1996). Assessing relationship standards: The Inventory of Specific Relationship Standards. *Journal of Family Psychology, 10,* 72–88.

Baucom, D. H., Epstein, N., Sayers, S., & Sher, T. G. (1989). The role of cognitions in marital relationships: Definitional, methodological, and conceptual issues. *Journal of Consulting and Clinical Psychology, 57,* 31–38.

Beach, S. R. H., Etherton, J., & Whitaker, D. (1995). Cognitive accessibility and sentiment override – Starting a revolution: Comment on Fincham et al. (1995). *Journal of Family Psychology, 9,* 19–23.

Berger, C. R., & Roloff, M. E. (1982). Thinking about friends and lovers: Social cognition and relational trajectories. In M. E. Roloff & C. R. Berger (Eds.), *Social cognition and communication* (pp. 151–192). Beverly Hills: Sage.

Berkowitz, L., & Devine, P. G. (1995). Has social psychology always been cognitive? What is "cognitive" anyhow? *Personality and Social Psychology Bulletin, 21,* 696–703.

Berscheid, E. (1994). Interpersonal relationships. *Annual Review of Psychology, 45,* 79–129.

Birchler, G. R., Weiss, R. L., & Vincent, J. P. (1975). Multimethod analysis of social reinforcement exchange between maritally distressed and nondistressed spouse and stranger dyads. *Journal of Personality and Social Psychology, 31,* 349–360.

Bradbury, T. N. (1989). *Cognition. emotion and interaction in distressed and non-distressed couples.* Unpublished dissertation, University of Illinois, Urbana-Champaign.

Bradbury, T. N., & Fincham, F. D. (1987). Affect and cognition in close relationships: Towards an integrative model. *Cognition and Emotion, 1,* 59–87.

Bradbury, T. N., & Fincham, F. D. (1989). Behavior and satisfaction in close relationships: Prospective mediating processes. *Review of Personality and Social Psychology, 10,* 119–143.

Bradbury, T. N., & Fincham, F. D. (1990). Attributions in marriage: Review and critique. *Psychological Bulletin, 107,* 3–33.

Bradbury, T. N., & Fincham, F. D. (1991). A contextual model for advancing the study of marital interaction. In G. J. O. Fletcher & F. D. Fincham (Eds.), *Cognition in close relationships* (pp. 127–147). Hillsdale, NJ: Erlbaum.

Bradbury, T. N., & Fincham, F. D. (1993). Assessing dysfunctional cognition in marriage: A reconsideration of the Relationship Belief Inventory. *Psychological Assessment, 5,* 92–101.

Bruner, J. S. (1957). On perceptual readiness. *Psychological Review, 64,* 123–152.

Budner, S. (1962). Intolerance of ambiguity as a personality variable. *Journal of Personality, 30,* 29–50.

Burgess, E. W., Wallin, P., & Shultz, G. D. (1954). *Courtship, engagement, and marriage.* New York: Lippincott.

Burgoon, J. K. (1993). Interpersonal expectations, expectancy violations, and emotional communication. *Journal of Language and Social Psychology, 12,* 13–21.

Buunk, B. P., & van der Eijnden, R J. J. M. (1997). Perceived prevalence, perceived superiority, and relationship satisfaction: Most relationships are good, but ours is the best. *Personality and Social Psychology Bulletin, 23,* 219–228.

Buunk, B. P., & Van Yperen, N. W. (1989). Referential comparisons, relational comparisons and exchange orientations: Their relation to marital satisfaction. *Personality and Social Psychology Bulletin, 17,* 710–718.

Carver, C. S., & Scheier, M. F. (1990). Origins and functions of positive and negative affect: A control-process view. *Psychological Review, 97,* 19–35.

Castro-Martin, T., & Bumpass, L. (1989). Recent trends in marital disruption. *Demography, 26,* 37–51.

Cherlin, A. J. (1992). *Marriage, divorce, remarriage* (2nd ed.). Cambridge, MA: Harvard University Press.

Christensen, A., & Nies, D. C. (1980). The spouse observation checklist: Empirical analysis and critique. *American Journal of Family Therapy, 8,* 69–79.

Crockett, W. H. (1965). Cognitive complexity and impression formation. In B. A. Maher (Ed.), *Progress in experimental personality research* (Vol. 2, pp. 47–90). New York: Academic Press.

Crouse, B., Karlins, M., & Schroder, H. (1968). Conceptual complexity and marital happiness. *Journal of Marriage and the Family, 30,* 643–646.

Davila, J., Karney, B. R., & Bradbury, T. N. (1999). Attachment change processes in the early years of marriage. *Journal of Personality and Social Psychology, 76,* 783–802.

de la Ronde, C., & Swann, W. B. (1998). Partner verification: Restoring shattered images of our intimates. *Journal of Personality and Social Psychology, 75,* 374–382.

Denton, W. H., Burleson, B. R., & Sprenkle, D. H. (1995). Association of interpersonal cognitive complexity with communication skill in marriage: Moderating effects of marital distress. *Family Process, 34,* 101–111.

Doherty, W. J. (1981). Cognitive processes in intimate conflict: II. Efficacy and learned helplessness. *American Journal of Family Therapy, 9,* 35–44.

Downey, G., & Feldman, S. (1996). Implications of rejection sensitivity for intimate relationships. *Journal of Personality and Social Psychology, 70,* 1327–1343.

Downey, G., Freitas, A. L., Michaelis, B., & Khouri, H. (1998). The self-fulfilling prophecy in close relationships: Rejection sensitivity and rejection by romantic partners. *Journal of Personality and Social Psychology, 75*, 545–560.

Dunning, D., Leuenberger, A., & Sherman, D. A. (1995). A new look at motivated inference: Are self-serving theories of success a product of motivational forces? *Journal of Personality and Social Psychology, 69*, 58–68.

Dunning, D., & McElwee, R. O. (1995). Idiosyncratic trait definitions: Implications for self-description and social judgment. *Journal of Personality & Social Psychology, 68*, 936–946.

Dunning, D., Meyerowitz, J. A., & Holzberg, A. D. (1989). Ambiguity and self-evaluation: The role of idiosyncratic trait definitions in self-serving assessments of ability. *Journal of Personality and Social Psychology, 57*, 1082–1090.

Eidelson, R. J., & Epstein, N. (1982). Cognition and relationship maladjustment: Development of a measure of dysfunctional relationship beliefs. *Journal of Consulting and Clinical Psychology, 50*, 715–720.

Ellis, A., & Grieger, R. (1977). *Rational-emotive therapy: A handbook of theory and practice.* New York: Springer.

Epstein, N., & Eidelson, R. J. (1981). Unrealistic beliefs of clinical couples: Their relationship to expectations, goals, and satisfaction. *American Journal of Family Therapy, 9*, 13–22.

Fazio, R. H. (1990). A practical guide to the use of response latency in social psychological research. *Review of Personality and Social Psychology, 11*, 74–97.

Fazio, R. H. (1995). Attitudes as object-evaluation associations: Determinants, consequences, and correlates of attitude accessibility. In R. E. Petty & J. A. Krosnik (Eds.), *Attitude strength: Antecedents and consequences* (Vol. 4, pp. 247–282). Hillsdale, NJ: Erlbaum.

Fincham, F. D. (1998). *Construct accessibility in marital research: Does it matter?* Paper presented at the Association for the Advancement of Behavior Therapy, Washington, DC.

Fincham, F. D., & Bradbury, T. N. (1987). The assessment of marital quality: A reevaluation. *Journal of Marriage and the Family, 49*, 797–809.

Fincham, F. D., Bradbury, T. N., & Grych, J. H. (1990). Conflict in close relationships: The role of intrapersonal phenomena. In S. Graham & V. S. Folkes (Eds.), *Attribution theory: Applications to achievement, mental health, and interpersonal conflict* (pp. 161–184). Hillsdale, NJ: Erlbaum.

Fincham, F. D., Bradbury, T. N., & Scott, C. K. (1990). Cognition in marriage. In F. D. Fincham & T. N. Bradbury (Eds.), *The psychology of marriage* (pp. 118–149). New York: Guilford.

Fincham, F. D., Garnier, P. C., Gano-Phillips, S., & Osborne, L. N. (1995). Preinteraction expectations, marital satisfaction, and accessibility: A new look at sentiment override. *Journal of Family Psychology, 9*, 3–14.

Fincham, F. D., & O'Leary, K. D. (1983). Causal inferences for spouse behavior in maritally distressed and nondistressed couples. *Journal of Social and Clinical Psychology, 1*, 42–57.

Fletcher, G. J. O., & Fincham, F. D. (1991). *Cognition in close relationships.* Hillsdale, NJ: Erlbaum.

Fletcher, G. J. O., & Fitness, J. (Eds.). (1996). *Knowledge structures in close relationships: A social psychological approach.* Mahwah, NJ: Erlbaum.

Fletcher, G. J. O., & Kininmonth, L. (1992). Measuring relationship beliefs: An individual differences scale. *Journal of Research in Personality, 26*, 371–397.

Fletcher, G. J. O., Rosanowski, J., & Fitness, J. (1994). Automatic processing in intimate contexts: The role of close-relationship beliefs. *Journal of Personality and Social Psychology, 67*, 888–897.

Fletcher, G. J. O., & Thomas, G. (1996). Close relationship lay theories: Their structure and function. In G. J. O. Fletcher & J. Fitness (Eds.), *Knowledge structures in close relationships: A social psychological perspective* (pp. 3–24). Mahwah, NJ: Erlbaum.

Fowers, B. J., Lyons, E. M., & Montel, K. H. (1996). Positive marital illusions: Self-enhancement or relationship enhancement? *Journal of Family Psychology, 10,* 192–208.

Harvey, J. H. (1987). Attributions in close relationships: Research and theoretical developments. *Journal of Social and Clinical Psychology, 5,* 420–434.

Helgeson, V. S. (1994). The effects of self-beliefs and relationship beliefs on adjustment to a relationship stressor. *Personal Relationships, 1,* 241–258.

Henderson, V. L., & Dweck, C. S. (1990). Motivation and achievement. In S. S. Feldman & G. R. Elliot (Eds.), *At the threshold: The developing adolescent* (pp. 308–329). Cambridge, MA: Harvard University Press.

Hendrick, C., & Hendrick, S. (1986). A theory and method of love. *Journal of Personality and Social Psychology, 50,* 392–402.

Higgins, E. T. (1997). Beyond pleasure and pain. *American Psychologist, 52,* 1280–1300.

Higgins, E. T., & King, G. (1981). Accessibility of social constructs: Information processing consequences of individual and contextual variability. In N. Cantor & J. Kihlstrom (Eds.), *Personality, cognition, and social interaction* (pp. 69–121). Hillsdale, NJ: Erlbaum.

Jacobson, N. S. (1985). The role of observational measures in behavior therapy outcome research. *Behavioral Assessment, 7,* 297–308.

Jacobson, N. S., & Moore, D. (1981). Spouses as observers of the events in their relationship. *Journal of Consulting and Clinical Psychology, 49,* 269–277.

Johnson, D. J., & Rusbult, C. E. (1989). Resisting temptation: Devaluation of alternative partners as a means of maintaining commitment in close relationships. *Journal of Personality and Social Psychology, 57,* 967–980.

Johnson, D. R., Amoloza, T. O., & Booth, A. (1992). Stability and developmental change in marital quality: A three-wave panel analysis. *Journal of Marriage and the Family, 54,* 582–594.

Karney, B. R., & Bradbury, T. N. (1995a). Assessing longitudinal change in marriage: An introduction to the analysis of growth curves. *Journal of Marriage and the Family, 57,* 1091–1108.

Karney, B. R., & Bradbury, T. N. (1995b). The longitudinal course of marital quality and stability: A review of theory, method, and research. *Psychological Bulletin, 118,* 3–34.

Karney, B. R., & Coombs, R. H. (2000). Memory bias in long-term close relationships: consistency or improvement? *Personality and Social Psychology Bulletin, 26,* 959–970.

Kelley, D. L., & Burgoon, J. K. (1991). Understanding marital satisfaction and couple type as functions of relational expectations. *Human Communication Research, 18,* 40–69.

Kelley, H. H., Berscheid, E., Christensen, A., Harvey, J. H., Huston, T. L., Levinger, G., McClintock, E., Peplau, L. A., & Peterson, D. R. (1983). Analyzing close relationships. In H. H. Kelley, E. Berscheid, A. Christensen, J. H. Harvey, T. L. Huston, G. Levinger, E. McClintock, L. A. Peplau, & D. R. Peterson (Eds.), *Close relationships* (pp. 20–67). New York: W. H. Freeman and Company.

Kelley, H. H., & Thibaut, J. W. (1978). *Interpersonal relations: A theory of interdependence.* New York: Wiley-Interscience.

Kelly, G. (1955). *The psychology of personal constructs.* New York: Norton.

Kenny, D. A., & Acitelli, L. K. (1994). Measuring similarity in couples. *Journal of Family Psychology, 8,* 417–431.

Kirkpatrick, L. A., & Hazan, C. (1994). Attachment styles and close relationships: A four-year prospective study. *Personal Relationships, 1,* 123–142.

Klohnen, E. C., & Bera, S. (1998). Behavioral and experiential patterns of avoidantly and securely attached women across adulthood: A 31-year longitudinal perspective. *Journal of Personality and Social Psychology, 74,* 211–223.

Knee, C. R. (1998). Implicit theories of relationships: Assessment and prediction of romantic relation-ship initiation, coping and longevity. *Journal of Personality and Social Psychology, 74*, 360–370.

Kunda, Z. (1990). The case for motivated reasoning. *Psychological Bulletin, 108*, 480–498.

Kurdek, L. A. (1992). Assumptions versus standards: The validity of two relationship cognitions in heterosexual and homosexual couples. *Journal of Family Psychology, 6*, 164–170.

Linville, P. W. (1987). Self-complexity as a cognitive buffer against stress-related illness and depression. *Journal of Personality and Social Psychology, 52*, 663–676.

Locke, H. J., & Wallace, K. M. (1959). Short marital adjustment prediction tests: Their reliability and validity. *Marriage and Family Living, 21*, 251–255.

Lydon, J. E., Meana, M., Sepinwall, D., Richards, N., & Mayman, S. (1999). The commitment calibration hypothesis: When do people devalue attractive alternatives? *Personality and Social Psychology, 25*, 152–161.

Markus, H., & Smith, J. (1981). The influence of self-schemata on the perception of others. In N. Cantor & J. F. Kihlstrom (Eds.), *Personality, cognition, and social interaction* (pp. 233–262). Hillsdale, NJ: Erlbaum.

Martin, R. (1992). Relational cognition complexity and relational communication in personal relation-ships. *Communication Monographs, 59*, 150–163.

Martin, R. W. (1991). Examining personal relationship thinking: The Relational Cognition Complex-ity Instrument. *Journal of Social and Personal Relationships, 8*, 467–480.

Miller, R. S. (1997a). Inattentive and contented: Relationship commitment and attention to altern-atives. *Journal of Personality and Social Psychology, 73*, 758–766.

Miller, R. S. (1997b). We always hurt the ones we love: Aversive interactions in close relationships. In R. M. Kowalski (Ed.), *Aversive interpersonal interactions* (pp. 13–30). New York: Plenum.

Murray, S. L., & Holmes, J. G. (1993). Seeing virtues in faults: Negativity and the transformation of interpersonal narratives in close relationships. *Journal of Personality and Social Psychology, 65*, 707–722.

Murray, S. L., & Holmes, J. G. (1994). Story-telling in close relationships: The construction of confidence. *Personality and Social Psychology Bulletin, 20*, 663–676.

Murray, S. L., Holmes, J. G., & Griffm, D. W. (1996). The benefits of positive illusions: Idealization and the construction of satisfaction in close relationships. *Journal of Personality and Social Psychology, 70*, 79–98.

Neimeyer, G. J. (1984). Cognitive complexity and marital satisfaction. *Journal of Social and Clinical Psychology, 2*, 258–263.

Newman, H. M., & Langer, E. J. (1988). Investigating the development and courses of intimate relationships. In L. Y. Abramson (Ed.), *Social cognition and clinical psychology* (pp. 148–173). New York: Guilford.

Nisbett, R E., & Ross, L. (1980). *Human inference: Strategies and shortcomings.* Englewood Cliffs, NJ: Prentice-Hall.

Pelham, B. W., & Swann, W. B. (1989). From self-conceptions to self-worth: On the sources and structure of global self-esteem. *Journal of Personality and Social Psychology, 57*, 672–680.

Pham, L. B., & Taylor, S. E. (1999). From thought to action: Effects of process-versus outcome-based mental simulations on performance. *Personality and Social Psychology, 25*, 250–260.

Raush, H. L., Barry, W. A., Hertel, R. K., & Swain, M. A. (1974). *Communication, conflict, and marriage.* San Francisco: Jossey-Bass.

Read, S. J., Vanman, E. J., & Miller, L. C. (1997). Connectionism, parallel constraint satisfaction processes, and Gestalt principles: (Re)Introducing cognitive dynamics to social psychology. *Personal-ity and Social Psychology Review, 1*, 26–53.

Ruvolo, A. P., & Rotondo, J. L. (1998). Diamonds in the rough: Implicit personality theories and views of partner and self. *Personality and Social Psychology Bulletin, 24,* 750–758.

Ruvolo, A. P., & Veroff, J. (1997). For better or worse: Real–ideal discrepancies and the marital well-being of newlyweds. *Journal of Social and Personal Relationships, 14,* 223–242.

Sanitioso, R., Kunda, Z., & Fong, G. T. (1990). Motivated recruitment of autobiographical memories. *Journal of Personality and Social Psychology, 59,* 229–241.

Schroder, H. M. (1971). Conceptual complexity and personality organization. In H. M. Schroder & P. Suedfeld (Eds.), *Personality theory and information processing* (pp. 240–273). New York: Ronald Press.

Scott, W. A., Osgood, D. W., & Peterson, C. (1979). *Cognitive structure: Theory and measurement of individual differences.* Washington, DC: Winston and Sons.

Seligman, M. E., Abramson, L. Y., Semel, A., & Von Baeyer, C. (1979). Depressive attributional style. *Journal of Abnormal Psychology, 88,* 242–247.

Shaver, P. R, Collins, N., & Clark, C. (1996). Attachment styles and internal working models of self and relationship partners. In G. J. O. Fletcher & J. Fitness (Eds.), *Knowledge structures in close relationships: A social psychological perspective* (pp. 25–62). Mahwah, NJ: Erlbaum.

Showers, C. (1992a). Compartmentalization of positive and negative self-knowledge: Keeping bad apples out of the bunch. *Journal of Personality and Social Psychology, 62,* 1036–1049.

Showers, C. (1992b). Evaluatively integrative thinking about characteristics of the self. *Personality and Social Psychology Bulletin, 18,* 719–729.

Sillars, A. L. (1985). Interpersonal perception in relationships. In W. Ickes (Ed.), *Compatible and incompatible relationships* (pp. 277–305). New York: Springer-Verlag.

Simpson, J. A. (1987). The dissolution of romantic relationships: Factors involved in relationship stability and emotional distress. *Journal of Personality and Social Psychology, 53,* 683–692.

Simpson, J. A., Fletcher, G., & Campbell, L. (2001). The structure and function of ideal standards in close relationships. In G. J. O. Fletcher & M. S. Clark (Eds.), *Blackwell handbook of social psychology: Interpersonal processes* (pp. 86–106). Oxford, UK: Blackwell.

Snyder, M., Tanke, E. D., & Berscheid, E. (1977). Social perception and interpersonal behavior: On the self-fulfilling nature of social stereotypes. *Journal of Personality and Social Psychology, 35,* 656–666.

Spanier, G. B. (1976). Measuring dyadic adjustment: New scales for assessing the quality of marriage and similar dyads. *Journal of Marriage and the Family, 38,* 15–28.

Sprecher, S. (1999). "I love you more today than yesterday": Romantic partners' perceptions of changes in love and related affect over time. *Journal of Personality and Social Psychology, 76,* 46–53.

Sprecher, S., & Metts, S. (1989). Development of the "Romantic Beliefs Scale" and examination of the effects of gender and gender-role socialization. *Journal of Social and Personal Relationships, 6,* 387–411.

Srull, T. K., & Wyer, R. S. (1989). Person memory and judgment. *Psychological Review, 96,* 58–83.

Swann, W. B. (1983). Self-verification: Bringing social reality into harmony with the self. In J. Suhls & A. G. Greenwald (Eds.), *Psychological perspectives on the self, Volume 2* (pp. 33–66). Hillsdale, NJ: Erlbaum.

Swann, W. B., De La Ronde, C., & Hixon, J. G. (1994). Authenticity and positivity strivings in marriage and courtship. *Journal of Personality and Social Psychology, 66,* 857–869.

Tangney, J. P., Niedenthal, P. M., Covert, M. V., & Barlow, D. H. (1998). Are shame and guilt related to distinct self-discrepancies? A test of Higgins' (1987) hypothesis. *Journal of Personality and Social Psychology, 75,* 256–268.

Taylor, S. E., Wood, J. V., & Lichtman, R. R. (1983). It could be worse: Selective evaluation as a response to victimization. *Journal of Social Issues, 39,* 19–40.

Tetlock, P. E. (1983). Accountability and complexity of thought. *Journal of Personality and Social Psychology, 45*, 74–83.

Tetlock, P. E., & Suedfeld, P. (1988). Integrative complexity coding of verbal behavior. In C. Antaki (Ed.), *Analyzing everyday explanation: A casebook of methods* (pp. 43–59). London: Sage.

Thagard, P. (1992). *Conceptual revolutions.* Princeton, NJ: Princeton University Press.

Thibaut, J. W., & Kelley, H. H. (1959). *The social psychology of groups.* New York: Wiley.

Thorndyke, E. L. (1920). A constant error in psychological ratings. *Journal of Applied Psychology, 4*, 25–29.

Tyndall, L. W., & Lichtenberg, J. W. (1985). Spouses' cognitive styles and marital interaction patterns. *Journal of Marital and Family Therapy, 11*, 193–202.

Vaillant, C. O., & Vaillant, G. E. (1993). Is the U-curve of marital satisfaction an illusion? A 40-year study of marriage. *Journal of Marriage and Family, 55*, 230–239.

van Lange, P. A. M., & Rusbult, C. E. (1995). My relationship is better than – and not as bad as – yours is: The perception of superiority in close relationships. *Personality and Social Psychology Bulletin, 21*, 32–44.

Vanzetti, N. A., Notarius, C. I., & NeeSmith, D. (1992). Specific and generalized expectancies in marital interaction. *Journal of Family Psychology, 6*, 171–183.

Vorauer, J. D., & Ross, M. (1993). Making mountains out of molehills: An informational goals analysis of self- and social perception. *Personality and Social Psychology Bulletin, 19*, 620–632.

Vorauer, J. D., & Ross, M. (1996). The pursuit of knowledge in close relationships: An informational goals analysis. In G. J. O. Fletcher & J. Fitness (Eds.), *Knowledge structures in close relationships: A social psychological perspective* (pp. 369–396). Mahwah, NJ: Erlbaum.

Weinstein, N. D. (1980). Unrealistic optimism about future life events. *Journal of Personality and Social Psychology, 39*, 806–820.

Weiss, R. L. (1980). Strategic behavioral marital therapy: Toward a model for assessment and intervention. In J. P. Vincent (Ed.), *Advances in family intervention, assessment, and theory* (Vol. 1, pp. 229–271). Greenwich, CT: JAI Press.

Weiss, R. L. (1984a). Cognitive and behavioral measures of marital interaction. In K. Hahlweg & N. S. Jacobson (Eds.), *Marital interaction: Analysis and modification* (pp. 232–252). New York: Guilford.

Weiss, R. L. (1984b). Cognitive and strategic interventions in behavioral marital therapy. In K. Hahlweg & N. S. Jacobson (Eds.), *Marital interaction: Analysis and modification* (pp. 337–355). New York: Guilford.

Wills, T. A., Weiss, R. L., & Patterson, G. R. (1974). A behavioral analysis of the determinants of marital satisfaction. *Journal of Consulting and Clinical Psychology, 42*, 802–811.

Wood, J. V., & Taylor, K. L. (1991). Serving self-relevant goals through social comparison. In J. Suhls & T. A. Wills (Eds.), *Social comparison: Contemporary theory and research* (pp. 23–49). Hillsdale, NJ: Erlbaum.

CHAPTER TEN

Language and Social Cognition

Gün R. Semin

Introduction

The mutual influence of language and social cognition is a classic problem not only in social psychology but also in human intellectual history. The theme is this: does language influence, shape, or perhaps even determine human cognitive activities, or alternatively, do cognitive processes affect language? A closer inspection of this research field suggests that some of the unspoken, meta-theoretical assumptions, by which our notions of language and cognition are shaped, constitute the key for a systematic understanding of the domain. Let us briefly review these assumptions that will be elaborated upon in the main body of this chapter.

The most commonly shared assumption by both scientists and lay persons alike is that cognition and language should be viewed from an *individual* perspective. In this approach, language is a tool for thinking, representation, and computation. Similarly, social cognition refers to individual processes: encoding, representing, thinking, retrieving, etc. For instance, if two cultures linguistically code the color spectrum differently, do they then perceive and represent colors incommensurably or not? Not surprisingly, thinking of language and cognition in this way leads to the fascinating and classic issues that have occupied many minds about the relationship between language and cognition and their mutual influence. Do linguistic tools influence cognitive processes, or vice versa?

However, language and cognition are not merely for representation, processing, and computation. Both are essential(ly) for action. Language is also a tool for doing. While it is true that language is a tool to construct and represent meaning, it is also true that language is a tool to transform reality by conveying meaning. All acts of communication entail a transformation of some reality. To bring about transformation is an essential feature of language use, like being able to invite somebody for a first dinner, a first dance, to get somebody to agree with your view or opinion, to get a body to approve a grant, a piece of legislation, or

The writing of this chapter was facilitated by the Netherlands Organization for Scientific Research, No. PGS56–381 Pionier Grant and Aandachstsgebied No. 575–12.020. I would like to express my thanks to Tony Manstead for his careful and constructive comments on an earlier version of this chapter.

a donation. Such transformation is only possible when language is used as a structuration device by which we strategically present aspects of reality or an idea in communication in order to *influence or shape the social cognitive processes of the recipient* to a message. The language–cognition relationship and their mutual influence acquire an entirely different complexion when considered in this way. In this view, assumptions about language and cognition originate within a transformational communicative context. Language refers to a tool that aids the strategic structuring of the representation of some reality or notion in communication. This strategic use is designed by the transmitter to effect a transformation in its recipient. In such a transformational context cognitive processes refer not only to the processes by which the transmitter gives strategic shape to the communicative act, but also to those processes that determine how the communicative act (the linguistic representation) is received by the recipient.

A third set of assumptions introduces an entirely different level of analysis. There are numerous cognitive tasks that exceed the capabilities of a single individual. These types of tasks, such as navigating a large ship (Hutchins, 1996), rely on knowledge that is distributed among members of the task group. This type of distributed knowledge and its communication is socially organized. In this particular instance, we have assumptions about both cognition and language that are defined in terms of task characteristics. Such tasks are often encountered in human society, and facilitate the coordination of socially distributed and socially constituted cognition. In other words, it is shared knowledge that is critical in terms of facilitating the achievement of the group's goal. An instance is successfully navigating a large vessel to its destination. Similarly, the transmission and reproduction of culture is an achievement that requires cooperative activities to facilitate the acquisition of capabilities that go beyond those of an individual. The developmental take on this is the Vygotskian notion of "zone of proximal development." This refers to the finely tuned interaction between caregivers and children where language is used as a tool for structuring and controlling action in order to produce interpsychological events critical for the child to succeed at a task beyond its capabilities.

Two distinctive features distinguish the three sets of assumptions about language and cognition. The first is the levels of analysis that are tacitly assumed, and which are respectively the *individual*, *inter-individual*, and *group* levels. Each level of analysis has a dramatic impact on the definition of the language–cognition interface. Equally, if not more importantly, the second distinctive feature of these three sets of assumptions is how action is conceptualized in relation to language and cognition. Whereas the first set of assumptions entails a disembodied individual, the second set involves a transformational context of influence and focuses upon language as a tool for action – namely a tool to effect transformation. The third set goes beyond individual actors and focuses upon communicative action as the primary objective to examine how socially distributed cognition is effectively maintained, as in the attainment of supra-individual goals or the transmission of task mastery and knowledge.

The main body of this chapter consists of an overview of the work on the relationship between language and social cognition from these three different types and levels of analysis. This is prefaced with a brief analysis of language and language use. This analysis furnishes an explanation of why each of the three levels of analysis has emerged and appears plausible, as well as how they relate to each other.

The Different Faces of the Language–Social Cognition Interface

Language and language use

The peculiar relationship between language and language use is best introduced by drawing upon the related metaphor of tool and tool-use. The use of this metaphor in the context of language is in itself not new (see, for example, Clark, 1997; Gauker, 1990; Semin, 1995, 1998; Vygotsky, 1981; Wertsch, 1991). My purpose in using this metaphor is to explicate the language–language use relationship, which I will then use to highlight how the different levels of analyses in investigations of the language–social cognition interface have arisen.

Tools have *structural properties* that have been engineered to optimize their use. For instance, hammers have a shaft and a peen, a hard solid head at a right angle to the handle, sometimes a claw, etc. Such structural properties are distinct from the variety of things that one can do with it, or its uses. Thus, while any tool has a finite set of structural properties that can in principle be identified, its uses are *indeterminate*. The same tools in the hand of one person may create a hut, in the hands of another a chalet, or a Chinese pagoda, etc. What is noteworthy is that the use of the very same tools can yield a great variety of unique outcomes. One can refer to the variety of uses that one can put tools to as their *affordances*, to use Gibsonian terminology (Gibson, 1979). Such affordances are possible only to the extent that human beings have the *capacity* to use them. Hence, "usability as a hammer" as an "affordance" is relational and manifested pragmatically only in the interface between tool and tool-user.

Where the tool and tool-use analogy falls short is in the following. While literal tools have a real existence independent of their use, linguistic tools do not have an existence independent of communication. Linguistic tools are *reproduced in communication*. In terms of social behavior, the fact that I utter a sentence in English contributes to the reproduction of English as a language. This is an unintended consequence (Giddens, 1979) of uttering that sentence. Let me elaborate. The use of language has two fundamental aspects (Bakthin, 1979; Giddens, 1976; Ricoeur, 1955). One is the communication of meaning and the other is a structure that carries this meaning. What is being proposed is that human verbal communication has two interrelated fundamental features, namely (a) the reproduction of a structure, without which (b) meaning, could not be conveyed.

Any speech act presupposes a structured system of signs that is understood by everybody. Language use displays traceable consistencies that are repeated and reproduced in every speech act. These reiterative and reproducible properties of language constitute the *structural properties of language* (syntactical and semantic) that simultaneously carry unique and situated meanings. Whereas "meaning" is subjective, the structural properties of language are intersubjective. For example, word meanings, syntactic rules, and the like must be shared in order to be able to convey meaning that is initially unshared or subjective. Language use then amounts to drawing on shared structure in order to convey a potentially novel and unique meaning. The same structure can convey a wide range of meanings to a great variety of actors. While structure is determinate in terms of its properties (specified by semantic and syntactic rules), its affordances and potential uses are indeterminate (Semin, 1998). Language use not only transmits meaning, but also reproduces and reinforces the structure (syntax and semantics).

Implications of the language and language use distinction

We can now take a new look at the three different levels of analysis adopted in examinations of the language–cognition interface in the light of the distinction between the structural properties of language and language use. This distinction is instrumental in understanding how these different and practically independent levels of analyses have emerged, namely the individual centered, transformational, and socially distributed approaches to language and social cognition.

The first level of analysis – the individualistic – relies on the treatment of language in terms of a structure that is disembodied, by attending to only those aspects of language that are repeated, reiterative, and reproducible, and not its non-reiterative, unique, and individual aspects. Language is regarded as an abstract set of "rules" that are "virtual and outside of time" (Ricoeur, 1955). This is treating language "without a subject," namely not as the property or production of any one particular speaker. The focus is upon language as an extra-individual and systematic set of abstract properties. Regarding language in this way makes it "subjectless" and "timeless" and presents the ideal assumption for examining the relationship between specific linguistic properties (e.g. lexical semantics, grammatical categories) and cognitive processes that are also conceptualized in a disembodied, timeless, and subjectless manner. The classic discussion of the mutual influence between language and thought (Whorf, 1957) and related work in the social cognition–language tradition is cast at this level (see section 1 below). The distinctive feature of all these "modern" versions of the language–social cognition relationship is their focus upon the individual as a unit of analysis for both language and cognition. This is a version that is also characteristic of more recent analyses (e.g. Hardin & Banaji, 1993; Hoffman, Lau, & Johnson, 1986; Hunt & Agnoli, 1991). In a sense, this has been the mainstream approach not only to understanding social cognition but also language: what are the human capacities that are responsible for the production and interpretation of language and what are the properties of language that can influence cognitive processes. This is the first part of the research reviewed here.

The second level of analysis relies on the assumption that language is a "medium for practical activity" (Ricoeur, 1955). The focus now is upon language use in terms of the situated doings of subjects in terms of the types of transformations that they intend in communicative contexts. This level of analysis requires both an understanding of the structural properties of language and the situated purposes that they serve. Language use presupposes a subject, acknowledges the presence of the "other," and is dialogical. Cognition in this context becomes intended activity and language the tool for the implementation of such action. Additionally at this level, extralinguistic factors such as conversational rules (Grice, 1975) become significant to understand transmission of meaning. This research is reviewed in section 2 below.

The third level of analysis has a similar focus upon language, namely as practical activity, except that it is not concerned with the production of language at any level. Rather, the focus is upon how language as practical activity is deployed in contexts that require the reproduction of new structures (navigation) as well as their situated realization (navigating a large vessel into the harbor). At this level, the focus is the role played by language as a medium by which cultural artifacts are reproduced and transmitted. Verbal communication is seen as a means by which joint solutions are achieved. Thought in this context refers to socially distributed cognition that is embodied – as is the coordination of social action through communication. This constitutes the third part of the overview.

1   Language and Social Cognition: Individual Centered Approaches

Linguistic relativity

An obligatory reference in any discussion of the language–social cognition relationship is to the influential but problematic issue of linguistic relativity and determinism. The most influential formulation of the relationship between language, thought, and culture is the one advanced by Benjamin Lee Whorf (1957), whose contribution derives from a long intellectual heritage. Whorf argued for a correspondence between the structural properties of language to represent aspects of the world and the implications of such structural properties upon thinking about the world. His classic observation was that "the world is presented in a kaleidoscopic flux of impressions which has to be organized by our minds – and this means largely by the linguistic systems of our minds" (ibid., p. 213). This argument is based on the following reasoning. If one notes differences in the formal meaning structure of two languages then this is also likely to be manifested in the "habitual thought" of the speakers of these languages. The observation at the heart of Whorf's "linguistic relativity hypothesis" is the following: "Users of markedly different grammars are pointed by their grammars toward different types of observations and different evaluations of external similar acts of observation, and hence are not equivalent as observers, but must arrive at somewhat different views of the world" (ibid., p. 221). The classic example is the often-cited difference in the encoding of time in the Hopi and English languages. In English, time is encoded in nouns (years, days, and hours), a *grammatical form* that is used for objects. Putting what is essentially cyclical and continuous into a discrete grammatical form means that we can do things with time, like measure it or count it. For the Hopi, time is represented as a recurrent event. Although they have words that we can recognize as years, days, etc., their grammar does not have a tense system like English and does not permit the emergence of an abstract notion of time as is the case in English. Whorf concluded that the experience of time is very different for Hopi and English-speakers.

The general linguistic relativism argument is that differences in linguistic categories (grammatical and lexical) across languages influence individuals' "habitual thought" patterns. Thus, *linguistic determinism* refers to the argument derived from linguistic relativity that there is a causal influence of semantic patterns on cognition. Language determines the very way we think about the social and physical world. There is a strong and a weak version of this hypothesis. The argument of the strong version, which is mostly regarded as a "straw man" (e.g. Gumpertz & Levinson, 1996, p. 24; Lucy, 1992, p. 3) suggests that concepts that are not coded linguistically are unattainable. The more widely accepted weaker version suggests that linguistically coded concepts are facilitated, thus more accessible, easier to remember, etc.

Hoffman, Lau, & Johnson (1986) illustrate how the presence or absence of a *lexical category* facilitates the activation of knowledge or information structures. These authors selected a number of personality descriptions in Chinese and English which were presented to Chinese and English native speakers. For some of these descriptions (e.g. attributes such as progressive, left-wing, tolerance, open-mindedness, Bohemian) English has an economic lexical category (i.e. liberal), but Chinese does not. For others (e.g. strong family orientation, socially skilled, experienced), Chinese has an economic lexical category (i.e. *shi-gu*), but English does not. A recognition memory test showed that accuracy of recognition was influenced by the availability of lexical category. Both Chinese and English subjects showed less recognition accuracy for items that were consistent with "their" economic category. When subjects were given previously presented items that were congruent with the category of their language, they were less confident in recognizing these. Moreover, they had greater difficulty in rejecting category-congruent new items. Recognition memory was superior over-all in the case of items for which the language did not have a category.

The above two examples are instances of how grammatical and lexical categories are related to thought. Whorf's position on this relation was primarily in terms of language influencing "unconscious habitual thought" rather than the potential to think. The precise nature of this relationship was however not further specified. There exists a variety of attempts to paint a clearer picture of this relation. It is to the credit of Lenneberg and his colleagues (e.g. Brown & Lenneberg, 1954) that the research agenda of how color lexically is coded and how it influences cognitive processes was set. This is a domain that has occupied center stage in the discussion of linguistic relativity and determinism in psychology. Also, the agenda defined more clearly what was to be understood by the term "cognitive processes." "Does the structure of a given language affect the thoughts (or thought potential), the memory, the perception, the learning ability of those who speak that language?" (Lenneberg, 1953, p. 463). Do linguistic structures influence non-linguistic categorization, memory, perception, thinking, etc.?

The lexical domain of color became a major one in debating whether or not the Whorfian hypothesis had any merit. Color was interesting because it constituted a domain for which there were objectifiable external referents. Earlier research suggested that if color is distinct-ively differentiated in the lexicon then it is more likely to be memorable. For instance, Brown and Lenneberg's (1954) classic study showed that colors that were more codable in English (had shorter names, and elicited more agreement in naming) tended to be the ones that were recognized and remembered more readily.

The early support for linguistic relativity came to an end with Berlin and Kay's (1969) seminal work. They showed that basic colors had a salience that was independent of language. This work provided the stepping-stone for E. Rosch's well-known studies that set a new landmark in color perception and memory. She showed that when the Dani (who only had two basic color terms) were asked to learn eight arbitrary names for eight focal color terms and a different eight arbitrary names for non-focal color terms, they learned the names for the focal colors better (Rosch, 1973). This and other research by Rosch was regarded as the critical turning-point for the linguistic relativity argument because it suggested that primary color categories had real psychological significance for the Dani, although they did not have any linguistic categories for them.

Currently, different views prevail about how to interpret the overall evidence. The weight of the recent work (e.g. Kay & Kempton, 1984; Lucy, 1992) suggests that under specific task conditions the availability of lexical categories leads to non-linguistic cognitive effects in classification and categorization tasks. This overview of the color domain is brief in view of the fact that there exist extensive reviews of the field (e.g. Brown, 1976; Lucy, 1992; Hardin & Maffi, 1997).

Language, memory, cognitive processes, and behavior

It is possible to conceptualize and examine linguistic relativity (with more experimental control) in terms of a single language that provides its speakers with different ways of talking and/or representing the same thing. This perspective opens the door to a very broad range of relevant research in social psychology. Below, indications are given of relevant literature in social cognition that has implications for how linguistic cues influence cognitive processes.

Probably the best-known studies on the effects of language upon memory come from eyewitness testimony research (Loftus, 1979). For instance, having been misleadingly asked about a blue car that was green in the video that they had seen, participants were more likely to remember it as blue than a control group that was given no color. Modifying verbal references to a car-collision implying differences in velocity (e.g. "smash" vs. "hit") has been shown to lead participants to remember that the cars were traveling at a higher speed in the "smash" condition than the "hit" condition. These participants were also more likely to erroneously report broken glass at the incident.

Another body of research addresses the influence of verbalization on visual memory. For instance, it has been shown that describing a previously seen face impairs recognition of this face, a phenomenon termed "the verbal shadowing effect" (e.g. Dodson, Johnson, & Schooler, 1997; Schooler & Engsler-Schooler, 1990). The explanation is based on a confusion between previously encoded visual and verbal encoding, because verbalization creates or activates a corresponding verbal representation that is in conflict with other representations in memory (Chiu, Krauss, & Lau, 1998). Earlier studies with visual forms have shown that verbalization interferes with visual recognition (e.g. Bahrick & Boucher, 1968; Ranken, 1963; Santa & Ranken, 1968).

A substantial body of research shows that verbal-framing influences problem representation and judgments (e.g. Kahneman & Tversky, 1984; Levin, Schnijttjer, & Thee, 1988). The effects of verbalization on memory and judgment are also underlined in studies by Higgins and his colleagues (e.g. Higgins & Rholes, 1977). They found that when participants read an ambiguous narrative about a person containing positive, negative, and neutral information and were asked to summarize this ambiguous information, having a negative attitude (like vs. dislike) influenced not only what participants wrote, but also their subsequent memory and judgments. The written summaries were congruent with recipients' attitudes as were participants' subsequent memory and judgments of the target person, which became more exaggerated over time. These effects were not found for a control group who did not write down a summary of the target (see also Higgins & McCann, 1984; Higgins, McCann, & Fondacaro, 1982).

Further, research on semantic priming (Neely, 1977; Meyer & Schvaneveldt, 1971) suggests that priming with lexical categories has cognitive and behavioral consequences. A typical example is the research by Dovidio, Evans, & Tyler (1986), who showed that priming with the label of a group activates group-related trait terms. The use of subliminal primes (us, we vs. they, them) has been shown to influence reaction times to traits in ingroup and outgroup related valence classification tasks (Perdue, Dovidio, Gurtman, & Tyler, 1990). In a related context, Devine (1989) showed that stereotypes of African Americans become activated even when verbal stimuli (related to African Americans) were presented subliminally. This suggests that verbal stimuli can have an effect upon the activation of knowledge structures in the absence of a participant's awareness along with some individual differences in the strength of the activated knowledge . The subliminal presentation of trait terms has been shown to influence recognition and judgment processes (e.g. Bargh & Pietromonaco, 1982). Indeed, it has also been found that verbal priming can influence behavioral responses, as in the case of performance on "Trivial Pursuit." Participants score higher when primed with the word "professor" than with the word "hooligan" (Dijksterhuis & Van Knippenberg, 1998). More recently, Dijksterhuis, Aarts, Bargh, & Van Knippenberg (in press) have shown that priming participants subliminally with words associated with "the elderly" (old, walking stick, bingo) can influence their memory performance (forgetfulness) as a function of their experience with the elderly. Even the subliminal priming of letters appears to have an effect on estimates of the number of words beginning with that letter (Gabrielcik & Fazio, 1984), which would suggest that the activation of knowledge structures in the most minimal sense can have judgmental consequences.

The more recent work sketched in this section has to do with the activation of knowledge by supraliminal or subliminal stimuli. One of the significant advances of this type of work – which was not directly conducted to examine the linguistic relativity hypothesis – is that it is concerned with the detailed examination of the processes that lead to the cognitive consequences of using, for instance, a prime to activate a stereotype. In that sense, despite the fact that this research is not conducted across different linguistic communities, it is more sophisticated in terms of uncovering process aspects of the cognitive and behavioral consequences of language.

Cognitive inferences mediated by interpersonal verbs

There is one domain in social psychology where the language–social cognition interface has been explicitly researched. This has been on the types of inferences that are mediated by interpersonal verbs. Interpersonal verbs (to help, to dislike, to cheat, to amaze, etc.) are the linguistic tools that do the hardcore work when it comes to describing interpersonal events and relationships. Broadly speaking, there are two general classes of interpersonal verbs, namely verbs of action (e.g. help, kick, and talk) and verbs of state (e.g. like, hate, and respect). Whereas the former refers to *observable* acts, the latter refers to *unobservable psycho-logical* states.

Interpersonal verbs as implicit qualifiers: the logic of generalization   The very first system-atic treatment of interpersonal verbs is to be found in a series of studies by Abelson (e.g. Abelson & Kanouse, 1966; Kanouse, 1971). This research examined the contribution of linguistic factors to how individuals form inductive and deductive generalizations from a given event or relation.

The conclusion across these diverse studies is that interpersonal verbs influence generaliza-tions systematically. Action verbs are found to lead to stronger inductive generalizations than do state verbs (action verb example: Jack buys *Newsweek*. Does Jack buy magazines? vs. state verb example: Jack likes *Newsweek*. Does Jack like magazines?). For deductive generalizations (e.g. Jack reads magazines. Does Jack like *Newsweek*? vs. Jack likes magazines. Does Jack like *Newsweek*?) the pattern they uncover is the reverse. Sentences with action verbs are found to give rise to much weaker deductive generalizations when compared to their role in con-tributing to inductive generalizations. Sentences with verbs of state produce a somewhat ambiguous pattern, although the overall pattern suggests that they produce a tendency to yield stronger deductive generalizations than inductive ones. An explanation advanced by Abelson and Kanouse is whether action and state verbs imply different types of quantifiers for sentence subject and object. For instance, does the sentence "Jack likes (buys) magazines" imply "all," "most," "many," "some," or just "a few" magazines? For this type example, Kanouse (1972) has shown that state verbs such as "like" imply a higher quantity than action verbs such as "read."

Interpersonal verbs as mediators of person attributions: the causal schema hypothesis   This research by the Yale group anticipated and foreshadowed what was to be termed "the causality implicit in interpersonal verbs" by Brown and Fish (1983). Brown and Fish's contribution had a major influence on further research development in this field. This was in part due to the fact that they introduced a way in which it was possible to systematically differentiate between different verb classes by examining the semantic roles that are associated with the sentence subject and object (noun predicates). For a group of verbs that have to do with overt and observable *actions* such as help, disagree, cheat, the relevant semantic roles are that of *agent* and *patient*. The agent role refers to somebody who causes or instigates an action. The patient role refers to somebody who is undergoing change. In the case of verbs of *state* (like, hate, trust) the relevant roles are those of *stimulus* and *experiencer*. The stimulus role refers to the originator of the experience and the latter role to the person who has a specific experience. Furthermore, Brown and Fish showed that sentences with action verbs lead to stronger causal attributions to the sentence subject, and sentences with state verbs lead to stronger causal attri-butions to the sentence object. For instance, when participants are given the sentence "John helped David, because *he* is a kind person" and asked to disambiguate the "he," then the predominant response is "John." Replacing the action verb "helped" in the example with the state verb "likes" leads to the reverse. Now the predominant disambiguation is to David.

According to Brown's (e.g. Brown & Fish, 1983) "causal schema" hypothesis a sentence with an action verb (e.g. "John helps David") activates an agent–patient schema, whereas a state verb sentence (e.g. "John likes David") elicits an experiencer–stimulus schema. These schemata are further coupled to the attribution theoretical principles of consensus and distinctiveness, whereby the agent-patient schema is associated with a low consensus–low distinctiveness schema and the experiencer–stimulus schema is associated with a high consensus–high distinctiveness schema (Rudolph & Försterling, 1997). Therefore, sentences with action verbs are easily generalized to other objects or patients, whereas sentences with state verbs are more easily generalized across subjects or experiencers.

Alternative explanations Brown and Fish advanced and rejected the possibility of a morphological explanation. According to this hypothesis adjectives derived from interpersonal verbs mediate the causal choices people make. In a stimulus sentence such as "John likes David" the morphologically related adjective is "likable" and refers to David, the sentence object to whom the causal attribution is made. Similarly, "helpful" refers to John in a sentence such as "John helps David," again the source to whom causality is attributed in the depicted event. An examination of the lexicon reveals that most adjectives derived from action verbs are subject referent and those derived from state verbs are mostly object referent. Brown and Fish reject this morphological hypothesis.

Hoffman and Tchir (1990) have pointed out that this hypothesis has not been directly tested and that the verb selection in Brown and Fish has methodological problems. They attempted to rectify this by a careful selection of action and state verbs that have only subject referent (action: help–helpful; state: resent–resentful) and object referent adjectives (action: tickle–ticklish; state: like–likable). Their first experiment provided ambiguous evidence for the morphological hypothesis. Ascription of causality does not seem to be clearly predictable from the attributive reference of the derived adjectives. In fact, only in the case of action verbs did they get a verb-type based causal inference pattern. Their second experiment indicated that "the relation between causal asymmetry embodied in interactive verbs and the attributive reference derived from those verbs was not fully explained by the third variable of role generality (i.e. distinctiveness and consensus)" (ibid., p. 772). In a later study, Semin and Marsman (1994), controlling in a completely balanced design for verb-derived adjectives, showed that the availability of derived adjectives does not influence the causal inferences that subjects make.

One of the alternative explanations is Fiedler and Semin's (1988) "antecedent-consequent event structure" account of implicit causality. When participants are given a stimulus sentence (John helped David) and asked "why," then they imagine the stimulus sentence context which consists of what happened before and after the stimulus sentence. The argument is that for action verbs the event preceding the stimulus sentence (antecedent) shows more frequent references to the stimulus sentence subject (John). In the case of state verbs the antecedent sentence has stronger references to the stimulus sentence object (David). The sentences that subjects generate about what happened after the event in the stimulus sentence had occurred (consequent) reverses this pattern. In this case, sentences with action verbs elicit more frequent references to the stimulus object (David). In the case of sentences with state verbs, the more frequent consequent response is to the sentence subject (John). The correlational data provide reasonable but not entirely convincing evidence, particularly for the consequences of action verbs and for the antecedents of state verbs.

Gilovitch and Regan (1986) propose a "volitional model" to explain implicit causality. They draw attention to the asymmetries in volition inherent in the semantic roles of agent-patient versus stimulus-experiencer. Whereas actions are under the volitional control of agents, experiences are under the control of stimuli. According to them this volitional asymmetry contributes to the differential elicitation of the semantic role schemata proposed by Brown and Fish (1983).

Kasoff and Lee (1993) advance an "implicit salience" argument to explain how causal inferences are mediated by interpersonal verbs. According to this view, "sentences that describe interpersonal events evoke mental representations in which subjects and objects differ in salience" (ibid., p. 878). The idea is then that people are more likely to attribute causality to the more salient object rather than the less salient one. In two studies they find evidence for this. In a secondary analysis of data from a variety of sources, they show that the correlations between salience and causality ratings vary between .26 and .94 for action verbs and −.04 and .61 for state verbs.

Conclusions   There is a remarkable paradox when one views this research in its entirety. All the studies that have been conducted with interpersonal verbs rely on correlational evidence. Mostly, they rely on the simultaneous measurement of implicit causality and some other dependent variable (DV). Such DVs include the dispositionality of the agent, the temporal duration of an event, the salience of an agent. Despite the fact that a variety of different inferences are made apart from event agency inferences, implicit causality is taken as the epistemically privileged anchor for explanations. However, there is no particular *a priori* theoretical or empirical reason to privilege implicit causality over any of the other properties of interpersonal verbs (e.g. sentence context, salience, event recurrence, etc.). It is also logically incoherent to suggest that *all* of these inferences be made at once when a participant is given a simple subject–verb–object sentence. The paradox is largely due to the fact that the diverse inferences are interpreted from an individual centered point of view and not considered in terms of what the main function of language is: it is not merely a tool for representational purposes but a device for communication purposes.

---

2   Language and Social Cognition: Language as a Transformational Device

The emphasis in this section is upon language as a medium for practical activity, or a medium to achieve particular ends (Chiu, Krauss, & Lau, 1998; Krauss & Fussell, 1996; Higgins, 1981). Language is not merely a tool for representing the world but a device by which changes in one's social world can be implemented. This is a conception of language in terms of a tool by which we can affect each other's behavior (Clark, 1997; Gauker, 1990). Such activity consists of the situated doings of subjects in order to achieve some transformation of social reality in communicative contexts. Cognition in this perspective becomes intended action with language as the tool to implement such action. A speaker, in trying to give public shape to a subjective goal, has to construct a linguistic representation. To this end, different linguistic tools have to be accessed to shape the desired or optimal representation of some aspect of reality. This way of looking at language means that we now have to consider how different lexical and grammatical categories are used as structuring resources that give shape to the representational space between a speaker and a listener. This contrasts strongly with the individual centered view of language, above. While linguistic relativity addresses lexical and grammatical categories as constraints on variation, the language use framework treats them as resources that facilitate variations in linguistic representations of the same event. Language is treated in this framework as a structuring resource for communication purposes. There are different ways in which a speaker can structure the public shape of a query in order to form a representation that will influence a listener's response.

The twin objectives are (1) to describe a model analyzing dimensions or properties of interpersonal language, and (2) to review two research domains showing how properties can be used as a structuring resource in formulating messages. The domain of language that is of particular relevance as structuring resources are interpersonal predicates, namely transitive verbs that refer to actions (to confide, to help, to cheat), to states (to like, to abhor, to respect) or feelings, and adjectives (friendly, trustworthy, unreliable) (Semin, 1998).

The linguistic category model (LCM)

The linguistic category model (Semin & Fiedler, 1988, 1991) was developed to identify properties or dimensions of interpersonal language that transcend specific semantic fields or word meanings. The model is based on a distinction between (a) systematic properties of language as a tool, and (b) psychological processes that entail using specific tools with differing properties to maximize some goal. The LCM is *not* a model of psychological processes. It therefore also involved a shift in methodological commitment, namely from one that privileges individual processes and properties to one that emphasizes the properties of "tools" by which communication is enabled (see Semin, 1998, p. 250ff.).

The LCM is a taxonomy of interpersonal predicates developed on the basis of a number of independent but converging linguistic criteria (see Semin & Fiedler, 1991) to differentiate between different verb categories and adjectives. A distinction is made between the following five categories. *Descriptive action verbs* refer to an invariant feature of the action (kick, push, talk). *Interpretative action verbs* provide a frame for a variety of actions (to help – an old lady cross a street, a friend in financial difficulty, etc.). *State action verbs* refer to the psychological consequences of an action (to bore, to thrill, to disgust). *State verbs* (to love, to abhor, to respect) refer to invisible psychological conditions. As a final category, *adjectives* (friendly, aggressive) refer to properties of individuals. Importantly, it has been shown that these categories have a number of inferential properties that vary systematically. Chief among these are (1) the degree to which a dispositional inference can be made; (2) the ease and difficulty of confirming and disconfirming statements constructed with these predicates; (3) the temporal duration of an interpersonal event depicted by these terms; (4) the likelihood of an event recurring at a future point in time (see Semin & Fiedler, 1991, 1992). These variables have been shown to form a concrete–abstract dimension in which the five categories are ordered systematically. That is, the first category mentioned above (descriptive action verbs) constitutes the most concrete one and adjectives the most abstract one, with categories two to four occupying – in that same sequence – intermediate positions in this dimension. Additionally, a second dimension is constituted by event agency, salience, and induced emotionality implied by interpersonal verbs (Semin & Fiedler, 1991).

What is central to understanding this model and its use is the distinction between semantic or meaning fields (e.g. the domain of economic transactions) and general properties such as event agency or the specific properties that are bundled in the abstraction–concreteness dimension. These constitute grammatically coded properties of the predicates represented by the LCM. It is by means of these dimensions that a number of different social phenomena have been analyzed by systematically examining situated messages that people generated in experimentally controlled or natural settings with regard to the types of predicates used. Instead of giving a comprehensive overview of all the diverse studies conducted with this model, I shall review just two domains that have attracted substantial research interest. The first is the so-called linguistic intergroup bias introduced by Maass and her colleagues (Maass, Salvi, Arcuri, & Semin, 1989) and the other is the question–answer paradigm (Semin, Rubini, & Fiedler, 1995).

The linguistic transmission of stereotypes

The linguistic intergroup bias (LIB) refers to a differentiated use of predicates in descriptions of ingroup and outgroup behaviors that contribute to the transmission and maintenance of stereotypes (e.g. Maass, Salvi, Arcuri, & Semin, 1989). Typically, this means that behaviors or events showing the ingroup in a favorable way and outgroups in an unfavorable way are represented with abstract language. In contrast, behaviors that depict the ingroup in undesirable ways and outgroup in desirable ways are communicated with concrete language. The use of abstract language conveys the suggestion that the properties in question are enduring, and likely to recur in the future. In contrast, concrete language suggests that the behavior in question is contextually determined and therefore transitory, and of no enduring significance. This is precisely what Maass, et al. (1989) found. The phenomenon is a stable one. It has been repeatedly demonstrated using different dependent variables (i.e. forced choice response formats for predicate choice and open-ended narratives). It has also been demonstrated in analyses of newspapers and television (Maass, Corvino, & Arcuri, 1994).

Systematic variations in predicate use in messages can serve a two-fold diagnostic function. On the one hand, the message structure can be an indicator of the psychological processes (motivational or cognitive) that have led to particular message structure. On the other hand, the message structure is important in order to examine its impact on recipients' inferences. Thus, message structure can be seen as both a dependent and an independent variable. If the aim is to investigate the psychological processes that lead to a particular message composition then message structure is a dependent variable. Message structure can also be an independent variable when the aim is to assess its impact upon recipients' inferences, judgments, and actions.

The work on the psychological processes responsible for linguistic intergroup bias is an instance for the dependent variable case. Two distinctive processes have been held responsible for the LIB. One is based on ingroup protective motives and social identity (Tajfel &

Turner, 1979). In this analysis, the LIB serves to maintain a positive ingroup image (Maass, Ceccarelli, & Rudin, 1996). The other process is assumed to be a cognitive one based on expectations (Maass, Milesi, Zabbini, & Stahlberg, 1995). The argument is that positive outgroup and negative ingroup behaviors are unexpected and behavior that is inconsistent with expectancies is described more concretely. In contrast, expectancy-consistent behavior is described more abstractly. The evidence is equivocal (Maass, et al., 1995, 1996) and suggests that the motivational and cognitive processes may be complementary.

When these types of messages become independent variables in a design that examines the impact of their structure upon recipient inferences, then we have the more typical question "How does language influence thought?" (Semin & De Poot, 1997a). Wigboldus, Semin, & Spears (in press) showed that when recipients were presented with messages produced by transmitters, messages that were expectancy-consistent were attributed more strongly to dispositional factors. In contrast, recipients found that events described in expectancy-inconsistent stories were due to situational factors. These effects were shown to be mediated by the level of abstraction in the stories.

The question–answer paradigm

The research done within the question–answer paradigm (Semin, Rubini, & Fiedler, 1995) is an instance of how strategic language use can contribute to the shaping of targets' answers and third parties' perceptions. This research dissects the continuous feedback loop in an interview exchange into separate stages in order to examine the distinct features of each step in the sequence. This gives rise to three interdependent questions. The first is whether specific expectations shape preferences regarding how a question is structured. Second, do particular question structures contribute to the shape of a target's answer? Third, how does a target's answer influence the perception and expectations of the respondent or a third party?

The first part of this research is based on how one can vary event agency in question formulation. The following four questions give a flavor of the possibilities:

1 "Did you dance with Stephen?"
2 "Did Stephen dance with you?"
3 "Why did Ed confide in Jeremy?"
4 "Why does Ed trust Jeremy?"

Changing the sentence subject or object positions in the question modifies implied event agency (in sentence 1 *you* and in sentence 2 *Stephen*). Implied agency is modified in sentences 3 (*Ed*) and 4 (*Jeremy*) by verb choice (action verb vs. state verb). Semin & De Poot (1997b) used a simulated rape victim interview scenario in which participants were given no expectation (control) or were led to expect that the victim was either trustworthy or untrustworthy. Participants selected questions that implied the agency of the perpetrator for the event if they expected the victim to be trustworthy. Participants who expected the victim to be untrustworthy chose predominantly questions implying victim agency. The control group was in between. The issue of how question formulation influences the message structure of answers was addressed by Semin & De Poot (1997a). When they analyzed the message structure in terms of abstraction–concreteness and implied agency, they found, as predicted, that questions formulated with action verbs gave rise to message structures that implied the agency of the respondent to the recalled autobiographical event. Furthermore, these narratives had a relatively concrete message structure. In contrast, autobiographical events prompted with state verbs were found to have a more abstract message structure and to imply the agency of "others" in the event (see also, De Poot & Semin, 1995; Semin, Rubini, & Fiedler, 1995; Rubini & Kruglanski, 1997). In a second step, Semin & De Poot (1997a) asked the respondents who generated these messages to judge implied agency, the likelihood of the event recurring at a future date, implied dispositionality, and perceived stability of the relationship between the persons described in the event. All these variables were known to measure inferences that are systematically mediated by the abstractness–concreteness of a message. There were no systematic effects on respondents' judgments with respect to these variables. These results suggest that respondents are not aware that the question structure influences the structure of the answers they give. However, when third parties were given the same task with the same narratives, by assigning a third party participant to each respondent–narrative, all the expected differences were shown to obtain. Events generated by state verb questions and which had an abstract message structure were perceived to be caused by others, more likely to recur at a future date, be less situationally determined, and to be indicative of a stable relationship, compared to the more concrete action verb generated narratives. Furthermore, it was shown that these inferences were directly mediated by the linguistic abstraction of the narratives. More significantly, these results suggest that the underlying properties tapped by the abstractness–concreteness dimension are insensitive to the specific narrative content or semantics, since each narrative was unique. More recent research in another domain confirms this general conclusion (Wigboldus, Semin, & Spears, in press).

Conclusions

An approach that regards language as a transformational device and investigates the tacit dimensions of language is in this sense a very significant development, in that it highlights not only message properties, but also message comprehension. The grammatical relationships induced by interpersonal verbs convey systematic information about dimensions such as time, causation, dispositionality, and distance of interpersonal relationship. These are significant in communicating and interpreting events, as we have seen. Dimensions that are coded in language and cut across lexical fields are critical in text construction and comprehension and are valuable features in how language shapes comprehension.

Furthermore, by focusing upon properties of language as properties of a tool, the transformational approach also introduces a perspective on how specific ways of structuring a "conversational opening" are likely to influence a response to such an opening. Thus, if you say "Thank you" after an event, then the most likely response is "You're welcome," although the recipient to the "Thank you" may not feel like making you welcome at all. What's more, an uninvolved outsider listening to this conversation may think that you *are* actually welcome. The difference between this example and the research on inferences mediated by interpersonal predicates is that the person saying "welcome" is well aware that she does not mean what she says. The predicate mediated research suggests that the person answering questions is neither aware that their response is being structured by the question and nor are they aware of its impact on listeners. One of the implications of viewing language as a structuring device is that it can be seen as a device that induces a powerful and tacit mindlessness (cf. Langer, 1989) into conversations, a mindlessness that we do not at all register as performers, but which is certainly recorded by an audience that judges us (Semin & De Poot, 1997a, 1997b).

3 Language and Social Cognition: Socially Distributed Knowledge

The focus here is on language and social cognition at the group level. Cognition in this context refers to knowledge that is socially shared and language use as communication plays a central role in achieving goals that exceed the capabilities of any single individual. As Hutchins (1996) notes, "Shifting attention from the cognitive properties of an individual to those of a system of socially distributed cognition casts language in a new light. The properties of language itself interact with the properties of the communications technology in ways that affect the computational properties of the larger cognitive system" (ibid., pp. 231–232). The type of cognitive activities that Hutchins is referring to is distributed across social space. In such situations, the kind of language that is used is critical in affecting the cognitive properties of the group. Thus, language or language use is a structuring device that will influence the group even if it does not affect the cognitive properties of the individuals. The general point raised by such a perspective is that there is a multitude of tasks in all human societies that cannot be achieved by individuals on their own. These kinds of tasks necessitate a social organization of distributed cognition. Such organization may or may not be appropriate to the task. Language becomes a very important factor as a tool for structuring and controlling action. Hutchin's empirical research focuses upon navigation, a group-task situation in which all members share a joint superordinate goal. He provides a great number of ethnographic instances of how language influences the cognitive properties of the group. For instance, in one illustration he shows how the structure of the lexicon constrains the cognitive process of the group, when the Marine commander phones the charthouse to find out the phase of the moon. The reply he gets is "gibbous waning." When receiving the answer there is confusion and the commander then wants to know whether it is "new," "first," "full," or "last." The answer then is "last," which is the nearest match to "gibbous waning" – with the following private comment of the commander in the chartroom after the phone exchange: "Rock is a great guy with a brain about this big [making a circle with the tip of his index finger matching the first joint of his thumb]. He must never have taken an amphib mission onto a beach at night. He might get by on a crescent moon, but on a gibbous waning he'll be dead" (ibid., p. 231). This example illustrates the limitations introduced by lexical capabilities, which are important determinants of the computations that have to be accomplished, the significance of such input for action. In other connectionist simulations, Hutchins (1996) investigated the implications of different communication constraints by creating the behavior of communities of networks.

In social psychology there is currently no work that investigates the link between socially distributed knowledge and language as a structuring device. It is likely that this domain will prove of considerable significance in the not-so-distant future.

The revival of attention on the social bases of cognition is seen in diverse approaches. For instance, Clark (1996) refers to the information that is shared between participants as "common ground." Similarly, Krauss and his colleagues (e.g. Krauss & Fussell, 1991) have examined the construction of common frameworks. The socially shared cognition "development" (Ostrom, 1984) is in fact a reassessment of the social bases of cognition. This development has a different emphasis from "socially distributed cognition" and the role that language and communication play in the social distribution of knowledge. The work that comes closest to this type of analysis comes from Vygotski's sociocultural approach. It is in particular the notion of the "zone of proximal development" that has commanded a considerable amount of attention in recent years. This is defined "as the distance between a child's actual developmental level as determined by independent problem solving" and the higher level of "potential development as determined through problem solving under adult guidance or in collaboration with more capable peers (Vygotsky, 1978, p. 86)" (Wertsch, 1991, p. 90). Clark (1997) refers to this type of action as "scaffolded action" in that it relies on some kind of external support. "Such support could come from the use of tools or from exploitation of the knowledge and skills of others; that is to say scaffolding . . . denotes a broad class of physical, cognitive, and social augmentations – augmentations that allow us to achieve some goal that would otherwise be beyond us" (Clark, 1997, pp. 194–195). In the context of the zone of proximal development, the primary caregiver walks the child through a difficult problem, by engaging in an exchange including verbal instructions. In tackling the same problem at a later point in time, the child conducts a dialogue but on her own. Language in this case also functions as a structuring device in that it shapes and controls the child's actions.

This closing perspective on the language–social cognition interface is intended to hint at a possible window for social psychological research. Such research could have considerable implications for an improved understanding of the social nature of social cognition. Moreover, this type of analysis is very likely to contribute to a clearer picture of the relationship between individual based approaches to socially shared cognition and socially distributed aspects of cognition as defined here.

Conclusions and Future Directions

An assessment of the interface between language and social cognition is simultaneously an invitation to consider and reassess a number of issues and assumptions that are in the heart of social psychology. One is undoubtedly what *is* social and what *is* psychological. The original linguistic relativity debate revolved around the question: what are the non-linguistic cognitive consequences of lexical or grammatical categories? Crudely put, this is a question about how the "social" influences the psychological, to the extent that language is a socially and not an individually constituted institution. The recent work on semantic priming, stereotyping, and automatic processes is precisely about how the social (linguistic primes) influences and shapes cognitive processes.

The work reviewed in sections 1 and 2 above on the properties of interpersonal predicates suggests that there are systematic ways in which interpersonal predicates vary with regard to the types of inferences they mediate. One potential implication of this conclusion is that in studies that use verbal stimuli about persons or social events we will have to be more careful about the nature of the stimuli we use. A majority of studies in social cognition proceed by using verbal stimuli and sometimes these stimuli may have some consistent "biases" that may contribute to the phenomenon under investigation. For instance, take the research on spontaneous trait inferences (Winter & Uleman, 1984; Winter, Uleman, & Cunniff, 1985). Here, all the critical stimulus sentences are constructed with action verbs. Would one get the same results if one were able to change the action verbs to state verbs and retain the same sentence otherwise? The answer is no, as Semin & Marsman (in press) have shown. The point is that the linguistic properties of stimuli require more attention than they have received to date.

Equally importantly, spoken and written language have qualitative differences that may systematically affect cognitive processes. Most of our research is based on written stimuli, although most of our interest is to extrapolate from that to phenomena that occur by other means of communication. For instance, the ease or difficulty of decoding written material may prove to be an important factor that has to be taken into account. This is illustrated by the observation that the algebraic development of the Greeks was stunted by their failure to develop an arithmetic notation based on symbols and their reliance on ordinary language, and an algebra that utilized letter symbols to represent unknown quantities (cf. Seanger, 1997, p. 132). One of the main arguments underlying this is that "Effective mathematical notation allows a maximum amount of information to be unambiguously displayed in foveal and parafoveal vision" (ibid.). Similar arguments have been raised in connection with the emergence of music notation (Levin & Addis, 1979, pp. 71–76).

There are a number of ways in which new directions are likely to evolve, but a significant and difficult avenue is the one that attempts to integrate the three views on the language–social cognition interface outlined in the three main sections of this chapter. In general, considering language and language use seriously in social cognition is likely to yield innovative syntheses. This can be achieved by systematic investigation of the constraints that are introduced by language and language use. In other words, a detailed examination of language furnishes the possibility of taming a significant source of variance, which if unattended can run wild.

REFERENCES

Abelson, R. P., & Kanouse, D. E. (1966). Subjective acceptance of verbal generalizations. In S. Feldman (Ed.), *Cognitive consistency: motivational antecedents and behavioral consequences* (pp. 171–197). New York: Academic Press.

Bahrick, H. P., & Boucher, B. (1968). Retention of verbal and visual codes of the same stimuli. *Journal of Experimental Psychology, 78*, 417–422.

Bakthin, M. M. (1979). *The esthetics of verbal creativity.* Moscow: Iskusstvo. Quoted in Wertsch (1994).

Bargh, J. A., & Pietromonaco, P. (1982). Automatic information processing and social perception: The influence of trait information presented outside of conscious awareness on impression formation. *Journal of Personality and Social Psychology, 43,* 437–49.

Berlin, B., & Kay, P. (1969). *Basic color terms: their universality and evolution.* Berkeley: University of California Press.

Brown, R. (1976). Reference: In memorial tribute to Eric Lenneberg. *Cognition, 4,* 125–153.

Brown, R., & Fish, D. (1983). The psychological causality implicit in language. *Cognition, 14,* 237–273.

Brown, R., & Lenneberg, E. H. (1954). A study in language and cognition. *Journal of Abnormal and Social Psychology, 49,* 454–462.

Chiu, C., Krauss, R. M., & Lau, I. Y.-M. (1998). Some cognitive consequences of communication. In S. R. Fussell & R. J. Kreuz (Eds.), *Social and cognitive approaches to interpersonal communication* (pp. 259–279). Hillsdale, NJ: Lawrence Erlbaum Associates.

Clark, A. (1997). *Being there: Putting brain, body, and world together.* Cambridge, MA: MIT Press.

Clark, H. H. (1996). *Using language.* Cambridge: Cambridge University Press.

De Poot, C. J., & Semin, G. R. (1995). Pick your verbs with care when you formulate a question! *Journal of Language & Social Psychology, 14,* 351–368.

Devine, P. G. (1989). Stereotypes and prejudice: Their automatic and controlled processes. *Journal of Personality and Social Psychology, 45,* 1096–1103.

Dijksterhuis, A. & Van Knippenberg, A. (1998). The relation between perception and behavior or how to win a game of Trivial Pursuit. *Journal of Personality and Social Psychology, 74,* 865–877.

Dijksterhuis, A., Aarts, H., Bargh, J. A., & Van Knippenberg, A. (in press). Unintentional forgetting: Direct experience as a trailblazer of automatic behavior. *Journal of Personality and Social Psychology.*

Dodson, C. S., Johnson, M. K., & Schooler, J. W. (1997). The verbal overshadowing effect: Why descriptions impair face recognition. *Memory & Cognition, 25,* 129–139.

Dovidio, J. F., Evans, N., & Tyler, R. B. (1986). Racial stereotypes: The content of their cognitive representations. *Journal of Experimental Social Psychology, 22,* 22–37.

Fiedler, K., & Semin, G. R. (1988). On the causal information conveyed by different interpersonal verbs: The role of implicit sentence context. *Social Cognition, 6,* 21–39.

Gabrielcik, A., & Fazio, R. (1984). Priming and frequency estimation: A strict test of the availability heuristic. *Personality and Social Psychology Bulletin, 10,* 85–90.

Gauker, C. (1990). How to learn language like a chimpanzee. *Philosophical Psychology, 3,* 31–53.

Gibson, J. J. (1979). *The ecological approach to visual perception.* Boston: Mifflin.

Giddens, A. (1976). *New rules of sociological method.* London: Hutchinson.

Giddens, A. (1979). *Critical problems in social theory.* London: McMillan Press.

Gilovich, T., & Regan, D. (1986). The actor and the experiencer: Divergent patterns of causal attribution. *Social Cognition, 4,* 342–352.

Grice, H. P. (1975). Logic and conversation. In P. Cole & J. Morgan (Eds.), *Syntax and semantics* (pp. 41–58). New York: Academic Press.

Gumpertz, J. J., & Levinson, S. C. (1996). Introduction to part 1. In J. J. Gumpertz & S. C. Levinson (Eds.), *Rethinking linguistic relativity* (pp. 21–37). Cambridge: Cambridge University Press.

Hardin, C. L., & Banaji, M. R. (1993). The influence of language on thought. *Social Cognition, 11,* 277–308.

Hardin, C. L., & Maffi, L. (1997). *Color categories in thought and language.* Cambridge, UK: Cambridge University Press.

Higgins, E. T. (1981). The "communication game": implications for social cognition and persuasion. In E. T. Higgins, M. P. Zanna, and C. P. Hermans (Eds.), *Social cognition: The Ontario symposium*, Vol. 1 (pp. 343–392). Hillsdale, NJ: Erlbaum.

Higgins, E. T., & McCann, C. D. (1984). Social encoding and subsequent attitudes, impressions, and memory: "Context-driven" and motivational aspects of processing. *Journal of Personality and Social Psychology*, 47, 26–39.

Higgins, E. T., & Rholes, W. S. (1977). "Saying is believing": Effects of message modification on memory and linking of the person described. *Journal of Experimental Social Psychology*, 14, 363–378.

Higgins, E. T., McCann, C. D., & Fondacaro, R. A. (1982). The "communication game": Goal-directed encoding and cognitive consequences. *Social Cognition*, 1, 21–37.

Hoffman, C., & Tchir, M. A. (1990). Interpersonal verbs and dispositional adjectives: The psychology of causality embodied in language. *Journal of Personality and Social Psychology*, 58, 765–778.

Hoffman, C., Lau, I. J., & Johnson, D. R. (1986). The linguistic relativity of person cognition: An English-Chinese comparison. *Journal of Personality and Social Psychology*, 51, 1097–1105.

Hunt, E., & Agnoli, F. (1991). The Whorfian hypothesis: A cognitive psychology perspective. *Psychological Review*, 98, 377–389.

Hutchins, E. (1996). *Cognition in the wild*. Cambridge, MA: MIT Press.

Kahneman, D., & Tversky, A. (1984). Choices, values, and frames. *American Psychologist*, 39, 341–350.

Kanouse, D. E. (1971). Language, labelling, and attribution. In E. E. Jones, D. E. Kanouse, H. H. Kelley, R. E. Nisbett, S. Valins, & B. Weiner (Eds.), *Attribution: Perceiving the causes of behavior* (pp. 121–134). New York: General Learning Press.

Kanouse, E. E. (1972). Verbs as implicit quantifiers. *Journal of Verbal Learning and Verbal Behavior*, 11, 141–147.

Kasoff, J., & Lee, J. Y. (1993). Implicit causality as implicit salience. *Journal of Personality and Social Psychology*, 65, 877–891.

Kay, P., & Kempton, W. (1984). What is the Sapir–Whorf hypothesis? *American Anthropologist*, 86, 65–79.

Krauss, R. M., & Fussell, S. R. (1991). Constructing shared communicative environments. In L. B. Resnick, J. M. Levine, & S. D. Teasley (Eds.), *Perspectives on socially shared cognition* (pp. 172–200). Washington, DC: American Psychological Association.

Krauss, R. M., & Fussell, S. R. (1996). Social psychological models of interpersonal communication. In E. T. Higgins & A. W. Kruglanski (Eds.), *Social psychology: Handbook of basic principles* (pp. 655–701). New York: Guilford Press.

Langer, E. J. (1989). Minding matters. In L. Berkowitz (Ed.), *Advances in experimental social psychology* Vol. 22 (pp. 137–173). NY: Academic Press.

Lenneberg, E. H. (1953). Cognition in ethnolinguistics. *Language*, 29, 463–471.

Lepore, L., & Brown, R. (1997). Category and stereotype activation: Is prejudice inevitable? *Journal of Personality and Social Psychology*, 72, 275–287.

Levin, H., & Addis, A. B. (1979). *The eye–voice span*. Cambridge, MA: MIT Press.

Levin, I. P., Schnijttjer, S. K., & Thee, S. L. (1988). Information framing effects in social and personal decisions. *Journal of Experimental Social Psychology*, 24, 520–529.

Levinson, S. C. (1996). Introduction to part 2. In J. J. Gumpertz & S. C. Levinson (Eds.), *Rethinking linguistic relativity* (pp. 133–144). Cambridge: Cambridge University Press.

Loftus, E. F. (1979). *Eyewitness testimony*. Cambridge, MA: Harvard University Press.

Lucy, J. A. (1992). *Language, diversity and thought: A reformulation of the linguisitic relativity hypothesis*. Cambridge: Cambridge University Press.

Maass, A., Ceccarelli, R., & Rudin, S. (1996). Linguistic intergroup bias: Evidence for in-group-protective motivation. *Journal of Personality and Social Psychology, 71*, 512–526.

Maass, A., Corvino, P., & Arcuri, L. (1994). Linguistic intergroup bias and the mass media. *Revue de psychologie social, 1*, 31–43.

Maass, A., Milesi, A., Zabbini, S., & Stahlberg, D. (1995). The linguistic intergroup bias: Differential expectancies or in-group-protection? *Journal of Personality and Social Psychology, 68*, 116–126.

Maass, A., Salvi, D., Arcuri, L., & Semin, G. R. (1989). Language-use in intergroup contexts: The linguistic intergroup bias. *Journal of Personality and Social Psychology, 57*, 981–993.

McCann, D. C., & Higgins, E. T. (1992). Personal and contextual factors in communication: A review of the "communication game." In G. R. Semin & K. Fiedler (Eds.), *Language, interaction and social cognition* (pp. 144–172). Newbury, CA: Sage.

Meyer, D. E., & Schvaneveldt, R. W. (1971). Facilitation in the recognition of word pairs: Evidence of a dependence between retrieval operations. *Journal of Experimental Psychology, 90*, 227–234.

Neely, J. H. (1977). Semantic priming and retrieval from lexical memory: Roles of inhibitionless spreading activation and limited-capacity attention. *Journal of Experimental Psychology: General, 1*, 226–254.

Ostrom, T. M. (1984). The sovereignty of social cognition. In R. S. Wyer & T. K. Srull (Eds.), *Handbook of social cognition* Vol. 1 (pp. 12–27). Hillsdale, NJ: Erlbaum.

Perdue, C. W., Dovidio, J. F., Gurtman, M. B., & Tyler, R. B. (1990). Us and them: Social categorization and the process of intergroup bias. *Journal of Personality and Social Psychology, 59*, 475–486.

Polanyi, M. (1967). *The tacit dimension*. London: Routledge.

Ranken, H. B. (1963). Language and thinking: Positive and negative effects of naming. *Science, 141*, 48–50.

Ricoeur, P. (1955). The model of the text: meaningful action considered as text. *Social Research, 38*, 530–547.

Rosch, E. (1973). On the internal structure of perceptual and semantic categories. In T. E. Moore (Ed.), *Cognitive development and the acquisition of language* (pp. 111–157). New York: Academic Press.

Rubini, M., & Kruglanski, A. W. (1997). Brief encounters ending in estrangement: Motivated language use and interpersonal rapport in the question–answer paradigm. *Journal of Personality and Social Psychology, 72*, 1047–1060.

Rudolph, U., & Försterling, F. (1997). The psychological causality implicit in verbs: A review. *Psychological Bulletin, 121*, 192–218.

Santa, J. L., & Ranken, H. B. (1968). Language and memory: reintegrative memory for shapes facilitated by naming. *Psychonomic Science, 13*, 109–110.

Schooler, J. W., & Engsler-Schooler, T. Y. (1990). Verbal overshadowing of visual memories: Some things are better left unsaid. *Cognitive Psychology, 22*, 36–71.

Seanger, P. (1997). *Space between words*. Stanford, CA: Stanford University Press.

Semin, G. R. (1998). Cognition, language, and communication. In S. R. Fussell and R. J. Kreuz (Eds.), *Social and cognitive psychological approaches to interpersonal communication* (pp. 229–257). Hillsdale, NJ: Lawrence Erlbaum Associates.

Semin, G. R., & De Poot, C. J. (1997a). The question–answer paradigm: You might regret not noticing how a question is worded. *Journal of Personality and Social Psychology, 73*, 472–480.

Semin, G. R., & De Poot, C. J. (1997b). Bringing partiality to light: Question wording and choice as indicators of bias. *Social Cognition, 15*, 91–106.

Semin, G. R., & Fiedler, K. (1988). The cognitive functions of linguistic categories in describing persons: Social cognition and language. *Journal of Personality and Social Psychology, 54*, 558–568.

Semin G. R., & Fiedler, K. (1992). The inferential properties of interpersonal verbs. In G. R. Semin & K. Fiedler (Eds.), *Language, interaction and social cognition* (pp. 58–78). Newbury Park, CA: Sage Publications.

Semin, G. R., & Greenslade, L. (1985). Differential contributions of linguistic factors to memory based ratings: Systematizing the systematic distortion hypothesis. *Journal of Personality and Social Psychology, 49*, 1713–1723.

Semin, G. R., & Marsman, G. J. (1994). "Multiple inference inviting properties" of interpersonal verbs: Event instigation, dispositional inference, and implicit causality. *Journal of Personality and Social Psychology, 67*, 836–849.

Semin, G. R., & Marsman, G. J. (in press). The mnemonic functions of interpersonal verbs: Spontaneous trait inferences. *Social Cognition.*

Semin, G. R., Rubini, M., & Fiedler, K. (1995). The answer is in the question: The effect of verb causality on locus of explanation. *Personality and Social Psychology Bulletin, 21*, 834–842.

Tajfel, H., & Turner, J. C. (1979). An integrative theory of intergroup conflict. In W. S. Austin & S. Worchel (Eds.), *The social psychology of intergroup relations* (pp. 33–47). Monterey, CA: Brooks/Cole.

Vygotsky, L. S. (1981). The instrumental method in psychology. In J. V. Wertsch (Ed.), *The concept of activity in Soviet psychology* (pp. 196–227). Armonk, NY: M. E. Sharpe.

Wertsch, J. V. (1991). *Voices of the mind: A sociocultural approach to mediated action.* Cambridge, MA: Harvard University Press.

Wertsch, J. V. (1994). The primacy of mediated action in socio-cultural studies. *Mind, Culture, and Activity, 1*, 202–208.

Whorf, B. L. (1957). *Language, Thought, and Reality.* Cambridge, MA: MIT Press.

Wigboldus, D. H. J., Semin, G. R., & Spears, R. (in press). How do we communicate stereotypes? Linguistic bases and inferential consequences. *Journal of Personality and Social Psychology, 78.*

Winter, L., & Uleman, J. S. (1984). When are social judgments made? Evidence for the spontaneousness of trait inferences. *Journal of Personality and Social Psychology, 47*, 237–252.

Winter, L., Uleman, J. S., & Cunniff, C. (1985). How automatic are social judgments? *Journal of Personality and Social Psychology, 49*, 904–917.

CHAPTER ELEVEN

Attitudes, Norms, and Social Groups

Joel Cooper, Kimberly A. Kelly, and Kimberlee Weaver

The concept of the attitude has had a long and venerable history in social psychology. In his seminal chapter in the original *Handbook of Social Psychology*, Gordon Allport (1935) called the attitude, "probably the most distinctive and indispensable concept in contemporary American social psychology." In all probability, it still is. At the very least, it is the most widely referenced concept in social psychology as the twentieth century draws to a close.

It is interesting that it was not always so. According to Allport, before the attitude concept gained acceptance, there was no agreed upon way to represent preferences, sentiments, and values. But the growth of the attitude concept gave social psychologists a way to discuss and measure such preferences. Cantril (1934) defined attitude as "a more or less permanently enduring state of readiness of mental organization which predisposes an individual to react in a characteristic way to any object or situation with which it is related." Current students of attitudes have generally conceived of attitudes in much the same way. Petty and Cacioppo (1996), for example, refer to attitudes as "a general and enduring positive or negative feeling about some person, object, or issue" (p. 7).

Despite the similarity in definitions of attitudes during the past seven decades, there have been interesting and subtle differences in the direction of research. In Allport's view, one of the benefits of the attitude concept was that it allowed researchers not only to examine the preferences of individuals, but also the dispositions and preferences of social groups and cultures. For Allport, the study of attitudes provided a meeting ground for the study of groups and individuals. In that vein, Festinger (1950) emphasized the integral interdependence of individual and group by noting, "an attitude is correct, valid, and proper to the extent that it is anchored in a group of people with similar beliefs, opinions, and attitudes" (p. 272).

During the intervening decades, the focus of attitude research has shifted from its coemphasis on individuals and groups to a predominant interest in the individual. With a few notable exceptions, attitude research has emphasized internal processes and has largely ignored the influence of groups on attitude formation and change. Consequently, it goes almost unnoticed that Petty and Cacioppo's (1996) definition of attitudes exclusively addresses the feeling of an individual toward a person, issue, or thing and does not refer to the social situation or social group.

In this chapter we will review research and theory that suggests that the social groups to which we belong play a major role in attitude formation, attitude–behavior consistency, and attitude change. We begin by examining the ways in which groups influence the formation of attitudes. We then look at the link between attitudes and behavior, paying special attention to the importance of reference groups in promoting attitude–behavior consistency. Finally, we explore two theories of attitude change: group polarization and cognitive dissonance. While polarization has always been studied from a "group" perspective, cognitive dissonance has primarily been studied at the individual level. However, both past and recent research can give us some insight into the ways in which group membership may play an important role in attitude change.

One recurring theme throughout this chapter is the idea that groups have the largest influence on attitudes when group identities are important, relevant, and salient. Many of the current models of social cognition place an emphasis on the fact that we often will act upon whatever attitude, information, or goal happens to be accessible at a particular moment in time. Like other types of cognitive structures, when group identities have been activated, they can influence how we form, act upon, and change our attitudes. This is particularly true when the group is important to us, and when group membership is relevant to the attitudinal issue.

Attitude Formation

People often seek information about objective reality by examining the actions of others. At other times people are concerned about being accepted by others, and comply with group norms in order to obtain social approval. These two forms of social influence are typically referred to as informational and normative social influence, respectively (Deutsch & Gerard, 1955). In this section, we will examine how both informational and normative social influence affect the ways in which people form attitudes. We will also explore the ways in which the salience of group norms and social identities can influence attitude formation.

Informational social influence

In situations in which the correct attitude or behavior is difficult to determine, people can look to those around them for clues as to what they should think and do. For instance, if people want to know if the ocean water is warm enough to go swimming, they might look to see if any other people are in the water. If people are uncertain about a particular attitudinal issue, they might behave in the same way. They could examine the attitudes of those around them, in order to learn what other people think. Hence, this type of influence is known as informational social influence.

Sherif (1935) demonstrated that in ambiguous situations, people look to the opinions of others for information. Sherif asked participants in a dark room to estimate the distance a small light moved. Due to a visual phenomenon known as the autokinetic effect, most people perceived the light to be moving, even though it remained stationary. At first, individuals' estimates of the distance the light moved varied. However, after repeated trials in which the participants heard everyone's responses, all of the participants in a given group began to make similar distance estimates.

Participants in Sherif's (1935) experiment apparently internalized the information they received from the other group members. When asked to judge the movement of the light in private, participants still responded with answers that matched the previous group consensus. This suggests that in cases where people are uncertain about what attitudes to hold, individuals may influence each other through their actions and responses until most group members hold similar attitudes.

The nature of the group: Ingroups and outgroups.   The nature of the group providing the information influences whether individuals will accept other group members' opinions. In a replication of Sherif's (1935) experiment, Abrams and his colleagues (Abrams, Wetherell, Cochrane, Hogg, & Turner, 1990) manipulated the degree to which participants saw themselves as members of a group. They placed confederates (outgroup members) in each condition, and then varied the distinction between ingroup and outgroup. The first group performed the autokinetic task anonymously in the dark, as had Sherif's participants. A second group received a label to distinguish them from the subgroup of confederates, and the third group both received a distinguishing label and performed a prior task with their own subgroup.

Abrams et al. (1990) found that participants' responses were less likely to converge with the responses of the confederates as the salience of their status as a distinct group increased. Conformity was lowest when the participants had previously distinguished themselves from the outgroup (confederates) by performing a task together. Conformity was highest when the distinction between ingroup and outgroup was not readily apparent. These results suggest that although groups can provide information people use to form attitudes, people are more likely to accept this information from ingroup members.

Normative social influence

The second type of influence that groups can provide is normative social influence. The most common example of normative influence is Asch's (1951, 1956) line-length experiments. In these experiments, participants were asked to judge the length of lines, after hearing responses from several other individuals. Occasionally, the other individuals (who were all confederates of the experimenter) would give an incorrect response. Sometimes this normative pressure led participants to agree with the incorrect estimates. Later experiments (e.g., Deutsch & Gerard, 1955) found that when participants gave their answers privately, they were much less likely to agree with the confederates.

Although the Asch experiment does not deal directly with attitude formation, experiments with similar designs have investigated the role of normative influence in the formation of attitudes toward objects as diverse as paintings (Argyle, 1957), flavors (Kelley & Lamb,

1957), and people (Raven, 1959). For instance, Raven (1959) asked participants to form an attitude about a juvenile delinquent named "Johnny Rocco." Although participants tended to feel that Johnny should be treated leniently, they were told that the majority of group members advocated harsh punishment. As in the Asch (1956) study, participants were more likely to conform to the judgments of other group members when their responses were public rather than private, indicating normative social influence as the basis for the attitude.

Ingroups and outgroups revisited.   As with informational influence, research has shown that normative influence is also dependent on the relationship people have with the group providing the norm. Abrams et al. (1990) replicated the Asch (1956) experiment using a straightforward ingroup, outgroup manipulation. When the confederates were members of the ingroup, the participants showed the usual pattern: They were more likely to conform publicly than privately. However, when the confederates were outgroup members, participants were more likely to conform privately than publicly. Although people may alter their behavior to publicly match ingroup norms, outgroup norms are more likely to influence private attitudes rather than public behavior.

Salience of group norms and social identities

When are groups most likely to influence attitudes? Psychologists working in the tradition of social identity and self-categorization theory have proposed that when a particular social identity is made salient, people will categorize themselves in terms of that social category (e.g., Turner, 1991). As Terry and Hogg (1996) point out, "When social identity is salient . . . a person's feelings and actions are guided more by group prototypes and norms than by personal factors" (p. 790). When people see themselves as group members, group norms will be more likely to influence the ways in which they form, act upon, and change their attitudes.

Groups can provide information and exert normative pressures on individuals, which will influence attitude formation. The influence of groups will vary, based upon whether people categorize themselves as a member of the group, or as an outsider. Groups will have the largest influence on attitude formation when group identity is salient. Yet even after attitudes have been formed, groups can influence the likelihood that people will act upon those attitudes.

Attitude–Behavior Consistency

How predictive are attitudes in determining behavior? In an early review of empirical research, Wicker (1969) called into question the assumption that there is a straightforward and direct relationship between attitudes and behavior. Wicker (1969) argued instead that the relationship between attitudes and behaviors was weak. The lack of empirical support for a simple

between attitudes and behavior led theorists to look more closely at the attitude–
lation in an attempt to develop better behavioral predictions.

since Wicker's (1969) review has pointed to the importance of social norms as
rsonal attitudes in determining whether people will act in accordance with their
In this section we will discuss both the automatic and more deliberate ways in
which social norms can influence the attitude–behavior relationship. Because they have
different perspectives on the role of group norms in the attitude–behavior relationship, we
will examine both the motivation and opportunity as determinants (MODE) model and the
theory of planned behavior (Ajzen, 1991).

Attitudes can affect behavior both automatically and deliberately. One area of research
that has investigated this dichotomy is the MODE model. Research conducted under the
MODE model (Fazio, 1986, 1990, 1999) has helped to outline the two processes through
which attitudes lead to behavior. According to the model, under some conditions people's
behavior is spontaneously or automatically guided by their attitudes, while under other
conditions people engage in effortful and deliberate thought about their attitudes when
forming behavioral intentions.

Automatic processing

Fazio argues that spontaneous or automatic attitude–behavior links occur when people hold
highly accessible attitudes toward certain targets. Highly accessible attitudes spontaneously
guide behavior in part because they influence people's perceptions of a particular target or
situation. For instance, if a teacher holds a positive attitude toward a student, the teacher will
likely interpret the student's behavior selectively, and in line with the positive attitude. This
selective attention to attitude-consistent information will lead to attitude-consistent behavior.
According to Fazio (1990; Fazio & Towles-Schwen, 1999), people are more likely to exhibit
attitude–behavior consistency when their attitudes are highly accessible and thus can guide
behavior spontaneously.

Although the emphasis of the MODE model is on how attitudes guide behavior, it
also acknowledges that social norms play a role in whether people will behave in attitude-
consistent ways. Like attitudes, the influence of norms can be either automatic or conscious.
For example, research has shown that the accessibility of norms from different reference
groups can spontaneously influence people's perceptions of attitude objects. For instance,
Baldwin and Holmes (1987) showed that norms of accessible reference groups influenced
participants' reactions to a description of sexual permissiveness. In their study, participants
were asked to visualize either the faces of two campus friends or the faces of two older family
members. Participants were then asked to evaluate a sexually permissive passage as part of an
allegedly unrelated task. Those who had visualized the faces of campus friends evaluated the
description more positively than participants who had visualized the faces of two older family
members. Apparently, the different reference groups brought to mind norms that the participants then used to evaluate the passage. The MODE model argues that people are more
likely to exhibit attitude–behavior consistency when their attitudes are both highly accessible
and in line with accessible social norms.

Deliberate processing: The theory of planned behavior

According to the MODE model (Fazio, 1990; Fazio &Towles-Schwen, 1999), other types of situations lead people to engage in effortful and deliberate reflection upon their attitudes when formulating behavioral intentions. A student making a difficult decision about which graduate school to attend would likely engage in this more effortful and deliberate processing mode, and would thus be likely to scrutinize his or her attitudes before making a decision. It is when people formulate behavioral intentions through effortful reflection that the relationship between a person's personal attitude and his or her behavior is not always straightforward. Although the MODE model acknowledges that in some situations people scrutinize their attitudes, research conducted under the MODE model does not address the role of deliberate processing in the attitude–behavior relationship.

The theory of planned behavior (Ajzen, 1991, see also its predecessor, the theory of reasoned action, Fishbein & Ajzen, 1975; Ajzen & Fishbein, 1980), on the other hand, was designed to describe the relationship between attitudes and behaviors in situations in which deliberate, effortful processing is required. The theory of planned behavior maintains that behavioral intentions, rather than attitudes, directly influence behavior. According to the model, behavioral intentions comprise both personal factors (i.e., the person's attitude and his or her perceived level of behavioral control) and social factors (i.e., social norms). These two types of factors are hypothesized to exert psychologically independent influences on the behavioral intentions that people form with regard to certain situations.

More specifically, the theory of planned behavior posits that behavioral intentions are determined by three types of beliefs: Personal beliefs about the consequences of a behavior (the person's "attitude"), personal beliefs about control ("perceived behavioral control"), and social, or normative, beliefs ("subjective norms"). According to the model, the individual's personal attitude is a function of beliefs the person holds about the consequences of a given behavior, and the person's evaluation of these consequences. Control beliefs are those that the person holds about his or her ability to perform the behavior. The person's social beliefs, on the other hand, are a function of the degree to which the person perceives social pressure to perform the behavior. This perceived social pressure, or subjective norm, is determined by the person's perceptions of how referent individuals or groups think that he or she should behave in a situation, and the degree to which the person is motivated to comply with these referent individuals or groups. According to the theory of planned behavior, researchers attempting to predict whether a college student will engage in binge drinking should assess the student's personal attitudes toward such behavior, the degree to which he or she feels a sense of control over the behavior, and his or her perceptions of what relevant referent others (e.g., peers, parents) would endorse with regard to binge drinking.

Are social beliefs important? The salience of personal and normative beliefs. The theory of planned behavior argues that the combined additive influence of attitudes, control beliefs, and social beliefs (subjective norms) leads to behavioral intentions, which in turn directly influence behavior. Although the theory acknowledges that the relative import-ance of one type of belief over the other will vary with the situation, it does not provide an analysis of the conditions under which each type of belief will be most important in predicting a behavioral intention, beyond stating that it is an empirical question (Fishbein & Ajzen, 1975).

In fact, Ajzen (1991) called into question whether social norms independently predict behavioral intentions at all. In a review of the literature, he noted that in the vast majority of the studies on the theory of planned behavior, both the attitudinal and the perceived control components of the theory were significant independent predictors of behavioral intention. In contrast, results for the subjective norm component of the theory were mixed. Some studies showed that subjective norms made a significant contribution to the prediction of intentions, yet other studies showed that subjective norms did not independently predict behavioral intentions. From this review, Ajzen (1991) concluded that, "personal considerations tended to overshadow the influence of perceived social pressure" (p. 189). Recent research conducted from a social identity/self-categorization perspective has suggested that this may be a premature conclusion (e.g., Terry & Hogg, 1996; White, Terry, & Hogg, 1994). In the next section we will review recent work that has helped specify the conditions under which people's behavioral intentions are influenced by the presence of social factors, most particularly social groups.

When do social factors influence behavioral intentions?   Recent research has begun to specify how people weigh personal and social factors when formulating behavioral intentions. These factors include social identification (Terry & Hogg, 1996; White, Terry, & Hogg, 1994), cultural factors (Abrams, Ando, & Hinkle, 1998), the accessibility of social norms (Fishbein, Chan, O'Reilly, Schnell, Wood, Beeker, & Cohn, 1992), and the accessibility of the collective or private self (Ybarra & Trafimow, 1998).

Social identification. Researchers working from a social identity/self-categorization theory perspective (e.g., Terry & Hogg, 1996; White, Terry, & Hogg, 1994), have raised the possibility that the lack of consistent support for the social norms component of the theory of planned behavior is due to the theory's conceptualization of social norms. Specifically, Terry and Hogg (1996) argue that the social component of the theory of planned behavior should be reconceptualized in light of recent theoretical and empirical development on social identity and self-categorization theory.

Social identity theorists define social identity as "that part of an individual's self-concept that derives from his knowledge of his membership in a social group (or groups) together with the value and emotional significance attached to that membership" (Tajfel, 1982, p. 255). According to social identity theorists, people are motivated to preserve a positive sense of themselves. One of the ways that people can achieve such a positive self-identity is from their memberships in social groups. Therefore, social norms should be most likely to predict behavior when group membership is a significant and valued part of an individual's self-concept.

In a set of studies, Terry and Hogg (1996) showed that social norms did make significant independent contributions to behavioral intentions, but only when the referent others were members of a group that was a part of the participants' social identity. Specifically, Terry and Hogg (1996, study 1) looked at the influence of attitudes, perceived level of behavioral control, and social norms on students' intentions to engage in exercise behavior. Consistent with the theory of planned behavior, analyses showed that both attitude and perceived level of behavioral control were significant predictors of behavioral intentions for all the students. Consistent with predictions derived from social identity and self-categorization theory, however, the group norm component significantly predicted students' behavioral intentions to engage in exercise, but only for those who strongly identified with the relevant group (peers at the university). In contrast, the group norm was not a significant predictor of intentions for those who expressed low levels of identification with the reference group.

In addition to showing that the behavioral intentions of the low identifiers were not influenced by the group norm, Terry and Hogg (1996) showed that personal factors exerted a larger influence on the behavioral intentions of low identifiers as compared to high identifiers. For example, Terry and Hogg (study 2) showed that students who did not identify strongly with their group were more influenced by their personal attitudes toward the behavior than were students who did identify strongly with the group.

Overall, the results from the Terry and Hogg (1996) studies suggest that the normative component of the theory of planned behavior may exert a greater impact than the personal component when a behavior is seen as normative for a group that is part of participants' self-concepts. These results are consistent with social identity and self-categorization theory, which posit that when a person categorizes him or herself in terms of a social category, he or she assimilates to the group prototype, and thus behaves as a member of that group (Turner, 1991; also see Hogg, 2001). Personal factors, on the other hand, play a larger role in determining behavioral intentions for those who do not identify strongly with a salient reference group.

Cultural factors. Other research has shown that cross-cultural differences may influence the relative importance of the personal and normative components of the theory of planned behavior in predicting behavioral intentions (Abrams et al., 1998). For instance, Abrams et al. (1998) measured the effects of personal and normative factors in employee turnover intentions in both British and Japanese samples. Results from two studies showed that the predictive influence of subjective norms on turnover intentions was significantly stronger for Japanese workers than it was for British workers. People in collectivist countries are generally more sensitive to their social ties and to the expectations of their referent others (Markus & Kitayama, 1991). Cultural differences in the emphasis placed on meeting group expectations appears to moderate the relative importance of personal versus social factors in people's formations of behavioral intentions.

Accessibility of social norms. Other research has indicated that the degree of social community organization can have an impact on the relative importance of social norms in predicting behavioral intentions. Fishbein et al. (1992), for example, showed that social norms were stronger predictors of safe sex intentions for gay men who lived in well-organized gay communities than they were for gay men who lived in less organized communities. Further research showed that the differential impact of social norms on intentions was due to the degree of attention that the men paid to the normative pressures, rather than due to the existence of different subjective norms in the different communities (Fishbein, Chan, O'Reilly, Schnell, Wood, Beeker, & Cohn 1993).

Accessibility of private or collective self. Variations in the accessibility of the private or collective self can also influence the weight people give to the personal and social components of intentions. Ybarra and Trafimow (1998), for instance, showed that when participants' private selves were made accessible in an experimental situation, they placed more weight on personal or attitudinal beliefs when forming behavioral intentions. In contrast, when their collective selves were accessible in the experimental situation, participants gave more weight to normative considerations when forming behavioral intentions. Research has also suggested a role for chronic accessibility or individual differences in the importance of personal and normative beliefs in behavioral intentions (Finlay, Trafimow, & Jones, 1997; Trafimow & Finlay, 1996).

The theory of planned behavior has been important in its emphasis on the significance of the social environment in determining whether or not people will behave consistently with their attitudes. Recent research on social identity variables has pointed to the possible utility of revising the social norms component of the theory of planned behavior to take into account research on the effects of social identification. Although the MODE model has not been as widely studied, it also acknowledges the means by which social norms can influence behavior. Examining both the deliberative and automatic processes should result in a better understanding of the conditions under which attitudes will predict behavior.

Attitude Change

Groups not only influence how people form and choose to act upon their attitudes, they also influence how and when people change their attitudes. In this section we will examine how groups influence attitude change in two different areas of research: One that has traditionally been studied from a group perspective, and one that has traditionally been studied from an intrapersonal perspective. We will begin by examining group polarization, one of the most actively researched topics in the study of group influences on attitude change. We will then take a close look at ways in which groups influence cognitive dissonance arousal and reduction.

Group polarization

One of the most robust findings in social psychology is that of attitude polarization following discussion with like-minded others. Specifically, research has shown that when group members with similar initial attitudes engage in group discussion to achieve consensus, the discussion strengthens the average individual inclinations of group members and leads to attitude polarization. The first attitude polarization studies examined attitudes toward risk. In these studies, groups comprised individual members who each personally supported a moderately risky approach to a choice dilemma and discussed the approach as a group in order to give a unanimous recommendation. Results showed that both the group consensus and the individual group members' postdiscussion private attitudes advocated greater risk than their average prediscussion recommendation (e.g., "risky shift" Stoner, 1968). The tendency to advocate more risk following group discussion was deemed "group polarization" when subsequent research showed that the polarizing effects of group discussion generalized to attitude issues other than those that involved risk (Moscovici & Zavalloni, 1969).

The most widely accepted theoretical explanations of group polarization findings have focused on the role of the group as a source of either informational or normative influence (see reviews by Isenberg, 1986; Lamm & Myers, 1978; Myers & Lamm, 1976). The most widely researched informational explanation, the persuasive arguments position (e.g., Burnstein & Vinokur, 1977), maintains that before expressing an attitude or choice, people perform a mental search for arguments either in favor of or against the attitudinal position or choice. According to this line of reasoning, when group members formulate their pretest attitudes, each member initially relies on a somewhat different set of arguments for or against the topic. Consequently, when the group members come together to discuss the topic, in the course of discussion they are exposed to supportive arguments that they had not thought of previously. Persuasive arguments theory maintains that the attitude polarization finding is a consequence of group members' exposure to this additional supportive information.

Support for the role of persuasive arguments in attitude polarization has shown that group members' postdiscussion ratings are influenced by the order in which they hear persuasive arguments (Kaplan & Miller, 1976). The fact that recency effects influence postdiscussion attitudes is consistent with the role of the group as a source of informational influence that is inherent in the persuasive arguments position.

In contrast to the persuasive arguments position, normative explanations of group polarization maintain that attitude polarization following group discussion is a result of social comparison processes (Jellison & Arkin, 1977; Sanders & Baron, 1975). Social comparison explanations hold that people are motivated both to see themselves in a socially favorable light and to present themselves in a socially favorable manner. Social comparison explanations of attitude polarization that focus on "bandwagon effects" maintain that people have a desire to be different from others in a valued direction (see Isenberg, 1986; Turner, 1991 for discussions of variants on this social comparison explanation). According to this explanation, participants in group polarization studies shift their attitudes to more extreme positions in order to hold a more favorable position than the rest of the group. Evidence in support of the social comparison explanation of polarization effects has shown that under certain circumstances participants' attitudes become polarized even when they are only given knowledge of the group norm and are not exposed to persuasive arguments per se (Blascovich, Ginsburg, & Veach, 1975; Myers, Wojcicki, & Aardema, 1977).

Although research has supported the role of both persuasive arguments and social comparison in accounting for attitude shifts in group polarization studies, reviewers have noted that neither perspective is able to account for all the results (see, e.g., Isenberg, 1986; Myers & Lamm, 1976). Additionally, recent research on the influence of other group variables in attitude polarization has shown that the persuasive arguments viewpoint and the social comparison explanations are not sufficient accounts of group polarization findings. Specifically, several studies examining predictions derived from social identity and self-categorization theory suggest that social categorization processes also play a significant role in group polarization.

Social identification theory/self-categorization theory.   Self-categorization theory also offers a theoretical explanation of group polarization. Group polarization effects occur through three steps: (1) categorization of the self as a member of a group; (2) identification of the prototypical characteristics, behaviors, and norms of the group that differentiate the ingroup from other groups; and (3) stereotyping of the self as a member of the group (Mackie, 1986; Mackie & Cooper, 1984; Turner, 1982, 1985, 1991). According to this theoretical explanation of group polarization, attitude polarization in response to information about one's ingroup or discussion with one's ingroup occurs as a result of people conforming to a polarized group norm (Hogg, Turner, & Davidson, 1990).

Categorization of the self. Research has been consistent with this social categorization explanation of group polarization. For instance, research has shown that participants exhibit attitude polarization in response to persuasive arguments only when the arguments are put forth by members of an ingroup. Mackie and Cooper (1984, study 1), had participants who were mildly in favor of retaining standardized tests as college admissions criteria listen to a taped discussion of three people presenting arguments either in favor of or against retaining such a policy. Participants were led to believe that they would participate in a similar group discussion later in the session, and that their group would compete with another group for a monetary prize. Half of the participants were led to believe that the discussants on the tape were members of their future ingroup (ingroup condition), whereas half of the participants were led to believe that the discussants were members of the group against which their group would be competing (outgroup condition).

Results showed that participants who were led to believe that the discussants were ingroup members exhibited more attitude polarization than those who had heard the identical discussion attributed to an outgroup. Although the persuasive arguments the participants heard were identical, only participants who categorized themselves as members of the group on the tape exhibited attitude polarization and changed their attitudes to become more in favor of retaining standardized tests.

Polarization of group norm. Mackie (1986; see also Mackie & Cooper, 1984) also examined the processes – polarization of the group norm and self-stereotyping – through which social categorization is postulated to drive the polarization effect. Consistent with the idea that when people categorize themselves as group members they perceptually distinguish their ingroup from other groups, Mackie (1986) found that participants tended to attribute more extreme attitudes to their own groups than did outside observers who heard the same discussion. Mackie (1986) speculated that this perceptual accentuation or polarization of the group norm may have led participants to perceive that their group was more unanimous in its position on the standardized test issue than would have been attributed by outside observers.

Conformity to polarized norms. Results from Mackie (1986) also suggest that the attitude polarization exhibited in group polarization is a consequence of participants conforming to polarized or extremitized group norms. For instance, in a set of two studies Mackie (1986) provided mediational analyses showing a significant correlation between participants' attitude change from pretest to posttest and the difference between participants' pretest and group norm estimates only for participants in the ingroup condition. These analyses suggest that for participants for whom the group was a salient ingroup, perceptions of the group's norm influenced their attitude change toward the issue.

Comparative context. Other research has shown that the context in which the group is embedded influences the degree and direction of group polarization. Specifically, self categorization theory maintains that group polarization is "conformity to a polarized norm which defines one's own group in contrast to other groups within a specific social context" (Hogg, Turner, & Davidson, 1990, p. 77). Hogg et al. (1990) reasoned that manipulating the social context by introducing other groups into the social environment would influence the degree and direction of the group defining norms. Results from this study showed that when groups were confronted with outgroups at one or another pole of a risky or cautious scale, the groups polarized away from the direction in which the outgroup was leaning. For instance, groups confronted with a risky outgroup polarized toward caution on choice dilemma decisions, whereas groups confronted with a cautious outgroup polarized toward risk.

The persuasive arguments, social comparison, and self-categorization explanations for group polarization all suggest different ways that groups can influence attitudes. Although group polarization researchers have always examined social influences on attitude change, other researchers have focused on cognitive influences. For example, cognitive dissonance researchers have only just begun to explore the many ways in which groups can influence dissonance-induced attitude change.

Cognitive dissonance

Although the first published study of dissonance, *When Prophecy Fails* (Festinger, Riecken, & Schachter, 1956), examined dissonance within a social group, very little subsequent work has looked at group influences on dissonance. In fact, of the thousands of dissonance articles that have been published over the last 40 years, only a handful have examined dissonance within a group context. However, by examining these few studies, we can find evidence that groups can influence both dissonance arousal and dissonance reduction strategies.

Dissonance arousal

Cognitive dissonance, as originally formulated by Festinger (1957), arises when an individual holds two inconsistent cognitions simultaneously. This situation creates psychological discomfort, which the individual is then motivated to reduce. After performing a behavior, people assess the consequences of that behavior, and whether or not they were responsible for any negative consequences (Cooper & Fazio, 1984). When people accept responsibility for causing aversive consequences, they experience dissonance arousal.

Groups can influence both whether people experience dissonance and how they reduce dissonance arousal once it occurs. In some situations, individuals may be able to avoid feelings of responsibility for negative outcomes (and thus avoid dissonance arousal) by diffusing responsibility throughout a group. At other times, people may compare their behavior to normative or group standards to judge whether their actions have been inconsistent, or have created undesirable consequences. Sometimes group membership alone is enough to create dissonance, if a group member is confronted by the knowledge that his or her group or a member of the group has committed a dissonant act.

Diffusion of responsibility.   As mentioned above, dissonance occurs when a person feels responsibility for creating an aversive outcome (Cooper & Fazio, 1984). Consequently, when people are able to escape feelings of responsibility for aversive outcomes, they should not show any evidence of dissonance arousal. When there are other people around who may serve as targets to blame, it is much more likely that people will diffuse responsibility for an outcome, and therefore not experience dissonance.

Zanna and Sande (1987) examined diffusion of responsibility by having students write counter-attitudinal essays by themselves, or as a combined group effort. In one condition, three students sat together in a room, writing their own essays. In the other condition, the students discussed their arguments, planned the essay, and wrote one final product. The researchers expected that students would feel less responsible for their actions when their essays had been created as a group effort.

The results of the experiment supported this hypothesis. When three students wrote separate essays in the same room, they showed the expected attitude change predicted by dissonance theory. After writing in favor of university funding cutbacks, they became more favorable toward the policy. In contrast, the students who wrote one essay together did not show as much attitude change as the students who had written their essays separately. Although writers of "group" essays believed their essays would be more persuasive, they apparently did not accept responsibility for the negative outcomes their persuasive essays might create. This responsibility could have been shared (and thus reduced), or even completely assigned to the other students who helped write the final essay.

According to Zanna and Sande's (1987) theorizing, and in line with the predictions of the "New Look" model of dissonance (Cooper & Fazio, 1984), dissonance arousal probably never occurred for these participants. If they did not feel responsible for creating an aversive consequence, then they should not have had any dissonance arousal. However, it is interesting to consider whether "diffusion of responsibility" might also work as a dissonance reduction strategy, once dissonance has been aroused. In some cases, people might first accept responsibility for their actions, then later decide to blame their actions on others.

Normative versus personal standards for behavior.   Groups can provide people with an "escape" from dissonance arousal, but they can also provide the information people use to determine whether they have behaved inconsistently. Stone, Cooper, and colleagues (Cooper, 1999; Stone, 1999; Stone, Cooper, Galinsky, & Kelly, 1999) have recently proposed that the salience of personal and normative expectations can help determine whether individuals will experience dissonance arousal. According to this self-standards model, when people assess their recent behavior, they compare that behavior to either normative or personal standards. If people decide that their behavior has failed to live up to the salient expectations, they will experience dissonance.

In most dissonance experiments, personal and normative expectations for behavior are the same; most individuals share societal behavioral norms. However, when an individual's personal expectations for behavior are salient, that individual may not experience dissonance, even if his or her behavior fails to conform to normative standards. For example, imagine a young man in Festinger and Carlsmith's (1959) boring task experiment. He has been induced to lie about the uninteresting nature of the experiment. If social norms are made salient, most individuals should feel dissonance, since lying goes against commonly accepted social norms. However, if the individual is an accomplished actor or con-artist, he might feel pleased at convincing the other student of something that was not true. In this case, if individual standards for behavior were brought to mind, the con-artist would not feel dissonance, since his personal standards for behavior do not preclude lying.

Several studies by Stone and his colleagues (Kelly, Stone, & Cooper, 1996; Stone et al., 1999) have shown that the salience of normative and personal standards influences dissonance arousal. In one experiment, Stone et al. (1999, experiment 2) manipulated the accessibility of self-standards. The experimenter asked participants to rate 10 psychology studies, and gave them a choice between two they had rated similarly. After the choice, participants were asked to write about a target person, either in terms of their own personal standards, or in terms of the normative standards held by "most people." When participants wrote from a personal perspective, those with high self-esteem experienced more dissonance than did those with low self-esteem. The manipulation apparently reminded high self-esteem participants of their own high standards for behavior, which they had recently failed to meet. There were no differences between the responses of high and low self-esteem participants in the normative condition, and their responses did not differ from a no-prime control group.

According to Stone et al. (1999), when normative standards are salient, everyone who shares those norms should experience dissonance, regardless of individual differences in personal standards for behavior. However, other research has shown that normative influences can differ, depending on the level of group identification (e.g., Terry & Hogg, 1996). If an individual is not closely identified with a group, that individual may not experience dissonance, even when failing to live up to salient group norms.

Normative standards across cultures. While individuals may vary in the extent to which they subscribe to cultural norms, norms themselves can vary from culture to culture. The vast majority of researchers who have studied dissonance have examined how people from Western cultures respond to different kinds of dissonant situations. Inherent in all of this research is the assumption that the participants will find their experimentally induced behavior unacceptable, and thus will be motivated to reduce dissonance. While lying to another participant (as in Festinger & Carlsmith's 1959 experiment) may go against the norms of many cultures, other commonly used dissonance paradigms may not induce the same level of dissonance in all cultures.

Heine and Lehman (1997) studied both Japanese and Canadian participants using the "free-choice" paradigm. The researchers asked the participants to rate a selection of popular CDs, and then offered participants a choice between two CDs they had rated similarly. The Canadian participants showed the usual dissonance effect: When later asked to rate the CDs, the Canadians rated the chosen CD higher, or rated the unchosen CD lower than they had before. The Japanese participants, however, did not show this typical "spreading of alternatives."

Heine and Lehman (1997) interpreted their results as suggesting that people from the Japanese culture are not as concerned about the inconsistency that arises when they "lose" the positive aspects of the unchosen alternative, and "accept" the negative aspects of the chosen alternative. This could suggest that the Japanese may not be as concerned with limited instances of personal inconsistency. However, Sakai (1999) offers another interpretation of their results. He points out that the researchers used CDs of Western rock and pop music in the experiment, all of which may have seemed very similar to the Japanese participants. Sakai points out that Festinger (1957) predicted that the more similar people find the alternatives, the less dissonance they will have after making the choice. If people cannot distinguish between two items, why should they worry about choosing one rather than the other?

Sakai (1981) has found that in the forced-compliance paradigm, Japanese participants can experience dissonance. After being induced to advocate that their school should put an end to coeducation, the Japanese participants rated the anti-coeducation policy more favorably. This and other research by Sakai and his colleagues (e.g., Sakai, 1997) suggests that in some circumstances, Japanese participants will behave like Western participants, and will be motivated to reduce their dissonance.

More research needs to be done on cultural differences in dissonance arousal before we reach any conclusive answers about how dissonance varies between cultural groups. However, given what we know about the ways in which norms differ across cultures, it seems very likely that we will find different patterns of dissonance arousal in different cultures. Non-Western cultures might indeed place less emphasis on minor instances of personal inconsistency. However, it seems just as likely that we will find circumstances in which people from non-Western cultures experience much more dissonance than would be expected from Westerners. For example, a young American woman may experience some dissonance if she decides not to follow her parents' wishes that she take up the family business. However, a young Japanese woman in the same situation might feel much more dissonance, if her actions are seen as highly inconsistent with the norms of a more interdependent culture. Researchers may need to re-examine the typical dissonance paradigms to see what assumptions they make about the norms and values of a culture. We may need different tools to examine different cultures.

Sharing of responsibility.   In some situations, group membership alone may be a cause of dissonance arousal. If your group, or a member of your group, acts in a way that is inconsistent with your beliefs, you may experience dissonance. Many times people find themselves at odds with the leaders of the religious or political groups to which they belong. When such a group brings about an unwanted consequence, it can have implications for the members of that group.

If a person feels that he or she shares some of the responsibility for what the group has done, that person should experience dissonance. Sakai (1997) explored this idea by creating a two-participant version of Festinger and Carlsmith's (1959) experiment. Using reasoning derived from Heider's (1958) balance theory, Sakai created a "unit relationship" by having some participants share proximity and a common fate with a confederate in the experiment. In this "grouped" condition, the researcher asked that one of the participants tell the waiting participant that the boring task was interesting. The confederate then offered to speak, but suggested that they both go tell the participant, and asked if this plan was acceptable. In the "ungrouped" condition the researcher asked the confederate to speak to the waiting participant. Sakai found that participants who shared a unit relationship with the confederate felt closer to their partners, felt more responsible for the negative consequences, and rated the boring task as more interesting.

Group membership can also lead to dissonance vicariously. Imagine that a member of your group acts in a way that normally arouses dissonance. For example, suppose that a member of a gun control group wrote an essay attacking legislation requiring locks on hand guns. Would you, as a person who belonged to the same gun control group, experience dissonance? Would you be motivated to change your attitude, even though you were not the person who wrote the essay?

Norton, Monin, and Cooper (1999) predicted that observing a group member engage in dissonance-producing behavior would cause dissonance to occur in the observer. In their first study, Norton et al. had students listen to a speech made by another person who was either a member of the student's own residential college (ingroup) or a different college (outgroup). The speech, which advocated an increase in college tuition, was contrary to the true attitude of the participant and for most members of the college community. The results showed that, for participants who were highly identified with their ingroup, observing a fellow group member make a counter-attitudinal speech produced attitude change. This occurred despite the fact that the student participant made no speech him or herself and never interacted with the ingroup or outgroup member. None the less, the act that normally produces dissonance in the essay writer also produced attitude change in the participant – provided that the essay writer was a member of the observer's ingroup and the observer was highly identified with that group.

In a second study, Norton et al. (1999) again had group members believe that a fellow ingroup member had agreed to make a speech that was contrary to the attitudes of most group members. However, in this study, the speech-maker made clear that he either was or was not personally in favor of the speech he had volunteered to make. Ingroup members who observed their fellow group member agree to write the speech then had their own attitudes assessed. As predicted, observers who strongly identified with their group changed their own attitudes in the direction of the speech in the very same condition that should have aroused dissonance in the speech writer – that is, when the speech-writer was personally opposed to the speech he wrote. Taken together, the results of the two studies suggest that group membership can cause us to experience dissonance vicariously. If a member of one of our highly valued ingroup acts in a dissonance-producing manner, then we too seem to feel the effects of dissonance arousal and change our attitudes accordingly.

Dissonance reduction strategies

Once dissonance has been aroused, it can be reduced in a number of different ways. In most dissonance studies, participants reduce their dissonance arousal by changing their attitudes. However, sometimes attitude change is not the easiest or most preferable option. If people are unable to change their attitudes, they can also manage dissonance arousal through forgetting (Cooper & Gonzalez, 1976), bolstering (Sherman & Gorkin, 1980), derogating others (Cooper & Mackie, 1983), trivializing actions (Simon, Greenberg, & Brehm, 1995), affirming the self (Steele, 1988), or misattributing the source of dissonance arousal (Fazio, Zanna, & Cooper, 1977).

Group identities can influence dissonance reduction in at least three different yet systematic ways. If people's attitudes are tied to a group identity, the only way in which they may change those attitudes is by reducing their affiliation with the group. When reducing group affiliation is not a practical option, people must use dissonance reduction strategies other than attitude change. Finally, group identities can serve to protect people from dissonance, and prevent them from needing to change their attitudes.

Changing group-related attitudes. Sometimes group-related attitudes are definitional in nature: They define the characteristics of group members (Cooper & Mackie, 1983). When people change attitudes that are definitional to their group identities, they distance themselves from the group. By reducing group affiliation, they also reduce the inconsistency they created by acting against group norms.

Several researchers have theorized about how this distancing may operate. Steele (1997) has proposed that when people's self-integrity is threatened by their actions in a particular self-concept domain, they may disidentify with that domain. By distancing themselves from the threatening domain, people are better able to maintain global self-esteem. For example, when people commit a dissonant act that is related to a group identity, they can disidentify with the group, which will result in less need for attitude change and will protect self-esteem.

Aronson, Blanton, and Cooper (1995) studied disidentification in cognitive dissonance by inducing participants to write essays against expanding services for the handicapped. Writing the essays under conditions of high choice threatened participants' views of themselves as compassionate individuals. When these participants were given the opportunity to change their attitudes, they did so. However, when the opportunity to change attitudes was not readily available, participants instead reduced the importance of compassion to their self-definitions. Although Aronson et al.'s (1995) study focused on self-identities rather than social identities, it seems likely that disidentifiation with social identities could occur in a similar fashion.

Indirect dissonance reduction strategies. When dissonance arousal is closely tied to group membership, one of two things can happen. If the group is not important to you, you can distance yourself from the group, and therefore distance yourself from the source of the arousal. Sometimes, however, the group is so important to your identity that distancing yourself from the group would threaten your self-esteem. When this occurs, dissonance needs to be reduced through some other means.

Bolstering of ingroup. The members of Marion Keech's cult, as described in *When Prophecy Fails* (Festinger, Riecken, & Schachter, 1956), provide an extreme example of such a situation. The members of the cult had given up their jobs, homes, friends, and family to join the cult; all other groups and roles were pushed aside. When Ms. Keech's prophecy failed to be fulfilled, the group members undoubtedly experienced extreme dissonance. However, distancing themselves from the group was not an option. Too many of their resources were at stake. Instead, group members responded to their dissonance by accepting Ms. Keech's declaration that their group had saved the world. In the language of cognitive dissonance theory, which Festinger later described (Festinger, 1957), the cult members appeared to be "adding consonant cognitions" to the dissonance equation. By spreading the good news about how the world had been spared, the cult members justified all of the actions that had led them to join the cult in the first place.

This "bolstering" response to a threat to group identity can be seen more systematically in an experimental study conducted by Sherman and Gorkin (1980). Sherman and Gorkin invited young women who considered themselves to be feminists into the laboratory, where they were asked to solve a brain-teaser. The correct answer to the problem required the participants to realize that the doctor in the question was female. Most of the women failed to solve the problem, because they assumed (in a very nonfeminist fashion) that the doctor was male. The women who failed to solve the problem experienced dissonance, yet they were unable to simply change their attitudes about feminism. Because their identities as feminists were important, the women needed to reduce dissonance in another manner. In this case, the women chose to "bolster" their feminist beliefs, and they responded in a more feminist fashion when later rating job applicants.

Derogation of outgroup. Bolstering is not the only way people can deal with dissonance when changing groups is not an option. Cooper and Mackie (1983) examined this same issue, from the perspective of social identity theory. If membership in a group is defined by holding a particular set of attitudes, group members will be less likely to change those "definitional" attitudes.

Cooper and Mackie (1983) decided to examine Reagan re-election supporters belonging to the "Youth for Reagan" group, since these students would presumably be unlikely to change their pro-Reagan attitudes. Under conditions of high or low choice, they asked group members to write one of two counter-attitudinal essays. Those who wrote essays in support of government-funded healthcare showed the pattern typical of dissonance studies: Students who wrote under conditions of high choice changed their attitudes while those writing under conditions of low choice did not. The other half of the participants wrote essays in support of the re-election of President Carter, an issue that clashed directly with their identities as Youth for Reagan. These participants did not show any attitude change, even in the high-choice condition.

According to dissonance theory, the students who wrote for Carter under conditions of high choice should have been experiencing dissonance. However, because they could not easily change an attitude so closely related to the very definition of their group membership, they needed to reduce their dissonance another way. Although there was no attitude change toward Carter per se, when participants were later asked to rate Carter supporters, those who had written high-choice essays in favor of Carter gave Carter supporters more negative ratings, as compared to students who had written low-choice or healthcare essays. This study shows that another way people can reduce dissonance without altering a definitional group attitude is by derogating an outgroup. Derogation and bolstering may be two sides of the same coin: Bolstering enhances ingroup identity, while derogation diminishes the outgroup.

Forgetting. A study of group identity by Cooper and Gonzalez (1976) shows that forgetting is yet another strategy that people can use to combat group-based dissonance. Members of an evangelical Christian group and non-evangelical Christians were invited into the laboratory and asked to read, memorize, and tape-record pro-Buddhist messages under conditions of high or low choice. After recording the pro-Buddhist message, non-evangelical Christians became more favorable toward Buddhism if they had recorded the message under conditions of high choice. Evangelical Christians did not change their attitudes toward Buddhism, regardless of the level of choice.

Although they did not show attitude change, the evangelical Christians in the high-choice condition remembered less of the pro-Buddhist paragraph than did other participants. It appears that the high-choice evangelical Christians may have deliberately tried to put the essay out of mind. Although some of the poor memory may have been due to an impoverished "Buddhism" schema, evangelical Christians did remember significantly more in the low-choice, as opposed to the high-choice condition.

Bolstering, derogating outgroups, and forgetting can all help people deal with group-created dissonance when leaving the group is not a viable option. Research will undoubtedly uncover other possible ways that people can deal with group-created dissonance. Although it has not yet been studied in a group-identity context, it seems that trivialization (Simon, Greenberg, & Brehm, 1995) may also provide a possible avenue for dissonance reduction when people are unable to disidentify with a group. For example, if individuals in Cooper and Gonzalez's (1976) study were asked to think about the importance of writing their essays "in the grand scheme of things," they might have decided that writing the essay was not important, which would have reduced their dissonance.

When group identities protect the self. Although groups can create dissonance for their members and can limit the possible methods of dissonance reduction, groups can also help reduce dissonance once it has been aroused. Steele's (1988) self-affirmation theory states that when people are able to affirm an important aspect of their self-identity, they should not need to change their attitudes following a dissonance manipulation. Because positive identity is in part derived from membership in social groups (Tajfel, 1982), group membership should be able to serve as an affirmation.

In a study by Steele, Hopp, and Gonzales (1986, cited in Steele, 1988), students with a business or science value orientation participated in a dissonance experiment. After dissonance had been aroused, but before attitudes were measured, the students were given an opportunity to put on white lab coats. When their attitudes were later assessed, business students showed the typical dissonance pattern – they changed their attitudes under conditions of high, but not low choice. The science students, however, had been given an opportunity to affirm an important social identity when they were asked to wear the lab coats. Because they had the opportunity to self-affirm, these students did not show the attitude change typical of dissonance experiments.

In addition to influencing existing dissonance arousal, group identities might also help prevent dissonance from being aroused. Important group identities may serve a protective function, insulating people from the negative impact of dissonant acts. If people focus on a social group to which they belong (one that has not been implicated in the dissonance-inducing attitude issue), they may be able to avoid dissonance arousal altogether.

Although most self-affirmation experiments have focused on affirmation after dissonance has been aroused, Steele and his colleagues (Steele, Spencer, & Lynch, 1993) have also described this self-protective function of affirmation. According to their theory, when self-resources are primed before the dissonant act is committed, people can be insulated from potential dissonance arousal. For example, when Steele et at. (1993) primed self-resources for high self-esteem participants by having them fill out a self-esteem scale, the high self-esteem participants did not change their attitudes during a later dissonance experiment. Group identities may serve the same protective function; when important group identities are salient, people may be less likely to experience dissonance.

Linville's (1985, 1987) theory of self-complexity also addresses the self-protective function of group identities. According to self-complexity theory, the more identities a person holds, the more resilient that person will be when faced with threats to the self. Social identities, along with personal identities may help protect people who are experiencing dissonance. As Linville points out, self-complexity theory brings to mind the saying "don't put all of your eggs in one basket." If your identity is only made up of one aspect (e.g., cult member) and that identity is threatened, you will experience emotional distress. However, if your identity is made up of many aspects (e.g., teacher, soccer player, Democrat, social club member), then when one of those aspects is threatened, you will still have many other aspects available to maintain your self-esteem.

On the basis of self-complexity theory (Linville, 1985, 1987), one could imagine that people with many social identities might be less likely to experience dissonance. First, people high in self-complexity have been found to be less emotionally reactive, and therefore they might not experience as much dissonance arousal. In addition, because they have so many potentially affirming identities that could be primed, the odds are greater that some cue in the environment will provide an affirmation opportunity. For example, if Democrats were induced to write anti-Democrat essays, those with many alternative social identities (father, teacher, tennis player, etc.) would have many other identities to turn to, if they had to distance themselves from their identities as Democrats.

As we have shown, groups can influence both dissonance arousal and reduction. Groups can influence dissonance arousal by providing the normative standards to which people will compare their behavior. Groups can also provide an easy target for blame, when people attempt to diffuse responsibility for outcomes. In addition, people may experience dissonance when they share a group identity with someone who creates an aversive outcome. Groups can influence the route to dissonance reduction by providing an opportunity for disidentification, or by blocking attitude change as a reduction strategy. Finally, groups can serve to protect us from dissonance, and can reduce the need for attitude change once dissonance has been aroused.

Today's attitude researchers are helping to bring back the "social" in the social psychological study of attitudes. Now that we understand so much about the intrapersonal aspects of attitudes and attitude change, it is time to pay attention to the interpersonal aspects. In many cases, salient norms or group identities may provide important information that will help us understand what attitudes people will form, when they will act upon those attitudes, and the conditions under which they will change their attitudes.

REFERENCES

Abrams, D., Ando, K., & Hinkle, S. (1998). Psychological attachment to the group: Cross-cultural differences in organizational identification and subjective norms as predictors of workers' turnover intentions. *Personality and Social Psychology Bulletin, 24,* 1027–1039.

Abrams, D., Wetherell, M., Cochrane, S., Hogg, M. A., & Turner, J. C. (1990). Knowing what to think by knowing who you are: Self-categorization and the nature of norm formation, conformity, and group polarization. *British Journal of Social Psychology, 29,* 97–119.

Ajzen, I. (1991). The theory of planned behavior. *Organizational Behavior and Human Decision Processes, 50,* 179–211.

Ajzen, I., & Fishbein, M. (1980). *Understanding attitudes and predicting social behavior.* Englewood Cliffs, NJ: Prentice-Hall.

Allport, G. W. (1935). Attitudes. In C. A. Murchison (Ed.), *A handbook of social psychology* (Vol. 2, pp. 798–844). Worcester, MA: Clark University Press.

Argyle, M. (1957). Social pressures in public and private situations. *Journal of Abnormal and Social Psychology, 54,* 172–175.

Aronson, J., Blanton, H., & Cooper, J. (1995). From dissonance to disidentification: Selectivity in the self-affirmation process. *Journal of Personality and Social Psychology, 68,* 986–996.

Asch, S. E. (1951). Effects of group pressure on the modification and distortion of judgments. In H. Geutzkow (Ed.), *Groups, leadership, and men.* Pittsburgh, PA: Carnegie.

Asch, S. E. (1956). Studies of independence and conformity: A minority of one against a unanimous majority. *Psychological Monographs, 70,* No. 9.

Baldwin, M. W., & Holmes, J. G. (1987). Salient private audiences and awareness of the self. *Journal of Personality and Social Psychology, 52,* 1087–1098.

Blascovich, J., Ginsburg, G. P., & Veach, T. L. (1975). A pluralistic explanation of choice shifts on the risk dimension. *Journal of Personality and Social Psychology, 31,* 422–429.

Burnstein, E., & Vinokur, A. (1977). Persuasive argumentation and social comparison as determinants of attitude polarization. *Journal of Experimental Social Psychology, 13,* 315–332.

Cantril, H. (1934). Attitudes in the making. *Understanding the Child, 4,* 13–15.

Cooper, J. (1999). Unwanted consequences and the self: In search of the motivation for dissonance reduction. In E. Harmon-Jones & J. Mills (Eds.), *Cognitive dissonance theory: Progress on a pivotal theory in social psychology* (pp. 149–173). Washington DC: American Psychological Association.

Cooper, J., & Fazio, R. (1984). A new look at dissonance theory. In L. Berkowitz (Ed.), *Advances in experimental social psychology* (Vol. 17, pp. 229–266). San Diego, CA: Academic Press.

Cooper, J., & Gonzalez, A. E. J. (1976). What to do with leftover dissonance: Blame it on the lights. Unpublished manuscript, Princeton University.

Cooper, J., & Mackie, D. M. (1983). Cognitive dissonance in an intergroup context. *Journal of Personality and Social Psychology, 44,* 536–544.

Deutsch, M., & Gerard, H. G. (1955). A study of normative and informational social influence upon social judgment. *Journal of Abnormal Social Psychology, 51,* 629–636.

Fazio, R. H. (1986). How do attitudes guide behaviors? In R. M. Sorrentino & E. T. Higgins (Eds.), *The handbook of motivation and cognition: Foundations of social behavior.* New York: Guilford Press.

Fazio, R. H. (1990). Multiple processes by which attitudes guide behavior: The MODE model as an integrative framework. *Advances in Experimental Social Psychology, 23,* 75–109.

Fazio, R. H., & Towles-Schwen, T. (1999). The MODE model of attitude-behavior processes. In S. Chaiken & Y. Trope (Eds.), *Dual process theories in social psychology* (pp. 97–116). New York: The Guilford Press.

Fazio, R. H., Zanna, M. P., & Cooper, J. (1977). Dissonance and self-perception: An integrative view of each theory's proper domain of application. *Journal of Experimental Social Psychology, 13,* 464–479.

Festinger, L. (1950). Informal social communication. *Psychological Review, 57,* 271–282.

Festinger, L. (1957). *A theory of cognitive dissonance.* Stanford, CA: Stanford University Press.

Festinger, L., & Carlsmith, J. M. (1959). Cognitive consequences of forced compliance. *Journal of Abnormal Social Psychology, 58,* 203–210.

Festinger, L., Riecken, H. W., & Schachter, S. (1956). *When prophecy fails.* Minneapolis, MN: University of Minnesota Press.

Finlay, K. A., Trafimow, D., & Jones, D. (1997). Predicting health behaviors from attitudes and subjective norms: Between-subjects and within-subjects analyses. *Journal of Applied Social Psychology, 27,* 2015–2031.

Fishbein, M., & Ajzen, I. (1975). *Belief, attitude, intention, and behavior: An introduction to theory and research.* Reading, MA: Addison-Wesley.

Fishbein, M., Chan, D. K. S., O'Reilly, K., Schnell, D., Wood, R., Beeker, C., & Cohn, D. (1992). Attitudinal and normative factors as determinants of gay men's intentions to perform AIDS-related sexual behaviors: A multisite analysis. *Journal of Applied Social Psychology, 22,* 999–1011.

Fishbein, M., Chan, D. K. S., O'Reilly, K., Schnell, D., Wood, R., Beeker, C., & Cohn, D. (1993). Factors influencing gay men's attitudes, subjective norms, and intentions with respect to performing sexual behaviors. *Journal of Applied Social Psychology, 23,* 417–438.

Heider, F. (1958). *The psychology of interpersonal relations.* New York: Wiley.

Heine, S. J., & Lehman, D. R. (1997). Culture, dissonance, and self-affirmation. *Personality and Social Psychology Bulletin, 23,* 389–400.

Hogg, M. A. (2001). Social categorization, depersonalization, and group behavior. In M. A. Hogg & S. Tindale (Eds.), *Blackwell handbook of social psychology: Group processes* (pp. 56–85). Oxford, UK: Blackwell.

Hogg, M. A., Turner, J. C., & Davidson, B. (1990). Polarized norms and social frames of reference: A test of the self-categorization theory of group polarization. *Basic and Applied Social Psychology, 11,* 77–100.

Isenberg, D. J. (1986). Group polarization: A critical review and meta-analysis. *Journal of Personality and Social Psychology, 50,* 1141–1151.

Jellison, J., & Arkin, R. (1977). Social comparison of abilities: A self-presentation approach to decision making in groups. In J. Suls & R. Miller (Eds.), *Social comparison processes: Theoretical and empirical perspectives* (pp. 235–258). Washington DC: Hemisphere Press.

Kaplan, M. F., & Miller, C. E. (1976). Judgments and group discussion: Effect of presentation and memory factors on polarization. *Sociometry, 40,* 337–343.

Kelley, H. H., & Lamb, T. W. (1957). Certainty of judgment and resistance to social influence. *Journal of Abnormal and Social Psychology, 55,* 137–139.

Kelly, K. A., Stone, J., & Cooper, J. (1996, March). *The role of self-attributes in dissonance arousal and reduction.* Paper presented at the 67th Eastern Psychological Association Conference, Philadelphia.

Lamm, H., & Myers, D. G. (1978). Group-induced polarization of attitudes and behavior. In L. Berkowitz (Ed.), *Advances in experimental social psychology* (Vol. 2, pp. 147–195). New York: Academic Press.

Linville, P. M. (1985). Self-complexity and affective extremity: Don't put all of your eggs in one cognitive basket. *Social Cognition, 3,* 94–120.

Linville, P. M. (1987). Self-complexity as a cognitive buffer against stress-related illness and depression. *Journal of Personality and Social Psychology, 52,* 663–676.

Mackie, D. M. (1986). Social identification effects in group polarization. *Journal of Personality and Social Psychology, 50,* 720–728,

Mackie, D. M., & Cooper, J. (1984). Attitude polarization: Effects of group membership. *Journal of Personality and Social Psychology, 46,* 575–585.

Markus, H. R., & Kitayama, S. (1991). Culture and the self: Implications for cognition, emotion, and motivation, *Psychological Review, 98,* 224–253.

Moscovici, S., & Zavalloni, M. (1969). The group as a polarizer of attitudes. *Journal of Personality and Social Psychology, 12,* 125–135.

Myers, D. G., & Lamm, H. (1976). The group polarization phenomenon. *Psychological Bulletin, 83,* 602–627.

Myers, D. G., Wojcicki, S. B., & Aardema, G. C. (1977). Attitude comparison: Is there ever a bandwagon effect? *Journal of Applied Social Psychology, 7,* 341–347.

Norton, M. I., Monin, B., & Cooper, J. (1999). *Vicarious dissonance: Experiencing the psychological discomfort of similar others.* Poster presented at the American Psychology Society (Denver, 1999).

Petty, R. E., & Cacioppo, J. T. (1996). *Attitudes and persuasion: Classic and contemporary approaches.* Boulder, CO: Westview Press,

Raven, B. H. (1959). Social influence on opinions and the communication of related content. *Journal of Abnormal Social Psychology, 58,* 119–128.

Sakai, H. (1981). Induced compliance and opinion change. *Japanese Psychological Research, 23,* 1–8.

Sakai (1997, March 1). *Does shared responsibility for negative consequences generate cognitive dissonance?* Paper presented at the Cognitive Dissonance Theory 40 Years Later Conference, Arlington, TX.

Sakai, H. (1999). A multiplicative power-function model of cognitive dissonance: Toward an integrated theory of cognition, emotion, and behavior after Leon Festinger. In E. Harmon-Jones & J. Mills (Eds.), *Cognitive dissonance theory: Progress on a pivotal theory in social psychology* (pp. 267–294). Washington, DC: American Psychological Association,

Sanders, G. S., & Baron, R. S. (1975). Is social comparison irrelevant for producing choice shifts? *Journal of Experimental Social Psychology, 13,* 303–314.

Sherif, M. (1935). A study of some social factors in perception. *Archives of Psychology No. 187.*

Sherman, S. J., & Gorkin, L. (1980). Attitude bolstering when behavior is inconsistent with central attitudes. *Journal of Experimental Social Psychology, 16,* 388–403.

Simon, L., Greenberg, J., & Brehm, J. (1995). Trivialization: The forgotten mode of dissonance reduction. *Journal of Personality and Social Psychology, 68,* 247–260.

Steele, C. M. (1988). The psychology of self-affirmation: Sustaining the integrity of the self. *Advances in Experimental Social Psychology, 21,* 261–302.

Steele, C. M. (1997). A threat in the air: How stereotypes shape intellectual identity and performance. *American Psychologist, 52,* 613–629.

Steele, C. M., Hopp, H., & Gonzales, J. (1986, cited in Steele 1988). *Dissonance and the lab coat: Self-affirmation and the free choice paradigm.* Unpublished manuscript, University of Washington.

Steele, C. M., Spencer, S. J., & Lynch, M. (1993). Self-image resilience and dissonance: The role of affirmational resources. *Journal of Personality and Social Psychology, 64,* 885–896.

Stone, J. (1999). What exactly have I done? The role of self-attribute accessibility in dissonance. In E. Harmon-Jones & J. Mills (Eds.), *Cognitive dissonance theory: Progress on a pivotal theory in social psychology* (pp. 175–200). Washington, DC: American Psychological Association.

Stone, J., Cooper, J., Galinsky, A., & Kelly, K. A. (1999). *Self-attribute accessibility and the multiple engines that drive cognitive dissonance.* Unpublished manuscript.

Stoner, J. (1968). Risky and cautious shifts in group decisions: The influence of widely held values. *Journal of Experimental and Social Psychology, 4,* 442–459.

Tajfel, H. (1982). *Social identity and intergroup relations.* Cambridge, UK: Cambridge University Press.

Terry, D. J., & Hogg, M. A. (1996). Group norms and the attitude-behavior relationship: A role for ingroup norms. *Personality and Social Psychology Bulletin, 22*, 776–793.

Trafimow, D., & Finlay, K. A. (1996). The importance of subjective norms for a minority of people: Between-subjects and within-subjects analyses. *Personality and Social Psychology Bulletin, 22*, 820–828.

Turner, J. C. (1982). Towards a cognitive redefinition of the social group. In H. Tajfel (Ed.), *Social identity and intergroup relations* (pp. 15–40). Cambridge, UK: Cambridge University Press.

Turner, J. C. (1985). Social categorization and the self-concept: A social cognitive theory of group behavior. In E. J. Lawler (Ed.), *Advances in group processes: Theory and research* (Vol. 2, pp. 77–122). Greenwich, CT: JAI Press.

Turner, J. C. (1991). *Social influence.* Pacific Grove, CA: Brooks/Cole.

White, K. M., Terry, D. J., & Hogg, M. A. (1994). Safer sex behavior: The role of attitudes, norms, and control factors. *Journal of Applied Social Psychology, 24*, 2164–2192.

Wicker, A. W. (1969). Attitudes versus actions: The relationship of verbal and overt behavioral responses to attitude objects. *Journal of Social Issues, 25*, 41–78.

Ybarra, O., & Trafimow, D. (1998), How priming the collective self affects the relative weights of attitudes and subjective norms. *Personality and Social Psychology Bulletin, 24*, 362–370.

Zanna, M. P., & Sande, G. N. (1987). The effects of collective action on the attitudes of individual group members: A dissonance analysis. In M. P. Zanna, J. M. Olson, & C. P. Herman (Eds.), *Social influence: The Ontario symposium* (Vol. 5, pp. 151–163). Hillsdale, NJ: Erlbaum.

CHAPTER TWELVE

Shared Cognition in Small Groups

R. Scott Tindale, Helen M. Meisenhelder, Amanda A. Dykema-Engblade, and Michael A. Hogg

Two of the earliest texts in social psychology were Le Bon's (1896/1960) *Psychologie des Foules* (*Psychology of Crowds*) and McDougall's (1920) *The Group Mind*. Both espoused as a central tenet the view that behavior in social aggregates was not simply a function of some combination of individual acts. Rather, they saw social behavior as being guided by forces defined by the aggregate – a "collective consciousness" or "group mind" – that could not be understood fully by simply understanding individual behavior or individual minds. Such ideas were not unusual for the times. Durkheim (1893/1984, 1965), Mead (1934) and other sociologists and social philosophers also saw collective or shared meaning as an integral component for understanding social behavior (see Farr, 1996). However, with the onset of behaviorism, psychology's focus moved almost exclusively onto the individual, and the notion of collective thought and meaning fell out of favor (Allport, 1924). In mainstream social psychology, focus on aggregates versus individuals has waxed and waned (see Steiner, 1974, 1986; Moreland, Hogg, & Hains, 1994 for reviews), but the key explanatory variables have remained mainly at the individual level. Thus, in recent social psychology textbooks, the early ideas concerning "collective cognition" are rarely mentioned except for historical context, if they are mentioned at all (e.g., Baron & Byrne, 2000).

However, social psychology has seen a recent resurgence of the notion of cognition at the level of the collective, typically referred to as "socially shared cognitions" (Resnik, Levine, & Teasley, 1991; Thompson & Fine, 1999). This resurgence has developed from a number of different directions. Probably the most central influence has been European social psychology, through the writings of Henri Tajfel and his colleagues (Tajfel & Turner, 1979, Turner, Hogg, Oakes, Reicher, & Wetherell, 1987; Hogg & Abrams, 1988; see Abrams & Hogg, 2001; Hogg, 2001; Reicher, 2001). Tajfel's social identity theory placed the group front and center stage for understanding a number of aspects of behavior. These ideas eventually influenced theory and research in most of the major areas of the field: person perception,

Preparation of this chapter was supported by NSF Grant #SBR-9730822 to the first author, a US Air Force Institute of Technology Ph.D. Fellowship to the second author, and a Loyola University Chicago Graduate Fellowship to the third author. We would like to thank Dick Moreland for his helpful ideas, insights, and suggestions.

stereotyping, prejudice, attribution, attitudes, self-concept, and so forth (see Abrams & Hogg, 1999 for recent summaries in each of these areas), as well as work on small groups (Hogg, 1996). Another European influence that promoted the notion of shared thoughts and beliefs was Moscovici's (1984) notion of "social representations" (see Lorenzi-Cioldi & Clémence, this volume, chapter 13). Drawing on Durkheim's (1965) notion of "collective representations," Moscovici argued that collectives rely on shared images and ideas to form the basis of "common sense." These shared meanings then become the cognitive context within which members of the collective communicate and coordinate their actions. Similar ideas have more recently been developed by Bar-Tal (1990) in relation to group beliefs and their impact on individual and collective behavior.

Another major influence on the shared cognitions approach came from theory and research on organizations (Thompson, Levine, & Messick, 1999). Theorists such as Weick (1979) argued that organizations are defined by the process of organizing, which is defined, in part, at the cognitive level. Thus, organizations are defined by the "sense making" and "heedful interrelating" (Weick & Roberts, 1993) that occurs, and the shared cognitions that result. The popularity of work teams in organizations has also spawned a strong research tradition in the study of group performance in organizations (Guzzo & Shea, 1992; Hackman, 1998). Within this tradition, the notion of common understandings (Helmreich, 1997), and shared mental models (Klimoski & Mohammed, 1994; Thompson, 1998) have played significant roles in recent theorizing.

Specifically within the small-group literature in social psychology, probably the biggest influence in moving the field toward a focus on shared cognitions was the "hidden profile" paradigm formulated by Stasser and Titus (1985, 1987; see also Stasser & Dietz-Uhler, 2001). Although this paradigm and its offshoots will be discussed in depth later, the basic finding that shared information in groups plays a much more significant role in group process and performance than does information that is not shared, shattered a number of the prior basic assumptions underlying group research. A number of researchers have followed up on this finding (e.g., Larson, Foster-Fishman, & Keys, 1994; Gigone & Hastie, 1993, 1996), and this body of literature helped to crystallize the idea of groups as information-processing systems (Hinsz, Tindale, & Vollrath, 1997; Larson & Christensen, 1993) with "social sharedness" as an underlying theme (Kameda, Tindale, & Davis, in press; Tindale & Kameda, 2000).

The notion of socially shared cognitions has permeated virtually all areas of social psychology. Thus, a comprehensive review is beyond the scope of the present chapter (see Thompson & Fine, 1999 for a more thorough treatment of socially shared cognitions in general). True to the theme of the present volume, we will focus almost exclusively on intragroup phenomena and how the shared cognitions resurgence has influenced theory and research on small-group process and performance. The remainder of the chapter is divided into two main sections. The first briefly discusses recent (and not-so-recent) ideas concerning how groups develop shared cognitions. Drawing on traditional (e.g., symbolic interactionism, social comparison, etc.) and more recent (e.g., models of evolution, communication, group identity, and dynamical systems) orientations, we will show that shared cognitions develop naturally in groups, often with little or no effort on the part of the constituent members. The second section discusses the effects that shared cognitions have on groups, in terms of both process and performance. We discuss both recent findings and some reinterpretations of earlier classic findings in the field. Although grounded in some of the earliest work in the field, the shared cognitions framework for studying groups is still evolving. Thus, we close the chapter with a few speculations as to where these ideas may be able to take the field.

How Shared Cognitions Develop

Common experience, learning, social interaction, and social comparison

Obviously, some of the cognitions, beliefs, knowledge, and so forth, that members of social groups share come from their shared experiences with the world around them. Human physiology is mainly constant in terms of how our sensory systems operate, so it is not surprising that we experience things in similar ways. In addition, the laws of physics are constant (at least at the level at which our senses operate) so that we fall *down* when we lose our balance, and feel *pain* when our flesh is exposed to fire, etc. (Although as is argued below, most – if not all – of the *meanings* we attribute to such common experiences are socially mediated.) In addition, all societies/cultures have in place mechanisms for teaching their younger members the shared *truths* as defined by them. Children learn math, science, history, and so forth, in schools or through family elders and are told that these ideas and procedures are both true and relevant. However, instruction and common experience are not the only ways that shared cognitions develop.

Some of the earliest discussions of shared social meanings in psychology and sociology stem from the symbolic interactionist approach (see Farr, 1996; Fine, 1990; Thompson & Fine, 1999). This perspective argued that collective meaning is an essential feature of social life and that social order depends on the subsequent shared interpretations based on those collective meanings. Even the definition of self was seen as dependent on our ability to take on the role of the other. By our ability to see the world through another person's eyes (so to speak), we develop a perspective of our place as an entity in the social environment. Symbolic interactionists contend that socially shared meaning develops through interaction among social actors, and is continually modified by those same interactions. Although the approach does not claim that all individual perspectives on a situation are identical, it does argue that the ability to share perspectives is what allows social interaction to exist in any meaningful way.

Moscovici's (1984) notion of social representation fits nicely with the symbolic interactionist perspective, though he attributes the basis of the idea to Durkheim (1964). Through interactions with others, we learn what beliefs and attitudes are considered "givens" in our social environment. Thus, social representations are seen as the basis of what is typically referred to as "common sense." Although some social representations have a physical basis for their existence (e.g., brick walls are hard – don't pound your fist against them), others are more purely social or cultural in nature (i.e., the Sabbath is a day of rest – do not work on that day). Many of the social representations concerning social groups (e.g., stereotypes) are learned through a combination of social consensus and subsequent experience biased by social perceptions. Although social representations are dynamic – they change over time as both situations and knowledge bases change – they remain the common-sense basis for interpretation and understanding for the people that share them. (See Lorenzi-Cioldi & Clémence, this volume, chapter 13.)

Recent work on the role of communication also shows that simply exchanging information increases the perceived validity of the information (Hardin & Higgins, 1995; Higgins, 1992). Higgins (1992) has argued that part of the rules associated with communication is that the speaker "tunes" his/her message to the recipient so as to improve comprehension. This can often lead to recipients perceiving a greater degree of convergence in meaning than may have been the case. During the continued exchange, both participants gradually shift their perspectives to match what has been communicated. Thus, information that has been shared through communication acquires some validity purely from the sharing. This change in meaning seems to occur even when the communicator intentionally distorts the communication to match expectations concerning the audience (Higgins, 1992). Such ideas are quite consistent with theories of cognitive consistency (Festinger, 1957; Heider, 1958). When we tell someone else that something is true, it becomes truer to us as well.

Another way in which social interaction leads to shared cognitions is through social comparison (Festinger, 1950, 1954). Festinger argued that when physical reality does not provide cues for appropriate behavior or opinion, people use social reality (i.e., the other people around them) as cues for appropriateness. Thus, people compare their behavior, beliefs, attitudes, etc. with those of others around them in order to reduce uncertainty. Although some have argued that in fact all such comparisons are social because our perceptions of physical reality are also heavily socially mediated (Moscovici, 1976), the evidence that social comparisons guide many if not most of our behaviors is well established (see Suls & Wills, 1991; Darley, 2001).

Probably the best empirical example of this process is the work by Sherif (1936) on the development of social norms. Using the perceptual illusion of the autokinetic effect (perceived motion of a stationary light in a darkened room), Sherif had participants in small groups publicly judge how far the light had moved. Within a fairly small number of trials, Sherif found a fairly large degree of convergence among the judgments within the group. Thus, in the absence of any "real" physical cues, group members used the judgments of others to modify their own judgments. Social comparison processes are probably even more prevalent in situations where new members are intentionally trying to "fit in" in a new group or organizational context (Levine & Moreland, 1991, 1999; Levine, Moreland, & Choi, 2001).

Recent ideas on naturally occurring shared cognitions

Latané (1981) formulated a theory of social impact that posited three key aspects of social influence associated with the influence source – strength (e.g., power, persuasiveness), immediacy (physical and/or social distance) and number of influence sources compared to the number of targets. Recently, Latané and colleagues (Nowak, Szamrej, & Latané 1990; Latané & Bourgeois, 2001) have adapted the theory, using a dynamical systems approach, to incorporate the dynamic and reciprocal nature of social influence. In addition to the assumptions specified above, the dynamic version of the model adds three more. First, it assumes that individuals (varying in strength and other attributes) are distributed in a social space. Where they are located in the space defines their immediacy in terms of other individuals within the space. Second, each individual is influenced by his/her own position (e.g., belief, attitude, preference) and by the other people in proportion to a multiplicative function of their strength, immediacy, and number. Third, a person will change his/her position if and only if the total persuasive impact (the pressure to change to a different position) outweighs the pressure to maintain one's own position (the strength of the initial position plus any supportive impact). Dynamic social impact is then taken to be the cumulative effect of the iterative, recursive influence present during interaction. The model makes no assumptions about intentions of the other people in the social space to influence someone.

Using computer simulations (SITSIM; Nowak & Latané, 1994), Latané and colleagues have discovered a number of consistent findings, which have then been tested in different experimental settings. The most central finding for current concerns is that people tend to cluster in the social space in terms of position similarity. In other words, a random distribution of positions within the space will soon become organized into "belief clusters." Second, the space will tend to consolidate in such a way that majority positions tend to become stronger (more prevalent) and minority positions weaker. However, unless the initial majority is extremely large, minority clusters remain even after thousands of iterations. Thus, diversity of opinion continues despite the consolidation process. An additional aspect of the simulations shows that people in clusters tend to become similar to each other on multiple issues – what Latané has called correlation. Each of these simulation results have received empirical support in a number of different social aggregates, even in situations where there are few if any reasons for people to change their positions to match those around them (Latané & L'Herrou, 1996). Thus, it appears that shared cognitions are a natural product of even limited social interaction (simply exchanging position information), and they form as a consequence of self-organizing principles of the social system.

Two other recent ideas, born from thinking about social psychology and groups in evolutionary terms, help to elucidate how and why shared cognitions develop. Kameda and Hastie (1999) have run a number of simulations exploring the potential adaptive value of different social decision heuristics or group decision-making strategies. In their work, they assumed that a small band of foragers is to choose one patch or area out of many (10 in their simulations) to search for food/resources. They also assume the patches differ in resource level, and that individuals/groups can only know the resource levels of different patches stochastically, based on environmental cues (using a Brunswik's lens model framework – Brunswik, 1956; Gigone & Hastie, 1996). They then simulated different group decision strategies and compared them both in terms of necessary computational resources to use the strategy and opportunity costs (resource differences between chosen patch and optimal patch). Although strategies with high computation demands performed best, they found that majority decision processes performed best of the low computations strategies – even better than "best member" (going with the most optimal individual choice) strategies. Research on group decision making has shown that majority processes are quite common (Kameda, Tindale, & Davis, in press) and often lead to post-decision convergence in individual member opinion. Thus, heuristically adaptive group decision strategies can lead to greater opinion sharing in groups.

On a more general scale, Caporael (1997) has argued that human evolution has at its core a social or group component. She argues that the notion of "repeat assembly" can be viewed as operating at many levels, not just in terms of genes. Given that one aspect of the human environment that has probably not changed from early evolutionary history is the social (face-to-face) group, it would not be surprising if a number of individual and group structural characteristics were "repeated," as part of human evolution, in order to promote the adaptiveness of group life. A full discussion of these ideas is beyond the scope of the present chapter, but one of the key aspects of her "core configurations model" is that "demes" (bands of individuals larger than the single family unit) require and promote a shared reality. In other words, one of the functions of social groups is to promote a shared construction of reality (see Hogg, in press a). The shared reality then allows for behaviors such as group movement, general maintenance of the group, and work group coordination. Shared language and language capabilities play a large role in such shared realities, and thus, these ideas are quite consistent with the aforementioned symbolic interactionist perspective. Another natural function of such social groups is the development of social identity, a topic to which we now turn.

Social identity and self-categorization

The social identity perspective in social psychology is a systematic attempt to develop a model of the social group and of group and intergroup behaviors that rests upon collective self-conceptualization – social identity (e.g., Hogg & Abrams, 1988; Tajfel & Turner, 1979; Turner, 1982; see Hogg, 2001). Developing out of the collectivist and "social dimension" agenda of post-War European social psychology (Tajfel, 1984), the social identity perspective is an integrated theoretical framework that has a number of distinct but compatible conceptual components. It integrates categorization processes (e.g., Tajfel, 1972), social comparison processes (see Hogg, in press b; Turner, 1975), self-enhancement motivation (see Abrams & Hogg, 1988), and people's beliefs about relations between groups (see Tajfel & Turner, 1979), in order to explain intergroup behavior and the collective self/social identity. More recently the categorization process has been more fully elaborated (self-categorization theory: Turner et al., 1987) as has the motivational role of uncertainty reduction (e.g., Hogg, in press c; Hogg & Mullin, 1999). This approach continues to generate a great deal of research, and has been influential in placing the study of groups back in the limelight of contemporary social psychology (see Hogg & Abrams, 1999; Moreland et al., 1994). Of particular relevance here, is that shared cognition lies at the heart of social identity processes.

People in groups categorize themselves and others in terms of relevant ingroup or outgroup prototypes. Prototypes form according to the principle of metacontrast – they optimize the balance between minimization of differences among people in the same group and maximization of differences between ingroup and outgroup (or non-ingroup). Prototypes define and prescribe the properties of group membership (perceptions, attitudes, feelings, behaviors) in such a way as to render the ingroup distinctive and high in entitativity (e.g., Campbell, 1958). Above all, prototypes are shared – they are shared representations of ingroup and outgroup properties. The process of categorizing someone as a group member perceptually assimilates them to the relevant ingroup or outgroup prototype, and thus deper-sonalizes them (i.e., they are not viewed as idiosyncratic persons, but as embodiments of the prototype). Categorization of self, self-categorization, has the same effect on self-perception, but more profoundly it transforms self-conception, attitudes, feelings, and behaviors. Self is experienced as collective self, and attitudes, feelings, and behaviors become group normative.

This analysis quite clearly identifies shared cognition as a fundamental feature of group life. In psychologically salient groups people form a shared representation of who they are and how they differ from people who are not in the group, or who are in specific outgroups. Information is selectively weighted and processed in order to clarify intergroup distinctive-ness and intragroup uniformity and entitativity. The resulting group representations deper-sonalize our perceptions of other people and transform our own self-conception, attitudes, feelings, and behavior.

Thirty years of social identity research have assembled substantial empirical evidence for the way that psychologically salient group membership produces effects based on the emergence or existence of shared cognitions. For example, patterns of attraction within groups become based on shared prototype-based criteria (Hogg, 1992), ingroup and outgroup perceptions become based on shared stereotypes (Oakes, Haslam, & Turner, 1994), and social influence processes produce and are guided by shared membership-defining norms (Turner, 1991).

The Impact of Shared Cognitions on Group Process and Performance

A number of recent reviews of the small-group performance literature have used a cognitive or information-processing model as an organizing framework for understanding how small task-performing groups operate (Hinsz, Tindale, & Vollrath, 1997; Larson & Christensen, 1993; Kameda, Tindale, & Davis, in press; Tindale & Kameda, 2000). Hinsz et al. defined group information processing as "the degree to which information, ideas, or cognitive pro-cesses are *shared*, and are *being shared*, among the group members . . ." (1997, p. 43, italics added). Kameda et al. (in press; Tindale & Kameda, 2000) coined the phrase "social sharedness" as a general theme underlying group information processing. The basic notion is that things that are shared among group members have a stronger impact on both group process and performance than do things that are not shared. We will restrict the present review mainly to cognitive aspects of "sharedness," and will borrow heavily from these early reviews. Our purpose is to show how shared cognitions at many levels influence the types of processes and outcomes exhibited by groups. (For related discussions of some of the same theory and research, see Stasser & Dietz-Uhler, 2001 and Kerr & Park, 2001).

Shared preferences

Much of the early research on group decision making or choice focused almost exclusively on member preferences as the legitimate inputs for aggregation (Kameda et al., in press). Social choice theorists (e.g., Arrow, 1963; Black, 1958) devised models of how these preferences should be aggregated in order to produce optimal group outcomes. In social psychology, the early work on small groups by Lorge and Solomon (1955), Smoke and Zajonc (1962), Steiner (1972), and others also devised models that used member preferences as the key inputs, although these models were more descriptive than prescriptive. Probably the most influential work on combining individual preferences in order to reach group decisions has been Davis's (1973) social decision scheme (SDS) theory (see Davis, 1973, 1982, or Stasser & Dietz-Uhler, 2001 for a description of the theory).

The SDS approach has generated a large body of research findings concerning the match between differing task demands and the related group consensus processes (see Davis, 1982; Stasser, Kerr, & Davis, 1989 for reviews). Although a number of factors have been found to influence group decision processes (Davis, 1982; Laughlin, 1980), one of the more consistent and robust findings from this research has been that "majorities/pluralities win" most of the time. This is particularly true when no "demonstrably" correct alternative exists (Laughlin & Ellis, 1986). When groups cannot demonstrate that a particular alternative is "optimal" or "correct" during discussion, "correctness" tends to be defined by the group consensus, and larger factions tend to define the group consensus. Majority/plurality type processes have been found for groups working on a variety of decision tasks/situations, including mock juries (Kameda, 1991; Tindale & Davis, 1983), risk taking (Davis, Kameda, & Stasson, 1992), duplex bets (Davis, Kerr, Sussman, & Rissman, 1974), choosing political candidates (Stasser & Titus, 1985), reward allocation decisions (Tindale & Davis, 1985), and promotion decisions (Tindale, 1989).

One limitation of the SDS approach is that it is restricted to decision situations with discrete decision alternatives. However, a number of recent models have been developed that describe preference aggregation for continuous response dimensions. Crott, Szilvas, and Zuber (1991) developed a model based on Black's (1958) work with single-peaked preference curves. Black showed that the median position among the group members dominates (in the game theoretic sense) any other possible position along the continuum, assuming member preference distributions are single peaked. Crott et al. (1991) found that a median model provided a good fit to group decision data from three different decision tasks. Davis, Au, Hulbert, Chen, and Zarnoth (1997) also found support for a median-based model (i.e., median of the $r - 1$ closest members, with $r =$ group size) using a civil trial mock jury task. In both of the aforementioned studies, the arithmetic mean of the member preferences provided rather poor fits to the data.

Recently, Davis (1996) proposed a social judgment scheme (SJS) model for groups reaching consensus on a continuous response scale. The model is a weighted linear combination of member preferences where the weights are an exponential function of the distances between a given member's preference and all other members' preferences. (See Davis, 1996, or Kameda et al., in press for a more complete description of the model.) The amount of weight given to any member decreases exponentially as an increasing function of the discrepancy of that member's preference from the other members of the group. Thus, members whose preferences are similar to one another receive larger weights and members whose preferences deviate from most other members receive very little weight. Although formulated recently, the model has fared well in empirical tests (Davis, 1996; Davis, Stasson, Parks, Hulbert, Kameda, Zimmerman, & Ono, 1993).

The models discussed previously all share two common elements. First, they all show the influence of social sharedness at the preference level. This is most clearly demonstrated with the majority/plurality models in that the largest faction of members that share a particular preference are able to put forth that preference as the group's decision. In other words, the preference that shows the greatest degree of sharedness among the members wins. However, both the Black (1958) median model and Davis's (1996) SJS model also emphasize the degree of preference sharing. The SJS model emphasizes shared preferences explicitly by giving more weight to those members whose preferences are similar (i.e., close to one another on the response dimension). It is easiest to see the sharedness aspect of the median model by comparing it to a model based on the mean. In a six-person group with four members whose preferences are quite similar and two members whose preferences deviate substantially from the other four, the median of the member preferences would fall within the range of the four similar members. However, the mean would be influenced to a much greater degree by the two deviant members. Thus, if most of the members of a group have similar preferences, the median will reflect the shared preferences of those members.

The second common element relates to the implications of such models for group decision outcomes. All three models will tend to exacerbate in the group response distribution those preferences that are dominant at the individual level. Thus, all three models are consistent with the group polarization effect (Myers & Lamm, 1976). Again, this is rather easy to see with the majority/plurality models. For example, assume a group size of five and a response distribution containing two alternatives (Plans A and B). If one randomly selects members from a population where 55% favor Plan A and 45% favor Plan B, a majority process predicts that 59% of the randomly composed groups would choose Plan A. If the population were 60% in favor of A, then groups functioning under a majority process and sampled from that population would choose A 68% of the time. These effects are even larger with larger group sizes (e.g., 62% and 73% respectively with 10-person groups). The relationship between the other two models and the exacerbation or polarization effect can also be seen by comparison to a simple average of the group member preferences (which is often how group polarization is defined – as a deviation from the mean of the pre-group discussion member preferences). Both the SJS and median models predict that group responses will be more influenced by members whose preferences are similar, relative to a simple average of preferences within the group. Thus, any skewness in the population distribution toward a particular end of a response continuum would be exacerbated in the group response distribution due to the higher likelihood of members having preferences in the smaller tail. In essence, all of these models give greater weight to preferences that are socially shared by a majority/plurality of members relative to the actual degree of preference sharing (i.e., the actual proportion of members who share the preference).

The above models do not make predictions concerning the individual-level preference structure after group consensus has been reached. However, a large body of research shows that group members tend to agree with, or move closer to, the group consensus choice after it has been made (e.g., Tindale & Davis, 1985; Tindale, Davis, Vollrath, Nagao, & Hinsz, 1990). Even in situations where consensus is not required, members are influenced by the positions held and arguments generated by other members (Sherif, 1936; Myers & Lamm, 1976). Thus, after group discussion, preference sharing tends to increase, regardless of whether the members must all agree on a single choice alternative or judgment position. In other words, the degree to which preferences are shared among group members both influences, and is influenced by, group decision making.

Shared information

The common knowledge effect. Although much of the early work on group decision making focused on preferences, some work did focus on the information distribution underlying those preferences (Graesser, 1982; Vinokur & Burnstein, 1974). Probably the best-known early attempt to understand groups at the information or argument level was Vinokur and Burnstein's persuasive arguments theory. In an attempt to explain group polarization, Vinokur and Burnstein argued that for any given issue, there is a population of arguments associated with it. They also argued that group discussion could be seen as members sampling arguments from that population. If there were more and/or more persuasive arguments favoring positions at one end of the continuum, then the sample of arguments would favor that end and would lead group members to move in that direction – thus, group polarization. One of the key assumptions of the theory was the importance of unshared or unique arguments. They assumed that shared arguments would have little impact when brought up during discussion because everyone already had that information. In contrast, they argued that unshared or unique information would affect member preferences and was crucial for polarization to occur.

However, more recent research has demonstrated exactly the opposite. Stasser and Titus (1985) designed a paradigm for studying the effects of shared and unshared information on group decision making that had a major impact on the field of small-group research. The paradigm has been referred to as the *hidden profile* technique and the basic finding has been called the *common knowledge effect* (Gigone & Hastie, 1996). Stasser and Titus had four-person groups choose one of three political candidates based on information profiles about the candidates. In some of the groups, all members were given complete information about all three candidates. However, in other conditions, some information was shared by all members and some information was only held by individual members. With complete information, most individuals typically preferred a particular candidate (e.g., candidate A). However, in the hidden profile (unshared information) condition, the positive information about candidate A was divided among the group members while the negative information about A was shared. This led individual members to prefer some other candidate at the beginning of discussion. Even though the groups, with a thorough discussion, should have been able to discover that candidate A was optimal, this rarely happened. Most of the groups chose an alternative candidate, and the group discussions contained mainly shared information. In addition, a majority model tended to describe the group decision processes at the preference level.

Stasser and Titus (1987) showed that a simple information-sampling model could account for the above effects. First, research has shown that the likelihood of a piece of information being recalled by a group is a function of the number of members presented with that information (Hinsz, 1990; Tindale & Sheffey, 1992). Thus, shared information is more likely to be recalled than unshared information at the group level. In addition, even with perfect recall, the probability that a piece of information gets brought up is also a function of the number of members who have it. Based on these assumptions, Stasser and Titus (1987) formulated their information-sampling model. The model (based on Lorge and Solomon's (1955) model A for predicting group problem-solving outcomes) basically assumes that the probability, $p(D)$, that a given piece of information will be discussed is 1 minus the probability that no one mentions the item during discussion. This can be mathematically described as $p(D) = 1 - [1 - p(M)]^n$, where $p(M)$ is the probability of any given member mentioning an item that he/she has, and n is the number of members having that item. When only one member knows a given piece of information $p(D) = p(M)$. However, as n increases, so does $p(D)$ so that shared information always has an advantage over unshared information in terms of it entering into the discussion content. Gigone and Hastie (1996), using a rather different paradigm, demonstrated similar findings and shed additional light on the processes underlying the common knowledge effect. Gigone and Hastie used a multi-cue judgment task, and varied whether the cues were shared or unshared among the group members. Each group made multiple judgments so that Gigone and Hastie could assess the degree of importance each cue had for predicting individual member and group judgments. Consistent with the Stasser and Titus (1985) findings, shared cues were more important for predicting group judgments than were unshared cues, with importance generally being a linear function of the degree of sharedness (i.e., cues increased linearly in importance as more members received them). Interestingly, cues that were actually brought up during discussion did not increase in weight as a function of their being mentioned. In addition, the effects of the cues on group judgments were totally mediated by the member preferences. Thus, it seems that the distribution of information in the group (i.e., information sharedness) influences group judgments only indirectly through member preferences (i.e., preference sharedness) (though see Winquist & Larson, 1998 for an exception).

Although very robust and often replicated (see Wittenbaum & Stasser, 1996; Stasser, 1999 for review), the common knowledge effect can be attenuated by some procedural mechanisms. First, Larson, Foster-Fishman, and Keys (1994) have shown that unshared information becomes more prevalent in group discussion over time. Thus, extending the discussion time of groups should help to insure that unshared information gets brought up during discussion. However, the opposite seems to happen when time pressures are put on the group. Groups focus on fewer alternatives and place more emphasis on shared information when under time pressure (Janis, 1982; Karau & Kelly, 1992). Recent work by Sawyer (1997) and Sheffey, Tindale, and Scott (1989) has shown that allowing group members to have access to informational records during discussion can attenuate hidden profile effects. Sawyer (1997) also found that instructing group members not to form a priori judgments helped to reduce the effects, although this has not always been found to be effective (Sheffey et al., 1989). Stasser and Stewart (1992) found that framing the task as a problem to be solved (implying a correct answer) led to greater sharing of unshared information during discussion. Finally, Stewart and Stasser (1995) demonstrated that assigning roles associated with the information distribution (e.g., "you are the expert on candidate x") led to more discussion of unshared information, but only when the roles were known by all of the group members.

Cognitive centrality of group members.   Work on the common knowledge effect has focused on the effect of shared *information* or *knowledge* per se on consensus. Little emphasis has been placed on group *members'* status or power as a function of degree of knowledge sharing with other members. For example, one member may share a substantial amount of information with other members, while another member may share only a portion of it. Since shared information has a greater impact on final group decisions, it seems likely that members having more shared information may acquire *pivotal power* in the group. This idea was tested in a recent set of studies by Kameda, Ohtsubo, and Takezawa (1997). Using a social network framework, Kameda et al. devised a model to represent the degree to which any given member was "cognitively central" in the group. Much like Davis's (1996) SJS model, which locates members' preference centrality, Kameda et al.'s measure of *cognitive centrality* defines members in terms of the degree of centrality in the *sociocognitive network*. The greater the degree of overlap between the information held by a given member and the information held by other members on average, the greater the degree of centrality for that member.

Kameda et al. (1997) ran two studies to assess whether cognitively more central members would be more influential in their groups, regardless of their preference status (i.e., whether they were in minority or majority factions). In Study 1, they had three-person groups discuss whether a defendant in a highly publicized trial deserved the death penalty. By coding contents of knowledge each member held prior to group interaction, they calculated a cognitive centrality score for each member in each group. They then used the members' cognitive centrality score to predict participation rates and opinion change after group discussion. Members' ranking in terms of centrality were positively related to their ranking in terms of participation. For members in minority factions, their degree of centrality also predicted (inversely) their amount of opinion change, though centrality was unrelated to opinion change for majority members.

In Study 2, Kameda et al. manipulated the information given to each group member to create two different situations. In one condition, the most cognitively central member of the group was a lone minority (in terms of preference) against a two-person majority. In the other condition, the most cognitively central person was part of the two-person majority, with the minority member being the least cognitively central. When the minority person was most cognitively central, the group went with the minority position (over the majority position) 67% of the time. When the minority person was most peripheral, the minority won only 42% of the time. In addition, groups were considerably more confident in the conditions where the central minority person's preference was chosen by the group. Thus, being the most central person in the group allows that person a greater degree of influence, even when he/she is a minority in terms of preference. Kameda et al. (1997) argue that such an enhanced social power accrues from perceptions of expertise for the cognitively central member in the focal knowledge domain.

Shared task representations

Research on the common knowledge effect tends to show that shared information plays a central role in group decision making. In addition, it shows that shared information and shared preferences tend to correspond with each other. Thus, the research on shared information has tended to fit nicely with the work on majority/plurality processes. However, there are a number of instances in the small-group literature where deviations from majority processes have been observed. Probably the most notable is the work by Laughlin and his associates (Laughlin, 1980; Laughlin & Ellis, 1986) on group problem solving. Problem solving, or "intellective" tasks are defined by Laughlin as tasks where a "demonstrably correct solution" exists, as opposed to decision-making tasks where "correctness" tends to be defined by the group consensus (Kameda et al., in press). A demonstrably correct solution is one where the group members can "demonstrate" a particular alternative is correct or optimal during the group discussion. Research has shown that majority/plurality models tend to severely under-predict group performance on such tasks. Models such as "truth wins" or "truth supported wins" (where either one or two members, respectively, who prefer the correct alternative can win out over incorrect majorities) provide much better fits to the experimental data (Laughlin, 1980). In defining demonstrability, Laughlin and Ellis (1986) argued that a key feature was a system of axioms or beliefs that were shared among the group members. This shared belief system serves as a background for the members understanding the logic behind the correctness of a given alternative. Thus, using the shared belief system, minority factions arguing for a correct alternative can win out over majorities favoring an incorrect alternative.

Tindale, Smith, Thomas, Filkins, and Sheffey (1996) generalized this notion and argued that whenever a "shared task representation" exists, alternatives consistent with the representation will be easier to defend and thus more likely to end up as the group's collective choice. Tindale et al. define a shared representation as "any task/situation relevant concept, norm, perspective, or cognitive process that is shared by most or all of the group members" (p. 84). Task/situation relevant means that the representation must have implications for the choice alternatives involved, and the degree to which a shared representation will impact on group decision processes will vary as a function of relevance. Its impact should also vary as a function of the degree to which it is shared among the group members. If no shared task representation exists (or if multiple conflicting representations are present), then groups will tend to follow a symmetric majority/plurality type process. However, when one does exist, the group process will tend to take on an asymmetric structure favoring the decision alternative that is consistent with the representation. Thus, majorities or minorities favoring the alternative consistent with the shared representation will be more powerful within the group.

Although the work by Laughlin (1980) on group problem solving is the strongest example of such effects, a number of others also exist. For example, much of the work on mock jury decision making (Davis, 1980; MacCoun & Kerr, 1988; Tindale & Davis, 1983) has shown that "not guilty" is an easier verdict to defend than "guilty," which is consistent with the shared processing objective of looking for "reasonable doubts" given to juries in all U.S. criminal cases. Thus, both majorities and minorities favoring not guilty are more powerful than comparably sized factions favoring guilty (Tindale et al., 1990). More recently, Tindale and associates (Tindale, 1993; Tindale et al., 1996) have shown that shared decision biases or heuristics can produce similar deviations from symmetric majority processes. For example,

Tindale (1989) showed that biased feedback procedures intended to produce conservative hiring or promotion practices allowed minorities voting against a job candidate's promotion to win out over majorities favoring promotion. Tindale, Sheffey, and Scott (1993) found that groups given the "loss" version of the standard "Asian Disease" problem (Tversky & Kahneman, 1981) would choose the riskier alternative even when a majority of the members favored the less risky alternative (see also Laughlin & Early, 1982).

A recent study by Smith, Dykema-Engblade, Walker, Niven, and McGrough (in press) also showed how a shared-belief system could be used by a minority to influence a majority. In the sample of students used by Smith et al., between 80–85% were in favor of the death penalty. However, the population of students at the university also had rather strong religious (Christian) convictions. In group discussions concerning the death penalty, Smith et al. found that minorities arguing against the death penalty were effective in moving majority members toward their position if they used religious arguments to substantiate their positions. Minorities had little if any influence if they did not rely on the shared religious convictions of the majority. Other minority influence research has also shown that if a local minority (a minority within the current discussion group) argues in favor of positions that are shared by the larger population, they are more effective than local minorities that argue for positions that are also less prevalent in the population (Clark, 1990). This analysis is consistent with the social identity idea that minorities are more effective if they can be viewed as sharing social identity with the majority (e.g., Turner, 1991; see Martin & Hewstone, this volume, chapter 9).

Recent research has shown that shared representations potentially operate in two different ways to affect group decisions. First, Smith, Tindale, and Steiner (1998), using a "sunk-cost" problem, found that sunk-cost arguments were persuasive, even if only a minority of members mentioned them as reasons for their decisions. Thus, arguments that are consistent with the shared representation can be especially influential in a group-decision context. Second, a recent study by Tindale, Anderson, Smith, Steiner, and Filkins (1998), continuing a program of research looking at the estimation of conjunctive probabilities by individuals and groups (Tindale, Sheffey, & Filkins, 1990; Tindale, Filkins, Thomas, & Smith, 1993), videotaped the group discussions for conjunctive probability problems. Earlier research had shown that minorities making non-normative ("erroneous") estimates were more powerful than majorities making normative estimates. The videotaped group discussions showed that groups rarely discussed strategies as to how to make the estimates, but rather simply exchanged information concerning their individual judgments. Quite often (greater than 60% of the time), groups went with a single member's judgment. When groups went with a single member's judgment as the group judgment, they were more likely to endorse the judgment of an incorrect member for conjunction problems that typically led to errors. For conjunction problems that typically did not lead to errors, groups were more likely to endorse the judgment of a correct member. These patterns were relatively independent of the preference distribution in the group. Thus, it seems that shared task representations can affect group decisions even when only preference information is exchanged. As long as a given individual preference is plausible within the shared representation, the group members will find it acceptable without thorough debate.

Collective efficacy

A topic that is just beginning to receive attention in the groups literature is collective efficacy (Bandura, 1997; Mischel & Northcraft, 1997). An extension of Bandura's notion of self-efficacy, collective efficacy is "a group's shared belief in its conjoint capabilities to organize and execute courses of action required to produce given levels of attainment" (Bandura, 1997, p. 477). As a relatively young area of research, there is still a number of conceptual and methodological issues that need to be resolved, but the early findings tend to locate collective efficacy as a critical aspect of group performance (e.g., Prussia & Kinicki, 1996). Much like self-efficacy, it is seen as a central component of various aspects of motivation. Both amount of effort and persistence are seen as a function of whether the group collectively believes it is good at or can accomplish a specific task.

One of the earliest questions addressed by this research was whether collective efficacy was really different from member self-efficacy. Most of the research findings to date imply that they are separate constructs. For example, Feltz and Lirgg (1988) assessed both members' self-efficacy and beliefs about team efficacy for seven collegiate hockey teams during a season. Early in the season, the average rating of member self-efficacy was a better predictor of team performance, but by the end of the season, collective efficacy was a better predictor of several different performance measures. Thus, it appears that accurate assessments of team efficacy take time to develop. Spink (1990) found similar effects with elite volleyball teams. He found that collective efficacy was particularly effective in terms of persistence and dealing with adversity (losses). Teams high in collective efficacy outperformed low efficacy teams after losses.

Although much of the research on collective efficacy has focused on sports teams, the concept has also been applied to organizational work teams. For example, Little and Madigan (1997) found a positive relationship between collective efficacy and performance in a field study of manufacturing work teams. These results are particularly interesting because they controlled for other factors such as members' technical job skills. Prussia and Kinicki (1996) tested whether collective efficacy, goal setting, and affective evaluations mediated the effects of feedback on task performance in a laboratory setting. By providing bogus performance feedback to the groups, they showed that both feedback and vicarious learning affected collective efficacy, but had no direct effects on performance after collective efficacy (and affective evaluations) were taken into account. The effect of goal setting on performance was also mediated by collective efficacy. A recent study by Peterson, Mitchell, Thompson, and Burr (in press) assessed the degree to which group efficacy and shared mental models (discussed more fully in a later section) would predict performance over time in classroom groups. Group efficacy was one of the stronger predictors of the variables measured and its relationship with performance was not mediated by measures of teamwork or liking for other group members. Collective efficacy has also been found to be important in social dilemma and public goods problems, wherein higher senses of efficacy in terms of being able to provide the good (even if illusory) increases cooperative behavior (Kerr, 1989; see also Kerr & Park, 2001).

Collective or group efficacy has also been viewed as an important aspect of leadership (see Chemers, 2001). One of the most important predictors of leadership effectiveness has been found to be the degree to which leaders can instill in group members perceptions of group efficacy. Such a finding is consistent with the findings of Prussia and Kinicki (1996) in that leaders are often in roles of providing groups with feedback. They are also often responsible for setting goals for and providing motivation to groups. It would seem that groups with effective leaders would be likely to form strong efficacy beliefs for their ability as a group to perform. However, some theorists have argued that collective efficacy might have a potential down side as well. Lindsley, Brass, and Thomas (1995) argue that very high levels of group efficacy could lead to overconfidence and complacency. Thus, having a leader that continues to set challenging goals for the group and focuses the group's attention on improvement strategies could be very important for avoiding these potential problems.

Shared metacognitions – transactive memory

Thus far, our discussion of socially shared cognitions has dealt mainly with things that group members share (e.g., preferences, information, etc.) irrespective of whether the members realize the degree of sharedness. Although group discussion may make certain aspects of sharedness apparent, it does not necessarily have to (thus, the hidden profile effect). However, recent trends in small-group research have begun to focus on not only the degree of sharing, but also whether members know what is shared and not shared among the group members (Hinsz, 1996; Hinsz, et al., 1997). In cognitive psychology, knowledge about what one does and does not know is referred to as "metacognition" (Metcalfe, 1996). Considering small groups as information-processing systems, metacognition at the group level can be viewed as members' knowledge of what other group members know. Shared metacognition is not really a new area in the groups literature, given it was a key aspect of the symbolic interactionism movement in sociology (Mead, 1934). However, it has only recently resurfaced in social psychology. Probably the best recent example of metacognition in groups is *transactive memory* (Wegner, 1987). Using an individual-level metaphor, Wegner argued that groups of individuals encode, store, and retrieve information much like single individuals do. Early on in a group's existence, much of the transactive memory system must be negotiated. For example, when new information enters the group, the group may discuss where and how it should be stored and who is to be responsible for it. This can be seen as parallel to memory encoding at the individual level when learning material in a new domain. Once encoded, information can then be retrieved by the appropriate memory cues – by asking the appropriate person. However, as the group's transactive memory system becomes established, new information is simply encoded by the member whose role within the system it is to deal with that type of information. Thus, over time, the transactive memory system can work almost automatically. Much like a chess master remembers board positions with ease, groups that have been working together for many years can encode and retrieve information as a group with little if any effort. This then frees up group members' time for other task relevant actions.

Wegner (1995) argues that groups can serve memory functions much like external memory aids. In fact, he has compared group transactive memory systems to computer networks in terms of things like data sharing, directory updating, and the like. Just as other aspects of collective tasks can be distributed among group members, memory storage can also be distributed. Wegner argues that group members can rely on other members to remember information that is more consistent with their areas of expertise or preferences. Thus, other group members can serve as memory aids for information not directly relevant to a given member's main duties or role within the group. In this way, the group can remember much more than any given member, yet each member has access to the entire information in the group by knowing which members know what. It is the shared metacognitive knowledge that allows each member access to the group's entire store of information.

Most of the research on transactive memory to date has focused on dating and marital relationships (e.g., Wegner, Erber, & Raymond, 1991) – partly because transactive memory systems develop over time, and they are therefore difficult to study in laboratory settings. However, recent work by Moreland, Argote, and Krishnan (1998) has demonstrated the usefulness of transactive memory in work groups. Moreland et al. hypothesized that training group members together as a group would help foster transactive memory systems, and thus, improve group performance. Moreland et al. report a series of studies that had three-person groups learn the various aspects of a radio assembly task. The studies contained two parts: a training session and a final performance session. In the initial study, the group members were either trained individually or trained together as a group. Then, all participants worked as three-person groups to assemble a radio. Moreland et al. found that groups trained together performed better than groups whose members were trained as individuals. In addition, they found that the performance increases were due to enhanced transactive memory systems rather than other potential mediating variables, such as cohesiveness or social identity. Memory differentiation, task coordination, and trust among members as to their respective levels of expertise were found to be the critical factors involved in the transactive memory system. In later studies, they showed that being trained in one group and working in another did not produce the same benefits. Thus, simply experiencing group work was not the key factor – actually working with the same people was of central importance (Moreland, 1999).

Hollingshead (1998a, b, 2001) has also isolated certain key aspects of transactive memory systems in intimate couples. She found that dating couples were better at a collective recall task than were pairs of strangers when no communication was allowed. She hypothesized that the main advantage for the couples was that they knew what the other person would expect them to remember. However, this advantage disappeared when communication was allowed, and in fact, strangers tended to outperform couples. Thus, explicit negotiation of the transactive memory system at encoding tends to improve its performance. The couples in the communication condition may have relied too heavily on implicit expectations whereas the strangers were forced to explicitly distribute responsibility. Hollingshead (1998b) also showed that non-verbal and paralinguistic aspects of communication can be important retrieval cues in a transactive memory system. Although couples performed better than strangers in both face-to-face and computer-mediated interaction settings, couples per-formed better in the face-to-face environment. A follow-up study showed that the lack of access to paralinguistic and non-verbal cues could account for the difference.

Shared mental models

A number of researchers have begun to borrow the concept of a *mental model* from the cognitive literature and apply the notion to small groups (Brauner, 1996; Cannon-Bowers, Salas, & Converse, 1993; Hinsz, 1996). A mental model can be seen as a template or mental representation of how a particular system operates. For example, a car mechanic may have a mental model of the internal combustion engine. Although engines in different cars may be designed slightly differently, the same mental model can be used as a template for understanding each of them. Cognitive psychologists have argued that mental models are important for understanding how people interact with various aspects of their environment (Rouse & Morris, 1986). In relation to task performance, a mental model allows the task performer to estimate the important variables and bring the requisite skills to bear on completing the task. In relation to groups, mental models have two major components: knowledge about the task and knowledge about the group and its members (Cannon-Bowers et al., 1993).

Sports teams are good examples where mental models can be applied to group performance. For example, each of the nine members of a baseball team must have an understanding of the rules of the game and the roles for each player in order for the team to work together. Thus, team players must have a mental model of the task (rules of the game) and the group (the roles of each player) in order to play effectively. However, this knowledge must be shared among the members in order for it to aid in team effectiveness. Two players who have different models of how to react in a given situation could each behave in ways that would interfere with the other's behavior.

Although research on mental models in groups is in its infancy, a number of interesting findings have already emerged. First, thorough group discussion tends to lead to a convergence of mental models among group members (Brauner, 1996; Hastie & Pennington, 1991). Hastie and Pennington have argued that deliberation (particularly *evidence-driven* deliberation) leads to a convergence in the stories that jurors use to make sense of the evidence presented, in order to make a verdict decision. Brauner (1996) had groups work on a city planning task, where the groups were composed of two teams – economic experts and social/environmental experts. During early discussions, it was clear that the two teams had different mental models of the task. However, after two group discussion sessions, a large degree of convergence was evident. This was in spite of the fact that the teams still differed in attitudes and social categories. Conversely, Tindale et al. (1993) found little convergence in cognitive frames among group members after discussing a risky decision task. However, groups in the Tindale et al. experiment typically reached consensus in less than four minutes. Thus, it appears that mental model convergence among group members takes time to develop. Another area where the usefulness of shared mental models has been demonstrated is negotiation. Thompson (1997) compared expert and novice negotiators and discovered that not only do experts reach better negotiation outcomes than novices, but they also show a greater similarity in their mental representations of the negotiation situation. Thus, experience in negotiation leads to similar mental models, which can help negotiators find mutually beneficial tradeoffs and areas of common interest.

Although mental models can be shared without member awareness of the sharedness, there are reasons to assume that a meta-knowledge of such sharedness could aid group performance (Klimoski & Mohammed, 1994). Again using a sports team metaphor, a particular player's knowledge that other players share his/her knowledge of the game allows the player to concentrate on only those aspects of the task important for his/her role, without worrying about what the other players will be doing. Thus, the transactive memory systems discussed above are often seen as key components in shared mental models, but other components are also important. Knowledge of who knows what is important for gaining knowledge when needed, but knowledge of who is going to do what and when is important for making sure that all parts of a task are coordinated and completed.

Cannon-Bowers et al. (1993) have delineated four separate aspects or types of mental models that may be important for team functioning. The "equipment model" involves knowledge of the function and operations of the equipment to be used, which should remain fairly stable over time. The "task model" involves strategies for task performance and the various contingency plans that may be necessary. They argue that these are only moderately stable. Third, members need a shared "team interaction model" so that they can coordinate their activities and have complete and efficient lines of communication. These are also seen as moderately stable. Finally, they define the "team model" as the knowledge, skills, preferences, and tendencies of the team members. These obviously change as a function of turnover in the group. Thus, they might remain stable for long-term groups with few member changes, but could change rapidly as members are replaced.

Like transactive memory, mental models take time to develop, particularly those associated with the team and team interaction. However, Cannon-Bowers et al. (1993) argue that training, using the shared mental models orientation, can aid groups in both developing and using their shared knowledge systems. Recent evidence for this has come from research on airplane crews using the training system known as crew resources management (CRM; Helmreich, 1997; Weiner, Kanki, & Helmreich, 1993). CRM attempts to teach cockpit and complete airline crews how to use their collective resources to operate efficiently in a crisis. It attempts to get all members of a team well versed in the expertise and duties of each member, and then to get them to effectively communicate (through both active participation and listening) the crucial knowledge they have to the other members of the team. Thus, the technique incorporates both task and group mental models. The key ideas are team based and assume that if low-status members don't provide their information, it can't be used. However, even if provided, if it is not listened to by the leaders of the team (pilots, copilots, etc.) then it can't serve its purpose. Through the use of simulators, research has shown that CRM can lead to improved safety and efficiency by airline teams (Helmreich, 1997). In addition, similar techniques are being used to train surgical teams in hospitals (Helmreich & Schaefer, 1994).

Shared identity

Although originally a theory of intergroup relations, social identity theory (e.g., Hogg & Abrams, 1988; Tajfel & Turner, 1979) more recently has begun to play a major role in understanding intragroup processes as well (e.g., Hogg, 1996). Both social identity (Tajfel & Turner, 1979) and related ideas on self-categorization (Turner et al., 1987) have been used to explore both new and old topics in the small-group literature. Since these theories and findings are well represented in a number of other chapters in this volume (see chapters by Abrams & Hogg; Hogg; Marques, Abrams, Páez, & Hogg; Reicher; and Worchel & Coutant) we will only touch on a few of the major findings here.

Earlier we discussed the notion of group polarization in terms of majority decision processes and preference sharing. However, a number of studies has shown that group identification also influences polarization (e.g., Hogg, Turner, & Davidson, 1990; Mackie, 1986; Mackie & Cooper, 1984). Where social identity is salient, for example in a salient intergroup comparative context, people categorize themselves in terms of the prototypical features of the ingroup, and assimilate themselves to the ingroup prototype – they exhibit normative behavior, or conform to the ingroup normative position. Since prototypes form according to the principle of meta-contrast, they not only capture ingroup similarity but they also accentuate intergroup difference. Thus, ingroup prototypes are typically polarized away from salient outgroups. Polarization is conformity to a polarized ingroup prototype or norm. Group interaction (or even just preference sharing) when a salient outgroup is present can, therefore, lead to more polarized attitudes within the group. The degree of polarization on a given issue can be predicted by the degree to which that issue clearly differentiates the ingroup from the outgroup.

Another traditional area in the small-group literature where social identity/self-categorization theory has been applied is group cohesiveness. Hogg and his associates have redefined group cohesiveness from a social identity perspective (Hogg, 1992; Hogg & Hains, 1996; Hogg & Hardie, 1991; Hogg, Hardie, & Reynolds, 1995). In contrast to early approaches to cohesiveness that focused on interpersonal attraction among group members, the social identity approach distinguishes between interpersonal attraction and attraction to the group, specifically attraction to the group prototype as it is embodied by group members. Of particular relevance here is the finding that when people identify (self-categorize) with a salient group, shared cognitions, in the form of shared ingroup prototypes, transform reciprocal patterns of mutual regard into consensual regard for more prototypical group members. One of the main problems with the group-cohesiveness literature has been a lack of consistent findings concerning how cohesiveness influences group outcomes like performance. This new conceptualization of group cohesiveness may help to clarify some of these issues in future research.

The notion of social identity has also been fruitfully used to help explain cooperation in social dilemma situations (Dawes, van de Kragt, & Orbell, 1988; Rapoport & Amaldoss, 1999). Groups that are allowed to discuss the dilemma situation before being asked to donate to some group-level good are much more cooperative than groups prevented from discussion. Dawes et al. (1988) have shown that group identity created through discussion is the likely cause of such cooperation. In addition, placing a group in a competitive situation with an outgroup will also increase cooperative behavior among the members of the ingroup (Rapoport & Amaldoss, 1999). One of the more interesting recent findings in the small-group literature is the "discontinuity effect" (Schopler & Insko, 1992). Their research has shown that while individuals playing a prisoners' dilemma game with communication are quite likely to cooperate, three-person groups playing against three-person groups are much more likely to defect. At least part of this discontinuity between individual and group behavior stems from efforts to protect the ingroup (fear of exploitation) and compete with the outgroup (greed). Since there is no group membership that is salient when individuals play the game, such intergroup forces are not operating, thus allowing for greater cooperation. The use of social identity/self-categorization theory to explain intragroup phenomena is still fairly recent, and we expect that the effects of shared identity on a number of small-group processes would be a profitable area for future research (for example, leadership – see Hogg, 2000; Hogg, Hains, & Mason, 1998).

Summary and Future Direction

Although the idea of socially shared cognitions in groups has a long history, its absence from mainstream social psychology for many years means that the potential yield in knowledge from such an approach is far from realized. We have attempted in this chapter to outline some of the key ideas and findings concerning shared cognitions in groups, but we feel the future will hold a much greater wealth of insight from this approach. Although there are many potential avenues for future research, we feel three might be particularly fruitful.

First, most of the research discussed here has tended to focus on one type of shared cognition – shared preferences, information, task representation, metacognition, and so forth. However, most group settings have the potential for sharing at multiple levels. One would expect some degree of consistency across dimensions, as some of the research has already demonstrated. Shared information tends to lead to shared preferences, as does a shared identity. However, Kameda et al. (1997) showed that members who share more information with other members can be influential even when they do not share the majority preference, and Tindale et al. (1996) have shown that shared task representations can he used advantageously by preference minorities. It would be interesting to see how other types of inconsistencies in degrees of sharedness impact on both group process and performance.

Second, very little work has been done on how sharedness at one level affects sharedness at other levels. Again, some of the research discussed here has shown interdimensional affects. Stewart and Stasser (1995) showed that giving a group a shared metacognitive framework in terms of member expertise increased the likelihood of unshared information being mentioned in the group discussion. Brauner's (1996) work on shared mental models also showed how discussion can lead to increased sharedness on some dimensions (cognitive models of the issue), while other dimensions (identity, attitudes) remained relatively unshared. Thus, further work on how different degrees of sharedness on one dimension affect sharing on other dimensions should prove interesting.

Finally, the processes by which shared cognition comes about on different levels is still relatively under-explored. Although we discussed a number of theories as to why shared cognitions should exist, studies of which forces are most salient, or which predate others in terms of time have received scant attention. Latané and Bourgeois (2001) hypothesize that the belief clustering predicted by dynamic social impact theory could lead to perceptions of group identity for members within those belief clusters. Obviously, many groups in society are formed around issues (political parties, environmental groups, etc.) and often members join groups because they expect to find like-minded people. However, the self-categorization processes associated with group identities can also lead to a greater degree of cognitive sharedness. It might be interesting to compare the effects of shared cognitions in interactive groups that formed in part on the basis of shared social identity, with those that formed on a different basis.

Studying groups on any level is not an easy prospect, in terms of time, resources, and the general complexity of the focus of study. However, we hope that by showing how cognitions emerge from group life, and how groups themselves are defined by their cognition, we will inspire a new generation of researchers to find the difficulties worth the effort.

REFERENCES

Abrams, D., & Hogg, M. A. (1988). Comments on the motivational status of self-esteem in social identity and intergroup discrimination. *European Journal of Social Psychology, 18*, 317–334.

Abrams, D., & Hogg, M. A. (Eds.) (1999). *Social identity and social cognition.* Oxford, UK: Blackwell.

Abrams, D., & Hogg, M. A. (2001). Collective identity – group membership and self-conception. In M. A. Hogg & S. Tindale (Eds.), *Blackwell handbook of social psychology: Group processes* (pp. 425–460). Oxford, UK: Blackwell.

Allport, F. (1924). *Social psychology.* New York: Houghton Mifflin.

Arrow, K. J. (1963). *Social choice and individual values* (2nd Ed.). New Haven, CT: Yale University Press.

Bandura, A. (1997). *Self-efficacy: The exercise of control.* New York: Freeman.

Baron, R. A., & Byrne, D. (2000). *Social psychology* (9th Ed.). Needhan, MA: Alleyn & Bacon.

Bar-Tal, D. (1990). *Group beliefs: A conception for analyzing group structure, processes, and behavior.* New York: Springer-Verlag.

Black, D. (1958). *The theory of committees and elections.* Cambridge, UK: Cambridge University Press.

Brauner, E. (1996). *Attitudes and mental models in group interaction.* Paper presented at the Nags Head Conference on Groups, Networks, and Organizations, Highland Beach, FL.

Brunswik, E. (1956). *Perception and the representative design of psychological experiments.* Berkeley, CA: University of California Press.

Campbell, D. T. (1958). Common fate, similarity, and other indices of aggregates of persons as social entities. *Behavioral Science, 3*, 14–25.

Cannon-Bowers, J. A., Salas, E., & Converse, S. (1993). Shared mental models in expert team decision making. In N. J. Castellan (Ed.), *Individual and group decision making. Current directions* (pp. 221–246). Hillsdale, NJ: Erlbaum.

Caporael, L. R. (1997). The evolution of truly social cognition: The core configurations model. *Personality and Social Psychology Review, 1*, 276–298.

Chemers, M. M. (2001). Leadership effectiveness – an integrative review. In M. A. Hogg & S. Tindale (Eds.), *Blackwell handbook of social psychology: Group processes* (pp. 376–399). Oxford, UK: Blackwell.

Clark, R. D., III. (1990). Minority influence: The role of argument refutation of the majority position and social support for the minority. *European Journal of Social Psychology, 20*, 489–497.

Crott, H. W., Szilvas, K., & Zuber, J. A. (1991). Group decision, choice shift, and polarization in consulting, political and local political scenarios: An experimental investigation. *Organizational Behavior and Human Decision Process, 49*, 22–41.

Darley, J. (2001). Social comparison motives in ongoing groups. In M. A. Hogg & S. Tindale (Eds.), *Blackwell handbook of social psychology: Group processes* (pp. 334–351). Oxford, UK: Blackwell.

Davis, J. H. (1973). A theory of social decision schemes. *Psychological Review, 80,* 97–125.

Davis, J. H. (1980). Group decision and procedural justice. In M. Fishbein (Ed.), *Progress in social psychology* (Vol. 1, pp. 157–229). Hillsdale, NJ: Erlbaum.

Davis, J. H. (1982). Social interaction as a combinatorial process in group decision. In H. Brandstatter, J. H. Davis, & G. Stocker-Kreichgauer (Eds.), *Group decision making* (pp. 27–58). London: Academic Press.

Davis, J. H. (1996). Group decision making and quantitative judgments: A consensus model. In E. Witte & J. H. Davis (Eds.), *Understanding group behavior: Consensual action by small groups* (Vol. 1, pp. 35–59). Mahwah, NJ: Erlbaum.

Davis, J. H., Au, W., Hulbert, L., Chen, X., & Zarnoth, P. (1997). Effect of group size and procedural influence on consensual judgment of quantity: The example of damage awards on mock civil juries. *Journal of Personality and Social Psychology, 73,* 703–718.

Davis, J. H., Kameda, T., & Stasson, M. (1992). Group risk taking: Selected topics. In F. Yates (Ed.), *Risk-taking behavior* (pp. 163–199). Chichester, UK: Wiley.

Davis, J. H., Kerr, N. L., Sussman, M., & Rissman, A. K. (1974). Social decision schemes under risk. *Journal of Personality and Social Psychology, 30,* 248–271.

Davis, J. H., Stasson, M. F., Parks, C. D., Hulbert, L., Kameda, T., Zimmerman, S., & Ono, K. (1993). Quantitative decisions by groups and individuals: Voting procedures and monetary awards by mock civil juries. *Journal of Experimental Social Psychology, 29,* 326–346.

Dawes, R. M., van de Kragt, A. J. C., & Orbell, J. M. (1988). Not me or thee but we: The importance of group identity in eliciting cooperation in dilemma situations: Experimental manipulations. *Acta Psychologica, 68,* 83–97.

Durkheim, E. (1964). *The rules of the sociological method.* New York: Free Press.

Durkheim, E. (1965). *Suicide. A study in sociology.* New York: Free Press.

Durkheim, E. (1984). *The division of labor in society.* New York: Free Press.

Farr, R. M. (1996). *The roots of modern social psychology: 1872–1954.* Oxford, UK: Blackwell.

Feltz, D. L., & Lirgg, C. D. (1988). Perceived team and player efficacy in collegiate hockey. *Journal of Applied Psychology, 83,* 557–564.

Festinger, L. (1950). Informal social communication. *Psychological Review, 57,* 271–282.

Festinger, L. (1954). A theory of social comparison processes. *Human Relations, 7,* 117–140.

Festinger, L. (1957). *A theory of cognitive dissonance.* Stanford, CA: Stanford University Press.

Fine, G. (1990). Organizational time: Temporal demands and the experience of work in restaurant kitchens. *Social Forces, 69,* 95–114.

Gigone, D., & Hastie, R. (1993). The common knowledge effect: Information sharing and group judgment. *Journal of Personality and Social Psychology, 65,* 959–974.

Gigone, D., & Hastie, R. (1996). The impact of information on group judgment: A model and computer simulation. In E. Witte & J. H. Davis (Eds.), *Understanding group behavior: Consensual action by small groups* (Vol. 1, pp. 221–251). Mahwah, NJ: Erlbaum.

Graesser, C. C. (1982). A social averaging theorem for group decision making. In N. H. Anderson (Ed.), *Contributions of information integration theory* (Vol. 2, pp. 1–40). New York: Academic Press.

Guzzo, R. A., & Shea, G. P. (1992). Group performance and intergroup relations in organizations. In M. D. Dunnette & L. M. Hough (Eds.), *Handbook of industrial & organizational psychology* (2nd Ed., Vol. 3, pp. 269–314). Palo Alto, CA: Consulting Psychologists Press.

Hackman, J. R. (1998). Why teams don't work. In R. S. Tindale, J. E. Edwards, L. Heath, E. J. Posavac, F. B. Bryant, E. Henderson-King, Y. Suarez-Balcazar, & J. Myers (Eds.), *Social psychological applications to social issues: Applications of theory and research on groups* (Vol. 4, pp. 245–268). New York: Plenum Press.

Hardin, C., & Higgins, E. T. (1996). Shared reality: How social verification makes the subjective objective. In R. M. Sorrentino & E. T. Higgins (Eds.), *Handbook of motivation and cognition: Foundations of social behavior* (3rd Ed., pp. 28–42). New York: Guilford Press.

Hastie, R., & Pennington, N. (1991). Cognitive and social processes in decision making. In L. B. Resnick, J. M. Levine, & S. D. Teasley (Eds.), *Perspectives on socially shared cognition* (pp. 308–327). Washington DC: American Psychological Association.

Heider, F. (1958). *The psychology of interpersonal relations*. New York: Wiley.

Helmreich, R. L. (1997). Managing human error in aviation. *Scientific American, 276*, 62–67.

Helmreich, R. L., & Schaefer, H. G. (1994). Team performance in the operating room. In M. S. Bogner (Ed.), *Human error in medicine* (pp. 123–141). Hillsdale, NJ: Erlbaum.

Higgins, E. T. (1992). Achieving "shared reality" in the communication game: A social action that creates meaning. *Journal of Language and Social Psychology, 13*, 141–154.

Hinsz, V. B. (1990). Cognitive and consensus processes in group recognition memory performance. *Journal of Personality and Social Psychology, 59*, 705–718.

Hinsz, V. B. (1996). *Metacognitions in groups and the potential of shared mental models*. Paper presented at the Society of Experimental Social Psychologists Pre-Conference on Small Groups, Sturbridge, MA.

Hinsz, V. B., Tindale, R. S., & Vollrath, D. A. (1997). The emerging conceptualization of groups as information processors. *Psychological Bulletin, 121*, 43–64.

Hogg, M. A. (1992). *The social psychology out group cohesiveness: From attraction to social identity*. London: Harvester Wheatsheaf.

Hogg, M. A. (1996). Social identity, self-categorization, and the small group. In E. Witte & J. H. Davis (Eds.), *Understanding group behavior: Small group processes and interpersonal relations* (Vol. 2, pp. 227–253). Mahwah, NJ: Erlbaum.

Hogg, M. A. (2000). *A social identity theory of leadership*. Manuscript submitted for publication, University of Queensland.

Hogg, M. A. (2001). Social categorization, depersonalization, and group behavior. In M. A. Hogg & S. Tindale (Eds.), *Blackwell handbook of social psychology: Group processes* (pp. 56–85). Oxford, UK: Blackwell.

Hogg, M. A. (in press a). Social identity and the sovereignty of the group: A psychology of belonging. In C. Sedikides & M. B. Brewer (Eds.), *Individual self, relational self, and collective self: Partners, opponents, or strangers*. Philadelphia, PA: Psychology Press.

Hogg, M. A. (in press b). Social identity and social comparison. In J. Suls & L. Wheeler (Eds.), *Handbook of social comparison: Theory and research*. New York: Plenum.

Hogg, M. A. (in press c). Subjective uncertainty reduction through self-categorization: A motivational theory of social identity processes. *European Review of Social Psychology*.

Hogg, M. A., & Abrams, D. (1988). *Social identifications: A social psychology of intergroup relations and group processes*. London: Routledge.

Hogg, M. A., & Abrams, D. (1999). Social identity and social cognition: Historical background and current trends. In D. Abrams & M. A. Hogg (Eds.), *Social identity and social cognition* (pp. 1–25). Oxford, UK: Blackwell.

Hogg, M. A., & Hains, S. C. (1996). Intergroup relations and group solidarity: Effects of group identification and social beliefs on depersonalized attraction. *Journal of Personality and Social Psychology, 70*, 295–309.

Hogg, M. A., Hains, S. C., & Mason, I. (1998). Identification and leadership in small groups: Salience, frame of reference, and leader stereotypicality effects on leader evaluations. *Journal of Personality and Social Psychology, 75*, 1248–1263.

Hogg, M. A., & Hardie, E. A. (1991). Social attraction, personal attraction, and self-categorization: A field study. *Personality and Social Psychology Bulletin, 17*, 175–180.

Hogg, M. A., Hardie, E. A., & Reynolds, K. J. (1995). Prototypical similarity, self-categorization, and depersonalized attraction: A perspective on group cohesiveness. *European Journal of Social Psychology*, *25*, 159–177.

Hogg, M. A., & Mullin, B.-A. (1999). Joining groups to reduce uncertainty: Subjective uncertainty reduction and group identification. In D. Abrams & M. A. Hogg (Eds.), *Social identity and social cognition* (pp. 249–279). Oxford, UK: Blackwell.

Hogg, M. A., Turner, J. C., & Davidson, B. (1990). Polarized norms and social frames of reference: A test of the self-categorization theory of group polarization. *Basic and Applied Social Psychology*, *11*, 77–100.

Hollingshead, A. (1998a). Communication, learning, and retrieval in transactive memory systems. *Journal of Experimental Social Psychology*, *34*, 423–442.

Hollingshead, A. (1998b). Retrieval process in transactive memory systems. *Journal of Personality and Social Psychology*, *74*, 659–671.

Hollingshead, A. B. (2001). Communication technologies, the Internet and group research. In M. A. Hogg & S. Tindale (Eds.), *Blackwell handbook of social psychology: Group processes* (pp. 557–573). Oxford, UK: Blackwell.

Janis, I. (1982). *Groupthink* (2nd Ed.). Boston, MA: Houghton-Mifflin.

Kameda, T. (1991). Procedural influence in small-group decision making: Deliberation style and assigned decision rule. *Journal of Personality and Social Psychology*, *61*, 245–256.

Kameda, T., & Hastie, R. (1999). *Social sharedness and adaptation: Adaptive group decision heuristics*. Paper presented at the 17th Subjective Probability, Utility, and Decision-Making Conference, Mannheim, Germany.

Kameda, T., Ohtsubo, Y., & Takezawa, M. (1997). Centrality in sociocognitive network and social influence: An illustration in a group decision-making context. *Journal of Personality and Social Psychology*, *73*, 296–309.

Kameda, T., Tindale, R. S., & Davis, J. H. (in press). Cognitions, preferences, and social sharedness: Past, present, and future directions in group decision making. In S. L. Schneider & J. Shanteau (Eds.), *Emerging perspectives on judgment and decision research*. Cambridge, UK: Cambridge University Press.

Karau, S. J., & Kelly, J. R. (1992). The effects of time scarcity and time abundance on group performance quality and interaction process. *Journal of Experimental Social Psychology*, *28*, 542–571.

Kerr, N. L. (1989). Illusions of efficacy: The effects of group size on perceived efficacy in social dilemmas. *Journal of Experimental Social Psychology*, *25*, 287–313.

Kerr, N. L., & Park, E. S. (2001). Group performance in collaborative and social dilemma tasks – progress and prospects. In M. A. Hogg & S. Tindale (Eds.), *Blackwell handbook of social psychology: Group processes* (pp. 107–138). Oxford, UK: Blackwell.

Klimoski, R., & Mohammed, S. (1994). Team mental model: Construct or metaphor? *Journal of Management*, *20*, 403–437.

Larson, J. R., & Christensen, C. (1993). Groups as problem-solving units: Towards a new meaning of social cognition. *British Journal of Social Psychology*, *32*, 5–30.

Larson, J. R., Jr., Foster-Fishman, P. G., & Keys, C. B. (1994). Discussion of shared and unshared information in decision-making groups. *Journal of Personality and Social Psychology*, *67*, 446–461.

Latané, B. (1981). The psychology of social impact. *American Psychologist*, *36*, 343–355.

Latané, B., & Bourgeois, M. J. (2001). Dynamic social impact and the consolidation, clustering, correlation, and continuing diversity of culture. In M. A. Hogg & S. Tindale (Eds.), *Blackwell handbook of social psychology: Group processes* (pp. 235–258). Oxford, UK: Blackwell.

Latané, B., & L'Herrou, T. (1996). Social clustering in the conformity game: Dynamic social impact in electronic groups. *Journal of Personality and Social Psychology*, *70*, 1218–1230.

Laughlin, P. R. (1980). Social combination processes of cooperative, problem-solving groups on verbal intellective tasks. In M. Fishbein (Ed.), *Progress in social psychology* (Vol. 1, pp. 127–155). Hillsdale, NJ: Erlbaum.

Laughlin, P. R., & Early, P. C. (1982). Social combination models, persuasive arguments theory, social comparison theory, and choice shift. *Journal of Personality and Social Psychology, 42,* 273–280.

Laughlin, P. R., & Ellis, A. L. (1986). Demonstrability and social combination processes on mathematical intellective tasks. *Journal of Experimental Social Psychology, 22,* 177–189.

LeBon, G. (1960). *Psychology of crowds.* (R. K. Merton, Trans.). New York: Viking Press. (Original work published 1896).

Levine, J. M., & Moreland, R. L. (1991). Culture and socialization in work groups. In L. B. Resnik, J. M. Levine, & S. D. Teasley (Eds.), *Perspectives on socially shared cognition* (pp. 257–279). Washington, DC: American Psychological Association.

Levine, J. M., & Moreland, R. L. (1999). Knowledge transmission in work groups: Helping newcomers to succeed. In L. L. Thompson, J. M. Levine, & D. M. Messick (Eds.), *Shared cognition in organizations: The management of knowledge* (pp. 267–296). Mahwah, NJ: Erlbaum.

Levine, J. M., Moreland, R. L., & Choi, H.-S. (2001). Group socialization and newcomer innovation. In M. A. Hogg & S. Tindale (Eds.), *Blackwell handbook of social psychology: Group processes* (pp. 86–106). Oxford, UK: Blackwell.

Lindsley, D. H., Brass, D. J., & Thomas, J. B. (1995). Efficacy-performance spirals: A multilevel perspective. *Academy of Management Journal, 20,* 645–678.

Little, B. L., & Madigan, R. M. (1997). The relationship between collective efficacy and performance in manufacturing work teams. *Small Group Research, 28,* 517–534.

Lorge, I., & Solomon, H. (1955). Two models of group behavior in the solution of eurcka-type problems. *Psychometrica, 20,* 139–148.

MacCoun, R., & Kerr, N. L. (1988). Asymmetric influence in mock jury deliberations: Jurors' bias for leniency. *Journal of Personality and Social Psychology, 54,* 21–33.

Mackie, D. M. (1986). Social identification effects in group polarization. *Journal of Personality and Social Psychology, 50,* 720–728.

Mackie, D. M., & Cooper, J. (1984). Attitude polarization: The effects of group membership. *Journal of Personality and Social Psychology, 46,* 575–585.

McDougall, W. (1920). *The group mind: A sketch of the principles of collective psychology with some attempt to apply them to the interpretation of national life and character.* Cambridge, UK: Cambridge University Press.

Mead, G. H. (1934). *Mind, self, and society from the standpoint of a social behaviorist.* Chicago, IL: University of Chicago Press.

Metcalfe, J. (1996). Metacognitive processes. In E. L. Bjork & R. A. Bjork (Eds.), *The handbook of perception and cognition: Vol. 10. Memory* (pp. 383–411). San Diego, CA: Academic Press.

Mischel, L. J., & Northcraft, G. B. (1997). "I think we can, I think we can . . .": The role of efficacy beliefs in group and team effectiveness. In B. Markovsky & M. J. Lovaglia (Eds.), *Advances in group processes* (Vol. 14, pp. 177–197). Greenwich, CT: JAI Press.

Moreland, R. L. (1999). Transactive memory: Learning who knows what in work groups and organizations. In L. L. Thompson, J. M. Levine, & D. M. Messick (Eds.), *Shared cognition in organizations: The management of knowledge* (pp. 3–32). Mahwah, NJ: Erlbaum.

Moreland, R. L., Argote, L., & Krishnan, R. (1998). Training people to work in groups. In R. S. Tindale, J. E. Edwards, L. Heath, E. J. Posavac, F. B. Bryant, E. Henderson-King, Y. Suarez-Balcazar, & J. Myers (Eds.), *Social psychological applications to social issues: Applications of theory and research on groups* (Vol. 4, pp. 37–60). New York: Plenum Press.

Moreland, R. L., Hogg, M. A., & Hains, S. C. (1994). Back to the future: Social psychological research on groups. *Journal of Experimental Social Psychology, 30*, 527–555.

Moscovici, S. (1976). *Social influence and social change.* London: Academic Press.

Moscovici, S. (1984). The phenomenon of social representations. In R. M. Farr & S. Moscovici (Eds.), *Social representations* (pp. 3–69). Cambridge, UK: Cambridge University Press.

Myers, D. G., & Lamm, H. (1976). The group polarization phenomenon. *Psychological Bulletin, 83*, 602–627.

Nowak, A., & Latané, B. (1994). Simulating the emergence of social order from individual behaviour. In N. Gilbert & J. Doran (Eds.), *Simulating societies: The computer simulation of social phenomena* (pp. 63–84). London: University College London.

Nowak, A., Szamrej, J., & Latané, B. (1990). From private attitudes to public opinion: A dynamic theory of social impact. *Psychological Review, 97*, 362–376.

Oakes, P. J., Haslam, S. A., & Turner, J. C. (1994). *Stereotyping and social reality.* Oxford, UK: Blackwell.

Perterson, E., Mitchell, T., Thompson, L., & Burr, R. (in press). Group efficacy and shared cognition predict performance over time in work groups. *Group Processes and Intergroup Relations.*

Prussia, G. E., & Kinicki, A. J. (1996). A motivational investigation of group effectiveness using social-cognitive theory. *Journal of Applied Psychology, 81*, 187–198.

Rapoport, A., & Amaldoss, W. (1999). Social dilemmas embedded in between-group competitions: Effects on contest and distribution rules. In M. Foddy, M. Smithson, S. Schneider, & M. Hogg (Eds.), *Resolving social dilemmas: Dynamic, structural, and intergroup aspects* (pp. 67–86). Philadelphia, PA: Psychology Press.

Reicher, S. (2001). The psychology of crowd dynamics. In M. A. Hogg & S. Tindale (Eds.), *Blackwell handbook of social psychology: Group processes* (pp. 182–208). Oxford, UK: Blackwell.

Resnick, L., Levine, J., & Teasley, S. D. (Eds.). (1991). *Perspectives on socially shared cognitions.* Washington, DC: American Psychological Association.

Rouse, W. B., & Morris, N. M. (1986). On looking into the black box: Prospects and limits in the search for mental models. *Psychological Bulletin, 100*, 349–363.

Sawyer, J. E. (1997). *Information sharing and integration in multifunctional decision-making groups.* Paper presented at the Society of Judgment and Decision Making Annual Meeting, Philadelphia, PA.

Schopler, J., & Insko, C. A. (1992). The discontinuity effect: Generality and mediation. In W. Stroebe & M. Hewstone (Eds.), *European review of social psychology* (pp. 121–151). Chichester, UK: Wiley.

Sheffey, S., Tindale, R. S., & Scott, L. A. (1989). *Information sharing and group decision making.* Paper presented at the Midwestern Psychological Association Annual Convention, Chicago, IL.

Sherif, M. (1936). *The psychology of social norms.* New York: Harper & Brothers.

Smith, C. M., Dykema-Engblade, A., Walker, A., Niven, T. S., & McGrough, T. (in press). Asymmetrical social influence in freely interacting groups discussing the death penalty: A shared representations interpretation. *Group Processes and Intergroup Relations.*

Smith, C. M., Tindale, R. S., & Steiner, L. (1998). Investment decisions by individuals and groups in "Sunk Cost" situations: The potential impact of shared representations. *Group Processes and Intergroup Relations, 2*, 175–189.

Smoke, W. H., & Zajonc, R. B. (1962). On the reliability of group judgments and decisions. In J. Crisswell, H. Solomon, & P. Suppes (Eds.), *Mathematical methods in small group processes* (pp. 322–333). Stanford, CA: Stanford University Press.

Spink, K. S. (1990). Group cohesion and collective efficacy of volleyball teams. *Journal of Sport and Exercise Psychology, 12*, 310–311.

Stasser, G. (1999). The uncertain role of unshared information in collective choice. In L. L. Thompson, J. M. Levine, & D. M. Messick (Eds.), *Shared cognition in organizations: The management of knowledge* (pp. 49–70). Mahwah, NJ: Erlbaum.

Stasser, G., & Dietz-Uhler, B. (2001). Collective choice, judgment, and problem solving. In M. A. Hogg & S. Tindale (Eds.), *Blackwell handbook of social psychology: Group processes* (pp. 31–55). Oxford, UK: Blackwell.

Stasser, G., Kerr, N. L., & Davis, J. H. (1989). Influence processes and consensus models in decision-making groups. In P. Paulus (Ed.), *Psychology of group influence* (2nd Ed., pp. 279–326). Hillsdale, NJ: Erlbaum.

Stasser, G., & Stewart, D. D. (1992). Discovery of hidden profiles by decision-making groups: Solving a problem vs. making a judgment. *Journal of Personality and Social Psychology, 63,* 426–434.

Stasser, G., & Titus, W. (1985). Pooling of unshared information in group decision making: Biased information sampling during discussion. *Journal of Personality and Social Psychology, 48,* 1467–1478.

Stasser, G., & Titus, W. (1987). Effects of information load and percentage of shared information on the dissemination of unshared information during group discussion. *Journal of Personality and Social Psychology, 53,* 81–93.

Steiner, I. (1972). *Group process and productivity.* New York: Academic Press.

Steiner, I. (1974). Whatever happened to the group in social psychology? *Journal of Experimental Social Psychology, 10,* 1467–1478.

Steiner, I. (1986). Paradigms and groups. *Advances in Experimental Social Psychology, 19,* 539–548.

Stewart, D. D., & Stasser, G. (1995). Expert role assignment and information sampling during collective recall and decision making. *Journal of Personality and Social Psychology, 69,* 619–628.

Suls, J., & Wills, T. A. (Eds.). (1991). *Social comparison: Contemporary theory and research.* Hillsdale, NJ: Erlbaum.

Tajfel, H. (1970). Experiments in intergroup discrimination. *Scientific American, 223,* 96–102.

Tajfel, H. (1972). Social categorization. English manuscript of "La catégorisation sociale." In S. Moscovici (Ed.), *Introduction à la psychologie sociale* (Vol. 1, pp. 272–302). Paris: Larousse.

Tajfel, H. (Ed.). (1984). *The social dimension: European developments in social psychology.* Cambridge, UK: Cambridge University Press.

Tajfel, H., & Turner, J. C. (1979). An integrative theory of intergroup conflict. In W. G. Austin & S. Worchel (Eds.), *The social psychology of intergroup relations* (pp. 33–47). Monterey, CA: Brooks/Cole.

Thompson, L. (1997). *A look inside the mind of the negotiator.* Invited paper presented at the 96th Annual Meeting of the Midwestern Psychological Association, Chicago, IL.

Thompson, L. (1998). *The mind and heart of the negotiator.* Upper Saddle River, NJ: Prentice Hall.

Thompson, L., & Fine, G. A. (1999). Socially shared cognition, affect, and behavior: A review and integration. *Personality and Social Psychology Review, 3,* 278–302.

Thompson, L., Levine, J. M., & Messick, D. M. (Eds.). (1999). *Shared cognitions in organizations.* Mahwah, NJ: Erlbaum.

Tindale, R. S. (1989). Group vs. individual information processing: The effects of outcome feedback on decision-making. *Organizational Behavior and Human Decision Processes, 44,* 454–473.

Tindale, R. S. (1993). Decision errors made by individuals and groups. In N. Castellan, Jr., (Ed.), *Individual and group decision making: Current issues* (pp. 109–124). Hillsdale, NJ: Erlbaum.

Tindale, R. S., Anderson, E. M., Smith, C. M., Steiner, L., & Filkins, J. (1998). *Further explorations of conjunction errors by individuals and groups.* Paper presented at the British Psychological Society Social Psychology Section Conference, Canterbury, UK.

Tindale, R. S., & Davis, J. H. (1983). Group decision making and jury verdicts. In H. H. Blumberg, A. P. Hare, V. Kent, & M. F. Davies (Eds.), *Small groups and social interaction* (Vol. 2, pp. 9–38). Chichester, UK: Wiley.

Tindale, R. S., & Davis, J. H. (1985). Individual and group reward allocation decisions in two situational contexts: The effects of relative need and performance. *Journal of Personality and Social Psychology, 48*, 1148–1161.

Tindale, R. S., Davis, J. H., Vollrath, D. A., Nagao, D. H., & Hinsz, V. B. (1990). Asymmetrical social influence in freely interacting groups: A test of three models. *Journal of Personality and Social Psychology, 58*, 438–449.

Tindale, R. S., Filkins, J., Sheffey, S., & Nagao, D. H. (1997). *Group member perceptions of group decision processes.* Poster presented at the Society for Judgment and Decision Making Meetings, Philadelphia, PA.

Tindale, R. S., Filkins, J., Thomas, L. S., & Smith, C. M. (1993). *An attempt to reduce conjunction errors in decision-making groups.* Poster presented at the Society for Judgment and Decision Making Meeting, Washington, DC.

Tindale, R. S., & Kameda, T. (2000). "Social sharedness" as a unifying theme for information processing in groups. *Group Processes and Intergroup Relations, 3*, 123–140.

Tindale, R. S., & Sheffey, S. (1992). *Optimal task assignment and group memory.* Paper presented at the Nags Head Conference on Groups, Networks, and Organizations, Highland Beach, FL.

Tindale, R. S., Sheffey, S., & Filkins, J. (1990). *Conjunction errors by individuals and groups.* Paper presented at the Annual Meeting of the Society for Judgment and Decision Making, New Orleans, LA.

Tindale, R. S., Sheffey, S., & Scott, L. A. (1993). Framing and group decision making: Do cognitive changes parallel preference changes? *Organizational Behavior and Human Decision Processes, 55*, 470–485.

Tindale, R. S., Smith, C. M., Thomas, L. S., Filkins, J., & Sheffey, S. (1996). Shared representations and asymmetric social influence processes in small groups. In E. Witte & J. H. Davis (Eds.), *Understanding group behavior: Consensual action by small groups* (Vol. 1, pp. 81–103). Mahwah, NJ: Erlbaum.

Turner, J. C. (1975). Social comparison and social identity: Some prospects for intergroup behaviour. *European Journal of Social Psychology, 5*, 5–34.

Turner, J. C. (1982). Towards a cognitive redefinition of the social group. In H. Tajfel (Ed.), *Social identity and intergroup relations* (pp. 15–40). Cambridge, UK: Cambridge University Press.

Turner, J. C. (1985). Social categorization and the self-concept: A social cognitive theory of group behavior. In E. J. Lawler (Ed.), *Advances in group processes: Theory and research* (Vol. 2, pp. 518–538). Greenwich, CT: JAI Press.

Turner, J. C. (1991). *Social influence.* Milton Keynes, UK: Open University Press.

Turner, J. C., Hogg, M. A., Oakes, P. J., Reicher, S. D., & Wetherell, M. S. (1987). *Rediscovering the social group: A self-categorization theory.* Oxford, UK: Blackwell.

Tversky, A., & Kahneman, D. (1981). The framing of decisions and the psychology of choice. *Science, 211*, 453–458.

Vinokur, A., & Burnstein, E. (1974). The effects of partially shared persuasive arguments on group induced shifts: A group problem solving approach. *Journal of Personality and Social Psychology, 29*, 305–315.

Wegner, D. M. (1987). Transactive memory: A contemporary analysis of the group mind. In B. Mullen & G. R. Goethals (Eds.), *Theories of group behavior* (pp. 185–208). New York: Springer-Verlag.

Wegner, D. M. (1995). A computer network model of human transactive memory. *Social Cognition, 13*, 319–339.

Wegner, D. M., Erber, R., & Raymond, P. (1991). Transactive memory in close relationships. *Journal of Personality and Social Psychology, 61*, 923–929.

Weick, K. E. (1979). *The social psychology of organizing*. (2nd Ed.). Reading, MA: Addison-Wesley.

Weick, K. E., & Roberts, K. H. (1993). Collective minds in organizations: Heedful interrelating on flight decks. *Administrative Science Quarterly, 38*, 357–381.

Weiner, E. L., Kanki, B., & Helmreich, R. L. (1993). *Cockpit resource management*. San Diego, CA: Academic Press.

Winquist, J. R., & Larson, J. R. (1998). Information pooling: When it impacts group decision making. *Journal of Personality and Social Psychology, 74*, 371–377.

Wittenbaum, G. M., & Stasser, G. (1996). Management of information in small groups. In J. L. Nye & A. M. Brower (Eds.), *What's social about social cognition* (pp. 3–28). Thousand Oaks, CA: Sage.

CHAPTER THIRTEEN

Group Processes and the Construction of Social Representations

Fabio Lorenzi-Cioldi and Alain Clémence

Social representations can be defined as commonsense knowledge about general topics (e.g., AIDS, computers, gender, health, intelligence, psychoanalysis, work) that are the focus of everyday conversation. The theory of social representations, originally developed by Serge Moscovici (1961/1976) on the basis of interdisciplinary and historical analyses, built on the premise that people use more than one mode of reasoning. This premise has its roots in Emile Durkheim's (1912/1995) important distinction between collective and individual representation. For Durkheim, individual representations were internal states that might not be shared with other people. In order for them to be communicated they had to be transformed into thoughts (words, images, and symbols) by the collectivity.

When the anthropologist Lévy-Bruhl (1925/1926) examined material collected from what he called "primitive" cultures, he used the notion of collective representations to distinguish between two modes of thinking: a rational one, typical of "civilized" cultures, and a "mystic" one, typical of "primitive" cultures. This distinction was also expressed by Piaget (e.g., 1932) when he characterized childish operative thinking and adult formal thinking. Whereas for Piaget the latter gradually replaces the former during the course of cognitive development, for Moscovici adults continue to reason in a childish way (mystic, representative), even if their thoughts are based on formal, rational, or logical principles (Moscovici, 1981). In everyday life, various kinds of constraints can lead us to make decisions or adopt positions without following logical rules. For a layperson, the content of thought becomes central in the organization of knowledge, while formal procedures are privileged in scientific thinking (Clémence & Doise, 1995; Moscovici & Hewstone, 1983). The general theoretical stance taken by social representations theory is grounded in this proposition (see Doise, 1990; Purkhardt, 1995; for critical discussions).

In this chapter, we describe a perspective based on social representations theory to analyze commonsense knowledge and group processes. By stressing both the social specificity of everyday thinking and the influence of scientific thinking upon it, social representations return to the central core of social psychology. First, we outline the present state of the theory of social representations. Particular attention is devoted to the anchoring process,

which is illustrated by research on rumor, in order to understand the diffusion of information among social groups. We then discuss the concept of group, by contrasting the social
cognition and the social representation approaches. By focusing on groups' social position
relative to other groups, we show how groups generate different social representations
of themselves and of the world. Gender and health are discussed as illustrations of these
processes.

A Dynamic Approach to the Processing of Meanings

Thinking in everyday life is oriented by the need to resolve abstract and/or obscure questions: How intelligent is my child? What are the origins of AIDS? Why are some people
more violent than others? To answer such questions, we rely on the way in which intelligence, the origins of AIDS, or violence are defined and discussed. Particularly, we rely on the
knowledge exchanged and shared around us in the groups in which we are embedded. We
can, of course, adopt an original position, but even then we have to refer it to common
points of reference, that constitute the shared knowledge environment within which we exist.
To understand this process, we need to understand the way in which reasoning is based in
cognitive functioning (categorization, inferences, etc.). However, it is probably more important to know how and why we give specific significance to some information relative to other
information. Cognitive processes are controlled and oriented by what Moscovici (1961/
1976) has called the normative meta-system, which operates through two sociocognitive
dynamics: objectification and anchoring.

Social orientations toward shared meanings

Objectification refers to the process of transforming abstract information into concrete knowledge, through communication. This process produces figurative, metaphorical, or symbolic
meanings, that become shared reference points for a specific domain. There is some debate
over the content and structure of these lay theories. The structural approach emphasizes the
idea that the content of a social representation is organized around a central nucleus composed
of a few consensual meanings (see Abric, 1984; Augoustinos & Innes, 1990), whereas the
dynamic approach maintains that social representations comprise different, contrasted
kinds of meanings, and that people's knowledge is made up of this network of variations
(see Doise, Clémence, & Lorenzi-Cioldi, 1993). However, both approaches have clearly
demonstrated the power of the process of objectification in transforming information which
is diffused in society. Other theoretical perspectives support this analysis (see Hardin &
Higgins, 1996; Levine, Resnick, & Higgins, 1993, on shared cognition, or the theory of the
epidemic diffusion of ideas documented by Sperber, 1990). The objectification process is
relatively well developed (see Flick, 1995; Jodelet, 1989; Markova & Farr, 1995; Wagner,
Elejabarrieta, & Lahnsteiner, 1995); therefore, in this chapter, we focus on and develop the
anchoring process.

Because social representations are elaborated through debate, different points of view
emerge during the transformation of abstract information into concrete meanings. Divergent

positions are publicly expressed by people who belong to different groups – groups which actively attempt to define abstract information from their own distinctive points of view. Individuals use normative rules grounded in the ideas, values, or beliefs of their own groups, to analyze ambiguous or mysterious aspects of changing lay theories – their thinking is anchored in, or positioned by, the perspective of their own group. This raises the question of precisely how positional differences among individuals are organized by variations between individuals and between the normative rules of different groups (Doise, Clémence, & Lorenzi-Cioldi, 1993). We argue that the social representations approach makes it possible to predict the sorts of inferences that people make, in ways that go beyond that offered by more purely formal (cognitive) analyses (see also Billig, 1985).

In contrast to early "normative" approaches to social cognition (e.g., Nisbett & Ross, 1980), social representations should not be considered to be false, weak, biased, or deficient forms of knowledge (see Bauer & Gaskell, 1999). More recent "pragmatic" approaches to social cognition may emphasize the functionality of commonsense representations in everyday life (Fiske, 1992; Fiske & Leyens, 1996), but still they tend to separate the personal and the social levels of analyses. In contrast, the social representations approach focuses precisely on the link between personal and social levels of analysis. Identities, attitudes, and attributions become expressions of specific social representations. As Moscovici (1998) puts it:

> Contrary to scientific and ideological representations, constructed following the demands of formal logic on the basis of fundamental terms all perfectly defined, [. . .], the representations of common sense are, in one or another, "cross-bred". That is to say that ideas, linguistic expressions, explanations of different origins are aggregated, combined, and regularized more or less like several sciences in a single hybrid science, like several idioms in a créole language. (p. 238)

Let us start with a discussion of the way the social representations approach tackles the phenomenon of rumors.

Rumors as an Anchoring Process

Consider the information below, which was run as a headline by the German newspaper *Kölnische Zeitung* when the German army captured the Belgian city of Antwerp in 1914 (Kapferer, 1987, pp. 52–53).

> With the advertisement of the capture of Antwerp, one made sound the bells.

This same event was heralded by a French newspaper *Le Matin* as: "According to the *Kölnische Zeitung*, the clergy of Antwerp was obliged to ring the bells when the fortress was captured." The English *Times* reported: "According to *Le Matin*, Belgian priests who refused to ring the bells after the capture of Antwerp were deprived of their offices," and the Italian *Corriere della Sera* reported: "According to the *Times*, the unfortunate priests who refused to ring the bells after the capture of Antwerp were sentenced to hard labor." Finally, *Le Matin* revisited the event, reporting: "According to the *Corriere della Sera*, it is confirmed that the barbarian conquerors of Antwerp have punished the unfortunate priests, who heroically refused to ring the bells, by hanging them on the bells, the head down."

This sort of transformation can quite easily be analyzed from a cognitive perspective. The initial information itself was ambiguous (where were the bells ringing?) and required more complete interpretation. To disambiguate the information people relied on knowledge stored in memory, in this case easily accessed and quickly retrieved stereotypical information about German troops. Consequently, new information was reinterpreted in the context of prior stereotypical knowledge with the result that the original stereotype may have been confirmed and strengthened (Sherman, Judd, & Park, 1989).

However, there is an inconsistency inherent to this line of reasoning. The notion of stereotypes assumes that, in 1914, French people shared the same representation of German troops. But we also assume that individuals differ in their representations. From a social cognition perspective this inconsistency is resolved by contrasting general beliefs with individual motives, knowledge, expertise, and so forth. Specifically, the meaning given to new information depends on the content and structure of prior knowledge. For instance, Vallone, Ross, and Lepper (1985) showed that individuals interpret media coverage of an issue on which they are strongly committed as biased against their own position. Fiske, Kinder, and Larter (1983) demonstrated that the use of prior knowledge to interpret information in a political arena depends on the expertise of the individual. Devine (1989) based her approach to stereotyping on the struggle between automatically activated stereotypes and personal beliefs (see Abelson, 1994, for a general discussion of these two coacting systems).

Automatic thinking appears to refer to public opinion or to consensual belief (a stereotype is easily accessible for everybody), whereas controlled thinking refers to individual variations and dissension (some people express a position against, and others in support of, the stereotype). Furthermore, some stereotypes are more automatic than other ones, and the strength of dissension differs according to the content under scrutiny. If the cognitive approach offers a powerful understanding of how people think about a problem, it neglects to explain why people consider the problem in the first place.

Emergence of different meanings

The social-communicative process associated with meaning transformation resembles that associated with the development and promulgation of rumors. The classic analysis of rumor conducted by Rosnow and his colleagues (Esposito & Rosnow, 1984; Rosnow, 1980, 1988; Rosnow, Esposito, & Gibney, 1988) is mainly concerned with the effects of personality traits (anxiety and uncertainty) and of message characteristic (ambiguity) on rumor circulation. The social representations approach deals not only with how information circulates and changes, but also with why this information itself interests people.

Representative thinking is based more on the specific content of the information than on format processes. Transformation of information depends primarily on the normative meta-system of a social context (often reduced to a question of relevance – see Sperber & Wilson,

1986), and variations between individuals in the meaning given to the information depend primarily on the normative principles adopted by specific groups.

Consider once again the announcement by the *Kölnische Zeitung* (see above). If the normative context is not given, we are unable to understand why the information was consensually interpreted by the French, Italian, and English media as reporting a barbarian action by the conquering Germans. The ambiguity of the information could have been resolved in many other ways and there is no reason why the French, Italian, and English media should necessarily have been in agreement. The specific outcome can only be predicted from knowledge of the wider historical context of the outbreak of World War I, in which relatively widely shared negative stereotypes of Germans had developed through widespread and heated debate about relations with Germany.

More generally, the emergence and diffusion of a rumor depends first on the need to understand an issue that has no clear and consensual meaning. If the issue becomes a focus of public debate, different groups propound different interpretations, and a process of normalization occurs (e.g., Moscovici, 1976; Sherif, 1936). The normalization process is not, however, a straightforward averaging process in which a compromise among divergent positions is reached. Groups vary in status, power, prestige, and so forth, and thus to the extent that a particular interpretation is closely associated with a particular group, marginalized groups (minorities) will have relatively little impact on the final representation – people would not want to become assimilated to a minority position through incorporation of minority perspectives (see Moscovici, 1980; Mugny & Perez, 1991; also Martin & Hewstone, 2001). However, ideas are very often dissociated from their authors, and thus their group origins, during their circulation in the sphere of public debate. Thus, group identity influences can often be weak, and what really matters in the construction of a shared representation is the content of the information itself.

The case of AIDS offers a good example of the construction of a social representation (see Herzlich & Pierret, 1988; Markova, 1992). The public diffusion of medical information about AIDS, allowed people to acquire new knowledge about AIDS and engendered substantial public debate about what was considered a strange and frightening disease. Different groups integrated medical information into their general theories. For instance some Catholic communities developed the idea that AIDS was a divine punishment for sexual promiscuity and drug abuse. Other people, at least in Western countries, gradually acquired new knowledge about the means of transmission of the disease. However, this scientific knowledge, that was now widely shared among laypeople, did not explain how the HIV virus responsible for AIDS emerged in the first place. Different groups used this information in different ways, depending on their ideological perspective, to answer this question. Extreme right-wing groups anchored scientific information in racist beliefs by claiming that the first cases of AIDS were observed in Africa. They believed that the disease was introduced to humans through Africans having sexual relations with monkeys that were contaminated by the virus. Another explanation was framed by Soviet propaganda and diffused among groups with a broadly anti-US socio-political agenda. Citing alleged experimental research conducted by scientists linked to the American government, members of these groups were convinced that the virus was produced in the laboratories of the CIA to contain demographic expansion in developing countries (see Grmek, 1990; Sontag, 1989). These two "theories" appeared at the beginning of the 1980s, shortly after the initial spread of the virus and of information about the virus. However, these "theories" continued to be publicly debated, long after the identity of their authors had faded. The disembodiment of these ideas, their dissociation from their group and ideological origins, would be expected to make them appear to many people to be more respectable and more worthy of serious consideration in making sense of AIDS.

Some support for this analysis comes from research conducted in Lausanne, a medium-size city in Switzerland (Clémence, 1997). Forty-one women and thirty-two men (mostly students) responded to a questionnaire measuring their knowledge about AIDS. Participants briefly described different aspects of AIDS, explained what they thought were the origins of the disease, and answered questions about HIV transmission and the fight against AIDS. Participants displayed appropriate knowledge about AIDS: 71% excluded all inappropriate risks of contagion (saliva, kissing, insect bites, sharing the same glass, sweat, sharing a swimming-pool, and shaking hands); 60% translated the AIDS acronym correctly; 96% strongly opposed the idea that AIDS was a divine punishment; and 72% expressed extreme sympathy with AIDS sufferers. Responses to the open-ended question about the origins of HIV offer more intriguing results. Responses were easily classified into three types of explanations: Two explanations corresponded to the "monkey" and the "laboratory" interpretations mentioned above, and the third was related to the idea of cleanliness. More complex and scientific explanations (e.g., virus mutation, alteration of the immune system) were grouped together.

As Figure 13.1 shows, a significant number of participants gave both the "monkey" and the "laboratory" explanations. These responses were not related to the educational level, age, or religion of the participants. The "hygiene" explanation was almost exclusively given by women (9 women, 1 man). The use of these explanations was, however, related to knowledge of the AIDS acronym. Specifically, participants who did not provide the correct translation

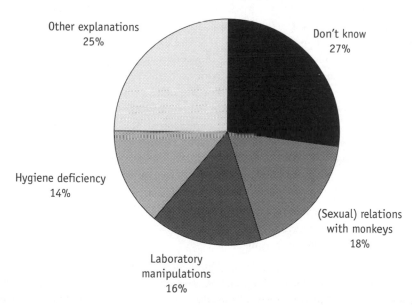

Figure 13.1. Explanations of the origins of AIDS.

of the AIDS acronym tended to adopt one of the three "rumors" (monkey, laboratory, hygiene) about the origins of AIDS. Moreover, those who cited the "monkey" explanation stressed the risk of being contaminated by saliva.

This study illustrates how minorities' speculations, that are in public circulation but are unattributed to their minority group origin, can influence common knowledge. It suggests that the efficiency of the anchoring process depends, at least in part, on the prior knowledge people have of a specific issue. Research on human inference has well documented the formal and pragmatic way in which individuals use prior knowledge to interpret or create new data (e.g., Hastie, 1983; Snyder, 1981). What is underlined here is the fact that such knowledge can protect us from the acceptance of new explanations (see McLeod, Pan, & Rusinski, 1995). However, we did not have the opportunity in this study to investigate why some participants were influenced by the "monkey" or the "laboratory" explanations. We need to go further, to examine how pre-existing beliefs orient the anchoring of new theories.

Alteration of meanings by groups

The anchoring process explains how groups with different belief systems arrive at different everyday explanations for threatening events of which the origins are unknown, obscure, or ambiguous. Consider, for instance, the Martian invasion of Earth reported by Orson Welles in a radio broadcast on October 30, 1938 (part of a dramatization of H. G. Wells's *War of the Worlds*). Listeners who were persuaded by this highly realistic broadcast were members of groups for whom such an invasion would fit well with their social representations. For members of closed religious communities, the invasion was interpreted as a sign of the end of the world; for patriots sensitive to military conflicts, it was an attack by a powerful foreign country; for anti-science movements, it was a catastrophic result of mysterious experimental research (Cantril, Gaudet, & Herzog, 1940).

In their classic research on rumor, Allport and Postman (1947) defined rumor as the alteration of a piece of information, resulting in a completely new signification. Their results suggested greater alteration when the information conflicted with beliefs to which a large group of people were strongly committed. For instance, participants made quite dramatic racial stereotype-consistent interpretive errors when information was actually stereotype-inconsistent – a flick-knife held by an elderly white woman was almost unanimously recalled as being held by a young black man. Subsequent research by Treadway and McCloskey (1989) has shown how a changed normative environment (since the mid-1940s) has reduced the tendency for participants to make such racially stereotypical recall errors. We suggest that this is evidence for anchoring rather than for social desirability effects.

Results of an experiment conducted by Rouquette (1975) illustrate how alteration is oriented by group beliefs. Using Allport and Postman's procedure, Rouquette transmitted a message to psychology students, stating that:

> A study conducted during June, 1973, showed that students who had received good marks in mathematics achieved higher final results in psychology. The study also revealed that more than 87% of young psychologists regretted having not had sufficient mathematical training.

Table 13.1. Transformation of a Message during Transmission: Final Statements of Chains According to the Attitude Position of the Participants in the Chain

Attitudes toward mathematics in psychology Positive	Negative
A study was done in June, 1973. Geography students are better at mathematics than psychology students. One possibility is that psychology students have been taught badly.	A study was performed among students on mathematics. One observed that they had better results.
There is a relation between success in mathematics and in psychology. 90% of people complain that they find it impossible to achieve success.	A study conducted in 1970 among psychology students showed that they do not want to be taught maths. 80% said that the lack of maths does not hinder their work.
It has been established that a math student is successful in psychology; it has been established that a math student is good at teaching; it has been established that a math student is good at mathematics.	A study was done in 1974 on the importance of mathematics in psychology. The aim of the study was to minimize the importance of mathematics.

Note: Adapted from Rouquette (1975, pp. 116–124).

Participants were classified on the basis of their attitudes toward the role of mathematics in psychology. Chains of five students were constructed: Half comprised students with a positive attitude toward mathematics in psychology (positive chains), and half comprised students with a negative attitude (negative chains). Participants were shown all stages of the progression of the message for each of the types of chain, and were asked to give a final interpretive statement.

Final statements (see Table 13. 1) show how the message was transformed in order to be anchored in participants' attitude toward mathematics. Those who expressed a positive attitude toward mathematics underlined the flawed training of psychology students and/or the good results of mathematics students; those who had a negative attitude toward mathematics in psychology stressed that psychology students did not want mathematics to form part of their education.

Rumor diffusion is linked to group cohesiveness, particularly to the extent to which people feel that their membership status is threatened (Miller, 1991). The diffusion of unverified information that originates in high credibility sources such as leaders (Kapferer, 1987) is often, therefore, regulated by the group's more marginal members. For these marginal members, the anchoring of beliefs in previous thinking is facilitated by a strong desire to belong and re-establish their membership credentials, and thus strong adherence to the group's normative attitudes – the classic case of zealotry or neophytism. Several studies corroborate this general process. For example, classical stories based on a supposed dreadful action by a stranger (kidnapping of young women by Jewish tradesmen, death of a child as a result of poison introduced into supermarket food by gypsies, etc.) are more strongly endorsed by more marginalized members of the community, such as elderly women or mothers at home with young children (Morin, 1969; Walker & Blaine, 1991). These observations raise the question of what function social representations may play in the construction of groups, and in interaction between groups.

The Construction of Groups by Social Representations

Doise (1972) has developed a dynamic model of group relationships based on the critical role played in intergroup relations by social representations of other groups, outgroups. Doise argued that all encounters with outgroups, and thus all intergroup behavior, must be based on some meaningful representation of the nature of the outgroup that allows one to predict and plan action. Because both groups often have no choice other than to follow their outgroup orientation (e.g., to cooperate or to fight), the representation of the other group usually closely fits its behavior. Anticipated intergroup definitions are consolidated because they are successfully tested during encounters (see also Abric & Kahan, 1972). Such a dynamic suggests that social representations are closely articulated with the construction of groups' identities.

Groups as social representations

Among different studies dealing with the construction of group identity and social representations (e.g., Breakwell, 1993; De Paolis, 1990; Elejabarrieta, 1994; Jodelet, 1991), Duveen and Lloyd have developed a genetic approach to social representations in order to account for the social construction of gender (1986; Lloyd, 1987; Lloyd & Duveen, 1990). For Duveen and Lloyd, social representations are generated and transformed by three types of processes:

> There are processes of *sociogenesis*, which concerns the construction and transformation of the social representations of social groups about specific objects, *ontogenesis*, which concerns the development of individuals in relation to social representations, and *microgenesis*, which concerns the evocation of social representations in social interaction. (Duveen & Lloyd, 1990, p. 6)

The authors have examined how children adopt, and participate in, the social representation of gender. Infants are born into a world in which gender differentiation is highly structured. Although biological characteristics are used by others to assign infants to a gender group, these characteristics initially have no gender signification for infants themselves. The same is true for the environment around them, where many objects (e.g., toys, clothes) are socially marked (De Paolis, Doise, & Mugny, 1987; Doise & Mugny, 1984) in the sense that they are connected with gender relations. Young children form relationships with objects and people, organized by the social representation of gender. They gradually discover the gender meanings and orient their activity in a manner congruent with a gender category. This ontogenetic process leads children to adopt the meanings of the gender categories and then to participate in their further elaboration. The differentiation between gender groups begins with knowledge of a common sign system furnished by the social representation of gender.

Chombart de Lauwe (1971, 1984; Chombart de Lauwe & Bellan, 1979) has analyzed material to support the view that childhood is a social representation constructed by adults. Adults create a common image of "childhood" on the basis of a selective transformation of their own memories, discussion with other adults, and, particularly over the last century, the incorporation of experts' views. This image is subject to change – for instance it has evolved from a "submissive child" model toward a more "autonomous person" model. Probably, for our purpose, the more interesting question is how do children interpret the models that adults present to them. Chombart de Lauwe and her colleagues suggest that children pursue two mixed goals: education and entertainment. First, children distil a limited number of simple prototypes of "heroes" or champions, for example the masculine adventurer, out of a large array of different and complex characters they encounter. Then, they social contextually anchor their heroes, by selecting models that are adjusted to their own social reality and by adding some of their own characteristics to the model. Thus, social reality constraints would generally make it difficult for girls, but easy for boys, to base their self-concept or identity on a masculine adventurer prototype.

The research by Chombart de Lauwe and Bellan illustrates how, through an anchoring process, a social representation generated by an outgroup (adults) organizes the construction of a social group (childhood) and contributes to the differentiation of subgroups (masculine and feminine childhood). The analysis of groups as social representations seems to offer a means of understanding how the content of social categories is elaborated. We now turn our attention to this question.

Mental and Social Representations of Groups

We have argued that the anchoring process depends primarily on group norms. However, group norms do not exclusively originate in the group member's activities, interactions, and thoughts within an ingroup frame of reference. Relations between groups have a critical impact. Groups are located in a network of intergroup relations that cause groups to vary quite dramatically in terms of their prestige, status, and power (see Hogg, 2001). This social positioning of a group with respect to all other groups has important consequences for the production of social representations. In this section, we discuss how the social positioning of groups impacts people's mental representations of groups and group membership.

Modern conceptions of category structure depart resolutely from an "all-or-none" Aristo-telian conception of group membership. Instead, categories are now thought to be structured around prototypes so that a cluster of modal or salient attributes determine inclusion in a group (e.g., Rosch, 1981). The group's members are distributed around these typical features. Since each individual's characteristics match the prototype to a differing extent, a certain amount of within-group heterogeneity or variability arises from comparisons between group members: not all category members are entitled to be members of the category to the same degree. As a result, groups are distinguished one from another by fuzzy boundaries.

Even greater intracategory heterogeneity is granted by recent exemplar-based models, in which a mental representation of a group need not include abstract features or summary judgments about shared or modal characteristics. Social categories consist of a number of particular instances or exemplars drawn from personal contacts, learned from the media, and so forth. Group membership is not abstracted at the time group members are encountered, but is computed later on by taking into account the whole set of known group members.

These mental representations of category membership have various psychological implications. The most important one, in the present context, is that exemplar-based representations of groups are internally more differentiated and varied than prototype-based representations, which, in turn, are more internally differentiated than Aristotelian-based representations (Linville, Fischer, & Salovey, 1989; Park & Hastie, 1987; Park, Judd, & Ryan, 1991). Whereas the Aristotelian approach advocates group members' homogeneity and interchangeability within the group, the prototype approach, and more so the exemplar approach, allow greater intragroup heterogeneity. For the prototype model, for instance, group membership expresses itself in degrees of discrepancy between the prototype – an ideal and not necessarily real member – and the various individuals, who are also potential members of other neighboring categories. The prototype approach has recently been applied by social identity theorists to analyze social-identity contingent structural differentiation, and concomitant behaviors, within groups (see Hogg, 1996, 2001).

From the standpoint of social representations theory, the question becomes how does the social position of a group provide content to these mental representations in everyday thinking. As one of us has quite extensively shown, a crucial moderator of content is the perceived social status of the target individual (either oneself or another person) to whom the category applies (Lorenzi-Cioldi, 1988; Lorenzi-Cioldi & Doise, 1990). Experimental and correlational data suggest that people elaborate different mental representations of a group according to the socio-structural position of the group. Members of subordinate groups often conceive of themselves and fellow ingroup members as interchangeable persons, that is, as *aggregates*. Their personal features derive to a large extent from features that are ascribed to their group as a whole. In contrast, members of dominant groups tend to conceive of themselves as a gathering of individuals endowed with a fair amount of uniqueness and interpersonal distinctiveness, that is, as a *collection* (cf. Boltanski, 1984; Bourdieu & de Saint Martin, 1978). Their identity is derived to a large extent from outside the group.

Collection and aggregate groups epitomize two opposing modalities of group membership. In an aggregate group, the emerging categorization model is Aristotelian, at best prototype-based: group members tend to possess all of the attributes that define the group at an abstract level. Conversely, in a collection group the model is exemplar-based, sometimes a mixture of exemplars and prototypes: each member endorses more or less strongly a subset of his or her group's attributes, or else, the group is made up of a juxtaposition of prominent instances. The group's features are then occasionally abstracted from consideration of the whole set of group members. (Note that Mullen, 1991, likewise, points to a tendency for individuals to apply different mental representations to groups differing by their size; that is, exemplar representations to majorities, and prototype representations to minorities.)

This distinction between social representations of dominant and subordinate groups has received significant empirical support (for a review, see Lorenzi-Cioldi, 1998). The important point here is that seemingly universal, antagonistic, and mutually exclusive mental representations of a group, such as those invoked by the Aristotelian, prototype, and exemplar-based approaches, become concurrent and compatible to a significant degree by taking into account the social positioning of perceivers and target group members.

The following sections show how social representations theory helps explain the emergence of these contrasting group representations.

Shared and group representations

Research in social and cultural psychology has documented that Western societies value social representations of the individual that stress "individualism"; that is, an individual's autonomy, freedom, and separateness with respect to other people (e.g., Lee & Ottati, 1993; Markus & Kitayama, 1991; Sampson, 1993). However, people with power and status have been found to personify more closely this culturally valued orientation (Guillaumin, 1972; see also Apfelbaum, 1979; Deschamps, 1982). Their self-representations match to a larger extent the culturally shared representation of an autonomous individual than do the self-representations of people with less power and status. They also come to define themselves mainly as "unique individuals," whose group membership makes only a minor contribution to their self-concept (i.e., the collection group). Less powerful and lower status individuals match the cultural norm less closely, and consequently they come to define themselves in terms of attributes which are associated with their group label as a whole (i.e., the aggregate group) (Lorenzi-Cioldi, 1998).

Research on sex-role stereotypes has demonstrated marked differences between men's and women's social representations of group membership, with respect to both content and structure. Studies conducted during the 1960s showed that descriptions of "men in general" matched closely those of "adult healthy persons" (sex unspecified), whereas descriptions of women comprised more group-specific characteristics (i.e., more relational and expressive characteristics; cf. Broverman, Vogel, Broverman, Clarkson, & Rosenkrantz, 1972; Hamilton, 1991; Lorenzi-Cioldi, 1988). Correlational research further reveals that such differences are not specific to gender. Questionnaire data gathered by Jackman and Senters (1980), for instance, showed a common tendency for women, African Americans, and low-SES group members, to perceive the social structure in categorical terms, and a tendency for the corresponding outgroup members to perceive it in more personalistic terms. Lorenzi-Cioldi and Joye (1988) used unobtrusive measures (sorting a large array of occupational labels) to demonstrate an analogous tendency among people with low socio-economic status or who came from impoverished cultural backgrounds. These people showed a pronounced tendency to sort the labels according to exclusive (i.e., bipolar) contrasts that uncovered stark status oppositions (e.g., blue vs. white collars, low-paid female vs. well-paid male occupations). Research on spontaneous self-perception (e.g., using the *Who-am-I?* test) has shown that less privileged group members are more likely than corresponding outgroup members to describe themselves in holistic and depersonalizing terms, especially ones that invoke relevant group labels (e.g., McGuire, 1984). This trend has been observed for a variety of asymmetrical group memberships, based on education (Deschamps, Lorenzi-Cioldi, & Meyer, 1982), ethnicity (Lorenzi-Cioldi & Meyer, 1984), and gender (Lorenzi-Cioldi, 1994).

This literature suggests that a shared social representation of the autonomous person is differently activated among different groups of people. By taking into account properties of social structure, one is able to predict that members of subordinate groups will attenuate their uniqueness (a tendency that emphasizes their collective identity), whereas members of dominant groups will accentuate their personal distinctiveness (a tendency that emphasizes their personal identity). We can now extend Markus and Kitayama's claim that "The notion of the autonomous individual in continuous tension with the external collective is 'natural' only from a particular cultural perspective" (1994, p. 570), to suggest that the poles of this tension, that is the individual and the collective, are likely to be represented in Western cultures by groups differing in social status. Only dominant group members are perceived as a gathering of individuals with more or less diverse characteristics (Lorenzi-Cioldi & Doise, 1990).

A series of studies was conducted to illustrate this idea (Lorenzi-Cioldi & Dafflon, 1998, in preparation). Specifically, these studies aimed at demonstrating that people, whatever their group membership, endorse to some extent representational content relating both to individual autonomy and uniqueness and to individual interdependence (i.e., individualistic vs. collectivistic representations for dominants and subordinates, respectively). To operationalize status differentials we used gender categories. The assumption that men have higher status and greater power than women is central to many social psychological analyses of gender stereotypes and behavioral differences between the sexes (e.g., Eagly, 1987; Ridgeway & Diekema, 1992; see Ridgeway, 2001). Although people in Western societies value individualism and independence, women are concurrently portrayed as having more relational, communal, and connected self and ingroup representations than men (Gilligan, 1982; Harding, 1986; Markus & Oyserman, 1989). Thus, men and women differ as groups regarding the proximity of their ingroup representations to the shared cultural representation: men match it more closely than women (Eagly & Mladinic, 1989; Kashima, Yamagushi, Kim, Choi, Gelfand, & Yuki, 1995). We therefore predicted that autonomy and independence would be more strongly endorsed by people to describe Western than non-Western cultures, and to describe men, and "persons in general," than women. Descriptions of women would embody average levels of both the shared (individual) and the ingroup (collective) descriptors.

To measure endorsement of the shared social representation of the autonomous person, participants rated their own culture (Occidentals in general) and the corresponding outgroup culture (Orientals in general). A symmetrical pattern of perceptions was hypothesized, with Occidentals being perceived to have higher levels of independence than interdependence, and Orientals higher levels of interdependence than independence. Gender was then used to distinguish between ingroup and outgroup perceptions within Western culture. Based on the assumption of gender status differentials, the shared dominant representation of the autonomous individual and the respective ingroup representations would coincide for judgments about male targets, and would conflict for judgments about female targets. Participants were thus expected to make stronger use of contents related to independence to characterize people in general and male targets, than female targets. For the latter, average levels of both independence and interdependence were expected. Accordingly, judgments of Occidental culture itself were expected to match those of people in general as well as male targets, while judgments of Oriental culture were not expected to match either those of people in general or those of female targets. Indeed, different cultures are likely to be judged by different standards (a social representation of individual autonomy for Occidentals, and a social representation of individual connectedness for Orientals), whereas men and women within Western culture should be judged in terms of both the shared cultural and the respective ingroup social representations.

Male and female Swiss participants were asked to judge the social desirability of various styles of behavior, by applying them to people in general, to men and women, to Occidentals and Orientals, and to the self (judgments about gender and cultural groups were collected in between-participants designs). Two styles of behavior with contrasting evaluative tones represented each social representation – the *individual* representation was operationalized by "independent" (positive tone) and "individualistic" (negative tone); the *collective* by "collectivistic" (positive) and "follower" (negative). Of particular interest here are the results concerning the ascription of each of the two representations (individual and collective, regardless of valence) to the sex-unspecified target, the gendered targets, and the cultural targets.

As predicted, "people in general" were described more in line with the individual than the collective representation, judgments of "men in general" closely paralleled those of "people in general," and self-descriptions showed that male and female participants perceived themselves similarly to their gender ingroup. Only men firmly described themselves in terms of the individual representation – women attributed to themselves intermediate levels of both the individual and the collective representations. As predicted, "Occidentals in general" were resolutely described by means of the individual norm, and "Orientals in general" were resolutely described by means of the collective representation.

Generally, the results point to a striking similarity between social representations of male targets, Occidental targets, and sex-unspecified persons (as well as men's self), and to a lack of similarity between perceptions of men and women. Social representations of female targets (as well as women's self) matched neither those of Occidentals and men, nor those of Orientals. These results lend provisional support to the conjecture that in Western cultures, where the dominant social representation refers to a self-contained person, only those who are likely to have more power and status, that is, men, are fully identified with this content. This shared social representation was attributed to a lesser extent to female targets, who were also equally well characterized in terms of the ingroup collective representation.

So far we have illustrated the process by which men and women come to be differentiated from one another, as a result of differential proximity to a shared social and cultural representation that emphasizes and values individual independence and autonomy. We now consider how more individualistic versus group-oriented self-representations are enacted by men and women.

Social Representations in Intergroup Contexts

As a consequence of the greater salience of group-defining features for subordinate relative to dominant group members, it is likely that self-representations of subordinate group members are more deeply embedded in ingroup–outgroup comparison than self-representations of dominant group members. Dominant group members are more likely to focus on interpersonal comparisons.

Gendered self-representations

Bem's (1981, 1993) gender-schema theory provides a basis for testing this idea. According to Bem, gender-schematic individuals display a readiness to organize information about themselves and other people in terms of a dichotomous male–female (ingroup–outgroup) categorization, in which masculine and feminine attributes (i.e., culturally shared social representations of masculinity and femininity) represent opposing ends of a single continuum. Gender-schema theory predicts individual differences in the use of gender to organize incoming information. In contrast, social representations theory predicts group differences in the use of gender schemas. Specifically, by virtue of their differential placement in the social structure (either "objective" or symbolic), women should display more gender-schematic perceptions than men.

This hypothesis was tested in an experiment using unobtrusive procedures to measure men's and women's self-descriptions on a series of masculine, feminine, and neutral attributes (Lorenzi-Cioldi, 1991). It was possible to compare the average latency of responses to schema-consistent information (i.e., acceptance of ingroup attributes and rejection of outgroup attributes) to the average latency of responses to schema-inconsistent information (acceptance of outgroup attributes and rejection of ingroup attributes). Gender-schema theory would predict that people make use of a gender-schema insofar as they process consistent information faster than inconsistent information. Consistent with social representation theory, the results revealed that it was women who behaved in a more gender schematic manner – they processed consistent information faster than inconsistent information. Men showed no differential processing of consistent versus inconsistent information.

Support for the differential salience of gender categorization also comes from other experiments, using a variety of procedures. For instance, Hurtig and Pichevin (1990; Pichevin & Hurtig, 1996) demonstrated the effectiveness of various moderators (numerical ratio of the sexes, dimensions of intergroup comparisons, and primes) to alter the perceptual salience of male but not female sex-membership. The latter remained highly accessible and thus readily available to all participants irrespective of their sex and of the context's characteristics.

Social representations and health

Research in health psychology provides other illustrations of the impact of an intergroup context on the construction of social representations. This research often rests on a pessimistic appraisal of people's current behavioral practices (Salovey, Rothman, & Rodin, 1998; Taylor, 1990). Medical statistics show that people often adopt behavioral practices that are detrimental to their health (drug abuse and cigarette smoking, inappropriate eating habits, etc.). Various cognitive models have been elaborated in order to promote beneficial health habits (e.g., Rothman & Salovey, 1997). However, the standard against which healthy versus unhealthy behavior is assessed, an implicit social representation of an ideal pattern of healthy behaviors, is rarely questioned. Surveys show that most of the attitudes and behaviors that promote healthiness are positively correlated with social status – lower status people tend to engage in an array of unhealthy behaviors that they often value because they are behaviors that promote collective socializing practices and activities within their group (e.g., Bourdieu, 1979). Yet, health-promotion programs are most often based on a de-contextualized representation of the risk factors involved in acquiring diseases (see McGuire, 1991). That is, they are based on individualistic principles that prescribe attitudes of self-responsibility, self-efficacy, and self-control – attitudes that have been shown to be unevenly distributed, or differently manifested, by members of different status groups (Gillioz, 1984).

Health-promotion programs are normative. They emanate from groups of medical experts and they fit the social representations of a specific group in the social structure; yet they are intended to be prescriptive for all members of society. This social representation is, once again, that of the autonomous and self-contained individual. Based on questionnaire data, and on factor analyses of opinions and behaviors, Gillioz (1984) outlined a multidimensional typology of health-related attitudes and behaviors. A gender logic and a social status logic prevailed in explaining different types of behavioral clusters, and the corresponding groups of people who most adhered to, or enacted, each type of behavior. The people most open to health recommendations issuing from medical experts were women, and medium to high status individuals, regardless of gender. It is noteworthy, given that health protection is linked to an individualistic social representation in terms of autonomy and self-containment, that it is women who take more action and take more care of themselves than do men. Possibly, this is because, in emotional terms, notions of femininity and healthy behavior coincide, whereas images of masculinity and healthy behavior do not.

Gillioz's (1984) analysis, based on the way a prevention program fits the expectations and actual behavior of a large sample of people in a city; is conceptually grounded in an account of the degree to which a dominant social representation (framed by medical discourse) matches social representations held by different groups of people in society. What this analysis shows is that "good" and "bad" health-related behaviors are homologous, to some extent, to "good" and "bad" social positioning. It then shows that health-promotion programs are usually grounded in a social representation of the individual and of ideal social relations that much better fits with social representations of dominant rather than subordinate group members. This analysis raises serious practical questions about the efficacy of many current health-promotion programs. The issue of course becomes even more provocative if we take a more global perspective and focus on issues involving deep cultural differences in social representations; for example, aboriginal health in Australia, birth control in India, and AIDS control in sub-Saharan Africa.

Conclusion: from Mental Representations to Social Representations

Social cognition perspectives on individuals' mental representations help clarify the way individuals think and act in unspecified circumstances. These thoughts and actions are formalized in abstract models of cognitive functioning, for instance gender-schemas. Social representation theory further explains why and when such general cognitive principles are activated and applied in specific social contexts. In this respect, social cognition and social representation approaches complement one another.

Because of their lack of emphasis on supra-individual, cultural and social dynamics, purely cognitive models tend to reify individuals' cognitive functioning. This reification has helped to develop a "good" model – an efficient and heuristic model – but has tended to detract attention from the study of the conditions that facilitate, hinder, or moderate the implementation of a plurality of cognitive principles. People are viewed as relatively mechanical information-processing modules that operate under specifiable, formal, and widely shared (at least in a given culture) cognitive principles. This perspective provides an intellectual environment in which debates often revolve around the formal properties of such cognitive principles – the dispute between Bem (1982), who propounds the notion of a gender-schema, and Markus and her colleagues (Markus, Crane, Bernstein, & Siladi, 1982) who propound the notion of a self-schema, is an illustration of this (see Lorenzi-Cioldi, 1994, for commentaries on this dispute).

Shweder and Sullivan, (1990) capture this situation beautifully in the following commentary:

> The basic idea of a central processing mechanism is that deep within all human beings is an inherent processing device, which enables us to think (classify, remember, infer, imagine), experience (feel, need, desire), act (strive, choose, evaluate), and learn. Not only is the central processing mechanism presumed to be an abstract, fixed, and universal property of human mental life; it is also presumed that this abstract, fixed, and universal form transcends and is sealed off from all the concrete, variable, and particular stuff, substance, or content upon which it operates [. . .]. One quick and dirty (and striking) indicator of the influence of [the central processing mechanism heuristics] on personality research is the strong inclination among social-psychological researchers to move very quickly – indeed, to rush – from the discovery of some local, context-specific, meaning-saturated regularity (e.g., an audience facilitation effect or a dissonance reduction effect) to the representation of it in the literature as a fundamental law or basic process. We suspect that this "presumption of basic process" is so commonplace because of the hegemony of the central processing mechanism *as an idea* [. . .]. It then takes about a decade for the latest "fundamental" or "basic" process to be unmasked as a "mere" local regularity. (Shweder & Sullivan, 1990, pp. 407–408)

Moving beyond formal properties of individuals' cognitive functioning, social representations theory draws attention to a variety of moderating factors in the way cognitions are enacted. In the examples presented in this chapter, social representations theory might explain why some information becomes a rumor, why some people – not people in general – endorse individualistic and/or collectivistic self-representations, why health-prevention programs are not always successful, and why some people display a gender-schema, while others do not. In the latter case, for instance, the theory demonstrates that gender-schematic processing of the information arises not solely from the match between the gender stereotypes and the male and female categories. Other factors, such as group positioning in the social structure, intervene to shape the individuals' self-representations.

As KihIstrom, and Cantor (1984) cogently pointed out:

We have treated the self as an object of knowledge – as a mental representation of a thing that exists in the physical and social world [. . .]. We have nothing to say about the self as knower, except, obviously, to identify it with the cognitive system that encodes, retrieves, and transforms information. But the matter of the self-as-knower is not simply a matter of information processing. [. . .] We identify our ideas, our precepts, our memories, and our actions as ours. This problem of consciousness and metacognition remains the great mystery. (Kihlstrom & Cantor, 1984, p. 40)

We believe that the mission of social representations theory is to fill this gap between our knowledge of the cognitive and the metacognitive aspects of social behavior. The concept of social representation is increasingly widely accepted in fields that study health-promotion programs, advertising, cultural differences, or social movements. Researchers are beginning to pay more, and more serious, attention to the content of knowledge – specifically, to knowledge in particular settings, and to the ways in which this knowledge is shaped during its transmission. By shifting scientific focus away from formal properties of psychological processes, toward more dynamic and concrete social issues, social representations theory takes the social psychological research process in a new direction. We may still be waiting for a unified theory of social representations that could be applied to all fields, but the relevance of social representations for future research is now quite clear.

REFERENCES

Abelson, R. P. (1994). A personal perspective on social cognition. In: P. G. Devine, D. L. Hamilton, & T. M. Ostrom (Eds.), *Social cognition: Impact on social psychology.* London: Academic Press.

Abric, J.-C. (1984). A theoretical and experimental approach to the study of social representations in a situation of interaction. In R. M. Farr & S. Moscovici (Eds.), *Social representations.* Cambridge, UK: Cambridge University Press.

Abric, J.-C., & Kahan, J. P. (1972). The effects of representations and behaviour in experimental games. *European Journal of Social Psychology, 2,* 129–144.

Allport, G. W., & Postman, L. (1947). *The psychology of rumor.* New York: Holt.

Apfelbaum, E. (1979). Relations of domination and movements for liberation: An analysis of power between groups. In S. Worchel & W. Austin (Eds.), *The social psychology of intergroup relations* (pp. 188–204). Chicago, IL: Nelson-Hall.

Augoustinos, M., & Innes, J. M. (1990). Towards an integration of social representations and social schema theory. *British Journal of Social Psychology, 29,* 213–231.

Bauer, M. W., & Gaskell, G. (1999). Towards a paradigm for research on social representations. *Journal for the Theory of Social Behaviour, 29,* 163–186.

Bem, S. L. (1981). Gender-schema theory: a cognitive account of sex-typing. *Psychological Review, 88,* 354–364.

Bem, S. L. (1982). Gender-schema theory and self-schema theory compared. *Journal of Personality and Social Psychology, 43,* 1192–1194.

Bem, S. L. (1993). *The lenses of gender.* New Haven, CT: Yale University Press.

Billig, M. (1985). Prejudice, categorization and particularization: From a perceptual to a rhetorical approach. *European Journal of Social Psychology, 15,* 79–103.

Boltanski, J. L. (1984). *Prime éducation et morale de classe.* Paris: Cahiers du Centre de Sociologie Européenne.

Bourdieu, P. (1979). *La distinction*. Paris: Minuit.

Bourdieu, P., & de Saint Martin, M. (1978). Le patronat. *Actes de la Recherche en Sciences Sociales, 20–21*, 3–82.

Breakwell, G. (1993). Social representations and social identity. *Papers on Social Representations, 2*, 198–217.

Broverman, I. K., Vogel, S. R., Broverman, D. M., Clarkson, F. E., & Rosenkrantz, P. S. (1972). Sex-role stereotypes: A current appraisal. *Journal of Social Issues, 28*, 59–78.

Cantril, H., Gaudet, H., & Herzog, H. (1940). *The invasion from Mars*. Princeton, NJ: Princeton University Press.

Chombart de Lauwe, M.-J. (1971). *Un monde autre: L'enfance*. Paris: Payot.

Chombart de Lauwe, M.-J. (1984). Changes in the representation of the child in the course of social transmission. In R. M. Farr & S. Moscovici (Eds.), *Social representations*. Cambridge, UK: Cambridge University Press.

Chombart de Lauwe, M.-J., & Bellan, C. (1979). *Enfants de l'image*. Paris: Payot.

Clémence, A. (1997). *A study on social representations of AIDS*. Unpublished manuscript, University of Lausanne, Switzerland.

Clémence, A., & Doise, W. (1995). La représentation sociale de la justice: Une approche des droits dans la pensée ordinaire. *L'Année Sociologique, 45*, 371–400.

De Paolis, P. (1990). Prototypes of the psychologist and professionalisation: Diverging social representations of a developmental process. In G. Duveen & B. Lloyd (1990). *Social representations and the development of knowledge*. Cambridge, UK: Cambridge University Press.

De Paolis, P., Doise, W., & Mugny, G. (1987). Social markings in cognitive operations. In W. Doise & S. Moscovici (Eds.), *Current issues in European social psychology*. Cambridge, UK: Cambridge University Press.

Deschamps, J.-C. (1982). Social identity and relations of power between groups. In H. Tajfel (Ed.), *Social identity and intergroup relations* (pp. 85–98). Cambridge, UK: Cambridge University Press.

Deschamps, J.-C., Lorenzi-Cioldi, F., & Meyer, G. (1982). *L'échec scolaire*. Lausanne, Switzerland. P.-M. Favre.

Devine, P. G. (1989). Stereotypes and prejudice: Their automatic and controlled components. *Journal of Personality and Social Psychology, 56*, 5–18.

Doise, W. (1972). Relations et représentations intergroupes. In S. Moscovici (Ed.), *Introduction à la psychologie sociale* (Vol. 2). Paris: Larousse.

Doise, W. (1990). Les représentations sociales. In R. Ghiglione, C. Bonnet, & J. F. Richard (Eds.), *Traité de psychologie cognitive* (Vol. 3). Paris: Dunod.

Doise, W., Clémence, A., & Lorenzi-Cioldi, F. (1993). *The quantitative analysis of social representations*. London: Harvester Wheatsheaf.

Doise, W., & Mugny, G. (1984). *The social development of the intellect*. Oxford, UK: Pergamon.

Durkheim, E. (1912/1995). *The elementary forms of the religious life*. New York: Free Press.

Duveen, G., & Lloyd, B. (1986). The significance of social identities. *British Journal of Social Psychology, 25*, 219–230.

Duveen, G., & Lloyd, B. (1990). Introduction. In G. Duveen & B. Lloyd (1990). *Social representations and the development of knowledge*. Cambridge, UK: Cambridge University Press.

Eagly, A. H. (1987). *Sex differences in social behavior: A social-role interpretation*. Hillsdale, NJ: Erlbaum.

Eagly, A. H., & Mladinic, A. (1989). Gender stereotypes and attitudes toward women and men. *Personality and Social Psychology Bulletin, 15*, 543–558.

Elejabarrieta, F. (1994). Social positioning: A way to link social representations and social identity. *Social Science Information, 33*, 241–253.

Esposito, J. L., & Rosnow, R. L. (1984). Cognitive set and message processing: Implications of prose memory research for rumor theory. *Language and Communication, 4,* 301–315.

Fiske, S. T. (1992). Thinking is for doing: Portraits of social cognition from daguerrotype to laserphoto. *Journal of Personality and Social Psychology, 63,* 877–889.

Fiske, S. T., Kinder, D. R., & Larter, W. M. (1983). The novice and the expert: Knowledge-based strategies in political cognition. *Journal of Experimental Social Psychology, 19,* 381–400.

Fiske, S. T., & Leyens, J.-Ph. (1996). Let social psychology be faddish or, at least, heterogeneous. In C. MeGarty & S. A. Haslam (Eds.), *The message of social psychology.* Oxford, UK: Blackwell.

Flick, U. (1995). Social representations. In J. Smith, R. Harré, & L. Langenbore (Eds.), *Rethinking psychology.* London: Sage.

Gilligan, C. (1982). *In a different voice.* Cambridge, MA: Harvard University Press.

Gillioz, L. (1984). La prévention comme normalisation culturelle. *Revue Suisse de Sociologie, 1,* 37–84.

Grmek, M. D. (1990). *Histoire du SIDA.* Paris: Payot.

Guillaumin, C. (1972). *L'idéologie raciste: Genèse et langage actuel.* Paris: Mouton.

Hamilton, M. C. (1991). Masculine bias in the attribution of personhood: People = male and male = people. *Psychology of Women Quarterly, 15,* 393–402.

Hardin, C. D., & Higgins, E. T. (1996). Shared reality. How social verification makes the subjective objective. In R. M. Sorrentino & E. T. Higgins (Eds.), *Handbook of motivations and cognition* (Vol. 3): The interpersonal context. New York: Guilford Press.

Harding, S. (1986). *The science question in feminism.* Ithaca, NY: Cornell University Press.

Hastie, R. (1983). Social inference. *Annual Review of Psychology, 34,* 511–542.

Herzlich, C., & Pierret, J. (1988). Une maladie dans l'espace public: Le sida dans six quotidiens français. *Annales ESC, 5,* 1109–1134.

Hogg, M. A. (1996). Intragroup processes, group structure, and social identity. In W. P. Robinson (Ed.), *Social groups and identities: Developing the legacy of Henri Tajfel* (pp. 65–93). Oxford, UK: Butterworth-Heinemann.

Hogg, M. A. (2001). Social categorization, depersonalization, and group behavior. In M. A. Hogg & S. Tindale (Eds.), *Blackwell handbook of social psychology: Group processes* (pp. 56–85). Oxford, UK: Blackwell.

Hurtig, M.-C., & Pichevin, M.-F. (1990). Salience of the sex category system in person perception: Contextual variations. *Sex Roles, 22,* 369–395.

Jackman, M. R., & Senters, M. S. (1980). Images of social groups: Categorical or qualified? *Public Opinion Quarterly, 44,* 341–361.

Jodelet, D. (Ed.) (1989) *Les représentations sociales.* Paris: Presses Universitaires de France.

Jodelet, D. (1991). *Madness and social representations.* Hemel Hempstead, UK: Harvester Wheatsheaf.

Kapferer, J.-N. (1987). *Rumeurs. Le plus vieux média du monde.* Paris: Seuil.

Kashima, Y., Yamagushi, S., Kim, U., Choi, S.-C., Gelfand, M., & Yuki, M. (1995). Culture, gender, and self: A perspective from individualism-collectivism research. *Journal of Personality and Social Psychology, 69,* 925–937.

Kihlstrom, J. F., & Cantor, N. (1984). Mental representations of the self. In L. Berkowitz (Ed.), *Advances in experimental social psychology* (Vol. 17). New York: Academic Press.

Lee, Y.-T., & Ottati, V. (1993). Determinants of in-group and out-group perceptions of heterogeneity. *Journal of Cross-Cultural Psychology, 24,* 298–328.

Levine, J. M., Resnick, L. B., & Higgins, E. T. (1993). Social foundations of cognition. *Annual Review of Psychology, 44,* 585–612.

Lévy-Bruhl, L. (1925/1926). *How natives think.* London: Allen & Unwin.

Linville, P., Fischer, G. W., & Salovey, P. (1989). Perceived distributions of characteristics of ingroup and outgroup members: Empirical evidence and a computer simulation. *Journal of Personality and Social Psychology, 57,* 165–188.

Lloyd, B. (1987). Social representations of gender. In J. Bruner & H. Haste (Eds.), *Making sense: The child's construction of the world.* London: Methuen.

Lloyd, B., & Duveen, G. (1990). A semiotic analysis of the development of social representations of gender. In G. Duveen & B. Lloyd (Eds.), (1990). *Social representations and the development of knowledge.* Cambridge, UK: Cambridge University Press.

Lorenzi-Cioldi, F. (1988). *Individus dominants et groupes dominés* [Dominant individuals and dominated groups]. Grenoble, France: Presses Universitaires.

Lorenzi-Cioldi, F. (1991). Self-enhancement and self-stereotyping in gender groups. *European Journal of Social Psychology, 21,* 403–417.

Lorenzi-Cioldi, F. (1994). *Les androgynes* [The androgynes]. Paris: Presses Universitaires de France.

Lorenzi-Cioldi, F. (1998). Group status and perceptions of homogeneity. In W. Stroebe & M. Hewstone (Eds.), *European review of social psychology* (Vol. 9, pp. 31–75). New York: Wiley.

Lorenzi-Cioldi, F., & Dafflon, A.-C. (1998). Norme individuelle et norme collective, I: Représentations du genre dans une société individualiste. *Swiss Journal of Psychology, 57,* 124–137.

Lorenzi-Cioldi, F., & Dafflon, A.-C. (in preparation). *Norme individuelle et norme collective, II: Représentations culturelles et sexuelles.*

Lorenzi-Cioldi, F., & Doise, W. (1990). Levels of analysis and social identity. In D. Abrams & M. Hogg (Eds.), *Social identity theory* (pp. 71–88). London. Harvester Wheatsheaf.

Lorenzi-Cioldi, F., & Joye, D. (1988). Représentations de catégories socio-professionnelles: Aspects méthodologiques. *Bulletin de Psychologie, 40,* 377–390.

Lorenzi-Cioldi, F., & Meyer, G. (1984). *Semblables ou différents?* [Similar or different?]. Geneva: International Labor Organization.

Markova, I. (1992). Scientific and public knowledge of AIDS: The problem of their integration. In M. von Cranach, W. Doise, & G. Mugny (Eds.), *Social representations and the social bases of knowledge.* Lewiston, NY: Hogrefe & Huber.

Markova, I., & Farr, R. (1995). *Representations of health, illness and handicap.* Chur, Switzerland: Harwood.

Markus, H., Crane, M., Bernstein, S., & Siladi, M. (1982). Self-schemas and gender. *Journal of Personality and Social Psychology, 42,* 38–50.

Markus, H., & Kitayama, S. (1991). Culture and the self: Implications for cognition, emotion, and motivation. *Psychological Review, 98,* 224–253.

Markus, H., & Kitayama, S. (1994). A collective fear of the collective: Implications for selves and theories of selves. *Personality and Social Psychology Bulletin, 20,* 568–579.

Markus, H., & Oyserman, D. (1989). Gender and thought: The role of the self-concept. In M. Crawford & M. Gentry (Eds.), *Gender and thought.* New York: Springer.

Martin, R., & Hewstone, M. (2001). Conformity and independence in groups – majorities and minorities. In M. A. Hogg & S. Tindale (Eds.), *Blackwell handbook of social psychology: Group processes* (pp. 209–234). Oxford, UK: Blackwell.

McGuire, W. (1984). Search for the self: Going beyond self-esteem and the reactive self. In R. A. Zucker, J. Aronoff, & A. I. Rabin (Eds.), *Personality and the prediction of behavior* (pp. 73–120). New York: Academic Press.

McGuire, W. (1991). Using guiding idea theory of the person to develop educational campaigns against drug abuse and other health-threatening behavior. *Health Education Research, 6,* 173–184.

McLeod, J., Pan, Z., & Rusinski, D. (1995). Levels of analysis in public opinion research. In T. L. Glasser & C. T. Salmon (Eds.), *Public opinion and communication of consent.* New York: Guilford Press.

Miller, D. (1991). "Snakes in the greens" and rumor in the innercity. *Social Science Journal, 29*, 381–393.

Morin, E. (1969). *La rumeur d'Orléans.* Paris: Seuil.

Moscovici, S. (1961/1976). *La psychanalyse, son image et son public* [Psychoanalysis, its image and its public]. Paris: Presses Universitaires de France.

Moscovici, S. (1976). *Social influence and social change.* London: Academic Press.

Moscovici, S. (1980). Towards a theory of conversion behavior. In L. Berkowitz (Ed.), *Advances in experimental social psychology* (Vol. 13). New York: Academic Press.

Moscovici, S. (1981). On social representations. In J. P. Forgas (Ed.), *Social cognition: Perspectives on everyday understanding.* London: Academic Press.

Moscovici, S. (1998). The history and actuality of social representations. In U. Flick (Ed.), *The psychology of the social.* Cambridge, UK: Cambridge University Press.

Moscovici, S., & Hewstone, M. (1983). Social representations and social explanations: From the "naïve" to the "amateur" scientist. In M. Hewstone (Ed.), *Attribution theory.* Oxford, UK: Blackwell.

Mugny, G., & Perez, J. A. (1991). *The social psychology of minority influence.* Cambridge, UK: Cambridge University Press.

Mullen, B. (1991). Group composition, salience, and cognitive representations: The phenomenology of being in a group. *Journal of Experimental Social Psychology, 27*, 297–323.

Nisbett, R. E., & Ross, L. (1980). *Human inferences: Strategies and shortcomings of social judgment.* Englewood Cliffs, NJ: Prentice-Hall.

Park, B., & Hastie, R. (1987). Perception of variability in category development: Instance versus abstraction-based stereotypes. *Journal of Personality and Social Psychology, 53*, 621–635.

Park, B., Judd, C., & Ryan, C. S. (1991). Social categorization and the representation of variability information. In W. Stroebe & M. Hewstone (Eds.), *European review of social psychology* (Vol. 2, pp. 211–245). New York: Wiley.

Piaget, J. (1932). *The moral judgment of the child.* Harmondsworth, UK: Penguin.

Pichevin, M.-F., & Hurtig, M.-C. (1996). Describing men, describing women: Sex membership salience and numerical distinctiveness. *European Journal of Social Psychology, 26*, 513–522.

Purkhardt, S. C. (1995). *Transforming social representations.* London: Routledge.

Ridgeway, C. L. (2001). Social status and group structure. In M. A. Hogg & S. Tindale (Eds.), *Blackwell handbook of social psychology: Group processes* (pp. 352–375). Oxford, UK: Blackwell.

Ridgeway, C. L., & Diekema, D. (1992). Are gender differences status differences? In C. L. Ridgeway (Ed.), *Gender, interaction, and inequality* (pp. 157–180). New York: Springer.

Rosch, E. (1981). Principles of categorization. In: E. Rosch & B. B. Lloyd (Eds.), *Cognition and categorization.* Hillsdale, NJ: Erlbaum.

Rosnow, R. L. (1980). Psychology of rumor reconsidered. *Psychological Bulletin, 87*, 578–591.

Rosnow, R. L. (1988). Rumor as communication: A contextualist approach. *Journal of Communication, 38*, 12–28.

Rosnow, R. L., Esposito, J. L., & Gibney, L. (1988). Factors influencing rumor spreading: Replication and extension. *Language and Communication, 8*, 29–42.

Rothman, A. J., & Salovey, P. (1997). Shaping perceptions to motivate healthy behavior: The role of message framing. *Psychological Bulletin, 121*, 3–19.

Rouquette, M. (1975). *Les rumeurs.* Paris: Presses Universitaires de France.

Salovey, P., Rothman, A. J., & Rodin, J. (1998). Health behavior. In D. T Gilbert, S. T. Fiske, & G. Lindzey (Eds.), *The handbook of social psychology* (Vol. 2, pp. 633–683). New York: McGraw-Hill.

Sampson, E. E. (1993). *Celebrating the other. A dialogic account of human nature.* London: Harvester Wheatsheaf.

Sherif, M. (1936). *The psychology of social norms.* New York: Harper.

Sherman, S. J., Judd, C. M., & Park, B. (1989). Social cognition. *Annual Review of Psychology*, *40*, 281–326.

Shweder, R. A., & Sullivan, M. A. (1990). The semiotic subject of cultural psychology. In L. A. Pervin (Ed.), *Handbook of personality: Theory and research*. New York: Guilford Press.

Snyder, M. (1981). Seek, and ye shall find: Testing hypotheses about other people. In E. T. Higgins, C. P. Herman, & M. P. Zanna (Eds.), *Social cognition. The Ontario symposium* (Vol. 1). Hillsdale, NJ: Erlbaum.

Sontag, S. (1989). *AIDS and its metaphor*. London: Allen Lane.

Sperber, D., & Wilson, D. (1986). *Relevance: Communication and cognition*. Oxford, UK: Blackwell.

Sperber, D. (1990). The epidemiology of beliefs. In C. Fraser & G. Gaskell (Eds.), *The social psychological study of widespreads beliefs*. Oxford, UK: Clarendon Press.

Taylor, S. E. (1990). Health psychology: The science and the field. *American Psychologist*, *45*, 40–50.

Treadway, M., & McCloskey, M. (1989). Effects of racial stereotypes on eyewitness performance: Implications of the real and the rumoured Allport and Postman studies. *Applied Cognitive Psychology*, *3*, 53–63.

Vallone, R. P., Ross, L., & Lepper, M. R. (1985). The hostile media phenomenon: Biased perception and perceptions of media bias in coverage of the Beirut massacre. *Psychological Review*, *90*, 293–315.

Wagner, W., Elejabarrieta, F., & Lahnsteiner, I. (1995), How the sperm dominates the ovum: Objectification by metaphor in the social representation of conception. *European Journal of Social Psychology*, *25*, 671–688.

Walker, C., & Blaine, B. (1991). The virulence of dread rumors: A field experiment. *Language and Communication*, *11*, 291–297.

CHAPTER FOURTEEN

How Language Contributes to Persistence of Stereotypes as Well as Other, More General, Intergroup Issues

Klaus Fiedler and Jeannette Schmid

The title of the present chapter provides a neat example for the various subtle ways in which language can induce beliefs and expectations. It uses several rhetorical devices that can have quite strong influences on communication partners, for they typically go unnoticed and thereby evade conscious control. The title uses *presupposition* and *nominalization* – two most prominent devices for reification and elimination of critical thought. Nominalizations like "persistence of stereotypes" take it for granted that stereotypes tend to persist, rather than being updated, and almost exclude the possibility of calling this premise into question (Bolinger, 1973). The same nominal phrase silently induces a restrictive theory which states that language contributes to stereotype persistence, as opposed to stereotype formation, or change. According to Grice's (1975) maxim of quantity, using a restrictive term can be taken as evidence that this restriction is substantive. Moreover, the title presupposes that language does contribute to stereotypes which in turn have to be conceived as a subcategory of other, more general, intergroup issues. All these linguistically induced assumptions are more likely to be encoded as veridical facts than to be discovered as potentially unjustified suggestions.

Language as a powerful symbol system offers such a rich repertoire of lexical terms and grammatical forms that virtually every utterance reflects a choice for this utterance, and against others. Moreover, language entails a gradient of connotative, evaluative meanings, such that any utterance conveys to some degree acceptance or rejection, approach or avoidance. It is thus no surprise that utterances about people and groups can have a potentially strong impact on social stereotypes.

The present chapter is organized as follows: An introductory section is devoted to illustrating the common social-interactional origin of both language acquisition and stereotyping, from a developmental or social-learning perspective. The methods and findings reviewed afterwards address two different but related topics: Language as a system and language as a toolbox to be used in social encounters or cultures. With respect to De Saussure's (1915) famous distinction, the former refers to "la langue" whereas the latter part is concerned with contextualized language use, or "le parole."

Language and Stereotyping from a Social-Learning Perspective

Although language is not given a systematic status in textbooks, monographs, and reviews of stereotype research (cf. Dovidio & Gaertner, 1986; Mackie & Hamilton, 1993), both representational systems, language and stereotypes, originate in the same process of social learning and interaction. Decades ago, pioneers in the psychology of stereotyping noted that ethnic stereotypes are often acquired during childhood, with little direct contact to the target groups (Brigham, 1971; Gardner, Taylor, & Feenstra, 1970). Such stereotypes are not based on first-hand experience but on second-hand information which is typically conveyed in humans' most effective symbol system, language. From an ontogenetic perspective, stereotypes are obviously encoded in language before they are encoded in children's memories.

Granting this central role of language in the learning and cultural sharing of stereotypes, the question arises whether language is only a medium for transferring cognitive representations from one person (parents, peers) to others (children, novices), or whether language adds something beyond the intended communication. As our starting example has shown, it is hardly possible to communicate without adding (actual or erroneously inferred) intentions, evaluations, interpretations, and simplifications. The essential need to be concise and informative rather than circumstantial, serves to simplify and accentuate original information in verbal communication. Thus, the Western European mother who never lived in a Turkish family but merely read a journal article about Turkish gender rules will presumably convey this knowledge to her daughter in a simplified and polarized fashion. The way in which she discourages her daughter from engaging in a close relationship with a Turk will leave little latitude for differentiation and cultural adaptation, and will induce more fear or xenophobia than when the daughter establishes a direct contact with Turks.

Without exaggeration, the acquisition of language and stereotypes not only coincides but also is identical in terms of basic learning processes. Learning the meaning of any word, such as "table," requires the (one-year-old) child to abstract from specific stimulus patterns elicited by particular objects and to acquire object constancy. Different tables produce different images on the retina and even the same table (perceived from varying angles, distances, illumination conditions, etc.) never reproduces the same sensory input. But the child has to understand all these different manifestations as belonging to the same abstract category, "table." This object constancy also converges in other sensory or operational modalities, such as touching the table surface, hearing knocking on table wood, lifting the table, using it as a place for eating and working, etc. Once this abstract word meaning is acquired different exemplars of the category can be recognized as "the same," or at least as more similar than before.

An analogous process can be assumed for the acquisition of generic word meanings, such as ethnic or national group labels (Japanese, Hispanics, Jews, Aboriginals), vocational categories (lawyers, professors, prostitutes), or groups defined by behavioral or habitual criteria (soccer players, homosexuals, juvenile delinquents). Learning of these categories involves abstracting from specific instances and ascribing the prototype or ideal type of that category to newly encountered exemplars. From a learning-theoretical point of view, there is basically no difference between language learning in general and learning of stereotype labels in particular.

A central defining feature of language (cf. Glucksberg & Danks, 1975), besides its generic infinity, is its reliance on arbitrary symbols that need not resemble the reference object. The sound pattern or graphical contour of the word "table" has no intrinsic similarity to the object table. It is this symbolic independence that creates the virtually unrestricted flexibility of verbal communication. Symbols used for denoting objects do not obey restrictive rules; any symbol will suffice, and human intelligence is flexible enough to figure out some resemblance between any two objects given the same arbitrary label. This arbitrariness points to a particularly intriguing aspect of social stereotypes. For any two persons, there are numerous ways of classifying them as same and different: Dagmar and Joshua may belong to different religions, sex groups, age groups, and professional groups, but they may be members of the same sports club, share the same hobbies, ethical and political values, and they may even be married. Treating Dagmar and Joshua differently or alike depends on the arbitrary choice of one categorization, perhaps dependent on which linguistic label happens to be activated. Categorization effects can even be obtained when meaningless fantasy terms are used to create artificial categories (e.g., "overestimators"), as evident from research on minimal groups (Tajfel, 1970).

Social learning does not take place in a vacuum, but in dynamic social interaction. It is learning by doing and instrumental learning. A young child who is only exposed to a radio receiver rather than to social interaction would hardly succeed in language acquisition. The same point holds, presumably, for stereotype acquisition. Just like the child uses words (table, ball, puppy) to get, express, avoid, or search something, stereotype terms are usually embedded in behavioral contexts. They come along with evaluations, behavioral intentions, approach or avoidance goals, specific topics or tasks, and local or temporal boundary conditions. This contextualized meaning of stereotypes constitutes their *surplus meaning* that often evades conscious awareness and is therefore hard to control or correct.

How Language as a System Affects Stereotype Maintenance

Language as a system has its own structural properties, independent of the language users' goals, perspectives, or personal styles. The constraints on information transmission imposed by these structural properties are relatively stable and inevitable. They include, among others, lexical, morphological, syntactical, semantic, and pragmatical constraints.

The role of sexist language in promoting anti-female stereotypes may illustrate this point. The lexicon supports the maintenance and reproduction of sexist attitudes in that it includes, for instance, many more terms applicable to promiscuous women than comparable terms for males. Thus, the lexicon makes lascivious, sexist talk about females a likely language game. A related example of morphological constraints would be the suffixes used to mark female expressions in many languages. While the generic, default terms are normally male, female forms are typically marked and thereby highlight the femininity of the person as an essential aspect (e.g., governor–governess; master–mistress).

An obvious manifestation of syntactic structure is the attention focus placed on the sentence subject – an almost inevitable consequence of the canonical order of sentence parts, from subject to predicate to object. The differentiation between active and passive voice has special importance in the possibility of shifting responsibilities for personal mishaps or interpersonal violence. This method has been investigated in the area of psychological accounts, for example in the context of rape trials (Henley, Miller, & Beazley, 1995). In the passive form "she was raped," the female target, rather than the male agent, is in the focal position, leading to decreased attribution of responsibility to the assailant and increased victim blame.

One pervasive source of semantic constraints is the associative network of word meanings. Numerous priming experiments demonstrate that conscious or unconscious priming effects can activate sexist knowledge in memory. This quasi-automatic influence is hard to control voluntarily (Blair & Banaji, 1996; Fazio, Sanbonmatsu, Powell, & Kardes, 1986; Wittenbrink, Judd, & Park, 1997). The greatest part of the present section will be devoted to semantic constraints.

Finally, the impact of pragmatic rules on the persistence of stereotypes can be illustrated with sexist jokes. The extent to which disparaging humor and culturally shared joke repertoires can contribute to gender stereotypes affords an intriguing research question (Hobden & Olson, 1994). One pragmatic reason why females are so vulnerable to anti-female jokes is that there is no way of disconfirming or objecting to the contents of a joke. Objections would only render things worse and increase the malicious effect of the joke.

The systematic distortion hypothesis

Central to the study of social stereotypes are the semantic constraints of trait adjectives, because stereotypes relate groups to traits, or traits to traits. (Virtually any trait category, like extrovert, can be reframed as a group, extrovert people). By definition, a stereotype states that some attribute or trait is more likely within a given group (or category) than in general (McCauley & Stitt, 1978). Stereotype research is thus about the learning and cognitive representations of trait contingencies. According to Shweder's (1975, 1982) systematic distortion hypothesis, this process is seriously biased toward the semantic similarities that exist between trait terms. People systematically confuse "likelihood" and "likeness"; they believe in correlations among those attributes that appear semantically similar. For instance, the correlation between *extroversion* and *leadership ability*, which is in fact close to zero, is drastically over-estimated just because the semantic meaning of the two terms, "extroversion" and "leadership ability," is rather similar. Shweder (1982) has made a strong point for his systematic distortion hypothesis, extrapolating from singular examples to whole arrays of trait terms. The general conclusion is that semantic similarities between traits constitute a much better predictor of subjective trait correlations than actually observed correlations.

A study conducted by D'Andrade (1974) illustrates the power of similarity-based illusory correlations. Observers of classroom interactions used the Bales (1950) categories to code the pupils' behavior over an extended period. These included behavioral categories like *asks for opinion, gives information, shows tension, agrees,* etc. Later on, observers were asked to judge the degree to which these behaviors correlated with each other. Judgments more clearly reflected the pairwise semantic similarities between the behavioral categories than the actually observed and encoded intercorrelations. Convergent evidence for this phenomenon comes from countless other studies on expectancy-based illusory correlations (Hamilton & Rose, 1980).

One interesting way in which illusory correlations can support stereotypes is through role labels. When the number of typical male and female attributes observed in two stimulus groups is the same, but the majority of members in both groups are labeled with different social roles (breadwinners vs. child raisers) associated with gender, observers believe they have seen more male traits in the group with the male label and more female traits in the female label group (Hoffman & Hurst, 1990).

To understand the underlying process, it is important to recognize the constructive nature of social perception. Most meaningful traits (emotionality, attraction, ability, hostility, credibility) are not amenable to immediate perception but have to be inferred or construed on the basis of fallible cues. That somebody is *emotional* is typically inferred from such cues as expressive voice, mimic reactions, crying and smiling, or disclosure of intimate states. As the symbolic meaning of these cues is much closer to *femininity* than masculinity, the stereotype that females are more emotional than males arises as a natural consequences of such cue overlap.

Verification and falsification of trait attributes

The semantic meaning of trait adjectives restricts the amount of evidence necessary to verify or falsify a stereotypical attribute. It takes more evidence to confirm that somebody is *honest* than to confirm that the same person is *dishonest*. As a general rule, evaluatively negative traits are often easier to verify than positive traits in the domain of morality-related social behavior, as Reeder and Brewer (1979), Skowronski and Carlston (1989), and others have shown. This asymmetry reflects the quantifiers that are implicit in the semantics of trait terms (Gidron, Koehler, & Tversky, 1993). To be honest means to act honestly most of the time, whereas to be dishonest means to cheat or to lie a few times, perhaps only once. Different confirmation thresholds can thus have obvious consequences for the likelihood with which positive versus negative stereotypes are inferred. Whereas negative stereotypes are easier to verify in the morality domain, positive inferences are more likely in the ability domain (Reeder & Brewer, 1979). Thus, a single observation of somebody juggling with seven balls is sufficient to infer juggling ability.

Other semantic components of trait terms concern the breadth of the behavioral domain within which a stereotype can be verified or falsified, and the frequency distribution of corresponding behaviors in social ecology (Hampson, John, & Goldberg, 1986; Rothbart & Park, 1986). As the stereotype "females are talkative" refers to a more specified class of behaviors than the stereotype "females are emotional," the latter should be more vague to test and falsify than the former, because of the unequal behavioral domains. Likewise, a stereotype referring to an infrequent, abnormal class of behaviors, such as "females are hysterical," is hard to correct because of the paucity of relevant occasions.

Linguistic categories and attribution

Semin and Fiedler's (1988) linguistic category model offers a comprehensive approach to understanding the lexical constraints imposed on interpersonal language. This model applies to verbs and adjectives that can serve the predicate role in sentences. Research in this framework has shown that semantic influences on stereotyping are not confined to trait similarities. Rather, it appears that entire implicit attribution theories are built into the semantics of particular word classes.

The linguistic category model (LCM) distinguishes four levels of abstractness that language offers to describing people and their behavior. *Adjectives* (friendly, dishonest) convey the highest abstractness; they abstract from particular behavioral episodes and from specific object persons and situations. At the second-most abstract level, *state verbs* (trust, detest) still refer to rather enduring states and therefore abstract from single, enumerable acts, but their meaning is already attached to specific object persons (i.e., the persons trusted or detested). Most state verbs refer to covert emotional states, but they can as well refer to cognitive states, or changes of states. *Interpretive action verbs* (to help, to insult) point to intentional actions with a clearly defined beginning and end. Unlike state verbs, the behavioral referents of action verbs are manifest and accessible to direct observation. *Descriptive action verbs* (to look at, to call) constitute the lowest level of abstractness and the highest dependence on contextual information. Whether looking at somebody reflects distrust, interest, or merely attraction, cannot be deduced from the linguistic term but has to be inferred from the context. Unlike interpretative action verbs, descriptive action verbs are defined by at least one physically invariant attribute (e.g., the voice for calling, a pen for writing), and they carry much less dispositional meaning and evaluation.

A summary of the semantic implications of these four classes is given in Table 13.1. When describing the behavior of a target person, abstract terms have stronger implications than specific terms about the subject person's personality, abstract terms suggest more temporal stability over time, but abstract statements suggest less voluntary control than specific statements, and less clear-cut situational references. Abstract statements are therefore more difficult to verify or falsify, and more likely to cause disagreement than specific statements. For example, the same dyadic behavior between Walter and Paul could be described as "Walter shouts at Paul" (specific, descriptive action verb) or "Walter is impulsive" (abstract, adjective). Clearly, the abstract term impulsive appears more informative about Walter, suggests a more stable disposition that exists independently of the situation, but implies less voluntary control (the imperative "Be impulsive!" sounds anomalous) than the former description. In contrast, the meaning of the specific term to shout depends on the concrete situational context. Once the specific term is contextualized (e.g., "Walter shouts at Paul on the soccer field"), the resulting statement becomes clearly verifiable or falsifiable, unlike abstract statements.

Because of these semantic implications, abstract descriptions of social behavior are more likely to suggest strong and stable dispositions in persons and groups than specific descriptions. However, since adjectives and abstract states are detached from specific situations and too vague to be tested critically, they do not invite verification attempts and reality tests.

Table 14.1. Taxonomy and Cognitive-Semantic Properties of Linguistic Categories (after Semin & Fiedler, 1988)

Verb class:	Descriptive action verbs	Interpretive action verbs	State verbs	Adjectives
Examples:	• Hit • Look at • Escort	• Attack • Monitor • Guard	• Hate • Distrust • Care	• Aggressive • Suspicious • Protective
Semantic implications:	Contextualized Local, unstable Reference to concrete action	Contextualized Local, evaluative Reference to action category	Decontextualized Stable, enduring Reference to internal state	Decontextualized Stable, general Reference to trait or disposition
Stereotyping implications:	Localization Highly verifiable Non-diagnostic Neutral	Internal causation Verifiable Intentionality Evaluative	External causation Difficult to verify Uncontrollability Emotional	Generalization Hardly verifiable Highly diagnostic Categorical

Relative to specific verbs, adjectives are thus relatively immune from falsification and therefore more suitable for inducing and communicating social stereotypes.

Semin and Fiedler (1992) have factor-analyzed the semantic ratings of linguistic categories on the semantic dimensions summarized in Table 14.1. Two dimensions were extracted that can account for the differences between abstract and specific terms. The first dimension contrasts abstract (adjectives) versus specific terms (descriptive action verbs) and represents a *dispositionality factor*, with highest loadings on subject informativeness, temporal stability, and a slightly negative loading on verifiability. The second dimension is *locus of causality*. The extreme poles on this dimension are represented by the two middle categories; interpretive action verbs (e.g., hurt, help) imply a cause within the sentence subject, whereas state verbs (e.g., admire, abhor) imply a cause within the sentence object or situation. This phenomenon of implicit verb causality (Brown & Fish, 1983; Fiedler & Semin, 1988; Rudolph & Försterling, 1997) generalizes over more than 80% of the entire lexicon and over many languages. It is primarily mediated by two semantic properties, emotion and controllability, which receive the highest loadings on the locus of causality dimension. The meaning of action verbs (prevent, influence) implies little emotion but high control in the sentence subject. In contrast, the semantics of state words (fear, desire), entail high subject emotion and little control.

Thus, with regard to social stereotypes, the two dimensions offer two ways in which verbs and adjectives can be used to convey attributions to persons and groups (see empirical evidence in the next section). On the dispositionality dimension, the two extreme categories, adjectives and descriptive action verbs, can be used to highlight either the stable, dispositional nature of some attribute (aggressive, jealous), or its local, unstable, neutral, situational character (to raise hands, to call). And on the locus of causality dimension, action verbs versus state verbs serve to convey the impression that social behavior originates in the sentence subject or object, respectively. Without overtly committing oneself to prejudice and group stereotypes, communicators can use these subtle tools to blame outgroups and excuse ingroup behavior (see next section) or to communicate evaluations without appearing partial (Hamilton, Gibbons, Stroessner, & Sherman, 1992; Maass, Milesi, Zabbini, & Stahlberg, 1995; Maass, Salvi, Arcuri, & Semin, 1989). Conversely, receivers can infer communicated attitudes from the words used to describe target persons (Von Hippel, Sekaquaptewa, & Vargas, 1997).

Since language users are hardly aware of the silent implications of linguistic categories, the stereotype-maintaining function of language is particularly hard to control. Indeed, there is evidence to suggest that the reasons underlying an abstract, adjectival language style are systematically misunderstood. As Wicklund and Braun (1990) have shown, people resort to static, dispositional descriptors suggesting predictability when they feel insecure or incomplete. For instance, when professional lawyers are compared with law students in their beginning semesters, the novices rather than the experts tend to ascribe static (stereo-)typical person descriptors to lawyers – a symptom of immaturity or incompleteness. However, when people are asked to infer others' expertise from their language style, the same static descriptors are mistakenly associated with experts rather than novices.

Consistent findings have been reported by other researchers showing that global, abstract language increases when people are high in need for closure (Rubini & Kruglanski, 1997; Webster, Kruglanski, & Pattison, 1997) or threatened by lethal symbols (Solomon, Greenberg, & Pyszczynski, 1991) and decreases with the familiarity and security of long-term close relationships (Fiedler, Semin, Finkenauer, & Berkel, 1995).

Two word classes serve to convey internal attributions to persons or groups, although for different reasons. *Adjectives* imply maximal dispositionality (stability and globality of attributes), whereas *action verbs* imply internal causation (personal control as opposed to emotional reactions). There is an intriguing analogy between the semantic properties of these two word classes and two major attribution theories. The manner in which adjectives mediate internal attributions reflects Kelley's (1967) attribution model. As indicated in Table 14.1, adjectives imply low consensus (high information about the sentence subject that cannot be generalized over other subjects), low distinctiveness (independence of situations), and high consistency (stability over time). In contrast, the manner in which interpretive action verbs induce internal attributions can be easily explained by Jones and Davis' (1965) correspondent inference model. The semantic properties of interpretive action verbs (hurt, encourage) include ability and intentionality (voluntary control) and an informative effect that is directed at specific goals or objects and cannot be generalized to many other objects (Brown & Fish, 1983). Given this almost perfect congruence with two major attribution theories, the attributional consequences of adjectives and action verbs are hardly surprising.

Evaluative language and accentuation

Stereotyping not only means to attribute dispositions but also to discriminate between different persons or groups. Accordingly, language not only serves an important function in the attribution paradigm but also in the categorization paradigm (Bruner & Goodman, 1947; Eiser & Stroebe, 1972; Tajfel, 1969). As a general rule, two stimuli tend to appear

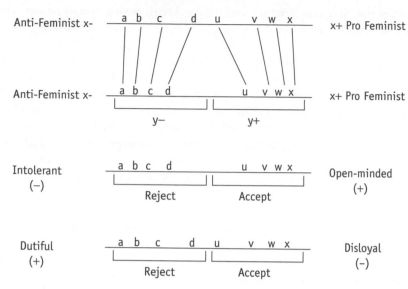

Figure 14.1. Graphical illustration of attitude accentuation. As pro-feminist statements (a, b, c, d) and anti-feminist statements (u, v, w, x) are correlated with different category labels (y– vs. y+), the difference between pro and anti positions is accentuated (upper part). When the judge is herself a feminist (middle part), pro and contra statements are correlated with acceptance vs. rejection. However, the resulting accentuation effect is reduced when the connotations of the judgment scale (+ vs. –) are incompatible with the judge's evaluative reactions (reject vs. accept; see bottom part).

more different if they are associated with different category labels than if they belong to the same category. For example, the difference between permissive versus restrictive educational attitude statements is accentuated (Eiser, 1971) when associated with different newspapers (fictitious labels: *The Messenger* vs. *The Gazette*). Likewise, political attitudes will appear more different when associated with different rather than same party labels, or the same behaviors will appear different when ascribed to different group labels.

Theoretically, this accentuation effect can be explained in terms of informational redundancy. When the task is to rate attitude positions on a judgment scale x, feminism (see Figure 14.1), the discrimination is enhanced when the relevant variable x (i.e., pro-feminist vs. anti-feminist attitudes) is correlated with another variable, y, that can result from a fully irrelevant classification (e.g., by age, race, or arbitrary groups). Consequently, statements not only differ in their attitude toward feminism (pro vs. anti) but also on the correlated dimension (e.g., association with different groups). The redundancy gained from such a superimposed categorization, y, facilitates the discrimination on the judgment dimension x, even when y is fully neutral or nonsensical.

An intriguing and almost universal source of accentuation is evaluation (cf. Eiser & Stroebe, 1972). Thus, for a woman who is herself a decided feminist, pro- and anti-feminist statements (dimension x) will be inevitably correlated with acceptance versus rejection on the valence dimension y, thus leading to accentuation. Therefore, involved feminists discriminate more between pro- and anti-feminist attitudes than people with a neutral attitude (Judd & Johnson, 1981). Accentuation of this kind is clearly relevant to understanding intergroup discrimination.

Most relevant to the role of language is that accentuation is moderated by semantic connotations. Discrimination on the judgment scale increases when the evaluative connotations of the scale labels are compatible with the judge's own attitude (Eiser & Mower-White, 1975; Oakes, Turner, & Haslam, 1991). For example, a pro-feminist judge should polarize more on a scale labeled "tolerant" (pro/positive) versus "narrow-minded" (anti/negative) than on a scale labeled "disloyal" (pro/negative) and "dutiful" (anti/positive). On the latter scale, a feminist's judgment would be deaccentuated. Evaluative language can thus be used, again in a subtle and hardly noticeable fashion, to accentuate or blur behavioral discrimination.

Methods of language analysis and diagnostic tools

The methods of language analysis differ in the unit of analysis as well as in the aspect of language they intend to assess. Some of them originate in straight linguistics while others owe more to social psychology.

A major part of language research uses content analytic methods (Holsti, 1968). Categories are developed that capture formal or thematic aspects of texts. One of the smallest possible text unit is individual words. If a lexicon of relevant words can be established beforehand, computer programs can be used to scan a text corpus, thus lightening the burden of the investigator, increasing coding objectivity and, due to the opportunity to scan large samples, enhancing the statistical power and reliability. Content-analytic methods can be used to establish contingencies, as for example between the co-occurrence of ingroup and outgroup references and evaluative adjectives. Such methods are often used to analyze samples from news media reports or TV shows. Their scope also encompasses long-term changes in language use, operationalized as an increase or decrease of relative frequencies of instances.

Greenwald, McGhee, and Schwartz (1998) have recently proposed the Implicit Association Test (IAT), a measure of stereotypes that is also located at the word level but that is sensitive to stereotypical word meanings in memory rather than the manifestation of words in text. It utilizes the compatibility principle that was already introduced in the above section on accentuation. The aim is to assess the latencies required to categorize stimulus words, using two response keys. For example, when applying the IAT to sexist stereotypes, respondents first have to assign female Christian names to the left response key and male names to the right response key. Then they have to assign negative attributes to the left key (previously associated with female) and positive attributes to the right key (previously associated with male). Then the respondents are presented with combined lists including female and male names as well as negative and positive attributes in alternating order. Assuming an anti-female stereotype, sorting response latencies should be faster in the compatible condition, when female names and negative attributes as well as male and positive terms have to be assigned to the same response key, than in an incompatible condition, where female and positive terms and male and negative terms have to be assigned to the same response keys.

The IAT has been applied to measure sexist and ethnic stereotypes (see Greenwald et al., 1998). Its heuristic appeal arises from the fact that it assesses an implicit aspect of stereotypical language (Lepore & Brown, 1997) rather than overt attitudes that can be controlled and corrected voluntarily.

Other language-analytic methods are not confined to lexical units but also use syntactical and pragmatical information. The linguistic category model (LCM; Semin & Fiedler, 1988) described previously is still based on words (predicates), but it classifies these words by syntactical categories rather than semantic meaning. Categorization by thematic rather than syntactic units is characteristic of Vallacher and Wegner's (1987) action identification theory. In this method of content analysis, descriptions of actions on a low level (giving the mechanical details) are distinguished from behaviors identified on a high level (the action's effect and implications).

Firmly in opposition to frequency analytic methods is discourse analysis. It treats language as reflexive, performative, and constructive (Edwards & Potter, 1992; Potter & Wetherell, 1987). Language is seen as not purely descriptive but as goal-directed. To understand discourse, expectations and interventions of the listener have to be taken into account. As discourse is strongly dependent on the context and the interaction goals, large intersituational as well as intraindividual variance must be expected.

These selected methods can be arranged on several dimensions: From word analysis to discourse, the recording unit size increases, as well as the control attributed to the sender over his/her language production. Also, the anticipated expectations of the recipient play an increasing role. The more complex the recording unit gets, the more interpretative effort is needed on the part of the researcher. This disadvantage is partly compensated by the advantage that larger recording units allow for richer and more context-sensitive coding.

How Rules of Language Use Affect the Stereotyping Process

The connection of language use and stereotypes can be constructed from two vantage points: (1) Stereotypes have implications for the way social groups communicate with each other. (2) Taking language as a starting point, communication rules can strengthen existing stereotypes.

The linguistic intergroup bias

When people describe the behavior of ingroup and outgroup members, systematic differences can be observed. The most prominent findings regarding implicit attributions of dispositionality come from Maass' and her colleagues' research on the linguistic inter-group bias (LIB; Maass, Salvi, Arcuri, & Semin, 1989). Their analyses demonstrate a tendency to describe positive ingroup behaviors and negative outgroup behaviors in more abstract terms than negative ingroup and positive outgroup behaviors. Similar results were obtained by Fiedler, Semin, and Finkenauer (1993) in males' and females' descriptions of male and female behavior. These findings lend themselves to an explanation in terms of an ingroup serving bias, or striving for positive ingroup identity (Tajfel & Turner, 1986). A global negative evaluation keeps the outgroup at its (inferior) place and ensures the necessary distance, while discounting negative ingroup behavior as local and context-dependent.

Apart from ingroup–outgroup differences, cooperative and informative communication is characterized by a general tendency to abstract from concrete details and to provide inter-pretations and evaluations beyond mere descriptions (Fiedler, Semin, & Bolten, 1989). The degree of this general abstraction tendency increases with the amount of shared knowledge. A related result is reported by Maass, Montalcini, and Biciotti (1998): The earlier in history a stereotype came into being, the more abstract is its description. A shift toward concreteness should occur, however, when the validity of statements is challenged (thus questioning the common ground) or when concrete language helps to communicate personal interests (Rubini & Kruglanski, 1997).

The tendency to communicate expected, commonly shared knowledge in abstract terms raises an alternative interpretation of the LIB. Most of the time, positive ingroup behavior and negative outgroup behavior are more in line with prior expectations than negative ingroup and positive outgroup behavior. However, when expectedness and group-serving biases are pitted against each other, the former overrides the latter. That is, when describing ingroups on negative but stereotypically expected dimensions, descriptions tend to be abstract rather than concrete. Thus, the basic variant of the LIB can be understood as a completely normal instance of cooperative language use, without any discriminative intention: What is already known can be said in general terms, but the unexpected and surprising must be particularized.

Intergroup perspective and actor-observer biases

In accordance with the general phenomenon of an actor-observer bias (Jones & Nisbett, 1972; Watson, 1982), behavior is more readily attributed to stable dispositions or traits from the perspective of an outgroup observer than from the actor's own ingroup perspective (Fiedler et al., 1993). This finding holds for the intergroup as well as the interpersonal domain, as evident in attributions of one's own and one's partner's behavior (Fiedler, Semin, & Koppetsch, 1991; Fiedler et al., 1995).

Mass communication

The mass media have been credited with an important role in the process of socialization and political attitude formation. Especially in magazines and TV, stereotypical depictions of minority groups and women have for a long time been an issue of heated discussions. It is feared that particularly children and adolescents are susceptible to these influences. Many content analytic studies have addressed the stereotypic contamination of media information. For instance, in an analysis of Italian newspapers, Maass, Corvino, and Arcuri (1994) have shown that the description of an anti-Semitic episode during a basketball game differed markedly between Jewish and Non-Jewish newspapers. Non-Jewish newspapers used less abstract words to describe anti-Semitic aggression (implying less internal, dispositional attributions).

Language use in the legal system

The attribution of guilt (or innocence) is part of the professional work of lawyers in court. Whereas the prosecution does argue from an outgroup position when referring to the defendant, the defense closes ranks with the defendant with the ultimate goal to influence the jury to see this person as a person much like themselves, as a member of the ingroup. Examining a witness gives attorneys unique opportunities to discredit witnesses and plant impressions in the jury. Closing speeches are the last chance of the two parties, prosecution and defense, to sway the jury or to immunize them against the arguments of the legal adversary. Keeping the semantic properties of word classes in mind, several strategies suggest themselves: (a) The causality-dimension (viz., the choice between interpretive action verbs and state verbs) can be used to attribute blame to other agents or even the victim. (b) Using the abstractness-dimension (adjectives), the behavior of the alleged perpetrator can be attributed to stable traits or situational pressures. (c) The abstractness-dimension also controls the attribution of credibility of the argument, for dispositional statements are hard to verify and may reduce a communication's credibility. When talking about linguistic strategies in the legal context, it is important not to misunderstand the word "'strategy'" as implying consciousness. It only denotes a systematic use of linguistic categories that can be linked with attributional consequences.

An analysis of protocols of the Nuremberg Trials (Schmid & Fiedler, 1996) and an experimental study with lawyers-in-training giving closing speeches for the defense and for the prosecution (Schmid & Fiedler, 1998) support these expectations. The defendant is on trial because of assumed negative actions that can be described concretely (e.g., defendant took victim's purse, descriptive action verb). The prosecution can try to imply dispositionality (the defendant is greedy, adjective), but since abstract statements are hard to verify, they prefer to apply the alternative strategy to induce internal attributions using interpretative action verbs (defendant stole from victim), suggesting intentionality and voluntary control. In comparison, the defense must try to downplay and distract from the typically negative behavior of the defendant in a criminal trial. As concrete positive terms are not applicable, they have to resort either to rather abstract, vague positive predicates (defendant is a responsible citizen) or to negative state verbs which suggest external causes or excuses for negative behavior (defendant detested victim). Moreover, the subject phrases of defense attorneys' statements often avoid direct references to the defendant and instead refer to co-defendants or fuzzy groups as a means of shifting blame and attributional focus.

The videotapes of the final speeches given by the lawyers-in-training were shown to laypersons who had to act in the capacity of a jury member. Their subsequent decisions were significantly influenced by language features (Schmid & Fiedler, 1998).

Stereotypes and the verbal interaction process

Someone who reads a paper or watches a TV show has only limited possibilities to interact with the sender, and a jury member has to listen to the arguments put forth by the lawyers. In contrast to this one-sided information flow, intergroup affairs are normally embedded in a dynamic interaction process that conveys symbolic meaning and emotional signs in multiple ways.

Speech accommodation.   It is a well-known phenomenon that speakers adjust their speech style to converge with or to diverge from their communication partners' style. The more effort they put in converging, the more favorably are they evaluated so that the listeners also start to converge (communication accommodation theory; Giles & Coupland, 1991). Accommodation takes place not only in speech, but also in paralinguistic and extralinguistic behavior. One of the functions of accommodation is identity maintenance. If someone converges with an outgroup member, he/she demonstrates a desire for integration, whereas divergence underscores social distance. In a similar vein, dialects and accents can improve or worsen the evaluation of the speaker. Nonstandard dialects may lead to the inference of incompetence and low social status (Ng & Bradac, 1993).

In the first part of this chapter, sexist language was introduced as an example of the way language as a system can further stereotypes. The socialization of gender roles not only consists of the learning of connotations and denotations of gender related vocabulary, but also includes gender differences in communicative behavior. Communication styles of men and women are expected to differ and exceptions may not be tolerated and may lead to negative impressions of the speaker (Mulac, Lundell, & Bradac, 1986). So-called female speech patterns have strong similarities to powerless speech, which not only gives the speaker a lesser chance to hold her own in an argument, but also raises a general impression of indecisiveness and weakness (O'Barr, 1982). Both the lexical and the conversational features of gender-related language can be interpreted as routinely used measures of intergroup control (Ng, 1990).

The communication game.   In contrast to communication approaches that focus on the encoding and decoding of message contents, other theories propose that the meaning of a message is negotiated between participants in conversation. Communication can be described as a game with rules, roles, and goals (communication game; Higgins, 1981). The rules reflect conventions of language use that have to be followed to achieve the desired effect. Of major importance is the tuning to the audience's expectations. An already familiar example of social tuning is that information that is quite well known to the audience will be conveyed on an abstract level.

Of course, skillfully excluding an audience to indicate distance is also an option in this game. Here the communication game approach converges with communication accommodation theory. However, communication game theory has a distinct link to social cognition: What and how speakers communicate not only determines the information conveyed to recipients but also affects the speakers' own memory (Wyer & Gruenfeld, 1995). Higgins and Rholes (1978) demonstrated that senders who were asked to convey a description of a target person to an audience that either liked or disliked the target not only tuned their message in a way that fit the evaluative expectations, but the senders' own subsequent impressions of the target person reflected the evaluative bias.

The question-answering paradigm.   In verbal interaction, the answers (given by politicians, patients, or applicants) are determined to a considerable degree by the questions asked (of journalists, diagnosticians, or personnel managers). This is the empirical message of the question-answering paradigm (Rubini & Kruglanski, 1997; Semin & Marsman, 1994; Semin, Rubini, & Fiedler, 1995). For instance, a teacher might ask a female student "Why did you *choose* physics as a major?" (using an action verb) or, alternatively, "Why do you *like* physics as a major?" (using a state verb). As noted above, action verbs trigger knowledge structures that induce internal attributions to the subject whereas state verbs induce external attributions. These knowledge structures give rise to systematically different answers. Answers to the "choose" question will typically refer to the respondent's own internal motives, goals, or talents. In contrast, answers to the "like" question will point to external factors, such as assets of the discipline, physics. Moreover, as state verbs are more abstract than action verbs, answers to state-verb questions will tend to be more abstract than answers to action-verb questions. The answers then can strengthen the attributions that already shaped the questions.

What are the psychological processes underlying this self-fulfilling circle? On the one hand, verbal interaction is generally affirmative (Snyder, 1984; Zuckerman, Knee, Hodgins, & Miyake, 1995), that is, conversation relies on a silent contract to cooperate with conversation partners' goals, which means to acquiesce most of the time. Thus, whether the question refers to advantages or disadvantages of a political party, either question will elicit a tendency to comply with the language game (i.e., let's talk about assets vs. deficits), and to find an affirmative answer for both suggestions.

On the other hand, the respondent may take the very fact that the question asks for advantages rather than disadvantages as conjectural evidence (Snyder, 1984) that the interviewer has relevant background information. And similarly, the response alternatives offered in questionnaires or interviews may serve as cues or demands as to appropriate answers (Schwarz, 1996).

Automatic processes.   Language forces people to step into the shoes of their predecessors and even walk a bit in the direction they took. Language use is partly routinized, without conscious effort or intent on the part of the individual, and the processes as well as their results are sometimes beyond the individual's control. In particular, trait inferences from behaviors occur spontaneously and independently of explicit goals or intentions (Newman & Uleman, 1989; Uleman, 1987).

Inference processes start with observed behavior and (sometimes) end up with stereotypes. These stereotypical concepts can in turn induce manifest behavior. Simple words presented incidentally or even subliminally can elicit subsequent actions, as many recent priming studies show. For example, priming the social category of the elderly can reduce the walking speed of people who are fully unaware of this influence (Bargh, Chen, & Burrows, 1996), and priming of the stereotype "professor" can increase performance on general knowledge tasks (Dijksterhuis & Van Knippenberg, 1998). Even the priming of ingroup or outgroup pronouns ("us" vs. "them") can he used to influence evaluative judgments (Perdue, Dovidio, Gurtman, & Tyler, 1990).

The priming paradigm attempts to quantify stereotypes as reaction time gains. It is not exactly clear, though, what is measured with such instruments. Their proponents hold that automatic associations are implicit indicators of stereotypical knowledge and prejudices.

A more skeptical account would be that these methods assess associative strength of concepts, but not necessarily the individual's belief in those stereotypes nor their behavioral dispositions.

Summary and Conclusion

The first part of this chapter was concerned with the various constraints that language as a system places on the way in which stereotype-relevant information can be conveyed in verbal communication. Apart from lexical, morphological, syntactic, and pragmatic constraints, the present section was mainly concerned with semantic influences on social stereotypes. Semantic similarities between trait terms lead to an overestimation of the actual correlation between traits, and the breadth of the related behavioral domain as well as the valence of the attribute have an impact on the possibility to verify and falsify a stereotype. Several techniques for the investigation of such semantic constraints on interpersonal language were presented.

The second part of this chapter dealt with the impact of language use on the stereotyping process. Several language approaches to stereotype formation and consolidation were introduced that can be ordered along a dimension of controllability. Theories of automatic processes in stereotype formation are located at the low-controllability end of this dimension, which is of central importance for understanding stereotype maintenance and change (see Brewer & Gaertner, 2001; Rothbart, this volume, chapter 7). Subtle language effects are so important because they evade the conscious attention and control of language users.

The enhanced accessibility of stereotypical word meanings and associations constitutes an essential aspect of semantic knowledge. However, this knowledge should be neither confused with the belief that a stereotype is true nor with actual discriminating behavior toward the target group or person. Nevertheless, as the present chapter has shown, there is a growing body of evidence which suggests that semantic, syntactic, and pragmatic factors can have notable influences on attitudes, judgments, and manifest behaviors.

REFERENCES

Bales, R. F. (1950). A set of categories for the analysis of small group interactions. *American Sociological Review, 15*, 257–263.

Bargh, J. A., Chen, M., & Burrows, L. (1996). Automaticity of social behavior. Direct effects of trait construct and stereotype activation on action. *Journal of Personality and Social Psychology, 71*, 230–244.

Blair, I. V., & Banaji, M. R. (1996). Automatic and controlled processes in stereotype priming. *Journal of Personality and Social Psychology, 70*, 1142–1163.

Bolinger, D. (1973). Truth is a linguistic question. *Language, 49*, 539–550.

Brewer, M. B., & Gaertner, S. L. (2001). Toward reduction of prejudice: Intergroup contact and social categorization. In R. Brown & S. Gaertner (Eds.), *Blackwell handbook of social psychology: Intergroup processes* (pp. 451–472). Oxford, UK: Blackwell.

Brigham, J. C. (1971). Ethnic stereotypes. *Psychological Review, 76*, 15–38.

Brown, R., & Fish, D. (1983). The psychological causality implicit in language. *Cognition, 14*, 233–274.

Bruner, J. S., & Goodman, C. D. (1947). Value and need as organizing factors in perception. *Journal of Abnormal and Social Psychology, 42,* 33–44.

D'Andrade, R. L. (1974). Memory and the assessment of behavior. In H. M. Block, Jr. (Ed.), *Measurement in the social sciences.* Chicago, IL: Aldine.

De Saussure, F. (1915). *Cours de linguistique générale.* Paris: Payot.

Dijksterhuis, A., & van Knippenberg, A. (1998). The relation between perception and behavior, or how to win a game of Trivial Pursuit. *Journal of Personality and Social Psychology, 74,* 865–877.

Dovidio, J. F., & Gaertner, S. L. (1986) (Eds.), *Prejudice, discrimination, and racism.* San Diego, CA: Academic Press.

Edwards, D., & Potter, J. (1992). *Discursive psychology.* Newbury Park, CA: Sage.

Eiser, J. R. (1971). Enhancement of contrast in the absolute judgment of attitude statements. *Journal of Personality and Social Psychology, 17,* 1–10.

Eiser, J. R., & Mower-White, C. J. (1975). Categorization and congruity in attitudinal judgment. *Journal of Personality and Social Psychology, 31,* 769–775.

Eiser, J. R., & Stroebe, W. (1972). *Categorization and social judgment.* London: Academic Press.

Fazio, R. H., Sanbonmatsu, D. M., Powell, M. C., & Kardes, F. R. (1986). On the automatic activation of attitudes. *Journal of Personality and Social Psychology, 50,* 229–238.

Fiedler, K., & Semin, G. R. (1988). On the causal information conveyed by different interpersonal verbs. *Social Cognition, 6,* 21–39.

Fiedler, K., Semin, G. R., & Bolten, S. (1989). Language use and reification of social information: Top-down and bottom-up processing in person cognition. *European Journal of Social Psychology, 19,* 271–295.

Fiedler, K., Semin, G. R., & Finkenauer, C. (1993). The battle of words between gender groups: A language-based approach to intergroup processes. *Human Communication Research, 19,* 409–441.

Fiedler, K., Semin, G. R., Finkenauer, C., & Berkel, I. (1995). Actor-observer bias in close relationships: The role of self-knowledge and self-related language. *Personality and Social Psychology Bulletin, 21,* 525–538.

Fiedler, K., Semin, G. R., & Koppetsch, C. (1991). Language use and attributional biases in close personal relationships. *Personality and Social Psychology Bulletin, 17,* 147–155.

Gardner, R. C., Taylor, D. M., & Feenstra, H. J. (1970). Ethnic stereotypes: Attitudes or beliefs? *Canadian Journal of Psychology, 24,* 321–334.

Gidron, D., Koehler, D. J., & Tversky, A. (1993). Implicit quantification of personality traits. *Personality and Social Psychology Bulletin, 19,* 594–604.

Giles, H., & Coupland, N. (1991). *Language: Contexts and consequences.* Oxford, UK: Open University Press.

Glucksberg, S., & Danks, J. H. (1975). *Experimental psycholinguistics: An introduction.* Hillsdale, NJ: Erlbaum.

Greenwald, A. G., McGhee, D. E., & Schwartz, J. L. K. (1998). Measuring individual differences in implicit cognition: The implicit association test. *Journal of Personality and Social Psychology, 74,* 1464–1480.

Grice, H. P. (1975). Logic of conversation. In P. Cole & J. L. Morgan (Eds.), *Syntax and semantics* (Vol. 3: Speech acts, pp. 41–58). New York: Academic Press.

Hamilton, D. L., Gibbons, P. A., Stroessner, S. J., & Sherman, J. W. (1992). Stereotypes and language use. In G. R. Semin & K. Fiedler (Eds.), *Language, interaction, and social cognition* (pp. 102–128). London: Sage.

Hamilton, D. L., & Rose, R. L. (1980). Illusory correlation and the maintenance of stereotypic beliefs. *Journal of Personality and Social Psychology, 39,* 832–845.

Hampson, S. E., John, O. P., & Goldberg, L. R. (1986). Category breadth and hierarchical structure in personality: Studies of asymmetries in judgments of trait implications. *Journal of Personality and Social Psychology, 51*, 37–54.

Henley, N. M., Miller, M., & Beazley, J.-A. (1995). Syntax, semantics, and sexual violence: Agency and the passive voice. *Journal of Language and Social Psychology, 14*, 60–84.

Higgins, E. T. (1981). The "communication game": Implications for social cognition and persuasion. In E. T. Higgins, C. P. Herman, & M. P. Zanna (Eds.), *Social cognition: The Ontario symposium* (pp. 343–392). Hillsdale, NJ: Erlbaum.

Higgins, E. T., & Rholes, W. J. (1978). "Saying is believing": Effects of message modification on memory and liking for the person described. *Journal of Experimental Social Psychology, 14*, 363–378.

Hobden, K. L., & Olson, J. M. (1994). From jest to antipathy: Disparagement humor as a source of dissonance-motivated attitude chance. *Basic and Applied Social Psychology, 15*, 239–249.

Hoffman, C., & Hurst, N. (1990). Gender stereotypes: Perception or rationalization? *Journal of Personality and Social Psychology, 58*, 197–208.

Holsti, O. R. (1968). Content analysis. In G. Lindzey & E. Aronson (Eds.), *The handbook of social psychology* (2nd ed., Vol. 2, pp. 596–692). Reading, MA: Addison-Wesley.

Jones, E. E., & Davis, K. E. (1965). From acts to dispositions: The attribution process in person perception. In L. Berkowitz (Ed.), *Advances of experimental social psychology* (Vol. 2). New York: Academic Press.

Jones, E. E., & Nisbett, R. E. (1972). The actor and the observer: Divergent perceptions of the causes of behavior. In E. E. Jones et al. (Eds.), *Attribution. Perceiving the causes of behavior* (pp. 79–94). Morristown, NJ: General Learning Press.

Judd, C. M., & Johnson, J. T. (1981). Attitudes, polarization, and diagnosticity: Exploring the effect of affect. *Journal of Personality and Social Psychology, 41*, 26–36.

Kelley, H. H. (1967). Attribution theory in social psychology. In D. Levine (Ed.), *Nebraska symposium on motivation* (Vol. 15, pp. 192–238). Lincoln: University of Nebraska Press.

Lepore, L., & Brown, R. (1997). Category and stereotype activation: Is prejudice inevitable? *Journal of Personality and Social Psychology, 72*, 275–287.

Mackie, D. M., & Hamilton, D. L. (1993). *Affect, cognition, and stereotyping: Interaction processes in group perception.* New York: Academic Press.

Maass, A., Corvino, P., & Arcuri, L. (1994). Linguistic intergroup bias and the mass media. *Revue de Psychologie Sociale, 1*, 31–43.

Maass, A., Milesi, A., Zabbini, S., & Stahlberg, D. (1995). Linguistic intergroup bias: Differential expectancies or in-group protection? *Journal of Personality and Social Psychology, 68*, 116–126.

Maass, A., Montalcini, F., & Biciotti, E. (1998). On the (dis)-confirmability of stereotypic attitudes. *European Journal of Social Psychology, 28*, 383–402.

Maass, A., Salvi, D., Arcuri, L., & Semin, G. R. (1989). Language use in intergroup contexts: The linguistic intergroup bias. *Journal of Personality and Social Psychology, 57*, 981–993.

McCauley, C., & Stitt, C. L. (1978). An individual and quantitative measure of stereotypes. *Journal of Personality and Social Psychology, 36*, 929–940.

Mulac, A., Lundell, T. L., & Bradac, J. J. (1986). Male/female language differences and attributional consequences in a public speaking setting: Toward an explanation of the gender-linked language effect. *Communication Monographs, 53*, 115–129.

Newman, L. S., & Uleman, J. S. (1989). Spontaneous trait inference. In J. S. Uleman & J. A. Bargh (Eds.), *Unintended thought* (pp. 155–188). New York: Guilford Press.

Ng, S. H. (1990). Language and control. In H. Ciles & W. P. Robinson (Eds.), *Handbook of language and social psychology* (pp. 271–285). Chichester, UK: Wiley.

Ng, S. H., & Bradac, J. J. (1993). *Power in language.* Newbury Park, CA: Sage.

Oakes, P. J., Turner, J. C., & Haslam, S. A. (1991). Perceiving people as group members: The role of fit in the salience of social categorizations. *British Journal of Social Psychology, 30,* 125–144.

O'Barr, W. M. (1982). *Linguistic evidence: Language, power, and strategy in the courtroom.* New York: Academic Press.

Perdue, C. W., Dovidio, J. F., Gurtman, M. B., & Tyler, R. B. (1990), Us and them: Categorization and the process of intergroup bias. *Journal of Personality and Social Psychology, 59,* 475–486.

Potter, J., & Wetherell, M. (1987). *Discourse and social psychology: Beyond attitudes and behaviour.* London: Sage.

Reeder, G. D., & Brewer, M. B. (1979). A schematic model of dispositional attribution in interpersonal perception. *Psychological Review, 86,* 61–79.

Rothbart, M., & Park, B. (1986). On the confirmability and disconfirmability of trait concepts. *Journal of Personality and Social Psychology, 50,* 131–142.

Rubini, M., & Kruglanski, A. W. (1997). Brief encounters ending in estrangement: Motivated language use and interpersonal rapport in the question-answer paradigm. *Journal of Personality and Social Psychology, 72,* 1047–1060.

Rudolph, U., & Försterling, F. (1997). The psychological causality implicit in verbs: A review. *Psychological Bulletin, 121,* 192–218.

Schmid, J., & Fiedler, K. (1996). Language and implicit attributions in the Nuremberg trials: Analyzing prosecutors' and defense attorneys' final speeches. *Human Communications Research, 22,* 371–398.

Schmid, J., & Fiedler, K. (1998). The backbone of closing speeches: The impact of prosecution versus defense language on juridical attributions. *Journal of Applied Social Psychology, 28,* 1140–1172.

Schwarz, N. (1996). Survey research: Collecting data by asking questions. In G. R. Semin & K. Fiedler (Eds.), *Applied social psychology* (pp. 65–90). London: Sage.

Semin, G. R., & Fiedler, K. (1988). The cognitive functions of linguistic categories in describing persons: Social cognition and language. *Journal of Personality and Social Psychology, 54,* 558–568.

Semin, G. R., & Fiedler, K. (1992). The inferential properties of interpersonal verbs. In G. R. Semin & K. Fiedler (Eds.), *Language, interaction and social cognition* (pp. 58–78). London: Sage.

Semin, G. R., & Marsman, G. (1994). On the information mediated by interpersonal verbs: Event precipitation, dispositional inference, and implicit causality. *Journal of Personality and Social Psychology, 67,* 836–849.

Semin, G. R., Rubini, M., & Fiedler, K. (1995). The answer is in the question: The effect of verb causality on locus of explanation. *Personality and Social Psychology Bulletin, 21,* 834–841.

Shweder, R. A. (1975). How relevant is an individual difference theory of personality? *Journal of Personality, 43,* 455–484.

Shweder, R. A. (1982). Fact and artifact in trait perception: The systematic distortion hypothesis. In B. A. Maher & W. B. Maher (Eds.), *Progress in experimental personality research* (Vol. 2). New York: Academic Press.

Skowronski, N. J., & Carlston, D. E. (1989). Negativity and extremity biases in impression formation: A review of explanations. *Psychological Bulletin, 105,* 131–142.

Snyder, M. (1984). When belief creates reality. *Advances in Experimental Social Psychology, 18,* 247–305.

Solomon, S., Greenberg, J., & Pyszczynski, T. (1991). A terror management theory of social behavior: The psychological functions of self-esteem and cultural world views. In M. P. Zanna (Ed.), *Advances in Experimental Social Psychology, 24,* 93–157.

Tajfel, H. (1969). Cognitive aspects of prejudice. *Journal of Social Issues, 25,* 79–97.

Tajfel, H. (1970). Experiments in intergroup discrimination. *Scientific American, 223,* 96–102.

Tajfel, H., & Turner, C. J. (1986). The social identity theory of intergroup behavior. In S. Worchel & W. G. Austin (Eds.), *Psychology of intergroup relations.* Chicago, IL: Nelson-Hall.

Uleman, J. S. (1987). Consciousness and control: The case of spontaneous trait inferences. *Personality and Social Psychology Bulletin, 13*, 337–354.

Von Hippel, W., Sekaquaptewa, D., & Vargas, P. (1997). The linguistic intergroup bias as an implicit indicator of prejudice. *Journal of Experimental Social Psychology, 33*, 490–509.

Vallacher, R., & Wegner, D. M. (1987). What do people think they're doing? Action identification and human behavior. *Psychological Review, 94*, 3–15.

Watson, D. (1982). The actor and the observer: How are their perceptions of causality divergent? *Psychological Bulletin, 92*, 682–700.

Webster, D. N., Kruglanski, A. W., & Pattison, D. A. (1997). Motivated language use in intergroup context: Need-for-closure effects on the linguistic intergroup bias. *Journal of Personality and Social Psychology, 72*, 1122–1131.

Wicklund, R. A., & Braun, O. L. (1990). Creating consistency among pairs of traits: A bridge from social psychology to trait psychology. *Journal of Experimental Social Psychology, 26*, 545–558.

Wittenbrink, B., Judd, C. M., & Park, B. (1997). Evidence for racial prejudice at the implicit level and its relationship with questionnaire measures. *Journal of Personality and Social Psychology, 72*, 262–274.

Wyer, R. S. Jr., & Gruenfeld, D. H. (1995). Information processing in social contexts: Implications for social memory and judgment. *Advances in Experimental Social Psychology, 27*, 49–91.

Zuckerman, M., Knee, C. R., Hodgins, H. S., & Miyake, K. (1995). Hypothesis confirmation: The joint effect of positive test strategy and acquiescence response set. *Journal of Personality and Social Psychology, 68*, 52–60.

Author Index

Subject Index